ROGER FALIGOT

Chinese Spies

From Chairman Mao to Xi Jinping

Translated by

NATASHA LEHRER

HarperCollins *Publishers* India

First published in French by Nouveau Monde as *Les services secrets chinois* in 2008 (fourth edition 2021), and in English by
C. Hurst & Co. (Publishers) Ltd in 2019

Published in India by HarperCollins *Publishers* 2022
4th Floor, Tower A, Building No. 10, Phase II, DLF Cyber City,
Gurugram, Haryana – 122002
www.harpercollins.co.in

2 4 6 8 10 9 7 5 3 1

P-ISBN: 978-93-5489-238-7
E-ISBN: 978-93-5489-551-7

Printed and bound at
Thomson Press (India) Ltd

MIX
Paper
FSC FSC® C010615

This book is produced from independently certified FSC® paper
to ensure responsible forest management.

To Jason Pan
and in memory of David Bonavia

"A commander's correct dispositions stem from his correct decisions, his correct decisions stem from his correct judgements, and his correct judgements stem from a thorough and necessary reconnaissance and from pondering on and piecing together the data of various kinds gathered through reconnaissance. He applies all possible and necessary methods of reconnaissance, and ponders on the information gathered about the enemy's situation, discarding the dross and selecting the essential, eliminating the false and retaining the true, proceeding from the one to the other and from the outside to the inside."

Quotations from Chairman Mao Zedong
Chapter 23—Investigation & Study, 1967
["Problems of Strategy in China's Revolutionary War" (December 1936),
Selected Works, Vol. I. p. 188]

CONTENTS

FOREWORD

The power of a country is usually reflected in its obvious economic and military strength, supported by a well calibrated narrative. Hidden behind this is the strength and professional efficacy of its intelligence agencies, which in turn is dependent on the attitude and policies of the government. This is particularly so in dictatorships—military or political. Dictatorships tend to lean heavily on their intelligence agencies to protect domestic interests and external goals. Dictators are fond of intelligence agencies, and yet are almost paranoid about their leadership. Loyalty to the leader is of utmost importance. It is not institutional, as in most democracies whose leaders sometimes do not have the same enchantment with secret intelligence as dictators do. Relationships between the head of government and the head of intelligence in a closed society can be enduring and functionally useful in preserving the leadership and maybe, the party; in a democracy this is dependent on how seriously the democratically elected government views the utility of the service to the country and sometimes, to the election prospects of the party in power. In a *communist* dictatorship, the intelligence is answerable to the party head and not to the government. Dissent is equated with treason and in China, the administration of the *Laogai* (the Chinese gulag) is one of the functions of internal security.

Chinese intelligence activity has a long history, going back to Sun Tzu and his famous fifth century BCE treatise, *The Art of War*; Indian intelligence similarly draws its inspiration from Kautilya's *Arthashastra*, composed in the second century BCE. The difference between the two is that in China the history has been unbroken, in India's case the *Arthashastra* receded into the background following the Mughal and the British invasions. The Communists, fighting their revolutionary war against the capitalist Chiang Kai Shek, relied on intelligence using tactics imbibed from Sun Tzu against their enemies, the British and French. The Chinese have had an unbroken system of gathering intelligence since the Shanghai Concessions of the 1930s.

This was similar to the Soviet pattern as their military intelligence was created by Leon Trotsky in 1918 and the GRU agency survives to this day. The Chinese apparatus was led by Zhou Enlai, who went on to become the Mao's deputy and the Chinese premier. As a revolutionary leader, Mao understood the importance of reconnaissance and the ability to identify what was irrelevant and incorrect and separate it from relevant and correct information. There is thus a long history and tradition of Chinese intelligence activity. In India, the initial post-British era leadership was, in contrast to Chinese experience and knowledge, quite innocent of such needs and practices. Perhaps even disdainful, and would adversely affect India's security interests.

Roger Faligot's *Chinese Spies: From Chairman Mao to Xi Jinping* is not only a history of Chinese espionage but also a history of the relationship between intelligence agencies and party leadership. Starting from the days of the Battle of Shanghai in the 1920s, Faligot covers Chinese secret operations relating to the New Silk Road, the current global economic wars, battles on the internet and against Islamist terrorism. He gives an engaging and detailed account of the rise of Communist China and the corresponding rise of its intelligence collection and operational capabilities, something that comes more easily when the two sides are engaged in military battles. Non-violence somehow introduces idealism but intelligence is about realism not idealism.

When China became a Communist republic in 1949, it had a functioning apparatus that was delivering intelligence and providing security. It was led by or had the involvement of senior party personalities that would matter in the governance of China. There was a continuity and Mao did not have to start from ground zero. Xi Jinping, in his quest to make China a global superpower, had to create what would be the most powerful army in the world. China's Strategic Support Force includes digital warfare capacities, and a new way of gathering intelligence and reconnaissance. Security, including internal security and secrecy, is even more paramount in Xi's China. Down the years there has been intrigue and counter-intrigue within the organizations and its leaders, for instance Zhou Enlai limiting Kang Shen's control. It was wise, for Kang Sheng, who had risen to head the internal security agency, Teke, was found to have installed listening devices in Mao's office.

Xi's strategic management of the seas dovetails into his Silk Road strategy, which has a great deal to do with territorial wars to correct "historic wrongs", this includes Taiwan retaking the Spratly Islands, what China calls Southern Tibet which is shorthand for India's Arunachal Pradesh, the Senkaku (Diaoyutai Islands) claimed by the Japanese, uniting Outer Mongolia with China, and recovering lost territories from the Russians. Naturally, the perceived "softer" options will be attempted first.

Along with its economy, China has also modernised its intelligence capacity in keeping up with its global ambitions. Faligot provides much-needed knowledge about the growth of both the Ministry of State security and the PLA's new services which makes them the largest intelligence organisations in the world today. This is crucial for India, since China is her neighbour and neither are on friendly terms.

Along the way, in China, there were crises like the Cultural Revolution that tore the country apart. The spies had their own revolt—Lin Biao, a close associate of the politically powerful Gang of Four, died in a convenient air crash while trying to flee China in 1971, which resulted in great international intrigue too. The inability of Chinese intelligence to predict accurately when Vietnam would attack the Khmer Rouge in Cambodia to get rid of Pol Pot was a setback that was worsened by the PLA receiving a drubbing at the China–Vietnam border in 1979. This was China trying to teach a lesson to the Vietnamese for having defeated America that ended up giving the former a bloodied nose.

Mao's meeting with US President Richard Nixon in 1972 was about countering the Soviet Union. Deng Xiaoping's opening of the economy in 1978, after the death of stalwarts like Mao and Zhou two years earlier, was just that. Deng's intelligence reforms led to the formation of the Ministry of State Security in June 1983, replacing existing arrangements. Clearly, Deng was not a liberalised economic reformer, he was going to ensure that his economic reforms would not lead to China adopting Western ideas of democracy and liberty. His Four Modernisations were not about democracy but the growth of Chinese power. However, Western powers had begun to assume that the opening up in China would lead to democracy and greater liberty in China. This narrative of opportunity in the West gave them justification for investing in China's economy. Profit was the opportunity. For Deng, it was the narrative of necessity—if Communism had to survive and become stronger, the economy had to do well.

Deng's intelligence reforms, however, did not prevent intelligence failure that did not foresee the protest that ended in the Tiananmen Square massacre of 1989, where about 10,000 were estimated to have been killed. Deng's reforms did lay the foundations for changes later, which in Chinese parlance essentially meant more power to the state. After the Tiananmen event had been brought under control, Chinese leaders met and some of the advice given by Deng to the Chinese Communist Party was to conceal their abilities, and never become leaders. The present Chinese leadership seems to think differently or that the time had come to claim leadership.

When a dictator reforms, he only becomes more dictatorial, for any lifting of the lid usually leads to losses. In pursuance of its desire to become a leading power and facilitate acquisition of economic intelligence and technology, China's legal reforms seek to ensure that its intelligence agencies can exploit private industry for access to secrets and technology abroad. The CCP promulgated several laws in recent years that require companies and individuals to actively support China's intelligence activities. The latest 2017 reforms by Xi Jinping stipulate that any organization or citizen shall support, assist and cooperate with state intelligence work in accordance with the law, and keep the secrets of national intelligence work known to the public.

The state would protect individuals and organizations who provide this. In any case, intelligence agencies have the authority to compel any entity to provide this support. There is a strong element of compulsion where Chinese society, companies and citizens are required to provide the government with intelligence, and refusal can invite harsh punishment. Beijing controls everything, not just the government and the economy, and the methods of this control include espionage, information warfare, industrial and foreign policies, and military power. It now also has the technological strength to create the world's first digital authoritarian state.*

If Chinese intelligence began to go global during Jiang Zemin's time (1993–2003), in Xi Jinping's ambitious hands, it is going into hi-tech and all that relates to the meta-world. The portion in the book on China's quest for hi-tech independence and supremacy is particularly significant for it shows tremendous foresight and a single-minded determination to seek this capability that is not restricted to any one leadership's time. It has been a national endeavour and worryingly for India, quite successful. There are other absorbing stories in the book about a failed coup and how the 2008 Beijing Olympics were managed. Sport and intelligence do mix.

Considerable research has gone into the writing of this book. There is enough mystery, intrigue, and history in it to make it one of the most fascinating narratives of Chinese history from the days of Mao to the present administration, and the contribution of intelligence services to China's growth and national ambition during the period.

14 January 2022
New Delhi

Vikram Sood
Former Chief, Research and
Analysis Wing (R&AW),
Government of India

---

* Nicholas Eftimiades, *Chinese Espionage: Operations and Tactics,* Vitruvian Press. Kindle Edition. pp. 5-6.

PREFACE

The word *Qingbao* in Chinese has two meanings: "intelligence" and "information".

The flimsy border between the two concepts facilitates the work of secret agents but complicates that of journalists. A Xinhua News Agency correspondent caught red-handed snooping in the military domain can swear on the memory of Chairman Mao that he was simply engaged in a straightforward reporting assignment, while a western journalist interviewing a supporter of the underground democracy movement is always going to be labelled an "imperialist spy". As for the writer or reporter researching the history of Chinese espionage who appears to have a good knowledge of Chinese... Let's not even go there.

The spy is Other. Intelligence owes much to psychology. A government "policy officer" from the Information Section of the Lao Zi Institute might also be an undercover "handler", working for one of the various different intelligence services that abound all over the world under some nebulous cultural title; or he might be a true man of letters who simply wants to share his love for Chinese history and philosophy. He could even be both. I have known several highly intellectual spies.

The concept becomes even more interesting when one studies the Chinese characters and roots of the word *Qingbao*, namely: 情报.

The original meaning of *Qing* 青 is "life light" and "heart". It can be translated as "the reality of the situation", "the way things are", the "situation" put in perspective.

The second character, *Bao* 报, originates from an ancient pictogram, simplified in modern times, meaning "a person, whose hands are fixed, kneeling, forced to confess". Quite a lot of meaning to unpack in a single character.

This is the original pictogram that is the basis of the character today:

INTRODUCTION

OLD RED SPIES NEVER DIE

In May 2017, Yao Zijian, aged 102, was guest of honour at an extraordinary ceremony in Beijing. As the oldest surviving Chinese spy, he found himself in the midst of a crowd of hundreds: parents and children of Chinese secret agents, who have fought on the "underground front" since the founding of the Chinese Communist Party—in the war of espionage.

The occasion was the ninetieth anniversary of the Central Committee Special Branch (*Zhongyang Teke*), the oldest of the Chinese secret services, set up in Shanghai on 11 November 1927 under the aegis of the future prime minister, Zhou Enlai. Later renamed the CCP Central Investigation Department (*Zhongyang Diaochabu*), it was for a long time the main political intelligence service, led until the 1980s by the remarkable Luo Qinchang (1918-2014).

Luo's son, General Luo Yuan, addressed a speech to the offspring of these "great soldiers of the covert war", lauding the qualities of the "nameless agents", who were unwaveringly "loyal, fearless, cautious when alone, alert, capable and helpful to each other … [T]he spirit that every Party member and soldier should learn from".[1]

This was more than an exercise in homage to the heroic underground militants who engaged in historic espionage, first against the French and British in the Shanghai Concessions, then against Chiang Kai-shek's Kuomintang and spies from Japan. As those in the audience were surely aware, this secret war is an ongoing reality under

President Xi Jinping today. The choice of the intelligence service to be honoured, the Diaochabu, was significant in this regard. In the 1980s, it had joined forces with the counterespionage branch of the Ministry of Public Security: the Gonganbu. Together the two services then formed a new Ministry of State Security, the *Guojia Anquanbu*, or Guoanbu for short. It was the Guoanbu, still in operation today, that organized the anniversary event in 2014. Its first leader, minister Ling Yun, died in March 2018 at the age of 100. The publicity afforded to this ceremony also had another, more immediate purpose, serving as the launch of a new campaign against "imperialist spies"—that summer, a draconian new anti-espionage law was passed.

In the twenty-first century, the Guoanbu considers itself to be a global intelligence player as significant as the Soviet KGB was in the twentieth. The Chinese intelligence services, an umbrella term including several other organisations beside the Guoanbu, rival the largest in the world: the American CIA, the Israeli Mossad, the Indian RAW, the French DGSE, Britain's MI6, and of course the other intelligence services in the region, such as the Taiwanese MJIB and the Japanese Naicho.[2]

This book explores the longstanding importance of intelligence in communist China. Its multiple origins go back to the fourteenth-century novel *Romance of the Three Kingdoms*, and Sun Tzu's famous treatise *The Art of War*, as well as the influence of both Russian communism and, paradoxically, enemy states: the French and British secret services fought by Zhou Enlai and his spies in the 1930s, in the Shanghai Concessions. *Chinese Spies* is an attempt to illustrate both the long history of the intelligence and security services since the creation of the Chinese Communist Party, and their ongoing role in politics today. In 2019, the CCP still preserves a Marxist intelligence tradition that dates back to the interwar period.

There is no equivalent to this unbroken tradition, apart from the Russian military intelligence service, the GRU, which was founded by Leon Trotsky in 1918 and retained its name even after the implosion of the USSR. A century later, until 2019, it played a major role in defeating the Islamic State (ISIS) in Syria. However, the ideological veneer of communism has disappeared from the Russian intelligence service, even though its good relations with the Chinese secret services are no doubt facilitated by the psychological behaviour patterns of President Vladimir Putin's agents, rooted in those of the Soviet organisations.

Our story opens with the Battle for Shanghai in the 1920s, and ends with cyber conflict, the secret operations surrounding the New Silk Road, the global economic wars underway today, the battles waging on the internet, and the war against Islamist terrorism.

As a result of these new challenges, there has been a formidable increase in the authority of the Chinese intelligence apparatus, specifically since 2017, when Xi Jinping, self-proclaimed "supreme leader" of the People's Liberation Army (PLA) and the "leadership core" of the party, enhanced his powers at the 19th CCP Congress, making him the most powerful Chinese leader since Mao Zedong and Deng Xiaoping. This was a synthesis of the dual political heritage that Xi boasts: a form of neo-Maoism tinged with the cult of personality, and a post-Mao pragmatism in the service of a triumphant modernization. According to "Xi Jinping Thought", the most important thing is to maintain the "mass line", at the same time as "deepening reform", and to revitalize the country through the "renaissance of the Chinese nation".

Chinese intelligence is distinguished from that of other countries in the degree to which it is influenced by politics. Each service is two-pronged, with a technical director, charged with handling daily operations, working alongside a political commissar, who is responsible for ensuring that the organization's ideological orientation conforms to the strategy decreed by the CCP.

Specifically, this orientation dovetails with the "Chinese Dream," in other words President Xi's aim of preserving the supremacy of the party, while also pursuing his global strategy. That strategy is in fact not only global, but interplanetary, too: Beijing has already proclaimed its intention to fly the red Chinese flag on Mars, the "red planet", in 2049, the centenary of the People's Republic of China.

China, a new "soft power" titan, prides itself on being the most effective pacifying force on the planet, with vast projects like the One Belt One Road initiative, an international infrastructure and investment scheme billed as a new Silk Road, or the Shanghai Cooperation Organization (SCO), which aims to shift the global economic and security centres from the West to a new axis led by the China–Russia partnership. This pact incorporates the former Muslim countries of the USSR, as well as Pakistan and India as recent members and Iran as an observer.

Meanwhile, President Xi is setting out to create what will be nothing less than the most powerful army ever seen in the entire history of humanity. Since early 2016, Xi Jinping has completely reorganized the People's Liberation Army, originally founded in 1949. He has simplified its command hierarchy, replaced the seven military regions with five "theatre commands", and fused two strategic armed forces, besides the land, sea and air armies: the People's Liberation Army Rocket Force (missiles, interplanetary rockets) and the Strategic Support Force (SSF), which includes for example the digital firepower required for cyber warfare. As we will see in later chapters, the SSF is an entirely distinct army of intelligence-gathering and reconnaissance.

Xi has also launched a new concept, the "strategic management of the sea", designed to be pursued in tandem with the Silk Road strategy. According to some Indian analysts, between today and 2050 the PLA could, theoretically, engage in up to six different wars: for unification with Taiwan; the "retaking" of the Spratly Islands, southern Tibet, and Diaoyutai (called the Senkaku Islands by the Japanese, who claim them as their territory); unification with Outer Mongolia; and the recovery of territories lost to Russia.

This is the context in which Chinese intelligence has evolved. Of course, there is also a role to be played by internal security, the administration of the *laogai* (the Chinese gulag), and the repression of dissidents, including Nobel Peace Prize laureate Liu Xiaobo, who died in July 2017. But the latter part of this book is focused specifically on Xi's reorganization of the secret services abroad and their activities. In the 1980s, Deng Xiaoping conceived of the services as going hand in hand with modernization. In the 1990s, Jiang Zemin allowed them to evolve from a community of regional intelligence services into a global apparatus, taking advantage of the temporary disappearance of the Russian KGB, which has reappeared today in a different form. Xi Jinping has now developed this massive apparatus to resemble that of a global superpower. We will see how he did this as we follow the evolution of both the Guoanbu and the PLA's new services. Together, in terms of both personnel and the range of organizations, they constitute the largest intelligence service in the world today.

PART ONE

1

THE BATTLE FOR SHANGHAI

At the beginning of the twentieth century, there were 400 million people living in China, which covered 11 million square kilometres. Various further parcels of once-Chinese territory had been annexed during consecutive foreign invasions. With the signing of the Treaty of Nanjing in 1842, the British had granted themselves Hong Kong, known as the "Fragrant Harbour". Other "unequal treaties" led to the granting of Concessions—entire areas of major cities—to the "long noses", as well as the imposition of war damages by foreign powers, which devastated the Chinese economy.

In 1900 in Beijing, the "northern" capital, foreign legations were besieged during the Boxer Rebellion, as it was called by foreign journalists. By the end of the fifty-five-day siege, the uprising had been crushed by an international expeditionary force, and the dowager empress Ci Xi, an ally of the Boxers, was toppled. The last Manchu emperor, Pu Yi, was forced to abdicate at the age of six in 1912. The new Republic of China, headed by nationalist leader Sun Yat-sen, quickly took shape as a dictatorship under the yoke of the northern warlord Yuan Shikai.

The history of modern Chinese espionage begins ten years after these events, in the French Concession of Shanghai, a port on the River Huangpu, which is an tributary of the Yangtze. Three hundred thousand Chinese people lived in the Concession. Indeed, the story of Chinese communism and its secret services is partly French; in the 1920s, Shanghai was nicknamed "the Paris of the Orient".

The French were not the only Westerners to have wrested a concession from the Manchu emperors. Shanghai's International Settlement belonged to the British and the Americans, whose jurisdiction was applied to its 750,000-strong Chinese population, while another million lived in the working-class Chinese neighbourhoods of Zhabei and Nandao. One doesn't need an abacus to work out that only 30,000 Westerners—"foreign devils", with their own police force, army and legal system—were imposing their rule on fully half the city's inhabitants.

These laws had a variable geometry, for the Western powers, like the Chinese bourgeoisie, turned a blind eye to the fact that Shanghai at the time was not only one of the most lively cities in the world, both economically and culturally; it was also a paradise for gambling, weapons and opium trafficking, and a hub for Western prostitute-trading, spying and myriad different kinds of fraud and corruption.

The powerful made accommodation with this extraordinary underworld: Yu Qiaqing, president of the Chinese Chamber of Commerce, was simultaneously a major businessman and a senior figure in the Green Gang (*Qing Bang)*, the all-powerful secret society that pulled the strings in this astonishing shadow puppet theatre. The head of this criminal organization, Du Yuesheng, had a powerful "blood brother", Félix Bouvier: the owner of both the Canidrome, Shanghai's greyhound racing track, and the Grand Monde Casino, where exiled Russian princesses, American arms dealers and Japanese spies played for high stakes, as immortalized in the 1932 film *Shanghai Express*.

"Mister Du", the Al Capone of Shanghai, also drew into his clan of influential characters people like the young nationalist general and future leader of the Republic, Chiang Kai-shek, and Étienne Fiori, who had previously worked as an intelligence officer in Morocco, and was now both head of the French Concession's Special Police Bureau and active in the criminal activities of the Corsican mafia, which was in cahoots with the Green Gang.

A short, swarthy man with slicked-back hair and a crooked smile, Fiori's principal criminal involvement was with the "Grande Combine", a white slave network that consisted of Corsicans "Shanghai'ing" young French girls and sending them to the largest brothel in the world, in exchange for opium bricks sent by Mister Du to Marseille.[1] But this trade was hardly reserved for the export market. Huge quantities were consumed in Shanghai's 800 opium dens, to which people were guided by some 3,000 "vagabonds", as the henchmen of the Green Gang were called.

This diseased, corrupt world was starting to provoke an immune response. Influenced by the Russian Revolution and their professors, young Chinese people—students at the Aurora University and members of the nascent Rickshaw Association union—were determined that the East would soon turn red.

Mao dodges the French police

In July 1921, twelve delegates representing fifty-seven militants from different provinces all over China met at a supposedly secret location, in the house of one delegate's relative: 160 Wantz Road in the French Concession.

In the small, dimly lit, smoky salon, ashtrays were passed around and tea was served before the participants launched into debates with two emissaries from the Comintern, "Maring" and "Nikolsky". "Maring", in fact a Dutch man called Henricus Sneevliet, communicated Moscow's position: it was an excellent idea to establish a communist party, but it was vital that it aligned with the Kuomintang, the nationalist party founded by Dr Sun Yat-sen to carry out the democratic revolution begun ten years previously with the overthrow of the last Manchu emperor. The first three days of discussion continued late into the night, relocating to the dormitory of the girls' school on Rue Auguste-Boppe, where the delegates eventually slept after these exhausting sessions (the schoolgirls were on holiday).

On the evening of a fourth day of fiery debate, a strange-looking man knocked at the front door, claiming that he was looking for someone called Li or Zhang, both very common names. Then, apologizing that he had the wrong address, he turned on his heels and left.

It was one of Fiori's police officers. Following the Russian envoy Maring's advice, the delegates made a hasty getaway, "like mice, with their hands on their ears", as a Chinese expression puts it. Their instincts were correct: ten minutes later Chinese policemen, led by a French officer, burst into the house.

The history of the Chinese Communist Party had barely even begun and it had already exposed a shadowy web of informants, secret police and spies.

Chinese people tend towards fatalism rather than growing discouraged. The following day, in the absence of the two Comintern representatives, the delegates relocated their meeting to a pleasure boat, which they sailed around a lake in Zhejiang, a province to the southwest of Shanghai. The motions proposed were as plain-spoken as Confucian aphorisms; they debated them while watching wild cranes in flight and the delicate gait of elegant ladies carrying parasols as they took their afternoon constitutionals.

Against this enchanting background, they ratified their decisions on this fifth day of talks, and baptized their new movement the Chinese Communist Party (CCP, or *Gongchandang* in Pinyin). Based on the Russian model, the younger version adopted a straightforward programme: to set up a red army, topple the bourgeoisie and establish a rule of the proletariat in which private property and class differences would be abolished. As Comrade "Lie-Ning" (Lenin) had insisted, each communist party had to be organized around the principle of "democratic centralism", within which factions were not tolerated, and professional revolutionaries were bound by a framework of iron discipline.

The leader of these Chinese Bolsheviks was an elected general secretary, a brilliant intellectual inspired by Enlightenment philosophy and the French Revolution of 1789: Chen Duxiu. Among the younger delegates, one man from Changsha, capital of Hunan province, was known for his brilliance and his reserve. In the future he would come to be known as Mao Zedong, "Red Sun", and he had almost ended up in a French prison.

The Comintern would have preferred the CCP to have chosen someone with greater flexibility than this young tub-thumper: someone open to the idea of a "united front" with the Kuomintang, for example. Nonetheless, Moscow agreed to provide for the needs and education of the new party as it suited it. Meanwhile, towards the end of 1921, Maring, who bore a certain distrust towards this group of intellectuals, met with Sun Yat-sen, who had established his government in the south, in Canton (modern-day Guangzhou). He offered

Dr Sun Moscow's aid, and even, without consulting his Chinese comrades, that of the CCP. This marked the beginning of the entente cordiale between the Kuomintang and the future USSR. The latter's objective, according to Lenin, was to unite a greater China, which had been ravaged by warlords, through a left-leaning government whose alliance would break the political isolation that plagued the nascent USSR.

The CCP—despite chafing at the bit, eager to start the revolution there and then—held back, encouraged by the promise of an even brighter future. Yet there was a moment when it seemed like this might never come to pass. Who was it who had betrayed the Party's inaugural meeting? And how to resolve the mystery, other than by setting up an investigation and creating a small spy network? This book is no less than the story of how that embryonic structure would one day become the biggest secret service network in the world.

Luo Yinong, a young student who came, like Mao, from Hunan, and who would later be sent to Moscow to be trained in the art of espionage and revolutionary insurrection, took charge of the inquiry into the infiltration of the Party meeting. This revealed that the intrusion of the French police had a simple explanation, and that the Comintern was to blame.[2] It seemed that two young emissaries from the Comintern's youth organization, bringing subsidies for their Chinese comrades, had been shadowed by Fiori's agents since their arrival in Shanghai. As far as can be ascertained, they were Henri Lozeray and Jacques Doriot, both from Saint-Denis, a suburb to the north of Paris. Realizing that they were being tailed by the police, the young men were careful to take a circuitous route on their way to joining the other delegates at the meeting. But their liaison agent must have been less prudent.

After they returned to France, via Moscow, these two men helped set up the Paris branch of the CCP, and, as we shall see, assisted a well-known militant, the true founding father of the original Chinese communist secret service. But let us leave them for the time being, as they board a ship to Vladivostok and then the Trans-Siberian express to Paris, via Moscow and Berlin.[3]

The Soviets' Chinese networks

The Soviets, meanwhile, as we shall see, did not remain idle. In Moscow, their secret service, the Cheka, set up by the Polish-born Felix Dzerjinsky, had as its emblem a gladiator sword and shield. The sword's razor-sharp blade represented the Cheka's highly efficient foreign intelligence service, the INO.[4] The shield represented the political police, whose job was to eliminate counter-revolutionaries and imperialist spies within Russia, beginning with those from the British Intelligence Service and the Deuxième Bureau (France's external military intelligence agency). The Cheka was conducting a ruthless war against both services. At stake was the very survival of the revolutionary state, which was surrounded by an ever-tightening circle of anti-Bolsheviks.

Since the beginning of the 1920s, the Cheka, renamed the GPU in 1922, had been investing hugely in China, with two objectives. The first was the recruitment of Chinese agents to inform Moscow of the intentions of, variously, warlords, the imperial powers who owned the Concessions, exiled White Russians preparing their return, Kuomintang nationalists, and informers who were traitors to the revolution. It was a huge programme. The Cheka's sponsoring of the security services of both the nascent CCP and the Kuomintang was also a strategy for controlling them.

The Cheka was not the only organization operating behind the scenes. At the same time, the Red Army's intelligence service, the Razvedoupr (better known as the GRU), headed by General Arvid Seibot, was also active. In every country in the world, the GRU was monitoring military potential as well as overseeing the military sections of the communist parties, which were themselves born of the Red Army. The Latvian-born Jan Berzin, head of the 3rd Directorate (Espionage), was soon to become head of the GRU, and would go on to intensify operations in Asia. In China, following an agreement with Sun Yat-sen, this sizeable service—which is still active today, under the same name—also oversaw, in an advisory capacity, the Huangpu Military Academy, which had been set up by Chinese nationalists. In 1927 the military attaché to the Soviet embassy in Guangdong was Colonel Semion Aralov, who had been the first head of the GRU in 1918, under Trotsky.

We have already heard of the third Russian organization present in China, more outwardly political than the Cheka or the GRU: the Comintern, founded in 1919 to foment the world revolution. Its clandestine activities were organized by the International Liaison Service (OMS), led by an old revolutionary called Iossip Piatnitsky. These activities included the transfer of funds and financing of parties, unions and committees, and the training of agents in clandestine skills, including encryption and broadcast of wireless messages, forging of documents, and developing cover stories for secret agents.[5]

The organization of the Soviet espionage service in China was taking shape. The first *rezident* of the Cheka in Beijing, Aristarkh Rylski (real name Aristarkh Riguin), was replaced in 1922 by the Armenian diplomat–spy Yakov Davtian, who undertook several missions to France under the name "Jean Jan". Not long after his arrival in Beijing, Davtian complained to his superior Meyer Trilisser, head of the INO in Moscow, that he was being weighed down by the enormous amount of work he faced. "The workload, though extremely interesting, is incredibly heavy and challenging. One has to demonstrate a great sense of responsibility. The distance from Moscow, the poor quality of the liaisons, the mutual incomprehension with the Centre—everything complicates our work. I have never worked so hard in my life—even at the INO—as I do here and my nerves have never been under such severe strain."

But Comrade Davtian reluctantly put a brave face on it, because China was, as he said, "the hub of world politics, not just world imperialism's Achilles heel but also ours". And even if Riguin and Davtian did not get on particularly well, the INO "residences", or intelligence stations, in Beijing, Tianjin, Mukden, Changchun, Harbin, Canton and Shanghai were thriving, as evidenced by the encouraging report penned by Davtian a year after his arrival: "The work is going well. If you have been following the documents that I have been sending, you will see that I have succeeded in extending our network all over China, meaning that nothing important can happen without us being alerted. Our network of contacts is expanding. Overall I can say that none of the White Russians living in the Far East can get by unnoticed. I know everything that happens, often even before it has actually taken place."[6]

On 11 February 1923, Davtian sent a message to the Centre, as Moscow intelligence headquarters is known: "I have significantly expanded our activities. We now have appropriate Residences in Shanghai, Tianjin, Beijing and Mukden. I have set up a significant administrative apparatus in Harbin. We have plans to infiltrate the Japanese intelligence service, and a wide network of informers in Shanghai."[7]

In Beijing, Soviet military intelligence (the GRU) was officially represented by General Anatoli Gekker, who was the Soviet Embassy's military attaché there until 1925. One of Gekker's official missions at the time was to help the Russian military advisors attached to the Kuomintang army to oversee the creation of a nationalist military intelligence training corps, and supervise an intelligence service nicknamed the "College" *(Zhongxue)*, run by a senior figure in the Kuomintang, a former teacher called Tan Pin-san.[8] The Soviets were thus overseeing both the nascent Chinese communist intelligence service and that of the nationalists, whose leader, Sun Yat-sen, continued to support an alliance with Moscow up until his death in March 1925.

This formally present military apparatus was just the tip of the iceberg. In practice, the great majority of GRU intelligence in China, like Cheka/GPU intelligence in the USSR, was collected by "illegals": undercover secret agents, whether roaming or permanently stationed. Traces of them can be found in the hundreds of French intelligence reports I have consulted, through which I have been able to create a real *Who's Who* of Russian espionage in China in the 1920s and 1930s. This has been a fairly complicated undertaking, given that we are talking about a world where everyone had multiple aliases, false names and "fake-genuine" passports, which abound in the archives of the French Consulates in Shanghai and Tianjin from the interwar period.

It was by no means only in China, in the French Concessions and the International Settlements of Shanghai and Hong Kong, that the Chinese Communist Party was establishing its underground network. In Paris, too, young militants on a work–study programme were being schooled in undercover techniques. They had to brave the French police force, the counterintelligence service and the external military intelligence service that had been instructed to root them out. Decorated with First World War medals, Police Chiefs Louis Ducloux and Charles Faux-Pas-Bidet from the Sûreté (French security service) and Colonel Henri Lainey, head of the counterintelligence and intelligence service (SCR), had to shift the focus of their work to combatting the rising tide of Bolshevism and its agents. The so-called "yellow peril" was still to come, but the political unrest in China and Indochina demanded a high level of vigilance and was a matter of great concern for the French Empire in Asia. For the militants from the Far East, learning how to foil the tails and traps mounted by master spies in the streets of Paris, Lyon and Marseille meant that they were already playing a role in this war of shadows.

Zhou Enlai's Hakkas come to Paris

China's Hakkas used to be a nomadic people; hence their name, which means "guest families". Over the course of many centuries, they fled the Mongols and sought refuge: on the plains of central China, south of the Yellow River, by the Pearl River in Hong Kong, in Canton, and elsewhere. They were as brave in battle as they were adventurous in their travels. Many left China. They constitute a distinct ethnic group, with their impenetrable dialect, and symbols and rituals very different from those of the rest of the Chinese diaspora. During the Qing dynasty of 1644-1912, their luxuriant hair was testimony to the fact that they refused to express allegiance to the Manchu conquerors by shaving their heads and keeping only a single plait. Women had the same rights as men, at least in terms of the right to work in the fields. A Hakka bowed down to no one. A Hakka was indomitable.

One sign of this was the fact that, unlike other Chinese peoples, Hakka fathers did not force their daughters to have their feet bound and atrophied in order to turn them into objects of desire. When they reached adulthood, Hakka women married only other Hakkas, for the bourgeois of Shanghai, the Mandarins of Beijing and the farmers of Changsha considered them hideous, with their "enormous" feet. The Hakkas are proud people. The legendary Hong Xiuquan, flamboyant leader of the Taiping Rebellion (1850-64), was a Hakka. Hong's vision was the establishment of a heavenly kingdom of peace on earth. This revolutionary spark triggered a civil war; according to the brothers Élisée and Onésime Reclus, France's most famous geographers at the time, the subsequent repression led to the loss of between 12 and 15 million lives in China.[9] The Taiping saga horrified the entire world and inspired Jules Verne to create a character called Wang, a philosopher, in *The Tribulations of a Chinaman in China*.

Had the men of the interwar French Special Branch and military intelligence officers actually read the anarchist Reclus brothers or Jules Verne? We can't know, but they had certainly been following the tribulations of the Chinese in France in July 1922. Whilst no doubt ignorant of the complex history of the Hakkas, detectives were keeping the effervescent world of France's Chinese student–workers under constant surveillance. Many of the Chinese students were engaged in propaganda in the diaspora for the defence of academic freedom, and they joined both the nationalist Kuomintang led by Sun Yat-sen, himself a Hakka, and a new group that had infiltrated them: the CCP, established in Shanghai with money from Moscow and help from the communists Doriot and Lozeray.

Under assumed names, these young Chinese in Paris engaged in clandestine activities, operating in secret cells. One of these Hakkas was little "Ten" from Sichuan, with a baby face and jet black hair flying in the wind—he was none other than the future Deng Xiaoping, who worked in the Renault factory and was nicknamed "Mister Mimeograph", because he spent his evenings printing out *New Youth* and *Red Dawn*, underground Chinese-language pamphlets. Who would have imagined then that he would become president of the People's Republic of China sixty years later? Or that, among the Hakkas in the Paris communist circle, there were no fewer than three future marshals of the People's Liberation Army? This trio would play a role in every chapter of the history of the secret services: Chen Yi, Ye Jianying and Zhu De.[10]

According to French secret police reports, the young communist Hakkas met for the first time in spring 1922, at the apartment of Henri Lozeray, alias "Gardon": 15 rue Goncourt, in Paris's 11th arrondissement. Lozeray, who worked as a typesetter, was head of colonial affairs in the Communist Youth, and though he had just missed the birth of the CCP in Shanghai, he was in the front row for the baptism of its European branch. The meeting in his apartment was organized by another Renault employee, a lathe operator nicknamed "Wu Hao". The future leader of Vietnam, Ho Chi Minh, was also there, under his given name, Nguyen Ai Quoc; the police had already built up a fat dossier on him, dating back to his attendance at the founding meeting of the French Communist Party. He worked retouching photographs and mending china, and went by the alias "Ferdinand". Ferdinand was in fact a Comintern agent, and his friendship with the Breton Jean Cremet, a rising star in the French Communist Party, did not fool the authorities as to his additional, clandestine involvement in the struggle.[11]

The Sûreté inspectors also staked out a building at 17 rue Godefroy, in the Gobelins neighbourhood of Paris near the Place d'Italie, where a small Chinatown was growing up. A young man calling himself Mr Stephen Knight, who dressed like an English gentleman and held a British passport, lived on the second floor. He claimed to be a businessman from Hong Kong. His description matched that of the Wu Hao who had been at Lozeray's apartment, and they were indeed one and the same person: the son of a bureaucrat from Zhejiang, southwest of Shanghai, a young man who had become radicalized early on. His real name was Zhou Enlai. Having broken off relations with his family, he had spent time in Japan before coming to Europe. In November 1920, Zhou, alias "Wu Hao", arrived in Marseille on board the *Bordeaux*, a French merchant ship. With a natural instinct for clandestine activity, for two years he ran Chinese communist cells in France, Belgium and Germany. After the occupation of the Chinese Legation in Paris by student–workers, the police arrested him, but, unaware of his true identity, merely decided to escort him to Marseille, from where he was to be expelled from France and sent back to China. He managed to jump unseen from the moving train in open countryside, and thus escaped his guards. The "revolutionary mandarin" was already proving himself a skilled escape artist.

Zhou surrounded himself with faithful Hakka comrades, also gifted in clandestine activity, and became close to a young man called Nie Rongzhen who, like Deng Xiaoping, hailed from Sichuan. He had studied with Deng at the University of Grenoble and then at Charleroi in Belgium, where he fell under the influence of Belgian socialists. Recruited by Zhou for his scientific mind, he was expert in encryption and wireless messaging. He worked as an engineer with Creusot and Renault. He would later became a marshal in the People's Liberation Army, and one of the founding fathers of the atomic bomb.

It is worth remembering that these Hakkas and future marshals, and the rest of the group that formed around Zhou, along with their children, will continue to feature in this singular tale, all the way up to the present day.

French counterintelligence did not depend only on informers. Pen-pushers at 11 rue des Saussaies in Paris were making shrewd estimations. They realized that Moscow must be subsidizing the Chinese, with French Comintern agents acting as intermediaries.

A seasoned radical named Suzanne Girault was responsible for transferring the money. Born in Switzerland, where she first met Lenin, she had worked as a primary school teacher in Russia, where she was recruited in 1919 by the International Liaison Service of the Comintern, the OMS. This was how she came to be responsible for handing over tidy sums to various revolutionary groups, including the Chinese, as was clear from documents seized by the French police during a search of her home, after a spy ring led by Jean Cremet was uncovered in 1927.

In summer 1924, Zhou Enlai returned to China. It was not until he reached Hong Kong that the French police discovered who it was who had been hiding behind the alias Stephen Knight, and that the English gentleman and the Chinese labourer Wu Hao were one and the same man.

The spies who inspired Man's Fate

Zhou Enlai arrived in Hong Kong on 1 September 1924. From there he continued on to Canton, where he joined the corps of officers running the Huangpu Military Academy, created at the instigation of the Russians and Sun Yat-sen, to participate in the formation of a nationalist army to fight the warlords of northern China.

Various comrades from his time in Europe joined him there, including Ye Jianying, Chen Yi and Nie Rongzhen. The academy was under the tutelage of Mikhail Borodin, permanent representative of the Comintern to China, and General Blücher, head of the Soviet military advisory mission. The CCP was gaining wisdom with age. With a membership of 30,000, it had joined forces with the Kuomintang, and several high-profile figures of the communist movement—such as Chen Duxiu and Mao Zedong—became part of the joint leadership, although it was dominated by nationalists.

Clearly, this double affiliation within the burgeoning national army led to a certain amount of ambiguity, with the "officer factory" at Huangpu training both communists and nationalists. Borodin had chosen a promising young general, Chiang Kai-shek, to run the school, with Zhou Enlai as head of the political department. Also in Borodin's entourage was another familiar gaunt figure from the Paris period: Nguyen Ai Quoc, the future Ho Chi Minh. The honeymoon between nationalists and communists reached its apotheosis when the head of the Academy and chief of the National Revolutionary Army, Chiang Kai-shek, sent his son, Chiang Ching-kuo, to study in Moscow.

This was rather surprising, considering that Chiang Kai-shek had set upon a secret plan: having defeated the warlords, he decided it was now time to get the communists out of the way. The Chinese bourgeoisie would have no scruples about supporting him, especially since the communists had been independently organizing major strikes in Canton, Hong Kong and Shanghai. When the mass strike in Canton began in 1926, Chiang decided to punish the communists. The arrest of Zhou Enlai and other leaders was a warning shot. Chen Duxiu, the CCP chief, thought that the communists needed to distance themselves from the nationalists, although Borodin, speaking in "his master's voice" (in other words, Stalin's), did not agree.

This did not prevent Borodin from taking precautions: in October 1926 he sent his bodyguard, Gu Shunzhang, to Vladivostok, to familiarize himself with espionage and revolutionary insurrection techniques. Comrade Gu was a quite extraordinary character: born in 1902 on the wrong side of the tracks in Shanghai, he spent his adolescence hanging around bars, smoking opium, having affairs with women, learning the ways of the underworld and being sworn into the Green Gang. He became a brilliant illusionist called Hua Guangqi, performing his wildly popular show in famous nightclubs and casinos such as the Grand Monde and the Sincere Department Store. Who would have suspected that Gu the magician had secretly joined the CCP?

After his return from the USSR, Gu, along with Kang Sheng, the new leader of the Shanghai district party, organized a communist patrol as protection against the increasing threat posed by the Kuomintang.

In March 1927, Chiang Kai-shek, head of the Kuomintang, established his army and government in Nanjing, the southern capital. Within weeks, on 12 April 1927, everything began to fall apart for the communists. Chiang had outflanked them. The massacre that took place was, as the American journalist Harold Isaacs titled his book, "the tragedy of the Chinese revolution". The young writer André Malraux was later to base his novel *Man's Fate* on these tragic events.

As the CCP was planning an insurrection, several thousand criminals from the Green Gang set about the slaughter of communist militants and sympathizers. The authorities and police in the foreign Concessions averted their eyes from the bloodbath that was taking place outside their walls in the Chinese quarter. Zhou Enlai, Luo Yinong, Gu Shunzhang and Kang Sheng managed to hide in the French Concession, where they spent their days planning the reorganization of the Party as they waited for things to calm down. Elsewhere in China, the picture was hardly more cheering: in September, in Hunan, Mao Zedong led the disastrous Autumn Harvest insurrection, whose few survivors later took refuge in the mountainous desert region of Jiangxi before founding their own red army. Then, in December 1927, another insurrection, the Canton Uprising, was crushed; some 15,000 communists were massacred.

The double game of Captain Pick

The situation was a catastrophe for the Soviets. Not only had the CCP been decimated in several large Chinese cities in the wake of its disastrous policy of allegiance with the Kuomintang, followed by a series of bold insurrections intended to make people forget this compromise; but worse, the Chinese police had burst into the Soviet embassy in Beijing, arresting diplomats and seizing cartloads of archives. The police also arrested the new head of the CCP, Li Dazhao, the "Chinese Lenin", who had taken refuge there. He was executed without trial on 28 April 1927.

Huge numbers of the Embassy documents have been amassed and decrypted, detailing the ways in which the Comintern and the Soviet government set up networks of secret organizations in China. We know today that the discovery of this setup owes a great deal to the interception of communications, uncommon at the time, by the British, who were already experts in the field. The organization responsible for wiretapping, the Government Communications and Cypher School (GC&CS), had set up wiretapping stations in every large garrison town across the British Empire from 1920. In China, these stations were located in Hong Kong and Shanghai.[12]

The humiliation suffered by Moscow only increased when Dai Li, the head of Chiang Kai-shek's intelligence service, had the documents translated and published as a book of selected extracts from the communications of the Soviet spies.[13] A report sent to Paris by the French intelligence service, which also consulted the documents, summarized the wealth of information that had been seized, and the naivety of the Soviet cadres who had neither encrypted nor destroyed the files after they had finished with them:

> Document numbers 7, 8, 9, 10, 11, 12, 13 and 14 deal with Soviet espionage and counterintelligence. N°7, dated 1925, outlines the general organization of the intelligence service in the south; among other things it reveals that at the time the Soviets were already preparing to send secret agents to Hanoi and Haiphong, Macao and Hong Kong. N°8 is a report on intelligence gathering in Kwantong [Guangdong, region of Canton] in November 1925.
>
> N[os] 9, 10 and 11 deal with counterintelligence in Kwantong and offer interesting information about the creation, development, organization and functioning of an organization in Canton that was closely modelled on the Russian GPU (Cheka).[14]

And since bad news often comes in twos, so it was that in May 1927, an agent considered one of the most important figures of the GRU in China defected. The Shanghai Municipal Police's Irish-born Chief Detective Inspector Pat Givens must have been thrilled to be able to "debrief" and "turn" this experienced GRU officer. But who was Evgeny

Mikhailovich Kojevnikov, also known as "Morskoy", "Dorodin", "Hovans" and "Captain Pick"?[15]

His public persona was that of a Tsarist officer who had backed the Bolshevik Revolution of 1917, before joining Borodin in China. From 1926 onwards he worked for the head of the GRU in Beijing. But in fact he had been recruited months earlier by Givens and was secretly reporting everything he knew about the activities of undercover spies employed at the Russo-Asian bank Dalbank, the role of correspondents for the press agency Tass, and Chinese communist activists.

His role as a double agent—one might call him an intelligence swindler—was detailed in a statement given some years later by Gu Shunzhang, the magician who became one of the most important figures in the CCP's intelligence service: "At the time I was Borodin's bodyguard, and a secret service agent in Hangzhou and Wuhan. I discovered that Eugène Pick, who worked for Borodin as a warrant officer, had stolen from his boss a notebook and a report about foreign ships docked in Hangzhou, and sold them to the French consul. Pick was working as a spy for several foreign consulates."[16]

Pick told his British handlers that on 18 April 1927 he had received orders from Borodin to have Chiang Kai-shek—responsible for the recent slaughter of communists in Shanghai—assassinated, and that, on 1 May, he had received a counterorder from the INO *rezident*, S.L. Wilde. It would appear that he let his guard down and was unmasked, for two weeks later, according to a leaked French counterintelligence report, Pick was almost kidnapped by a commando unit led by a certain "Pockmarked Chen".

It was under his pen name "Captain Eugène Pick" that the Russian defector compiled *China in the Grip of Bolsheviks*, in which he divulged a list of dozens of Soviet operatives active in China.[17] There is no doubt that references to these agents, often accompanied by anti-Semitic allusions, were not written by Pick alone, but were the fruit of a collaboration between the British, French and Kuomintang secret services. Indeed, according to Russian archives, Pick was no more than a low-ranking subaltern who had been drafted as an informer by British Intelligence from the start.[18]

It barely mattered. This blisteringly polemical publication was a powerful propaganda weapon. The book, which had a considerable impact all over the world, bolstered the image of Chiang Kai-shek as poised to bring down the "Red Dragon". André Malraux drew on Pick's book for certain episodes in his *Man's Fate*, including the failed assassination attempt on Chiang and some elements of the Baron Clapique character (note the similarity of the Baron's name to that of the Captain). In 1933 Malraux won the Prix Goncourt. The same year, Hergé was working on a Tintin book, *The Blue Lotus*, in which Dawson, the unlikeable chief of the British Police Force who is persecuting the young reporter Tintin, bears a remarkable similarity to Pat Givens. It was Givens the Irishman who, until 1936, was responsible for rooting out communist agents, for which he received the Order of Brilliant Jade from Chiang Kai-shek himself in recognition of his loyal service. It was also Givens, head of Special Branch, who had manipulated the entire Pick affair from beginning to end. As we shall see, Malraux embellished his novel's plot with anecdotes that he heard from another communist defector whom he met in Shanghai in 1931: the deputy general secretary of the French Communist Party, Jean Cremet.

Special operations

The inscrutable "Zhao Rong", alias Kang Sheng, was one of several CCP leaders who went to ground in the French Concession, which Dai Li's nationalist police were not authorized to enter—even when the chief spy of the Kuomintang came to ask the corrupt police chief Étienne Fiori and his Chinese police inspectors for their assistance. (The latter were allowed to enter the International Settlement thanks to Givens's Special Branch.) Chief Inspector Huang Jirong was, like Dai Li, a member of the Green Gang. "Pockmarked Huang", as he was nicknamed, would surely have been proud to know that he was the inspiration for the main character in Josef von Sternberg's film *Shanghai Express*, with Marlene Dietrich in the role of the bewitching Shanghai Lily.

Kang Sheng did leave the French Concession to see another film, a Harold Lloyd picture, at the Carlton Theatre on Park Road. This served as a cover for his secret assignation with "Wu Hao", who was preparing to leave for the USSR on a mission. Wu Hao was of course the indefatigable Zhou Enlai, who handed over responsibility for the secret service to Kang for the duration of his absence. The young intellectual, son of a landowner from northern Shandong—homeland of Confucius—wasted no time, since Luo Yinong had given him the task of establishing networks and infiltrating the enemy.[19]

While communists were being shot and decapitated in the Chinese district of Zhabei, Kang managed to pull off the infiltration of the century. This highly cultivated, well-turned-out young man became personal secretary to Yu Qiaqing, president of the Chamber of Commerce, with the aid of servants also originally from Shandong, who helped him find a job with the wealthy businessman. Yu was a member of the Green Gang, and, like all the other stalwarts of industry, finance and commerce, sided with the boss, his friend Du Yuesheng, who had given the green light for the murder of communists as demanded by Chiang Kai-shek.

As they drank tea, smoked opium and chatted about their flourishing businesses, Yu and Du had no reason to suspect that the young intellectual in gold-rimmed spectacles, handwriting sales orders and invoices in the next room, was the head of a communist spy ring. How could they have known he was the very person responsible for setting up a new network, in preparation for the communist revenge?

In August 1927, Zhou Enlai and his wife, Deng Yingchao, left Shanghai for Dalian disguised as a pair of antique dealers. From there they took the train for Moscow. Under the alias Chen Guang, Zhou moved with his young wife into the Hotel Lux, a crumbling palace that hosted heads of the Comintern and secret agents preparing to leave on mission, including the Frenchman Jean Cremet (room 27) and the German Richard Sorge (room 19). To further cover his tracks, Zhou was also given a Russian moniker, "Moskvin".[20]

Soon after their arrival in Moscow, the couple were sent for espionage training at the GRU spy school on Lenin Hills, where they learned the latest spy skills, coding and wireless broadcast techniques.[21] In spring 1928, the two "antique dealers" took part in the Chinese Communist Party Congress held in a Moscow suburb, inside a GPU-owned sanatorium. Stalin claimed it was organized outside China for security reasons, but no one fell for this: it was a clever way for Moscow to retain control of the Chinese sister party's new direction. Eighty-four delegates took part, along with 100 observers, most of them students at Moscow's Sun Yat-sen University, where young Chinese people were inducted into the joys of Marxism-Leninism. The Congress reluctantly backed the main tactics of the Comintern leadership, which had met just before to hammer out its strategy: "The Party must prepare for a new revolutionary dynamic. The principal mission that currently falls to the Chinese Communist Party is the conquest of the masses. No more playing with uprisings … The Party must control the activities of partisan detachments, and consider that these units will serve as a basis for a vast mass movement that will extend to all the Chinese people."[22]

In other words, the CCP—which, in spite of significant losses, now had 40,000 members—should encourage the setting up of military organizations in both cities and the countryside. Although Mao Zedong, who first set up the rural bases, was absent, the way was now open for his Long March to power in twenty years' time. In the meantime, Zhou Enlai and the "urban" leaders Li Lisan, Zhang Guotao and Xiang Zhongfa were to return to China with the following objective: to create an efficient combat structure, with the secret services as the vanguard.

When he came back to Shanghai in November 1928, Zhou Enlai took over the transformation of the small protection service there, now renamed the "Central Committee Special Branch" (*Zhongyang Teke*), or Teke for short, to carry out "special operations" work (*Tewu Gongzuo*).[23] Gu Shunzhang, the magician, was conjured up to supervise these missions alongside Zhou, flanked by the new CCP general secretary, a former mariner called Xiang Zhongfa, who had been leader of the Red Gang (*Hong Bang*), a Triad, or traditional secret society, and bitter rival of the Green Gang.

The Teke established secret bases across the whole of China, including Hong Kong. But Shanghai remained at the heart of this underground war. One Chinese specialist of international affairs told me in 2008 that intelligence officers still considered—not without a certain nostalgia—that there was a direct link between today's service and the original organization founded by Zhou Enlai at this time. The Teke was comprised of four sections: the 1st Section was responsible for close protection of leaders, making available apartments where they could sleep and organizing meetings; the 2nd was responsible for intelligence and counterintelligence; the 3rd, the "Red Guard", was a squadron whose advance guard was known as the "dog-beating squads" *(Dagou Dui)* and dealt with the elimination of traitors. Lastly, the 4th section was responsible for communication.

From this time on, under Kang Sheng's leadership the Teke also became principally responsible for security, a secret police force tasked with surveillance of its own party. Kang excelled at spying on his own friends. The writer and novelist Han Suyin, daughter of a Hakka-origin Chinese father and a Belgian mother, first sat down to interview Zhou Enlai in 1956 for a biography that she eventually published nearly thirty years later. Her description of this police function is very telling:

> The Teke kept records of every member of the Party, gathered all kinds of information, punished betrayals, managed radio stations. It also organized protection teams and vigilante commandos who carried out extra-judicial killings of those who were suspected of betraying the interests of the Party, of allowing leaks of information or of having caused the arrest or death of comrades.
>
> Secrecy, a characteristic which Zhou had begun cultivating during his stay in Paris, became an essential element of the communist structure.[24]

To prevent leaks, Teke agents were not allowed to have any kind of relationship with other party militants. The organization was so compartmentalized that even its name was not known. For residents of Shanghai, it was known by the macabre name "Wu Hao's dagger"; few will have got the reference to Zhou's nom de guerre. But the name was clearly justified by the violence with which the Teke executioners assassinated dissidents, resistance fighters, deserters and other opponents. Kang Sheng and Gu Shunzhang's men did not stop at killing traitors or informers: they would massacre the entire family. In this, they were not so very different from Chiang Kai-shek's henchmen, but they also revived an ancient Chinese tradition of exquisitely refined torture, the principle being that the more slowly the death is administered, the more it will inspire terror.

The jewel in the Teke's crown was the 2nd Section, responsible for intelligence and infiltration. Multiple connections branched out, exploiting the famous *guanxi*—relationships based on family, community and geography—to infiltrate Shanghai's powerful cultural and artistic milieus. Within this world, the Teke constituted a small army of messengers, people smugglers, and informers. The eyes and ears of Wu Hao were focused on martial arts clubs, cultural and religious groups, the worlds of music, theatre and cinema, "flower girl" brothels, and Russian cabarets where some of the "*polusky* girls" were "white of skin but red of heart". Kang Sheng, though obsessed with antique Chinese eroticism from the Ming era, was also a habitué of the modern world of Shanghai's film studios. This was where he met up with a childhood friend from Shandong, possibly a former lover, now a cinema starlet called Lan Ping ("Blue Apple"). Later she became rather more famous as Jiang Qing, better known as Madame Mao.

By exploiting all these adroitly woven threads, a spider's web of connections, the clandestine CCP system set itself an ambitious goal: to use the endemic corruption in the city to infiltrate Chiang Kai-shek's Kuomintang and the foreign police forces.

Gemo spies on the counterattack

Chiang Kai-shek is generally seen as a fine tactician and a peerless political animal, who successfully supplanted his rivals within the Kuomintang, but as a weak strategist. He may have won the battle for Shanghai for now. But would he be able to conquer the north? Unify China at the expense of the communists? Win the war? It was already shaping up to be a protracted conflict, according to the embryonic theory being developed by Mao, who would come to be recognized in the long term as the better strategist of the two.

In any case, the Generalissimo—or "Gemo", as he was commonly known—had crushed the communists in Shanghai and intended to pursue the country's reunification by conquering the north. If he was to succeed in governing the entire country, Chiang was going to have to rely on master spies as fierce and implacable as their enemies. The Gemo's closest comrades were two brothers, Chen Guo-fu and Chen Li-fu. They were, like him, from Zhejiang, with links to the Green Gang, and responsible for the political intelligence of both the Kuomintang and the Blue Shirts, a militia group inspired by European fascist movements.[25]

The most powerful of the Gemo's service heads was Dai Li. Born in 1897 in the Year of the Rooster, he too was from Zhejiang. Like the Chen brothers, he had lost his father at a young age, and by the time he was fourteen had become a foot soldier in the service of a warlord. He ended up at the Huangpu Military Academy, where he befriended several communists before later becoming their executioner.

Dai set up a new secret service, the Bureau of Investigation and Statistics (*Diaocha Tongzhi)*, which, when it was subsequently reorganized and put under the control of the military, was renamed the *Juntong*, though it was still known to the wider public as the "BIS". A trusted member of the Green Gang, Dai became captain of the military police in 1927 and played a key role in the collapse of the communists in Shanghai. Friendly and polite with a face described as "squirrel-headed", Dai was capable of appalling brutality. Throughout China, talk was rampant of the torture suffered by those who fell into his hands, including being given heroin overdoses. All of which earned him his nickname abroad, the "Chinese Himmler". Rumours spread, wildly amplified by communist propaganda, which may be explained by the fact that several prominent communist prisoners had chosen "submission" and defection over dying in excruciating agony.

Nowadays, more balanced biographies have been written about Dai Li.[26] He is credited with having set up a network of 100,000 agents in China, and of having organized a vast machine whose tentacular system extended well beyond China, thanks to another former Huangpu officer, General Tang Yueh-liang, who organized the international secret service using a network of military attachés. A system of influence was built up, with Soong May-ling, Chiang Kai-shek's wife, at its head. It aimed to make Roosevelt's USA shift from its position of neutrality to supporting the Kuomintang against the Japanese. Dai Li was also a pioneer in intercepting communications. With the help of an American encryption and decryption expert, Herbert O. Yardley, he was able to set up a state-of-the-art service. During the 1920s, it was largely the ability of Chiang Kai-shek's services to intercept communications that enabled him to crush the warlords. The only problem was that this highly sophisticated service was riddled with communist agents.

Chen Geng and the Breton of Shanghai

With hindsight, it cannot be denied that Stalin's policy of dispersing the CCP for a time within the Kuomintang was beneficial to communist espionage. Some militants never identified themselves as communists and remained hidden, like moles, within the labyrinthine nationalist structures: the Blue Shirts, the BIS, the national army, the communication service, and so on.

This deep penetration was controlled by Chen Geng, a militant at the head of the 2nd Section—the Teke's secret intelligence service. Born in Hunan in 1904 in the Year of the Dragon, to a wealthy landowning family, he was, thanks to a personal tutor, well read in Confucian philosophy, including the virtues of "filial piety". This had not prevented him from running away from home at the age of thirteen to join the republican army. After a period as a union leader on the railways and as a strike organizer, he joined the CCP. He trained as an officer at the Huangpu Military Academy, from which he graduated as a cadet in its first graduating class. During the military campaign in the north, he experienced an event that was to play a key role in his later life: during an ambush he saved the life of the Gemo, Chiang Kai-shek himself.

But Chen Geng was only hero for a day: in 1926 he was sent along with Gu Shunzhang to the USSR to complete the GPU training programme. When he returned to China, after taking part in various failed uprisings, he took over Teke intelligence in Shanghai under the alias "Mr Wang". His first mission was to throw light on a mystery: the 14 April 1928 arrest on Gordon Road of Luo Yinong—a fierce, longstanding militant, responsible for setting up the embryonic intelligence service—and his subsequent assassination, which took place immediately after he was handed over to the Chinese police. With the help of Gu Shunzhang's contacts in the police and his old friends in the Green Gang, Chen discovered that a German-speaking woman had approached the British Special Branch and offered to hand over hundreds of activists in exchange for a considerable sum of money. To prove her good faith, she had given Pat Givens's men Luo's address. The traitor was a woman called He Zhihua. She was the ex-wife of Zhu De, the former warlord who became a communist general and was amongst those who had spent a period in Paris. She had lived with Zhu in Germany, at the time of the "student–workers". After a stay in the USSR, she joined the secretariat of the CCP leadership in Shanghai, which gave her access to the list of party members. In an utter betrayal of communist ideals, she was planning to sell out her former comrades and use the money to begin a new life abroad.

The revenge of the "dog-beating squads" was not long in coming. Killers turned up at the traitor's home, and found her in bed with her new husband. They emptied their Mauser 7.65 pistols into the couple. Riddled with bullets and seriously wounded but still alive, He Zhihua abandoned her husband's corpse and vanished. The Teke killers, however, managed to recover the list of names and, most significantly, to broadcast the chilling message that "Wu Hao's dagger" never slept. It knew neither pity nor remorse.[27]

Of all the infiltration operations conducted by Dai Li's service, however, the most successful was silent: the encrypting and communications service. The militant responsible for these missions was Li Kenong. Li is worth considering in a little more depth, because he would later become one of the most important figures in the world of Chinese espionage.

Behind his dark glasses, Li Kenong had the soul of a journalist. He was born in the impoverished eastern province of Anhui in 1899 in the Year of the Pig. With his portly figure, moustache and cheerful demeanour, he was known as the "smiling Buddha". In his youth he went to France on the work–study programme and it may have been during that period that he became one of the first of Zhou Enlai's agents. In any case, he was to spend thirty years working as a spy in the service of the "revolutionary mandarin".

After his return to China, Li worked as a journalist. In 1926 he had become deputy editor of the *National People's Daily* and a supporter of Chiang Kai-shek's northern campaign, although he was secretly now a militant communist. He returned to Shanghai in 1928, where he continuing working both as a journalist and for the Teke. He contrived to be taken on as Chiang Kai-shek's personal cryptographer. As an expert in this field, he succeeded in joining the General Staff of the nationalist army, and thus was able to send "Wu Hao" and Kang Sheng copies of the telegraph messages that sat on his desk. He was part of a network that included Qian Zhuangfei, another communist mole, who had become secretary to Xu Enzeng, the head of the Kuomintang's BIS secret service.

Meanwhile, Nie Rongzhen, who had also been in Paris and was now a specialist in wireless communication, was charged with setting up a radio post in Hong Kong. In May 1930 he arrived in Shanghai, also under cover of being a journalist, and joined Chen Geng's staff, as he explained in his memoirs:

> Apart from me, other people with specific responsibilities included Chen Geng, Li Qiang and others ... It was a nerve-wracking and exciting time. We managed to place several highly competent comrades in key enemy departments—Li Kenong, Qian Zhuangfei and Hu Di. With their help we had real-time access to information on different organizations, and we knew which comrades the enemy had uncovered. Occasionally we even received detailed information of planned attacks on us by Chiang Kai-shek's troops.[28]

Another aspect of the responsibilities of "Mr Wang", alias Chen Geng, was to provide the logistical support of his intelligence service to operatives from Moscow. Though this mission would seem to contradict the tight security regulations in place, it was ordered by the Comintern as part of its plan to set up a Far Eastern bureau, and to provide support to Comintern personnel attached to the GRU who were sent to China on missions by General Berzin. These included Jean Cremet and Richard Sorge, who met in January 1930. Cremet was largely based in Shanghai's International Concession, working with the Far Eastern Bureau as an itinerant inspector to other communist parties in the region (Japan, Philippines, Dutch East Indies, and so on). As his reports to the Centre make clear, he was dispatched to help Ho Chi Minh set up a communist party in Indochina, Hong Kong and Macao. He was also sent to convince Chen Duxiu, the former head of the CCP who had broken with the movement in 1927, to return to the fold and visit Stalin in Moscow. This feels rather like it must have been a trap, bearing in mind Chen's links with the exiled Trotsky.

Cremet was posing as a wealthy Belgian trader named René Dillen, in whose name he had a fake passport. He was active until the spring of 1931, after which he vanished from Moscow's sight—going to ground after the defection of Magician Gu (see below). In around summer 1930, he was sent to negotiate the purchase of arms in Shanghai, which he escorted back on board a junk destined for the Guangxi 8th Red Army Corps, a maquis organized in Hakka territory by Deng Xiaoping, an old comrade from the Paris days. During the voyage, however, the extraordinary Breton communist vanished during a storm. "He was drawn to the depths, to the kingdom of the Dragon King", as they say in Chinese. He drowned on the high seas.

In Moscow there was fury: what had happened to him? Another French comrade, Joseph Ducroux, who was familiar with Asia, was sent to try and find him. In fact, by this time leaning towards Chen and Trotsky's position, Cremet had decided to organize his own disappearance, with the help of Clara and André Malraux. He was one of the first significant Comintern defectors under Stalin's rule.[29]

Richard Sorge, meanwhile, was somewhat luckier—at least for the time being. He set up a new Soviet surveillance post in Shanghai. Although he was the object of criticism from within the GRU regarding his usefulness, he did help organize the visit of several senior members of the CCP to the USSR, including Zhou Enlai and Wang Ming.[30] Sorge went on to spy on Japan, where he was captured and hanged in 1944, though the information he had gleaned three years previously had been sufficient to warn Stalin that Hitler was preparing to invade the USSR.

Gu the magician defects

Joseph Ducroux drew a blank in his investigation into the disappearance of his comrade, with whom he had once worked in the Colonial Affairs Department of the French Communist Party. All those he consulted, whether Chinese or Indochinese, were unable to offer any answers as to what might have happened to Cremet. He had simply vanished.

Ducroux wrote an unpublished memoir in the 1950s, in which he recalled how the hunt for Cremet unfolded: "On my way from Paris to the Far East, I stopped in Moscow in February 1931 and was housed in a private house in the city, where only Abramov [head of the OMS] and a French comrade came to visit. I had no direct contact with the Communist International. During one of our many meetings, Abramov confided in me that it was some time since the Comintern had had news of Cremet, since his departure [from Moscow] in 1929. He told me the name he had been travelling under, which I have forgotten. He had a Belgian passport. Abramov asked me to go round all the hotels in Shanghai and Hong Kong to see if I could find any trace of him, which I did, not without encountering numerous obstacles and with no success in either city. I could not, of course, visit every single one of the many hotels in these two major international ports. But those I did visit offered up no trace of the man who was travelling under a Belgian alias. I drew a complete blank on Cremet."[31]

Frustrated, Ducroux continued his travels and went on to Singapore, where he was enlisted to help the nascent South Seas Communist Party (covering Malaysia, the Dutch East Indies and Burma). He was, in other words, taking over Cremet's abortive mission. On 27 April 1931, he moved into the famous Raffles Hotel in Singapore under the name Serge Lefranc.

Ducroux probably had no idea of what had taken place in Shanghai since he had left the city—a shocking event with implications that reverberated through the Teke and the wider CCP. The magician Gu Shunzhang had defected from the party. On 25 April 1931, after leaving the city with other party leaders, the illusionist went to Wuhan, as usual, to perform the magic tricks that served as a cover for his missions. While he was there, surrounded by children of all ages, he was spotted in the street by a nationalist informer, a former member of the CCP, who alerted local Kuomintang agents. They threw themselves on Gu, seized him, and a local BIS officer sent telegrams to Nanjing to announce the fantastic news. The nationalists' worst enemy, one of the most important figures in the CCP, had been caught like a rat in a trap. But the head of the BIS, Xu Enzeng, had left the office to go dancing with his mistress's sister; this gave Qian Zhuangfei, head of encryption but more importantly a communist mole at Kuomintang headquarters, time to alert the other main informer in the Shanghai Central Telegraph Bureau, Li Kenong. Li in turn alerted Chen Geng, head of the 2nd Section. During the hours that followed, Zhou Enlai, Kang Sheng, Chen Yun (Kang's new deputy), Li Qiang (head of the communications section), and Xiang Zhongfa managed to find safe houses for some 500 activists. They also ordered Li Kenong and Chen Geng to leave town.

Nie Rongzhen found himself once again on the frontline, as he recounts: "We were lucky enough to have had comrade Qian Zhuangfei working in the office of the BIS in Nanjing, who helped us avoid an even greater disaster. When Qian, who was extremely clever and capable, learned that Gu had defected, he went straight to Shanghai to alert the Central Committee of the urgency of the situation.

"I went straight over to see comrade Zhou Enlai, but he was not at home. I told our "sister" Deng [Zhou's wife] and warned her to flee. Given the circumstances, it was vital that we act before the enemy did. It was Zhou Enlai himself who took care of everything. Every office of the Central Committee and every one of the comrades whom Gu knew was moved to a new location. All links with Gu were broken. Working day and night it took us only two days to complete the job."[32]

Zhou and his comrades were right to act as they did. Gu Shunzhang immediately switched his allegiance to the services of Chen Lifu and Xu Enzeng, the master spies of the nationalist movement. In addition, he agreed to head up a special anti-communist section, and to author an instruction manual for the fight against the communist secret service. In the hours that followed, roundups made it clear that the magician really had revealed everything he knew about the underground organization of the CCP. In spite of all the precautions that the communists had taken, there were multiple arrests in different cities. On 21 June 1931, Xiang Zhongfa, general secretary of the party since the 1928 Moscow Congress, was captured hiding out in a jewellery shop on Avenue Joffre with his mistress, a cabaret dancer. He too offered to defect to the Kuomintang, but he was shot before a counterorder pardoning him, signed by Chiang Kai-shek, reached his jailers.[33]

As part of his planned response, Zhou Enlai decided to restructure CCP intelligence. The leadership of the special services was now made up of a group of five militants. Kang Sheng, now the man with the most power, surrounded himself with four others who had been trained in the USSR and whose ideological commitment was unswerving: Chen Yun, Guang Huian, Ke Qingshi and Pan Hannian.

"I remember Kang Sheng during that period," recalled Guan Shuzi in an interview with the author half a century later in Taiwan. He too had defected to the Kuomintang, later on. "I had just returned from studying at Sun Yat-sen University in Moscow. I was lying low in the Hotel Normandie in Shanghai. I met Kang in an apartment that belonged to the underground. He was very affable and distinguished, though he chain-smoked throughout. We had to deal with another big problem for Moscow: Hilaire Noulens, head of the Comintern's Far Eastern bureau, had been arrested. I had seen Noulens very recently: he had the biggest bunch of keys that I had ever seen in my life, for all the secret apartments he looked after."[34]

Indeed, at around the same time that the Party's general secretary was killed, Moscow learned of a further damaging failure in the wake of Gu Shunzhang's defection. On 15 June, Hilaire Noulens and his wife had been arrested in Shanghai as Comintern agents. The couple remained tight-lipped and gave nothing away, and were sent to prison. It was not until 1991 and the collapse of the Soviet Union that their son revealed their real names: Yakov Rudnik and Tatiana Moisseenko. But from their papers, deciphered by the police, dozens of Western-born Soviet agents were identified in Shanghai. Many fled to the USSR. Curiously, the best known of the spies identified at the time, Richard Sorge, remained under surveillance but was never arrested.

However, a suspicion persists: on 1 June 1931 the Frenchman Joseph Ducroux, alias "Lefranc", had been arrested in Singapore. Special Branch officers found on him a badly encrypted notebook, with a PO Box address in Shanghai: HILANOUL BP 208. Was Ducroux in fact indirectly responsible for the collapse of the Comintern's Shanghai bureau? Or had he been amongst those denounced by Gu Shunzhang, and the British officers had simply waited before arresting him, as a final kick to the collapsed anthill?

On 6 June, there had been another setback: Nguyen Ai Quoc (later Ho Chi Minh) was arrested in a Kowloon district of Hong Kong. Ducroux had met with him before leaving for Malaysia, but his details were also discovered in Hilaire Noulens' papers, duly combed through by the detectives working for Pat Givens, the British police chief in Shanghai.[35] Her Majesty's colonial police were active throughout the Shanghai–Singapore–Hong Kong triangle.

For Kang Sheng, Gu's defection was not all bad. It meant that he could extend his realm, and assume complete control of the Teke's 4th Section, responsible for encryption and communication. Zhou Enlai also gave him the green light to hand over responsibility for revenge executions to Guang Huian, making him the new head of the 3rd Section. Guang, nicknamed "Little Shandong", started by ordering the killing of three women: Gu's wife and two Cantonese servants. "Wu Hao's dagger" was pitiless. Gu's entire family was buried alive in caverns dug and sealed beneath the city, as a telegram from the French secret service revealed:

> Gu Shunzhang defected, his whole family assassinated, the affair uncovered after the arrest of Wang Liao De Zi, an accessory to Zhou Enlai, who confessed to the June 1931 assassination of 11 people. The corpses were found at the corner of 37 Ai Dang-li and Prosper Paris Road, at number 33 in the same block in the French Concession, and in the International Settlement, at 6 Sien Teh Feung Passage.[36]

During the following two years, the battle for control of Shanghai continued with escalating violence. The ongoing struggle between the Kuomintang secret services and those of the CCP, told in all its detail, would fill several volumes.[37] It foreshadowed the settling of accounts that ultimately led to the victory of communism in 1949, not only in Shanghai but across the whole of China.

On 7 January 1933, according to the French Sûreté, a meeting of communist cadres took place in Zao-ka-dou, where the restructuring of the Chinese GPU was agreed upon: there was to be an investigation group set up to spy on party traitors; units to provide protection for active members of the party; and a "dog-beating squad" to eliminate traitors.

These decisions are an indication of the level of infiltration that the clandestine CCP was once again facing. Two months after this meeting, Chen Geng, former head of the 2nd Section, was arrested, having gone into hiding at the home of the great writer Lu Xun. He was described by the French as the "head of the 2nd Section", although he had in fact been replaced two years previously by another exceptional agent, Pan Hannian.[38] Arrested on Peking Road on 24 March 1933, Chen was sentenced a week later and handed over to the Chinese police. "Mr Wang" was so important in the eyes of the Kuomintang that he was transferred to Nanchang, where he was interrogated by Chiang Kai-shek himself. But at the end of the interrogation the nationalist leader, recalling how Chen had saved his life during the battle for the north, decided to release his prisoner, asking him to negotiate an accord with the "red generals" in his camp. In May, Chen Geng "escaped", and fled to the Soviet zone of Jiangxi. He remained a communist and was a commander during Mao's Long March.

Six months later, a report by the new French chief of police, Louis Fabre—Fiori finally having been removed from office for corruption and collusion with the Green Gang—brought news of Gu Shunzhang, who had become head of a special anti-communist brigade. The French report gave details of the Blue Shirts, the 3,000-strong paramilitary organization led by the Chen brothers, and revealed the organizational structure of their special services:

1. An intelligence service composed of: a) a military intelligence section (Wang Pai-ling); b) a secret intelligence service (Kou Chien-chung, Kuomintang Central Committee);
2. An executive department (Gu Shunzhang), charged with carrying out terrorist activities, which recruits mainly from graduates of the Huangpu Military Academy. Made up of secret cells in Shanghai, Hong Kong, Canton, Beijing.

At the head of the nationalists' blacklist of people to bring down was Zhao Rong, better known as Kang Sheng. Kang had been single-handedly running the urban special services in Shanghai, but now it seemed his time was up. Zhou Enlai had joined forces with Mao. Kang Sheng, master shadow-puppeteer, went to Moscow to join Stalin.

Kang Sheng goes to Moscow

At the beginning of 1933, Kang Sheng was sent to Moscow to join the Comintern leadership. The revolution in Europe was floundering with Hitler's rise to power. It was imperative that it be revived in Asia. Kang was to be trained in new Soviet methods of state security and espionage. He was also involved in agitprop, as propaganda was called in those days. Agitprop, disinformation and deception were all weapons as important as intelligence-gathering.

Towards the end of 1933, Kang published an article in the Comintern journal entitled "The 6th Kuomintang campaign and the victory of the Chinese Red Army". Perhaps this was a straightforward analysis seeking to trigger worldwide proletariat solidarity with the Chinese revolution. But it may have been intended to obtain support from Stalin and his strategists for the leaders who had renounced urban insurrection in favour of a rural-based guerrilla movement—not least the new communist warlord, Mao Zedong, and his army of peasants.

The following year, Kang Sheng coauthored a short book with his comrade Wang Ming, another Chinese attached to the Comintern leadership, who was to become the next interim general secretary of the CCP, after completing his Soviet training. *Revolutionary China Today* was published in several languages via Willi Münzenberg's propaganda arm of the Comintern.[39]

Kang Sheng was expected to painstakingly copy the new Soviet methods. The techniques of the GPU, the secret police, were what a powerful Chinese movement needed. Kang must surely have approved of what André Malraux had written two years earlier: "The International had no choice ... Its aim was to give the Chinese proletariat, as quickly as possible, the class-consciousness it needed in order to attempt to seize power ... I have to admit that a Russian-style secret service, but even stronger, was certainly one possible solution."[40]

Kang focused on the surveillance of Chinese students at both Sun Yat-sen University and the KUTV, the Communist University of the Toilers of the East. As instructed, he spied on the Trotskyist followers of the former CCP leader, Chen Duxiu.[41] But most of all "Master Kang" learned to blend in. He became immersed in the type of collective paranoia instituted by Stalin, which was to leave a permanent mark on China.

In 1935, the Chinese "Grand Inquisitor" even came close to depriving the world of one of its great communist leaders, Ho Chi Minh. Kang was part of the commission of inquiry into the errors made following the destruction of networks in Hong Kong, Shanghai and Singapore in 1931. The troika charged with studying Nguyen Ai Quoc's dossier was made up of Dmitri Manuilsky, technical head of the International; Vera Vassilieva, head of the Indochina Section; and

Kang Sheng. Manuilsky remained neutral in the affair, all the more so since he certainly risked being blamed himself, for having dispatched the two Frenchmen involved in the debacle, Cremet and Ducroux. Nguyen Ai Quoc faced the blame for his friendship with Borodin, the former Comintern envoy to China who had subsequently been purged; or for his escape from a British jail in Hong Kong in 1932. Or had he been working all along as an agent of the British Intelligence Service? It was clear that Kang Sheng loathed him, and it took all the diplomatic skills of Comrade Vassilieva, arguing that his arrest had simply been a consequence of his inexperience, to save him at the eleventh hour.[42]

Meanwhile Stalin's rival, Sergei Kirov, was assassinated in Leningrad on 1 December 1934, a prelude to the Moscow Trials. Kang Sheng redoubled his efforts, and was rewarded by being allowed to take part in a devastating purge in the ranks of the Asian communists in Muscovite exile. In his room in the Hotel Lux, where he was living with his wife Cao Yi'ou and his mistress Su Mei (who also happened to be his wife's sister), Kang even set up his own miniature GPU, the "Office for the Elimination of Counter-Revolutionaries". Hundreds of young Chinese people in Moscow who believed in communism were denounced, sent to the gulag or shot in the neck by the men of Lavrentiy Beria, the head of the new NKVD. Among them, presumably condemned for being a "Trotskyist", was Xin Ouyang, former head of the 2nd Bureau of the Shanghai Teke, once headed by Kang Sheng.

Undoubtedly, the Moscow Trials were the inspiration for the mass purges known as the Yan'an Rectification Campaign, presided over by Kang in 1942 with Mao's authorisation. By the mid-1930s, Kang Sheng had been completely integrated into the apparatus of Stalin's secret police. They trusted him. In particular, he was given the responsibility of keeping an eye on an embarrassing guest, "Nicholas Elizarov", who was in reality Chiang Ching-kuo, son of the nationalist leader Chiang Kai-shek. In 1925 he had been sent to Moscow to study, during the period when the USSR backed the Kuomintang. The bloody conflict between the Kuomintang and the communists in 1927 had meant that he was now more hostage than guest. He had even been forced to write a tract denouncing his father, the supposedly cunning and cruel Chiang Kai-shek. But Stalin spared both father and son: there was every indication that he would soon likely obliged to renew the USSR's alliance with Chiang against the Japanese, and so, in mid-April 1937, the young Chiang was sent back to China with his blonde Russian wife, whose name—Fayina Ipatevna Vakhreva—long remained a state secret.

Not long after Chiang's departure, two other well-known Chinese sons arrived, Mao's own children. Two months earlier, Kang Sheng had been sent to France on another delicate mission. It was not his first visit. In 1936 he had spent several months in Paris during the government of the Popular Front, before going to Spain as a delegate of the Comintern to inspect the International Brigades, set up to fight on behalf of the Spanish republicans.[43] But this time, in the winter of 1936–7, he was sent to try and find two "illegal emigrants", the children Mao had had in the 1920s with his second wife Yang Kaihui: Anying and Anching. This was one of the new tricks Stalin had up his sleeve: in order to keep the CCP leaders on a tight rein, he detained members of their families, like trophies. The trouble in this case was that, while Chiang Kai-shek had always felt real affection for his son, Mao Zedong seems to have been much less attentive to his offspring.

It is true that in the meantime, between October 1934 and October 1935, Mao had led the Long March, the strategic retreat of 12,000 kilometres to evade the Kuomintang army, and the exodus of an army of 120,000 partisan fighters, supervised by many Hakkas, of whom only 20,000 remained by the time the marchers reached Yan'an in Shaanxi province. There, in deepest rural China, an embryonic communist state was established. In January 1935, the Zunyi Conference was held, during which Mao managed to seize power of the CCP and distance himself from Soviet theories on how to conduct the revolutionary war. Urban insurrection had only led to failure. The spearhead of the revolution was to be the peasantry.

Zhou Enlai joined forces with Mao and took over diplomacy. The names of several of his generals are already familiar to us: Zhu De, Chen Yi and Ye Jianying had been with Zhou in Europe and were to play important roles, as was Chen Geng, the former head of intelligence in Shanghai. The nascent state lacked only a head of the secret services, and an iron-willed interior minister. Stalin sent Kang Sheng, along with several Soviet advisors to the Comintern, to prepare for the final victory, and the advent of what can only be called the Chinese surveillance state. With remarkable irony, Kang Sheng was to use the methods he learned in Moscow to eventually purge the Soviets and their supporters from within Mao's secret service.

2

MAO'S SECRET SERVICE

On 1 November 1995, a low-key but moving celebration took place in Beijing. On behalf of President Boris Yeltsin, renowned Sinologist and Russian ambassador to China Igor Rogachev bestowed on a Chinese secret agent Russia's highest distinction, in recognition of his contribution to the defence of the USSR. This was a doubly posthumous ceremony, for both the Chinese spy being honoured and the Soviet Union were dead, the latter having been dissolved at the instigation of Yeltsin himself. But the Russian officials had not forgotten those who had worked for the victory of the USSR against the Third Reich, during what they call the "Great Patriotic War". And this was an excellent opportunity to enhance the newly revived Sino-Russian friendship.

The name of the secret agent, who would have been 100 years old in 1995, was Yan Baohang, and the services he had rendered were truly significant: in May 1941, he was one of those who warned the Kremlin of Hitler's imminent attack on the USSR. Four years later, the information from his espionage of the Japanese army enabled Stalin to launch his lightning attack on Japan.

Yan's son, Yan Mingfu, accepted the medal on his father's behalf with tears in his eyes. Yan Mingfu had himself headed an important political intelligence department, the "United Front Work Department" (*Tongzhan Gongzuo Bu*), until June 1989, when he was dismissed for expressing sympathy with the students demonstrating for democracy on Tiananmen Square. Later he chaired an NGO involved in the "business of charity". A man of strong principles, Yan Mingfu was proud of the father he had followed into the world of professional intelligence. He, like his father, was born in Manchuria. In 1941, when he was only ten years old, his father—a lawyer as well as a secret communist—became part of the inner circle around Chiang Kai-shek's wife, Soong May-ling, and the nationalist general Zhang Xueliang. Zhang, despite being a prominent member of the Kuomintang, claimed the distinction of having kidnapped Chiang Kai-shek in December 1936, in order to coerce him into joining forces with the CCP against the Japanese. Indeed, it was under the twin influences of the Soviets and, soon after, the Americans, that nationalists and communists sealed a new alliance, the Second United Front, to fight Hirohito's army, which invaded the country after an initial attack on Shanghai in August 1937.

Moscow agreed to support this alliance, handing over some $450 million to Chiang Kai-shek between autumn 1937 and November 1940. In return, the Chinese Red Army was reorganized and placed under the command of the Kuomintang Military Affairs Commission. The 8th Route Army fought in the north-west, while the New Fourth Army operated south of the Yangtze River.

This explains why Zhou Enlai was in Chongqing, the capital of a "united" China at war with Japan, in spring 1941. Zhou, leading the nascent communist diplomatic service, had instructed Yan Baohang to gather as much information as possible from those in the nationalist inner circle he had managed to infiltrate. In 2005, Yan Mingfu, who waited ten years after the ceremony honouring his father to reveal the details of the affair, divulged that his father had made many high-level contacts, "including important government figures, Madame Chiang Kai-shek and Sun Ke, the son of Dr Sun Yat-sen, and many others."[1]

Diplomatic cocktail parties offer an opportunity to exchange specialist information amid banal small talk. So it was that, one fine day in May 1941, Yan Bahoang was invited to a dinner in honour of the German military attaché—the Reich had not declared war on China. In the course of this soirée, he overheard Sun Ke say that Adolf Hitler planned to launch Operation Barbarossa around 20 June. Yan discreetly had the information confirmed, before reporting the conversation straight back to Zhou Enlai, who, in turn, sent a coded telegram to Mao Zedong's Yan'an communist headquarters. From there the information passed through the usual channels: the Comintern, via the Soviet permanent envoy to Mao. According to the Chinese, this was how Stalin was able to make preparations to prevent an even bigger disaster than the one that eventually took place that summer.

That was not all: Yan Baohang did not rest on his laurels. Four years later, Chen Geng, who had been former chief of the special services in Shanghai in 1931 before becoming head of the Red Army Military Committee's political department, asked Yan to obtain information on the Japanese army in Kwantung, in the north-east, to find out about any planned attack by its elite troops on the USSR in the near future. Yan managed to obtain extremely precise information on troop deployment, defence plans, weapon types, the details of troop numbers and units, and names of army generals.

It was thanks to Yan's intelligence-gathering that Stalin's troops succeeded in crushing the Japanese army in August 1945. On 8 August, just two days after the Americans dropped the first atomic bomb on Hiroshima on the 6th, and the day before they dropped the second on Nagasaki, the USSR went to war against Japan. Eighty Soviet divisions—half a million men supported by an artillery of 26,000 weapons, 3,700 tanks and 500 planes—carved the Kwantung army led by General Yamada Otozo into pieces. With vital help from Chinese spies, the Soviets were at last able to take their revenge for Tsarist Russia's defeat in the Russo-Japanese War of 1905.[2]

This episode reveals two important facts: firstly, that the Chinese communists were continuing to work closely with the Comintern and the Soviet secret services; and, secondly, that Zhou Enlai, at the time of Japan's surrender, was still in control of the CCP's external, political and diplomatic intelligence. However, he had been forced, at Mao's insistence, to cede to Kang Sheng control of the party's police, counterintelligence and internal repression services. As we shall see, this was an unfortunate choice that almost led the party to self-destruct.

Kang Sheng sets up the secret police

On 29 November 1937, there was great excitement in the walled city of Yan'an, where Mao Zedong had his headquarters. Aeroplanes were never seen flying over the city, but that day a Tupolev TB3 bomber from Moscow landed on an improvised and icy runway. On board was Kang Sheng, the Chinese Grand Inquisitor; Wang Ming, whom the Russians wanted to impose as general secretary of the CCP; and two Chinese intelligence specialists who were later to become ministers in the People's Republic of China, Chen Yun and Zeng Shan.[3] Not to mention, of course, Kang Sheng's wife and mistress, the sisters Cao Yi'ou and Su Mei. Following strict instructions from the Kremlin, Kang and his team, together with Mao, were to take over the anti-Japanese resistance in Yan'an.

One biography of Zeng Shan includes a very telling image: a photograph of all the plane's passengers—except the women—and the welcoming committee. In the centre, Mao, relaxed and corpulent, cigarette in hand, is wearing a worn, badly buttoned jacket, with a Red Army commander's cap on his head. To his left is Kang Sheng, in a fancy uniform and an elegant cap adorned with a red star, recognizable by his schoolteacher's posture and his intellectual's steel-rimmed spectacles. On the right, Wang Ming, the Russians' man, looks away, beyond the frame.

In the days that followed, it came as no great surprise when Kang Sheng received orders from Mao to take over the leadership of the Political Protection Bureau, which had been headed since 1935 by Wang Shoudao, a fellow militant from Hunan. In the summer of 1938, Kang was ordered to restructure and take over the CCP's new secret service, the innocuously named "Social Affairs Department". In Chinese it was called *Zhongyang Shehuibu*, *Zhongshebu* or *Shehuibu* for short; in English it is known as the SAD. "The CCP had consolidated intelligence and CI (Counter-intelligence) into the Social Affairs Department in approximately 1936, but Kang was responsible for the final shape of the department after 1938," explained Matt Brazil, an Australian specialist of Chinese intelligence. "Three organizations were integrated into SAD: the Special Branch (above); the Political Protection Bureau, which provided Red rear area security before the Long March and security for Mao during it; and the Guard Office (*Baowei chu*) which provided protection to Mao in [Yan'an] and a local constabulary and CI service. Under Kang and his deputy Li Kenong, SAD expanded into every province where the CCP had control. SAD had elements doing military security, political security, economic security, international intelligence, and domestic intelligence. SAD's members were paid more and had privileges and access to food unavailable to other party members."[4]

In other words, the SAD was branching out in all directions. Kang Sheng was surrounded by a group of private secretaries, his "trusted men": Xiao Li, Fu Hao—future ambassador to Japan—and Zhao Yaobin, a chief of staff who defected to the nationalist camp in 1949.[5] The sisters Cao Yi'ou and Su Mei followed Kang Sheng around like two little poodles, but also filled filing cards with information about all the comrades—small pieces of card bound by vegetable twine that would later prove very useful to party archivists.

Kang Sheng first contrived to push his deputy director Li Kenong, considered to be "Zhou Enlai's eyes", from his inner circle. At first glance, Kang's chosen mode of organization was taken from the Soviet model: Section 1 dealt with administration and personnel; Section 2, intelligence; Section 3, counterintelligence; and Section 4, intelligence analysis. There was also a general affairs department, part of the officers training corps. Two additional special sections were set up, for security and the "executions department" (*Zhisibu*) respectively. External liaisons were managed by another former comrade from Shanghai, Pan Hannian, who was responsible for complex liaison operations with the Japanese intelligence services, with the purpose of obtaining information on the Kuomintang.[6]

Relations with the Triads were also tricky. Some of the secret societies had sold themselves to the Japanese, such as the "Hong Five Continents Society" (*Wu Zhou Hong Men*); others were semi-patriotic (such as the Green Gang of Shanghai), while others still were patriotic and ready to collaborate with the communists. The Long March and the move to Yan'an would have been impossible had Mao not maintained some kind of allegiance to the longstanding Elders Brothers Society (*Gelaohui*), whose members included Zhu De, the other military leader of the Long March, and Deng Xiaoping's own father.

"In other words," explains the Korean historian Park Sang-soo, a specialist in rural secret societies, "if the backbone of the Long March was the astonishing Hakka community, its logistics were guaranteed by the secret society *Gelaohui*, to which many of those who later became high-ranking members of the Communist Party belonged."[7]

The highly sensitive work of dealing with these relationships with secret societies and Triads fell to the second-in-command at the SAD, Li Kenong, who took over personally when he returned to Yan'an in 1941 after three years of special activities as Zhou Enlai's deputy and with the 8th Route Army. It was Zhou who insisted that he be included in Kang Sheng's inner circle.

Kang Sheng set up an intelligence school at the Date Garden to train his secret agents and his political officers. Wu Defeng, his director, received instructions to spread the party line: "We must forget what we studied in Moscow and develop our own Chinese-style intelligence."[8] Among the school's teachers were the unionist Wu De, future mayor of Beijing, who taught economics, and Chen Yun. Chen Yun, a Jiangsu militant born with the century, was, as we have seen, part of the group that had reorganized Shanghai's special service, the Teke, after the defection of Magician Gu. After returning from Moscow with Kang, he was given the important role of running the CCP's Organization Department. From 1940 onwards he was in charge of the Central Finance and Economics Department. Chen could be considered the founding father of the Chinese communist economic intelligence system. After 1949 he was one of the principal architects of the first Five-Year Plan.[9] In the West it is a widespread misconception that the Chinese, unlike the Japanese, did not engage in this early period in what's now known as "economic intelligence" and commercial and financial espionage. Chen's role proves otherwise—that a large part of communist espionage strategy has been devoted to economic intelligence since the very birth of the PRC.

Under Kang Sheng, the SAD—the CCP's new secret service—dealt with the most minute details of political and economic life, while maintaining agents in the military, political, economic and international intelligence agencies. On top of that, in 1943 Kang took control of the Commission for Work Behind Enemy Lines, for which SAD operatives and military intelligence officers worked. With Mao's support, Kang Sheng was constantly expanding his power beyond the political police. The poetically named "Date Garden" soon came to be feared by CCP cadres as a horrific, nightmarish lair: not only was it Kang's headquarters, but it also had interrogation rooms and prisons built into the clay hillside, where suspects were interrogated until they pronounced their self-criticism and committed a formal confession to paper. This would earn them, depending on the case, either a bullet in the back of the neck, or the right to be presented at a public "struggle session", during which they would self-flagellate and endure public abuse.

This extension of Kang's domain continued: increasingly greedy, he took control of all communications, imposing at the top his henchman Li Qiang, former chief of the clandestine radio station in Hong Kong and Shanghai. This gave him access to the contents of all reports sent back to Moscow by Soviet agents in Yan'an. Along the way, Kang also succeeded in getting Deng Fa, chief of security, demoted, and Luo Ruiqing, head of military intelligence, removed.

Somehow, as early as 1938, Kang had also managed to seize control of the Red Army Secret Service (*Qingbaoju*). This was something of a paradox, given he had neither participated in the 12,000-kilometre Long March, nor ever commanded a military unit, unlike the famous "marshals" Zhu De, Lin Biao, Chen Yi, Peng Dehuai, Deng Xiaoping, Ye Jianying and Luo Ronghuan. This strategic service, headed by Ye Jianying, the "Heroic Sword", was the precursor to the Second Department of the General Staff of the People's Liberation Army, represented by military attachés in embassies around the world, after the foundation of the PRC in 1949.

Army chiefs did succeed in forcing Kang Sheng to share power over both the garrison regiment, which was responsible for protecting Yan'an, and the Second Department of the party's Central Military Commission, which guided war strategy. Naturally, Mao himself presided over the latter.[10] But this hardly made any difference, since Kang Sheng contrived to bypass every obstacle and continued to widen his circle of influence. In 1943 he gained control of the operational intelligence services of the two main armies, the "Eighth Route Army" and the "New Fourth Army", which distinguished themselves in every major battle against the Japanese.

In order to build on this sprawling edifice of power in Yan'an, Kang pulled off two masterstrokes. First, he isolated the Soviet delegates under his charge who had come to China as agents of Stalin, to report on how the Chinese comrades' operations were progressing. The Comintern envoy Peter Vladimirov (real name Vlasov) was no longer "the eyes of Moscow" in Yan'an, and more of a hostage. Then, by making a definitive alliance with Mao, Kang prevented Wang Ming, a former fellow exile in Moscow, from usurping Mao, which was what the Kremlin wanted. He decided to have him poisoned, in small doses, like in some ancient legend. Kang Sheng, despite having been imposed by the Soviets in the first place, was now actively opposing them.

The Soviet representative Vladimirov kept an explosive diary throughout this period. In it he complained of being quarantined to the point that he was only allowed to see Kang Sheng and Xiao Li, his private secretary. He saw Mao rarely. Kang was becoming more anti-Soviet by the day. On 4 February 1943, after rejoicing that the German troops had been crushed at Stalingrad, Vladimirov noted in his diary:

> I was not mistaken in my previous conclusions. Kang Sheng has a strong influence on the Chairman's moods. Mao Zedong is indifferent to the practical problems of socialism. He is crammed with Kang Sheng's inaccurate stories about our country; in this case this is the only source of his information. As for Kang Sheng, he is only too glad to slander us. He is a rabid enemy of the Soviet Union, he sullies the Bolshevik Party and spares no efforts to prevent the Chinese Communist Party from consolidating ideologically.

In over 500 pages of entries, the hapless Vladimirov describes the long drawn-out collapse of Yan'an, the crucible of the revolution, under the dual aegis of Mao and Kang—these revelations are all the more surprising coming from a cadre moulded in the steely ideological rigidity of Stalinism.[11]

More contradictions were to come, and Vladimirov was not the only one to notice them. But Kang Sheng had another trick up his sleeve: the "Queen of Hearts". Since December 1937, the former cinema actress known as "Blue Apple", who hailed from the same village as Kang—Zhucheng, in Shandong—and who was even rumoured at one time to have been his mistress, had become part of his inner circle. After joining the CCP, she came to Yan'an and was introduced by Kang to Mao. The chairman immediately fell under her spell. From then on he had eyes only for her; all his other lovers were dismissed, and she reigned unchallenged, just as the favourite concubine of the emperor would have done in earlier eras.

Despite criticism from Yan'an leaders opposed to their marriage, the young woman soon became the third Madame Mao, better known by her new name, Jiang Qing (Azure River). For good measure, Mao's unfortunate second wife, He Zizhen, was sent to the USSR, where she was locked up in an asylum for the insane; various other women of Mao's entourage, including the American journalist Agnes Smedley, were also dismissed.

It is almost an understatement to say that Jiang Qing had great admiration for Master Kang (*Kang Lao*), as she called Kang Sheng. This only enhanced Kang's status as powerful shadow master, since she was not only Mao's wife but also his private secretary, with political as well as personal influence. The only people who were permitted to see Mao at any time of the day or night were Kang Sheng and Mao's male private secretary, who was later to be given a key role during the Cultural Revolution of the 1960s. This was Chen Boda, who had been head of the propaganda section of the CCP's Central Party School. Leadership of the school was later handed over to none other than Kang Sheng himself.

In 1942, Kang, marrying his ideology with his policing techniques, launched an internal campaign as head of the secret services to purge the party of dangerous influences, including Wang Ming, the man Stalin had wanted to replace Mao. The purpose of this "rectification movement" (*zhengfeng*) was to engender self-criticism, a crackdown on spies, and elimination of counterrevolutionaries of all kinds. It recalled the Stalinist purges and the Moscow trials that Kang had both witnessed and participated in six years earlier, during his persecution of the Asian community at Soviet universities.

Starting with the closed world of writers who criticized Yan'an bureaucracy, the campaign rallied political leaders including Chen Yun, Zhu De, Ye Jianying, Liu Shaoqi and several other major Chinese communist figures. It initially focused on group discussions about "rectifying work style", and Mao's writings on art and literature. But it also foreshadowed the "struggle sessions" and the public trials and humiliations of the Cultural Revolution, whose most prominent leaders were Jiang Qing, Kang Sheng and Chen Boda.

Kang Sheng, inventor of Maoism

Between 1942 and 1944, encouraged by Mao, Kang Sheng began hunting down spies and forcing the party's "deviationist" elements to submit to self-criticism, change their ideological viewpoints and commit to "thought reform". Writers targeted included Ding Ling and Wang Shiwei (assassinated in 1947 by the communists), while the hunt began for all "deviationist" cadres who backed Moscow's preferred faction instead of rallying behind Mao.

Kang Sheng followed the Leninist precept that "the party strengthens itself by purging itself", with his own innovation of mass meetings. On 8 June 1942, he organized a demonstration, during which various leaders spoke in favour of extending the campaign. This could be seen as the launch of a new stage in the history of Marxism—the invention of the Mao Zedong cult of personality, and the birth of Maoism.

On 16 December 1942, while cadres were "struggling" to reform their thinking, Kang Sheng caused a sensation at an open-air meeting, where he declared that political "deviation" was inextricably linked to being a spy.

"This is the great revelation," he explained in his high-pitched voice. "There is a close link between the twin crimes of espionage and deviationism. One is not a deviationist, as we have tended to believe, by chance or by error. It is, ineluctably, dialectically, because one is a Japanese agent or a Kuomintang spy—or both. We must begin a ruthless hunt to root out these two plagues from Yan'an because, by fighting against deviationism, we weaken the clandestine plots of our enemies, and vice versa."

Kang's tirade opened the way to appalling abuses. Kang Sheng launched a reign of terror in Yan'an and other areas under communist control, and a huge and diverse range of techniques of repression began that are still employed by the political police in 2019. These included the setting up of the "Central Case Examination Group" to discuss a suspect's fate; the *bigongxin* method of forcing a false confession in order to build a case against the accused; *sixiang gaizao*, thought reform or brainwashing, permitting the accused to work on correcting their mistaken thinking (this would have its moment of glory during the Korean War); and reform through labour, which prefigured the Chinese gulag, the *laogai*.

As Kang Sheng was convinced that at least 30 per cent of each organization was made up of spies and counterrevolutionaries, the "social workers" of counterintelligence, as they were sometimes called, had a quota to fulfil—to which end Kang established an inquisitorial system, utilizing techniques of punishment and interrogation inspired by the millennia-long Chinese tradition of torture, updated by twentieth-century Stalinism for the requirements of the era. Among the popular tortures practiced by Kang Sheng's gang were "the *bamboo cut*: bamboo spikes were driven under the fingernails. *Passing a horsehair through the eye*: a hair from a horse's tail was inserted into the penis; *Passing through a woman*: water from a narrow hose was pumped into the vagina at great pressure; *Giving the guest a drink*: a large quantity of vinegar was forced down the throat; after the first few retchings, the pain was excruciating; *Beam pulley*: the victim was suspended by his arms and lashed with leather thongs; *Pressing incense*: with the prisoner suspended from a rafter by his arms, smoldering incense was applied to the armpit; when withdrawn it tore out a piece of burning flesh; *Pulling down the road*: the prisoner was bound and tied to a horse's tail, then dragged to his death as the horse was whipped; *Assisting production*: the prisoner dug his own grave and was pushed in and buried alive."[12]

There was madness in the air at Yan'an, as Vladimirov noted in alarming reports he sent to Moscow: "24 June 1943: Kuomintang spies are being arrested. How many spies are there? And what gives Mao Zedong the right to suspect any communist of treason? And what sort of right is it, the right to supreme wisdom?

"30 June 1943: Kang Sheng displays a special attitude towards all kinds of shady characters. There is the impression that no real danger threatens the real Japanese spies, Kuomintang, and other agents in the Special Area, if they respect Kang. How many dubious characters of all kinds enjoy the confidence and protection of leading CCP functionaries! But honest communists are not among those whom [Kang's] department favours ... Kang Sheng is unpopular in the party, but he has planted his people there too. Secret reports as well as denunciations through 'exposing speeches' at meetings—this is all the intra-party life of the CCP."

On 6 September 1943, Mao and Kang Sheng launched a campaign of "spy reform" during which, as Vladimirov explains, "everyone—young or old—was busy spy-hunting or exposing himself." At this stage of the inquisition, the CCP was running out of money.

Nonetheless, when certain leaders let it be understood that it was time to put an end to such practices, they clearly ran the risk of being denounced as spies themselves. Even Zhou Enlai became suspicious in the eyes of Kang Sheng. He had after all been in contact with the Kuomintang in Chongqing. Perhaps his collaboration had begun in 1927, at the Huangpu Military Academy. Maybe the 1931 betrayal of Gu Shunzhang in Shanghai had not in fact been an unfortunate accident. And Zhou was in contact with the US Army Observation Group, a mission sent to Yan'an by President Roosevelt in September 1944 to coordinate the war against the Japanese, known as Colonel Barrett's Mission Dixie.

However, it was almost impossible to attack Zhou, who had the full support of both Mao and the Soviets. This became clear after an unfortunate fall from a horse in Yan'an led him to be hospitalized in the USSR—though even this did not stop the SAD from attacking those in his circle, including Qian Zhuangfei, who had once saved the leadership of the party by informing the Shanghai leadership of Gu the magician's defection. The unfortunate Qian was caught, tortured and executed. The very elements that had made the mathematical expert a hero—for having infiltrated Chiang Kai-shek's communications department—were now turned against him. Kang Sheng was convinced that the double agent had become triple agent. Without a doubt, the violent attack on the unfortunate Qian was because he had undertaken his mission as a communist mole in 1931 under the direction of Chen Yun and Zhou Enlai, without Kang Sheng being informed.

Meanwhile, Zhou succeeded in obtaining the last-minute release of Chen Muhua, a member of the diplomatic apparatus he had set up, who later won fame for her foreign affairs activities in Africa, where she promoted trade links and established a family planning programme. Kang accused her of spying. Her real error was being related to a Kuomintang general.[13] But Kang had crossed a red line on this occasion; he was attacking far too many spies and counterrevolutionaries, even going so far as suspecting one of Mao's sons.

Mao made it clear to Kang that it was important to know when to bring a rectification campaign to an end, explaining that suspects should not actually be killed. How many died in Yan'an? Around

2,000, I am told in Beijing. It's hard to know. For comparison, the Sinologist Jean-Luc Domenach claims that, during the May–July 1940 purge in Hebei alone, 360, 1,200 and 2,000 executions took place in three neighbouring districts.[14]

The communists were now largely under the thumb of Moscow. On 22 December 1943, George Dimitrov, the Bulgarian who had overseen the official cessation of Comintern activities worldwide, sent a telegram criticizing the campaign and demanding that Mao guarantee both the life of the chairman's rival Wang Ming and Zhou Enlai's position. The Moscow leadership even suggested that Kang was "a spy charged with destroying the CCP from top to bottom", and wondered how the most loyal pro-Soviet could have become such a traitor, turning completely against his former mentors. In this pervasive atmosphere of paranoia and spy mania, it is not entirely beyond the bounds of possibility that, as one Beijing researcher has suggested—not without malice—"one day we will find out that Kang Sheng was unwaveringly faithful to the Russians, that he was their spy, and that his mission was to make the Chinese Communist Party implode".

This reaction from the Kremlin was understandable. Two months earlier, Vladimirov had managed to send his doctor, Orlov, to visit Wang Ming; Orlov realized that Wang was being poisoned in a series of small doses. On 2 January 1944, Mao sent a telegram to Dimitrov to reassure him about Zhou Enlai's position, but explained that, because Wang Ming had previously been captured by the Kuomintang and released under suspicious circumstances, he could not be trusted. A few days later, according to Vladimirov, Mao invited Wang to the Peking opera, where the leader went back on his inopportune remarks and expressed his gratitude to Comrade Stalin. The Soviets had just saved Wang Ming's life: he would be sent back to the USSR in 1950.[15] This allowed them to preserve their alliance with Mao without going directly against Kang Sheng.

Nevertheless, trouble was now brewing for Kang, orchestrator of the first great Chinese purge. The CCP leadership was now openly in opposition to him, with the sharpest criticism coming from Zhou Enlai, on 6 September 1944. Hatred of the man known behind the scenes as the "party's hangman" was such that Mao had to force him to undertake his own self-criticism in March 1944: "It was a subjectivist mistake, only 10 per cent of the comrades criticized were really spies!" was the substance of his explanation. Meanwhile, insidious rumours were circulating about him—concerning his three-way marriage with Cao Yi'ou and Su Mei; the fact that he had vouched for Jiang Qing's "political virginity"; and the mysterious circumstances of his entry into the party and his clandestine life in Shanghai while living under the roof of a Green Gang chief.

Kang was relieved of his position as coordinator of the intelligence services—which now passed entirely into Li Kenong's control—and sent back to his native Shandong to set up a programme of "agrarian reform". He went on to lead another violent purge in that province. The Yan'an Rectification Campaign was to have another perverse effect: long after the People's Republic of China had been established, party members who had lived in Yan'an back when it was the epicentre of the fight against spies were suspected of playing for both sides. There is, after all, no smoke without fire.

Zhou Enlai's alternative secret service

Even in the midst of this political maelstrom, Zhou Enlai had managed to keep Kang Sheng from sole control of all the intelligence services. Li Kenong, Zhou's eyes and ears, had been deputy leader of the SAD. Now, in spite of the rumours that swirled around him about his relationships with the young Red Pioneer boys with whom he was often seen, he had taken over as head of the entire service.

Zhou Enlai had gathered around him a few trusted people he knew from either Paris or Shanghai, to set up, with Ye Jianying's support, a new, distinct military intelligence service: the 2nd Department, which was independent of the pre-existing Red Army Secret Service. Its head was one of Li Kenong's comrades, Liu Shaowen, who liaised with Chen Geng, head of the Red Army Military Committee's political department.

The service had been established specifically in order to keep important aspects of intelligence out of Kang Sheng's destructive orbit, and it is at the root of an unusual arrangement that continued right up until Xi Jinping's reform of the People's Liberation Army in

2017 (see Chapter 14): the existence of two separate and competing Chinese military intelligence services: the 2nd Department of the army general staff (*Er Bu*, or PLA2), and, closer to Zhou's original creation, the General Political Liaison Department (*Zongzheng lianluobu*).

Meanwhile, two civilian organizations, still active today, were given increasing powers under Zhou, with Mao's endorsement. The first was the ILD, the International Liaison Department of the Communist Party (*Zhonglianbu*), which reported to the Central Committee of the CCP. Wang Jiaxiang, the son of a peasant with Soviet intelligence training, set up the ILD at the communist base of Jiangxi in 1931, before taking over from Kang Sheng at the Comintern in Moscow. The ILD was in fact a kind of miniature Chinese-style Comintern, and over the years it managed relationships not only with the liaison services of other communist parties around the world, but also with various third-world liberation movements. Wang was reappointed head in 1951, and remained in post until 1966. Even then, he continued until his death in 1974 to maintain contact with various interested political parties around the world, whether of the left, centre or right, as well as working for the party leadership in an advisory capacity.

The second service, which also reported to the CCP Central Committee, was called the "United Front Work Department" (*Tongzhan Gongzuo Bu*). Through discreet and painstaking work within social, political, cultural, economic and religious organizations, the UFWD brought significant segments of the population over to the CCP's cause. Both within China and overseas, it targeted Chinese people who were beyond the Kuomintang's sphere of influence, or prepared to break away. Even today, it continues its mission to rally overseas pro-Taiwanese Chinese (*Huaqiao*) to the Beijing cause. In other words, as far back as the 1940s, Zhou Enlai and his colleagues had set out to influence foreign parties and governments and obtain the support of public figures to help build a "new China". Zhou chose a longstanding friend to head the UFWD: Li Weihan, better known by his nom de guerre "Luo Mai", as André Malraux calls him in his first "Chinese" novel, *The Conquerors*. Li, one of the student–workers from the Paris days, now wore two hats, as both a syndicalist and a secret agent in Shanghai. With the UFWD he would set up a major apparatus for influencing international opinion towards Chinese communism.

To his credit, Li Weihan and his UFWD did pull in some big fish in the United States, including General Li Tsung-jen, former vice-president of the Chinese nationalists, who agreed to return to China in 1965. Before that, and even more significantly, rocket engineer Qian Xuesen was brought back into the fold. Trained in the US, Qian was working at the Caltech Aircraft Propulsion Laboratory in 1950 when the FBI was alerted to the fact that he was sending books and technical journals to China—though of course this was not technically espionage, in the sense that these materials were freely available. In any case, the Chinese services would hardly have asked a scientist of his calibre to risk prison when the plan was to invite him back to China to launch the missile industry and become part of the team developing the atomic bomb, an obsession of Mao's since 1945. The situation was extremely risky, however: this was at the height of Senator McCarthy's anti-communist campaign, which culminated in the death sentence and execution of the Rosenbergs as members of the Soviet spy ring that had infiltrated the Atomic Center at Los Alamos.

In 1955 Qian did return to Beijing to work on the development of Chinese missiles, and later the famous anti-ship missile *Silkworm*. He was not the only one: eighty-four Chinese scientists trained in the US returned to China because of the UFWD's persuasive tactics. On 5 November 1960, thanks to Qian, the Chinese would launch their first R-2 rocket, a precursor to the *Dongfang* ("East is Red"). Marshal Nie Rongzhen, who had worked for Zhou's technical service in Paris and Shanghai, joined the technical team developing communist China's strategic weapons. He opened a bottle of champagne, in the presence of Qian, and declared: "This is the first Chinese missile to fly over the horizon of its motherland, marking a turning point in its history."[16]

One of those collaborating with Qian and Nie, Qian Sanqiang, should arguably be considered the real father of the Chinese atomic bomb. Born in Zhejiang in 1907, he was working in a European laboratory when Japan attacked China in 1937, a member of Irène and Frédéric Joliot-Curie's atomic research team in Paris, part of the CNRS (National Centre for Scientific Research). Qian Sanqiang and his wife, the physicist He Cehui, witnessed the splitting of uranium and thorium nuclei under the action of neutrons, and they also had occasion to meet other atomic scientists linked to the underground Soviet intelligence, including Bruno Pontecorvo who, after his move to Moscow, would go on to help the Chinese make their own atomic bomb.[17]

In 1947, the Chinese couple discovered the principles governing the tripartition and quaternary fission of uranium. This led to an enhanced understanding of nuclear fission both in France and in Moscow, where the results of their experiments were sent. Chinese leaders were undoubtedly delighted when these eminent scientists returned to China in 1948, on the eve of the Red Army's victory over the Kuomintang; it meant that, when the time came, they would no longer have to depend on the goodwill of Soviet scientists.[18]

In December 1949, Chiang Kai-shek retreated and fled to Taiwan. In Chinese tradition, a defeated general and his army change sides. This was the case with former intelligence officers from Dai Li's nationalist secret service, the BIS. The rout had evidently been hastened by Dai Li's death in a plane crash on 17 March 1946, and his immediate replacement by General Mao Feng, father of Chiang Kai-shek's first wife. The crash has sometimes been blamed on the communist services, but was probably simply due to heavy fog.[19] Multiple defections followed. The most famous defector was Shen Zui, a former BIS cadre and Dai Li's aide-de-camp who, at the request of Zhou Enlai, and to obtain clemency from his communist jailers, wrote "confessional materials" (*jiadai cailiao*) which were then turned into widely circulated books describing the depravity of Shen's former bosses in the nationalist secret services.[20]

However, the publishing of propaganda books is clearly not the best way to influence democracies or turn the public mood in one's favour. Zhou Enlai and the now victorious CCP's Chinese secret services knew that they had to exercise great subtlety in their use of agents of influence, and to exploit the goodwill of high-profile cultural figures without their knowledge.

Pearl S. Buck, the Gong sisters and Eleanor Roosevelt

In 1937, ten years before the start of the Cold War, FBI chief J. Edgar Hoover, the unassailable leader of US counterintelligence, opened a file on the novelist Pearl S. Buck. Even when she won the Nobel Prize for Literature the following year, for a body of work that included several novels set in China—*East Wind: West Wind, The Good Earth, Sons, The Mother, A House Divided*—she remained under surveillance. Hoover was not keen on writers, and on his orders the "Untouchables", a notorious Chicago-based team of federal law enforcement agents, amassed a wealth of documentation on Buck, a passionate advocate for human rights and the Chinese cause. As the records show, despite his legendary paranoia, Hoover was not wrong on one point: Buck did try to influence the wife of the president, Eleanor Roosevelt, to abandon her relationship with Madame Chiang Kai-shek and back the Chinese communists: "They are the ones who have the true support of the people. You have to talk with Zhou Enlai," the novelist insisted.[21]

Buck urged Mrs Roosevelt to pay attention to Soong Ching-ling, widow of the late nationalist leader and founder of the Kuomintang, Sun Yat-sen. A graduate of Wesleyan College, Madame Sun Yat-sen never became a communist, but in 1926, newly widowed, she visited Moscow, just after Chiang Kai-shek had taken control of the Kuomintang and contributed in large part to the increasing corruption spreading through the party, thanks in particular to his links with the Green Gang. Madame Sun participated in many propaganda campaigns via multiple committees, leagues and anti-imperialist fronts, all orchestrated by the astonishing Willy Münzenberg, leader of the Comintern's media empire. In the United States, she also had the "Chinese lobby" to deal with, led by her own sister, Soong May-ling—Madame Chiang Kai-shek—and other members of the wealthy Soong family.[22]

Buck had no trouble convincing the First Lady that Madame Sun Yat-sen was the only one in the family pursuing her husband's ideals with real integrity. She pointed out the criminal activities of the Kuomintang, telling Mrs Roosevelt about Dai Li, the head of the special services, then still very much alive and active, and nicknamed the "Chinese Himmler".

Eleanor Roosevelt's circle was largely female. It included another remarkable Chinese woman, who was also part of Zhou Enlai's inner circle of special agents: Gong Pusheng. Daughter of one of Sun

Yat-sen's generals during the revolution of 1911, Gong had been a brilliant student at Columbia, where she and her youngest sister, Gong Peng, had led the non-communist student movement. Thereafter the fates of the two Gong sisters had seemingly drawn apart. "Little Sister" Peng, who loved tales of honour, outlaws and warlords, like the picaresque *Romance of the Three Kingdoms*, had gone to Yan'an in 1935, where she became Zhou Enlai's secretary in Chongqing. She worked mostly in press relations, through which she made many friends, including the American journalist Edgar Snow. She undertook multiple liaison missions abroad for the CCP, and after she married a party leader named Qiao Guangua, Zhou sent the couple to Hong Kong to set up the New China News Agency, which served both as an organ of propaganda and as an intelligence post. In 1949, when the People's Republic was founded, Gong Peng became director of the intelligence section at Zhou's Ministry of Foreign Affairs (*Waijiaobu diaocha xinwensi*), a post she held until 1958.

Meanwhile, "Big Sister" Gong Pusheng was playing a major role in the United States. She had become a member of the Human Rights Committee at the League of Nations in New York and, as requested by Zhou, had inveigled her way into friendships with the elite of the Democratic Party. Naturally, she gathered valuable intelligence that she passed on to the Chinese secret service.

Like her younger sister, Gong Pusheng was extremely pretty. She was also a passionate feminist. She and Eleanor Roosevelt got on well and she soon became a close friend and confidante of the First Lady. The FBI was aware of her relationship with the president's wife, but because they thought of her primarily as the daughter of a nationalist general, it apparently did not occur to them that she might also be a secret member of the CCP. Pearl Buck, who did not hide her dislike for Chiang Kai-shek's clan, was kept under much closer surveillance. The pro-Kuomintang lobby remained very powerful in the United States, and kept a close eye on her. Ultimately, despite the urging of Pearl Buck, Soong May-ling and Gong Pusheng, in 1943 Eleanor Roosevelt was forced by her husband to cancel a trip to China, during which she had been planning to meet Zhou Enlai. But Zhou was to have the last word.

The mystery of The Blue Lotus

The *Blue Lotus* affair is quite simply one of the strangest episodes involving Comintern agents, the Chinese secret services and Zhou Enlai's network of influence in the arts world.

Hergé originally found fame in 1930 after his first Tintin volume, *Tintin in the Land of Soviets*, was published serially in the children's supplement of a right-wing Belgian Catholic newspaper. At the time, in line with his editor and readership, he made no attempt to hide his dislike of communism. But *The Blue Lotus*, the book that really made him famous five years later, was quite different.[23] Hergé did a vast amount of reading while working on this volume, the most deeply researched of all his works.[24] It tells the story of Tintin in China, bravely engaged in a fight against drug traffickers in cahoots with both the Japanese secret services, headed by the cunning Mitsuhirato, and the imperial powers who reigned over the International Concession—the story's police chief, Dawson, was modelled on Patrick Givens, the Irish-born head of the Shanghai Special Branch and the bane of the Shanghai communists.[25]

Perhaps people believed that Tintin's allies in the Sons of Heaven secret society, and his friend Chang, represented the Chinese people as a whole when faced by the cataclysm of war, Western imperialism and the Japanese. In any case, the book delighted both the Kuomintang and the CCP, particularly in the wake of their new anti-Japanese alliance. The facts were drawn directly from real news stories: the famous train attack on 18 September 1931, which triggered the Japanese invasion of Manchuria, is carried out in the comic book by the spymaster Mitsuhirato. This character—"A true Japanese knows everything honourable, sir!"—was inspired by Colonel Doihara Kenji, also chief of the real-life secret society the Black Dragon Sect (a black dragon features on the cover of *The Blue Lotus*).

Public opinion in the mid-1930s was hostile to the Japanese, and many books released at that time were strongly influenced by Willi Münzenberg's Comintern propaganda service. Indeed, Brussels was the hub of these operations, for it was there, in February 1927, that Münzenberg founded the League Against Imperialism, presided over by Albert Einstein, with Ho Chi Minh, Sun Yat-sen's widow and André Malraux—who, as usual, made a speech—in the front row. As we've seen, Madame Sun Yat-sen, like the Gong sisters, was a major figure in the international networks of influence set up by Zhou Enlai and his special services, and in 1928 she attended another Brussels meeting of the League Against Imperialism, where an array of well-known participants showed their support for Chinese communism.

Among Madame Sun's friends in Belgium was Lou Tseng-Tsiang, a former prime minister of her husband. In 1926, after his wife died, Lou took orders and became a Benedictine monk at the abbey of St André in Bruges, taking the name Dom Pierre-Celestin Lou. It was through him that, on 1 August 1934, Hergé first met Zhang Chongren, a young student at the Royal Academy of Fine Arts in Brussels. Zhang Chongren, who had come to Brussels from Shanghai three years previously, helped design *The Adventures of Tintin in the Far East* (the original title of *The Blue Lotus*), serialized later that year in the *Petit Vingtième*. To help him with his research, Dom Pierre-Celestin Lou lent Hergé the book he himself had published the previous year, *The Invasion and Occupation of Manchuria*.

Zhang does not appear to have been a right-wing student or linked in any way to the Kuomintang. But we do know that his close friend in Brussels, a biology student named Tong Dizhou from Zhejiang, was a graduate of Fudan University, founded by Zhang's uncle. Tong went on to establish the People's Republic of China's Institute of Oceanology in 1950 and served as its first director. He later became vice-president of the Academy of Sciences and gained renown in the 1960s for cloning carp.[26] He became an important regime figure at the instigation of the United Front Work Department (UFWD), the secret service that we know persuaded large numbers of scientists to return to the fold.[27] Was he secretly a member of the CCP the whole time he was in Brussels, or was he brought round to the cause later? In any case, Tong was to become one of the communist regime's senior scientific figures.

Similarly, his old friend Zhang went on to be closely associated with communism, whatever he may later have wished people to believe. In the wake of the communist victory, he would meet Marshal Chen Yi, who led the troops that took Shanghai in 1949. The subsequent repression of counter-revolutionary elements in the city was implacable: 100,000 Shanghai residents were executed, including many members of the secret societies referenced in *The Blue Lotus*. The leader of the Green Gang, Du Yuesheng, fled the city. He died in Hong Kong in 1951.

Zhang, meanwhile, was to be well regarded by the communist authorities. In the 1950s, Chen Yi, now mayor of Shanghai, organized a committee to select artists for patronage, appointing two familiar figures: Pan Hannian, the secret service man and former intimate of Kang Sheng and Li Kenong; and Madame Sun Yat-sen, now vice-president of the People's Republic of China (PRC). The committee chose Zhang as an official artist. He received many commissions for his sculptures and paintings, including a huge sculpture of "six characters: a worker, a farmer, a soldier, a young man, a woman of the people and a child, all standing together about to hoist a large flag bearing the five-star emblem of the PRC. The sculpture symbolized the union of the entire people, which had brought about political change. Its meaning was immediately understandable; everything was concentrated in this sculptural form."[28]

Zhang would later recount that some bureaucrats complained that he did not have enough "political thought", and that perhaps someone else should have been chosen. But at the time, the CCP claimed that his work was promoting "socialist realism". He continued to create glorifying statues such as that of Shen Yumin, a heroine of the CCP in Shandong. "At that point I was well known as a sculptor. In 1954, I created a statue of a revolutionary activist, a hero of the People's War, for a Moscow exhibition of sculpture from socialist countries, the only Chinese work to be selected."[29] In other words, whatever political ideology he may have held in the mid-1930s, Zhang at least ended up an important member of the PRC, legitimizing its ideals through art.

In 1966, he fell victim to the plight of many artists during the turmoil of the Cultural Revolution. This was not because he was hostile to the regime, but because his protector Chen Yi, now foreign minister, was first in the Gang of Four's line of fire; even his friendship with Zhou Enlai failed to protect him. It was only with Deng Xiaoping's political reforms from 1981 that Zhang was rehabilitated. At this time Hergé tried to find his old friend, whom he had made the hero of *Tintin in Tibet*. The novelist Han Suyin, Zhou Enlai's biographer and friend, helped Hergé find Zhang and persuaded Deng—a fellow Hakka—to allow Zhang to visit Belgium. There was a moving reunion in Brussels. Tintin-lovers were delighted. The CCP was also delighted; the tales of "Ding Ding", as the plucky reporter was called in Chinese editions, were promoting the very slogans Zhang had advocated: "Use foreigners to serve China!" (*Yang wei zhong yong*); "Use foreign power to enact Chinese propaganda!" (*Liyong waili wei wo xuanchuan*). It is this "future" context—the closeness of Zhang to both Hergé and to the communist regime—that is rather telling when we look at the political ideas in *The Blue Lotus*.

In 1934, when Zhang first met Hergé, the young Chinese artist told him which Chinese slogans should appear on the walls of Shanghai in his drawings for the book. He did the calligraphy for him. As Benoît Peteers correctly points out in his biography of Hergé, *The Blue Lotus* is dotted with innumerable inscriptions, drawn by Zhang himself, which underline the political significance of the story.[30] Their translation reveals certain surprises: "Abolish the unequal treaties!" "Down with imperialism!" [*Dadao Diguozhuyi!* 打倒帝国主义!] "Boycott Japanese goods!"

Obviously this messaging was subliminal and entirely beyond the understanding of the thousands of children and adults who, like me, have read and adored the story. But it does explain the general context in which the book was conceived.

When Tintin leaves Shanghai, he goes "deep into Chinese territory". "From the moment he gets there, we can't touch him!" says the Japanese general on his tail, Haranoshi. This was territory freed from enemy threat—the enemy being the Japanese, the French and British imperialists and the Kuomintang. The flooded village Tintin visits there is called Hou Kou; in 1931, when the story is set, the region of Jiangxi was one of Mao's first rural *soviets*, where the nascent Red Army was under the command of one of his old Hakka friends—none other than Zhang's future patron, Chen Yi. Chen was one of the former Paris student–workers, a member of Zhou Enlai's underground. He liquidated 2,000–3,000 communists hostile to Mao in the Hou Kou region.[31] Hergé would not have known about these events, given the lack of broadcast news and so on at the time. So was this setting a random choice, or evidence that Hergé had access to insider communist knowledge, coming from Chen via Zhang?

Hergé was presumably not manipulated into including these details in his book, but perhaps his platform was harnessed by the CCP propaganda machine and its policy of a "united front". The anti-Japanese line of *The Blue Lotus*, which provoked fury from the pro-Japanese lobby in Brussels, suited the Kuomintang. In 1939 Madame Chiang Kai-shek invited Hergé to visit China at her expense, but with the outbreak of war in Europe he never took up the invitation. He lost touch with Zhang, who meanwhile lived through the throes of Shanghai's occupation under Hirohito's troops.

A number of mysteries about Hergé have remained unresolved by the many books published about him, notably those overseen by the Hergé Foundation for its centenary celebrations in 2007, and indeed the details described above remained unknown until the publication of this book in French in 2008. This was partly because of Hergé's celebrated reputation in the world of children's literature, with his renowned Tintin series, and partly because it was hard to imagine that a writer–illustrator known for his far-right politics during the Second World War had once been a communist sympathizer, and perhaps had even been unknowingly manipulated by Chinese communists.

Probably the main reason why the *Blue Lotus*/communism story took so long to emerge is simply that no one thought to investigate the context in which Zhang Chongren and Hergé became friends, nor to analyze how much influence Zhang had on the Belgian writer. I myself, as one of many investigative journalists whose youthful career ambitions can be traced back to reading *The Blue Lotus*, understand only too well how society might have preferred to stick to the touching, apolitical tale of an international friendship between Hergé and Zhang Chongren, and their fictional counterparts, Tintin and Chang Chong-chen.

The precise nature of *The Blue Lotus*'s political dimension may never be clear. But the fortunes of Hergé's friend Zhang were also those of China in his age: Chen Yi, Zhang's protector, had now taken Shanghai, and in September 1949 Mao had proclaimed the People's Republic of China in Beijing. A new era of Chinese intelligence was opening up.

1949, the birth of the spy state

By 1949, the military defeat of Chiang Kai-shek was complete. Chiang withdrew with his army to Formosa (Taiwan), which, with the help of the Americans—and particularly the CIA—would become a stronghold for the dreamt-of "reconquest of mainland China". Since that time half a century ago, these two Chinas have been engaged in an extraordinary covert war.

The "Bamboo Curtain" fell across the Taiwan Strait in the south, and the Great Wall in the north. As with communist regimes in Eastern Europe, security services—secret police and intelligence agencies—were set up and played a key political role. Under the CCP, they organized and administered surveillance of the largest national population in the world, and, until the 1970s, worked for the global export of the communist revolution, in concentric circles beginning in Asia.

However, multiple setbacks hampered Mao Zedong's dreams for the People's Republic of China: the Tibetan rebellion, backed by the CIA and the Indian intelligence services, which was crushed in 1951 and led to the young Dalai Lama's flight to India; the Korean War (1950–3), in which China lost a million men, and with it Mao's hope for military conquest of Taiwan; the 1953 death of Stalin, for—although the two leaders had never really got on—Mao had copied his methods of controlling the population and the planned economy; Nikita Khrushchev's arrival at the Kremlin, which precipitated a schism with the Chinese that slowed their technological progress, notably in their naval fleet and the development of the atomic bomb; the disastrous error of the 1958–62 economic programme known as the "Great Leap Forward", which would claim the lives of 30 million Chinese; Japan's recovery, after a period as little more than a vast American aircraft base on the PRC's eastern flank; the secret war on China waged from Hong Kong by Taiwan and the West; the British counterinsurgency operations against Chinese guerrillas in Malaysia and Singapore, and the American operations against Filipino Huks; the Sino-Indian Wars of the 1960s; and the French war in Indochina (1945-54), followed by the American conflict in Vietnam (1955-75).

It was in this challenging international context that the Chinese special services emerged and grew. They received guidance from various Soviet comrades in the MGB (the transitional name of the former NKVD and future KGB), including Colonel Ivan Raina, deputy director of the 1st Directory. But the Chinese kept the Soviets at a respectable distance, including them only very indirectly in their intelligence operations—not least because they were well aware that the Soviets had embedded operatives in certain Chinese intelligence networks.

The two communist countries' services agreed on the exchange of information gleaned in capitalist countries of the West, but it was out of the question for the future KGB to wield authority over its Chinese counterpart as it was doing in Eastern Europe. In a show of goodwill during Mao's 1949 trip to Moscow, Stalin pointed out various American imperialist agents within Mao's entourage, including the journalists Edgar Snow, Anna-Louise Strong and Sidney Rittenberg. Rittenberg, less fortunate than the other two, was held prisoner by Chinese counterintelligence for several years, while Mao tried to use Snow as an intermediary with the CIA; this was absurd, since Snow was not working for them. According to recent accounts, Stalin went on to insist that Mao receive a list of all Chinese agents working for the Soviets, though it is hard to believe that Moscow was not also maintaining networks of "illegals", at least in border zones.[32]

The Soviets were undoubtedly reassured by the fact that Kang Sheng had been replaced by Li Kenong as head of the SAD. Li was now responsible for foreign intelligence, management of agents, and the top-secret archives of the triumphant CCP. It was a sign of his importance that he attended meetings of the Party's political bureau as an observer.

The SAD developed a network of regional offices throughout China, whose function was counterintelligence. These offices reported to the departments, sections and teams set up at all administrative levels of the CCP: provinces, municipalities, and districts (*xian*). Li Kenong was promoted to the rank of colonel general (three-star general) in the new People's Liberation Army (PLA). As deputy chief of staff, he was also responsible for military intelligence (the PLA2 and PLA General Political Liaison Department) as well as intercepting communications, carried out by an undercover section of the Meteorological Bureau. The operational command of these services fell to General Li Tao. This apparatus was able to operate abroad through a network of military attachés and with the support of journalists from the military section of the New China News Agency (*Xinhua*). The intelligence services were very involved in the wars in Indochina and Korea (led by General Liu Shaowen, successor to Li Tao), as well as in the Beijing-instigated insurgency conflicts that were unfolding throughout Asia.

Luo Ruiqing's Gonganbu

Eventually, most of the security service was incorporated into the Ministry of Public Security, the Gonganbu. Set up on 20 October 1949, the Gonganbu had 308,808 officers; its headquarters were located at 14 Dongchang'an Avenue in Beijing, not far from Tiananmen Square, from where it still operates today. The ministry dealt with internal security, the police, and counterintelligence, particularly in small towns where the SAD did not have an office, as well as running the newly founded Chinese gulag system of "re-education camps", the *laogai*.

The Gonganbu only carried out foreign missions in border countries. For example, Ling Yun, a veteran of the SAD and former Yan'an investigator who became head of the Gonganbu in Guangzhou, set up a spy operation in Hong Kong. In the 1980s he was to become minister for state security—the Guoanbu, the new spy agency created at the instigation of Deng Xiaoping, which has become increasingly active in the twenty-first century.

For ten years, the Gonganbu was headed by Luo Ruiqing, an important figure in the revolution who, like most of the founding cadres of Gonganbu, came out of the Red Army—military security was often the first to take over liberated areas. He was nicknamed the "Chinese Dzerzhinsky", a reference to the founder of the Russian Cheka (the KGB from 1954). An effigy of Dzerzhinsky, a Polish Bolshevik and friend of Lenin, sat not only on Luo's desk, but also in the interrogation centres of the secret police.

Born in 1906 in the Year of the Horse, into a family of wealthy Sichuan landowners, he attended the Huangpu Military Academy, where he became acquainted with Zhou Enlai. On 1 August 1927, he took part in the Nanchang uprising, which was a failure—albeit a legendary one, since that was when the PLA first came into being.

Luo trained in counterintelligence techniques with the GPU in the USSR, after which Moscow sent him to Paris to tackle the French Deuxième Bureau. In Paris—capital of his beloved French Revolution and home to his idol, the Jacobin Saint-Just—he went underground. After he returned to China in 1938, he was appointed political commissar of the 6th Army. After being wounded and sent to the USSR for treatment, he took over command of the 5th Corps. During the Long March, his role in the secret services expanded and he became both head of political security and deputy head of foreign intelligence. 1938 saw his first clash with Kang Sheng, which robbed him of the role of head of military intelligence.

Despite everything, Luo's role in the secret war against the Japanese was considerable and in 1945 he reappeared as a member of the CCP Central Committee. Thus began a race to see who would take over the leadership of the CCP's many security institutions after the party took power in Beijing.

Though he did not descend into the same frenzied hunt for spies as Kang Sheng had before him, Luo Ruiqing nonetheless created an iron-fisted police state under the direct control of Mao and Peng Zhen, head of the political-legal commission that oversaw all the security services. On 1 January 1951, announcing his ministry's annual figures, Luo boasted that he had arrested 13,812 "spies" between January and October 1950.[33] He also created the "Second Department" (*Gong An Er Chu*), an elite group of investigators in charge of high-level political affairs, which examined senior figures under suspicion, or particularly complex espionage cases. The Second Department also handled the interrogation of Pu Yi, last emperor of China, captured by the Russians and handed over to the Chinese in 1950. This particular service followed to the letter the directives of the CCP Central Committee's Political Defence Bureau (*Zhengzhi Baoweiju*).

Jean Pasqualini, the Corsican-Chinese journalist imprisoned as a spy between 1957 and 1964, was among those interrogated by the 2nd Department. He painted a complex portrait of Luo Ruiqing to me, one that recognized Luo's complicated relationship with Mao: "Mao's real problem was that he never actually had full control of every aspect of power, unlike Stalin. In particular, he never had a security chief who was entirely in his hands. Luo Ruiqing was not a Maoist.

He was 100 per cent communist, responsible for hundreds of thousands of deaths. But it truly was all for the cause! He entirely lacked any personal ambition. Luo realized that after each campaign of mass internal repression—the Yan'an Rectification movement and the 1954 repression, for example—Mao was strengthened, and he was trying to stop this trend. He focused on drawing attention to external rather than internal risks: the Taiwanese and the Americans, against whom effective counterespionage needed to be developed.

"Luo Ruiqing was very popular with his staff, with the security people. Firstly, they knew he was not acting out of personal ambition. And secondly, he treated them well. He lived relatively modestly. He did not treat his agents like minions. Everyone I met in prison had a lot of respect for him."[34]

Tensions with KGB comrades

"Imperialist spies" were not the only targets. Chinese leaders kept a close eye on the Soviets, particularly the MGB/KGB *rezident* in Beijing from 1947 to 1958, Ivan Zaitzev. Nikolai V. Roschin, Soviet ambassador to the PRC, was in charge of coordinating Moscow's intelligence operations in China. Unlike other sister countries, and although the leader of the Gonganbu was considered to be pro-Soviet, the Chinese regarded security advisors with suspicion. They realized that, despite past agreements, Lavrentiy Beria, head of the NKVD in Moscow, was setting up new spy networks in China. The first tension arose when a man called Kazakov was arrested in Shanghai; though a Chinese citizen, he was a Soviet agent.

Yet not everything to do with the Soviets was cause for concern. For example, they helped to establish the Nanjing Foreign Language School for the training of intelligence personnel. The best students were sent to the Institute of International Relations and the future-KGB training school in Moscow, to learn the latest techniques of intelligence gathering. Among these top students was Lieutenant Cao Gangchuan, a graduate of the Russian-language school in Dalian. By the end of the century, he was to become head of the Commission for Science, Technology and Industry for National Defence (COSTIND), and in 2007 he was named armed forces minister.[35]

Alexander Panyushkin, former head of the Chongqing NKVD office, returned for a year to Beijing to serve as ambassador. In 1956, during a visit to Britain, the newly appointed head of the KGB, General Ivan Serov, asked the British secret services for permission to open a KGB *Rezidentura* in Hong Kong to keep southern China under surveillance, which he was denied. Serov did send somebody to Hong Kong, however: a counterespionage expert, Colonel Yuri Voronin, to set up an anti-British intelligence service, at the request of the Chinese.

Tensions grew between Beijing and Moscow in the wake of the 1953 deaths of Stalin and Beria. In 1958, several incidents took place in which Chinese police officers refused orders by Soviet comrades to arrest their fellow Chinese. As a result, the Soviets called for the dismissal of Li Kenong, head of the Social Affairs Department.

According to information provided to me by Iliya Sarsembaev, a Moscow-based specialist in Sino-Soviet relations, Khrushchev sought to defuse the emerging rivalry between Beijing and Moscow: he sent Mao a list of Chinese agents who had been working for the Russians for 27 years, a much longer list than the one delivered by Stalin. Some of these agents were CCP members who had been sent to the USSR for training in the 1920s: "A number of them stayed behind in the Soviet Union after graduation, took nationality, and became intelligence and counterintelligence officers in the NKVD, creating a large, reliable and powerful network of Chinese agents, loyal to Marxism-Leninism and Stalin. This network, set up during the 1920s and '30s, was an effective long arm for the Soviet Union until the late 1950s, and played an important role in foreign policy under Stalin, to whom they provided quality intelligence. However, many of these [Chinese-born Soviet nationals] were accused of Trotskyism and became victims of the 1936-7 purges. Later, on Khruschev's personal orders, these agents' names were handed over to Mao, as testimony to the fraternal friendship between the Russian and Chinese peoples."[36]

But the Chinese were not only suspicious of the Russians. They were also closely monitoring the embassies of the new Warsaw Pact people's republics, as evidenced by an amusing anecdote that was recounted to me by a specialist in Hungarian affairs.

Fooling around at the Hungarian embassy

In 1956, the Beijing representative of the Hungarian State Security Agency (AVO), József [P.] Szabó, officially a press attaché, was enjoying a romantic intrigue with the wife of the Hungarian ambassador, Ágoston Szkladán. Liu Lantao, one of the heads of the UFWD Chinese secret service, was sent to Budapest as part of a delegation led by Vice-President Marshal Zhu De. He asked the head of the AVO, Mihaly Farkas, who had been Kang Sheng's comrade in Moscow, "Is your AVO Resident's fooling around with the ladies a constituent part of your intelligence operations?" He explained to Farkas the true purpose of Szabó's extravagant expenses on hotel rooms, or "conspiracy apartments", rented by case officers to debrief their agents—or, it seemed, for other, personal uses.

Szabó was ousted from the AVO. But every cloud has a silver lining: he went on to become a journalist and eventually head of Hungarian radio. The Hungarians, meanwhile, did not forget this episode, taking note, like the Soviets, of the fact that the Chinese were monitoring secret agents of fellow communist countries as closely as they were those of the imperialist nations.[37] The Soviet ambassador in Budapest at the time, Yuri Andropov—future head of the KGB and one of the main architects of the ultimate break with the Chinese—never forgot this lesson.

Farkas, the head of the AVO, failed to foresee the anti-Soviet uprising in Hungary. He was arrested in October 1956, expelled from the party and thrown into prison. The cuckolded ambassador in Beijing was replaced by Sándor Nógrádi, a former Comintern agent active in France in the 1930s, who was later appointed head of Hungarian state radio Magyar—in other words, as Szabó's boss. The AVO was dismantled in October of the same year.

The Chinese intelligence chief's visit to Budapest had another unexpected result. Liu's reports, like those of the military attaché Colonel Zhang Bingyu, fed Mao's concerns that the Budapest uprising, like that in East Berlin the same year, coupled with Khrushchev's report on de-Stalinization, held serious risks for Chinese communism. Mao ordered Zhou Enlai to set up an institute to predict potential future disasters. The Institute of International Relations (*Guoji guanxi yanjiusuo*) was set up as part of the Foreign Affairs

Ministry. Its other main function was to train spies for the SAD and the Xinhua News Agency.

Xinhua News Agency: a nest of spies

The New China News Agency (*Xinhua*) began to play an important role in international intelligence gathering. Liao Chengzhi, nicknamed "Liao the sailor man", because of his former role in the dockers and seamen section of the Comintern, founded the agency in the Yan'an era; it became a state agency in 1949. Its "international" sections, along with those of the PLA, were responsible for collecting foreign intelligence abroad, some of which was used for propaganda purposes—a journalist's investigation of poverty or the situation of African Americans in the United States, for example. The rest of the news and reports remained unpublished, entering the circuit of confidential reports seen only by leaders, access to secrets being controlled according to a hierarchy of importance within the CCP. Twice a week, Xinhua's Department of International Affairs published an internal magazine called *International Affairs* (*Guoji Neican*). It drew on articles from Xinhua's foreign correspondents all around the world, which were never published.

The use of the Xinhua agency as a cover for the secret services was particularly significant in Hong Kong. Set up by "Little Sister" Gong Peng and her husband, Qiao Guangua, at the request of Zhou Enlai, Xinhua served as a sort of embassy, or even a shadow Chinese government, in the British colony. The deputy director of the agency was always a Chinese intelligence operative, until Hong Kong was returned to China in 1997. Moreover, in the 1950s and '60s, a series of Xinhua correspondents were identified as working as liaison officers with Third World guerrilla movements, in Africa, Asia and Latin America. Others, in small numbers, defected, which enabled counterintelligence agencies to study Xinhua's internal organization system and its integrated intelligence role.

Franco-British secret agents and Australian "surveyors"

The number one problem for Western intelligence—supported by Taiwanese and Japanese postwar intelligence services—was to understand how this new China and its special services functioned. As part of the Cold War agreements, the CIA relied heavily on its allies' secret services. That was how the French Foreign Service of Documentation and Counterintelligence (SDECE) became widely known. Jacques Locquin, an outstanding journalist and former Resistance member, was named head of the SDECE's Political Affairs Section at the end of the Second World War: he later became a correspondent for Agence France-Presse in Beijing. In 1957, Locquin helped former French foreign minister Edgar Faure write *The Turtle and the Serpent*, a book conceived as a kind of memorandum for General de Gaulle, who had not yet returned to power, to help him decipher the intentions of the "enigmatic Chinese". But the Gonganbu caught the intrepid reporter in a honey trap, or what Mao's agents called "the beautiful woman stratagem" (*meiren ji*). Locquin was expelled from China as an "undesirable element". Jean Pasqualini, "Mao's prisoner", as he titled his autobiography, was not so lucky. He was thrown into a Gonganbu jail on trumped up charges of spying for France and was not released until January 1964, when General de Gaulle recognized Mao's government.

Despite these successful interventions, Chinese counterintelligence was working according to very imprecise hypotheses, as Pasqualini explained to me: "When the Gonganbu men arrested me, they claimed that I was spying for the SDECE. I denied it, and nothing they did in their interrogations changed that. They could not force me to confess, because it wasn't true. I was actually working for British intelligence. My MI6 handlers were Edward Youde in 1953—he went on to become ambassador in Beijing—and John Fretwell the following year. I never had any direct contact with them; I used to bring my information to the Indian High Commission in Beijing, which was collaborating with the British. It was more discreet."

During his time in prison, Pasqualini found himself in the political detention centre known as the Basket of Herbs (*Caolanzi*), which was so important that it was located inside the Imperial City in the heart of Beijing, north of Mao's residence in the Zhongnanhai complex. This was where Pasqualini crossed paths with two CIA agents who had been caught up in the action at the beginning of the 1950s, Richard Fecteau and Jack Downey, whose plane—which belonged to the CIA's front company, the Civil Air Transport—was shot down in November 1952 while they were on a mission sending armed anti-communist guerrillas into Manchuria. Several nationalists who had already been parachuted in had been arrested and forced to send radio messages drawing the CIA men into a trap. Luo Ruiqing's secret services waited two years to announce the men's capture. Then, after a grand show trial, the two Americans were held prisoner for almost two decades, before their release in 1971. Their plane, a highly symbolic bit of war booty, is still displayed prominently at the PLA Museum in Beijing. During the 1954 trial, the Chinese announced that in January 1953 eleven more Americans had been arrested, after another plane was shot down. Those operatives were luckier than Fecteau and Downey, and were released only two and a half years later. The Gonganbu also announced that, between 1951 and 1954, 106 American and Taiwanese agents parachuted in to train anti-communist guerrillas had been killed, and 124 captured. It was not until 1960 that the CIA was persuaded their operation had achieved nothing. Eventually it was brought to an end, along with CIA backing for the Tibetan armed resistance.[38]

Half a century later, James Lilley, China specialist at the CIA and later ambassador to Beijing, made an assessment that was widely shared in the CIA: "Downey and Fecteau's capture was one of the most glaring examples of the CIA's failed covert policy in the early 1950s. Shortly after the two CIA officers were lost in Manchuria, those of us working clandestinely in Asia recognized that covert operations, including missions like Downey's into China, were not revealing much about the closed-off Middle Kingdom. Contrary to CIA predictions, our missions were unable to locate or exploit the kind of discontent among the Chinese population that could be used to establish intelligence bases in China."[39]

Unable to undertake deep surveillance work in the Chinese theatre, and without the kind of sophisticated satellites and communications interception systems that exist today, the Americans asked the Australians to undertake brief missions in China. Several journalists, academics and businessmen accepted the role of "honourable correspondent"—a voluntary intelligence collaborator. This was both less expensive and less dangerous than trying to set up guerrilla bases. Since its inception in 1957, businesspeople and retailers of all stripes had been attending the Canton Fair, the showcase of China's burgeoning economy. Many agreed to gather pertinent intelligence there. The MO9, as the Australian service was called at the time, even employed a real businessman and created a small company, tailor-made for these operations.

Recently opened archives in Canberra indicate that, throughout the Cold War, first the MO9 and then its successor the ASIS, alongside the Australian Foreign Affairs Department, ran a formidable "sweeping" operation in China with the help of Australian visitors, managing to turn the Chinese espionage system against the Chinese themselves.

This is how it was described by Timothy Kendall, author of an excellent book on China through the eyes of Australians, *Ways of Seeing China*—although his account could also easily describe similar strategies deployed by other democracies: "Throughout the Cold War, the Australian Government relied on this network of 'surveyors' to map the communist terrain and generate new information about China. I use the word 'surveyor' because they were not professionally trained intelligence officers but, for the most part, ordinary citizens—passive intelligence gatherers who collected data that was then used by Australian strategists and allied nations. Most of the information they gleaned was security-related data: it focused on standard of living, visibility of Chinese security personnel, ports in China, warships, the presence of Russians in Chinese cities, the attitude of China towards Taiwan and so on."[40]

Australian surveyors managed to create a massive patchwork of intelligence that two or three professional spies would never have been able to gather in China, in the midst of great political turbulence. However, there were some hiccups. During the Labor government of the early 1970s, the Australian secret services had the bright idea of recruiting a student on a university exchange as an "honourable correspondent". He was given all the necessary espionage equipment: camera, video camera, invisible ink. But on his return from China he was filled with guilt and sank into a depression. Worse, he told all his friends what he had been made to do, then went to the Chinese Embassy in Canberra to apologize for having spied on his friends. Not only that, but by dint of complaining, he even managed to persuade MO9 to pay him AU$4,000 in damages.[41]

The fall of Pan Hannian

The paranoia typical of police systems in totalitarian countries like China, vastly amplified by Kang Sheng, continued to be felt in the early PRC of the 1950s, to the point that the hunt for imperialists or nationalists spying for the Kuomintang affected some communist cadres well respected for their role in the revolution. One of the earliest instances was the case of Chen Bo, alias Bo Lu, known as the "Sherlock Holmes of Yan'an". In 1950, after he became head of the Canton Gonganbu, he and his colleague Chen Kun were arrested by some associates on the charge of spying for MI6 and the Kuomintang. They were sentenced to twenty years in prison.[42]

The most famous case, however, took place in Shanghai: that of Pan Hannian, who, twenty years earlier, had been involved in the early secret war alongside Zhou Enlai and Kang Sheng. Pan, a superb secret agent, had made his career in the SAD, becoming deputy head of Asia, while also serving as deputy mayor of Shanghai under Chen Yi. He was part of the team that enthusiastically carried out Mao's instruction of December 1950: "In the repression of the counter-revolutionaries, take care to strike with safety, precision and severity."

The crackdown was led with an iron first by Xu Jianguo, the head of the local Gonganbu known as the "executioner of Shanghai", who had been trained by Kang Sheng at the SAD. Had Pan Hannian fallen out with the master of Shandong's security men, who had begun to resurface in the mid-1950s? Was he framed for trying to loosen the repressive stranglehold over his hometown, with its 100,000 dead, as some in China now believe? Or was he caught, as others suppose, in Zhou Enlai's wrath?

Whatever the case, on 3 April 1955, while attending a rally, Pan was arrested, along with the Gonganbu deputy director, Fang Yan. He was accused of having spied for the Japanese and the nationalist camp, and specifically of having allowed Kuomintang nationalists to escape the vengeance of proletarian justice. From the records it appears that he had been in contact with both the Japanese secret services and those of the former Kuomintang leader, Wang Jingwei, who had turned to collaborating with the Japanese occupation, and was known as the "Chinese Pétain" as a result.

The problem for Pan, who was expelled from the CCP, is that all of this was true—but he had been acting at the request of Zhou Enlai. All these events had taken place in 1940, at the same time as Europe saw Hitler and Stalin sign the Nazi–Soviet pact and divide Poland. Mao and Zhou saw no harm in maintaining a similar strategic relationship with the Japanese, against whom they were officially at war, if the mutual assistance between the Japanese and communist services meant that they were weakening their common enemy, the Kuomintang. This was how Pan Hannian had come to be exchanging information with Li Shiqun, the head of Wang Jingwei's secret services. Since March 1940, Wang—a former left-wing rival of Chiang Kai-shek within the Kuomintang—had settled in Nanjing, where he had become leader of a so-called "national government", but had in fact gone over to the Japanese occupying forces. This "Napoleon of the Ningbo" gave himself the title of *Zongcai*, a Chinese version of Il Duce or the Führer. A motley band of former communist representatives, disgraced nationalists, opium traffickers, brothel keepers, and criminal elements from the underworlds of Shanghai and Nanjing had joined General Wang.

Among them were the two heads of Wang's new secret services: a couple of shady crooks, Ding Mocun and Li Shiqun, trained in the art of intelligence in the USSR. Back in Shanghai, under cover of a "Social Information Agency" (*Shehui Xinwenshe*), they had established the "Red Guard", the Teke's shock troops led by the magician Gu Shunzhang before his defection. Ding and Li were arrested in May 1934 on their way to assassinate a senior Kuomintang leader. To save their skins, they joined Chen Lifu's Blue Shirts and fought against their former comrades. In 1938, they followed one of them—Zhou Fohai, co-founder with Mao of the CCP, who had also turned nationalist—to join the ranks of the collaborationist Wang Jingwei.[43] Now in the pay of this Japanese vassal, Ding and Li set up a new secret service that collaborated directly with Kempeitai, the "Japanese Gestapo". Theirs was a dizzying trajectory, perhaps, but nothing out of the ordinary in 1930s China. It had not ended well: Ding, "the little devil", was shot in 1947 by the Kuomintang, while Li Shiqun ended up being poisoned by his Japanese handler.

Meanwhile, at Zhou Enlai's behest, Pan Hannian had managed to make secret contact with Li Shiqun, and they exchanged information useful to both sides. Naturally this story, not officially disclosed by the Gonganbu's 2nd Department investigators, did not help his case in 1955.

There was worse to come: Pan had also been in direct contact with the Japanese themselves. In 1940, when he was "exchanging" with his old Red Guard friend turned fascist, Pan Hannian also made contact with Lieutenant General Kagesa Sadaaki, a Japanese intelligence officer in the Nanjing government, to propose a ceasefire between the communist army in the north and the Japanese troops.[44] Kagesa had been a senior official in Japan's 2nd Bureau *(Rikugun Johobu)*, becoming first head of the 7th Section (Asia), then the 8th (strategic propaganda), before being assigned to the occupation troops in China. All of which is to say that he was a master in espionage and manipulation.

It's hard to know which of the two, the Japanese spy or the communist operative, was manipulating the other, but what is clear is that the ceasefire plan submitted by Pan to the Japanese came to nothing. Meanwhile he had been compromised in the eyes of the CCP secret service apparatus, and supporters of Kang Sheng also drew attention to his file, in order to make him appear to be a "Japanese agent".

A committed activist for the cause and an exceptional spy, Pan Hannian was sent to the *laogai* for twenty years; it is only today, long after his death, that books are being written that seek to rehabilitate his reputation.[45] It is hard to avoid the suspicion that the fall of Pan Hannian was a veiled attack against Zhou Enlai, who, in 1955, opened up Chinese diplomacy to the global Non-Aligned Movement, when he attended the Bandung Conference.

Zhou would never have made it to the conference had he taken up his seat on the Indian aeroplane the *Kashmir Princess*, which was taking his delegation to Indonesia on 11 April 1955. In an attack blamed on the Kuomintang and the CIA, the plane exploded after it had passed Natuna Island and was approaching Malaysia. Reportedly, British agents from the Hong Kong Special Branch, working together with special agents from Li Kenong's SAD, had got wind of a planned attack and persuaded Zhou to travel on another plane flying over Burma. The CIA abandoned an alternative plan to poison Zhou Enlai in Bandoeng.[46]

The SAD under Li Kenong

After the founding of the PRC, the Ministry of Public Security—the Gonganbu—had continued the repression of counter-revolutionary elements. But, unlike other "socialist" countries, the Chinese did not yet have a true state-run foreign intelligence service. They maintained a structure subsidiary to the leadership of the CCP. The SAD, located at 15 Gongxian Hutong, was now considerably weakened, because all the elements responsible for counterintelligence had been integrated into the Gonganbu. Mao made this decision to avoid criticism over having kept the leaders of the Yan'an Rectification Campaign in office.

Zhou Enlai insisted that Li Kenong be kept in his post in foreign intelligence. According to one of his Chinese biographers, Li's first job was to co-write with a team of veterans an internal history of the communist special services from 1927 to 1949, a task that took him six months.[47]

Meanwhile Kang Sheng, his rival and boss, was eclipsed. Various different theories have been put forward to explain why he was removed from the top post in the intelligence services. One explanation is that his role in the Yan'an purges had attracted the wrath of many senior officials, some themselves victims of his frenzy. Kang, the man known abroad as the "Chinese Beria", was sidelined from the leadership and, depending on which version of events we follow, either retired to his native Shandong to establish a political stranglehold from which he planned to bounce back, or, somewhat less likely, was struck by acute paranoia and symptoms of schizophrenia and placed in a mental asylum. This was the theory put about by Mao's doctor, Li Zhuisui.[48]

Rumours swirling around the American intelligence community hinted that Kang's fall was linked to the death of Stalin, or that of the real Beria in the same year. Those who tended towards this interpretation pointed out that, during his training in Moscow, Kang had been part of a pro-Stalinist faction, and was now suffering the same fate as some of his counterparts in the new Eastern European states. But, as we have seen, Kang Sheng's ambition had long been to establish an autonomous Chinese system hostile to Moscow. In this, he had the support of Mao Zedong and Zhou Enlai—the difference being that both of those men had to show diplomacy in the matter.

Around this time, Maurice Oldfield, head of the MI6 station in Singapore—and director of the British secret intelligence service in 1973-8—obtained information indicating that not only did Kang Sheng remain a close and influential associate of Mao, but also that it was he who had convinced the chairman, in the early 1950s, to break with the USSR, when Moscow was seeking to wield control over China through its advisors and scientists.[49]

There is one other possible explanation, which I explored with Rémi Kauffer in our biography of Kang Sheng,[50] with the help of certain people in the French intelligence services and their links with missionary networks and the Chinese "Church of Silence": that Kang Sheng had in fact been tasked with seeking out and bringing back Chinese scholars from around the world, for the purpose of developing a Chinese atomic bomb. Many clues point to the viability of this explanation.

In 1956 Kang Sheng returned to the public eye. In the meantime, Li Kenong had been developing the SAD's intelligence networks and, under the wing of his friend Zhou Enlai, was appointed deputy minister of foreign affairs. This led to the two men appearing in Geneva in 1954 during the negotiations for peace in Indochina.

To modernize the service, and encourage people to forget the Kang Sheng era, the name of the service was changed. No longer the SAD, in 1955 it became the CCP Central Investigation Department (*Zhongyang Diaochabu*), or Diaochabu for short, with one branch of the SAD separating out into the Legal and Administrative Work Department.[51]

In the 1950s each embassy had its own "Bureau of Investigation and Research", which dealt with intelligence gathering. One fact became clear over the years: the Diaochabu did not have the rigid structure of the Soviet KGB; its jurisdiction fluctuated, as much for those with posts in the service—such as agent recruiters and case officers (*gongzuo dandang guan*)—as for its coordinators, who were subordinate to the central directorate of the CCP.

Intelligence was collected and examined by the CCP's 8th Bureau, a vast centre of analysis that in 1965, on the eve of the Cultural

Revolution, signalled a change in direction towards the outside world, altering its name to the China Institute for Contemporary International Relations (CICIR). This institute was set up almost at the same time as the Foreign Affairs College, which was responsible for the training of secret agents. The simultaneous establishment of these two institutions was obviously backed by Zhou Enlai, who was now at the helm of China's international and diplomatic policy-making.

On 9 February 1962, after a thirty-year career in special affairs and intelligence, Li Kenong died in Beijing from the consequences of the brain damage he had suffered after a fall three years earlier. He had been seriously ill for quite some time. When his close associate Chen Geng, former head of the Teke in Shanghai, had died in March 1961, Li had been unable to travel to the funeral, although his name was on the Funeral Committee list. Officially, Li retained his position as deputy army chief of staff, in charge of overseeing military intelligence alongside the head of Diaochabu. However, in reality, the Diaochabu had now for some time been run by cadres from the Yan'an period: Kong Yuan, former secretary of Kang Sheng in Shanghai and a close associate of Zhou Enlai, assisted by Zou Dapeng and Luo Qingchang. In the gathering storm of the Cultural Revolution, the Chinese secret services were about to experience new and terrifying levels of turmoil.

3

THE SPIES' CULTURAL REVOLUTION

Tens of thousands of Red Guards stood screaming and brandishing *Little Red Books* of the thoughts of Chairman Mao, their hearts bursting with emotion for the man they called the "Red Sun in the hearts of the people of the world". They waved banners warning against "Soviet revisionists" who were accused of having destroyed Marxism-Leninism, and flourished placards with slogans attacking the "American imperialists" bombing Vietnam. Sometimes the sound of stamping grew muffled as, egged on by Chairman Liu Shaoqi, the "Chinese Khrushchev", they trampled to the ground an old teacher accused of being a "Mandarin", or kicked a "degenerate" cadre who had got caught up in "bourgeois ways". From the distance, in the direction of a university campus that had descended into anarchy, came the sound of shots, perhaps exchanged between rival Red Guards, or squadrons from the People's Liberation Army (PLA) sent in by Marshal Lin Biao, Mao's closest comrade-in-arms, in an attempt to put a stop to the chaos that these leaders themselves had triggered.

The violent clashes, pitched battles and mass demonstrations in Tiananmen Square that began in the summer of 1966 must have seemed quite bizarre to the thousands of workers hard at work like ants 8 metres below the ground, breaking stone with pickaxes and jackhammers as a revolutionary storm swirled through the streets of the capital. At least, that is how I imagined it forty years later on a guided tour of Dixia Cheng, the vast city beneath Beijing that Mao Zedong, Zhou Enlai and Lin Biao built during the Cultural Revolution as protection in the event of a nuclear or chemical attack ordered by the Kremlin.

The launch of a vast KGB disinformation campaign in China led to a renewed burst of activity on this vast, secret project. A legendary Russian agent named Victor Louis was, unwittingly, the cause. He wrote regularly for the press in the West, publishing scoops from impeccable sources with the help of his friend Yuri Andropov, the new head of the KGB. In March 1969, he stoked Chinese paranoia in the wake of several border incidents on the banks of the Amur River, which saw the two Red Armies, Russian and Chinese, engaging in skirmishes. *Dazibao*, wall posters denouncing Soviet "social-imperialists", began to appear on buildings all over Beijing. Meanwhile, behind closed doors, Zhou Enlai met with his Russian counterpart, Prime Minister Alexei Kosygin. Passing through Beijing airport, Kosygin was on his way back from Hanoi, where he had paid homage to the coffin containing Ho Chi Minh's embalmed body, as the second Indochina war continued to rage. Zhou was hoping to defuse the Sino-Soviet clashes, because, as Victor Louis revealed, he feared a Soviet nuclear attack on Beijing.[1]

Dixia Cheng: the underground bunker city

"It was during this time that we literally buried the secret services!" a source told me in 2007. The underground city, Dixia Cheng, was built by 40,000 civilians and soldiers to house 300,000 people, or 40 per cent of Beijing's population at the time. The miners of the revolution dug down as far as 20 metres below ground, over an area of 85 square kilometres.

I made my way down the long corridors with a friend, a Japanese filmmaker. Our guide was a young female soldier in combat fatigues, whose choice of words was shaped by 1960s ideology—an impeccable Red Guard, forty years after the fact. The sense of mystery was only enhanced by portraits on the walls of Mao, Zhou and even Lin Biao, "the young tiger of the forest", once Mao's heir apparent but now long erased from history. Photographs of Sukhoi planes, Soviet tanks and American B-52 bombers were displayed along the dank, clammy walls. There were vintage posters, the kind one can pick up in flea markets the world over, denouncing "social-imperialist jackals" and "American paper tigers". We smiled at the images of French and Japanese planes that belonged to the "lackeys of US imperialism". The French were much less hated than the Japanese, the mere sight of whom inflamed the Chinese. France was the homeland of the Paris Commune and General de Gaulle, who recognized the PRC in the 1960s, before it took over China's seat at the UN in 1971. But this relatively positive view of the French did not prevent the Red Guards from posting *dazibao* on the walls of the French Embassy at the beginning of the Cultural Revolution in 1966, calling its nationals "dog heads" and provoking mockery on the part of General de Gaulle, who responded with mild irony, "To be called dog heads by Pekingese rather takes the biscuit."

The first level of Dixia Cheng is 8 metres underground, a warren of streets built as an exact replica of Beijing's open arcades, with a filtration and aeration system designed to cope with a possible chemical attack and nuclear radiation. Here the militia, the secret services, the Gonganbu and army reservists would hide, weapons and gas masks at the ready, scanning their *Little Red Books* as they awaited the enemy strike.

Next is an even deeper second floor, 20 metres below the ground, with shelters for the civilian population, shops, puppet theatres to keep children occupied, nurseries, hospitals, cinemas, covered markets, and dormitories as far as the eye can see. Street signs with numerical names were designed to make it easier for civil protection troops and the army to find their way quickly through the maze of streets. Under the dark eyes of our young Red Guard, I noted down the number 01–8001 in the gallery where we stood, indicating that we were walking in the direction of Tiantan Park and the Army Library.

A European journalist who has lived in Beijing for many years told me that once upon a time her apartment, which previously belonged to a senior party functionary, had had a trap door leading straight down to a shelter connected directly to the Zhongnanhai ("Central and Southern Seas") government complex that stands to the west of the Forbidden City. When I put this to our guide, at the mere mention of Zhongnanhai she responded by holding up a hand and shaking it, clearly shocked: "*Mimi*! *Mimi*! It is secret!"

There are several entry points to this historical site. Different exits lead out of the underground city not far from the Forbidden City into Xidawo Changlie, a former Xingfu Dajie carpet factory, and into the Chongwen and Qianmen neighbourhoods. Today the underground city has taken on an entirely new dimension. With the destruction of several old neighbourhoods in preparation for the 2008 Olympic Games, many of the underground galleries have been filled in or taken over as the basements of hotels or shops, and for a new underground train line leading directly to the Olympic stadiums.

Some of these galleries have been updated, reinforced and rebuilt in utmost secrecy, under cover of the Olympic building programme, by special PLA engineering and military security units. The rapid transport systems, constructed like light railways, can move troops from one part of the underground city to another in case of unrest, or exfiltrate leaders from the underground garrison at Zhongnanhai and the Baiyi Building of the Central Military Commission (CMC), with its underground levels and twelve floors above ground, which have been entirely renovated in order to conform to anti-seismic and anti-terrorism standards.

At the same time, work on a new underground city beneath Beijing, designed for civilian activities, began in the summer of 2006 and was completed in 2012. The CMC directed the project, overseeing the triumvirate in charge of the works—the CCP, the PLA and Beijing City Hall—to construct seven or eight more advanced anti-nuclear shelters, though this still only provides room to shelter 10 per cent of the population in the event of an attack. The Chinese dream is that this invisible city will be the largest in the world, with reinforced command centres at Beijing's four cardinal points, a doubling of evacuation points to 150, and an underground transport network for troops or refugees in twenty neighbouring districts, connected to railway stations and airports. At the time of writing the first edition of this book, the authorities were considering the viability of constructing similar underground cities in Shanghai, Nanjing and eventually other cities of over 1 million inhabitants.

We have come a long way from the purely defensive construction built at the time of the Cultural Revolution. Politically, though, we are not far today from the system of the 1960s, when the best protected underground position, apart from that of Mao Zedong himself, was the area housing the headquarters of Kang Sheng, who had once again become head of the secret services.

The mysteries of the Bamboo Garden

Having retired to his native Shandong in the early 1950s, Kang the "shadow master" was recalled to Beijing a few years later, from where he would play a leading role in communist China's largest ever purges, similar to the "rectification campaign" he had carried out in Yan'an in 1942.

The subterranean city tunnels led to the Bamboo Garden in the north of Beijing, not far from the Drum Tower. This was the former residence of a Ming emperor's head eunuch and, later, a Qing emperor's cousin—a group of pavilions ornamented with red lacquer, surrounded by a Tao garden planted with bamboo and filled with winding paths, rocks and fountains. It was here that Kang Sheng established his headquarters. There were many strange goings-on in and around the different pavilions. Underground bunkers were filled with piles of artworks that had been looted from temples or old houses by bogus Red Guards in Kang's pay. There were alcoves filled with hundreds of erotic books from the Ming period—a taste Kang shared with Mao—with titles like *The Prayer Mat of Flesh* and *The Plum in the Golden Vase*. These were particularly relished by Kang, not least because he had had such works banned. He spent hours listened to tape recordings of thousands of women during orgasm, real or simulated. He watched pornographic plays, of which many exist in the traditional Chinese repertoire, performed by androgynous actors from the Beijing Opera in the roles of elegant women, *hua dan*, who excelled at imitating the sexual pleasure of aristocratic ladies, courtesans or simple peasants. It is unclear if Kang enjoyed these plays because of his own erotic perversions, or whether it was related to his obsession with the administrative evaluation of the most private areas of people's lives. After all, this was at a time when the minister of health, who was the wife of the Gonganbu chief, obliged women to post the dates of their periods on the front doors of their homes.[2]

The men in green jackets running around the Bamboo Garden were not thinking about sex. They were busy at work in the underground listening stations, with their encrypted communication systems and red telephones that allowed the secret services to communicate instructions to provincial officials. Kang Sheng, who was always dressed in white—the traditional colour of death—used these telephones to call his native Shandong, to find out how the revolution was taking shape and whether, for example, the house of Confucius had been destroyed yet, as per his orders. He would call the leader of the local Red Guards, whom he trusted implicitly, for the simple reason that this was his own son, Zhang Zishi.

Today the Bamboo Garden is a tranquil boutique hotel—though still run by the secret services—where I went for a drink with my Japanese filmmaker after our underground tour. It was nothing like what it had been in Kang Sheng's time—a buzzing hive of activity, the centre of operations for the Cultural Revolution throughout China. By following the thread of national events, we can unravel some of the most important episodes in the battle for power and overall control of the secret services in the 1950s–60s. In China, of course, power and control of the secret services were, and still are, one and the same thing.

Kang Sheng was rising through the ranks once again, using both political and ideological means. As surprising as it seems to us today, at the time, Deng Xiaoping and Kang Sheng were entirely in agreement when it came to dealing with the thorny issue of relations with the USSR. Unlike Mao, they both had international experience that gave them a global perspective. Both regretted the fact that, since the death of Stalin in 1953 and the rise of Khrushchev, the global revolution had softened, with a new emphasis on peaceful coexistence with the United States.

Act I: Kang Sheng and the Sino-Soviet split

In the 1950s Kang Sheng returned to Moscow with Peng Zhen, formerly of Yan'an Special Services, who had become mayor of Beijing in 1951. Representing the International Liaison Department (ILD) of the CCP, the two were there to set in motion a break with the

Soviets. The head of the Soviet ILD, Yuri Andropov, who later became head of the KGB, was well informed. He understood that Mao was trying to unite the CCP around his leadership by fostering hostility toward Moscow. Mao criticized the Kremlin leadership under Khrushchev for its malleability and its reformism—the very same charges he would soon level in China against Chairman, Liu Shaoqi, as well as Deng Xiaoping, Peng Zhen and the head of the Party's Organization Department, Yang Shangkun.

From 1956—when Kang Sheng first accused Tito's Yugoslavia of being behind the "counter-revolutionary rebellion" in Hungary—to the 1960s—when he personally attacked Khrushchev—Kang, the former (and soon to be reinstated) head of the secret services, appears to have been the main actor responsible for the escalation of the Sino-Soviet split.

"You are not qualified to argue with me," Khrushchev once yelled at him. "I am the general secretary of the Communist Party of the Soviet Union and you are just an alternate member of your political bureau."

With piercing eyes behind his metal-rimmed spectacles, Kang Sheng replied in the broken Russian that he had picked up in Moscow, "Your credentials are much more shallow than mine. In 1931 I was a member of the Politburo standing committee. In 1935 I was an alternate member of the executive of the Comintern. At that time, you were not even a member of the Central Committee."[3]

The Soviets' loathing of Kang Sheng was all the more intense because, like Zhou Enlai, Deng Xiaoping and Liu Shaoqi, he had once been an approved agent of the GPU, the KGB's predecessor, from which he had learned everything he knew about espionage techniques: dissimulation, disinformation, manipulation—and, as was to become quite clear, how to turn a situation completely on its head.

Many members of the Chinese leadership thought that Kang Sheng was pushing the anti-Soviet line too hard. But the purpose of these and subsequent attacks was to impress both Mao and Khrushchev; Kang was playing a game of both internal and international politics. He and Mao agreed on many points, including the most important of all: that China should become the new centre of world revolution. But to achieve this, they had to revive the revolution in China itself.

Act II: The Shanghai Gang and the Shandong Mafia

Kang Sheng was part of the group of ideologues based in Shanghai who launched the campaign against revisionist tendencies within the party in the fields of art and literature. As in the Yan'an era, political positions were critiqued through culture. It might seem that a play or a novel was being strongly criticized, but it was actually the author's protector politicians who were being targeted. The four leaders of this Shanghai group, whose name is etched into the historical memory of that terrifying era, were known as the Gang of Four.

Jiang Qing, the film actress known as "Blue Apple" in 1930s Shanghai, was the gang's figurehead. She was Mao's official wife; like an emperor of old, he also lived with other concubines provided by Kang Sheng and Wang Dongxing, chief of his personal security team. Madame Mao, like Kang, was from Shandong, and it was she who helped Kang make his successful return to the top brass of the party and the secret services.

Zhang Chunqiao was also from Shandong, and nicknamed the "Old Eunuch". He had studied at the Shaanbei Academy, formerly run out of Yan'an by the SAD—in other words, the secret services. There he had become Ke Qingshi's secretary. Ke was the activist who had helped Kang Sheng restructure the Shanghai intelligence service in 1931 after the defection of Gu the magician. In 1960, Ke became mayor of Shanghai, with Zhang as his head of propaganda. In 1965 the Old Eunuch recruited a young journalist from the daily newspaper of the CCP's Shanghai Committee, the *Jiefang Daily* (or *Liberation Daily*), to launch the first attacks on intellectual circles deemed to be counter-revolutionary.

The third member of the Gang of Four was Yao Wenyuan, son of Yao Pengzi, a well-known writer in the 1920s. Yao Junior worked as a secret agent for Pan Hannian, that other spymaster, and a friend of Zhang Chongren, of *Blue Lotus* fame. This was before Pan's imprisonment on trumped up charges of spying for the Kuomintang.

The last member of the gang, and the most important in the CCP hierarchy, was Chen Boda, the main advisor of the Cultural Revolution Group. Originally from Fujian, near Shanghai, he had been Mao's secretary in Yan'an and, along with Kang Sheng, the architect of the cult of Maoism. In the 1960s, the two men continued the deification of the chairman with a particular stroke of genius: they selected quotes from Mao's abundant writings and collected them into a small book with a red plastic jacket, called Chairman Mao's *Little Red Book*. Every good revolutionary learned these aphorisms by heart and was able to chant them like Buddhist sutras or Muslim *suras*.

As Stephen Fitzgerald, Australia's first ambassador to the People's Republic of China (PRC), wrote in his memoirs, "The Cultural Revolution was also the struggle between Beijing and Shanghai."[4] It was in Shanghai that the first attacks were made—on a theatre production, with the purpose of persecuting top-ranking officials including the mayor of Beijing, Peng Zhen, and the PLA chief of staff, General Luo Ruiqing.

Act III: The overthrow of Luo Ruiqing

The undermining of CCP top brass was possible only through an alliance with the army leadership. Mao Zedong and the defence chief, Marshal Lin Biao, together plotted the overthrow of Luo Ruiqing. Luo, a veteran of the Long March and head of the Gonganbu at the founding of the PRC, was army chief of staff as well as deputy prime minister. He also controlled a large part of the security apparatus. Clearly, his downfall would help Kang gain a stranglehold over the coveted secret services.

In early 1966, Lin Biao ordered Luo's arrest. He suffered such horrific treatment in March of that year that he tried to commit suicide by throwing himself from the window of his interrogation cell. With two broken legs, he was transported by the Red Guards to the site of a mass meeting, where he was forced to make his own self-criticism.

Kang Sheng concocted a dossier on him, garbed in the language of betrayal, accusing him of "illicit intercourse with foreigners", presumably the USSR. Throughout the Cultural Revolution, until his health deteriorated from opium and cigarettes, Kang Sheng excelled in compiling incriminating files on his enemies, put together from murky cases that often went back to the 1930s.

This was the second time in thirty years that Kang had robbed General Luo of the top job in the secret services. The battle for control of these services raged all the way through the bloody turmoil of the Cultural Revolution (1966–76). Kang Sheng relied on the help of Wang Dongxing, one of his former deputies, to stop Luo, strengthen his ties with Mao, and take apart the special services even as he was clawing back its overall leadership. Wang, one of Mao's longstanding bodyguards, had been deputy head of the Gonganbu since 1955, and head of the 8,000-man 8341 (*basansiyi*) Unit, also known as the "Central Safeguard Regiment" (*jingwei tuan*), established in 1938.[5] On every journey out of Beijing, Mao Zedong and Zhou Enlai were protected by a hundred of these elite guards. On 16 July 1966, combat swimmers from the 8341 Unit helped Mao swim 15 kilometres down the Yangtze River.

Our history so far has shown us that one political-security elite managed to maintain power from the 1920s. Many of the political leaders during the 1960s had been secret agents in the pre-1949 underground, and intelligence professionals were more likely to reach the higher echelons of the Party apparatus.

This provided Kang Sheng with useful biographical details for the records he kept on leaders who might one day fall from the top of the tree. This was all part of the cycle of battles between factions and groups, bound together by so-called "invisible relations" (*touming guanxi*), but nonetheless often in opposition to one another. This phenomenon was naturally rooted in Soviet communism, but was also influenced in the PRC by specifically Chinese forms of historical despotism.

The KGB in the eye of the hurricane

The Russians, naturally, were still exerting a strong influence. Their experts had been sent home in the wake of the Sino-Soviet split, which Kang Sheng had of course orchestrated. After becoming head of the KGB in 1967, Yuri Andropov had hopes of converting the Soviet embassy in Beijing, which he would run as ILD chief for a few more months more, into the control tower of the Chinese revolution.[6] In the USSR itself, some Chinese were still considered friends. They remained in Moscow and were approved as Soviet agents, although obviously, as a front, they had to denounce the "social-imperialist" Russians before the Chinese regime, to avoid a similar fate to that of Luo Ruiqing. To my knowledge, only one of the trainees from the 1930s remained in the USSR as a specialist on the Chinese secret service desk. With his Russified name "Djancha", this former GPU agent was absolutely committed to the Soviet cause. In 2008, his son, Sergei, was still living in Moscow, where he ran a travel agency specializing in travel to China.

In the mid-1960s, the Beijing activities of the KGB and the military intelligence GRU were considerably scaled back, and even getting hold of the *Jiefangjunbao*, the PLA newspaper forbidden to foreigners, was not easy.[7] Soviet diplomat–spies were trailed by dozens of Chinese agents wherever they went. The most common tactic to avoid this was to leave the embassy in the trunk of an ordinary cadre's car, then be dropped off and get lost in the crowd. But given the constant presence of the Red Guards, for anyone who did not belong to one of the Central Asian or Mongolian ethnic groups, it was impossible to avoid being spotted for long.

The journalist Alexei Antonkin, who chose to work for the USSR's TASS news agency rather than for the KGB, was useful to the Beijing embassy when it came to obtaining confidential documents such as the "Communications of the Central Committee of the Party", dated 16 May 1966, or the "Report of the Working Group of the Central Committee for the Examination of the Errors of Luo Ruiqing". Antonkin also managed to procure the list of the newly elected Central Committee members, enabling the team of analysts at the Soviet embassy to take note of the rise of women, dignitaries, agents for the intelligence services around Kang Sheng and Wang Dongxing, and theorists like Chen Boda and Zhang Qunqiao—all to the detriment of the more moderate faction around Liu Shaoqi—the "Chinese Khrushchev"—and Deng Xiaoping.

Antonkin received instructions from his TASS supervisors ordering him to write articles about how the Chinese people were "hostile to Mao". Like his KGB comrades, he drew from one of the most informative sources in the PRC, the "wall newspapers", or *dazibao*: "The best source of information, and the least used by reporters other than those working for the Chinese press, were quite under the radar: the *dazibaos* plastered all over the walls of the city. I found all kinds of *dazibao* in the Haidian district, a short way away from the University of Beijing. Some were more interesting or revealing than others. Among the plethora of *dazibaos*, I was able to find information that was in line with official guidelines. Internal conflicts in factories, universities, different administrations and banks were plastered all over the walls ... I took useful information from *dazibaos* in Haidian and on Wangfujing [the busiest commercial street in Beijing] which spoke of peasant and monk revolts in Lhasa and other parts of Tibet—which was a first—making it clear that the Chinese army had put down these revolts before they spread."[8]

KGB agents, likewise struggling to put together the different pieces of the puzzle, encountered further difficulties, to the point that Alexander Sakharovsky, head of the KGB First Chief Directorate and so in charge of foreign intelligence, wrote in a directive: "The KGB *Rezidentura* in Beijing is operating under siege conditions."[9] Indeed, Fedor Vasilyevich Mochulsky, resident in Beijing since 1965 under his official title of "embassy advisor", went through some very tense periods when he was subjected to intimidation by Kang Sheng's men. Several Soviet agents were expelled by force in two successive waves: Yuri Kossyukov and Andrei Krushinsky in 1966; and Nikolai Natachin, Valentin Passchuk and Oleg Yedanov the following year. When Yuri Andropov was promoted to head of the KGB in 1967, the Chinese protested using their habitual jargon: "This is a sudden and significant change in leadership within an important instrument of the fascist dictatorship in the hands of the revisionist Soviet ruling faction," proclaimed *Beijing–Information* on 12 June 1967.

In order to find out what was going in China, Yuri Andropov had to step up his "K Line" activities—K for *Kitai*, the Russian word for China. But how could the K Line act, having lost its internal networks? The KGB's First Directorate was clear: the initial objective was to recruit Chinese people during diplomatic meetings held outside China. This was a particularly difficult operation given that Chinese diplomats circulated in groups and lived together under the watchful eye of agents from the CCP's secret service, which was once more in the hands of Kang Sheng.

The second objective was to set up a special KGB *Rezidentura* in Hong Kong, one of the preferred points of entry into southern China. The Taiwanese special services had made it their main point of infiltration, but like the American services, their spies were regularly expelled from the British colony, because London did not want to provoke its powerful neighbour. (This "friendliness" by the British did not prevent the 1966 Hong Kong riots, which were plotted in Canton by the Chinese secret services.) Hong Kong also remained the privileged place where refugees from China were "debriefed", having swum across the Pearl River to escape the bloody turmoil of the Cultural Revolution. The head of the KGB office in Hong Kong, Stepan Tsumayev, was expelled in 1972. It was not until 1977, during the interim era of Hua Guofeng's leadership, that new KGB operatives returned to the British colony. They would include Yevgeni Zhemchugov and *Rezident* Mikhail Markovich Turchak, who was stationed in North Korea before becoming first bureau chief in Beijing (1976–81), then head of the China Section in the KGB's 6th Department.[10]

The third objective of the KGB First Directorate was to recruit agents from among the Uyghur, Tajik and Kazakh minorities, in Kazakhstan and other border states, who would be able to blend in with the local population, particularly in the region around Xinjiang (former East Turkestan), which had a large Muslim population and had been independent until its annexation by China in 1949.

The fourth objective was to work closely with intelligence services such as the Mongolian Foreign Service, which could run agents relatively unnoticed in Inner Mongolia, which was under Chinese control. The papers of KGB defector and MI6 agent Vassili Mitrokhin, held at the Churchill Archives Centre in Cambridge, confirm this programme. Studying this archive enables us to see how the KGB was obliged to proceed in a circular fashion during the Cultural Revolution, having recalled its "illegal" agents from China and lost several along the way. The KGB's collaboration with the Mongolian and North Korean secret services therefore proved very useful. It was necessary to cooperate with the Border Guard Intelligence Service in Kazakhstan, Manchuria and Xinjiang in order to send in undercover, pro-Soviet Chinese agents, but also to monitor and study the activities of Chinese agents abroad, including in enemy countries such as Japan and the United States. Between 1966 and 1969, according to a report filed by Krestyaninov, who was stationed in Canada, the KGB managed to identify a network of eleven Chinese secret service agents run out of New York by Siu Minchen, a translator at the UN, his wife Tsin Fen, an academic, as well as Den Yuishu, employed at the University of Maryland, Yan Tsiuya-yun at the University of Georgia, the Kuomintang consul general in Los Angeles, Tsian Yishen, and Tsen Yisan, an actress living in New York.[11]

In 1969, a Chinese restaurateur in New York named Min Chiausen was murdered, along with her friend Wang En-ping. According to the investigators, Miss Min, borrowing the name of another Chinese woman who had died in an accident in 1952, had been sent undercover to the United States by Li Kenong's service. No one knew who killed her. New York triads? Kuomintang agents? Might it even have been the Russians?

The KGB, meanwhile, also had an operative working against the Chinese in France: Ronald Lebedinsky, a KGB specialist on China, who was posted to Paris in 1974. Andropov's service was in a race with the Chinese services to recruit Madame Mao's former husband Ma Jiliang, alias Tang Na, who had been running a well-known Chinese restaurant in the city, La Fontaine de Jade, since 1961.[12] Shortly before his death in 1988, the Guoanbu—the post-Mao intelligence agency—contacted Ma Jiliang to write his memoirs, presumably fishing for details on relations between his ex-wife and Kang Sheng. For Madame Mao, at the start of the Cultural Revolution in 1966, was right in the eye of the hurricane.

The disintegration of the special services

In August 1966, Mao stood in Tiananmen Square and addressed the young Red Guards: "We are right to revolt!" This was the launch of the fight against artists, teachers and intellectuals, a campaign of cultural annihilation particularly dear to Madame Mao's heart. At the end of the summer, the witch-hunt of party functionaries began. Kang Sheng attended all the mass meetings and rallies in his customary white suit as a representative of the "Central Case Examination Group", a kind of super-secret police. He simultaneously launched the pursuit of counter-revolutionaries within the intelligence services.

However, even as the crusade against anti-party elements began to grow, it was vital that the ensuing anarchy should not lead to the total destruction of the secret services. On 8 September 1966, Kang Sheng, in accord with Wang Dongxing, posted a Central Committee directive attempting to limit the Cultural Revolution's attacks on the services: "Codes, telegrams, confidential documents, files and secret archives are the essential secrets of the Party and the State; the safeguarding of all of these elements is the responsibility of all cadres, revolutionary masses, students and revolutionary teachers. The Red Guards and the People's Liberation Army Reservists must cooperate with the Government and Party organizations and the People's Liberation Army in assuming the glorious responsibility of protecting secrets of the Party and the State."

But the leadership had unleashed something it was unable to control. The Chinese security and intelligence apparatus began to fall apart, like all the other institutions disrupted by the Cultural Revolution. Luo Ruiqing was its first sacrificial victim. In the winter of 1966, three "revisionist" leaders, Liu Shaoqi, Deng Xiaoping and Yang Shangkun, were arrested and subjected to a barrage of intense criticism and humiliating self-criticism in mass meetings where collective hysteria prevailed over Marxist-Leninist orthodoxy. Yang Shangkun's was a particularly curious case: as head of the Central Committee's General Affairs Office, Yang, who came from a wealthy Sichuan family and had been trained by the GPU in Moscow, was accused of having bugged Mao's office on behalf of the Soviets. Only in the aftermath of the Cultural Revolution was it discovered that he had indeed bugged the Zhongnanhai office as far back as the 1950s, but with Mao's agreement—just as Richard Nixon had recording devices hidden, presumably for posterity, in the Oval Office. In that case, of course, the bugs proved to be the president's own downfall when the Watergate scandal emerged.[13]

If someone was not suspected of being a KGB spy, they were suspected of working for the CIA. Liu Shaoqi's wife, Wang Guangmei, was accused of being a "spy for the imperialist services" and, in the charming words of Madame Mao, of being "Sukarno's whore", on the grounds that she wore an evening gown and a pearl necklace during an off-duty trip to Indonesia where she met that country's president. During a mass rally in April 1967, Madame Mao did everything she could to humiliate Wang and force her to self-criticize, which she refused to do, in spite of the wondrously crafted file on her produced by Kang Sheng.

China, with its 800-million-strong population, was inflamed by the Red Guards' revolts. The public security service, the Gonganbu, did not escape the fire. Of the 250,000 functionaries at the Ministry for Public Security, as it was officially known, heads of committees in Beijing, Shanghai and elsewhere were dismissed from their posts. In 1966, every Gonganbu deputy minister, with the exception of Kang Sheng's ally Wang Dongxing, was purged for being a "double agent". Two of the imprisoned leaders—Ling Yun and Liu Fuzhi—were to resurface after the Cultural Revolution and avenge themselves in the 1980s by setting up new secret services, while three others died in prison.[14] Meanwhile, 225 heads of the Gonganbu's central offices and 34,480 functionaries were fired. 1,500 were killed. The Gonganbu Red Guards even published their own newspaper called *The Red Security Officer* (*Hongsi Gongan*) recounting their exploits.

The public security minister himself, however, Xie Fuzhi, opted to remain loyal to Mao and Kang Sheng. This led him, with a certain irony, to oversee the destruction of his own organization, whilst simultaneously orchestrating his and his wife's promotion within the new system. His wife Liu Xiangping was appointed minister of health. As the ship began to sink, a good number of the Gonganbu's forces found a lifeline in the army, headed by Mao's ally Marshal Lin Biao.

At this rate, the entire Chinese intelligence universe was in danger of imploding, as Kang Sheng was only too aware. Working out of the Bamboo Garden, he set about strengthening his own networks. Many others were also finding ways to hang on to their positions. Lin Biao's army, Zhou Enlai's diplomatic service and Wang Dongxing's special units all preserved entire sections of the system. Zhou guaranteed the decent treatment of some jailed functionaries. This was the case for some political figures, including Deng Xiaoping, and for some intelligence agents.

The collapse of the Diaochabu

After the death of Kang Sheng's rival Li Kenong in 1961, Kong Yuan, who had been Kang's secretary at the CCP's Shanghai Organization

Department in the 1930s, took over as head of the Diaochabu, the CCP's intelligence department. Kong was a close friend of Zhou Enlai and Deng Xiaoping—so close indeed that in September 1939 Kong and Deng had married two women who were themselves close friends in a joint celebration at Yan'an, with a small party organized by Mao. Zhuo Lin, Deng's new wife, was a secret agent behind Japanese lines.[15]

From 1961 onwards, Kong Yuan's task had become increasingly challenging, for the Diaochabu was now responsible not only for the investigation and monitoring of party cadres, but also for intelligence missions abroad under various diplomatic or journalistic guises. Kong, who had been deputy minister of foreign trade, had begun planning to enlarge the role of economic intelligence within the service.

The Cultural Revolution broke this momentum. Kong's deputy in the Diaochabu, Manchu Zou Dapeng, was arrested and murdered by the Red Guards in April 1966. In November, it was Kong Yuan's turn to be removed from office; his wife, Xu Ming, principal private secretary to Zhou Enlai, did not support the Red Guard attacks—she committed suicide. Kong's other deputy, Luo Qingchang, also a private secretary to Zhou Enlai, replaced him for a while, and the service was put largely under military supervision, although its external operations were still coordinated by a special office in Zhou Enlai's foreign affairs department. What was left of the organization appeared to be dormant.

Given the abuses of the Gang of Four, it is hardly surprising that several Diaochabu officials posted abroad during the Cultural Revolution attempted to defect. In April 1967, following new skirmishes between rival factions of the Red Guards, the Diaochabu headquarters in the West Garden (*Xiyuan*) were stormed by the PLA, and the service completely shut down.[16] Many leaders were sent to the countryside for "rectification" of their incorrect ideas. Most were sent—not by chance—to Shandong province, Kang Sheng's stronghold; this allowed him to maintain control over his former secret agents, who were now forced to work in the fields in what were called May Seventh Cadre schools. These labour camps were intended as a way of sorting the wheat from the chaff and enabling the ultimate redeployment of "re-educated" functionaries.

The archivists of the Diaochabu and their files were largely absorbed into the 2nd Department of the PLA, responsible for military intelligence, under the authority of Marshal Lin Biao. But not entirely: Kang Sheng took several loyal functionaries into his own networks and secret archives to examine incriminating charges against fallen leaders. Certain other leaders, including Luo Qingchang, were under the protection of Prime Minister Zhou Enlai, and were able to continue their investigations. This was very similar to the situation back in the 1940s: while Kang Sheng was engaged in witch-hunts, Zhou Enlai strove to maintain at any cost the autonomous networks so useful for his diplomacy.

* * *

For Kang Sheng's Central Case Examination Group, barely any pretext was needed. In mid-April 1967, a 50-year-old woman, Su Mei, was found dead in her Beijing apartment. Deputy director of the political department at the Academy for Political and Legal Cadres, which trained security officials, Su was none other than the sister-in-law and former mistress of Kang Sheng. At first it was thought that she had committed suicide. When the autopsy showed that she had been the victim of a murder covered up as suicide, Kang had a file drawn up on the woman who had conducted the autopsy, and arrested the head of the Academy where Su had worked. Once more, it was innocent people who were paying the price. Soon rumours began circulating in elite circles: Kang Sheng had ordered the murder of his ex-lover and sister-in-law to keep her from revealing awkward details about his CCP membership and his relationship with the Green Gang, the mafia that ruled Shanghai during the 1930s.

In the academic world where Su Mei had worked, however, the intelligence sector was somewhat protected, just as scientific research, particularly in the field of nuclear physics, was safeguarded. Scientists were preparing for the launch of the first Chinese space satellite, *Dong Fang Hong 1*, nicknamed "East is Red", in 1970. It was a similar situation for the first think-tank established in China, linked to the Diaochabu. According to historian Matt Brazil, "the only one of these institutes [Mao] kept open was the just established (1965) China Institute for Contemporary International Relations (CICIR). Although it continued to function, CICIR had to send some staff to the countryside while others remained in Beijing to analyse important events like the US escalation in Vietnam, the USS Pueblo crisis, the Soviet invasion of Czechoslovakia, and the border crisis with the USSR. By 1969 Mao allowed CICIR to be restored. The Foreign Ministry's Institute of International Relations did not reopen until 1973, underlining the critical role of CICIR during this period when Mao recognized the USSR threat and the opportunity for an opening to America."[17]

Despite the difficulties in obtaining intelligence from within China, just as the KGB was still able to operate until 1967, the CIA too launched a wide-ranging analytical programme called POLO, whose archives have been open to researchers since 2007. These offer another perspective on the disintegration of the Chinese secret services during the Cultural Revolution. On 28 November 1969, John Kerry King, deputy director of the CIA's Office of Political Analysis, gave the green light to the distribution of a memo ("POLO XXXVII") describing the destruction and rebuilding of the Chinese security apparatus.

According to the memo, "By September 1965, the only [remaining] leaders of organs of the political–security apparatus were those who had been working for Mao personally—constituting a de facto apparatus within the apparatus. Mao's personal apparatus 'possibly' included: Kang Sheng of the secretariat; Wang Dongxing from the Central Committee staff office; Luo Qingchang and Yang Qijing, of what remained nominally of the old Social Affairs Department or equivalent [actually the Diaochabu–NdA] (Luo was a SAD man assigned to Zhou Enlai's secretariat)."[18]

In December 1970, a new CIA report ("POLO XLII") threw some more light on the changes that were taking place: "The security area would be concerned with both political security (the Party, especially the leadership) and public security (the populace). The chances are that the de facto political security directorate, subordinate at first to Mao directly and then (like the staff office) to the Politburo standing committee, has now been reabsorbed by this de facto secretariat. Kang Sheng and Wang Dongxing, as officers of the Cultural Revolution Group, may supervise themselves as heads of security area, and may concurrently head some of the departments of this area, e.g. a reconstituted Social Affairs Department or (a later name) Political Security Department."[19]

The CIA was finding it increasingly hard to get a grip on all these developments, since Mao Zedong and Kang Sheng, beginning to be wary of Lin Biao's military networks, were making plans to infiltrate them. This was the mission given to General Guo Yufeng, an official at the PLA's Political Department. In 1967 he was catapulted in as head of the CCP's Organization Department, which—with the help of Kang Sheng's wife, Cao Yi'ou—was putting together incriminating files on members of the anti-party faction. Meanwhile Kang, afraid that Lin would become increasingly empowered if the PLA were instructed to restore order against the Red Guards, had also instructed Cao to infiltrate undercover agents into the marshal's entourage.[20]

The Maoist faction similarly seized control of the PLA's 2nd Department in 1967, appointing General Shen Shazi as Chief of this military intelligence division. Shen's deputy, Xiong Xianghui (about whom more later), was also head of the 3rd Department in charge of communications; he was one of the most senior Chinese secret agents and a friend of Zhou Enlai. He was also responsible for guarding the PLA 793 Foreign Language Institute of Zhangjiakou, which trained military intelligence officers and analysts in communication interception, and which also later imploded in the wake of the Cultural Revolution. Thus, despite being nominated Mao's heir apparent at the 9th Congress of the CCP in 1969, Lin Biao now found himself surrounded by spies trying to glean information about him to prepare for his fall at the instigation of Chairman Mao himself.

The principal consequences of these upheavals were that many of the PRC's intelligence missions around the world became impossible to maintain. Xinhua News Agency journalists or embassy diplomats who were deported at the time were not necessarily spies, as people thought they must be. In fact it was often the opposite; precisely because they were mere supporters of the Cultural Revolution abroad, who had not been trained as special agents, they were easily detected as they sought to foment revolution in Africa, Latin America and elsewhere. According to a CIA report, "a message sent to one embassy in mid-December (and probably representing a circular directive to all overseas installations) had stipulated that between one-third and one-half of all mission personnel should return for retraining and direct participation in the 'Cultural Revolution'".[21]

In January 1967, 600 of the 2,200 embassy staff—both spies and genuine diplomats—returned to Beijing. A first "reprogrammed" group was sent off to Burma, to engage in the new common mission: to foment revolution, handing out Chairman Mao badges, copies of his *Little Red Book*, and other magazines and books translated into different dialects, published by the Foreign Languages Press in Beijing. The campaign was so ridiculous that in the opposing pro-Soviet camp, Markus Wolf, head of the East German intelligence service, received orders from Moscow to count the number of posters of Mao that had been plastered onto walls in Zanzibar.[22]

In other parts of the world, however, Kang Sheng's group did help trigger uprisings, just as in the 1920s the Soviets had encouraged, advised and armed the Chinese communist insurgency. There were clear parallels between the failed uprisings of 1927, which led to Chiang Kai-shek's reign of "white terror", and the attempted September 1965 uprising by the Indonesian Communist Party, supported by Beijing, which led to nothing but a bloodbath. One million Indonesians were murdered by Suharto's army; he seized the moment and usurped Sukarno.

May '68 and Kang Sheng's Little Comintern

While Kang Sheng had brought the Diaochabu secret service to its knees, he was still relying on the other two services of the CCP's Central Committee, now stripped down and affiliated with the world of intelligence: the International Liaison Department (ILD) and the United Front Work Department (UFWD).

The ILD was largely answerable to the umbrella of organizations controlled by Zhou Enlai. Wang Jiaxiang, its founder and chief after the "Liberation", suffered terrible retribution at the hands of Kang Sheng, as did Li Weihan, another figure from the same service. The entire Wang family was persecuted; some were murdered, others starved and made homeless. Wang's wife, Zhu Zhongli, was locked up for six months in a windowless cell in the ILD building and tortured by Cao Yi'ou, Kang Sheng's wife, who was running the department alongside her husband. Like Madame Mao and Lin Biao's wife Ye Qun, Cao took enormous pleasure in persecuting other women and seeing them suffer. Many functionaries were also purged by one of Kang's deputies, Wang Li, former head of the Diaochabu's 9th Department, who formed his own group for rooting out "counter-revolutionaries".[23]

Kang Sheng wanted to transform the ILD into a "little Comintern", a new International for training national, pro-Chinese-communism sections throughout the world. This required a deepening of the Sino-Soviet split, achieved by creating schisms in traditional, pro-Moscow communist parties abroad. Kang and his faction had been trying to improve relations with Albanian and Romanian communists, and had been making overtures since the early 1960s towards Hungary and East Germany. A CIA report even suggested that at one point it looked like the latter might go over to the Chinese camp.[24]

As far as Western Europe was concerned, local counterintelligence agencies identified the Chinese embassy in Switzerland as the main hub for making links with smaller parties, where Marxist-Leninist communists praised the thought of Chairman Mao to the skies. Former cadres from pro-Soviet parties broke with Moscow and agreed to set up pro-China groups. They attracted younger activists to this beating heart of the new revolution. As head of China's ILD, Kang Sheng personally received Maoist delegations. They were fascinated by this revolution in which a rebellious youth was rising up against the adult world and Soviet "revisionism" was being torn apart alongside capitalism. "Run, Comrade, the old world is behind you!"

But the main European leader of this pro-Chinese protest movement, the Belgian Jacques Grippa, was no longer very young himself. During the Second World War he had been leader of the Armed Partisans, the resistance wing of the Belgian Communist Party. In the '60s, at the time of the Sino-Soviet spit, he chose the Chinese camp and laid the foundations for a textbook Maoist movement. I interviewed him on several occasions in Brussels and he told me how he had met up with Kang Sheng and the men from the Chinese secret services, in Switzerland and elsewhere. On two occasions he visited Beijing, the new Mecca of communism, caught up in the whirlwind of the Cultural Revolution. But as a realist, he felt sympathy for the losers of this story: Liu Shaoqi and Deng Xiaoping. Grippa was pro-

Chinese, but hostile to the excesses of the Cultural Revolution—and resolutely unimpressed by Kang Sheng.

A similar rift occurred within the French Communist Party. Marxist-Leninist groups formed; to a great degree these constituted the crucible of what became the Parisian intelligentsia in the 1980s and 1990s. Yet, after the cataclysmic surge of May '68 up until the early 1970s, French Maoists neither rode the crest of the revolutionary wave at home, nor resorted to terrorism as in neighbouring Italy. This might have been because of the Chinese leadership's special attitude towards the French government. They made clear to French Maoist comrades who came to the PRC, hailed as the "heirs of the Paris Commune", that the CCP had no desire to see de Gaulle overthrown; for he had recognized the PRC and left nationalist Taiwan adrift. Although portraits of Mao loomed over the Sorbonne during the events of May '68, and in spite of the wild claims propagated by the interior minister Raymond Marcellin, in fact the Chinese secret services did not encourage the protests, and orthodox Maoists remained on the sidelines, compared with other leftist groups.

Kang Sheng himself told a visiting delegation of the Marxist-Leninist Communist Party of France (PCMLF) that they were right in urging their supporters to vote neither for de Gaulle nor for Mitterrand in the 1965 presidential elections. Writer Régis Bergeron recalled his meeting with Kang Sheng during that trip: "He can't simply be described as a security chief, because he was such an ideologue. That's why he was in charge of the ILD. We met him in August 1966, when the Red Guards were marching through Beijing. He was tired. He only slept four hours a night. All his actions were measured. He was thin as a rake, with the demeanour of an intellectual. Every issue we raised, his secretary took out a new sheet of paper. He spoke Chinese; like Zhou and Deng, he spoke barely three words of French. His interpreter, Madame Ci, had studied at the Sorbonne. She had been the interpreter during conversations between Mao and Malraux."[25]

Raymond Casas, a former resistance fighter for the French "franc-tireurs", as well as an ex-member of the French Communist Party, also took part in this curious adventure. He took notes during meetings. During a dinner organized by the Chinese, he heard about Kang Sheng's visits to Paris in 1925 and 1936, and his meetings with leading communists like Marcel Cachin and Jacques Doriot. "Kang Sheng told me he was in Paris when the Popular Front came to power in 1936," Casas recalled. "He told me, 'I was in Paris on 1 May 1936. I saw forests of red flags with the hammer and sickle hanging from the windows of apartments and shops. It was hard to believe. I left Paris in late 1936. It was the Spanish Civil War.'"[26] Casas told me that Kang Sheng had realized the Maoists should hold back from criticizing de Gaulle, since in 1945 de Gaulle had entered into a tripartite alliance with the French Communist Party, led by Maurice Thorez. However, the French Maoists were not all in agreement. Those from the small Federation of Marxist-Leninist Circles (FCML), the group around Georges Frêche, who was later elected the socialist president of the Languedoc-Roussillon Regional Council, did call on its members to vote for de Gaulle in 1965, calling Mitterrand "a CIA agent".[27]

Amidst all this Maoist activity in Europe, the Soviets were monitoring the Chinese in Switzerland, for which purpose a special section, the "Twelfth", was created. As former Russian diplomat Nikolai Poliansky recalled, "We had to allow nothing to slip past us of the activities of the Chinese in Switzerland, whether it was the activities of the Chinese embassy in Bern, the work of the Association of Swiss-Chinese Friendship, the arrival of delegations, or the Maoist activities of various leftist youth organizations like the Revolutionary Marxist League in Lausanne. It was well known that every Soviet embassy in Europe had its own specialist in Chinese affairs (there had even been a special decision on this passed by the Central Committee of the CP). In Bern, this specialist was the third secretary, Valeri Ivanovich Sysoev, a KGB agent who spoke Chinese and had worked at the embassy in Beijing. He was responsible for all intelligence-gathering on Chinese activities in Switzerland."[28]

In Lausanne, the KGB succeeded in infiltrating an undercover agent into a pro-Chinese group, an abattoir worker called Marcel Buttex. In February 1970, Buttex was arrested and sentenced for spying for the Soviets.[29]

Bogus defectors and the phony party in the Netherlands

Meanwhile, two extraordinary episodes in this secret war took place in the Netherlands. Along with Switzerland, the Netherlands was considered an ideal base for the Chinese secret services. As early as the 1950s, in an operation called Red Herring, a China counterespionage section called the *Binneenlandse Veiligheidsdienst* (BVD) had been working with the CIA to detect the presence of major intelligence agents in the country, such as Zou Dapeng, second in command at the Diaochabu, who was killed during the Cultural Revolution.

From 1960 onwards, Xie Li, the Chinese chargé d'affaires at The Hague, was also under close surveillance. He, like Zou, disappeared in the turmoil of the Cultural Revolution. Their target, as part of the "united front work", had been the Chinese community in the former Dutch colony of Indonesia, with the ultimate objective of wresting this diaspora back from the nationalists in Taiwan.

In 1963, Xie Li was replaced by Li Enqiu, a stern man with links to Maoist groups in the three Benelux countries, where Jacques Grippa was also a major figure. On 16 July 1966, Dutch police in The Hague found a seriously injured Chinese man sprawled on the pavement not far from a compound housing Chinese diplomats. The BVD opened an investigation in conjunction with the Belgian police. The man, Xu Zicai, was a Chinese engineer, a specialist in transmissions, who had made the mistake of asking for political asylum. He was hospitalized, and then, in a dramatic twist, kidnapped semiconscious from the hospital by a commando unit. Two weeks later on 29 July, a van emerging from the Chinese embassy compound was intercepted by the police, who discovered Xu's corpse in the back. He had been beaten to death. A few days later, Li Enqiu was expelled from the Netherlands. But his career was not over. He was sent to Czechoslovakia as an ambassador.

Another diplomat, Liao Heshu, took over the Chinese secret service in The Hague. He was constantly monitored by the BVD until 24 January 1969, when he went to the police and announced he wanted to defect to the West and talk to the CIA. This was a triumph for Cleveland Cram, chief of the CIA station in The Hague. He organized Liao's transfer to the United States for a debriefing. But this turned out to be disappointing: Liao passed on information about the death of Xu Zicai and about the operating methods of Chinese services in Europe, but that was it. James Angleton, head of counterintelligence at CIA headquarters in Langley, who had already been burned by certain Soviet defectors, realized that Liao Heshu was a bogus defector, sent by Kang Sheng to penetrate the CIA. For once Angleton's instincts were right. To keep the Chinese ignorant of the fact that their double agent had been unmasked, the CIA gave Liao a minor job translating unimportant documents, while keeping him under close surveillance.

A joint operation by the CIA and BVD was rather more fruitful. They set up a phoney Marxist-Leninist party with the purpose of infiltrating the PRC by inveigling Kang Sheng with invitations. This extraordinary operation, baptized "Mongol", was exposed in 2004 by Frits Hoekstra, a former BVD agent, who was at the time responsible for the communism section of the Dutch secret services. In his memoirs, he recounts how a Dutch Marxist-Leninist communist party (the MLPN) was created in the 1960s with 600 members, the secret purpose of which was overseen by four surveillance officers from the BVD, who also produced the party newspaper *De Kommunist*. They not only fooled Beijing and received money from Tirana, then allied to the Chinese, but even succeeded in weakening the Netherlands's traditional pro-Moscow communist party.[30]

Chris Petersen, the general secretary of the MLPN—in reality a BVD informer by the name of Peter Boevé—managed to get himself invited by the CCP leadership to Beijing; he has an indelible memory of the incredible food provided. Boevé was a mathematics teacher, recruited as a BVD informer in 1957 at a youth festival in Moscow; he had travelled to China to study Mao Zedong's ideology. Subsequently, as a guest of the Albanians and the Chinese, he met all of the CCP top brass, including Zhou Enlai and Kang Sheng. As a result of these meetings, in 1969 the Chinese embassy in The Hague offered Boevé more funding for *De Kommunist*—thereby saving the BVD a fair amount of money. This almost comical operation was not unique. While researching this book, I came across a story from Australia, in which the CIA and the Australian Security Intelligence Organization were engaged in a similar infiltration operation in the same period, registering fake students at Beijing University.

Xiong Xianghui and the "American" card

While the CIA and Chinese services were crossing swords in the Netherlands, in Britain, one extraordinary Chinese man was responsible for setting up the PRC's London embassy at 31 Portland Place in 1965. MI5 was keeping a close eye on Xiong Xianghui, who was undoubtedly one of the most remarkable Chinese secret agents of the twentieth century. The details of his story were brought to light in his memoirs, published in 2006 a year after his death at the age of eighty-seven. It is a sign of the times and of the extent to which Chinese diplomacy has opened up that his book, which reveals a great deal about the history of Chinese intelligence, can now be bought openly in Beijing, from the People's Liberation Army Publishing House shop and other bookshops in the capital.

The title of Xiong's memoir could hardly be more straightforward and direct: *My Career as an Intelligence Officer and Diplomat.*[31] Born in 1919 in the Year of the Goat, Xiong was the son of a Shandong judge. He became involved in politics in 1936, secretly joining the CCP while still a student. He soon came to the attention of Zhou Enlai, who exhorted him to join the staff of one of Chiang Kai-shek's generals, Hu Zongnan. In yet another triumph for the CCP's special services, which excelled at infiltration, Xiong succeeded in becoming Hu's private secretary, a position he held for a decade. His masterstroke came in 1947, as he was preparing to leave on a mission to the United States with his wife Chen Xiaohua—the only person privy to the fact that he was a mole. Just before his departure, he learnt some vitally important information: a jubilant General Hu told him that the nationalists were planning to annihilate the communists with an attack on Yan'an, headquarters of the revolution. Duly warned by Xiong, Mao Zedong and his troops retreated into the mountains, and Yan'an was nothing but a ghost town by the time the Kuomintang soldiers showed up.

Following two years of secret service activity in the US, Xiong returned home after the communist victory and joined Zhou Enlai's nascent diplomatic service. Zhou entrusted him with the post of deputy director of the Chinese People's Association for Cultural Relations with Foreign Countries, where he worked alongside several other intelligence officials, including Zou Dapeng. He accompanied Zhou Enlai to Geneva during the 1954 discussions on Indochina. It was on this occasion that London and Beijing decided on a mutual exchange of envoys. Xiong went to the British capital in 1962 and remained there until the Cultural Revolution, when he returned to China and became one of the deputy directors of the Diaochabu.

With Zhou's agreement, Xiong was one of the signatories of a petition protesting the fact that Marshal Chen Yi, then foreign minister, had been labelled "revisionist". When Xiong in his turn became a target of the Red Guards, and all his comrades were sent to the countryside to undergo rectification, Zhou reminded Mao that Xiong had once saved his life in Yan'an; as a result, he was allowed to remain in Beijing to continue his intelligence missions. One of these was to infiltrate Lin Biao's staff, where he became deputy director of the PLA's 2nd Department.

This was a hugely important position. Xiong was charged with a top-secret mission that risked incurring the wrath of the man who was considered to be Mao's future successor. In this role, Xiong took part in a transformation of PRC strategy whose effects would be felt worldwide. He became secretary of a small group of marshals charged with drawing up plans for a radical change of diplomacy, to be presented to Mao: in the midst of the Cultural Revolution, they had looked closely at the consequences of the Sino-Soviet clashes, and were afraid of the very real possibility of all-out war with Moscow. Notwithstanding Lin Biao's fiery speeches antagonizing both the USSR and the US, two of the marshals, Chen Yi and Ye Jianying, proposed making diplomatic overtures towards the US. Chen and Ye, who had been part of the network of Hakkas around Zhou Enlai in Paris in the 1920s, had a broader and more tempered perspective on the outside world. Through them and Agent Xiong, Paris was about to become the centre of some surprising intrigue.

Chen Yi wrote a report proposing that the Chinese "play the American card" against the Soviets. Xiong reported this idea to Mao. But how would they be able to hold talks with Washington without the Soviets finding out? Ought they to take advantage of the negotiations on Vietnam already instigated by Nixon? Ultimately the Chinese used various strategies to pass information to the Americans, some more successful than others. Mao, for example, floated the idea during a meeting with André Malraux, organized by Zhou Enlai. Unfortunately, Malraux, de Gaulle's minister of culture, was listening to his own voice as usual, and failed to hear what was being said to him.

So Mao tried another tack: an interview with the journalist Edgar Snow, who had achieved a certain amount of fame for his 1937 book about the Long March, *Red Star Over China*. Not long before he died, Stalin had hinted to Mao that Snow was a CIA agent. Twenty years later, this made him seem the ideal intermediary for passing information to Nixon. This was a fatal error, for when his book was first published, the Americans had in fact labelled Snow a communist.[32] Snow was unable to pass any information on to Nixon's administration, which believed him to be an agent passing on communist disinformation.

Meanwhile, Henry Kissinger, alerted to the Chinese plan, put out several hooks to lure in Beijing. He used a special navy unit, independent of the CIA, to contact the Chinese services. As early as 1970, the Chinese learned of the Americans' desire to negotiate, thanks to several moles, including one in the CIA and another in the French diplomatic service, both of whom were only unmasked ten years later. Attempts were also being made in the opposite direction: in The Hague, the Chinese embassy summoned "their" Marxist-Leninist man Chris Petersen to ask him what he thought about Beijing's overture towards the United States. The BVD agent lost no time reporting this to his Dutch handler and the CIA was quickly alerted.

Once more, Paris became the hub for clandestine Chinese talks. In 1968, Kissinger had relied on the services of former resistance fighter Raymond Aubrac to contact Ho Chi Minh—godfather to Aubrac's son[33]—about a possible ceasefire in the Vietnam War. But Ho Chi Minh died in 1969. He was not going to be able to help his old comrade Zhou Enlai now.

This time, at Kissinger's request, contact with Chinese secret agents was made by General Vernon Walters, an interpreter during the Kennedy–de Gaulle discussions and now military attaché in Paris. He was careful to ensure that the head of the CIA's Paris office, David Murphy, was kept in the dark about what was going on. Murphy, suspected of being a KGB agent, was on the blacklist drawn up by James Angleton, head of counterintelligence at Langley. This was quite the circus of spies: Liao the bogus defector, Petersen the faux-Maoist working for the CIA, and the CIA's Paris station chief, in the pay of the KGB.

Luckily for the Chinese, however, they had another player in this double-bluffing ring: Cao Guisheng, an advisor at the Paris embassy who was in fact the Diaochabu's station chief. He was just as high-flying a spy as Xiong Xianghui. In 1954, Cao was Hanoi correspondent for Xinhua, the classic cover for Chinese secret agents. He flew to Geneva to join Zhou Enlai's delegation for the Indochina negotiations—a meeting that was swarming with intelligence specialists. The head of Diaochabu himself, Li Kenong, was present. The only known photograph of the spymaster in Europe was taken at the conference, featuring his familiar black-rimmed glasses. It also shows Zhou, standing next to Pierre Mendès-France. Xiong Xianghui and Gong Peng, then director of foreign affairs intelligence, were in attendance, too.

Cao was trusted and he was Anglophone. He was put in charge of liaising with Walters. He set up the meetings between Zhou and Kissinger. First, on 25 July 1970, Kissinger attended a secret meeting with Huang Zhen, the Chinese ambassador to France, at Huang's residence. Soft music was played, the air was filled with perfumed incense, and Kissinger was served apricots, smoked tea and Shaoxing wine to break the ice.

The strategy worked. A year later Kissinger travelled to Beijing, where he held talks on 9 July 1971 with Zhou Enlai. "For us this is an historic occasion," he declared. "Because this is the first time that American and Chinese leaders are talking to each other on a basis where each country recognizes each other as equals."[34]

Caution remained the watchword, however; it would not take long for the KGB to learn about the talks. Andropov put about a rumour that Kissinger was a Soviet agent, with the express purpose of derailing the Sino-American discussions.

The Chinese would have been hard pressed to endorse this manoeuvre, particularly as Kissinger ended up doing them an immense service at the expense of Moscow. Right at the end of his trip, a meeting took place whose significance was not recognized at the time. Kissinger met one of the four marshals, "Heroic Sword" Ye Jianying, at Beijing airport, and revealed intelligence so top-secret that even US intelligence officials were in the dark about it. He drew from memory an extremely detailed picture of the Soviet troops deployed along the Chinese border. He recalled land units, missiles, and strategic forces, the exact number and names of the divisions, the four kinds of tactical missiles at the Soviets' disposal—the SS-1B SCUD, the SS-12—and so on. Marshal Ye was stunned. His own spies could never have dreamed of receiving such valuable intelligence. To avoid leaks, Kissinger insisted that even the CIA must not know the Chinese were being given this information. The Hakka marshal beamed: "Thank you very much indeed. This will be very useful. And it is a great indication of the US desire to improve our relationship."

Kissinger's trip opened the way for Richard Nixon's 1972 visit to Beijing. Among others, Edgar Snow was present on that occasion, at last recognized by the White House as a great observer of China and an unparalleled analyst of Chinese affairs.

The Sino-American entente cordiale had immediate consequences for intelligence; the services on both sides agreed to set aside past differences and disputes. As we know, the Diaochabu station chief in The Hague, Liao Heshu, had "defected" to the West. Since it was the CIA who had received him and realized that he was a phoney defector, the organization saw no harm in returning him to Beijing. In exchange, the Chinese finally released their two favourite prisoners: Richard Fecteau and Jack Downey, whose spy plane had been shot down in 1952.

Even more spectacular was the deployment of overt special services liaison officers, with the opening of respective embassies in 1973; James Lilley became the first CIA official formally attached to the US embassy in Beijing, while a Diaochabu agent was attached to the Chinese embassy in Washington.

"The Chinese eventually agreed to a deal in which each country could station one intelligence officer in its diplomatic mission in the other country's capital city," Lilley explains in his memoirs. "This placement of declared agents would be an indication of the closeness of the relationship since the CIA reserved that practice for its allies. As Kissinger had promised, I was revealed to the Chinese. The deal, however, was not entirely reciprocal. My understanding is that the Chinese did not inform us directly of the identity of my Chinese counterpart in Washington. Only later did we presume that the Chinese 'declared agent' was an English-speaking diplomat named Xie Qimei, a senior Chinese officer in the Ministry of Foreign Affairs."[35]

The end of the Mao era

Sino-American relations had fundamentally changed. This was exactly what Marshal Lin Biao had so opposed—but he had lost his life in a plane crash on a flight to the USSR in September 1971, after a failed putsch against Mao. After this, the Cultural Revolution took an even more unexpected turn.

According to the official story, Lin and his clan had tried to organize a coup, code-named Project 571. After the plan was uncovered, the official version went that Lin, his wife Ye Qun and his relatives fled, aboard a Trident plane that crashed in Mongolia. But some elements of the story remain unresolved even today.[36] Under the leadership of Wang Dongxing, an "Investigation Group of Lin Biao's anti-party faction" was set up with people from Unit 8341, the political security wing of the PLA, and the investigator–archivists of the Gonganbu. Three leaders of the latter were members of the Group: Yu Sang, Hua Guofeng and Li Zhen—the minister of security, who was to die in mysterious circumstances the following year.[37]

In the wake of the plane crash, the CIA looked into the disappearance of more than 100 generals who had been in on Lin Biao's attempted coup.[38] Naturally, military intelligence had to be reined in. This task fell to the elderly general Liu Shaowen, who had helped Zhou Enlai set up his own intelligence network to rival Kang Sheng's in the 1940s.

The staff of the Diaochabu, the party's investigative service—which had been absorbed into the PLA's control—now regained its autonomy under the leadership of another close friend of Zhou, Luo Qingchang. Marshal Ye and his advisor, the former Diaochabu director Kong Yuan, were helping to reorganize the service, which had managed to avoid falling under Kang Sheng's thumb.

Kang was now seriously ill with cancer. His final public appearance is described in the memoirs of Étienne Manac'h, the French ambassador in Beijing at the time. On 30 September 1974, Manac'h noted his impressions of the reception given in honour of the PRC's twenty-fifth anniversary: "The ceremony and the meal were brief. Just before we got up from the table, two people in wheelchairs were brought out in front of us. They were dignitaries who were being kept away from the jostling at the exit. The first, who stopped for a moment at our table to shake the hand of [Foreign Minister] Ji Pengfei, was Kang Sheng. His body was slumped and his eyes deeply sunken in his emaciated face."[39]

He may have been dying, but this did not stop Kang from trying to set up a third force, hostile to both Deng Xiaoping's faction and to the Gang of Four; he had collaborated in turn with both clans. Even on his deathbed, Kang wanted to send Mao a "file" on Madame Mao and Zhang Chunqiao claiming that they had both been spies for the Kuomintang since the 1930s.[40] It's true that during the early 1970s, at the time of Lin Biao's fall, there did exist within the security apparatus a group of people who, according to Hong Kong-based historian Ting Wang, indeed constituted a sort of "third force" led by Kang Sheng.[41]

Kang Sheng died on 16 December 1975, closely followed in January 1976 by Zhou Enlai, and then Mao Zedong that September. The following month, October 1976, the moderate group supporting Wang Dongxing and Deng Xiaoping was responsible for the arrest of the Gang of Four. Hua Guofeng succeeded Zhou Enlai as prime minister and Mao as party chairman, and eventually became head of the military commission that commanded the PLA, with the support of the indomitable Marshal Ye.

Even before this transition, however, another leader vilified by Kang Sheng had re-emerged. On 12 April 1973, after six years under house arrest and being sent with his wife to work in a factory in Jiangxi, Deng Xiaoping had made an appearance at a dinner given by Zhou Enlai, in honour of Prince Norodom Sihanouk of Cambodia. For months, Mao had been wanting to restore order in China. So Deng was pulled from the tractor factory and, under Zhou's guidance, helped to restore state power and, specifically, its central bureaucracy. Under Deng, who became Zhou's deputy, there was a clear shift in focus towards economic development and his "Four Modernizations": industry and commerce, education, the military, and agriculture.

Yet it was Hua Guofeng who became the nominal leader in 1976 after Mao's death, leaving Deng frustrated and chomping at the bit.

He, like the CIA and the French SDECE, must certainly have thought that Hua was only playing the same intermediate role played by Beria after Stalin's death, and that he would simply disappear after securing the real transition of power.[42] This threatened not to be the case.

Hua Guofeng, whose name means "Vanguard of China", was imposed on the CCP in a strange way that for some reason was never officially acknowledged. Many rumours circulated, with some claiming that Mao had issued a specific injunction before he died, rather like the clause in Lenin's will demanding that Stalin be removed from the Politburo.

But this was rather different: one of the most insignificant figures of the CCP rose to become a member of the group investigating the Lin Biao affair, then minister of security (head of the Gonganbu), then head of the CCP's central school, then general secretary and president of the party itself, as well as of its military commission—all at the express request of Chairman Mao. In other words, unexpectedly, Hua turned out to be Mao's heir—not Lin Biao.

"Contrary to what has often been said, Hua Guofeng was not just anybody," a French expert in China who has gone into the question told me. "I am convinced that he was actually Chairman Mao's biological son. This explains not only their physical resemblance, but also Hua's posting in Hunan, Mao's native province [see below], and his inexplicable promotion to the rank of security minister and president, all as a result of a secret clause that only a small number in the Politburo were privy to."

This is certainly a convincing explanation as to why we know so little about Hua's origins, other than that he was born in Shanxi in 1920 or 1921, named either Su Zhu, or Liu Zhengrong, and that he was an illegitimate child or possibly an orphan when he joined the Long March at the age of fourteen. He is one of the few heads of state, along with the North Korean Kim Il-sung, about whose early life we know almost nothing.

In 1977, a covert organization called 637 Headquarters, which backed Deng Xiaoping, circulated an illicit and devastating document entitled *Fire on Hua Guofeng*. This mini-biography recounted how Hua Yu, the new president's mother, had married a communist railway worker whom she then named as the father of her son. The family settled in Yan'an, headquarters of the revolution. In 1937 Hua Yu became one of Kang Sheng's mistresses after the latter returned from Moscow. Shortly afterwards, according to an investigation carried out by Beijing Mayor Peng Zhen in the 1960s, Kang had the unfortunate railwayman killed. If true, this is the crux of the story: Mao married Jiang Qing, Kang Sheng's former mistress, and Kang—perhaps as compensation—was given Hua Yu, mother of Mao's son, as his mistress.

This theory, however, is unconfirmed speculation. What we do know is that, once Mao came to power, he appointed Hua Guofeng party secretary of the Xiangtan prefecture in Hunan province, where Shaoshan, Mao's birthplace, is located. According to the official story, the two men did not meet until 1959, when Mao made a pilgrimage home to Hunan. Not long afterwards, Hua was promoted to govern Hunan province. During the Cultural Revolution, his violent suppression of the Changsha Red Guards earned him the nickname the "Hunan Butcher". In 1975, after Hua's appointment as deputy prime minister and head of the Gonganbu, Muslims banned from praying in mosques began rioting in Yunnan, a province bordering Vietnam. Hua sent in the military to violently crush the rebellion.[43]

On 8 January 1976, Zhou Enlai died, and Mao made Hua prime minister soon after. Deng Xiaoping was put under house arrest after a demonstration in Tiananmen Square, held in memory of Zhou Enlai and aimed at strengthening Deng's position. Meanwhile, a fake will and testament, written by the KGB but ascribed to Zhou, was circulating abroad, in which Zhou supposedly denounced the Cultural Revolution. Mao, at the heart of all these different machinations, named Hua his successor.

1976 was the Year of the Dragon, when the Heavens remove the emperor's mandate, leading to great upheavals. Zhou's death in January had been followed by the Tiananmen political earthquake in April and an actual earthquake in Tangshan in July, which claimed at least a quarter of a million lives. Mao Zedong died on 9 September 1976 after a long illness. A month later his widow, along with the rest of the Gang of Four, was arrested by commandos from Unit 8341, the army's political security unit. State security forces, with the support of the army under Marshal Ye's leadership, were poised to bring Deng Xiaoping to power.[44]

However, Hua Guofeng's and Wang Dongxing's reign in Zhongnanhai, government headquarters, continued. Having gained power in mid-October, they were trying to expand the prerogatives and activities of the Diaochabu, the party's intelligence bureau, which was re-established on 28 July 1978 under the leadership of Luo Qingchang. Their goal was to consolidate their position and, with Luo's help, remove their rivals. Deng Xiaoping, already in a strong position within both the party and the army, was opposed to this. No doubt he did not want this organization, which had caused him and many other functionaries so much trouble, to regain the upper hand. Deng planned for the majority of intelligence officers in the international service to leave their embassies, so that espionage would once again be done by undercover agents, working as journalists (as had already been the case) and, from the 1980s, businessmen.

By the late 1970s, however, the lack of professionalism in the post-Cultural Revolution intelligence service led to some serious failures by the new Chinese diplomatic service. Two spectacular events bore witness to this.

The Khmer Rouge and the Black Panther

On 5–9 November 1978, Wang Dongxing visited Cambodia—or "Democratic Kampuchea"—accompanied by Luo Qinchang, head of the re-established Diaochabu. Mao's former bodyguard reminded the Khmer Rouge leaders of the PRC's ten-year friendship. With Kang Sheng, Wang had helped Kaing Khek ("Deuch") and Nguon Kang ("Ta Mok") to set up the terrible secret police S–21 (Nokorbal), responsible for the deaths of hundreds of thousands of Cambodians. Ta Mok and Pol Pot thanked Wang and China for sending so many advisors to Cambodia.

But scarcely had Wang and Luo returned home before a Vietnamese liberation offensive began, which led to the overthrow of the Khmer Rouge and, on 7 January 1979, the fall of Phnom Penh. Prince Norodom Sihanouk had been a Khmer Rouge hostage, but was hostile to the Vietnamese; the Chinese just managed to fly him out in time. Wang Dongxing was now sidelined, and Pol Pot's men embarked on a new guerrilla war. On 13 January, Ieng Sary, another prominent

Khmer Rouge leader who had fled to Thailand, arrived in Beijing asking for $5 million in financial aid. Deng Xiaoping was open in his assessment of what the Khmer Rouge had done in Cambodia: "As we have already said, domestic counterintelligence activities created a negative atmosphere, slowing down many activities and causing social problems as well as many other problems. We must recognize that the massive scale of counterintelligence activities has created negative elements that need to be eliminated. A thorough study of this political aspect should be undertaken and concrete measures taken."[45] These were highly euphemistic words; Deng was well aware that the man standing in front of him was one of the leaders behind a genocide that is estimated to have claimed some 2 million lives.

Chinese intelligence chiefs, having proved themselves unable to keep the government properly informed, were also on the receiving end of fierce criticism, for even as Vietnam was launching its assault, Chinese intelligence was confidently informing Beijing that the Khmer Rouge would easily be able to repel the assailants and protect the capital. At the Chinese embassy in Phnom Pen, there were some excellent and trustworthy operatives, including the Indochina specialist Cao Guisheng, the man who had organized Kissinger's visit to Paris—he had been dispatched to Phnom Penh towards the end of 1976.

What happened? Were the Chinese agents blinded by their ideological closeness to Pol Pot and his followers? Whatever the reason behind this failure, the poor analysis of the situation—based on flawed intelligence—proved catastrophic for the PRC. One thousand Chinese military advisors fled Cambodia via Thailand, leaving 4,000 civilian advisors in the clutches of the Vietnamese army. In addition, contact was momentarily lost with the Khmer leadership, which vanished into the jungle to organize its guerrilla warfare under Ta Mok, accompanied by a single Chinese agent, equipped with one defective satellite radio.

Coupled with the routing of the PLA on the Vietnamese border, this was a serious setback. Nonetheless, Deng Xiaoping continued to support the Khmer Rouge for another ten years as it fought the new government installed by Hanoi. Details of Diaochabu operations in Cambodia were revealed in 2010 when a Sino-Cambodian defector called Vita Chieu published his memoirs in Taiwan. He revealed that the head of Cambodian missions under Kang Sheng, Cai Xiaonong, had been killed. His successor, Wang Tao, was under orders from Deng Xiaoping to curb relations with the Khmer Rouge.[46]

* * *

Another, no less resounding fiasco took place in a country far less obviously close in ideology to Maoist China: the Shah's Iran. In August 1978, Hua Guofeng travelled to Iran at the head of a delegation that also included Qiao Shi, an intelligence expert from the ILD who would become an important figure over the next two decades.

The two men had signed an agreement in Romania and Yugoslavia linked to China's break with Albania, a hitherto Maoist state. Its leader, Enver Hoxha, believed that Hua Guofeng and China's other new leaders had betrayed the world revolution, just as Khrushchev had. The Albanian secret service, the Sigurimi (*Drejtorija e Sigurimit të Shtetit*, State Security), which was set up with the help of Kang Sheng, now began shadowing Chinese agents. When Hoxha published his 800-page "diaries", he castigated these agents, and railed against the envoys "of the Xinhua agency, these Chinese secret service agents, in various countries of the world. The employees of this so-called news agency are engaged in all sorts of tasks, they collect information on everything, on state institutions, economic and social organizations, the organization of the army and details of the military, political parties, well-known individuals, and general aspects of the life of the country where they have been sent. In other words, they are engaged in undercover intelligence work."[47]

After withdrawing their intelligence bases from Albania, the Chinese had negotiated with Ceauşescu and Tito to redeploy them in Romania and Yugoslavia. Their 1978 trip to Tehran had a similar purpose. It was the Shah's twin sister, the shady Ashraf—nicknamed the "Black Panther"—who oversaw the negotiations, alongside General Nasser Moghadam, the new boss of SAVAK, Iran's dreaded secret police. Their objective was to create a regional intelligence base that the Israeli Mossad would also be invited to join. In the end, however, Hua's public declarations of the PRC's eternal friendship with the Pahlavi dynasty fell rather flat; just a few months later, on 16 January 1979, the Iranian revolution spread. The Shah flew into exile with his family; he would not return.

With the subsequent accession to power of Ayatollah Khomeini, the Americans lost their electronic interception base in Mashad. They invited the Chinese to join forces with them by putting up electronic listening devices along the Russian border. When the Iran–Iraq War broke out in 1980, Deng Xiaoping—seeking the mullahs' forgiveness for China's support for the Shah—supplied Silkworm rockets to the new regime.

It was Hua Guofeng who came out weakened by these two failures, and by the new balance of power within the CCP. Wang Dongxing was demoted from the leadership of his elite military security unit, 8341 (restructured as 57001), and was eventually removed from power. In December 1978, Deng Xiaoping defeated Hua at the CCP Central Committee Plenum. Now in control of both the party and the army, Deng, who had been nicknamed "Little Cannon" as a short, stocky student, was ready to launch. He would soon begin the Four Modernizations programme, and usher in a massive intelligence agency appropriate for this newly awakened China: the Guoanbu.

4

DENG XIAOPING'S DEEP-WATER FISH

The last emperor of China, Pu Yi, was completely swamped in his oversized uniform. This was the ultimate humiliation for the fallen sovereign, who as a child in the early twentieth century had played in the Forbidden City, and who rose to the dragon throne at the age of eight. The young man had been kidnapped along with his concubines by the Japanese secret services under Colonel Doihara—the inspiration for the spy Mitsuhirato in Hergé's *The Blue Lotus*—who sent him to reign over the puppet state of Manchukuo. The Soviets captured Manchukuo in 1945 and, five years later, handed the puppet emperor over to the new communist People's Republic.

This was how, in 1950, the "Son of the Dragon" found himself the prisoner of Mao Zedong. Seated across from him was a Gonganbu inquisitor, jovial and inflexible by turn. He handed him a cigarette, paper and calligraphy brushes. Pu Yi had no choice but to accept Zhou Enlai's edict that "Today the emperor is the people!" He was forced to recount episodes from his debauched life, to show that he was submitting and thus prove his allegiance to the people. This is how Pu Yi learned what the "New Democracy" was, to use the title of Mao's book, which he was given to study as part of his "re-education".

Bernardo Bertolucci portrayed this episode in his Oscar-winning film *The Last Emperor*, made during the Deng Xiaoping era (1978-89). China's new openness in that time is evident in the fact that the great

Italian director was given permission to film with Peter O'Toole, John Lone, Joan Chen and the other actors in the real Forbidden City. Filming in Beijing was made possible thanks to Ying Ruocheng, the rather unusual deputy minister of culture at the time, who also played the role of governor of the detention camp in the film. This was not entirely coincidental. Ying, considered one of the greatest English-speaking actors in China, was born into an influential Manchu family in Beijing. His father founded the liberal newspaper *Ta Kung Pao*. He himself was a national theatre actor and a translator of Shakespeare, as well as an "honourable correspondent" for the Guoanbu, the new Chinese secret service, founded four years before Bertolucci's film was made.

"'Honourable correspondent' is a laughable title for the role. Ying was a top-ranking state security official. He was given the entirely honorary rank of 'deputy minister'," a French diplomat who knew him at the time told me twenty years later.

"He used to be invited to cocktail parties at the French embassy, in the late 1990s when Pierre Morel was ambassador, and we were warned by our own secret services that he had a high position in the Chinese intelligence service. It's true that he used to down a lot of whisky during those embassy dos, which meant that people didn't take him very seriously. But he must have picked up lot of intelligence anyway. And he was such a good actor that Bertolucci invited him back to play the lama Norbu in *Little Buddha* in 1993. The Chinese must have appreciated him rather less in that, given that it was a story of reincarnation and made allusions to the Dalai Lama."

In fact, probably quite the opposite was true—it was precisely in a case like that of Bertolucci's *Little Buddha* that a high-flying "correspondent" like Ying, working on the fringes of the Guoanbu, could prove invaluable, identifying political and cultural figures who backed this film, clearly shot through with support for Tibetan "separatists".[1] Similarly, he managed to gather a great deal of useful information when he acted in the television series *Marco Polo* in the United States, or toured his productions of Elizabethan plays around the UK, Germany and France.

However, Ying's life—he died at the end of 2003 at the age of seventy-four—had not always been easy. During the Cultural

Revolution, he had been incarcerated in Qincheng Prison No. 1 in Beijing, which was run by the 5th Gonganbu Department under Wang Dongxing. This was where disgraced dignitaries and spies were locked up. Among his fellow prisoners was Zhang Langlang, an unlucky art student accused of being a French secret agent, whose only crime was to have studied French in high school.

Ling Yun, the eye of the serpent

Qincheng Prison N°1 was a garrison similar to the one where Pu Yi had been imprisoned in 1950, and where he had been interrogated, just like in the film, by the counterintelligence agent Ling Yun, who was a victim of the purges during the Cultural Revolution (see Chapter 3). Ling had been in Qincheng at the same time as our future Guoanbu agent, Ying Ruocheng. Did friendship grow out of this coincidence? Was this the reason that Ling, promoted to chief of the new secret services twenty years later, invited Ying to become an "honourable correspondent"?

Ling Yun was born in 1917 in the Year of the Snake, in the city of Jiaxing, Zhejiang province, south of Shanghai. His given name was Wu Peilin—Ling Yun was a nickname meaning "noble ambition". He joined the CCP at the age of twenty, eager to help kick out the Japanese occupiers, and went to Yan'an in 1939. Three years later, he became head of interrogation at Kang Sheng's Social Affairs Department (SAD), right in the middle of the rectification campaign. Methods were brutal at SAD headquarters, and Ling must have excelled in the art of extracting confessions, because after the "Liberation" in 1949 he was promoted to head of the Gonganbu bureau, the new Ministry of Public Security, in Jinan, capital of Shandong—homeland of Kang Sheng. By now Kang had been sidelined, and Ling's appointment suggests that he may have been instrumental in keeping him under surveillance.

The following year, 1950, Ling took over the leadership of the SAD's 2nd Intelligence Bureau, which Li Kenong ran as the party's investigation service. As an extension to counterintelligence, the Fushun War Criminals Management Institute was set up and was now taking the lead in the mission to "re-educate" nationalist generals and other leaders of the old regime. This was how Ling found himself sitting opposite the last emperor, Pu Yi, though he did not, in fact, give him an especially hard time. His interrogations of nationalist Dai Li's former secret agents were much more fruitful. Indeed, they laid the groundwork for new operations against Taiwan, where Chiang Kai-shek and his troops had fled, leaving behind numerous spies and sleeper agents on the mainland. Many moles dug themselves in deep, awaiting better days and instructions from Taiwan to go ahead and destabilize the communists in power.

Sometimes investigations were conducted very judiciously. In 1949, Mao had imprisoned the only American to join the CCP, who had even offered his services to the Department of Social Welfare: Sidney Rittenberg. Stalin had personally told Mao that Rittenberg and Edgar Snow were CIA agents. Rittenberg, under his Chinese name Li Dunbai, was jailed for espionage in 1949 and remained in jail until 1955, when, after a lengthy investigation into his case, Ling Yun came to his cell to apologize in person before his release. This was not necessarily wise, however, for when Ling later got in trouble during the Cultural Revolution, Rittenberg—now imprisoned again on charges of being an "American" and "Zionist spy"—saw his sentence increased because of that old episode. Ling, too, was later accused of being an "American-Zionist viper", who had once released a CIA and Mossad spy.

Up until this low point during the Cultural Revolution, Ling Yun's career had followed a remarkable trajectory: after serving as head of counterintelligence in Canton and as head of the 1st Gonganbu bureau (internal security), he had become deputy minister of the same bureau, and been elected the representative for Shandong in the National People's Congress. Ling Yun had also overseen the modernization of Qincheng prison. Then the Cultural Revolution took place, and alongside it the destruction of the Gonganbu. In January 1968, he was arrested with Feng Jiping, head of the Beijing Gonganbu, along with many other security executives.[2] The counterintelligence specialist found himself behind bars in Qingcheng prison at the instigation of his former comrades, Kang Sheng, Xie Fuzhi and Wang Dongxing. On 13 January Kang Sheng gave instructions to the inquisitors: "This group of counter-revolutionary special agents, working for the enemy, has sold the most intimate secrets of the Party and the country, the government and the army, and, if they are guilty, they deserve ten thousand deaths. In dealing with them we cannot simply deploy the same methods used for ordinary criminals."

Ling Yun must have known what to expect from an interrogation, but he surely never imagined becoming the victim of his own colleagues from the bureau. Meanwhile, Kang Sheng advocated that "to prevent them from committing suicide they should be handcuffed" and "as enemies be subjected to extremely severe shock interrogations".[3]

In February, Kang received his first report. He wanted the interrogations to intensify, in order to force answers out of this "group of counter-revolutionary double agents": "Were they organized into a group of double agents at the instigation of Luo Ruiqing [the former Gonganbu boss turned army chief], and Peng Zhen [Beijing's mayor]? They often gave intelligence to the enemy—in what way did they benefit from this?" he scrawled with a furious brushstroke, in the margins of the reports he sent back with comments after reading them.

The interrogations and torture continued for two months, until Kang Sheng and Xie Fuzhi claimed that they were now clear about the Gonganbu group. Its members remained in detention, handcuffed almost the entire time, until the end of the Cultural Revolution. Several, including the deputy ministers Xu Zirong and Xu Jianguo, died in prison. Ling Yun was released in August 1975. Surprisingly, like many other officials who suffered at the hands of Kang Sheng, he prostrated himself in front of Kang's funeral bier on 21 December 1975, and his name even appeared on the Funeral Committee's list—a very useful document that contains the names of many in the intelligence community. One might suspect that Ling had secretly maintained a kind of esteem, a cold admiration, for Kang, who was after all the one who had given him his first leg up in the secret service.

In the years that followed, Ling Yun found himself at the heart of special operations. He travelled a great deal, accompanying various leaders, and was responsible not only for organizing their security but also for helping them with their overtures to the outside world. At the end of the Cultural Revolution, China had been left staggering, like a blind man who has just recovered his sight. Its leaders were well aware that they would have to build a new intelligence service, and Ling Yun was part of this recovery and reconstruction. He became deputy minister of the Gonganbu in 1978 and was elected to the Shanghai assembly (though this parliament obviously did not have the same function as in democracies). He accompanied Hua Guofeng during state visits abroad. In October 1979, at the head of a large delegation, the two men visited Western Europe—Great Britain, France, West Germany and Italy. Various directors from the Chinese security services took the opportunity to make purchases, including buying computers in France and Germany, which would prove very useful in the future. In Britain, Hua and Ling were received by Queen Elizabeth; in France, they met President Valéry Giscard d'Estaing and Jacques Chirac, then mayor of Paris.

However Ling's most significant trip took place earlier that year. In January 1979, he accompanied Deng Xiaoping to the United States. Ling appreciated the opportunity to collaborate with the FBI and the services in charge of Jimmy Carter's security, along with those of other VIPs including Deng. Meanwhile, the Chinese intelligence services had got wind of a Taiwanese plan to assassinate Deng while he was in Washington. Chiang Kai-shek had been dead for four years and his son Chiang Ching-kuo had replaced him; trained in Moscow, he maintained the authoritarian regime of the Kuomintang with an iron fist, and its secret services were just as powerful as those in the PRC. Everything was a state secret, including the real name of his blonde Russian wife, Faina Epatcheva Vakhreva. Chiang was directly in charge of the special services that entrusted this mission to the United Bamboo Gang, a powerful triad based in Taiwan with several international branches. Though the Gang did not succeed in killing Deng, it did assassinate Henry Liu, a writer living in the US, who had made the mistake of writing a critical biography of Taiwan's new president.

Another concern for those responsible for Deng's protection was the rumour that a US Maoist group, of all things, was planning to disrupt Deng's visit. The Revolutionary Communist Party reproached Deng for betraying Mao and opening China up to capitalist ideology. It organized a large demonstration in Washington DC called the "Deng Demo". The skirmishes that took place led to several criminal prosecutions, and Bob Avakian, the party leader, fled to France, where he went into hiding. In the late 2010s, the organization has been concentrating its efforts on the "fight against fascism"—that is, opposing Donald Trump's presidency. Thus Avakian still carries the torch for one of the world's last remaining Maoist parties.

For Deng Xiaoping, his week in the US as Carter's guest went extremely well, and on the flight home he and Ling toasted their success with champagne. A colour photograph shows the two men positively glowing: the Little Helmsman, as Deng was known, and Ling the "big bear", puffed up in his blue Mao tunic, large bifocals perched on his nose, lips stretched in a voracious smile. Ling Yun, "Noble Ambition", had truly won the jackpot. He was now the most important spymaster in the PRC.

The clean break from Maoism

The reformers upon whom Deng relied, the leaders Hu Yaobang and Zhao Ziyang, were in agreement: it was necessary to erase the past and undertake a thorough appraisal of the crimes committed during the Cultural Revolution, in order to lead China on the road to reform, particularly with the plan to create a modern secret service. Hu Yaobang, general secretary of the CCP's Central Committee and its overall number one (under Deng's tutelage), was charged with delivering a very long-winded speech on 9 November 1978 about Kang Sheng's role in the Cultural Revolution. It was a kind of post-mortem detailing many of the crimes of which Kang had been found guilty.

Li Junru, one of Hu's distant successors in this post, and an important advocate of Chinese reformist ideology in recent years, has told me that, like many other major statements during that time of great change, Hu's speech took place in front of the Central Party School in Beijing, of which he was then deputy director.

The party's investigation department, Luo Qingchang's Diaochabu, had produced a fat report bringing together all the testimonies against Kang Sheng, dating back to the 1930s. Everything was there: the fact that, in 1966, Chairman Liu Shaoqi had asked for a review of the case of former "Moscow agents", which brought to light the troubled past of Kang Sheng; how former leaders Chen Duxiu, Li Lisan, Zhang

Guotao and Wang Ming had been considered deviationist because of files on them compiled by Kang; and how Kang had organized the Yan'an purges: "At the time, both Liu Shaoqi and former prime minister Zhou Enlai said that Kang Sheng was not the ideal man for such important work. They also suggested that he be investigated. But most members of the Central Committee had by then been dispersed all over the country, and a special investigation was not possible."[4]

Subsequently, Hu explained in his speech, Kang pursued similar operations, labelling as "counter-revolutionary" anyone who stood in his way, particularly in Shandong, which had now became his personal fiefdom: "Recognizing the need for special security, for secrecy, and for granting 'high security' protection to those involved in intelligence work, the Central Committee made the Department of State Security an impenetrable and independent kingdom."

Hu Yaobang's listing of these files in his speech ran to many pages, but the students and functionaries in the audience, shocked by the revelations about the "Chinese Beria", remained alert throughout. The testimonies confirmed some of the craziest rumours, and explained the horrific events that had taken place during the Cultural Revolution, which, according to even the lowest estimates, had led to the deaths of between 1 and 2 million people. Alongside the trial of the Gang of Four, the speech delivered by Hu Yaobang inevitably brought to mind Khrushchev's 1956 "secret speech", which heralded the era of de-Stalinization in the USSR.

However, in the CCP of 1978, things were not yet quite so advanced. Hu Yaobang, while playing the transparency card by denouncing the leaders of the previous decade, relied on a kind of demonization not so different from the "Kang Sheng method"—for example, voicing the suspicion that Kang had always been a "Kuomintang agent". This was always the explanation for the party's and special services' self-destruction during the Cultural Revolution: whoever benefited from the crime must inevitably have been working for the Kuomintang.

"Kang Sheng's corpse will stink for all eternity!"

In the course of his seemingly interminable speech, Hu Yaobang described Kang Sheng as the "fifth man" in the Gang of Four. The reality, as we have seen, was a little more complex. Hu's concluding words first summed up the new impetus that the group around Deng Xiaoping hoped to give to politics, and to the remodelling of the intelligence services: "Last year we reviewed a large number of cases that had built up over the past few years. Many unresolved issues have now been clarified and many of our comrades have been released. At the same time, we have rehabilitated many people, functionaries as well as ordinary people, whether or not they were members of the Party, all victims of false, fabricated accusations. If we cannot bring those who have died back to life, we can at least restore their reputations, and posthumously confer honours upon them with the appropriate ceremony. As the Chinese proverb says, 'Disgrace based on injustice will be changed into glory'. The dead can now rest in peace. As you know, comrades, our comrades suffered a great deal, both morally and physically, before passing away. Some were tortured to death. Others committed suicide. Still others were poisoned or murdered by other means. Some died of hunger, others were locked up in insane asylums and died of despair. Those who had once held a position in the Party or the government were rehabilitated fairly quickly, but there are still millions of lowly functionaries and ordinary people awaiting justice. Some died long ago, and their bodies have long rotted away, but the label of 'enemy agent' still sticks to them. Their families still suffer. Even if the Organizational Department were larger, there would not be enough people to re-examine and settle all these cases one by one. We therefore hope that each province and district will undertake case reviews, so that we will be able to resolve all the outstanding cases as quickly as possible, and release those who remain in detention as soon as we can, and leave nothing hanging. To carry out this task we cannot rely solely on functionaries; we need the help and cooperation of the masses. With their help the work will be done quickly."[5]

Hu Yaobang then refocused his attacks on Kang, who had died three years previously: "It is odious that Kang Sheng perpetrated so many crimes. The worst of which was that by the end he was even keeping Chairman Mao, National Assembly Speaker Zhu De, Prime Minister Zhou Enlai, and Vice-Chairman Deng Xiaoping under surveillance. He had bugging devices installed in Chairman Mao's library and office. Everyone remembers that Prime Minister Zhou Enlai was in hospital for a long time. One of the reasons was of course the state of his health, and the fact that he was in need of rest. But another reason is that he could no longer remain at home. Prime Minister Zhou Enlai once said to Field Marshal Ye Jianying, with bitter irony, 'I cannot live at home. I have no choice but to move into the hospital ... there at least I can say what I want.'

"In September Chairman Mao summoned Kang Sheng and ordered him to end his campaign of dirty tricks. Kang Sheng denied everything. But later, in December 1972, during repair work in Chairman Mao's office, eavesdropping devices were discovered. Chairman Mao was furious. He summoned Kang Sheng and demanded an explanation. Kang Sheng not only vehemently denied any responsibility, but he also took the precaution of eliminating the three technicians involved, thus covering one crime by another.

"Chairman Mao once told the Central Committee, 'I am surrounded by far worse people than Lin Biao. They are not men but devils.' He was of course referring to Kang Sheng's spies. From 1969 to 1975, Kang Sheng spent 230 million yuan on purchasing sophisticated spy equipment imported from abroad. This equipment was not used against our enemies but against our own revolutionary comrades. During the last ten years, as head of our intelligence system, he turned our secret services into a kind of Gestapo, independent of the Central Committee. His henchmen were able to arrest and punish whomsoever they wanted. They could eliminate a man without orders. They could do and they did whatever they wanted.

"In 1971, after the Lin Biao–Chen Boda incident, Kang Sheng was put in charge of investigative work in the Special Cases Section of the Central Committee. Acting behind the back of Prime Minister Zhou Enlai, then head of the section, he took over virtually intact the network of special agents set up by Lin Biao in Guangzhou, Wuhan, Hangzhou, Shanghai, Hainan, Shenyang and Beidaihe. He also brought into his network all those who supported the Lin Biao–Chen Boda faction. In the latter half of 1972, he brought all of these elements together, along with 500 men drawn from his own security network, to form the Special Actions Group. Kang Sheng's office served as their base and they were under his direct control. Kang also set up his own network of special agents in each of the country's fifty-four major cities. Every branch was under the responsibility of people in whom he had absolute confidence. Their task was to monitor the activities of Party officials and to report back regularly to Kang Sheng. It should be noted here that no bureau chief at the Central Committee had as much [room for manoeuvre] as Kang Sheng. Chairman Mao had always insisted that bureau chiefs should not have too many secretaries. Nonetheless Kang Sheng had not only a large number of secretaries but also a dozen liaison officers at his disposal. What did they do? Nothing special. They did the work of any special agent. They transmitted secret reports. They sought to destroy other people. Although Kang Sheng was responsible for a single department, one office was clearly not enough. He needed two additional annexes so that all his 'office staff' would be comfortable. Only then could he broaden his sphere of influence, claim absolute power, and commit every imaginable crime.

"Kang Sheng's power reached its zenith around 1974; everyone in the government felt it. Many comrades in the Party's central apparatus noticed that 'it is better to enter hell than Kang's office.' The idea was even expressed in verse:

More frightening than drawing your own last breath
Is being called to Kang's office, the Kingdom of Death.

"Everyone was afraid of Kang. They considered him more important than King Yama, the god who judges and governs the dead in Buddhist hell. He and his henchmen were able to arrest and kill people as they pleased. They set up a torture chamber. It was said of Kang Sheng that he was an ugly man who 'never said anything bad, and never did anything good'. Without Kang Sheng and his network of agents across the country, without a spy in every district, the Gang of Four would never have been able to seize power without killing all of the Party leaders first."

Clearly, by focusing on Kang Sheng's evil deeds, Hu could leave Mao's reputation unblemished and his aura preserved. The Gang of Four trial took place between November 1980 and January 1981 and was broadcast on television. Jiang Qing, Mao's widow, was sentenced to life imprisonment,[6] and those who led the Cultural Revolution with her were also given long prison sentences. The trial—conducted, naturally, in the Stalinist tradition—also served as an occasion for accusing Kang Sheng of a slew of further crimes, even though he had by then been dead for several years. This was a kind of sideshow to the main event—the trial of the Gang of Four—and the announcement of Kang's posthumous punishment was in keeping with the whole spectacle: on 31 October 1980, on the eve of the trial, the CCP Central Committee announced his expulsion from the party, as well as that of his sidekick, Xie Fuzhi (d. 1972), the former head of the Gonganbu.

As we've already noted, Deng Xiaoping's rejection of the Maoist period was reminiscent of the "thaw" that began with the USSR Communist Party's 20th Congress in 1956 and the de-Stalinization it heralded. But unlike Khrushchev, who had been with Stalin all the way, Deng himself had suffered under the rule of Mao, the Gang of Four and Kang Sheng's secret police. Even after the Cultural Revolution had ended, he was still tormented by the daily sight of his son Deng Pufang, confined to a wheelchair after being thrown from a high window by the Red Guards in 1968.

This led Deng to commit to a three-fold reform of the intelligence services, in parallel with the major political and economic overhaul that he was planning. This troika of reform was conceived with the help of Zhao Ziyang, and with the support of Hu Yaobang. First, Deng wanted to cast Kang Sheng back to the underworld, where he was commonly held to be the demon master. In Hu's words, "One might be fearless when facing the king of the underworld, but quite terrified by the boss Kang" (*bupa yanwang, zhipa Kang laoban*). Hence Hu's highly critical speech and the posthumous revocation of Kang's party membership.

Second, Deng decided to demote the CCP's secret service wing, the Diaochabu, to a minor political function, and to integrate its "external intelligence expertise" into a large, modern espionage and counterintelligence service. Finally, in tune with the country's modernization projects, the opening up of China towards the outside world required a strategic reorientation of this new secret service—and indeed all the other services dependent on the party, foreign ministry and army—towards economic, scientific and technological research. With these three moves, Deng Xiaoping "revolutionized" Chinese intelligence.

The Chinese KGB

On 6 June 1983, Prime Minister Zhao Ziyang announced the establishment of a new Ministry of State Security, or *Guojia Anquanbu*. The Chinese officials to whom I have spoken call it for short either *Anquanbu* or *Guoanbu*; I have adopted the latter term to facilitate reading and pronunciation.

"In order to guarantee the security of the state and to reinforce counterintelligence," Zhao declared at the first session of the 6th National People's Congress (1983–8), "the State Council submits for the approval of this session plans to establish a Ministry of State Security to take the lead in these tasks."

Though considerably smaller in scale, with at this stage around 7,000 cadres, the Guoanbu was hoping to become the Chinese KGB. Under the direction of "Noble Ambition" Ling Yun, it had the same role as that Soviet service: foreign intelligence, and counterintelligence. It was created through a merger of part of the CCP's Diaochabu, responsible for intelligence in embassies around the world, with a huge number of counterintelligence officials from the Gonganbu, the "public security" ministry. The Gonganbu continued to maintain units for uncovering spies and dissidents in the provinces, at the lowest level of the pyramid, while the deputy ministers who assisted Ling Yun at the new Guoanbu—Hui Ping and Wang Jun—were drawn from there. Zhou Shaozheng, who almost became the leader of the Guoanbu but ended up merely a deputy minister, came from the Diaochabu. Born, like Ling Yun, in Zhejiang, Zhou was a specialist in technological intelligence and a former diplomat in Central America. Given his background in party intelligence, he represented the most political wing of the new ministry.

Ling Yun was anointed by Deng Xiaoping and his daughter Deng Rong—"Daddy's Ear", as she was nicknamed—who had close links to the military intelligence lobby through her husband, Colonel He Ping, military attaché in Washington. Ling also enjoyed the support of two men from Canton, both born in the same district: Marshal Ye Jianying—whose son would soon be appointed head of one of the PLA's intelligence services—and Liu Fuzhi, another counterintelligence specialist from the Gonganbu.[7]

Liu played an important role in the establishment of the new national spy administration. After serving as Marshal Zhu De's secretary in Deng Xiaoping's 8th Route Army, he had honed his counterintelligence skills in the 129th Division of the 8th Army and then in the Social Affairs Department. Subsequently he had become chief of staff to Luo Ruiqing, who would later become first head of the Gonganbu. Like Ling Yun, Liu had also served as deputy minister of the Gonganbu, during the Cultural Revolution, under Xie Fuzhi.

Liu was all but forgotten from 1967 to 1971, but as a qualified lawyer, he helped to reform criminal law in the new China, which led to him being appointed minister of justice in May 1982. He had great influence on Deng, as well as on Hu Yaobang and Zhao Ziyang, both in the choice of new structures and in the appointment of Ling Yun. Once the central counterintelligence function had been stripped from the Gonganbu, Liu became its head—minister of public security. It was his idea for the new Ministry of *State* Security—the Guoanbu—to absorb part of the Diaochabu, which would maintain the party archives, as well as continuing an internal inspection role both at home and within embassies abroad. Kong Yuan, who had been head of the Diaochabu until the Cultural Revolution, also continued to keep a close eye. He was now responsible for the overhaul of military intelligence, and helped Ling Yun to set up the new State Security.

Beijing's Western Park (*Xiyuan*), one stop after the zoo on the 332 bus and one before the Summer Palace, is an extensive royal park within the Imperial City. It housed the former Diaochabu buildings, now extended and modernized to accommodate the Guoanbu. Satellite photos today show the full extent of this secret ministry. At the beginning of the 1980s, it brought together a dozen large departments.

The 1st Bureau was responsible for internal affairs and security in the provinces, working in tandem with local Guoanbu offices, for example in Beijing (headed by Ming Buying) and Shanghai (under Ding Shenglie), as well as with the 1st Bureau of Liu Fuzhi's Gonganbu, headed until 1990 by Tan Songqiu. Though fewer in number than the Gonganbu's, the Guoanbu also had its own border guard units and camps reserved for its specific prisoners within the *laogai*, the Chinese gulag. In April 1983, one of these Guoanbu concentration camps welcomed some new prisoners: members of a Taiwanese intelligence network in Tianjin known as "the Society of the Continent" and the lawyer Huang Hanson, sentenced to ten years in prison for "espionage". This heralded the start of a long list of State Security prisoners sent to the *laogai*.

The 2nd Bureau was responsible for foreign intelligence, first and foremost in the already very active bases of Tokyo, Bangkok and Singapore. Its agents were given diplomatic cover in embassies as "advisors" or "second secretaries". In the Japanese capital, analysts led by Kamakura Sadame, head of the Naicho (Cabinet Intelligence & Research Office), took note of Chinese advisor Guan Zongzhou's arrival at the embassy in April 1983—just as the Guoanbu was being set up—under Ambassador Song Zhiguang, who had himself been the first intelligence officer at the newly opened Chinese embassy in Paris twenty years earlier.[8]

In France now, the embassy advisor Zhu Guanghai was being watched by the DST, a domestic intelligence branch of the national police. Officers soon realized that since his posting in Gabon, Zhu had devoted himself to "African affairs". Paris was indeed at the time the capital of Francophone Africa, but it turned out that this was not the only reason for Zhu's interest. In 1984 he was posted to the London embassy in Portland Place as a "second advisor", where he coordinated spy missions under the watchful eye of MI5. The Guoanbu in London went on to develop recruitment operations for English-speaking members of the African elite, coordinated from 1987 onwards by another Africa specialist—officially also a second secretary—Huang Xiugao.

The 3rd Bureau focused particularly on infiltration in the three places over which the PRC intended to recover sovereignty in the longer term: Hong Kong, Macao and Taiwan. Deng Xiaoping did not want to die without standing at least once on Hong Kong soil free from the British colonial yoke. A large delegation of Guoanbu officials was registered at the Xinhua News Agency there, which acted as a de facto embassy, stopping short of an actual parallel government.

The 4th Bureau was responsible for technology, in other words the technical aspects of espionage both for roaming or permanently stationed international operatives and for counterintelligence. The 5th Bureau was responsible for local intelligence—not to be confused with the 6th Bureau, which ran counterintelligence. These two Bureaus were in turn supported by the 7th, which carried out surveillance missions and special operations. All worked closely with the Political Security Bureau, whose 2nd Section focused on foreign diplomats stationed in Beijing or the consulates of other major cities such as Shanghai and Guangzhou. Special ops officers received training at the former Diaochabu secret agent training camp in Nanyuan, south of Beijing.

The 8th Bureau was responsible for research, largely through open sources, and took over the China Institutes of Contemporary International Relations (*Xiandai Guoji Guanxi Yanjiusuo*), a subsidiary division of the Diaochabu. Despite CICIR members' regular denials of any association with the intelligence services, on 20 February 1984 Cheng Zhongjing, director of the CICIR, was appointed as an advisor to the Guoanbu leadership, with Wu Xuewen, who had been expelled from Japan for espionage, as his deputy. Cheng was also director of the College of International Relations at Tsingua University (*Guoji Guanxi Xueyuan*), a training school for intelligence agents being posted abroad that was situated near the Summer Palace.

The 9th Bureau was responsible for dealing with the risk of infiltration by undercover enemy agents, and of Guoanbu agents defecting or being "turned" by the enemy. It also analyzed how enemy services protected themselves from Chinese operations. As we shall see later in the chapter, the 9th Bureau found itself with much to do following the defection of a senior Guoanbu official in 1985.

The 10th Bureau, destined for major development, oversaw research in scientific and technological intelligence. It worked with specialist state agencies such as the State Scientific & Technological Commission and the intelligence division of the huge Commission for Science, Technology and Industry for National Defence (COSTIND). The 11th Bureau managed the stock of information technology equipment that was being built up. Some of its computers had been purchased a few years earlier by the number two at the Gonganbu, Li Guangxiang. Li, a specialist in the fight against Taiwan, travelled to West Germany to study how the federal police, the Bundeskriminalamt, had carried out a massive population registration programme during the fight against the "Red Army Faction", the Baader-Meinhof Gang famously inspired by the Maoist revolution.

Finally, the 12th Bureau was the Office of Foreign Affairs (*Waishiju*), located in Beijing on the same premises as the Beijing Gonganbu bureau on Dongchang'an Avenue, and run by the extraordinary Yu Zhensan. It was responsible for liaisons with foreign intelligence services, including officials from various Western agencies—David Gries of the CIA, Dr Herms Bahl ("Dr Queck") of the West German BND, Nigel Inkster of MI6, and Thierry Imbot from the French DGSE—who were all, of course, under close surveillance.[9] The KGB *rezidentura*, headed by Viktor Kracheninnikov, which had made a comeback after the Cultural Revolution, was no exception to this rule.

The Guoanbu's Office of Foreign Affairs worked with its Office of Political Security to monitor diplomats, journalists and the first trickle of tourists, increasing in number now that tourist visas were being issued. Indeed this was one of the reasons given for the very creation of Guoanbu; no sooner had Ling Yun taken office than he announced: "The intelligence agencies and secret services of some foreign countries have increased their spying activities against China's state secrets and are now sending agents to subvert and destroy our country."[10]

It would be a few more years before a broad economic intelligence agency developed. But since the 1980s, this area of espionage had become something of an object lesson. In autumn 1984, Western diplomats stationed in Beijing began taking notice of a newly created school for industrial espionage, as evidenced by an article in a well-informed specialist newsletter:

> Diplomats are showing considerable interest in a new training institute going into operation in China. What you might call a school for spies. Not the usual kind of cloak and dagger espionage, like we see in novels. This institute is training a Chinese elite to do industrial espionage. What they want is know-how, and their main targets are Japan, the United States and a few Western European countries (specifically West Germany, France and Great Britain). Some of these very sophisticated spies are being sent abroad as businessmen for state-trading enterprises, and others are attached to Chinese embassies overseas. Most of them, however, go abroad as students studying for advanced degrees.[11]

Another sign of the times was the establishment in February 1982 of the Ministry of Foreign Economic Relations and Trade (MOFERT), headed by Chen Muhua—we might remember from Chapter 2 that

Zhou Enlai had removed him from the clutches of Kang Sheng in Yan'an, after Kang claimed he was "a Kuomintang spy". MOFERT's international sector—as well as that of its successor, MOFTEC—offered important cover for roaming Guoanbu agents, as Deng Xiaoping had suggested.[12]

All this training appears to have been rather necessary, because—according to several intelligence and security specialists who were fighting the new Chinese services at the time—they were not very good at what they were doing. As one French expert put it, "The Chinese needed this training school. Industrialists seemed to think that they weren't very good at economic espionage. For example, where the Japanese divide the task up between them—they go into a lab and make sure to take photos and notes about everything—the Chinese would stick together and barely dare to ask any questions."

One analyst in the Japanese intelligence service, the Naicho, put it this way: "The Guoanbu was training new cadres, who needed to know at least two languages, and to learn to be very proactive when it came to intelligence research. But the first thing they needed to do was to tour the embassies to monitor the Chinese diplomats, whose own attitude left a lot to be desired. Many were recalled to Beijing following a Guoanbu investigation and subjected to an in-depth interrogation.

"The service didn't have a large budget, which it was not happy about. It had no planes, and few cars and computers. In fact, amongst some of the older leaders, the Gonganbu still had a better reputation, even though the Guoanbu had been set up as a part of a programme of political and economic liberalization. It's a good service, [the equal of others in the East Asian region]. It just needed to develop considerably."[13]

This presumably explains why, all of a sudden, dozens of Chinese translations of books about foreign intelligence services began to appear in Beijing.

A literary interlude

In June 2007, I entered a group of buildings from the 1950s that were so dilapidated they appeared all but abandoned, in the Fangzhuang district of southern Beijing. The doorman was eating a bowl of rice and reading the newspaper. He casually passed me the phone so that I could speak to Mr Zhang Meirong, director of the Qunzhong Publishing House, whose offices were just upstairs. If I had a manuscript to leave, Mr Zhang suggested that I write to him. But I had already written to him, to announce that I was coming to see him. After a little discussion, a beefy young man led me down a maze of dark corridors to the publisher's offices. He was wearing a bright red T-shirt bearing the inscription "Chinese Public Security"—the Gonganbu. When I asked him if he was part of the police, he proudly told me that he was. This didn't really surprise me, given that Qunzhong Publishing House is more or less a satellite of the Gonganbu and Guoanbu. It specializes in non-fiction books about the police and the secret services, and novels about private detectives and espionage. Stories about terrorism became very popular in China after 9/11.

While he served me tea, Mr Zhang told me how much he loved France. I explained to him that the book I had come to discuss had already been published—by him—under the title: *Youyongchi—Faguo mimi jigou*—the translation of my book *La Piscine: The French Secret Service Since 1944*.[14] I told him that I had only discovered a few months earlier that it had been published in Chinese in 1987, and as I was the book's co-author, I would be most grateful if I could obtain a few copies. *Meiyou wenti*! No problem! I was sent off to see Madame Zhang Rong, director of the collection and head of fiction in translation.

She too offered me tea, in good English, and invited me to lunch, for it was not far off midday. But first she had to call the stock department. She absolutely adored France. She had been to Paris and Nice. As far as the book was concerned, there should be no problem at all! She went away, came back, served me tea. She was waiting for a call. If there is a problem, she assured me, it's sure to be easily solved. I took the opportunity to request a catalogue. Of course! No problem at all. Then the phone rang—the conversation lasted a while. Now Madame Zhang's tone changed. There appeared to be a small problem: "Unfortunately, since the book was published in 1987," she told me, "there are no copies available." Not even a copy in the archive that could be photocopied—or even just for me to take a look at? No.

Comrade Zhang presumably thought that I understood only English, for this was not what had been said during the telephone call

I had just overheard. Rather, I understood that the book was classified as *neibu* (secret) for foreigners. This was really a little odd, given that I, a foreigner, had written it. She told me that another edition had been brought out the same year by the publishing arm of the University of Public Security (*Zhongguo Renmin Gongan Daxue Chubanshe*), if I wanted to try to obtain it there. That was the end of our conversation. "By the way," she added, "I am afraid that there is no catalogue available." It appeared that I was no longer invited to lunch, either.

It was not long before even the edition of my book "pirated" by the Gonganbu no longer existed, either—it never had. I still do not know what actually happened: was the Qunzhong Publishing House ordered not to grant my request following an outside intervention? Or were they simply worried that I had come to claim the copyright stolen from me, my co-author, and our French publisher? I suppose I should have been grateful. After all, the important thing is to have played a part in the education of the masses, and the training of China's special agents, in the spirit of friendship between peoples.

Many of the books on intelligence that I found in bookshops on that trip were originally published in the 1980s. The Qunzhong Publishing House had published *Spy, Counter Spy*, the autobiography of the British MI6 agent Dusko Popov; another publisher had brought out a translation of James Bamford's *Puzzle Palace*, about the American National Security Agency, with whom Deng Xiaoping's services collaborated against the Soviets. I found *The KGB* (*Ke Ge Bo*) by the American John Barron, and *GRU: The Most Secret of the Soviet Services* by the Frenchman Pierre de Villemarest. All of these texts, and others like them, form part of a Guoanbu apprentice agent's reading list, while at the same time appealing to a broad audience, for the Chinese are very fond of tales about spies. This was the background against which *La Piscine* was published.

I have already lost face with this story of *La Piscine*, but I must make another self-criticism—about my book with Rémi Kauffer, *Kang Sheng and the Chinese Secret Service*. Published in 1987 in France, this book was also the subject of a curious Chinese translation, this time at the request of the Central Party School's publishing arm. Despite this official commission, the translator, who had suggested the addition of a new, updated preface, told me that we would need to wait for permission to publish it. The material must have been too sensitive—we never got the green light. Printed and bound, the book was, I was told, circulated to a few hundred important comrades at the party summit, within the Central Party School, and in some special departments. Some of the people I met clearly knew the book well. "But why are you so interested in such a vile person?" I was once asked.

These fine scholars must have jumped when reading the book's final chapter. For it is only today, twenty years later, that I can reveal the end of this story. In 1985, a senior functionary in the Guoanbu, known as "the adopted son of Kang Sheng" defected, and handed over all his secrets to the CIA.

Operation Jade Powder

The three counterintelligence services—State Security (the Guoanbu), Public Security (the Gonganbu) and the army intelligence (still the PLA2)—shared the running of the largest Beijing hotels, some of which they actually owned. This allowed them to spy on the travellers and businessmen who were beginning to arrive in ever larger numbers, with the hope of investing in Deng Xiaoping's China.[15]

In the 1980s, there was extensive surveillance at the Beijing Hotel, a stone's throw from Tiananmen Square. Bugs and hidden surveillance cameras were installed in the restaurant, the lobby and the bar, at reception, and in the bedrooms. The monitoring was not always very discreet. Bernard Gérard, head of the DST, used to tell French executives a funny story at conferences to make it clear what they were up against. A Breton businessman called his boss in Brittany from his room at the Beijing Hotel. Wanting to talk about the terms of a contract that they were negotiating, the two men spoke to each other in their native Breton. Suddenly, a female voice cut into the conversation: "Speak French!" Stubbornly, the two businessmen continued talking in Breton—which is unfortunately not on the curriculum of the Institute of Foreign Languages where Guoanbu officials are trained. Suddenly, the line was cut. Thus the head of French counter-espionage received a new piece of technical information: a large room in the basement of the Beijing Hotel housed an army of "telephone ladies", who swap places depending on the languages being spoken, in order to monitor all conversations taking place in every room in the building.

A little earlier, in the autumn of 1985, one of a group of CIA agents who had come to the hotel's bar for a drink was caught on camera. What created a stir was the sight of the affable Chinese man who sat facing him, whom he obviously knew well: this was Yu Zhensan, head of the Guoanbu's Office of Foreign Affairs, situated just two blocks away. The men of the 9th Bureau—the Guoanbu's internal security—wasted no time in alerting their superiors at the central office in Xiyuan, in the Fragrant Hills Park. But Ling Yun saw no cause for panic: after all, this was precisely what Yu and his Office were meant to do—discuss and "exchange" with the intelligence representatives from foreign services.

However, a few weeks later in November, Ling must have been kicking himself. Yu Zhensan left for a visit to Hong Kong, apparently for both professional and personal reasons—later it was thought that he had a Western mistress there. In fact, it might well have been she who was responsible for the dramatic twist that ensued when Yu disappeared, and a rumour began to circulate that "a senior Guoanbu official had defected and been picked up by the CIA". The operation to exfiltrate him from Hong Kong, somewhat delayed because of ill health, had been codenamed "Operation Jade Powder".

On 24 November 1985, an extraordinary piece of information ostensibly of no relevance to this development appeared on the teletype machines. The FBI had arrested a Chinese mole in the CIA called Larry Wu-Tai Chin—from his name in Pinyin, Jin Wudai—who had apparently been furnishing state secrets to the Beijing services for thirty years. The consequences of this affair would be great. It triggered an earthquake not only at CIA headquarters in Langley, and in Washington, but also at Xiyuan, the Guoanbu headquarters in Beijing.

Meanwhile, Yu Zhensan's defection remained relatively unknown to the wider public. In early summer 1986, Rémi Kauffer and I were in Hong Kong researching our book on Kang Sheng. Back then the last few junks were still moored in the Fragrant Harbour, where we got wind of the affair and gathered some information about Comrade Yu's background. This provided the material for the final chapter in the Kang Sheng book, even though at the time there were significant gaps in our knowledge of the affair. We did, however, discover that Yu himself had been responsible for the arrest of Larry Wu-Tai Chin, first identified as a mole in 1983. On 17 September 1986, teletype machines tapped out an AFP dispatch from Hong Kong: "A Chinese spy has escaped to the United States, having sold out an agent who had been working for Beijing from within the CIA, the US intelligence service, for 30 years, it was reported in a Hong Kong magazine on Wednesday.

"Yu San, head of the Foreign Affairs Office of the Chinese Ministry of Security, was described in January by reliable sources in Beijing as being in hiding abroad. According to *Pai Hsing* magazine he has claimed asylum in the United States.

"His first 'gift' to the CIA was to reveal that Larry Wu-Tai Chin, 63, employed by the CIA for thirty years, was one of the most important spies working for Beijing, according to *Pai Hsing*. Mr Yu offered up this information to the CIA during a secret visit to Hong Kong in November 1985. Mr Chin, a US citizen of Chinese origin, was arrested by the FBI, the US Federal Police, on 22 November. Having been sentenced to life imprisonment for spying, he committed suicide in prison in February.

"The magazine further reports that Yu—also known as Yu Zhensan—is currently in McLean, near Washington, D.C., where he is being interrogated and will remain a guest of the CIA for two years."

When I met Lu Keng, the editor of the bi-weekly *Pai Hsing*, in Hong Kong it was clear that his sources were unimpeachable. A Kang Sheng victim during the Cultural Revolution, he had spent ten years in jail, but by 1986 had built up a cordial relationship with the new party leadership and in particular with the general secretary, Hu Yaobang, whom he had interviewed several times.

Over the course of months and years, Yu Zhensan's extraordinary life story was gradually revealed. Forty-something years old, his original name was Yu Qiangsheng, and he was part of the Chinese nomenklatura, a key member of the bureaucracy, with longstanding links to both the CCP and the Kuomintang—in fact, both to Mao Zedong's close entourage and to Chiang Kai-shek's family. There were several other major figures in the China of this period who also had forebears in both camps, which was hardly surprising given the interactions that occurred in the 1920s and 1930s between the two parties.

Looking at the Yu family tree is rather enlightening. A wealthy Chinese man named Yu Mingzhen, from Shaoxing, Zhejiang province, had two sons: Yu Dachun and Yu Dawei, both fierce Kuomintang militants who followed Chiang Kai-shek to Taiwan in 1949. Yu Dawei served as the nationalist minister of defence between 1954 and 1965, and his son, Yu Yang-ho, married Chiang Kai-shek's granddaughter—the daughter of Chiang Ching-kuo, who had succeeded his father as president of Taiwan.

But his brother, General Yu Dachun, had children who had remained on the mainland. His son Yu Qiwei, also known as Huang Jing, was a veteran communist activist. In 1931 in Qingdao, Shandong province, he met somebody through his sister Yu Shan, a beautiful singer and actress at the Beijing Opera. This somebody, known as "Crane of the Clouds", went on to become the film actress "Blue Apple"—before gaining notoriety as Jiang Qing, mistress of Kang Sheng and then wife of Chairman Mao. The future Madame Mao lived with Yu Qiwei—some even claim they were married—until the CCP sent him to Beijing, at which point Jiang Qing decided to move to Shanghai to pursue her career in cinema. There she married another figure in the entertainment industry, Tang Na, who went on to open a restaurant in Paris, and who became, in the 1980s, an "honourable correspondent" for the Soviet secret services.

This glamorous circle—Jiang Qing, Kang Sheng and Yu Qiwei—met up again in Yan'an in 1935, along with Yu Shan. Despite Mao's marriage to Jiang Qing, Yu Shan became one of his many mistresses. In 1949, when Madame Mao was in hospital in the USSR—just as the triumphant communists were setting up shop in Beijing—it was Yu Shan who was sharing the chairman's bed. Some comrades actually confused her with Madame Mao, heard of but never seen.[16]

Yu Qiwei, Jiang Qing's former lover, had stepped aside for Mao, though he had remained a friend of Kang Sheng. In another blinding political crossover, he went on to marry a very unusual journalist, Fan

Jin. She, along with her friend Gong Peng, was part of Zhou Enlai's famous circle of female Chinese spies in the United States, which had played an influential role around Pearl S. Buck and Eleanor Roosevelt.[17]

Yu Qiwei and Fan Jin had two sons. The younger, Yu Zhengsheng, became a high-ranking figure in the CCP. After serving as party leader in Shandong and Hubei, then as minister of construction, he made a notable entrance into the Politburo in 2002, later becoming secretary of the Shanghai City Council in October 2007, replacing Xi Jinping.[18] Between 2012 and 2017, he was a member of the Politburo Standing Committee, the highest ruling body of the CCP. However, his career was nearly ruined in the 1980s, because his older brother was none other than Yu Zhensan—the Guoanbu double agent who handed himself over to the CIA in 1985. Fortunately for Yu Zhensheng, his father-in-law, General Zhang Aiping, was defence minister at the time.

One last aspect of this complex family tree is worth our attention: when the propaganda activist Yu Qiwei died of a heart attack in 1958, Kang Sheng agreed, at Madame Mao's behest, to make Yu Zhensan his "adoptive son". This explains how Yu became a counterintelligence agent, and how—though he had not participated in any of the violent abuse that was Kang's trademark—he managed to climb the ladder in the Foreign Affairs Office, joining first the Gonganbu in 1974 under Deputy Minister Yu Sang (no relation), then the Guoanbu when it was set up in 1983. In this key position, Yu Zhensan knew all the tricks of the trade when it came to recruiting foreign agents.

The CIA mole and the Chinese priest

At the FBI, the defector Yu Zhensan was codenamed Planesman. It was not until the Bureau's head of Chinese affairs, I.C. Smith, finally met him in late 1986 that the extraordinary saga of "Kang Sheng's adopted son" came to light. Smith's memoirs, published in 2004, quote extensively from my book, and confirm the accuracy of the Yu family tree that Rémi Kauffer and I had drawn up:

> If one accepts the writings of Faligot and Kauffer, Planesman was not just an ordinary Chinese citizen employed by the [Gonganbu]. He was one of China's "golden youth", the offspring of China's political elite. I became convinced that the "golden youth" were in a better position

> to see the hypocrisy of the Communist system under which they lived ... I believe Planesman saw this hypocrisy and at some point decided to hit back in his own way.
>
> His actions were simply audacious. He strolled around [Guoanbu] headquarters, routinely photographing documents on desks, pulling files, and making inquiries, and being the son of those with influence, he benefited from special treatment. He even pilfered the desk of his supervisor, whom he referred to as the "Beijing Bitch", where he was able to gain access to the most secret of the information contained within the [Guoanbu].
>
> ... Planesman in the flesh was a gregarious, animated individual who spoke in fractured English, but who seemed to have a very real zest for life. When we met at last after Operation Eagle Claw was over, he confirmed my long-held suspicion that he was the ultimate risk taker. I had the impression he would have paid the CIA to allow him to be their spy.[19]

Operation Eagle Claw, the FBI's codename for the unmasking and arrest of Larry Wu-Tai Chin, was probably—at least until the 2007 Chi Mak case—the most stunning FBI catch on record of someone found spying for the Chinese intelligence services.

Born in 1924, Larry Wu-Tai Chin joined the CIA in 1948 as a translator at the US Consulate in Shanghai. The SAD, headed by Pan Hannian, willingly allowed him to leave with the Americans in 1949. If he managed to be recruited and to rise through the ranks, he could be a very important double agent.

The young Chinese interpreter was transferred to the US Consulate in Hong Kong. During the Korean War, he participated with the US services in the interrogation of Chinese prisoners of war who had come to the aid of Kim Il-sung's army. He was recruited into the Chinese intelligence services in Okinawa, Japan, in 1952 by a certain Mr Wang, who was probably Liao Chengzhi, nicknamed "Liao the sailor man". As we know, this former Comintern agent, also an expert on special ops in Taiwan for the ILD, founded the Xinhua News Agency and turned it into a nest of spies.[20]

At the time of his recruitment, Larry was working in the Foreign Broadcast Information Service, then part of the CIA. The FBIS listened in on and transcribed broadcasts from regional radio stations in China, which enabled it to draw up a picture of how Chinese society was evolving using only "open sources". Larry was initially stationed at FBI headquarters in Santa Rosa, California, and then at CIA headquarters in Langley, where he had access to confidential documents and information about US projects in South-East Asia during the Vietnam War.

In the summer of 1970, Larry sent a key document to Beijing containing evidence that Richard Nixon had decided to enter into negotiations with the Chinese. We now know how decisive this diplomatic turn would be for the balance of global power. Knowing the intentions of the White House in advance was hugely useful to Mao and Zhou. Naturally, like so many communist spies captured during the Cold War, the Chinese mole within the CIA used this episode as an argument in his defence after Yu Zhensan sold him out, claiming that he had acted in the interests of peace and "friendship between peoples". The French diplomat Bernard Boursicot, imprisoned around the same time for espionage, told me that his Chinese handler encouraged him to use this line of defence in case he was ever caught.

Between 1978 and 1981, Larry made five trips to Canada. He had two handlers; the first was Ou Qiming, an intelligence veteran who had been imprisoned during the Cultural Revolution. They almost always met in clothes shops or Chinese restaurants in Toronto. The second was Zhu Entao, who later became deputy head of the Gonganbu and the Chinese representative at Interpol. In between these meetings, Larry received microfilms, which were sent by special courier to Hong Kong the same day. Using the "invisible banking system"—one with no accounting records or book-keeping, run on coded messages and personal phone calls—his account would be immediately credited with what the Chinese call "flying money" (*fei qian*). The FBI discovered that, after each of these trips, a sum of $7,000 was deposited into a Hong Kong bank account belonging to one Larry Wu-Tai Chin.

In January 1981, he retired. According to the usual rules, he was not allowed to return immediately to China. In November of that year, he travelled to London where he met with his handler, Ou Qiming, to prepare for his return, due to take place in early 1982. Plans were underway for secret festivities in his honour in Beijing. Counterintelligence officials from the Gonganbu, including, I was told, its then deputy head Ling Yun, were planning to roll out the red carpet in his honour. Comrade Larry was to be given the title of "service chief". This was not merely an honorific. It entitled him to a larger pension and a "golden parachute" bonus of $40,000, to be deposited in his Hong Kong bank account.

It was then, according to I.C. Smith of the FBI, that Larry made a fatal error. After a sweep of his apartment, US counterespionage agents discovered that he had kept the key of his room (number 533) at the Qianmen Hotel. The FBI believed it had discovered his handler, a Chinese woman to whom he paid mysterious visits in New York. In fact she was his mistress. In intercepted telephone conversations, the two were heard discussing various technical devices that intrigued the FBI, but turned out to be sex toys. A double agent leading a double love life was almost bound to get tripped up eventually. The FBI's discovery of this secret, and the threat of its revelation, will have made it much harder for Chin to resist pressure during interrogations.

It was thanks to an anonymous source that the FBI found the real figure handling Chin: "Our source", explains Smith, "reported that Chin's escape contact was a Catholic priest in New York named Father Mark Cheung. Amazing. I was taken aback by the very audacity of the Chinese but at the same time admitted a grudging admiration for their shrewdness. The priest, an ethnic Chinese, had been recruited to work for the Chinese Ministry of Public Security [the Gonganbu] and spent years establishing his cover serving parishes in the South Pacific and Hong Kong. In an emergency, Chin was to meet with Cheung in the confessional of his Transfiguration Church in Chinatown. Cheung later returned to Hong Kong and, after an interview by FBI agents during which he was completely uncooperative, reentered China never to resurface."[21]

This source who helped the FBI to identify the priest was still in Beijing. It was, of course, Yu Zhensan, alias Planesman. But from the beginning of 1983 to the end of 1985, there was no question of arresting Larry Wu-Tai Chin, for this would endanger Yu, their source at the heart of the Guoanbu. They first had to wait for him to defect.

Finally, on 22 November 1985, Larry was arrested. This operation was far from straightforward for the CIA, which was understandably embarrassed by the public disclosure of this obvious failure by its own counterintelligence service. This was during Ronald Reagan's presidency, when the CIA had an agreement with Deng Xiaoping's intelligence services to jointly intercept Soviet communications, and both countries were involved in joint operations supporting the Mujahedin in Afghanistan against the Soviet military. Bill Casey, head of the CIA, nonetheless finally gave the green light for the arrest of the mole in his ranks. Operation Eagle Claw finally swooped.

During the first days of his interrogation, Larry Wu-Tai Chin, a narrow-faced man whose glasses were constantly sliding down his nose, remained silent. But when one of the FBI agents mentioned the name of his longstanding handler, Ou Qiming, he cracked.

Between 4 and 7 February 1986, Larry's case was heard in the Federal Court of Alexandria in Virginia. Journalists following the trial were disappointed: the Chinese agent remained silent, and neither the CIA nor the FBI wanted to release information about how they had caught him, because to do so would expose the role of Yu Zhensan. Yu was put under witness protection; he assumed a new identity and was sent to live in a safe house near San Francisco. He apparently remained in contact with his cousins in Taiwan. Larry Wu-Tai Chin admitted to having handed over documents, but he claimed that all had been declassified. This did not quite fit with his admission that he had received around $180,000 from Beijing. As we know, he argued in his defence that he had fostered good relations between the United States and China, citing his reports of the expected Nixon thaw. But to no avail.

On 7 February, Larry was sentenced to a long prison sentence for spying. Two weeks later he committed suicide in his cell, suffocating himself with a plastic bag that he fastened tight around his head with his shoelaces. In 2014, a reliable source in Taipei told me that on the eve of his suicide, he had received an authorized visit from a Chinese consul, who led him to understand that if he died without revealing his secrets, Beijing would provide for the needs of his family. This final interview was discreetly recorded by the FBI.[22]

While going over the details of case, Kauffer and I stumbled upon an extraordinary chain of events: the whole thing had started when Larry Wu Tai-Chin told his handlers about the arrival in Beijing of a new undercover CIA officer, in a diplomatic post. Chinese counterintelligence chiefs sent Yu Zhensan to try and recruit him, but instead Yu used the contact with the CIA to go over to the Americans himself. He began to hand over intelligence—sporadically in the case of Larry, whose name he did not know, though he was aware of his existence. This enabled the CIA to identify Chinese moles within the agency. In other words, thanks to Yu's perfidy, Larry had signed his own death certificate when he faithfully reported to his Chinese paylords that a new US agent was in town.

Bernard Boursicot and the Beijing Beauty

Before his defection, Yu Zhensan delivered a dossier on another spy—one in the French embassy whom he had actually handled in Beijing. Three months after the suicide of Larry Wu-Tai Chin, on 6 May 1986, Bernard Boursicot went on trial in Paris accused of spying for China. This was the first case of its kind in Western Europe, in contrast to the multiple espionage trials that had taken place in the United States. Previously only spies for the Eastern Bloc had been tried and convicted.

Boursicot's case was unusual, not least because he had been recruited to the Diaochabu—CCP intelligence—by his Chinese lover, a woman called Shi Peipu, a singer at the Beijing Opera. As it turned out, his lover was a man. Both were denounced by Yu Zhensan; according to some sources, Boursicot was also denounced by a second, less important, Chinese spy who handed the information to MI6.[23] He was arrested by the French DST.

Boursicot and his lover became a public laughing stock, fuelled by the mockery of the examining magistrates. The prosecutor appeared to be having much fun at their expense: "By what curious acrobatics was Shi Peipu able to convince Boursicot that he was female?" The presiding judge, Versini, was even more brutal: "What on earth did you get up to in bed?" It was certainly a unique case; its only historical parallel is the story of the knight of Eon, a hermaphrodite spy sent by the French King Louis XV to the English court in the eighteenth century. David Cronenberg even made a moving film about Boursicot, *M. Butterfly* (1993), starring Jeremy Irons as the French diplomat/spy.

But beyond a romantic tragicomedy treated as a burlesque worthy of Monty Python, the Boursicot affair was also a case study for both Chinese and Western counterintelligence. The French DST, with the help of intelligence provided by the Americans, intercepted Shi and Boursicot.

I have interviewed Boursicot dozens of times, including for this new English-language edition of my book. Born in 1944 in Brittany into a modest family, Boursicot left France at eighteen to take up a post as a teacher in the newly independent Algeria. He had not only a burgeoning interest in the developing world, but also a passion for cinema, and despite his modest background he was adopted as the protegé of Henri Langlois, founder of the Cinémathèque française, who introduced him to the work of film-makers like Akira Kurosawa and Joris Ivens. Ivens was at the time in preproduction for his 1976 propaganda film about the Chinese revolution, *How Yukong Moved the Mountains*. It is one of the longest films ever made, at 763 minutes.

General de Gaulle had recently officially recognized the PRC. After passing the foreign service examination as an accountant, Boursicot was lucky enough to be posted there in October 1964. Western diplomats tend to stick together, but the young Breton was burning to discover China, which had undergone such a huge transformation, into a society of the common people. All he wanted was to get out on his bicycle and explore Beijing. Sometimes, his boss and eventual friend, the consul Claude Chayet, invited him to cocktails, where a few local people from Beijing were permitted to meet foreigners.

It was at one of these affairs, in the run up to Christmas 1964, that Boursicot met an intriguing and attractive young man, finely built, not tall, but with a striking face and wearing a Mao-collared suit. Shi Peipu was a member of the Writers' Union and the author of opera libretti and plays. Bernard was irresistibly drawn to this talented young man, who had trained with Mei Lanfang, a Beijing Opera actor who was world-renowned for his performances in the great female roles traditionally played by men.

Over the following months, Boursicot and Shi together explored ancient China, the worlds of the Tang and Ming dynasties, of the last Manchu emperor, and of the Forbidden City. Then, in May 1965, there was a dramatic development: on one of their walks, Shi took his hand and revealed to him that he was actually a woman. When Shi Peipu was born in 1938, into an aristocratic family in the northern province of Shandong, Shi's mother had feared that her mother-in-law, the matriarch of the house, would insist that her husband take a third wife unless she gave him a son. She decided to raise her daughter as a son: to dress and educate her like a boy.

Shi begged Boursicot to keep her secret: it was vital that everyone still believed she was a man. "This revelation changed my life, my entire way of seeing the world," Boursicot told me twenty years later. "It became impossible for me to conceive of life without Peipu."[24]

A few weeks later, Boursicot lost his virginity to Shi. It was very different from what he had imagined. He allowed himself to be guided, confident that certain caresses and gestures of modesty were linked to the complexity of Chinese tradition. Returning to the bedroom from the bathroom, he noticed blood beading on his lover's thigh.

"Now you are my wife," he whispered in her ear, bursting with joy. In December 1965, when the French foreign ministry told him that he would be changing jobs and returning to Europe, they met for one last time. Shi Peipu, in tears, told him that she thought she was pregnant.

"It will be a boy, and we shall call him Bertrand. I'll be back soon, I swear it," Bernard told her. He was inconsolable.

A Breton in China

After a period in Saudi Arabia and Paris, Boursicot returned to Beijing in September 1969 as an archivist and officer responsible for the diplomatic pouch, a subordinate but sensitive administrative position, given that all embassy secrets now passed through his hands.

The Cultural Revolution was in full swing, and Mao Zedong was trying to wrest power back from his rivals. In governments around the world, the political earthquake was being watched with apprehension. Diplomats at the British embassy found themselves under attack, as did journalists: Reuters correspondent Anthony Grey was accused of spying and held under house arrest for two years until his release in October 1969.[25]

In the French embassy, the newly arrived ambassador, Étienne Manac'h, a Breton like Boursicot, warned his diplomats to take care.

Despite the chaos, Bernard, criss-crossing Beijing by bicycle in his Mao suit, eventually located Shi. His first question to her was about their child:

"Where is our son Bertrand?"

"He is being brought up by farmers in Xinjiang," she told him. "It is far too dangerous to go and see him now."[26]

In order for them to continue seeing each other, Shi Peipu requested permission to teach the young diplomat Chinese and Mao Zedong Thought. The report by DST commissioner Raymond Nart describes an apparently comical but actually serious consequence: "One evening, a week after [the discovery of] Shi Peipu, while he was at her apartment, a crowd of local people burst in, grabbed Shi Peipu and dragged her away."

In late spring 1970 Bernard met an official from the Ministry of Public Security called Kang. Of course, this was a trap laid by the Chinese secret services, and Shi Peipu told Boursicot that two men from the Beijing municipality were going to replace her as his "teachers". "Kang" and his accomplice "Zhao"—their real names were Kang Gesun and Peng Zhe—were from the Diaochabu, which had a special section for compromising and recruiting foreigners stationed in China.

"Kang was my case officer from 1970 to 1981," Boursicot told me. "He was Muslim. I remember he didn't eat pork. Zhao was the political commissar and he taught me Marxism-Leninism. In 1981 Kang told me, 'We were very lucky to have recruited you, because there wasn't much left of the intelligence service during the Cultural Revolution.' That was when I realized that Kang was very high up in the intelligence world."[27]

Kang and Zhao drilled him on Marxism-Leninism, Maoism, and love of the common people. *Wei renmin fuwu!* He had to learn this expression—serve the people. Boursicot could not have asked for more. All he wanted in exchange was to enjoy his romance with Shi Peipu and retrieve his son; even, perhaps, to take them both back to France one day. If we are to believe the DST interrogations, Boursicot began passing diplomatic documents to the Chinese in the spring of 1970, and continued to do so up until May 1972, when he was posted to Dublin as an archivist-cryptographer. He resumed his espionage activities in April 1979, when he was posted to the ghostly embassy in Outer Mongolia. He lived in a suite in a hotel in Ulaanbaatar, where he stored archives in a safe.

"During the interrogations," Boursicot has explained, "the DST commissioner Raymond Nart told me, 'You should have come to us, you would have been given fake documents to deliver to them, and instead of going to court, you would have been given the Légion d'Honneur!' Frankly, would I have had fewer problems if I had become a double agent? Well yes, of course I would, but I was politically committed. I thought I would be able to help the country out of its isolation. There was one major condition, however: I never gave the Chinese information about my own country, France."

This was confirmed by the DST investigation. It would have been treason if he had handed over documents in French stamped "secret" or "highly confidential". The Chinese were in any case mainly interested in the Americans' intentions in Vietnam, and in their sworn enemies, the "Soviet revisionists", with whom they had been in a seven-month border dispute in 1969 over the Amur River.

Thanks to his work, Boursicot was finally given permission to visit his son Bertrand, or Dudu by his Chinese name, and was even able to spend holidays with him and his mother. The documents he delivered to his handlers came from other French embassies around the world, from the foreign ministry, and the various embassies in the PRC where he served. The Chinese were increasingly eager for documents about the USSR's military capacity, so Boursicot, in Ulaanbaatar, began cutting out articles from the French daily newspaper *Le Figaro*, typing them out in his own words, and—using a stamp filched from the ambassador—adorning them with a beautiful "TOP SECRET" stamp in red ink. Mao's agents were very happy.

They also received some more serious intelligence about the Soviet economy, the revival of Japanese militarism, the Indian elections, ethnic problems in Mongolia, Richard Nixon's trip to Beijing, and various news roundups on Hong Kong and China. The collaboration ended when Boursicot left Ulaanbaatar in March 1981. As the DST commissioner Nart noted, "Boursicot told us that during a visit to France with Shi Peipu—and this had nothing to do with any intervention from Kang or anyone else in the People's Republic—one day in Paris the two made the decision to break off relations with the Chinese cadre."

The Chinese knight of Eon

Boursicot was arrested in Paris at 11.40am on 30 June 1983, near the École Militaire metro station, by a team of police officers who took him to DST headquarters. He was led down to the basement, fearing the worst. The investigators, led by divisional commissioners Raymond Nart and Yvan Bassompière, took turns questioning him. For them, it was a perfect Chinese espionage case that would throw light on the modus operandi of the new Chinese secret services: the Guoanbu, or State Security, which was barely known to the DST; its creation had only been announced by Prime Minister Zhao Ziyang three weeks earlier, on 6 June.

Questions flew thick and fast about the disappearance of about 100 documents from the embassies in Beijing and Ulaanbaatar, right around the time when Boursicot had been there. But Raymond Nart also had another question: who were the Chinese people living with him on Boulevard du Port Royal, Monsieur Shi Peipu, and his son Shi Dudu?

Bernard Boursicot, almost relieved, answered: "I didn't do any of it for money!"

"But who is Shi Peipu?" the DST officers repeated. Shi had not yet been arrested. The diplomat hesitated, because of course his big secret was not the fact that he had been spying for China, but his rather unusual love affair.

"Shi Peipu is a woman," he confessed eventually. "And Shi Dudu is my son!" he added with pride. At this stage of the discussion, it was clear that he had nothing left to hide. He had spent too long pretending and concealing things, and wanted to explain himself. People in the DST would understand what had happened to him. He had done nothing serious. At last he would be able to live openly with his Chinese wife and their son. He would be released, probably with an official reprimand from the French foreign ministry. But that was not too bad.

The following day, 1 July 1983, the DST investigators arrested Shi Peipu at the diplomat's apartment. Because of her heart problems, they agreed to interview her there.

Shi recounted her version of the story to Commissioner Bassompière. Her account was almost identical to that of her "husband". She explained how she had grown up in Shandong and begun taking singing lessons in 1945 with the great teacher Mei Lanfang. She soon found herself immersed in an underworld where the worlds of the arts and the secret services collided—a remarkably common trope in Asian spy stories, as we have seen.

She explained how, thanks to the Deng regime's liberalization policy, in October 1982 she had managed to get herself invited to France by an academic institution. Security services agreed to allow her and her child to join Boursicot in Paris. Shi remained in contact with Wang Erqing, a cultural attaché at the Chinese embassy on Avenue George V and the darling of the French Sinophile world. He was even once the subject of a French television documentary.

The day after Shi's first interrogation, the examining magistrate Bruno Laroche accused Bernard Boursicot of "handing over intelligence information to agents of a foreign power". He charged Shi Peipu with being his accomplice—this was somewhat strange considering the chronology of events, for if anything it had been Boursicot who was Shi Peipu's accomplice, rather than the other way round.

The judge also ordered a medical examination to determine Shi's sex, for "she" was now claiming that "she" was a man—which the doctors confirmed. The news was made public on 13 July. In his cell in the Fresnes prison, Boursicot fainted when he heard the unbelievable news on the radio: "The Chinese Mata Hari is actually a man!" The news made the front page of all the newspapers, as the DST expected, tearing the Franco-Chinese couple apart, and hinting none too subtly at the homosexual overtones of the affair. The truth was not confirmed to Boursicot himself until he saw Shi Peipu in the hallway after a meeting with Judge Laroche.

"I don't believe it. I want to see," Boursicot insisted. Shi unbuttoned his trousers.

A week later, the Frenchman tried to cut his throat with his razor. How could he have been tricked like this? During the first medical examination, Shi had given a "technical" explanation of how the French diplomat had been tricked. American journalist Joyce Wadler, then New York correspondent for *The Washington Post*, explained it ten years later in her book on the case, *Liaison*. She quotes the statement Shi Peipu made to the judge:

> As concerns our sexual relations, these always took place in the dark as Boursicot always showed the greatest *délicatesse* toward me. I want to stress that this was my first sexual experience, and according to Boursicot, the same was true for him. Since I did not have a female sexual organ Boursicot could not penetrate me. When we made love, I kept my legs lightly pressed together, so that Boursicot may have had the impression that he was penetrating me.

During the trial, medical expert Dr Jean-Pierre Campana described how Shi had managed to conceal his genitals during a relationship that had lasted eighteen years: "Shi Peipu hid his penis inside the folds of his scrotum, which if the thighs are squeezed tightly together can be confusing because of the pubic hair. Of course, this allows only a fleeting and superficial penetration and requires a very credulous partner."

Wadler quotes the doctor's statement, which was published in *The New York Times* during the trial, detailing Shi's manipulation: "Then, as the examination is ending, the prisoner, without being asked, says that he would like to explain something to the doctors. Easily, smoothly, he pushes his testicles up into his body cavity. The skin of the scrotal sack hangs slack, like curtains. The man now pushes his penis between his legs, toward his back, bisecting the skin of the scrotum, and squeezes his legs tightly together. The penis is hidden, while the skin of the scrotum resembles the vaginal lips, beneath a triangle of pubic hair. Pushed between the empty scrotal sac, the penis has also created a small cavity so that shallow penetration is possible."[28]

However in his statements to psychiatrists, Shi Peipu insisted that he had never deceived his lover about his sex. Having tricked him once already, with this statement Shi Peipu now betrayed for a second time the man whose love had got them in this mess in the first place.

Shi was well rewarded for giving evidence against Boursicot: in February 1984 he was released on bail by the Court of Appeal. The Chinese authorities were putting pressure on the French by various means, and high-up ministers were keen to smooth out these "diplomatic" difficulties. Meanwhile, Boursicot remained behind bars.

"A magnificent setup"

During the trial, the prosecutor summarized the DST's position, arguing that the case was "a magnificent setup by the Chinese intelligence services" and claiming that Shi Peipu had come to France in 1982 in order to "reactivate Boursicot, because he was on his way to becoming a 'cadre B', that is, a fully fledged diplomat."[29]

In his own testimony, the DST commissioner Raymond Nart did eventually acknowledge Boursicot's extenuating circumstances: "You have to understand that espionage is a martial art in China and that the Chinese, with the assumption that one launches an attack on a defeated army, quickly spotted Boursicot in his first post: he was nineteen years old, immature, with sexually undefined tastes, and they threw Shi Peipu at him." He sagely concluded, "Such a fragile character as Boursicot should never have been posted to Beijing. The tragedy of this case is that it is not the instigators being judged, nor the reckless people who sent Boursicot first to China and then to Ulaanbaatar."

While the prosecutor left the jury to decide on Shi Peipu's sentence—he had recently suffered a heart attack—he demanded that Boursicot serve at least five years "because of his mentality". Henri Leclerc, Boursicot's lawyer, argued that "if any intelligence was handed over to the enemy, it must be recognized that it was very low level", but he was ignored. The court sentenced both of the accused to six years in prison. *Libération* captured the feelings of many with its headline: "Boursicot case: a verdict as cruel as Chinese torture."

On the whole, though, the great and good of Paris seemed more sympathetic to the androgynous Chinese artist than to the French diplomatic archivist. President Mitterrand pardoned Shi Peipu in 1987, and he settled in Paris. This was the first time a convicted foreign spy had escaped being declared *persona non grata*. Shi often returned to Beijing, where he was friends with the deputy mayor and had an apartment near the Forbidden City. Boursicot, rather less fortunate, had to wait to be released from prison, and was only given permission much later to return to China for a visit. Without his knowledge, a small group of former colleagues at the Beijing embassy, including his loyal friend Claude Chayet, had worked behind the scenes to secure his release. The ambassador, Étienne Manac'h, was not among them—he was not willing to stoop to the aid of a junior official, even though he was a great friend of China and particularly of Zhou Enlai, who once said of Manac'h that he was a "great bridge between the West and China".

Despite this sad double epilogue—the suicide of Larry Wu-Tai Chin and the imprisonment of Bernard Boursicot—Yu Zhensan's revelations enabled Western intelligence services to learn a great deal, both about how to proceed with the new Chinese KGB and about its own battle strategy. It was Ling Yun, the head of the Guoanbu, who lost face in these cases. In August 1986, the Chinese fought back by sentencing a Chinese-origin American citizen, Roland Shensu Loo, to twelve years in prison for spying for the CIA and the Taiwanese secret services. Around the same time, John Burns, a *New York Times* correspondent, was deported, officially for reporting from a no-go zone. The Guoanbu established strict guidelines on dealing with foreigners; Shanghai call girls were permitted to dance with tourists and businessmen on condition that they did not give out state secrets. Forbidding all contact with them would have prevented the security services from being able to engage in the classic operations known as the "beautiful woman stratagem" (*meiren ji*), the erotic recruitment of Western, Japanese and Korean businessmen and diplomats.

It took decades for me to discover that, when Yu Zhensan was debriefed by his CIA hosts, he told them that at the beginning of Boursicot's handling, the Chinese services were sufficiently prudish to doubt that their trick would work—they believed that Boursicot would quickly realize that he was in a homosexual relationship. The unexpected success of the operation encouraged the Guoanbu to increase this kind of honeytrap over the following decades.

Meanwhile, a senior official named Guan Ping replaced Yu Zhensan as head of the Ministry of Foreign Affairs. Yu, who served for a long time as an advisor to the American, British and Taiwanese secret services, died in 2013. He had been living in the Chinatown of an American city, under the false identity that the CIA had given him. Before he moved there a rumour had circulated—perhaps on his protectors' initiative—that he had been murdered by Chinese agents in his safe house.

Ling Yun quit the intelligence world in 1985. That long-serving spymaster died in 2018 just after turning 100 years old. His replacement was a politician, rather than an intelligence professional. Jia Chunwang was born in 1938 in Beijing, and graduated in Physical Sciences from Tsinghua University, the Chinese MIT. He was the son-in-law of Bo Yibo, a famous CCP leader and veteran of the anti-Japanese war, who had served as finance minister in 1949 and was a major supporter of the economic reforms instigated by Deng Xiaoping. Jia's only relationship to the security services came from his recent co-optation onto the Discipline Commission. His meteoric rise up to the top echelons of the Communist Youth League had impressed leaders like Hu Yaobang; perhaps his appointment was already on the cards during his July 1985 trip to Washington, accompanied by Ling Yun, at the head of a youth delegation.[30]

As a member of the CCP's Beijing Municipal Committee, Jia knew Fan Jin, mother of the defector Yu. Obviously, he did not care to have this fact raised, and when John Burns of *The New York Times* had the audacity to try to question the Guoanbu's new boss about the Yu Zhensan affair, he was promptly expelled from China.

The Guoanbu was sensitive on the matter because it feared other defections would follow the Yu case. The 9th Bureau went round all the Chinese embassies and repatriated any agents at risk of defecting. Despite these precautions, in September 1986, one of the heads of the service, nicknamed "Fu Manchu", proposed to the French that he defect to the West. That November, Du Bingru, the commercial attaché at the West German embassy, offered his services to the BND.

Despite this series of misfortunes afflicting Jia's special services, he was described as being affable, and fascinated with the West. He spoke English and, just as Zhou Enlai had in the early days, he had great admiration for the French intelligence services and the CIA. He was also on the frontline of China's new offensives in economic, scientific and technological intelligence—Deng Xiaoping's dream. This was how the pool of "deep-water fish" (*Chendi yü*) developed: the Guoanbu term for the thousands of exceptional special agents, hidden in the deepest strata of society—the cultural, scientific, economic and military worlds of the enemy, each a significant piece of the puzzle.

A Chinese-style National Security Council?

Setting up yet another spy station to throw light on an ever-changing world would not be enough for a country as big as China. Deng

Xiaoping was all too aware of this, especially given the major upheavals of the mid-1980s. These began with the rise to power of Mikhail Gorbachev, who became general secretary of the Soviet Union's Communist Party in March 1985, leading a reform team focused on *glasnost* (political transparency), and *perestroika* (economic restructuring).

Gorbachev became president in 1990, and soon talks between him and US President Ronald Reagan were cleansed of the bitter taste of discord, evolving into cordial agreement. Was the anti-Soviet alliance between China and the US about to fade, or even collapse?

Every day senior Chinese leaders were given a bound file of materials assembled from special service reports, including: "reference materials" (*cankao ziliao*) from the Xinhua News Agency and its "confidential newsletters from abroad" (*guoji necan*); reports from the international section of the Chinese Academy of Social Sciences; dispatches from military attachés that were scrutinized by the 2nd Department (PLA2); analyzes from the Ministry of Foreign Affairs; and "investigation documents" (*Diaocha ziliao*) from the China Institute for Contemporary International Relations (CICIR).[31]

The political-legal commission that coordinated all of the Chinese secret services—led by two survivors of the Cultural Revolution, Peng Zhen and Chen Xidian—was unable to centralize and analyse all these sources. That would amount to stacking one bureaucratic structure on top of another. That was why, when the Guoanbu was created in 1983, Deng Xiaoping—perhaps inspired by his own "American dream"—decided to set up a kind of National Security Council, a simpler version of the one at the White House.

"It does not matter if a cat is grey or black as long as it catches mice!" Deng would say, as a way of justifying opening up to a market economy under socialist rule. But the remark could equally be applied to geopolitics and international relations. What was the point of the considerable risks taken by China's "deep-water fish"—deep-cover or sleeper agents—if the intelligence they gathered, even when duly cross-checked, did not help Deng Xiaoping, Hu Yaobang and Zhao Ziyang to make decisions?

Deng gave a former diplomat, Huan Xiang, the job of establishing the International Studies Research Center (*Zhongguo Guoji Wenti Yanjiu*

Zhongxin), under the aegis of the State Council of the PRC—in other words, the government. Headed by Huan's deputy, Xu Dachen, a specialist on German affairs, the ISRC's role was to analyze a dozen or so hundred-page summary reports, usually sent out daily to those in the ruling elite. The ISRC was also expected to merge with the Diaochabu's similarly named Institute of International Studies, to further synthesize the information, intelligence and analysis being transmitted to government at Zhongnanhai.

The purpose of all this was to give Deng and his team a clearer view of the outside world—that is obvious. The real question is: why did he choose Huan Xiang?

Huan, who was close to Zhao Ziyang, was first noticed by Zhou Enlai. A well-travelled, open-minded journalist with a gift for languages, he was born in the western province of Guizhou in 1910 in the Year of the Dog. He studied both in Shanghai and at Waseda University in Japan. He had a remarkable career as a journalist (notably at the *Wenhui Bao* daily in Shanghai) and as a diplomat; in the early 1960s, he set up the PRC's embassy in the United Kingdom with the master spy Xiong Xianghui. He went on to become ambassador himself.

He never talked about the Cultural Revolution; the years between 1965 and 1976, when he basically disappeared, were a particularly terrible period for him. Afterwards he returned to political life, becoming the ambassador to Belgium, Luxembourg and the EEC. By the time he was eighty, still as fresh as an imperial carp, Huan's immense reputation earned him the privilege of being named advisor to the Chinese Academy of Social Sciences and vice-chair of the Foreign Affairs Committee at the National People's Congress. There he was one of ten members including the spy–ambassador Fu Hao, an expert on Japan.

But Deng Xiaoping chose Huan Xiang because, in the mid-1980s, he had come up with some audacious hypotheses about the way the world was turning and the changes that were to be expected, especially in the wake of the US–Soviet summit called by Reagan and Gorbachev in early 1986. The question was whether China's alliance with the United States would survive. His analysis had revolved around the evolution of the Star Wars system that Reagan wanted to set up, in order to force the Soviets to negotiate the end of nuclear proliferation and bring to an end the arms race threatening to exhaust both superpowers' economies.

"The two largest military powers are weakening and in the process of decline," Huan had said at a symposium in 1986. "They are developing militarily towards multipolarization. If the Star Wars plan develops, then multipolarization will become bipolarization, which risks becoming permanent. If that were to happen, if second-tier countries want to put in place a Star Wars plan, it will be very difficult. The position of these countries will rapidly decline."

In other words, only the end of the Cold War could save China and allow it to develop into a major power; otherwise, it would lag behind the two great "partners" in a latent conflict that had already been going on for half a century.

On 28 February 1989, Huan Xiang, the "Chinese Kissinger", died at the age of eighty, having revolutionized the leadership's vision in many different ways. He did not live to see the end of the Cold War or the fall of the USSR. With his death, and the decline of his research centre, the strategic intelligence of Deng Xiaoping's team began to falter, as the staggering events of Tiananmen, completely unanticipated by the Chinese secret services, began to unfold.

5

55 DAYS AT TIANANMEN

Deep in the bowels of Beijing's underground city, Dixia Cheng, a ghost train rattled ahead with a dreadful clanging, carrying soldiers in military fatigues, faces smeared in black, armed with 7.62mm-calibre Type-79 submachine guns. Dixia Cheng had never been used to shelter the population in the event of a nuclear attack as Mao had intended twenty years earlier. On this evening, 3 June 1989, a convoy of special troops was on its way to crush the capital's inhabitants: students, and residents of the *hutongs*—the alleys around Tiananmen Square—who had come out in support of the protesters. Carved out of polystyrene, the Goddess of Democracy, a ghostly simulacrum of the Statue of Liberty, stared out of the shadows at Mao's portrait, which loomed swollen-faced and with a proud smile over the Gate of Heavenly Peace.

In silence, the soldiers poured out of the underground tunnels via the exits at Zhongnanhai, the government palace at the Central and South Lakes, to the west of the Forbidden City. This was the regime's stronghold, right behind Tiananmen Square. The soldiers were paratroopers of the 15th Airborne Division, the vanguard of the Air Force's rapid response unit and expert in attacking the enemy from behind, as well as in law enforcement. This was the unit that had re-established order in Wuhan in 1967, in the middle of the Cultural Revolution. They were supported by the People's Armed Police, a paramilitary police force, whose training had proved insufficient when it came to quelling the student unrest, but who knew Beijing well. Primarily, the paratroopers were supported by commandos from Unit 84835, from the far-flung military district of Ningxia. Their speciality was "decapitation"—the art of taking out an enemy unit's leader.

Their mission was a surprise raid to retake control of Tiananmen Square, occupied by the protesters. The element of surprise was only relative, given that shootings had already taken place in various different suburbs. To the west of the city, the repeated sound of gunfire suggested the worst.

Thirty years later, the full extent of the tank battle that took place in the heart of the capital has still not been fully understood, nor acknowledged by the CCP. Tanks from the 21st Corps were firing at tanks of the First Cavalry Regiment, part of the 38th Army Corps, a Beijing unit that was not prepared simply to stand by doing nothing while the Tiananmen Commune was crushed.

Ivan Vladimirovich Grigorov, an advisor at the Soviet embassy in Beijing, witnessed these events. He hurried to the scene on the night of 3–4 June, where he observed clashes between PLA units, confirmed by other witnesses. That night he sent the Kremlin a report, some details of which were supplied by sources at the highest level of the Chinese secret services.[1] For the previous fortnight, Grigorov, the KGB *rezident* in Beijing since January 1987, had been under orders to send Moscow detailed and accurate information, several times a day, about what was going on in the Chinese capital. He was familiar with PRC politics, having been part of the Soviet delegation responsible for organizing a ceasefire with China following the border conflict on the Amur River (Ussuri).

His dispatches were read not only by Vladimir Kryuchkov, head of the KGB, but also by Mikhail Gorbachev, general secretary of the Communist Party of the Soviet Union. Gorbachev had been deeply offended by the inauspicious welcome the Chinese had afforded him just two weeks earlier, on 15 May. That day had witnessed the first Sino-Soviet summit since the longstanding split thirty years earlier. Yet, instead of receiving Gorbachev with pomp and ceremony in Tiananmen, the Chinese had organized a low-key welcome ceremony at the airport. There was a good reason for this. For the previous forty-eight hours, 3,000 students had been waging a hunger strike at the square.

Tiananmen has been the iconic location of student demonstrations since the protests against the Treaty of Versailles in 1919. It was where Mao Zedong had declared the communist victory in 1949. This "sacred ground", as a senior leader has called it, has frequently borne witness to the struggle between what could be called the yin and yang of Chinese politics: the bright revolt of youth, against the dark forces of communist power. In 1966, young people brandishing their *Little Red Books* had cheered the Great Helmsman in Tiananmen, unaware of how they were being manipulated by Mao and Kang Sheng. In 1976, Chinese youth had marched there in memory of Zhou Enlai, demanding the opening up of the country—a strategy deployed by Deng Xiaoping to prepare the ground for his return to power. In 1986, young people had demonstrated on the square in support of student movements in other cities. The unintended consequence of those protests had been the fall of the reformist general secretary, Hu Yaobang, who had been forced to resign.

Deng Xiaoping against Mikhail Gorbachev

On 16 April 1989, Hu suffered a heart attack and died. The following day, thousands of students gathered in Tiananmen Square to show their support for his reforms, demanding that his agenda be pursued and the "fifth modernization" continue its progress. As celebrated dissident Wei Jingsheng declared, this was democracy in action. And so began the "55 Days at Tiananmen."[2]

The leaders who lived at Zhongnanhai were reluctant to act against the students, many of whom were the children of party cadres, and not least because international television stations, CNN and ABC in particular, were broadcasting these images of China in turmoil around the clock. On television screens around the world young people were shown with their hands outstretched towards the Goddess of Democracy, represented by the gigantic polystyrene statue that stood facing Mao's enormous portrait.

Unlike his predecessors during the Cultural Revolution, Grigorov was not barricaded inside the Soviet embassy compound. He was able to go out and find out what was going on, with the help of his agents and contacts—from the local newspaper-seller to a scientist at the Academy of Sciences, to the Soviet students there to witness the rebellious spirit of their Chinese companions. Along with Ivan Fedotov, an embassy advisor, Grigorov had been diligently gathering intelligence for the increasingly astonishing reports sent back to Moscow. Some information came directly from the Chinese secret services. Much water had flowed under the bridge during recent years, and there had been a considerable thaw in the formerly icy relations between the Chinese special services and the Russian "organs", as the KGB and the military GRU were known.

A month of peaceful demonstrations had already gone by. From senior members of the party up to the top brass, with Deng Xiaoping at the helm, the Chinese leadership had underestimated the rise of Gorbachev, a reformer whose policy of *perestroika* was clearly influencing the younger Chinese generation. Deng wanted somehow to conjure a market economy while maintaining the one-party system, and he feared a Russian-style political revolution. Since 1987, he had had no official position, except for the presidency of the all-powerful CCP Central Military Commission, which controlled the PLA and its 3 million soldiers. Another old-timer, Yang Shangkun, a veteran of the Long March and victim of the Cultural Revolution, was deputy leader of the Commission and the recently appointed president of China. Both Yang and Prime Minister Li Peng—a protégé of Zhou Enlai and a Hakka like Deng—supported Deng's wariness of the Soviets. Meanwhile, at the other end of the political spectrum, Zhao Ziyang, Hu Yaobang's successor as general secretary of the CCP, felt a great deal of respect for Gorbachev.

Gorbachev himself was not unconcerned by what was going on in the PRC: "I have a lot of admiration for the Great Wall," he said to a group of journalists during his trip, "but walls are bound to fall sooner or later". His words were bold, though perhaps not as audacious as those of the journalist who shot back, "Even the Berlin Wall?" Perhaps, was Gorbachev's response.

Fearing for Gorbachev's safety, bodyguards from the 9th Section of the KGB decided to cut short his three-day stay in Beijing. He left for Shanghai, where the situation was calmer and the local leader, Jiang

Zemin, had a better relationship with the city's students. (This did not stop him from deciding to shut down a local magazine, considered too reformist by his mistress, the head of propaganda Chen Zhili.)

A drama was playing out behind the scenes. On the eve of Gorbachev's visit, on 14 May, a secret meeting had been held of the Politburo's Standing Committee, the five men who officially led the CCP and China. On that occasion, the policy of taking a moderate line with the students, as advocated by Zhao Ziyang, had apparently won out. Why not enter into discussions with them, rather than crack down on them? The party leaders known as the "Immortals"—Deng Xiaoping, Yang Shangkun, Bo Yibo, Peng Zhen and Chen Yun—were responsible for maintaining socialist principles and keeping alive the memory of the Long March; they acquiesced to Zhao's suggestion. But they remained busy behind the scenes.

Deng wanted to know more. He was receiving information from the all-powerful security coordinator, Qiao Shi, who was getting contrasting but disturbing reports from his agents. He was a practical man: after Gorbachev had returned to Moscow, Qiao went with Zhao Ziyang to Tiananmen Square at daybreak, to talk to the students. On 15 May, the leaders in Zhongnanhai received shocking news from agents of the Gonganbu: 1 million protesters had come out in support of the hunger strikers. A delegation travelled the 800 metres separating Tiananmen from Zhongnanhai, with a list of grievances to be handed to the leadership, but they were set upon by truncheon-wielding Gonganbu agents. In the afternoon, a senior party official, Yan Mingfu, who was director of the United Front Work Department, went alone to meet the demonstrators, promising them that they would be allowed to return to their campuses. He praised them for advocating reform, and even suggested they take him hostage in order to guarantee that they would be able to leave Tiananmen Square without risk.[3]

Qiao Shi, puppet master?

Grigorov knew Qiao Shi well. Along with Jia Chunwang, the head of the Guoanbu, Qiao was one of his principal interlocutors. It was Qiao, the head of the party's security services, who had telephoned

Ambassador Oleg Troyanovsky two days previously to explain that the welcoming ceremony for Raisa and Mikhail Gorbachev would be held at the airport. After the ceremony, a convoy had taken them to the Diaoyutai guest residence, where Qiao himself had kept an apartment, until his recent move to Zhongnanhai with his wife.[4] The obvious purpose of this chosen location was to prevent any contact between Gorbachev and the Tiananmen demonstrators, who were waving placards in Russian and Chinese to cheer comrade "*Ge-Er-Ba-She-fu*" and his policy of reform.

Qiao Shi had been pointing out since the beginning of the year to whoever was prepared to listen—both diplomats and journalists—that "outside forces are at work", without specifying whether he was referring to the CIA or the KGB. After Gorbachev's return to Moscow, Qiao Shi had gone out to Tiananmen Square with a megaphone to tell the students to return home, without success.

I have not been able to consult, as Grigorov did, the huge file on Qiao Shi in the archives at Yasenovo, Russian foreign intelligence headquarters. But over the years I have studied his little-known career in detail, attempting to better understand his growing political importance as one of Deng Xiaoping's preferred militants, and his complexity as a man who was both ideologically rigid, yet open to the reforms called for by Hu Yaobang and Zhao Ziyang. Events were soon to make this clear.[5]

Aged sixty-nine, with a long face and tortoiseshell-rimmed tinted glasses, perfectly manicured fingernails, a well-cut Western suit and expensive shoes (paired with 5-yuan socks), Qiao Shi was a man of contrasts. He was quite tall, he liked to run and swim, and he had managed to climb discreetly right to the upper echelons of the secret services. Some found him cold and austere, a man of few words with a fixed smile; his appearance suited his position, according to some foreign reporters. But others saw him quite differently, finding him "warm, personable and friendly."[6]

Was he a Janus? Qiao Shi—which literally means "the high stone"—was a nom de guerre that referred to his height and impressive girth. Back in 1940, when he joined the underground Shanghai Communist Party and became secretary of a cell, the 16-year-old was still known as Jiang Zhaoming. He was born in December 1924 in the

Year of the Rat, in Zhejiang city in the region of Dinghai, south of Shanghai. He swiftly made his way to the top of the Communist Youth League. At St John's Anglican University (*Sheng Yuehan*), one of the best-known universities in China, he studied European civilization and learned to speak fluent English. Its alumni include members of the Soong family, and many other well-known figures: Rong Yiren, the communist billionaire who encouraged CCP leaders to negotiate with the students of Tiananmen; the great writer Lin Yutang, author of *The Importance of Living*, who escaped to Taiwan; Raymond Chow, the Hakka producer of kung fu films by Bruce Lee and Jackie Chan; and the Chinese-American architect Ieoh Ming Pei, who built the Louvre Pyramid in Paris.

Going to university with such impressive classmates was bound to open the eyes of Qiao, as a young student who was curious about everything, as passionate about Shakespeare as about Marx. He was very busy, since he was also operating as an undercover agent at the University of Tongji, whose arts and sciences campus was moved to Shanghai in 1946. In 1943, the Japanese invaded the Western concessions in Shanghai, where the communists had taken refuge from the Kuomintang. Liu Changsheng, one of the heads of the CCP's intelligence service in southern China, gave Qiao Shi a leg up. Aided by his young wife, Wang Yuwen, Qiao was now active in the sensitive area of "secret party communications".

Family ties were the traditional gateway into the Chinese elite or power, as we saw in the case of the defector Yu Zhensan. The same was true of Qiao, giving him unexpected opportunities to become an activist. Chen Bulai, a well-known journalist with links to Chiang Kai-shek, was none other than Qiao's wife's uncle. He became Chen's secretary, and thus managed to gather vital information that established his reputation as an excellent secret agent in leading communist circles.

The civil war and the anti-Japanese resistance were the prelude to the eventual communist victory, and this was a useful period for the capable Qiao, now a youth leader in Hangzhou, in his native Zhejiang. From 1954 to 1964, he worked as a technical manager at the Anshan Metallurgical Company, before becoming head of the Institute of Studies at the Jiuquan Steel Company. This was a highly sensitive position, for among its other activities the company was secretly manufacturing weapons for the PLA. There was just one shadow that fell over this perfect picture: Qiao's wife—now simply called Yu Wen—was caught up in the turmoil of the anti-rightist campaign in 1957; her imprisonment slowed her husband's rise.[7]

The turning point in Qiao Shi's career came in 1964. Around the time that China detonated its first atomic bomb, he entered the ILD, the central party's political intelligence service that maintained contact with "brother parties" abroad and, equally importantly, gave support to third-world liberation movements. Qiao owed this post to the backing of his first mentor, Liu Changsheng, who went on to become the president of the China–Africa People's Friendship Association. Qiao became head of the Chinese–African Solidarity Committee, in charge of aiding pro-China guerrilla movements in Congo, Burundi and Zimbabwe. This was not really about countering Soviet revisionism in Africa, and was still a long way away from the Chinese focus on African investment that has characterized Beijing's relationship with the continent in the twenty-first century.

In Beijing, the Cultural Revolution had swept away everything in its path. Liu Changsheng was murdered by the Red Guards in 1967.[8] As we know, it dethroned Peng Zhen, the Beijing mayor and another of Qiao's protectors. Happily for Qiao, he had several other cadres from the special services keeping an eye out for him, in particular Luo Qingchang, the untouchable head of the Diaochabu, who had Zhou Enlai as his protector. Strengthened by these various patrons, Qiao Shi was trying to be all things to all people. Ten years later, he turned up as deputy head of international relations, while his wife, Yu Wen, became head of the ILD's Research Bureau, then deputy director of the party's propaganda department.

Most important of all, in the aftermath of the Cultural Revolution, Qiao Shi had the protection of two former party leaders who had the distinction of being economists developing relationships—*guanxi*—in the intelligence field: the first was Bo Yibo, who became deputy prime minister in 1978 and was the father-in-law of Jia Chunwang, future head of the Guoanbu; the second was Chen Yun, who invented the concept of economic intelligence. Chen had begun his political life as an activist in Shanghai, working undercover for Zhou Enlai's and Kang Sheng's Teke.

Qiao Shi travelled a great deal in the entourage of the new president, Hua Guofeng: to Romania, Yugoslavia and Iran, countries whose own special services were interested in cooperating with the Chinese against the Soviets. The overthrow of the Shah obliged Qiao to renegotiate agreements with the Savama, the new Iranian secret police serving the Ayatollah. But he excelled in behind-the-scenes negotiations, and this minor inconvenience was not enough to stop his rise to the top.

In April 1982, at the age of fifty-eight, Qiao became head of the ILD.[9] In this capacity, he made technical-oriented trips to Algiers, Tehran and Pyongyang, where he established a close collaboration with his North Korean ILD counterpart, Kim Yong-nam, and the head of state security, Kim Byong-ha. His rise coincided with that of a veritable "security lobby", reinforced abroad with the creation of the Guoanbu and at home in the PRC by the founding of the People's Armed Police (*renmin wuzhuang jingcha* or PAP), headed by Lieutenant General Li Lianxiu. This paramilitary police force was set up for the internal security and protection of the leadership, working with the central guards regiment under the control of the Central Military Commission.

It is said that it was Qiao Shi who had first suggested this idea to Deng Xiaoping. Inspired by the suppression of demonstrations in Poland and Hungary, he even proposed that the PAP be armed with equipment appropriate for street fighting and the low-intensity curbing of public demonstrations. As violence unfolded in Northern Ireland, he watched newsreels to see how the Royal Ulster Constabulary dealt with nationalist protests, and suggested that the Chinese copy their methods and adopt the same ammunition: water cannon, CS gas, and rubber and plastic bullets.

Qiao Shi was carving out a kingdom within this shadowy realm. A formidable player of the game, he knew better than anyone how to navigate between different factions, managing to gain both the trust of the conservatives (Peng Zhen, Bo Yibo and Chen Yun) and the understanding of the reformers (Hu Yaobang and Zhao Ziyang). On the one hand, he was a supporter of the old order; on the other, he backed economic reform. Qiao Shi—the most conservative of the reformists, and the most liberal of the traditionalists—was biding his time. Most importantly, he was about to gain control of the party apparatus that controlled all the security services.

"Intelligence men are climbing higher and higher in the Chinese hierarchy of power," James Yi, a Chinese intelligence specialist in the British Hong Kong administration, told me in 1986. "One day, Qiao Shi might well get to be number 1."[10]

His powers were indeed rapidly growing. Peng Zhen handed him control of the political committees—in other words, security, as it is understood in the PRC: the Ministries of Justice, State Security (the Guoanbu) and Public Security (the Gonganbu), and the National Minorities Section, whose senior advisors included his wife Yu Wen and Pu Yi, the "last emperor", recycled into a new role. Among the other areas he controlled were arms sales to Syria, Iran and Korea; backing for the Khmer Rouge and the Afghan Mujahedin; and counter-insurrection in Tibet, as well as special operations against the Dalai Lama in India and other parts of the world. Alternating firmness and flexibility, this man of two faces continued to occupy the best position: the centre. "Qiao Shi is the Emperor of the golden mean," was the word on the streets. In early 1989, he also took the helm of the CCP's Central Party School and, exploiting the death of the "Chinese Kissinger", Huan Xiang—which had gone largely unremarked—he increased his influence within the Chinese national security committee, the International Studies Research Centre, which answered to the State Council (i.e. the government).

Meanwhile, the student demonstrations were just beginning. True to his centrist tendencies, Qiao Shi initially intended to attempt conciliation. Wan Runnan, a reformist businessman and managing director of the Stone computer company, contacted him through Li Chang, an influential member of the Party Discipline Commission, proposing to join the negotiating intermediaries. Qiao Shi, as we have seen, was not against dialogue, and was opposed to a show of force against the students. This was the context in which he went to Tiananmen Square with Zhao Ziyang on 19 May.

But their positive disposition towards the students could not last forever. As head of the intelligence services, Qiao was directly accountable to Deng Xiaoping and the Politburo Standing Committee, of which he was now third in command. Guoanbu correspondents in foreign postings, as well as his own children living in Europe and America, provided him with a sense of the reaction abroad. His daughters were studying in the United States: Qiao Xiaoqian was at medical school in Houston, Texas, where she joined the Tiananmen student support movement; his younger daughter, Qiao Ling, was a high school student, who also enthusiastically supported the protests. His son Jiang Xiaoming—also called Simon X. Jiang—was studying at Cambridge's Judge Business School; Jiang's wife, Qiao Zhoujin, was a producer for the BBC World Service's China section.

The message from Qiao's children was clear: a violent repression would horrify the world. However, as a counterpoint, the security services were sure that simply giving in on certain clauses in economic contracts would be enough to appease opinion in the West on the regime's response. The question was whether Qiao Shi would opt for repression, and how he would advise Deng Xiaoping.

The "blue-haired dogs" and martial law

The briefs that Qiao Shi had received regarding China's internal situation, handed to Deng Xiaoping and other leaders, had indicated the probability of a large number of demonstrations in Lhasa. In March, martial law had been imposed on Tibet.

Shortly before that, in February, Qiao Shi had issued a warning, in which he mixed rhetoric about the struggle against corruption, smuggling and trafficking with condemnation of "sabotage by foreign intelligence services" and "the small minority of those who brandish the banner of 'democracy' and 'liberty', spreading rumours and trying to provoke unrest". There had been public executions in Canton, broadcast on television to celebrate the Year of the Snake. The "blue-haired dogs" of the Gonganbu, as they were nicknamed, had sent alarming reports from all over China that the "democratic" movement had now spread to 116 cities. Wang Fang, the Gonganbu chief, was a hard-boiled man, who had taken over the post at the end of 1986 after Ruan Chongwu's dismissal for failing first to predict the student protests, then to suppress them with force, leading to Hu Yaobang's dismissal as general secretary. Wang Fang, who had been a prosecutor at the trial of the Gang of Four, obviously wanted to avoid his predecessor's fate.

He had sent a memorandum to Qiao Shi containing information on eighty-eight autonomous workers' organizations, as well as embryonic so-called counter-revolutionary political parties (which were in fact democratic) and the self-defence militias that had recently come into being. "Autonomous workers' organizations" had emerged in nineteen provinces. In fact, the number was almost certainly higher, because the Gonganbu regional offices were not particularly precise; central government received reports that simply read: "Various autonomous workers' federations have sprung up in Wuhan."

These mushrooming organizations had been catalogued as one of four types of structure, which triggered cold sweats in senior officials within the Chinese state apparatus. The largest number were those whose purpose was to protect the protesters. They were called "picket teams" (*jiucha dui*) or "dare-to-die" units (*gansi dui*). They would also play an active role during martial law, preventing incitement by the secret services. There were also the "sympathy brigades" (*shengyuan tuan*): groups of workers who supported the students. The third category were the small parties and groups such as the "patriotic democratic league" (*aiguo minzhu lianhe hui*).

Finally, there were federations of autonomous workers (*gongzilian*), mini-unions that not only defended the interests of the working classes in the big cities, but also helped the students to organize. The Beijing Workers Autonomous Federation was set up, forming shock groups to provide protection for the burgeoning democratic movement. They were called the "Black Panthers" or the "Flying Tiger Corps", and would later be seen on the outskirts of Tiananmen Square.[11]

By mid-May, the worst nightmares of the leaders had begun to come true: students and city workers were in the process of forging an alliance, though the picture was still far from complete.

Qiao Shi was not concealing information, but Prime Minister Li Peng was wary of him. After all, Qiao had tried to negotiate with Yan Mingfu, head of the United Front Work Department (UFWD) and son of the master spy who had once warned Stalin of Hitler's plan to attack the USSR in 1941. Yan was clearly an intelligence connoisseur. But, like Qiao Shi, he was arguing for negotiation and forbearance towards the students. This would end up costing him dear.

Li Peng was setting up parallel networks in direct contact with the Gonganbu and military intelligence circles, in order to supersede Qiao's networks. Their coordinator was Luo Gan, a kind of private secretary for the special services (*tewu*). He was a broad-girthed, energetic man, with metal-rimmed round glasses, who shared with Qiao Shi a passion for swimming and playing tennis, and, also like Qiao, had been trained in industrial espionage. In 1989, he had managed to integrate the entourage around the conservative leader Li Peng, and ended up becoming Minister of Labour, secretary general of the State Council, and a kind of general factotum, overseeing Li's move to Mao's former residence in the Zhongnanhai complex, where the new leader loved to swim in the pool. Luo visited him every day to report back.[12] A huge fan of foreign cinema, he regularly reviewed footage of student protests set up by fake TV crews in the pay of the Gonganbu. Luo Gan wanted just one thing: for his master to bring about the fall of Zhao Ziyang and give the green light for suppression of the student protests.

On the morning of 17 May, there was a meeting of the Standing Committee at Deng Xiaoping's home. In addition to Zhao Ziyang, Li Peng, Qiao Shi, Hu Qili and Yao Yilin, Deng invited two important senior figures, Yang Shangkun and Bo Yibo. Conversation was tense.

> Zhao Ziyang: The fasting students feel themselves under a spotlight that makes it hard for them to make concessions. This leaves us with a prickly situation. [...]
>
> Yang Shangkun: Can we still say there's been no harm to the national interest or society's interest? [...]
>
> Li Peng: I think Comrade Ziyang must bear the main responsibility for escalation of the student movement, as well as for the fact that the situation has gotten so hard to control. [...]
>
> Deng Xiaoping: If our one billion people jumped into multiparty elections, we'd get chaos like the "all-out" civil war we saw during the Cultural Revolution.[13]

It appears from the minutes that Qiao Shi did not utter a word during the meeting. According to other sources, he agreed to the idea of sending the PLA onto the streets of Beijing, but with one caveat: to ensure that no blood was shed. In any case, the vote created a stalemate for the leadership: Zhao Ziyang and Hu Qili, a propaganda expert, were opposed to martial law; Li Peng and Yao Yilin, a conservative economist from the Chen Yun school, were in favour. Qiao abstained, which meant deadlock. They had to refer the decision to Deng Xiaoping, who, encouraged by Li Peng, gave the nod. Just as in Tibet, martial law was about to be declared. Despite this dramatic decision, immediately after the meeting, Zhao Ziyang and Qiao Shi, besieged by photographers, went to meet hunger strikers in hospital.

On 19 May 1989, the government announced the imposition of martial law and ordered troops from twenty-two divisions to march in the direction of Beijing. Many generals were extremely surprised, having failed to foresee that armed repression was going to being used against the students. On 20 May, a group of generals sent a message to Deng Xiaoping and the Central Military Commission: "We demand that troops do not enter Beijing, and that martial law not be established in the city." Deng dispatched officers for a meeting, while Yang Shangkun, president of the PRC, made a series of telephone calls to the generals. The febrile atmosphere calmed down a little.[14]

On 21 May, in order to reassure the dissident generals, Yang ordered the soldiers not to fire on innocent civilians, even if provoked. The next day, student leaders suggested ending the hunger strike, but their decision was thwarted under pressure from the many protesters who had recently arrived in Beijing from the provinces. Many of the 50,000 students now in Tiananmen Square were from outside the city. Gonganbu reports suggest that, over the course of the three days preceding the imposition of martial law, 165 trains filled with students had arrived in Beijing from other parts of the country, and that 319 schools and universities were represented at the square.

Generals from Yang Shangkun's faction were growing increasingly impatient. Among them was General Xu Xin, a senior ally of Li Peng, who was deputy chief of staff of the PLA. He was in charge of intelligence—nominally led by the head of the PLA2, General Xiong Guangkai—and military security, which monitored troops and infiltrated the student movement. Some soldiers began to defect, taking off their uniforms and sporting T-shirts emblazoned with the image of the Goddess of Democracy, but it was impossible to know if they were true children of the people who had naively decided to join the demonstrations, or agents of the secret services. Many of them were both, if one is to believe the testimonies and documents available today.

The military security sector, which monitored the troops' morale, was under the leadership of General Yang Baibing, head of the PLA General Political Department. Yang controlled the army secret police, called the Security Department (*Baoweibu*), in liaison with General Chi Haotian, who was not only army chief of staff but also Yang Shangkun's son-in-law. Within this pyramid of "political commissars", Yang Baibing exerted a disproportionate influence on the various military regions, and most importantly Beijing. Many commissioners who spoke up against the repression were dismissed from their posts; some were even shot.

But the troops of the Beijing Military Region were a problem. For the moment, they were still hesitant in the face of demonstrators chanting, "You are the army of the people, you must stand by the people!" In any case, they had no ammunition—either because at that point no one wanted things to escalate towards violence, or because they were not to be trusted. General Yang Baibing inspired confidence only within his own faction: he was the half-brother of President Yang, who, like Deng Xiaoping, hated this young people's movement with a passion, for it reminded them of the Cultural Revolution, when they had both been banished. The two Yangs, as well as Generals Chi Haotian and Xu Xin, constituted the kernel of PLA leadership that would eventually turn its military might against the people.

To be clear: Deng, as a young man, had once been a student activist in France, which got him into trouble with the French police. But the French cop of the 1920s was not as violent as the Chinese "blue-haired dog" of today. In any event, his main memory of a young people's revolutionary movement was of Red Guards throwing his son Deng Pufang from the top of a building, leaving him a wheelchair-bound paraplegic who was now the head of the China Welfare Fund for the Disabled.

On 21 May, Deng invited the inner circle of retired leaders, the so-called "Immortals", to talks, since it was becoming apparent that the current younger leadership was not going to be able to bring the situation under control. His decision was blunt and delivered with force: "During the recent upheavals, Zhao Ziyang has quite patently revealed his position," he said. "It is clear that he stands on the side of the agitators: in plain language one might say that he is actively fomenting divisions within the party by standing with the agitators. He is happy that we are still in control. Zhao Ziyang bears responsibility for this unrest and we have no reason to hang on to him. Similarly, Hu Qili is no longer fit to remain on the Standing Committee."

It was then that Chen Yun, Kang Sheng's former comrade in the Shanghai secret service, suggested someone to replace Zhao: "Comrade Jiang Zemin, the mayor of Shanghai, would make an excellent candidate. He is a modest man and very respectful of party discipline."

It was indeed said that Jiang knew how to deal with demonstrations in his city. But in Beijing the situation was grave. It was imperative that the Chinese leadership begin to rally military officials and prepare to take Tiananmen Square. A little later, Deng Xiaoping went to Wuhan to convince the leaders of the military region and several others that he was in control in Beijing.[15]

On the morning of 2 June, at Deng's behest, all the senior figures of the CCP met, though only three members of the Standing Committee remained: Li Peng, Yao Yilin and Qiao Shi. Prime Minister Li shared the latest news: "Yesterday, the Beijing Party Committee and the Ministry of State Security [the Guoanbu] submitted reports to the Politburo. These two reports offer us ample evidence that, following the imposition of martial law, there is a plan by the organizers of this unrest to occupy Tiananmen Square, and for it to serve as a command post for a final confrontation with the party and the government. The square has become the focal centre of the student movement and, in a way, of the whole nation."

The premier explained what was going on. "Dare-to-die" units had been formed to stop the military, and "thugs" had attacked the Beijing Public Security Bureau. One of the Flying Tigers groups was sending messages fine-tuning the details of their tactics, and illegal organizations including the Beijing Students Autonomous Federation and the Beijing Workers Autonomous Federation had set up loudspeakers through which they were broadcasting criticism of the CCP and fake news from the Voice of America. Employees of the US embassy, including CIA agents, were taking advantage of the situation to conduct "aggressive" intelligence missions and liaise with the Student Federation; the Chinese Alliance for Democracy had become an instrument of the United States and was providing secret agents for the Kuomintang to act against China. The aim of these people, the "dregs of our nation", was to forge "a coalition of reactionary forces, both from within China and abroad, to overthrow the Communist Party and subvert the socialist system".

"Those goddamn bastards!" burst out Wang Zhen, a veteran of the Long March, who had captured Xinjiang, the Chinese "Far West", and was a member of the martial law monitoring committee. "Who do they think they are, trampling on sacred ground like Tiananmen so long? They're really asking for it! We should send the troops right now to grab those counter-revolutionaries, Comrade Xiaoping!"

Deng agreed: "The causes of this incident have to do with the global context. The Western world, especially the United States, has thrown its entire propaganda machine into agitation work, and has given a lot of encouragement and assistance to the so-called democrats or opposition in China—people who are in fact the scum of the Chinese nation," he echoed Li.

It was left to President Yang Shangkun to detail how soldiers had comported themselves, arms at the ready: "Troops have moved into the Great Hall of the People, Zhongshan Park, the People's Cultural Palace, and the Public Security Ministry [Guoanbu] compound. The thinking of all officers and soldiers has been thoroughly prepared for a clearing of Tiananmen Square."

Qiao Shi had now decided on his response: "The facts show that we can't expect the students on the Square to withdraw voluntarily. Clearing the square is our only option, and it's quite necessary. I hope our announcement about clearing will meet with approval and support of the majority of citizens and students. Clearing the square is the beginning of a restoration of normal order in the capital."

Deng Xiaoping concluded the meeting thus: "I agree with all of you and suggest the martial law troops begin tonight to carry out the clearing plan and finish it within two days. As we proceed with the clearing, we must explain it clearly to all the citizens and students, asking them to leave and doing our very best to persuade them. But if they refuse to leave, they will be responsible for the consequences."[16]

A tank battle in central Beijing

At the beginning of the siege, around 200,000 soldiers from twenty-two divisions of thirteen PLA corps were transferred to the Beijing area. US satellites and communications intercepted by the National Security Agency, particularly from Australia, can give us an idea of troop movements up to the level of a battalion.[17]

The soldiers were under the command of the Martial Law Headquarters, which was technically under the command of General Chi Haotian, but was in fact led by three senior party members: Deng Xiaoping, Yang Shangkun and Wang Zhen. Although Deng was eighty-five, he wanted personally to supervise the manoeuvres, first from the resort town of Beidaihe and then from his West Hills home, near to which a mobile command post had been installed.

At 9pm on 3 June, the army was given the green light. Troops were ordered to arrive at Tiananmen Square at 1am, and to have it cleared by 6am. After the first clashes on the edges of the square, including between rival PLA units, the special forces gained entrance to the square through the tunnels of the underground city, via Zhongnanhai. British journalist Gordon Thomas describes how "troops were being ferried by underground train from Zhongnanhai to the Great Hall of the People. All entrances to the nuclear shelter tunnels in the city had been opened so troops waiting there could make their way up into the city."[18]

Meanwhile, regular units and armoured vehicles began their assault. The outline of the battle plan drawn up by Chi Haotian and his generals shows an attack from the west by the units of the Beijing military region, from the south-east by the Shenyang and Jinan military region units and the 15th Airborne Brigade of the Canton military region, and from the northern suburbs by Shenyang units.

Fighting lasted throughout the night and into the following day, 4 June. Along Everlasting Peace Avenue, *Chang'an Dajie*, which bisects Beijing north of Tiananmen, the least experienced soldiers of the 38th Corps became stranded. The 27th Corps, composed of older and more aggressive soldiers, made swifter progress. On the other hand, about fifty armoured vehicles remained immobilized for a long time near Nanyuan airport, on the south–north axis, as did vehicles approaching Tiananmen Square from the south. Battle raged at the Muxidi Bridge, and the PLA lost many vehicles, including armoured tanks.

According to various sources, there were between 200 and 3,000 victims (264 according to the authorities, including twenty soldiers and officers; 2,600, according to the Beijing Red Cross; and up to 10,000, according to reports in the Soviet press). The operation lasted for three days, with men from the security services mingling with civilians in the square in order to hunt down, and in some cases shoot dead, dissidents. At the Minzu Hotel, plain-clothes Guoanbu men chased a Chinese man into the lobby and shot him, without the slightest concern for the terrified clientele.[19]

Though this marked the beginning of a widespread and brutal repression, it could not conceal the enormous tensions in the ranks of the army and secret services that were beginning to emerge. "Interviews with embassy officials and Russian students studying in Beijing at this time confirm the fact that the night of 3–4 June was witness to scenes of fierce fighting in the city," according to Iliya Sarsembaev, a specialist in Sino-Russian relations. "The sound of cannon fire from tanks resounded through the streets, and in the morning dead bodies in PLA uniform could be seen lying in the streets alongside burned-out tanks. The Chinese government refuses even today to acknowledge that there was any fighting between PLA regiments. Some Chinese students say that, since the beginning of June, soldiers had been arriving in Beijing who were not [majority-ethnic] Han and spoke little, if any, *Putonghua* (Mandarin). These regiments came from Inner Mongolia and Xinjiang, and the soldiers had neither relatives nor friends in Beijing."[20]

This tallies with the description of the command structure sent by the KGB *rezident* Grigorov and his team on the morning of 4 June. This report to Vladimir Kryuchkov, head of the KGB, confirmed the messages that were pouring into Moscow of a major schism between the different army units:

> Engaged: Initially, troops of the five army corps that make up the Beijing Military Region.

- The 24th Army Corps (based in Chengde, east of Beijing Hebei Province encircling the Beijing area), and their 1st Armoured Division (Tianjin);
- The 27th Army Corps, General Staff in Shijiazhuang (Hebei) including the 13th Cavalry Brigade (tanks);
- 38th Regiment (Baoding headquarters, Hebei), with the 6th Tank Division (Unit 52884), stationed in Nankou, Beijing;
- 63rd Army Corps (Taiyuan headquarters, Shaanxi);
- 65th Army Corps (Zhangjiakou headquarters, Hebei);
- Special protection forces of the government and the leaders: the Central Guard Unit (57003) of the Military Region, under the command of the Central Military Commission.

As the situation has worsened in recent days, Beijing soldiers have received reinforcements from Lanzhou Military District regiments (controlling the Shaanxi, Gansu, Qinghai, Ningxia and Xinjiang military districts):

- The 21st Corps, Lanzhou MR Regiment, based in Baoji (Shaanxi);
- Special Units 84835 (Qingtongxia, Ningxia Province);
- Units from Hohhot (Inner Mongolia);
- Border Guard Defense Regiments dependent on Gonganbu;
- Brigade No. 205 with Uyghurs and Mongols;
- Units of the People's Armed Police (PAP).

Note that the tanks that fired on the soldiers of the RM of Beijing belonged to the 21st Corps. They attacked in particular armoured vehicles of the 6th Division belonging to the 38 Corps.

Journalists had similar information, but sometimes concerning units other than those mentioned in this report. For example, Patrick Sabatier, Beijing correspondent for the French daily *Libération*, wrote: "People tell me they have witnessed skirmishes, including armoured vehicles, between soldiers of the 28th and 27th Corps in the western part of the city. Others say they have seen wounded soldiers in the south-east of the city. Diplomatic sources confirm that clashes have taken place in the southern suburbs around the Nanyuan military airport, between units of the 27th and 16th Corps. Leaflets have been distributed throughout Beijing, claiming that old Marshal Nie Rongzhen, one of the most senior military leaders in the country and a longstanding comrade of Mao, who survived the Long March, has called the president, General Yang Shangkun, who is also the chief of the martial law troops, a 'thug'".[21]

Nie Rongzhen's position was all the more significant given that his relationship with Deng Xiaoping went back to their student days in Paris; he had been controller of Zhou Enlai's clandestine radio base in Shanghai, and was considered the military father of the atomic bomb and China's strategic missiles.

It was clear even from the scant information broadcast by journalists on the ground, details of which converged, that the mood in the army was anything but unified. Soldiers were defecting, abandoning their weapons and melting into the crowds. The case of the 38th Army Corps is particularly significant because many of these soldiers had family in the city, and many of the students in Tiananmen Square had taught in these units, meaning that soldiers and students were already fraternizing—to such an extent that General Yang Baibing, head of the PLA's political department, threatened to shoot generals from the Beijing military region, and in particular those from the 38th Corps, if they refused to fire on the students.

The insubordination came from the top: General Xu Qinxian, commander of the 38th Army Corps, had been on sick leave since the imposition of martial law in order to avoid having to lead his troops into combat. He was later court-martialled and imprisoned. Many other soldiers from his unit also tried to take sick leave to avoid being on patrol in Beijing. According to PLA internal security documents, 3,500 officers were investigated in the months following the massacre for insubordination. One hundred and eleven of these officers were punished, as well as 1,400 conscripts who had deserted.[22]

In contrast, Yang Baibing's nephew, General Yang Zhaojun, leader of the 27th Corps, was highly dedicated in his duties. He commanded the same group that his father Yang Shangkun had led during the 1979 war against Vietnam.[23] These men—many of them former convicts from the Chinese interior who had escaped *laogai* camps, and most of whom did not speak Mandarin—slaughtered protesters with zealous enthusiasm.

Meanwhile, General Xu Xin's intelligence services had infiltrated young spies into the student protests to track the movement's leaders: Wang Dan, the Uyghur Wuer Kaixi and Chai Ling. Wang Dan was picked up by the Guoanbu when he went back to his university dorm to fetch some belongings. The other two disappeared, and were right at the top of the list of twenty-one activists that the security services were desperate to find. These were the same special services from General Xiong Guangkai's army who, on 3 June, had sought to incite the demonstrators by leaving a bus full of weapons for them to find, in the hope that they would use them. Later on, they left guns next to the corpses of students to make it look as if they had fired at soldiers.

As with the PLA, not everybody in the civilian security and intelligence community reacted in the same way. We have seen Qiao Shi, the coordinator of the security services, vacillating and trying to negotiate with the students alongside Zhao Ziyang, before eventually rallying to Deng Xiaoping's position. On 5 May, students from the Institute of International Relations (*Guoji Guanxi Xueyuan*), where analysts and spies are trained by director and Guoanbu advisor Chen Zhongjing, had marched with banners.[24] In June, some newspapers criticized the Gonganbu head, Wang Fang, for failing to control his troops. In fact, the "blue-haired dogs" fulfilled their role in crushing the uprising with little if any soul searching. The chief of Beijing Public Security, Su Zhongxiang, refused to attack the students and resigned from his post, but that was all. Yan Mingfu, head of the UFWD, who had a knack for addressing the students, was dismissed.

Meanwhile, the PAP, set up with the specific purpose of suppressing demonstrations, proved incapable of doing so. It underwent a serious purge and its leader, General Li Xianxiu, was dismissed. Qiao Shi was going to have to reorganize it. A few years later, in 1991, the Central Guards Division (Unit 57003), led by General Yang Dezhong, was also reorganized, because too many officers had sympathies for the dismissed general secretary Zhao Ziyang; indeed, in late May 1989 there had been an attempted coup to get him reinstated.[25]

On 7 June 1989, in an event unprecedented in the history of the Chinese Communist Party, the head of the special services, Qiao Shi, was appointed interim general secretary of the CCP. However, Qiao did not take long to cede his uncomfortable position to the leader of the party's Shanghai branch, Jiang Zemin. He knew him well, for it was Jiang who had recruited him into the world of espionage in the late 1940s. In contrast to the top brass, and the "Immortals" who had by now taken over the leadership of the party, Jiang seemed to be the most personable of the ruling elite.

However, what was expected of Qiao Shi was something quite different to the political management of the crisis: he was required to crush the student movement and neutralize dissidents who were fleeing and seeking asylum abroad. Qiao Shi suppressed the uprising with determination, while always thinking forward towards the future. It was a strange dance he was required to perform. If the rumours are to be believed, it was on his orders that the security services allowed some dissidents to slip into Hong Kong—those whose faces had been seen on television and were now familiar worldwide.

Although he had ostensibly pledged allegiance to the new general secretary, Jiang Zemin, Qiao Shi continued to defend his own interests. Prime Minister Li Peng was responsible for keeping to the hard line; Jiang Zemin had the challenge of navigating the situation under the watchful eye of Deng Xiaoping; but Comrade Qiao allowed himself the possibility of switching allegiance at any moment. "The cunning hare has three exits to his lodgings," as the Chinese proverb has it.

On 9 June 1989, the fifty-fifth day of the Tiananmen revolt, the CCP claimed that order had been re-established in Beijing. Deng Xiaoping appeared on television garbed in a Mao suit—he had not been seen since his meeting with Gorbachev on 16 May—and officially thanked the army, "the Great Wall of Iron and Steel", for restoring stability in China. But the extent of the massacre was no secret to the foreign embassies in Beijing; a diplomatic cable sent from the British ambassador Sir Alan Donald to the UK Foreign Office on 5 June 1989 (declassified in December 2017) noted a "minimum estimate of civilian dead 10,000". Moreover, Donald added, there had been insubordination in the 27th Army Corps punished by execution, and soldiers had fired dum-dum bullets, even though they are prohibited under international law.[26]

Operation Yellowbird

The Western intelligence services in Beijing and Hong Kong did not wait for the tragic denouement of Tiananmen and the indignation of world opinion before acting. But political condemnations are one thing, and realpolitik is quite another. Thus the extraordinary episode known as Operation Yellowbird, the rescue of dissidents, was less about professional agents on a mission than about individuals standing up for those demanding democracy.

The rescue of astrophysicist Fang Lizhi and his wife Li Shuxian was one case that was in fact approved by the White House. George H.W. Bush's request to meet the man known as the Chinese Sakharov earlier that year, during his state visit to Beijing, had been refused. A little earlier, in January 1989, Professor Fang had sent an open letter to the Chinese leadership demanding the release of certain political prisoners, including the most famous of them all, Wei Jingsheng, Deng Xiaoping's "Man in the Iron Mask". Fang was already in the government's sights, on the blacklist of people whose arrest had been ordered by Qiao Shi. On the afternoon of 7 June, the professor and his wife managed to get to the American embassy and ask for asylum. Embassy employees explained that this was impossible, but they did give them the phone number of an American journalist, who agreed to hide them in his room at the Jianguo Hotel. The US State Department was immediately informed and the message was conveyed to the uppermost echelons in Washington. The response was categorical: "Send them straight back to the embassy."

It is not hard to imagine the headache this presented for Ambassador James Lilley, the former CIA agent who had opened the first CIA station in Beijing back in 1973. Lilley's diplomatic mission was the most closely monitored of all, and now he was being asked to play James Bond in a besieged Beijing, while the current head of the CIA in China had just gone on leave. In conversation with Bill Webster, the CIA chief at Langley, Lilley assured his boss that there was no risk that the army would be sent into Tiananmen Square.

His intelligence reflexes kicked in, and with the plain-clothes marines in charge of the embassy's security, Lilley managed to locate the Fangs and hide them in the embassy without the Chinese getting wind of it: "Fang's presence in the embassy was initially top-secret information that was known only to very few people," Lilley explained in his memoirs. "This was a very sensitive situation for me and it was vital to keep it under wraps until the situation in Beijing improved. So you can imagine my surprise when White House spokesman Marlin Fitzwater announced during a press conference that Fang and his wife had taken refuge in the US embassy. Although I thought the Chinese would eventually discover that they were there, I did not expect the US government itself to tell them. Apparently, there was confusion among decision makers in Washington about Fang's presence at the embassy, and Fitzwater simply thought he was being precise. The Chinese government hit the roof."[27]

Relations between Beijing and Washington turned as cold as they had been in the days of the Cultural Revolution, before Nixon and Mao broke the ice. As long as Fang Lizhi was sheltering in the embassy, a thaw was impossible. The question was how to bring out the Chinese professor without anyone losing face. As Lilley reported, relations between the Guoanbu and the CIA had once again resumed, for the purposes of exchanging intelligence about the USSR: all was well so long as nobody mentioned the Tiananmen massacre and its aftermath. However, at the same time, the CIA station in Hong Kong was reporting that a special anti-terrorist unit was apparently preparing to storm the US embassy and seize the dissident couple. The Chinese ambassador to Washington was summoned to the State Department and duly lectured about the dire consequences of such an action, were it to materialize.

Sometime around Halloween, at the end of October, the Chinese special services began to increase their surveillance of the embassy, perhaps afraid that Fang Lizhi was going to try and escape the premises in a mask or disguised as a pumpkin. The reality, of course, was rather more mundane. As a result of the agreement between Bush and Deng, whose purpose was to restore cordial relations, Fang and his wife were eventually able to leave the PRC on 25 June 1990.

One mystery remains, however: the Jianguo Hotel, where the Fangs originally took refuge, was one of the hotels under the direct management of the Guoanbu, and therefore under close surveillance. Had the intelligence service really not known that the dissidents were hiding there? Or was an order given at a higher level to let them slip away? Could it have been on Qiao Shi's orders?

The French network in Hong Kong

Similar questions also arose with regard to other dissidents, who left via the unofficial French network in Hong Kong that allowed dissidents to flee China. This was quite a remarkable setup, which had only come into existence on 4 June.

In the summer of 1989 a junk entered Macao waters, accompanied by a Portuguese navy speedboat. As a dinghy drew up alongside the junk, the captain explained that there was an injured passenger on board—nothing too serious. A Chinese coastguard had fired on them with a machine gun, and they'd made a narrow escape.

The small boat had in fact made this secret voyage from the mainland several times, but this was the first time it had been hit by a bullet. On the beach, a welcoming committee was waiting. Four Europeans and half a dozen Chinese men helped the injured man to disembark.

The officials—a Portuguese naval security officer, a British Special Branch inspector and two French diplomats—were acting without their governments' knowledge. The man whom they were welcoming to Macao was a well-known dissident, a film director who had been active in the Tiananmen movement. His name was Su Xiaokang and he was a professor at Beijing University. His television documentary, *The Elegy of the River* (*He Shang*), about the backwardness of China, had made something of a splash in June 1988 before later being attacked for its "nihilism".

Su had taken the ferry to Hong Kong, where, together with the French, Special Branch officers and their boss John Thorpe had given him protection. They were used to debriefing refugees in "conspiracy" apartments: what was your role in the movement? What relationship did you have with the authorities? How did you get here? They had to root out bogus dissidents and the Guoanbu spies who were also using this escape route. British counterintelligence grilled people with the same methods as those used during the Second World War, when they interrogated Resistance fighters from occupied France. After this screening, several people, including two French diplomats, Jean-Pierre Montagne and François Fensterbank, provided the dissidents with fake-genuine passports, before they were flown to France, accompanied by a member of the network.

Dozens of such trips were made, with hundreds of rescued dissidents seeking asylum in Europe, Japan and the USA. There was no doubt that the Chinese security services could have arrested some of these student or political leaders, but—apparently on the orders of either Qiao Shi in Beijing or Ye Xuanping, the governor of Guangdong and son of the Hakka marshal Ye Jianying—they were allowed to slip through the net. This was the case for one of the most famous student leaders, Chai Ling, who escaped on an Air France flight, carrying a false passport and wearing make-up so as to pass for the accompanying French diplomat's girlfriend. The Uyghur student leader Wuer Kaixi and his girlfriend Liu Yan, dissident Yan Jiaqi and his wife Gao Gao, as well as many others, fled through Hong Kong with the help of this network.

A few years later in Hong Kong, François Fensterbank explained the context in which this escapade was undertaken: "You have to remember the atmosphere at the time. François Mitterrand declared after the Tiananmen massacre that 'a government that shoots its youth has no future!' We deduced from that that we had some kind of moral green light to help fleeing dissidents. But we no longer had a secret service station in Hong Kong. The former head of the DGSE in Hong Kong, a captain who had moved from public service to private industry, came through from time to time, that was it. So that left a few of us to set it up ourselves. Because we loved China and we loved freedom. We had no training as secret agents—we were improvising. Fortunately, I had read some John Le Carré novels and now the British were helping us in real life. But they had to be careful not to draw attention to themselves, and after a while Special Branch made it clear that it was going to have to lower its profile because the Beijing government was attacking London, accusing it of maintaining a subversive base in Hong Kong."

Contrary to what Chinese leaders claimed, the CIA played only a modest role in Operation Yellowbird, which, although it was attributed to the US agency, was in fact cobbled together by a group of generous-hearted amateurs. Although it was secret, the escape network surfed on a wave of tremendous popular support in Hong Kong immediately after the massacre of 4 June. One million weeping people demonstrated in Hong Kong. Paradoxically, this was an opportunity for the young people of Hong Kong to show that they felt for the first time fully Chinese. It was also a moment to reflect upon the potential danger in Hong Kong's forthcoming return to the PRC, scheduled for 1997.

Nearly eighty dissidents settled in the British colony, with others fleeing further afield. The Yellowbird network had come together with the help of the entertainment world, some of whose most prominent figures helped to raise money to support the underground resistance. These included film stars and singers such as film producer John Sham, kung fu actor Jackie Chan, and Anita Mui, whose song *Big Bad Girl!* was a huge hit with Hong Kong teenagers.

It was no secret that many figures from the Hong Kong entertainment business were in cahoots with the Triads. Sham, Chan, Mui and many others were in contact with Charlie Heung, a well-known film producer. Officially, of course, he denied he had anything to do with the largest of the Triads, the Sun Yee On (New Virtue & Peace), which had 50,000 members. Except, that is, for the fact that it had been founded by his father in 1921, and many of the Heung brothers had been involved in criminal Triad affairs, and some even convicted. A British police chief with whom I spoke at the time told me that Charles Heung was the "Dragon Head", the Big Boss, of the Sun Yee On. He had been refused entry to Canada because of his links with drug trafficking.[28]

Still, Heung loved to be photographed for the gossip columns, standing with CCP figures like the governor of Canton, Ye Xuanping. Making the most of his links with the security services, the Sun Yee On helped him set up escape routes across China, for a fee. There is every reason to believe that the Sun Yee On was playing for both sides: helping the democrats by aiding fleeing dissidents, at the same time as helping communist leaders who wanted to avoid trials in Beijing of people who, thanks to CNN, had featured in TV news bulletins the world over. Other students and workers were not so lucky. They were either executed or sent to the *laogai*.

"We found ourselves on Kadoree Road, the street where all the stars live, in the popular district of Mong Kok. We were in Charlie Heung's sumptuous villa, with the main people behind Operation Yellowbird,"

Fensterbank told me. "That's where everything was decided. It was astonishing to see the motley crew that ended up helping the dissidents escape—including members of Special Branch and the Triads, who were normally sworn enemies."

In a striking epilogue, Chun Wong, a Triad boss, was arrested for drug trafficking in 1990. He was a "426", a senior official of the Sun Ye On, from the Tsim Sha Tsui East neighbourhood, where he had climbed the ladder to the very top of the organization controlling the brothels where young Hong Kong prostitutes worked.

US authorities had demanded his extradition for heroin trafficking, but he was released on an impressive $650,000 bail. The first surprise was that Special Branch gave the green light for his release, contrary to agreements in force between the US and the UK. Even more surprising were some of the people who contributed money to his bail—figures such as Anita Mui, John Sham and various other Hong Kong celebrities.

The reason for this only came to light in October 1995 after Chun, nicknamed the "Shim Sha Tsui Tiger", was killed in a motorcycle accident in Thailand after going on the run. Newspapers revealed that he had played a central role in organizing Operation Yellowbird. Figures as controversial as Stanley Ho had given money to the operation and, I was told in Macao, the famous "master of the casinos" had even provided accommodation to fleeing dissidents.

A French intelligence officer, stationed in Asia some time after this episode, confirmed to me in 2007 what an important role the French diplomats had played in saving the dissidents. He also told me that the Chinese services had acted with no compunction against certain members of the Western community in Hong Kong involved in opposition politics. As evidence, he cited the mysterious deaths of the wives of no fewer than three consuls, Swiss, Mexican and American, each of whom fell from a high building in Hong Kong. The first, "Mrs B", married to the Swiss consul, worked for an NGO in Hong Kong. She had visited Tibet just a few months before her death, where she had witnessed at first hand the repressive tactics of the Chinese regime.[29]

The global hunt for dissidents

In the aftermath of the Tiananmen Square massacre, Chinese special services sent teams of "cleaners" all over the world to neutralize dissidents who had fled abroad. Additional teams were posted in embassies, for not everyone could be trusted: many diplomats posted abroad had expressed qualms about the massacre. Some had thought that the Diaochabu, the CCP's investigation bureau, had been dissolved in 1983 when the Guoanbu was established; but its representatives were still placed in embassies to coordinate the hunt for dissidents and monitor colleagues who aroused suspicion.[30]

In West Germany, a delegation of some fifty Chinese officers arrived and asked their local counterparts to help them monitor the dissidents. They went all over the country to gain the support of the LfV, the regional branches of the federal counterintelligence service (Bundesamt für Verfaßungsschutz). But there was little eagerness to help the Chinese on display. In Munich, on the other hand, the BND, in charge of foreign espionage, agreed to take on trainees, and went even further, selling the Chinese bugging equipment, at a time when across Europe there was an embargo on selling arms to the PRC.

In France, at the time of the massacre, appalled DST technicians had carried out an operation on their own initiative: they flooded the Chinese embassy on the Avenue George V with faxes protesting against the repression of human rights in China, on behalf of various fictitious organizations.[31]

A "diplomat" named Cao Guoxing, accompanied by his driver and second secretary, Bai Zhangde, was very active in the Chinese embassy in Paris. He received reinforcements of some twenty Guoanbu agents, who were sent under commercial or diplomatic cover. Agents from the French DST and the Renseignements Généraux (internal intelligence bureau) kept a close watch on the two men and wondered if the lower-status Bai was not in fact in charge. Whether or not this was the case, he organized some remarkable operations on French soil, including the undercover infiltration of the Chinese students' union's local Marseille chapter. In general, Cao and Bai's methods were efficient: subtle threats when students went to deal with administrative formalities at the Consulate, constant pressure on individuals, a variety of hints and warnings. For Bai, the record seemed satisfactory: over time, students who supported the protests returned to the ranks, or at least significantly dialled down their activities. Having exerted pressure a little too conspicuously on students, Bai was nearly expelled from France.

Meanwhile, "deep-water fish" melted into Paris's Chinatown. According to the information I was able to gather at the time, they were aided by Chinese gangs who, for tactical reasons, were helping Beijing. This was facilitated by the fact that, in some cases, they had helped the students get to Europe. In addition—and this is to the great discredit of the profession—some journalists posted to Paris, including the correspondent for the Shanghai daily *Wenhui Bao*, were principally working as Guoanbu agents, to whom the French foreign office felt obliged to give journalist accreditation. Counterintelligence watched, appalled, as the China-loving Parisian press gave them ample column inches to criticize French democracy.

Meanwhile, the comings and goings of the "cleaners" did not go unremarked, as in the case of Liu Wen, who had been head of the Gonganbu Criminal Affairs Bureau since March 1988, and head of the national bureau for liaison with Interpol. He had visited France half a dozen times to oversee the hunt for the dissident "criminals", and he constantly altered his identity at border crossings, which rather intrigued the officers of the French Air and Border Police, as well as French internal intellgience, since his official status was with the international police.[32] The French were more flexible at the time than the American authorities, and they left Liu alone do his job. Zhu Entao, the official delegate to Interpol, was delighted to be able to operate so easily on French soil.

In the United States, the FBI had banned him from entering the country after a spying scandal in which he had been implicated five years before—the FBI believed he was controlling the Guoanbu mole Larry Wu-Tai Chin at the level of Gonganbu counterintelligence headquarters. The Americans were probably right, for the Guoanbu was doing everything it could to try to infiltrate the dissident movement. For example, in June 1989, during a Chinese Alliance for Democracy convention in the United States, a delegate called Shao Huaqiang announced publicly that he had been recruited as a spy by the Guoanbu before leaving China. His recruiters had given him the mission of infiltrating the Alliance and proving it had financial ties with Taiwan.

The hunt for dissidents in the US was complicated by the fact that the FBI was closely monitoring the Chinese diplomatic mission. In 1988 it protested—in vain—against the opening of a consulate in Los Angeles. It was later proved right, when it emerged that, as in France, the consul's education department was serving as a cover for Guoanbu agents monitoring Tiananmen refugees. This was corroborated in May 1990, when Xu Lin, a third secretary attached to the Department of Education in Washington, defected. He later explained to the Foreign Affairs Committee of the US Congress that he had refused to draw up lists of dissidents, as demanded by the Guoanbu. He also explained in detail how China's secret agents operated abroad.

In Britain, three first secretaries in the Chinese embassy decided to seek asylum from the Home Office. But the latter was being kept busy by other Chinese dissidents. Jiang Xiaoming, Qiao Shi's son, and his wife had disappeared from Cambridge. In fact, they had been given a safe house by British counterintelligence, who had discovered that so-called dissidents were planning to kidnap them. Qiao Shi was indebted to Her Majesty's Secret Service—nothing could surprise anyone at this point.

That diplomats and secret service agents were defecting to the West was bad enough for the Chinese. It was even worse when it happened in federal Russia, as with Wang Fengxiang, the Chinese consul general in St Petersburg, in March 1993. The Guoanbu, having learned that he had gone to see the head of the new police force, General Arkadi Kramarev, was trying to get him repatriated. But under Boris Yeltsin, Russian intelligence collaboration with the Chinese was far from consistent. Wang was already in Sweden by then, as the Chinese learnt too late. In Stockholm, they were unlikely to be able to recover him, since in early 1991 the Swedish government had declared *personae non gratae* three Chinese diplomats who were harassing dissidents; a Swedish diplomat had been expelled from Beijing in turn.

Paris and the mystery of Ma Tao

After Tiananmen the Chinese secret war also got hot in France, which—along with the United States—was considered the main haven for Chinese dissidents. They tended to meet in Paris, either at the Federation for a Democratic China (FDC) or at Democracy House, financed by Pierre Bergé and set up in the summer of 1989 with the support of various public figures including Yves Montand, Lucien Bodard, Simon Leys and Bernard-Henri Lévy.

On 14 July that year, during the bicentennial celebrations of the French Revolution, Chinese dissidents paraded down the Champs-Élysées in black headbands, one hand raised in a fist, the other pushing a bike like the ones that had been crushed beneath the caterpillar tracks of PLA tanks on Tiananmen Square. The architect Ieoh Ming Pei, who had once been Qiao Shi's classmate at the University of Shanghai, had just completed the Pyramid in the courtyard of the Louvre. He had also designed the Bank of China Building in Hong Kong, the colony's tallest building, and the Xiangshan Hotel, in a suburb of Beijing. Now he excoriated the Chinese leaders: "I have worked in China, despite many frustrations, out of love for my country, and in the hope that things would improve. Will I ever be able to work in China again?"

The authorities in Beijing were particularly irritated by a series of initiatives in France in the spring of 1990: there was the monthly magazine *Actuel*, and the Paris-based, pro-Taiwanese Chinese-language daily *Ouzhou Ribao* (*Europe Journal*). The latter chartered a radio ship, *The Goddess of Democracy*, to broadcast into the PRC from the China Sea, setting sail from La Rochelle on 17 March. Paris-based dissidents Chai Ling, Wan Runnan, Liu Binyan and Yan Jiaqi gave interviews to the media, and it emerged that a high-ranking Chinese official at UNESCO, Zhao Fusan, had defected.

Several mysterious events took place that spring: a car exploded not far from the Chinese trade mission in Neuilly. A burglary took place at the editorial office of *Actuel*, and documents and CD-ROMs were stolen that belonged to the journalist Christophe Nick, one of the organizers of the *Goddess of Democracy* project. Nicolas Druz, editor-in-chief of *Europe Journal*, claimed that he was being followed. A Paris-based human rights activist working on China and Tibet had his apartment broken into. The French police were on red alert. Something was going on.

More and more evidence suggested that the Federation for a Democratic China (FDC) had been the target of infiltration by undercover agents spying on its members and provoking rivalries within it, through a well-orchestrated whispering campaign. The official Chinese press was publishing vitriolic articles attacking Wan Runnan, the former head of the Stone computer company, who was close to Zhao

Ziyang. Wang Fang, the Gonganbu minister, claimed that both Wan and Zhao were CIA agents, because of their contacts with the Hungarian-born American financier George Soros. In Paris, where Wan was president of the FDC, the criticisms were of a completely different nature.[33] He found himself under attack for being maladroit, for having confused political activity with business. The rumours were of such magnitude that many dissidents involved in Democracy House wanted him to step down as president. Some even went so far as to suspect him of double-dealing—of maintaining "close ties" with Chinese secret service agents in Paris.[34]

A detailed report by French internal intelligence in March 1993 analyzed these problems. It described "an investigation into smuggling and Mr Wan Runnan's and his relatives' links with Beijing agents and the community of illegal immigrants, which was entrusted by the FDC's Board of Directors to a dissident." Wan was criticized for the opacity of his management of "a vast group of political associations and commercial companies, in which appear both Chinese officials and other members of the Chinese community involved in suspicious activities."

As well as locking down the management of the FDC, "at the end of 1991, Mr Wan Runnan launched a support fund theoretically intended to finance the FDC (the Global Fund for Democracy in China) which only increased the tension, with the board of directors questioning the secrecy surrounding the fundraising and the exact destination of the money. ... An investigation has established that the foundation has two bank accounts, both opened in November 1991, while that of the FDC proper was closed on 28 December 1990, shortly after Mr Wan Runnan took office.

"This gives credence to the thesis that funds raised for the benefit of the FDC were diverted by Mr Wan Runnan (in 1991 and 1992, the headquarters of the FDC in Paris received nearly $200,000, of which $90,000 were destined for 'secret operations' in mainland China)."

The report gave precise details of the different Chinese businesses in France linked to the affair, implicating a large number of people from both the political and the business worlds, and even what could be considered a "Chinese mafia".[35]

Meanwhile another dissident in Wan's entourage was attracting attention: a student, born in Beijing on 9 April 1966 in the middle of the Cultural Revolution, who had come to live in France in 1988: "The activities of another dissident, Mr Ma Tao, a close acquaintance of Mr Wan Runnan, appear to be particularly suspicious. Ma Tao is a young man, short of stature, who almost always wears a beige raincoat, with a fringe of jet-black hair falling over his eyes. He is very active in the FDC, but, more significantly, he became first general secretary and then president of Democracy House, before being expelled in October 1992. His peers are convinced that he works for the Guoanbu as an undercover agent within the movement for democracy."

It was about this time that some dissidents, who knew my and Rémi Kauffer's book *The Chinese Secret Service*, contacted me to suggest that I investigate the Ma Tao case on behalf of the Tiananmen activists. Either the Paris-based groups that had been set up for the defence of human rights were indeed being corrupted by spies and rumour-mongers, or Ma Tao was the victim of a conspiracy being run from within the Chinese embassy.

At the time I did not have the French intelligence dossier quoted above, so I had to try and work out what was going on through snippets of interviews with dissidents from Democracy House and a few police sources. Apart from having apparently sold testimonies of activists at Democracy House, which would have enabled people to obtain refugee status, Ma Tao was accused of being an undercover agent working for Qiao Shi. It was claimed that he was the son of a senior Guoanbu official, charged, according to the testimony of one of his friends in Beijing, "with training agents before they leave for the West". Even more incriminating, the young man was discovered to hold a foreign bank account in France at Credit Lyonnais, at the Rue St Dominique branch (account number 73304A 81301)—while domiciled at 14 Dongchang'an Avenue, Beijing, as evidenced by the photocopy of a cheque shown to me by one of the dissidents. 14 Dongchang'an Avenue is the address of both the Beijing office of the Gonganbu and of the Guoanbu Bureau of Foreign Affairs. This was the very same office in Beijing that, on 7 January 1990, had officially banned the FDC from all Chinese territory. It was too good to be true. How could an undercover agent have been so careless?

There was only one solution: to interview Ma Tao as part of a documentary on Chinese dissidents in France. The interview took place on 30 October 1993. I was accompanied by a cameraman who filmed the interview using both a floor-mounted and a shoulder-mounted camera.

Ma Tao explained to me the structure of the Federation for a Democratic China: "The FDC has fifteen branches. In Paris, we coordinate, with our newsletter from the administrative liaison—we keep an eye on things. We have 2,400 members, including 120 in France and 600 in the United States. We are going through a bad patch at the moment. People are less motivated than they were. The FDC remains in contact with underground groups: a Chinese social democratic party, a Christian democratic party, and a Free Trade Union."

He told me a little bit about his background. "I am twenty-six. I was born in Beijing. While I was at high school, I started studying at the Institute of Foreign Languages. I began learning French when I was twelve, then I went on to study French language and literature at Beida (Beijing University). In the 1970s [when he was only a young person] I went to study in Wuhan (central China), paid for by the French. I then got a grant to come to France to do a DEA [MPhil] in October 1988 at Paris VIII University. I received my degree on 7 November 1989. While I was writing my dissertation I was also going on demonstrations all the time. The following year I became one of the founding members of the FDC."

At this point, I unfolded an organizational chart of the Gonganbu with the name of his father Ma Jinshuan (马 进 拴) on it, and asked him if it was true that he was involved with the upper echelons of the security services (the Guoanbu and Gonganbu sharing offices, and often personnel, in Beijing). Ma Tao remained unflustered, though he admitted to finding the question a little "personal".

"My father is a university professor, but previously he was head of the Gonganbu's 'management, resources and administration'. That's right! When he was fifteen, in 1947, he was involved in the anti-Japanese struggle, and he became a member of the CCP. He went to school in Hebei in a liberated zone. After 1949, he joined the Ministry of Public Security [the Gonganbu]. Now when he writes to me he tells me to concentrate on my studies. He has no idea about my activities with the FDC. It would hurt him. My mother works in a nursery. I have two sisters. One went to a special engineering school and works in a factory; the other lives in Tianjin, and works in finance and banking."

As I knew that Ma Tao had obtained a passport from the Chinese embassy, I asked him what he thought of the surveillance that it carried out.

"In 1989 and 1990, a student turned up who had been sent by the Chinese secret service. This was often the case. There were several functionaries at the embassy who were in the services. For example, the embassy driver is actually a spy. Cao Guoxing, from the Education Department, runs the party in France (he studied in Beida before me). I had interviews with him in 1989. He told me: 'You must be very careful!' He himself was very uncertain after what happened."[36]

Ma Tao was certainly a curious character. I lost track of him after this interview. Was he indeed a spy who had been given the task of infiltrating the dissidents? Or was he just the naive victim of a conspiracy born of jealousy between militants and of rumours deliberately circulated in Beijing, intended to destroy the democratic movement in exile? The answer is surely obvious: Deng Xiaoping, Li Peng, Qiao Shi and the others had little to fear from these dissidents. Many of the exiles would have liked to go into business in the West or in Taiwan, or even to return to the PRC. The evolution of the Chinese economy would soon mean that they could do so—on condition that they drop any pretension of hoping for the "fifth modernization": democracy.

As I was writing this, I glanced up at a colour photograph showing a large banner. The writing on the banner shows that the picture was taken at a demonstration in Paris in support of the dissident Wei Jingsheng, the inventor of the "fifth modernization". Dressed in his beige raincoat, Ma Tao is standing in front of the white banner with a microphone in his hand, while a French activist holds a megaphone. The young Chinese man was probably calling for the release of Wei Jingsheng—which took place only in 1997, after eighteen years of imprisonment—and declaring, prophetically, that one day the CCP would collapse, as the communist party had collapsed some years earlier in East Germany.

A setback for Qiao Shi in the GDR and Romania

At the end of 1989, while his services were harassing Chinese democrats and dissidents around the world, the spy-teacher Qiao Shi was recharging his batteries in the various bastions of socialism, which were also going through huge social and political upheavals. But, according to Chinese analysts, they were holding firm.

The previous year, Qiao Shi had toured Poland, Hungary and East Germany. The East Germans were following the situation in China very closely, afraid of a similar scenario, as we can see in documents of the Stasi archives, now accessible to the public. In June 1989, Erich Mielke, head of the Stasi—or the MfS (*Ministerium für Staatssicherheit*), to give it its official name—launched a programme for monitoring potential opponents, focusing particularly on Protestant circles, afraid that pacifists were being inspired by the Chinese protesters.[37] Mielke feared that the movement in Tiananmen Square would trigger a wave of revolt behind the Iron Curtain. When the demonstrations did begin, Honecker decided to use the "Chinese method" of repression that had worked so well in Beijing.

But nothing worked in Germany. The Berlin Wall came down, sounding the beginning of the end for communism in Eastern Europe. On 7 November 1989, Berliners marched through the streets of the divided capital with cries of "*Die Mauer muß weg*! The wall must go!" On 11 November, Defence Minister Heinz Kessler summoned his generals to prepare an offensive: "We must use the Chinese method!"

In the shadow of the East Berlin reformers, the politician Hans Modrow and Markus Wolf, head of the secret services, who had plotted Honecker's fall with the Soviets, realized that they had lost control of the situation. With the fall of the Berlin Wall, the East German services were paralysed. As Mielke had feared, the demonstrators stormed Stasi headquarters and began seizing archives. The head of the Stasi in Beijing, a military attaché, defected. He refused to offer his services to the Guoanbu. He was expelled, and later returned as a businessmen working for a company headquartered in reunified Germany. The Chinese still keep him under surveillance, suspecting him of being an "honourable correspondent" for the BND, the German intelligence service.

It could have been even worse. In November 1989, Qiao Shi attended the Romanian party congress at the head of a CCP delegation, and praised the "seventy years of glorious revolutionary struggles of the Romanian Communist Party", wishing it "renewed success during these new historical developments". Admittedly, relations between the two parties went back a long way. Kang Sheng, Qiao's predecessor at the head of the secret services, had established good relations through a former classmate from the NKVD school in Moscow, a Romanian called Emil Bodnaras.

Qiao Shi himself had travelled to Romania in both March and August 1978, as part of Hua Guofeng's entourage. As we know, one of the main purposes of these trips was to establish a regional intelligence base, in liaison with the Romanian Securitate and the DIE (*Departamentul de Informatii Externe*), to replace that of Tirana after China broke with Enver Hoxha's Albania. In fact, in March of that year, Nicolae Ceauşescu had sent Ion Patan, his deputy prime minister and minister of foreign trade, to Beijing, to propose the establishment of a Sino-Romanian intelligence centre in the West. To which Hua had replied: "You may not believe me, but we do not have any spies in the West, although we do have a great many patriots."

This was the usual double language of Chinese phraseology. Hua knew perfectly well that the situation was soon going to change drastically. Furthermore, it was clear that he was joking when, during his visit to Bucharest that August, accompanied by Qiao Shi, he had offered the Romanians the latest system for developing photos—conceived by Kodak and copied by Chinese intelligence—in order to save the Romanians from having to buy the licence.[38]

In November 1989, after a gruelling year, Qiao Shi met up with his Romanian friends again. The trip went well, with Ceauşescu calling on the Chinese leadership to promote a new summit of communist countries. The events in Tiananmen and the fall of the Berlin Wall had shaken the Romanian dictator. Chinese analysts continued to believe that the situation in Romania was stable—but hardly had Qiao Shi arrived back in Beijing before the situation began to deteriorate, to such an extent that a Romanian Securitate unit came to Beijing to beg Qiao to help save the Romanian regime and draw up an escape plan for Ceauşescu and his wife.

It was too late: in December the revolution broke out, and Nicolae and Helena Ceauşescu were executed after a show trial. This was yet another humiliation for the PRC's leaders, in a year that ended as badly as it had started—particularly after they discovered that the

Romanian revolution had not been triggered by dissidents in the West, but by Mikhail Gorbachev's intelligence services. In Beijing, the KGB *rezident* Ivan Vladimirovich Grigorov would continue to taunt them.[39]

6

OPERATION AUTUMN ORCHID, HONG KONG

"Mr Xu had a heart attack out of the blue while we were making love. He died in my arms."

"You are lying to us, Madame Liu! The autopsy has shown that sexual intercourse did not occur!"

This extraordinary exchange took place in the Tokyo police headquarters, between detectives from the crime squad and a 38-year-old Chinese woman, who insisted she was cheating on her Japanese husband and was in an adulterous relationship with her Chinese lover.

Initially, circumstances seemed to confirm her words. But in fact things were not quite what they seemed. In March 1991, detectives discovered the corpse of Xu Yuanhai in a love hotel in Tokyo's red light district: Kabukicho, a neighbourhood of nightclubs, sex shops, "soaplands" (Japanese bath-house brothels), and the slot machine industry that is fought over, with American punches and the honed blades of sashimi knives, by Japanese Yakuza gangsters and Chinese bandits.

"That's right! Undercover agents would arrange rendez-vous in the dodgy neighbourhood of Shinjuku, deep in the mysteries of the floating world," laughed Kodama Michinao. It was 1996, and we were at the small Kabukicho bar where he used to meet CIA agents and Taiwanese spooks during the Cold War.[1]

With his razor-sharp moustache, Kodama-san was the spitting image of Mitsuhirato in *The Blue Lotus*, and indeed, before he became president of the Association of Private Detectives, he had been a

Japanese secret agent in Shanghai. With the spy and Manchu princess Yoshiko Kawashima, future tutor of the last emperor Pu Yi, he had taken part in the famous Shanghai Incident of 18 January 1932; in a dark, deserted alley, five Japanese monks were attacked. The beating was imputed to Chinese foot soldiers and used to justify the invasion of the city by 70,000 Japanese troops. It was the plot of *The Blue Lotus*, except that the Operation was codenamed Golden Lily.

During the Cold War, Kodama diligently trailed Chinese communist spies. "They were everywhere!" he told me. Only a few blocks away from the dive bar where we were sitting was the spot where Xu the spy had died in Madame Liu's arms five years earlier.

While the *mama-san*, the matriarch who ran the bar, served us another shot of whisky from Kodama's personal bottle, he told me the tragic saga of a Chinese man who had fallen deeply in love. His tale was embellished with multiple details from reliable sources that I was subsequently able to cross-check, point by point. For 4,000 yen, Xu had rented a small studio in the love hotel for a few hours, to engage in a bout of phoenix and dragon. Given the housing crisis and the small size of Tokyo apartments, it is common for married couples to use love hotels to have some intimate time together, away from the rest of the family.

Naturally, I am summarizing. After the autopsy, the background of 58-year-old Xu Yuanhai, director of the Sino-Japanese Friendship Association, left investigators with some serious reservations about Madame Liu's version of events—the pillow talk on this particular futon seemed to have been of a particular flavour: the spice of an espionage case. Xu had been an advisor to the Chinese embassy in Tokyo since 1986. According to Japanese experts, his title there, head of general affairs, loosely disguised his actual role as station chief for the Guoanbu, the ministry of state security responsible for foreign espionage, run since 1985 by Jia Chunwang.

Attached in turn to diplomatic missions in Pyongyang, Hanoi and Hong Kong, before being posted to Japan, Xu was one of the operatives who had been deployed by the Guoanbu in concentric circles all over Asia since its creation. In North Korea, these Guoanbu spies both supported and spied on the dying dictator Kim Il-sung, as they drew up plans for a palace coup. In Vietnam, they patched things up with the new generation of leaders while closely studying the capitalist effervescence filling the streets of Ho Chi Minh City. In Hong Kong, they prepared for the handover of the British colony, while maintaining it as a platform for a planned economic conquest.

By 1991, the year of his death, Xu Yuanhai had become an important roving emissary. In this role he was responsible for the student sector, charged with recruiting agents from among Chinese students on his frequent visits to Japan. Some honed their skills as spies by grassing on their comrades; two years after the Tiananmen tragedy, anyone disseminating dissident ideas was kept under close surveillance. In Japan, as in France and the United States, the Chinese embassy's education department played a key role in this area.

The Guoanbu's mission in Japan, as in other countries, was to put pressure on the local branch of the Federation for a Democratic China. In Shanghai, Ding Shenglie, head of the local Guoanbu station, arrested a Japanese foreign student called Yoshizaki Masami. Terrified at being threatened with imprisonment, he agreed to spy on Chinese dissidents upon his return to Japan. At the end of 1990, Chinese "diplomats" in Tokyo even managed to force the Japanese government to expel some of the Chinese students. They knew that the Japanese had more of a taste for commercial entente cordiale than for human rights, a Western concept whose appeal was in decline. Yang Zhongmei—one of the most high-profile Tiananmen dissidents in Japan—recalled a young student recruited by Xu who committed suicide under mysterious circumstances in November 1991.

The beautiful Madame Liu's background was no less murky. The wife of a Japanese travel agent, she had arrived in Japan only a year before Xu's death. According to the Hong Kong weekly *Far Eastern Economic Review*, she had previously worked in Beijing for the 3S research group, a specialist branch of the CCP founded in 1984.[2] "3S" stood for (Agnes) Smedley, (Edgar) Snow and (Anna-Louise) Strong, the trio of American journalists who had been close to Mao, and who had become heroes of the PRC—despite Stalin's suspicions that Strong and Snow were CIA agents.[3]

The 3S research group was set up to combat the negative image of the PRC in some foreign media. Madame Liu joined it after a stint working with the former foreign minister, Huang Hua. As a young man, Huang had been Edgar Snow's interpreter, and helped him write his bestselling book *Red Star Over China*. Huang also worked for the Social Affairs Department (*Zhongshebu*) and the Xinhua News Agency. Later, he succeeded his mentor Zhou Enlai as foreign minister. Even in China, the world of the elite is small: Zhou's widow, Deng Yingchao ("Abundant Brightness"), was honorary president of the 3S when Huang was president. From January 1992, Hua was also president of the Chinese Association for International Friendly Contact (*Zhongguo Guoji Youhao Lianluo Hui*), a front for military intelligence. The circle was complete.

Madame Liu was not just any Chinese woman looking for a good catch when she arrived in Japan in 1990. She was ostensibly there to galvanize support for a new organization, the Research Association for International Friendship. But Japanese counterintelligence learned that this was a cover, as was her speedy marriage to a Japanese citizen from the prefecture of Chiba, which usefully gave her Japanese nationality.

What with all the "covers" piled up on him in the Shinjuku love hotel, Xu Huanhai probably needed air. He did not survive the heart attack he had following a hearty lunch at the Japanese Foreign Correspondents' Club with a Japanese journalist and Madame Liu. When they looked a little closer, investigators were unable to exclude the possibility that the pair of spies had been in the habit of polishing off their lunch meetings with a little post-prandial tangle between the sheets. On this occasion, though, they probably hadn't had time.

Be that as it may, Zhong Jingeng, Xu's successor at the embassy, imposed a blackout on the case and hung some of the spy networks out to dry. Unfortunately for Beijing, the case revealed to Japanese counterintelligence several elements of its own strategic intelligence.[4] Firstly, Tokyo learned that the Chinese special services had launched a vast offensive of concentric-circle dissemination in Asia, and that Japan was one of the favoured targets. Secondly, this tragedy revealed the growing use of party organizations, such as the United Front Work Department and friendship associations, as fronts for intelligence operations.

The use of these organizations as fronts—at the behest of Qiao Shi, head of the CCP's security sector—was part of a charm offensive whose purpose was not only to enable China to improve its image in the early 1990s, but also to further advance its position on the world stage by accelerating its economic development. One aspect of Xu's spy career, analyzed by Japanese counterintelligence, was his work for several years at the Xinhua News Agency. This confirmed that the press agency was being used, in the absence of an embassy in Hong Kong, as a cover for Beijing special agents, who were becoming more numerous and more active in the British colony as the hour of the handover, planned for the summer of 1997, approached.

Deng Xiaoping: take Hong Kong and die

In late 1989, in the wake of the Tiananmen massacre, Deng Xiaoping—undoubtedly shocked by the events of 4 June—organized a meeting with his loyal inner circle: President Yang Shangkun, Qiao Shi, and the new general secretary Jiang Zemin. The student massacre had triggered a deep and concrete animosity towards China across the entire globe, with an embargo on the sale of arms and sensitive technologies to the PRC. Moreover, the communist countries of Eastern Europe were tumbling, one after the other, like a ship of fools. China, now a forsaken junk, was feeling more and more isolated, beyond its few friends like Burma and North Korea.

With a hesitant brush, the father of the revolution laid down on a piece of rice paper a sort of last will and testament, in the form of six fundamental precepts. These twenty-four Chinese characters would allow communist China to bounce back:

– Observe calmly and analyze coolly. *Leng jing guan cha* 冷静观察
– Confirm (our own) positions. *Wenzhu zhen jiao* 稳住阵脚
– Deal with changes with confidence. *Chen zhe ying fu* 沉着应付
– Conceal our real abilities. *Tao guang yang hui* 韬光养晦
– Make contributions. *You suo zuo wei* 有所作为
– Never become the leader. *Jue bu dang tou* 决不当头

These precepts were addressed to the CCP and its individual bodies, as well as to state-owned enterprises (and the growing private sector that relied on them), strategic institutes, research and development centres, and civil and military intelligence services.

They were the precise opposite of the exuberant principles of Marxism-Leninism that had led to disastrous famines and massacres under Mao, but which had also managed to preserve the supremacy of the party in all decision-making, even when it came to economic choices. Deng's six precepts made implicit reference to the great classics of concealment and manipulation found in Chapter 13 of Sun

Tzu's *The Art of War* and in *The 36 Stratagems*, another ancient text that had influenced the art of clandestine warfare and secret diplomacy through the centuries, given a new lease of life by the modern secret services of the PRC.

One of Deng's main objectives in setting forth these principles was to ensure that the handover of Hong Kong took place in the best possible conditions, by obscuring the memory of the Tiananmen crackdown and taking the opportunity to try and seduce Taiwanese public opinion. By 1989, Hong Kong was almost halfway to the handover deadline, the agreement with the British having been signed five years earlier.

There had been a tremendous sense of justice and relief on that occasion. On 26 September 1984 in Beijing, Ambassador Sir Richard Evans and China's deputy foreign minister Zhou Nan had signed a three-page text putting an end to the humiliation of the 1842 Nanking Treaty that had ceded the Perfumed Harbour to the British. "It is my dearest wish to live until the handing back of Hong Kong. After that I will be able to take a well-deserved retirement," Deng once said to the British foreign minister Sir Geoffrey Howe.

Not only had Deng insisted on the principle of supporting reunification with Hong Kong—"one country, two systems"—but he had also emphasized the reassuring signs of openness at that time: "We must allow a small dose of capitalism in China to help socialist development," he had said. Throughout 1984 and beyond, he had lavished a pampering welcome on visitors from Hong Kong.

The most notable example was that of the wealthy ship-owner, Sir Yue-Kong Pao, who had fled the communists in 1949. He was invited to Beijing and received as a brother by Deng, who sent his disabled son, Deng Pufang, to reassure the people of Hong Kong of his good intentions. The young Pufang, such a visible victim of the Cultural Revolution, was the living symbol of what the Chinese and the Hong Kong population shared: a longing to forget the lethal follies of the political maelstrom triggered by Mao twenty years earlier.

Was Deng being sincere, or was he simply a good tactician? This was, after all, the same man who had once said, "It doesn't matter if a cat is grey or black, as long as it catches mice." He was also the man who sent in the savage infantrymen of the 27th Corps to attack the students in Tiananmen Square. We can get closer to the bottom of

Deng Xiaoping's rule (1989–97) if we look at this era's formidable mechanisms of clandestine activity, particularly in the region of Hong Kong, whose triumphant reclaim by the PRC in 1997, just months after Deng's death, marked the opening of a new, ambitious era in Chinese global espionage.

Hong Kong: nest of spies

The principles of "keeping a low profile" and "concealing your true abilities" had first been set in motion by the communist and other secret services half a century earlier, in the wake of the communist victory. British Special Branch was first set up in 1933 as an anti-communist squad within the Criminal Investigation Department of the then Hong Kong police, in charge of the anti-communist struggle. In 1949, alongside MI5 and under the direction of Peter Erwin, it developed into a political police force, charged with fighting Chinese communists.[5] London realized that Mao, now in Beijing, had given up the idea of sending the PLA to invade Hong Kong when Marshal Lin Biao and his troops stopped 20 kilometres short of the Perfumed Harbour, red flag flying proudly in the breeze, weapons in hand. The British colony would be useful as an interface with the capitalist world, the CCP had decided. Similarly, Macao was allowed to remain a Portuguese colony, a gambling empire and huge den of money laundering, with integrated banking circuits for the benefit of special operations.

Thus the return of Hong Kong to the mother country was postponed. This did not mean that the Chinese stopped trying to provoke incidents to weaken the colonizers' hold on the region and their "imperialist subversion". This was a typical Cold War tactic: on both sides of the Bamboo Curtain, the subversive element was always the "Other".

The British did not take their eyes off the people they believed might be fomenting revolution in Hong Kong. In 1950, according to a Special Branch document that I was able to consult, the CCP established intelligence posts in Canton to work in Hong Kong and Macao, in liaison with the Xinhua News Agency headed by Hu Qiaomu. This operation served both as the regional department of the Gonganbu service created by Li Ru, an intelligence expert trained in the USSR, and as an international intelligence office linked to Shing Sheung Tat's Social Affairs Department (SAD).[6]

Before the communist victory, it had been the other way around: intelligence surveillance of Canton was organized out of Hong Kong, by Zhou Enlai's friends, Gong Peng and her husband Qiao Guangua, again under cover of working for Xinhua. Their leader, and the founder of the news agency, Liao Chengzhi—"Liao the sailor man"—played an important role in the secret battle for Hong Kong during this period.

In the 1950s, the situation was tense. Special Branch investigators reported that the Chinese communist police officer Lo Au Fung was planning the assassination of police officers in the New Territories—Hong Kong's largest region, alongside the smaller regions of Kowloon Peninsula and Hong Kong Island. Border incidents were also being triggered. Investigators seized confidential documents from the CCP. These were "secret guidelines for local CCP members" with instructions on "what actions to follow in the event of deteriorating relations between Hong Kong and Beijing". The main points were:

a) The organization of party cells must be tightened. Party members working in British government departments must prevent the destruction of archives and equipment in the event of war.
b) All party contacts must be changed and cadres must go underground.
c) Efforts must be made to provoke anti-American feelings.
d) A campaign is to be launched to encourage young men to return to China and join the armed forces. Chinese people living overseas with university degrees should be encouraged to return to the homeland.
e) Families of party members must be sent home to China.
f) Party members must refrain from visiting bookstores, reading newspapers or party literature in public, and attending open meetings.

The directives also dictated the course of action for awakening dormant networks, which were to be renewed continually up to the 1997 handover and beyond.

Similar instructions were given to underground militants when riots erupted in the colony in 1967. In April that year, the Cultural Revolution spread to Hong Kong; unions organized strikes to protest the conditions of workers in the Kowloon Chinese quarter on the peninsula. It began on 28 April with strikes at two artificial flower factories. The crackdown was brutal. Hundreds of workers were arrested by the police, triggering riots. In Beijing, the British embassy was set on fire. The head of Special Branch, Sir John Prendergast, who had worked for British intelligence in Kenya, Cyprus and Yemen, reported back to London that the two epicentres of the rioters were the import-export company China Resources (*Huaren Jituan*), which hosted Chinese intelligence spies, and the Xinhua News Agency in Sharp Street, which seemed to be the hub of underground diplomacy in Hong Kong, a kind of alternative Chinese embassy. Meanwhile, one of the journalists, Xue Bing, was arrested on 11 July, and in the words of the magazine *Beijing Information*, "not even taking into account the Chinese protests, the fascist British authorities in Hong Kong sentenced Xue Bing the following day". Zeng Zhaoke, who taught at the police academy in Hong Kong, was expelled for spying. Based in Canton, for the next twenty years he continued his surveillance work and advised Deng Xiaoping.

To complicate matters further, all over Hong Kong, conflicts were breaking out between different communist factions in the region, which thousands of Chinese people fleeing the Cultural Revolution had reached by swimming across the Pearl River Delta. These refugees were an important source of intelligence for the CIA, for Australian China-watchers, for the extraordinary Jesuits who produced the newsletter *China News Analysis* (CNA), founded by Hungarian priest Father László Ladány, and for British China experts, including Professor Ride, who was married to the cousin of Alexandre de Marenches, head of the French secret services, the SDECE. The French had two legendary officers in Hong Kong, vice-consul Roger Aimé and his wife Suzy, who ran the SDECE station in Beijing.[7]

"The biggest obstacle, though, in intelligence gathering remained the restrictions that the British Special Branch had placed on CIA activities in the 1950s, including the prohibition on recruiting agents inside communist organizations in Hong Kong," recalled James Lilley, who worked in Hong Kong before becoming the CIA's first station chief in Beijing.

"Contact with employees of Chinese communist-front organizations based in Hong Kong, such as the Bank of China, China Travel

Services, China Resources Company, and the New China News Agency—the organizations that outwardly handled the mainland's investment, tourism, trade, and propaganda, respectively, but that were also intelligence fronts—were off-limits.

"So, while China was reeling from the early stages of the Cultural Revolution, the CIA contingent in Hong Kong's downtown Central district had to content itself mainly with refugees fleeing domestic battles in China's major cities."[8]

Lilley remains discreet about the special operations conducted by the British, Americans and Taiwanese to deepen the divisions and settling of scores between rival factions of the Red Guards and CCP leaders. This was particularly an issue in southern regions such as Canton, where foreign special services sent out weather balloons packed with anti-Maoist leaflets. They also set up fake trade unions and political organizations to intensify the discord. Psychological warfare reached its height when the black radio stations—fake radio stations that people believed to be broadcasting from inside China—began to spread damaging rumours about PRC leaders.

The cherry on the cake was the production of a fake little red book, entitled *Thoughts of President Liu Shaoqi*, published in Hong Kong and circulated on the other side of the Bamboo Curtain to counter the influence of Mao's original *Little Red Book*, which had been produced by the spymaster Kang Sheng and Mao's private secretary, Chen Boda.[9]

This fictitious book by the so-called Chinese Khrushchev had a double purpose: to widen the gulf between the pro-Liu faction and the pro-Mao faction, and—in the event that Chinese security discovered the document had been printed and distributed at the instigation of the CIA and MI6—to hint at evidence of a conspiracy by the "imperialist secret services" in support of the deposed president Liu, and thus cultivate an atmosphere of paranoia. It is unclear whether this misinformation really did have the effect of intensifying the massacres desired by Mao and Kang Sheng. But one thing was clear: the Americans had a tendency to be influenced by their own propaganda. The CIA's China archives, declassified in 2007, show that some analysts were absolutely convinced that Wang Guangmei, Liu's wife, was an American spy, as per Kang Sheng's accusation.

OPERATION AUTUMN ORCHID, HONG KONG

The British SCOPG versus the democrats

In the 1970s, after the mysterious death of Marshal Lin Biao, tensions relaxed somewhat. The British reinforced their security apparatus, but also developed a new approach towards the Chinese in tune with Richard Nixon's thaw. Beijing and London renewed diplomatic relations. In 1971, John Addis was the first British ambassador appointed to China since the Cultural Revolution. He was later replaced by Edward Youde, a former Beijing-based MI6 secret agent and case officer of the French journalist and British agent Jean Pasqualini—the British were just as happy as the Chinese to appoint former spies as ambassadors. Youde had not even really cut his ties with the espionage world: in 1980 he was named Margaret Thatcher's intelligence coordinator. She also appointed him the last governor of Hong Kong, but he died before he could take up the post.

Meanwhile, in 1974, Maurice Oldfield, director-general of MI6, who had once led anti-communist operations in Singapore, sent a new representative, John Longrigg, to establish links with the head of the Diaochabu's Hong Kong office. This was the deputy director of the Xinhua News Agency, Li Jusheng. Longrigg's renewed MI6 station was then under cover of the anodyne-sounding British Forces Headquarters Study Group.

The strengthening of intelligence operations in Hong Kong in this period was no longer aimed at combatting the CCP, but rather at establishing a massive surveillance operation of the Hong Kong population, especially those who were considered a potential risk to the now good relationship between London and Beijing. This included the criminal Triad organizations—including the most famous, the Sun Yee On, which was sometimes manipulated by Beijing—and political opponents of the future handover. If this surveillance of the masses is surprising to readers, it is important to remember that the British system of administration in Hong Kong bore no relation to the democratic system of government in the United Kingdom itself. Along with Northern Ireland, Hong Kong was one of Britain's last foreign settlements, and the British Empire had never disseminated civil liberties in these spheres of influence—although it did leave behind a legal and constitutional system that would obstruct Beijing after the handover in 1997.

In the 1970s and 1980s, a network for monitoring and spying on the civilian population had been set up called the Local Intelligence Committee. It included the Hong Kong governor's political advisor, a Foreign Office official; the head of Special Branch (John Thorpe, who helped save Tiananmen dissidents, as seen in Chapter 5); Longrigg, the MI6 station head; a representative from MI5; the local director of the British communications interception service (GCHQ) and its antenna, the Composite Signals Organisation Station (run from Little Sai Wan with the Australians); and the head of the Joint Services Intelligence Staff.[10]

This system, just as Orwellian as the PRC's surveillance machine, also had a body specialized in the surveillance of citizens who wanted to democratize Hong Kong, called the Standing Committee on Pressure Groups, or the SCOPG—an innocent acronym that, as in all oppressive systems, hides a nastier reality. Its head, Barrie Wiggham, was assisted by another psy-ops specialist, Lieutenant-Colonel Johnny Johnstone, who had formerly been in charge of psychological warfare in Northern Ireland—that other large British testing ground for population control.[11]

In theory, the SCOPG could have monitored groups like the Triads, who were very powerful in the colony. In fact it was the unions, environmental groups and political organizations advocating independence for Hong Kong who were in the sights of this secret committee: the Christian industrial committee, the professional teachers' union, the environmental protection committee, newly formed political parties, and so on. Their mail was opened, their phone lines tapped, undercover agents infiltrated their organizations, and moles were recruited from within. Both British and Chinese-born individuals were targeted.

Take, for example, the activists of the Revolutionary Marxist League, a small group linked to Trotsky's Fourth International, founded in 1975 in Kowloon. Its young Chinese members were Marxists, but in the tradition of CCP founder Chen Duxiu, who was loathed in Beijing because he had gone over to Trotsky's camp in the 1920s. To the British government they were subversive communists, and to Beijing they were dangerous agitators—they were, in other words, dissidents against both regimes. On 22 April 1976, they occupied the premises of the Xinhua News Agency to show their support for demonstrators in Tiananmen Square, and their solidarity with jailed dissidents. The British authorities accused them of unlawful assembly and sentenced them to three months in prison. For the same offence in the PRC, they could well have been executed, but this form of British democracy certainly left something to be desired. One could even say that it foreshadowed the authoritarianism of the Tiananmen crackdown to come, in eleven years' time.

Britain's harshest critics say that it betrayed Hong Kong twice. Firstly, by failing to institute democracy as the people of Hong Kong might have hoped for, and secondly by offering the whole colony to Beijing on a silver platter in 1997, despite the fact that, according to international treaties, the PRC should only have been able to obtain the mainland "New Territories", not Hong Kong Island itself or even the Kowloon Peninsula. London did not seem too concerned with respect to the rights of the Hong Kong population after the handover.

In November 1996, I went to see for myself how preparations for the handover were advancing.[12] It was enough just to see the huge Bank of China tower, built by Ieoh Ming Pei, architect of the Louvre Pyramid. Its majesty crushes the small parliament building below, the Victorian-era Legislative Council on which democratically elected MPs had only been sitting for the last few years. Democracy had been brought to Hong Kong only at the last moment, thanks to the last governor, Christopher Patten—it came too late, though Patten had done what he could in the face of the Chinese secret services' campaigns against him.

I went to visit Emily Lau in the parliament building, the Hong Kong democrat boasting the strongest mandate, who, during those last months of freedom in the lead up to 20 June 1997, would travel around the world to persuade both influential political figures and the general public of what was at stake: "This is a matter of life or death for Hong Kong," she would say. "We cannot separate economic interests from fundamental freedoms."

Operation Autumn Orchid

The next day, I found myself in the elevator of the Central Plaza Tower, one of Hong Kong's tallest buildings (after the Bank of China), going up to the sixty-ninth floor. The place was full of people visiting the offices of various Chinese, European and Japanese companies. To get to the floor I wanted, or any floor higher than the sixty-ninth, I had to find another elevator on this floor.

When the elevator doors opened, it looked as though the tower was only half built. Up here there were no plaques engraved with the names of companies. There were cardboard boxes and miles of brown paper everywhere. The paint on the walls was not dry. I saw a guard in a sand-coloured uniform fast asleep on one side of the hallway. I tiptoed past in the opposite direction to avoid being caught on CCTV, though there must have been many other cameras that I didn't spot. I hurried on, trying to memorize as many details as possible—the clatter of telexes, computer screens. But I did not have time to see much. A guard shouted out to me in a mixture of broken English, Cantonese and Mandarin:

"Forbidden to be here. Just here offices!"

"Indeed," I answered. "It is these offices I have come to see." I asked if it was possible to see a manager.

"Impossible, there is nobody. Offices empty."

The angry guard was sweating under his black cap. He grabbed his walkie-talkie and yelled something into it; I realized that he was calling for back-up. The doors of the elevator were closing. I hurried back down while the security men were making their way up.

An informant had tipped me off: on these floors of the Central Plaza, a central eavesdropping apparatus had been installed by the Chinese special services and the PLA, where they were using scanners to intercept cell phones and emails—exciting new technologies back in late 1996!—as well as telexes and faxes. In every building on Hong Kong Island, companies were serving as fronts for fallow secret service organizations. Six months before the handover to China, the structures that were being set up to take over the controls were right there in front of my eyes.

The CCP in Hong Kong, which was of course underground, oversaw a whole web of organizations: the familiar United Front Work Department, tasked with rallying undecided or hostile Chinese to the motherland's objectives; the Hong Kong and Macao Affairs Office of the PRC's State Council; the Xinhua News Agency and its Hong

Kong Macao Working Group, which rivalled that Office; the military intelligence service, the PLA2 or later the PLA3 (I had seen one of their devices in Central Plaza for intercepting communications from businesses and the British Army); the Gonganbu, which had infiltrated the former Royal Hong Kong Police Force; the CCP's ghostly investigations department, the Diaochabu; and, last but not least, the Guoanbu. No less than three Guoanbu Central Offices, the First, Second and Third—led respectively by He Liang, Zhan Yongjie and Guo Dakai—were running various intelligence operations in Hong Kong and Macao, assisted by some sixty officials based in Beijing and Guangzhou. The Guoanbu's regional office (*guoanju*) in Guangzhou was headed by a prominent executive, Shen Hongying, who had organized a large exhibition in Shenzhen at the end of 1995 to which foreigners were invited, showcasing the Chinese technologies used by the PRC's security services.[13]

In December 1994, a rather more discreet ceremony had been held, typical of Chinese intelligence: a presentation of awards, and both collective and individual recognition for services rendered in the secret war. Overseen by Qiao Shi, the ceremony decorated leaders of Operation Autumn Orchid (*Qiu Lanhua*), whose given mission over the course of the previous decade had been to oversee the recovery of the two colonies: Hong Kong in 1997, and Macao in 1999. Autumn Orchid's agents had infiltrated all levels of Hong Kong society with various goals, which were all deemed to have been achieved.

The substance of the mission had been to establish files on all the colony's officials, covering the extent of their allegiance, neutrality or hostility towards Beijing; to spy on foreign political and economic organizations based in Hong Kong; to identify journalists' sources around sensitive subjects; and to infiltrate the media, in order to disseminate information favourable to the CCP.

To this end, popular Chinese enterprises in Hong Kong, such as China Resources (*Huaren Jituan*), the Bank of China and the Steam Navigation Company, were brought in, and social organizations were also used. For example, Yeung Kwong, the general secretary of the HKFTU union, with 170,000 members, was both a delegate to the National People's Congress and a member of the Hong Kong Macao Working Committee (HMWC), run by the Xinhua News Agency.

Unfortunately for Qiao Shi, all these intertwined relationships and covers had ended up being revealed in April 1991, when Xu Jiatun, the head of Xinhua, defected. Unable to accept the Tiananmen crackdown in 1989—and the fact that his friend, the CCP general secretary Zhao Ziyang, had been placed under house arrest—Xu had been contemplating this decision for a long time.

As the deadline for the June 1997 handover approached, it was becoming increasingly obvious that many of Xinhua's deputy directors were also high-ranking intelligence officers working for State Security—the Guoanbu. An integral part of Operation Autumn Orchid, they were codenamed the Chrysanthemum Group (*Luhua Xiaozu*).

A few months after the handover, various Guoanbu services had expanded their presence within the Xinhua agency, under the supervision of its deputy director. There was the coordination department, headed by Zou Zhekai; the research bureau, headed by Yang Huaji; the sports and culture service; and of course the Social Affairs Department, whose name recalled the communist secret service in the era of Kang Sheng. The Chrysanthemum Group was overseen by the Xinhua security section, which was based near a Happy Valley racecourse where the head of the Guoanbu worked.

Other Xinhua functionaries were engaged in outright political espionage. For example, Shen Zaiwang, head of Xinhua's International Affairs Division, was an expert in intelligence regarding the Japanese community in Hong Kong. He had studied Japanese at Beida (Beijing University) and had lived for a period in Japan, as confirmed to me by a Japanese journalist, who had him constantly on his tail.

Rebound base for economic espionage

The extensive work of compiling digital files, coordinated by the deputy directors of Xinhua, had major implications for the world of finance and commerce. The Guoanbu used genuine Hong Kong companies to send industrial spies overseas to gather intelligence on the West; several of these have been identified by counterintelligence services in France, the United Kingdom and the United States. These Western services complained that economic decision-makers in the West had been insufficiently on guard against the trainees they were taking on from Hong Kong, even going so far as to suggest that they were hoping, through them, to gain a foothold in the Greater China market. One major advantage for the operation was that, after 1997, these very special trainees would be able to return from the West, Japan, or South-East Asia to settle in Hong Kong, with the perfect cover of seeming democrats who had worked for capitalist enterprises.

Many long-established private companies also represented the interests of the various political factions of the CCP, as well as covering sector-specific intelligence missions. Nicholas Eftimiades, a former US officer in the Defense Intelligence Agency, cites a specific example in his book *Chinese Intelligence Operations*: China Resources, which provided a cover for military intelligence operations in Hong Kong although it was theoretically part of the Ministry of Economy.[14] I have visited the company, which is based in Wanchai. It had so many different businesses under its umbrella that it was exceedingly difficult to disentangle the wheat from the chaff. At the time, Western and Japanese security services were particularly interested in the Investigations Department, headed by Xin Changjiang, and its many subsidiaries dealing with the growing role of communications in the new globalized context, intensified by a tremendous surge in information technology.

Apart from the Guoanbu, the other major intelligence structure—with which it sometimes collaborated—was the military intelligence wing, the PLA2. As part of the preparations for taking over Hong Kong, the PLA's special services set up ad hoc departments ten years before the transfer of sovereignty. Significantly, the head of this military intelligence department, General Ji Shengde, was none other than the son of Ji Pengfei, a former foreign minister who had been appointed in 1983 to head the Hong Kong and Macau Affairs Office of the State Council. Family dynasties were a major element of the Chinese strategy for taking over Hong Kong.

The local PLA2 leader at the time of the transition, General Zhou Borong, had had solid Western training. Formerly a British naval attaché, he was named deputy chief of staff—in other words, head of military intelligence—as soon as the 42nd Corps of the PLA marched into Hong Kong.

The Guangzhou division of the 42nd Corps centralized the information coming in from businesses such as China Resources, which would systematically have at least one deputy director from military intelligence. One of this deputy director's duties was to ensure that no remnants of the British Army remained undercover in the former colony after the handover. Former Gurkhas were particularly targeted. Originally from Nepal, these ex-soldiers often served as bodyguards to Hong Kong tycoons. Arms deals were also monitored.

Some of the PLA2 underground units also served to protect the garrison that housed the 6,000 men of the 42nd Corps, and ensured that its soldiers did not engage in black market or criminal activity with the Triads. Military security went over the entire Prince of Wales barracks with a fine tooth comb to verify that the British, who had been headquartered there before the transfer to the PLA—had not bugged it before leaving. (This was an entirely justified suspicion.) Finally, the PLA was also using its Liaison Office, part of the Political Department, to duplicate the PLA2's clandestine operations in Hong Kong.

In addition to the different CCP and State Council (undercover military intelligence) structures, the colony also hosted certain key people whose intelligence experience now served them as political strategists. The most important was a close friend of Qiao Shi, the godfather of the Beijing secret service. His name was Li Chuwen, and he was going to carry out the most important operation of all: lifting up the new, Chinese head of the Hong Kong executive, after the departure of the British.

"Mister Li" and the Hong Kong tycoon

On 20 December 1984, the British prime minister Margaret Thatcher, accompanied by her foreign secretary, Sir Geoffrey Howe, landed in Hong Kong. This was a visit of huge significance, for immediately after their visit to Hong Kong they were going to Beijing to sign the accord agreeing to hand over the colony to the PRC. Upon their arrival in Hong Kong, they were welcomed by the British governor and a Chinese man with a triumphant smile on his lips who spoke excellent English. Unlike the other Chinese officials present, dressed in their

Mao-collared tunics, this man wore a tweed suit and a tie. He was the deputy director of the Xinhua news agency, Li Chuwen.

Li had long been known as the Zhou Enlai of Hong Kong, in reference to his previous diplomatic work. He could simply, like his predecessor Li Jusheng, have coordinated the intelligence services at the heart of Xinhua. But he had higher ambitions, whose origins can be traced in his unusual background.

"He started off life as a clergyman in Shanghai. He abandoned the religious life and became a communist power behind the throne," I was told in 1986, by an analyst working for British intelligence in Hong Kong. Flicking through file cards filled with information scrawled in a myriad of Chinese characters, my source removed his glasses and paused for a moment before saying, with a sly little smile: "Unless, of course, he started out as a secret communist, charged with infiltrating the Shanghai church. It was one of the functions of the CCP's United Front Work Department to send undercover agents into churches, to turn priests and recruit religious agents, who would be sent away from China to gather intelligence for Beijing, while claiming that they were being persecuted by the Reds. Whatever the case was here, Li Chuwen played a major role in Hong Kong."

Li, like Qiao Shi, was born in Zhejiang province, and like him he had studied at St John's University in Shanghai. It is quite possible that they knew each other there. It was Qiao Shi who had recruited the young Jiang Zemin into the underground CCP. In the 1990s, Li became one of Jiang's closest Shanghai-based advisors; but forty years earlier, he had studied in the United States, graduating with a degree from Yale.

After university, he became secretary of the Chinese section of the YMCA, which had been set up in Shanghai in 1904 by businessman Charlie Soong. Its premises hosted meetings of Sun Yat-sen's revolutionary party, and thirty years later one of Soong's daughters, Chiang Kai-shek's wife Soong May-ling, drew the movement into the Kuomintang's orbit after founding the "Movement for a New Life", an outgrowth of the fascist blue-shirt movement. Madame Chiang's movement rallied its members from youth groups and Christian circles, including the YMCA, to support Kuomintang nationalism.

A few months prior to the communist victory in 1949, Wu Yao-tsung, the YMCA propaganda officer in Shanghai, expressed his support for communism in the press. In fact Wu was a long-time Marxist, only pretending to have recently discovered the benefits of communism. He called for the YMCA and its sister organization the YWCA to "join the struggle of the new China under the banner of the New Democracy". While various religious denominations, both Christian and Muslim, were persecuted by General Luo Ruiqing's Gonganbu, Wu Yao-tsung encouraged Protestant circles to back the new Mao regime as part of the "Patriotic Church" movement. This was another example of a successful "united work front", like so many in the history of Chinese communism.

Needless to say, the communist special services recognized the advantages in a structure with Western origins, like the YMCA, claiming both independence from the "imperialist system" and autonomy from the CCP. When the Korean War broke out in 1950, Wu Yao-tsung, representing the "Protestant Patriots", coined the slogan "Support for Korea, Resistance against America". Later he went to Europe to participate in a World Congress for Peace, organized by the USSR and the PRC. In 1954, under the auspices of the CCP's Office of Religious Affairs, he was named president of the National Committee of the Three-Self Patriotic Movement of the Protestant Churches. Li Chuwen was moving in the same circles during this period. In those years, the Protestant pastor was sitting on the YMCA world committee in Geneva, and later, in the 1960s, he became vice-president of the Chinese Peace Committee.

Over the next decade, Li reinforced his position as a shadow diplomat, or, more accurately, as a strategic guardian of Shanghai's foreign policy. He was responsible for foreign relations on the municipal revolutionary committee and represented the Huangpu metropolis in the National People's Congress. He then went to Hong Kong, where he became deputy director of the Xinhua News Agency, a post that served as cover for his secret job as a political intelligence coordinator. This is a good example, often overlooked by observers, of activities of a regional intelligence service abroad, in this case in Shanghai, being transferred to Hong Kong, a sister city and economic rival.

With his English gentleman's suits, his well-travelled open-mindedness and his language skills, Li Chuwen always stood out alongside the usual glum-looking party officials. He was fluent in English and French, but his Cantonese was poor, because of his Shanghai origins. Emily Lau, the future democratic deputy, told me that when she was still a reporter for the *Far Eastern Economic Review*, Li had given her lessons in Mandarin Chinese, the Beijing lingua franca. Other sources report his good relationship with the US consul, John Gilhooley, who was head of the CIA in Hong Kong in the 1980s.

As the great turning point of the handover dawned, Li had built up many powerful positions as an *éminence grise*: he was foreign affairs advisor for the Shanghai Municipal Government and honorary president of the Shanghai Institutes for International Studies (SIIS). The latter, founded in 1960, was officially connected to the Ministry of Foreign Affairs in Beijing, but in reality forged Shanghai's international policies independently, from its base in an old, elegant house in the former French Concession.

Li had more than one trick up his sleeve. He was also interested in economic affairs, as was obvious during the Shanghai Top Management Forum, which took place in November 1995 in conjunction with the American Chamber of Commerce, and to which former US secretary of state Henry Kissinger was invited, along with other world leaders.

Li reached the very top of the Hong Kong echelons of power. In 1992 he became senior advisor at both Xinhua in Hong Kong and at the PRC State Council's Hong Kong and Macao Affairs Office. It suited him to wear these two hats, because both organizations were competing to manage the handover, and were having difficulty agreeing on a trustworthy candidate to lead the postcolonial executive after the handover. It was Li himself who eventually settled the matter, mentioning to Jiang Zemin, both a friend and a member of Deng Xiaoping's inner circle, the name of the Shanghai tycoon Tung Chee-hwa.

C.H. Tung, as he was called in English, had an impressive background. His father, Tung Chao-yung (C.Y. Tung), was born in 1911 in the city of Dinghai, Zhejiang province, where Qiao Shi was also born. Tung Senior, a small boat-owner in Tianjin, was interested in shipping and shipbuilding. He settled in Shanghai and set up his first company, the Chinese Maritime Co. He married the beautiful Koo Lee-ching, who gave him two sons and three daughters; Tung Chee-hwa, the future governor of Hong Kong, was born in Shanghai in

1937. He was still in the cradle when the Japanese invasion left the family destitute. They fled with the troops of Chiang Kai-shek, who was a friend of Tung Senior.

In 1945, with Japan suffering the after-effects of Nagasaki and Hiroshima, the Tungs decided they wanted to profit from Shanghai's economic revival. The new expansion of trade justified the development of maritime communications. Tung Senior began to build up his fleet. He bought an old boat, *The Heavenly Dragon*, which would become his flagship and the first Chinese boat to drop anchor in European ports.

Tung Senior built a maritime empire on the Chinese mainland and at the same time set himself up in business in Hong Kong. This was an excellent strategy. In 1949, he followed the Kuomintang to Taiwan, where he installed his companies, while at the same time diversifying his affairs in Hong Kong: Maritime Transport Ltd, the Orient Overseas Container Line, and the Island Navigation Corporation. His friendship with Chiang Kai-shek played an important role, not least because the Tung Group was considered Taiwan's national merchant shipping company.

Ten years later, by then the owner of a fleet of ships, Tung built the largest tanker in the world—the 70,000-tonne *Oriental Giant*—followed by his first new boat in France. He also purchased the *Queen Elizabeth*, which he wanted to make into a floating university for the United Nations to train maritime specialists.

Meanwhile, the young Chee-hwa was learning to read at St Stephen's School in Hong Kong. He was sent to secondary school in Portsmouth and gained a degree as a marine engineering technician in Liverpool while the Beatles were still playing the Cavern Club. He met and married a Chinese nurse called Chiu Hung-ping, with whom he had three children. I have never heard any rumours of him taking concubines or mistresses, unlike many Hong Kong tycoons, for whom such women were a sign of opulence and power, social as well as sexual. C.H. Tung was a reserved man who hated being in the public eye.

For ten years, he worked in the USA for an electronic equipment manufacturer, before returning to Hong Kong in 1969. His leadership qualities came not so much from his lineage but from his capacity to adapt to any role that economic circumstances might force on him. His father gave him a decade to learn how to manage the Orient Overseas Container Line, based in Taiwan and Hong Kong since 1979. When Tung Senior died in 1982, C.H. Tung and his brother, C.C. Tung, by now living in New York, succeeded their father at the head of an apparently thriving empire, the Orient Overseas Holdings (OOH). The company had overtaken its two great rivals, the Worldwide Group, owned by Yue-Kong Pao, and Wah Kwong Shipping, owned by the Chao family.

In fact OOH was going through a stormy period. Its new super-tanker, the 560,000-tonne *Seawise-Giant*, was too big for the needs of the global market, which was suffering in the aftermath of the oil crisis. As for the *Queen Elizabeth*, the emblem of an era, it had caught fire and sunk in 1971. An investigation revealed it to be a case of arson. On top of this, C.H. Tung was experiencing the full-blown repercussions of the recession. He first tried to raise funds in Taiwan but, unsuccessful, he turned to his friend Henry Fok Ying-tung. Was communist China ready to bail out the Tung empire? Henry Fok was definitely the right person to talk to.

The billionaire's ties with mainland China dated back to the Korean War, and he now chaired the pro-Beijing Chinese Chamber of Commerce. As vice-chair of the Preparatory Committee for the Hong Kong Special Administrative Region, he was well placed to sponsor Tung. He had built his colossal fortune on casinos, in association with another famous tycoon, Stanley Ho, who was based in Macao and had links to the Triads. The Fok family's close ties with the PRC were such that Henry Fok's own son, Thomas, was arrested in the US for illegally selling missile-making electronic technology to a China-based firm, which earned him several months in jail.

Thanks to Henry Fok's intervention, in 1986 the PRC agreed to loan C.H. Tung $120 million. It was the Bank of China that came to Tung's rescue, though his parent company OOH was still located in Taipei. In practice, it was Henry Fok who headed the "investment syndicate". Li Chuwen and Xu Jiatun, the head of Xinhua in Hong Kong, naturally played a hidden role, too. After he defected to the US, Xu hinted in his gossip-ridden memoirs at the help the Hong Kong billionaire had received, without naming him.[15]

From then on, according to the communist expression, Tung was "shackled", particularly since the investment had helped him to diversify, enabling him to set up Orient Overseas (International) Ltd, a branch that was trying to develop a fleet of container carriers. At the time, Tung simply said, "I would like to thank Mr Fok and the foreign banks who helped me out." He did not name the Bank of China, but financial analysts noted that, soon after, the shipping tycoon began to invest in the PRC.

In 1989, for the first time, Tung returned to his family's hometown of Shanghai, for a meeting with Jiang Zemin. Jiang had been promoted to the leadership of the party on 4 June, immediately after the Tiananmen massacre. "Let historians judge these events," Tung said cautiously of Tiananmen. He could not challenge his new friends. He had chosen his camp, while back in Hong Kong there was a huge movement of solidarity with the students and dissidents.

Jiang Zemin and Qiao Shi followed Li Chuwen's advice and made a choice of their own: C.H. Tung was going to be the next leader of Hong Kong. Under a glass bell, of course. But they recognized the need to proceed diplomatically. The trick was not to give a clear indication of the government's preferred candidate. In autumn 1995, a rumour was published in several gazettes that former Gonganbu chief Ruan Chongwu was to be appointed chief executive. Naturally, it was the special services themselves that circulated this lie. The idea was to frighten the people of Hong Kong with the prospect of being ruled by the former head of the terrifying public security ministry. Now governor of the island of Hainan, Ruan had been dismissed as minister at the same time as the reformist leader Hu Yaobang. People were quick to imagine a bloodbath in Hong Kong, and the leadership exploited this: it was an old trick, using fear to make another option appear more attractive in comparison. The media began to focus their spotlight on other potential candidates.[16]

At a reception in January 1996, Jiang Zemin publicly shook C.H. Tung's hand—the white knight had been anointed by the leadership. Three tycoons—Henry Fok, Li Ka-shing and Walter Kwok—believed he was the ideal candidate. Even his great business rival George Chao Sze-kwong, president of the Hong Kong Shipowners Association, thought it not such a bad idea: "In the long run, I am optimistic for the arms market but now we all have to be patient," he was quoted as saying in the *South China Morning Post*.

Modesty incarnate, C.H. Tung assured him that he would like a better idea of the challenges facing Hong Kong in the year 2000. In June 1996, he resigned from his position as advisor to the last British governor, Chris Patten. In the press, at cocktail parties, in ministries all over the world, people listed all the international connections that made this reserved man the perfect candidate to guarantee, in short, that Hong Kong would remain Hong Kong. Qiao Shi and Li Chuwen's special services were doing all they could to make this plain. Tung counted among his foreign friends Prince Rainier, who had appointed him honorary consul of Monaco. In the US, he had close ties with former president George H.W. Bush (1989–93), who had been head of the US Liaison Office in Beijing in the 1970s and director of the CIA before his election to the White House.

The British, meanwhile, appreciated Tung's role in the successful handover, in tandem with Anson Chan, the chief secretary in the British colonial government at the time. Tung was also said to be liked by the Queen, who received him from time to time. His ties with Taiwan were obviously important to Chinese leaders, especially when it came to a potential future rapprochement with the PRC, in which the Tung clan might play a useful role; his father had, after all, been close to Chiang Kai-shek. John Y.K. Peng, Tung's brother-in-law, was president of Taiwan's Chinese Maritime Transport Ltd and of Associated Industries China Incorporated. He would guarantee a direct line of communication with the government in Taipei.

Though C.H. Tung was said to have no political leanings, this was not really the case. He dreamed of a system modelled on that of Singapore, whose former prime minister Lee Kuan Yew (1959-90) was an example to him. Might Deng Xiaoping's "One country, two systems" become "a police state with two different economies", C.H. Tung-style?

To guarantee the continuation of a British-style administration, Tung asked Anson Chan to remain as chief secretary in the new government of the Hong Kong Special Administrative Region. That would reassure the British, apart from Chris Patten. To show that he was not planning to mess with the Chinese system, he chose as his justice secretary Elsie Leung, a lawyer, member of the National People's Congress (NPC) and founding member of the pro-communist Democratic Alliance for the Betterment and Progress of Hong Kong. She was quick to say that the media would not let her get away with anything untoward.

On 15 November 1996, I made my way to the Hong Kong Convention Centre, where some high-profile electors, selected by Beijing, were meeting. Outside, fewer than 100 democrats and dissidents were protesting against what they believed to be a farcical, rigged election of the chief executive. A large police deployment prevented them from getting anywhere near the tall building, while they were filmed by the Security Wing—the new Hong Kong political police—and photographed from every angle by Guoanbu secret agents. Journalists were being herded by Zhou Shanshan, the high priestess of the Xinhua News Agency. Dissidents and supporters of Martin Lee and Emily Lau's Democratic Party booed the Chinese foreign minister, Qian Qichen, who had come to guarantee the legality of the election. It was like witnessing a fight between a mouse and an elephant.

In a room hung with large purple banners, like a CCP congress, 202 of the 400 selected electors gave their vote to Tung. Judge Yang Ti Liang received eighty-two votes. He was thought of as an honest candidate, but far too "British" to be in with a real chance. He remained in the running for the second round, as did Peter Woo Kwong-ching (fifty-four votes), who was in favour of a good deal with Beijing. Simon Li Fook-sean (forty-three votes) had received support from the Chinese community in Fujian Province, but was out of the race. His overly pro-Western stance was a turnoff.

Jean-Philippe Béja is a China expert and was then head of the French Centre for Research on Contemporary China, based near Hong Kong's Lyndhurst Terrace. The day after the election, he told me, "Tung Chee-hwa received too many votes the first time for the smooth operation to be convincing. Everyone knew that the vote was manipulated."

This was so true that, the day following the vote, Jiang Zemin discreetly sent his *éminence grise* Li Chuwen to Hong Kong, to ensure that criticisms about the election did not risk sullying the image of their candidate. Presumably they judged that this was not the case. In order to test public opinion, a few days later C.H. Tung let it be known that, after 1997, the CCP would be legalized in Hong Kong. Observers became tangled up in speculation: was this merely a way of saying that the other parties would disappear? Or was it, on the contrary, a way of indicating that democracy was going to function effectively, and that the CCP would have to take its place among all the others?

A period of strategic manoeuvring began, until, on 11 December 1996, C.H. Tung was elected the first chief of Hong Kong's postcolonial executive, by 320 of 400 council members. It was hardly a shock result.

Immediately after his election at the Convention Centre, the electors wanted one thing only: to quit the building, as if they had a bad conscience, leaving the new master of Hong Kong alone with his thoughts. The previous day, at a small gathering at his home on The Peak, Tung had remarked astutely, "I may well find myself very much alone as chief executive." But that would be to ignore his new friends: Li Chuwen, Jiang Zemin and Qiao Shi, the men who had helped him become the elected leader of Hong Kong, independent of Beijing.

In case he was entertaining any doubts, in March 1997 a close acquaintance of Li Chuwen was suddenly named "special advisor" to Tung. Paul Yip (also known as Yip Kwok-wah) had taken part in the riots of 1967 and had been a member of Hong Kong's underground CCP branch. A former teacher, Yip was now the wealthy owner of various companies including the Renful Security Company, which employed ex-police officers to provide protection for senior Chinese officials in Hong Kong. He reported, of course, directly to the Guoanbu.

Tung's career had been exemplary. It was an excellent illustration of the path of a number of Hong Kong businessmen, who were prepared to invest in Beijing so long as nothing stood in the way of them increasing their wealth as they always had. Friends of Hong Kong's new chief executive liked to remind him that his father, the patriotic Tung Chao-yung, had given him a name that summed it all up: Chee-hwa (*Jian Hua* in Mandarin) means "build China". For C.H. Tung, this came to mean "unify China".

Hong Kong, hub of the Red Princes

Among Tung's friends were several of the so-called "Red Princes", children of the Beijing elite, who were the owners of some very unusual businesses. These company heads were family members of eminent CCP members and other Chinese leaders, who had chosen the colonies of Hong Kong and Macao as the main bases of their operations, their import-export businesses and prospecting companies.

By the mid-1990s, the ageing offspring of the communist revolution, the children of Mao Zedong's comrades and veterans of the Long March, were middle-aged. In some cases Mao had turned against his former comrades and banished their families during the Cultural Revolution. The Red Princes had then seen their influence rise during Deng Xiaoping's economic revolution in the early 1980s, and realized that Hong Kong would be the ideal base for lucrative financial operations. They had a direct line to the Beijing administration to facilitate Hong Kong investments in China.

They drove Mercedes and lived on The Peak or in other exclusive residential neighbourhoods. The princes had mistresses and concubines on both sides of the former Bamboo Curtain. If we are to believe the gossip, these "Red Princesses" also had complicated and expensive love lives. They and their children haunted the hottest spots in Hong Kong: cabarets, casinos and restaurants like the Royal Jockey Club, the Volvo Club and David Tang's China Club. They rejoiced that Hong Kong had been returned to the motherland, while very much hoping that the CCP was not going to kill the goose that laid the golden eggs.

"Preserving the Hong Kong economy will be a matter of survival for the Beijing regime. And not just because so many Red Princes—the sons of senior communist cadres—are running private companies here," Professor Lau Siu Kai, director of the Department of Sociology at the Chinese University of Hong Kong and member of the Preparatory Committee for the HKSAR, told me at the time. This preservation was possible up to a point, partly thanks to the very presence of these elite sons and daughters, playing capitalists while growing rich off the back of socialism. However, the risk was that they would introduce there the corruption already widespread on the Chinese mainland. Hong Kong, with the exception of areas controlled by the Triads, had been relatively free of such problems under the British.

Meanwhile, there was a great deal of rivalry between the Red Princes. They represented various and differing political views, largely dependent on their parents' positions in the struggle between opposing factions within the CCP and the *guanxi*, the complex web of social relations that characterizes Chinese society. But from the signing of the treaty with the British to the final handover, they had prospered in relative harmony. They were all in the same junk, as it were, even if they did not always agree on which direction to take.

By the late 1980s, Chinese investment in Hong Kong had grown significantly. This was primarily due to the huge conglomerate, the China International Trust & Investment Corporation (CITIC), founded in Beijing in 1979 by the Shanghai-born "red capitalist" Rong Yiren, also vice-president of the PRC. It was Deng Xiaoping himself who had given Rong the responsibility of setting up the CITIC, a capitalist business group in communist China, directly answerable to the State Council.

The CITIC came to Hong Kong in 1987 with Larry Yung—Rong's son—at the helm. Like a greedy dragon, the CITIC began to devour strategic Hong Kong companies. It bought a local listed company, Tyfull, which in turn bought 20 per cent of Hong Kong Telecommunications in 1990. Then the CITIC bought 46.2 per cent of Dragonair, the Hong Kong airline. It was also one of three shareholders of Asia Satellite Telecommunications Ltd, which managed communication satellites in the region. Among the CITIC's senior executives were several Red Princes, including Deng Zhifang, Deng Xiaoping's second son, who also owned several real estate companies, a growing sector in both Hong Kong and the PRC.

Wang Jun, president of the CITIC, was also head of Poly Technologies, one of the principal companies owned by the PLA, which under Deng Xiaoping had also became involved in the private sector. His father, Wang Zhen, was a former vice-president of the PRC, a close friend of Deng Xiaoping, and one of the most hard-line of those within the conservative faction of the CCP. This dogmatist, head of the Central Party School since 1980, was one of the most fervent supporters of the harsh crackdown on the Tiananmen protesters. But the CITIC, one of the most powerful state-owned enterprises in China, was swarming with secret agents.

A few years later, Agnès Andrésy, the Hong Kong-based publisher of the *Arcanes de Chine* newsletter, wrote a detailed account of the Red Princes: "The commercial status granted to these shadowy figures allows them to act and move freely without attracting attention. Similarly, the leadership of the CITIC is known to harbour within its ranks a large number of Chinese secret agents from the 2nd Department of the General Staff, one of the many general intelligence cells in China. It was Deng Xiaoping himself who demanded this particular function back when he was the PLA's chief of staff in 1978; even though Rong Yiren was [CITIC's] CEO, most of those close to him had been carefully selected by Deng, now an old man. In 1979, CITIC's vice-president, Xiong Xianghui, was the number one in the Chinese intelligence services, while the director-general, Mi Guojun, was both a member of the 2nd Bureau and in charge of a cell of the Chinese general intelligence bureau within the Ministry of Foreign Affairs.

"The CITIC was the cover of choice for intelligence activities. It made contact with people, established partnerships and furnished logistical assistance to the PLA and to the companies involved in the military-industrial complex. After Poly Technologies, it became the umbrella group for the arms-dealing China Poly Group, officially its subsidiary. The current CEO of the CITIC, Wang Jun, was recruited from within the Chinese secret services."[17]

Poly Technologies was involved in arms sales in association with Saul Eisenberg, a businessman who worked on joint ventures between China and Israel. It was a haven for the Red Princes. In 1988, the top ranks of the company included Wang Xiaochao, son-in-law of President Yang Shangkun, who would coordinate the Tiananmen crackdown the following year; Wang Zihua, son-in-law of Zhao Ziyang, general secretary of the CCP, who would be deposed during those events; and General He Ping, son-in-law of Deng Xiaoping. The scions of these theoretically rival dynasties were perfectly able to live and let live when it came to hard cash. The lure of profit and the instinct to stay onside easily outweighed differences of opinion on policy.

* * *

Yet another Red Prince was the CEO of Hong Kong's Everbright Company Ltd: Wang Guangying, brother-in-law of the former chairman Liu Shaoqi, who had been overthrown during the Cultural Revolution and horrifically abused by the Red Guards. Liu's wife had been attacked by the Red Guards for being an "imperialist spy"; yet now her brother was leading an important Hong Kong enterprise. How the world was changing under Deng Xiaoping, as China set forth on the path of capitalism.

The military-industrial lobby was one of the most powerful in Hong Kong. The Poly Group (including Poly Technologies) was at the top of the pyramid, run by the "spy" Wang Jun and He Ping, former deputy military attaché in the United States. Reporting to the PLA, Poly's import-export turnover at that time was around $500 million a year. He Ping was married to Deng Xiaoping's favourite daughter, Deng Rong. The couple were both attachés at the Chinese embassy in Washington in the 1980s, charged with cultivating valuable arms trading relationships and with establishing a pro-China lobby populated by well-known American figures.

But in 1996, US police arrested seven people in San Francisco suspected of having brought approximately 2,000 Kalashnikov AK-47 assault rifles and 800 handguns into the United States. The cargo was seized in the port of Oakland, California, thanks to a patient FBI intelligence operation that brought to light the leading role of two Chinese state-owned firms in the affair: Norinco (North Industries Corporation) and Poly Technologies. Norinco had ten offices around the world, including in Hong Kong. Two of those who worked in the San Francisco office, Zhang Yi and Lu Yilun, ended up in jail. Even more seriously, the investigation led directly back to the two companies' directors, He Ping and Wang Jun. This was one of several episodes in the Jiang Zemin era that tarnished relations between Beijing and Washington, as we will see in the following chapters.

* * *

Family loyalty was very strong in the Deng Xiaoping clan. Even He Ping's brother, He Zheng, worked for the China Poly Group (*Baoli*). Some of its activities were chilling: in January 1990, He Ping made a secret visit to Bangkok to sell weapons that would be used to strengthen the Khmer Rouge's military capacity in Cambodia. Fifteen years after the Cambodian genocide, the Chinese were still supporting the Khmer Rouge, by now global pariahs. Closely linked to Poly Technologies was a company called Hing Lung Hong, headed by a Macao national, Ieong Chong-pio, and a Hong Konger, Mickey Lai. The company also sold weapons to the PLA and in 1989 it began selling arms to Iraq, including the famous Silkworm missiles.

At the heart of these technology transfer operations was COSTIND, the Commission for Science, Technology and Industry for National Defence, headed until January 1997 by Ding Hengao, whose wife Nie Li was its deputy director. Nie, who was responsible for the espionage ship development programme, was the daughter of Nie Rongzhen, Deng Xiaoping's comrade in Paris in the 1920s and the founder of the Hong Kong communist secret service in the early 1930s. Alongside Ding and Nie were other prominent directors: Zhang Pin, son of former defence minister Zhang Aiping, and Deng Nan, the youngest daughter of Deng Xiaoping.

Clearly, the most successful Red Princes were those linked to the military-industrial lobby, which played an important role in weapons and technology proliferation. They were also supported by the secret services, which made money out of their operations, with sizeable commissions. All this was exposed in 1997, in a scandal that tarnished the White House, the Clintons and US Vice-President Al Gore: Chinagate.

* * *

Chinagate was a shady affair in which it was revealed that John Huang, former US under-secretary of commerce and one of those responsible for Democratic Party finances, was involved in a corruption scandal at the heart of the party, whose re-election committee was said to have received some $4.5 million from the Sino-Indonesian group Lippo, the Sino-Thai group Charoeun Popkhand, and San Kin, a Chinese group based in Macao. The intermediary was a Chinese-American called Charles Yan Lin Trie. The scandal, which resurfaced in 2008 during the US presidential campaign, exposed links with COSTIND and more specifically with Poly Technologies. Charles Yan Lin Trie, who owned a Chinese restaurant in Arkansas and knew the

Clintons, managed with Hillary Clinton's help to engineer a meeting at the White House between Bill Clinton and Wang Jun, head of the CITIC and the Poly Group, who was subsequently identified as a Chinese intelligence operative.

In such a context, donations made to the Democratic Party for its election campaign were considered bribes to obtain new arms sales—as was the fact that the US had turned a blind eye to the sale of Chinese arms and other sensitive technologies to countries like Pakistan, North Korea and Iraq. Here again, the Chinese were also using their arms trading networks as conduits for political-military intelligence. This affair, which is explored in detail below, reflected a new phenomenon: with the collapse of the Soviet empire, and the evisceration of the KGB, now limited to regional activities, the Chinese intelligence community, with the Guoanbu at its head, was beginning to develop global ambitions.

The case of the Varyag *aircraft carrier*

Without a doubt, one of the most picturesque examples of the Chinese special services using Hong Kong- and Macao-based businesses as a front was the purchase of the aircraft carrier *Varyag*. This was a Ukrainian ship destined for the scrapheap, until Beijing decided to buy it, with the idea—always considered and always rejected—of owning, like the Indians, a "seafaring giant" that could extend the reach of the PRC's air force far beyond Chinese seas.

This episode took place in 1998—one year after the handover of Hong Kong, the death of Deng Xiaoping, and the retirement of Admiral Liu Huaqing, vice-chair of the Central Military Commission, who had long cherished the dream of building a combat fleet worthy of the PRC's global ambitions. Persistent rumours and naval intelligence analyses from several countries suggested that the Chinese were hoping to launch a 44,000-tonne aircraft carrier by 2010.

This was not the first time that the Chinese had bought an aircraft carrier in order to study it in detail, from every angle. In 1985, China had purchased the *Melbourne* from the Australians; they then stripped it for parts in the port of Dalian. Later, Beijing bought two ships from the former USSR, the *Minsk* and the *Kiev*, which were turned into "tourist attractions".

The *Varyag* was a magnificent ship: 55,000 tonnes (displacement), with a span of 307 metres, large enough to carry 2,500 sailors and thirty-five planes. It had just one defect: because of the collapse of the USSR, it had never actually been completed. A Macao company, the Agência Turística e Diversões Chong Lot (the Chong Lot Travel Agency Limited), bought it for $20 million, but without its nuclear-powered engines. Officially the plan was to turn it into a floating casino, like the smaller ones owned by the gambling mogul Stanley Ho. Offshore gaming was not just about money laundering; it was a hub for all kinds of trafficking, including by North Koreans. Portugal surrendered its former colony to China in late 1999, so the field was wide open. The only problem was that the Turks, undoubtedly encouraged by the Americans, did not want to allow a military ship to enter its territory. This led to fifteen months of disagreement between Ankara and Beijing, before the *Varyag* at last set sail for the PRC in November 2001.

I tried to arrange a meeting with representatives from Chong Lot, based—according to the register—on Avenue Mario Soares in Macao, at the premises of the Bank of China. I came across a PO box and the address of the parent company in Hong Kong. Going through the register at the Chamber of Commerce, I discovered that Chong Lot is a subsidiary of another firm based in Hong Kong, called the Chinluck (Holding), as well as being connected to a third Hong Kong company, Goldspot Investments Ltd. Many of the shareholders of these companies were PLA officers with addresses in Beijing.[18] Within the parent company Chinluck (Holding), the connection was even plainer: three of the five directors were Chinese resident in Shandong, where the high command of the North Sea fleet is located.

In 2005, Chong Lot's chairman, Zheng Zhenshu, gave an interview to the Xinhua News Agency, in which he welcomed the passing of a new law prohibiting Taiwan from seceding from China. This was a strange political intervention from a business leader interested in developing tourism in Macao and Hong Kong—unless, of course, he was driven by a patriotic commitment to a not-too-distant future "reconquest" of Taiwan, aided by his helping the PLA equip itself with an aircraft carrier.

Ultimately, though, the *Varyag* did not sail all the way to Macao. It made it to Dalian, where it remains in dry dock under close surveillance, as can be seen in satellite photos. The Chinese have arranged their ports in such a way as to allow an aircraft carrier to anchor. They have purchased adaptable equipment for naval aviation, starting with the Russian Sukhoi Su-33, and others. In the first ten years after it docked, the Varyag sailed under a new flag as "001" Liaoning. Redesigned and modernized, it became the first aircraft carrier manned by the PLA Navy. By 2012, its first training operations began, with the brand-new Shenyang J-15 fighters. Then, six years later, China's first domestically built air carrier ("002") engaged in sea trials, pending a commission in 2019.

Greetings to our tens of thousands of spies!

The strategic expansion of the PRC and its secret services now had a new ruler: President Jiang Zemin (1993-2003). Deng Xiaoping died on 19 February 1997; he had revolutionized his country, largely succeeding in carrying out the "Four Modernizations", but he did not live to see Hong Kong back in the hands of the Chinese as he had long dreamed.

For the last decade of the twentieth century, he promoted Jiang, his successor as the "third-generation" leader of the People's Republic of China—though subsequently he regretted that Jiang had effectively brought the "Shanghai mafia" into government at Zhongnanhai. Deng also promoted Hu Jintao as the future leader of the "fourth generation". With these two men at the helm, China would modernize even further, expanding its secret services like never before.

At the beginning of 1997, multiple initiatives were set up. Deputy Prime Minister Zou Jiahua went to Paris to help plan the first French presidential visit to the PRC in fifteen years; Jacques Chirac was passionate about Far Eastern civilizations. Though it was not his first trip to China, it was his first as president. But Zou had multiple strings to his bow. A relative of Marshal Ye Jianying, he was deputy minister of COSTIND and highly knowledgeable in strategic affairs. A friend of former prime minister Li Peng, the "Beijing hangman", he was also chief of the group managing intelligence.

Though 1997 would bring multiple unexpected developments, Zou was doing well at the beginning of the year. Hong Kong newspapers covered the report he presented at a conference organized by the Guoanbu, the PLA2 and the United Front Work Department to "strengthen intelligence work". Under the title "Greetings to comrades from the special task front", Zou explained that these special working bodies had now established intelligence agencies in more than 170 cities across fifty countries worldwide. Subsidiaries of Beijing intelligence services were listed as general bases, stations and substations.

The deputy prime minister also gave us a clue as to the sheer number of secret agents running these intelligence and counterintelligence posts by the early Jiang years of the late 1990s: "Tens of thousands of nameless heroes who cherish and loyally serve their homeland are fighting quietly in their special posts abroad, in a complicated environment."[19]

PART TWO

7

GLOBAL INTELLIGENCE

FROM JIANG ZEMIN TO AFGHANISTAN 2021

On 26 June 1999, at the Institute of Far Eastern Affairs of Munich's Ludwig-Maximilian University, the Bavarian police came upon a horrific scene that bore all the hallmarks of a suicide.

It was only three days later that the *Münchner Kurier* reported that a woman had been found dead in an apartment belonging to the Department of Chinese Studies. It was not until 3 July that an announcement appeared in the *Süddeutsche Zeitung* at the instigation of the professors and students of the Institute in memory of their deceased colleague:

> In namenloser Trauer um
> *Violetta Zhang*
> 13–11.1965—26.6.1999
> Die Professoren, Mitarbeiter und Studierenden am *Institut für Ostasienkunde* der Ludwig-Maximilians-Universität München

The blond, blue-eyed, German-born Violetta's Chinese surname came from a failed marriage to a Shanghai man called Zhang Zhongping. She had died at thirty-four, in such impenetrable circumstances that the investigation eventually concluded, "Cause of death: unknown."

The police commissioner in charge of the criminal investigation was a woman known as Stephanie "Glück". Violetta's partner effectively put Glück on trial in a document describing her investigation as riven with professional incompetence, or worse, as a deliberate attempt to conceal what had really happened. Following this, in 2006, a summary judgment by a Bavarian court prohibited the publication of the police commissioner's real name. It is, however, possible to discuss the unsolved circumstances of Violetta's death, and I believe it is important to do so.

According to the author of the document, the journalist Armin Witt, there were multiple question marks surrounding Violetta's death that warranted further investigation. Witt was not alone in thinking so: the German television channel RTL II, where he worked, made a documentary reconstructing the events, which asked troubling questions: why had the authorities—the emergency services, police and judicial investigators—failed to agree among themselves the precise time the corpse had been discovered? According to the police report, Violetta cut her wrists, but the autopsy report, which I have seen, fails to mention this. There was no blood at the scene, either on the body or in the small studio within the Institute where she was found slumped on a leather sofa. Why had the other residents on the premises that day not been interviewed? Why did the forensic report say that a syringe had been found plunged deep into her chest? Did Violetta really write the suicide note left propped up prominently on the table? ("Dear Armin, you are right, I see it now. I am leaving you, I can no longer bear my life. It is nobody's fault. I beg you to forgive me. I have a great deal of love for you. Violetta.") Just two days previously, she had told her family—as they later testified—that it was "thanks to Armin that I've put my life in order".[1]

To understand what really happened, we must go back to early 1998, and Armin and Violetta's holiday to Shanghai, where Violetta had previously studied Chinese. As a student of the Tang era, she had long dreamed of a boat trip on the China Seas, and once in Shanghai the couple began planning a trip for early 1999 on board the *Galaxy*, a yacht that Armin had bought in Yugoslavia. The couple made contacts through the German consul in Shanghai, Krüger, and a friend of theirs who was the military attaché at the German embassy in Beijing. They were also thinking about setting up a tourism business between Germany and Hainan Island in southern China, where the *Galaxy* was to anchor.

But, four months prior to Violetta's death, this plan fell apart. Perhaps the Chinese authorities had grown suspicious of Armin, who was a journalist but had entered China on a tourist visa; or of Violetta, who spoke Chinese too well; or of the fact that they were in possession of classified nautical charts, and had brought with them a book full of stories about networks of Chinese people living overseas, written by a man called Sterling Seagrave, who was regarded with suspicion by Beijing.

This is not to mention the fact that, though it is open to visitors, Hainan Island is highly guarded, because of its numerous military installations and electronic interception stations. It was here, for example, that Chinese fighter planes forced down (and later dismantled for parts) a US Navy spy plane EP-3E on 1 April 2001. Moreover, at the time, Hainan's governor Ruan Chongwu—a former Gonganbu chief—had a particular interest in West Germany, and for good reason: from 1978 to 1983, he had been an advisor at the Chinese embassy in Bonn, in charge of scientific and technical intelligence. Of course, as a reformer close to Hu Yaobang, Ruan, who held the Gonganbu portfolio until 1986, wanted to give a positive image of the police as being close to the people. It is more than reasonable to suppose that, for the Guoanbu's Hainan chief Wang Yunji, and his bosses in Beijing, this pair of unfortunate tourists might well have been "honourable correspondents" working for the German Federal Intelligence Service (BND).

Was Violetta Zhang unaware that she had this reputation, or had she indeed been contacted by the BND, because of her knowledge of China? Was she being monitored by Guoanbu agents at the consulate on Romanstraße in Munich—who were particularly active, given that the BND headquarters was on their doorstep in nearby Pullach? Some may have thought that, since she had a Chinese surname, Violetta had an obligation to the country, and thus that she had somehow betrayed it. Whatever the facts of her activity in China, she was made to pay dearly for this supposed disloyalty.

The case bore all the signs of a state-sponsored crime dressed up as suicide, and of an official cover-up intended to avoid challenging and thus falling out of favour with a foreign country. Assuming that Zhang was indeed killed by the Chinese, the German intelligence services, having fully got the message, were hardly about to declare a major diplomatic incident over her death. Armin Witt believes that Violetta may have discovered something she should not have known about, to do with either her Institute or ChinaForum, the academic society that she oversaw, as the Institute's secretary, and which had been infiltrated by the Chinese services. Witt was also suspicious about the exact role of her ex-husband, Zhang Zhongping, who was now living between Munich and Sweden, where he worked for a telephone company.[2]

I have looked closely into the details of the affair. It is undoubtedly the case that the Chinese secret services have frequently tried to infiltrate foreign institutes and China research centres—the Chinese watching the China-watchers, as British and American observers like to say. This is particularly true in instances where they are convinced that false covers are involved, just as those they themselves provide for their own agents, as diplomats, journalists or academics. In West Germany, this suspicion was not entirely unfounded, for there were several former BND employees working in research institutes in Frankfurt, Hamburg and Munich.

In the Jiang Zemin era (1997-2004), the Chinese were certainly targeting these organizations, making contacts and setting up academic exchanges. At the time, Ms Lu Yaokan, an analyst from the China Institute for Contemporary International Relations (CICIR)—the Guoanbu analysis centre—and a leading Germany specialist, was locking down the West German scene and even wrote memoranda about these various institutes, such as the Federal Institute of Orientalism and International Studies.[3]

In Beijing, as the CICIR's head of European strategy, with a focus on German affairs, Lu was responsible for following cases such as that of Violetta Zhang. Along with Professor Feng Zhongling—who specialized in both France and Germany[4]—she analyzed and participated in the selection of intelligence targets in Germany on behalf of the Guoanbu, to whom she reported directly.

The Guoanbu think-tank

However, Lu and her boss Geng Huichang—who was appointed head of the Guoanbu in September 2007—had more pressing concerns than the death of Violetta Zhang, although it had put the Chinese services in a very awkward position. In the Haidian district of Beijing, another death—this time probably a genuine suicide—had just struck at the heart of the CICIR. This was a small world, comprising some 400 analysts who put their all into giving a serious, intellectual image to the think-tank, as far removed as possible from the special services. "We only deal with issues to do with international relations, we have nothing whatsoever to do with intelligence," a francophone specialist at the CICIR called Ms Gao Ying was to claim, shamelessly, a decade later.

Given these efforts to distance the think-tank from the Guoanbu, the death of Qiu Guanghui on 26 September 1998 was extremely compromising—not only because of the conditions that led him to end his life, but, even more problematically, because he was acting head of the Guoanbu's 8th Bureau, which oversaw the CICIR. In other words, he was the interface between it and the training schools for future officers and intelligence agents.

Qiu's career had followed a traditional course. Born in 1956, he had studied strategy at the PLA Military Command Academy, while his wife taught at the Academy of Diplomacy. In the early 1990s, as a specialist in counterintelligence, he travelled to Hong Kong, Australia and Japan on a "material acquisitions" trip, a term that barely disguised its real purpose of technological espionage. During his mission, he indulged in his passion for gambling. In the feverish, smoky atmosphere of the casino, he lost enormous sums of money that he claimed as expenses. In an echo of Graham Greene's *Our Man in Havana*, Qiu justified his huge expenses by inventing fictitious agents paid by him—a common practice by intelligence crooks in services around the world.

In thrall to his addiction, he lost HK$2 million in Macao gambling dens, on the eve of the handover of the Portuguese colony to the Chinese in 1999. Somehow, he managed to conceal what had happened. Two years later, he was transferred to the Xishan centre in west Beijing. He became both a member of the CCP committee within the Guoanbu, and head of the bureau that oversaw the CICIR. The purpose of the CCP committee within each ministry was to ensure the ideological purity and proper application of the leadership's directives within each institution. The secret service did not escape such regulation. Qiu was thus well placed to conceal his own actions.

Eventually, though, he ran out of luck. In an attempt to eradicate endemic corruption, the tail end of the twentieth century saw the launch of multiple investigations, which impacted on many Chinese functionaries. The word on the street was that Jiang Zemin was using the opportunity to disguise corruption within his own faction, the so-called "Shanghai clique". In September 1998, an officer from the PLA's Political Department, Major Jiang Shengmao, found himself accused of having misappropriated funds from companies run out of General Staff headquarters. Such were the misadventures that arose from the privatization of part of the PLA. Jiang committed suicide.

Next was the turn of Qiu, the inveterate gambler. During the course of an investigation into a Hong Kong Chinese company, military security realized that Qui had taken US$1.2 million to fuel his habit. He fiercely denied the accusation and explained that secret missions can be extraordinarily expensive, but he was summoned to appear before the Party Committee and the Guoanbu Disciplinary Committee. On 25 September, the Guoanbu's new boss, Xu Yongyue, fired him. At home the next day, he swallowed a large number of pills and turned on the gas.[5]

This episode illustrates the prevailing climate during the remodelling of the security services at the turn of the millennium. Exactly which empire was Qiu ruling over? The CICIR was just one of around 2,500 think-tanks set up during the Deng/Jiang era. Until recently, though, it had been one of the most prestigious.

The whirlwind of the Cultural Revolution had stirred things up so much that it is easy to overlook the fact that the CICIR, created in 1965, was one of the few research institutes that Mao had left partially open throughout the 1960s and '70s.[6] Its analysts studied the war in Vietnam; the crisis between the United States and North Korea after the seizure of the spy ship USS *Pueblo* by Kim Il-sung's Coast Guard; the French May '68 student uprising, which jeopardized the presidency of General de Gaulle, China's closest friend in Europe; the Soviet invasion of Czechoslovakia in the summer of 1968; and the Sino-Soviet border incident of 1969—the same year that some of those sent to the so-called May 7 re-education schools in the countryside came back to join their comrades in Beijing.

When Deng Xiaoping returned to power, the CICIR had fallen under the control of the State Council, in other words the government. As a cover, genuine students were invited to join the think-tank; nowadays, it is possible to study for a two-year Master's degree or a three-year doctorate in International Relations. Control of the institute passed from the Diaochabu to the Guoanbu after the latter was established in 1983, and today it remains answerable, in both administrative and budgetary terms, to State Security.[7] In the jargon of the special services, it is registered as an "open" (*gongkai*) organization, in order to facilitate intelligence gathering through multiple networks.

While the CICIR's 400 or so members provide sophisticated analyses of even the slightest geopolitical events, its real influence stems from the fact that its researchers, experienced professors and young professionals have links with thousands of academics and policymakers all over the world, and organize academic exchanges with many strategic research centres abroad. When I was working at such an institute in Japan in 2000, I realized that one of the tricks often employed by both the Chinese and the North Koreans is the exchange of researchers between two institutions, using the visiting card of a foreign research centre to gain entry to the most closed circles of the host country, as well as third countries.

Beijing's CICIR is one of the rare examples anywhere in the world of a think-tank presenting itself as 100 per cent academic, but having become 100 per cent integrated into the intelligence service. Over time it has answered variously to the 8th, 11th and 13th Bureaus of the Guoanbu. "The Institute of Contemporary International Relations is the analysis section of the MSS [Guoanbu]," according to Nicholas Eftimiades, a specialist on Chinese affairs affiliated first with the CIA and later the DIA (Defense Intelligence Agency).[8]

In addition, for specific missions or targeted research, the CICIR frequently co-opted both academics and members of the CCP, PLA or state secret services. Gao Ying told me that she returned to her university in summer 2007 after completing a three-year stint at CICIR, where she produced reports on international terrorism under Professor Li Wei.[9] Li, a great traveller, was director of antiterrorism research at the CICIR, and head of the Counterterrorism Bureaus (*fankongbuju*) of both the Guoanbu and the Gonganbu. He was one of the most senior members of the anti-terrorist strategy group for the 2008 Beijing Olympics.

CICIR researchers are not afraid to go into the field, even on highly dangerous missions—for example, into Taliban-held areas of Afghanistan—and they are even sometimes called upon to act as intermediaries in conflicts between warring factions. Sending an agent to a foreign country for short periods of time is difficult for the counterintelligence service, which is more used to dealing with the routines of permanently stationed Guoanbu officers working under diplomatic cover in foreign countries.

In the 2000s, increasing numbers of analysts from these services and think-tanks began accompanying high-level political and commercial delegations on missions abroad. During 2007, for example, several missions to Africa were organized by Xu Weizhong, a CICIR expert on African energy issues.[10] Making the most of the PRC's increasing openness toward other countries, CICIR analysts also began organizing conferences in China to which representatives of foreign institutes were invited. It was up to the host organization to seduce invitees into committing to a regular exchange of information, and to set in motion a mechanism for recruiting foreign researchers, subsidized by a variety of benefits in kind: money, sex, organized tours, publications of articles and books, or the gratifying status of being baptized a "friend of China".

Jiangnan Social University in Suzhou, Jiangsu province, is another higher education institution for the training of Guoanbu cadres. I have been unable to verify the claims of certain American observers, including the journalist David Wise, that the university teaches espionage techniques, martial arts and surveillance methods.[11] On the other hand, it is clear from its website that its students produce a large number of studies on various economic and geostrategic issues related to national security: in 2017 this included subjects like the Colour Revolutions in Georgia and Ukraine and their implications for Chinese security, Beijing's involvement in the fight against ISIS, and the security implications of the One Belt One Road strategy. Clearly the Guoanbu expects its officers and functionaries to gain a good knowledge of the country's geopolitical strategy before beginning to undertake intelligence missions.

In liaison with the CICIR, many of these analysts take part in international conferences arranged with other organizations, such as the China Institute of International Strategic Studies (CIISS), an offshoot of military intelligence (PLA2); the Academy of Social Sciences; the Shanghai Institute of International Studies; and many others. These institutes, which are like echo chambers, are truly Chinese centres of analysis, and regularly organize meetings on topics that allow their researchers to corroborate information and investigate major trends.

"We have frequent meetings with people from the CICIR or the United Work Front Department, which plays a very important role in foreign intelligence, for example in my field of expertise, the United States," explained Professor Liu Jianfei, director of the Foreign Affairs Division at the CIISS, another first-level organization reporting to the Central Party School, which functions as a training academy for senior civil servants honing strategic policy.[12]

In the course of this long discussion with Professor Liu—at an old-fashioned pavilion at the Friendship Hotel in Haidian district—I began to understand that the work of strategic intelligence researchers is structured according to a system linked closely to espionage. Walking through Haidian, north-west of Beijing, one realizes that all the main civilian intelligence agencies, such as the CICIR, are based there. The CICIR was initially housed in a building under military control, then at Tsinghua University—the Chinese MIT—before moving to a brand new building boasting conference rooms and a library of 500,000 reference works on international relations, as well as various rooms for smaller meetings.[13]

The CICIR also produces publications, including its internal newsletter, *Research in International Relations* (*Guoji guanxi yanjiu*), which is classified and intended for Guoanbu directors and government or party members. There is also a monthly magazine, *Contemporary International Relations* (*Xiandai Guoji Guanxi*), intended for a wider audience. The think-tank publishes books, including one on terrorism written by Professor Li Wei, and *The Global Strategic Resource Survey*, a crucial topic for a Chinese economy hungry for new energy resources.[14] In this respect, the Guoanbu is clearly emulating the CIA, which also publishes reference texts for the general public. Researchers are increasingly sought after by Chinese media, and, exploiting the new policy of openness, it is not uncommon to see analysts on the China Global Television Network (formerly CCTV) explaining events in Darfur or Iraq. Some have even become well known abroad, such as Professor Yan Xuetong, a graduate of the University of California, Berkeley, who often appears on CNN talking about global security, and travels frequently all over the world. He decided to leave the CICIR, which he believed was increasingly losing out to other think-tanks, including some with links to the military, whose reports and analyses were going into far deeper detail. He took up the directorship of a rival international studies institute in 2007.

In 1993, in the wake of the huge geopolitical upheavals triggered by the end of the Cold War, the CICIR was remodelled; new leaders were appointed, and four sub-institutes were added to the seven that already existed (see Appendix VI). These area studies institutes largely correspond to the same divisions in both the Ministry of Foreign Affairs and the Guoanbu. In terms of the concrete application of special operations, the central administration is particularly interested in Division 7, because its researchers study the biographies of international heads of state. A "headhunter" selects the figure to be researched, then seeks the help of secret service stations abroad for an intelligence operation. In the mid-1990s, Zhang Liangen, an expert on France, was looking at President Jacques Chirac and his relationships with the United States and Japan; Africanist Liu Yueming was compiling information on Togolese President Gnassingbé Eyadéma, then the doyen of African leaders; and Chen Shuangqing was investigating whether the Israeli prime minister and leader of the Likud party, Benjamin Netanyahu, was likely to continue the peace negotiations with the PLO initiated by the Oslo Accords (1993–5).

Jiang Zemin and the supervision of the special services

During this period, General Secretary and President Jiang Zemin was continuing down the path first mapped out by Deng Xiaoping, seeking to develop intelligence and analytical structures that would, for the first time, permit the PRC to compete on a level with the Americans. He asked his chief of staff and right hand, Zeng Qinghong, to set up a new National Security Council in Beijing.

The respected academic Ding Yifan—former Paris correspondent for the newspaper *Enlightenment Daily* (*Guangming Ribao*), and now senior fellow and deputy director of China's Institute of World Development, which is part of the State Council's Development Research Centre—distilled for me in 2007 this attempt to create a single organization for coordinating the entire PRC intelligence system, as well as offering a detailed vision of the global situation:

> There is a fundamental difference between the vision and the strategy of Jiang Zemin and that of President Hu Jintao today. Jiang used to have a good relationship with the United States, unlike today's situation [in 2007], which is marked by a challenging relationship with the Bush administration. On top of that, Jiang's vision was global, while Hu and Prime Minister Wen Jiabao are primarily focused on strengthening positions in Asia, with the purpose of creating a single market with an ASEAN free trade area. With his global vision, Jiang Zemin wanted to create a National Security Council, but it has to be said it did not function particularly well.[15]

There may very well have been an administrative bottleneck—a hallmark of the Chinese system, inherited from dynastic China's highly centralized imperial structure and then combined with a neo-Stalinist tradition, which greatly inhibited development of the entrepreneurial spirit common to all Western intelligence services. But, alongside the structural changes that accompanied the growing need for knowledge and decision-making tools, within the Chinese communist system the weight of the political framework and factional battles remained significant.

Jiang Zemin's takeover of the entire array of Chinese secret services took place in two stages, tied to the fourteenth (1992) and fifteenth (1997) party congresses as deadlines for remodelling them. During the 14th Congress, Jiang Zemin and Deng Xiaoping got rid of the Yang brothers, Shangkun and Baibing, who had helped them bring down the Tiananmen opposition, but since then had held on to a disproportionate amount of influence: it was even rumoured that, with those two at the head of the army, there was a risk of another attempted coup, similar to that attributed eleven years earlier to Marshal Lin Biao. The two Yangs were craftily ousted, and at the same time the structure of military intelligence also began to be modified, in light of the Chinese conviction that a new era of war and intelligence had begun with the First Gulf War of 1991, following Saddam Hussein's invasion of Kuwait. For good measure, the Yang brothers' main ally, Prime Minister Li Peng (the "Beijing hangman"), was also deposed—with one essential condition, which he had imposed to guarantee himself a trouble-free retirement: that Luo Gan, his personal secretary and security specialist, be allowed to hold on to his central position in his preferred fields.

Change was also in the air for Qiao Shi, forced to cede control of the security and special services sector. But Qiao was pushed not only out but up, appointed chairman of the National People's Congress, a far more prestigious position than head of the secret services. Abroad, Qiao Shi was nicknamed the Chinese Andropov, a reference to the former head of the KGB who had become a reformer in the USSR and catapulted Mikhail Gorbachev to power in 1987. For the old Chinese guard, this appellation was hardly a compliment, given that 1992 saw the implosion of the USSR, the dismantling of the KGB, and the collapse of the communist party's power. Faced with a post-Tiananmen situation in which the dynamic of reform seemed to have stalled, Qiao Shi—who had been genuinely ambivalent about Tiananmen—wanted to give greater weight to the role of parliament and, concomitantly, to reduce the influence of the CCP.

This debate was made more challenging in the early 1990s, when the leadership established something of a personality cult around Deng Xiaoping and his achievements, using him as a cover to advance their own agenda. Developments in Poland had further coloured Zhongnanhai opinion against the relative reformist Qiao. Everything Deng Xiaoping obsessively feared was contained in a single word: Solidarność. After all the upheaval in the USSR and China, the Solidarity movement was Deng's nightmare come true: the underground movement led by Lech Wałęsa was supported not only by the majority of Poles, but also by confederations of international unions, Pope John Paul II's Vatican, liberal intellectuals everywhere, and the CIA. It forced the Polish communist party to negotiate and then give up power in 1989.[16] And all this had taken place with almost no violence.

Jiang Zeming understood only too well what had so concerned his mentor. In the 1990s, China's strategy of openness to the world—including a cordial commercial agreement with the United States—was accompanied by major crackdowns on crime and dissent, waged by Tao Siju, the Gonganbu minister; his wife, Chen Fanfang, was head of the Gonganbu's 1st Bureau. In 1991, Eric Meyer—a Beijing-based journalist and former correspondent for, amongst others, the Brussels newspaper *Le Soir* and the French radio station France Inter—wrote an article about this crackdown: "Tao Siju announced the establishment of 'intervention brigades', capable of sniffing out in advance any planned sabotage or demonstration," Meyer explained.

> However, on November 13, *Public Security News* published a demand for an increase in both equipment and people for domestic and foreign espionage purposes. This might seem extreme, even bizarre, given that Beijing was already teeming with spies and informers in every shop and on every street corner, who trailed for the slightest reason any passing stranger, whether student or businessman, and any Chinese person they might speak to.
>
> ... According to the Hong Kong newspaper the *South China Morning Post*, China has triggered a huge expansion of its secret troops installed in its embassies abroad, undercover as diplomats or journalists, including in the United States and the USSR.
>
> ... Which all suggests two things: one, that espionage remains today one of the most solid pillars for guaranteeing the survival of this dictatorial regime, and two, that China is willing to pay for all this work, lavishly, and seemingly without limit.[17]

Although they had been undercover together in Shanghai in 1949, Jiang Zemin and Qiao Shi had never liked each other. Qiao had a better reputation within the party and seemed to delight in the fact that Jiang had been general secretary during the events of June 1989. There was a popular joke at the time: "When the course of the river drops (*Jiang*), the great stone gains in height (*Qiao Shi*)." Zhongnanhai had used Qiao Shi to organize the hunt for dissidents, but this danger had faded over the years. Now Jiang and his Shanghai clique thought they could push him out, with the help of old conservatives anxious at the idea of a new reformist project emerging.

As we know, they were ultimately successful in robbing Qiao of the security portfolio, after the 14th Congress in 1992. But he would not be got rid of with a single backhand swipe. As well as becoming head of the National People's Congress, he managed to maintain control of his invisible web of relationships—his *touming guanxi*—within the world of intelligence. He also manoeuvred some of his men into key posts, such as Wei Jianxing, now in charge of security issues, who also took over the Party Discipline Commission in 1992. There was also the Qiao loyalist Ren Jianxin, secretary of the political-legal commission that oversaw intelligence and judicial affairs. The commission's two deputies were Luo Gan and Jia Chunwang, head of the Guoanbu.

This led to a rather complicated cohabitation, bearing in mind the struggle between Luo Gan and Qiao Shi in the wake of Tiananmen for control of the People's Armed Police (PAP), then estimated at 800,000 men, which passed from the administrative supervision of the Gonganbu to the Central Military Commission. Jiang took over leadership of the CMC after Deng Xiaoping's death in 1997,[18] and needed to promote the rise of his own men, most of whom were linked in some way to the Shanghai clique. The most important of these men was Zeng Qinghong, whose qualities were not dissimilar to those of Qiao Shi, and who had been assigned to set up a security council.

Zeng, a Hakka from Shanghai, had come to Beijing with Jiang Zemin, for whom he worked as a private secretary at the time of Tiananmen. He was the son of Deng Lujin, a heroine of the Long March, and General Zeng Shan, who had been the leader of the first Chinese *soviet* in Jiangxi and at Kang Sheng's side when he arrived in Yan'an from Moscow in 1937.[19]

Between 1993 and 1997, Zeng was head of the CCP's powerful General Affairs Department, within which an expansion was taking place of some functions traditionally dependent on the secretariat. This expansion needed to take into account various different factions. The department began by increasing its staff to 350 civil servants, employed in political research, economic policy, party archives and the personal security of the leadership.[20]

Like Mao, Jiang Zemin attached great importance to the Central Security Bureau and its regiments, reorganized after Tiananmen under the leadership of Yang Dezhong, who had been Deng Xiaoping's bodyguard, and You Xigui, his personal minder from Shanghai, who ended up being promoted to general. You's constant presence at Jiang's side, especially on overseas trips, was a sign that he not only physically protected leaders, but also played the role of advisor and overall linchpin of political intelligence.

Another organization gaining momentum in the Deng–Jiang transition era, in terms of both intelligence and decision-making, was the Political Research Bureau (*Zhengce yanjiushi*), headed by Teng Wensheng, formerly a Diaochabu head; Teng had been responsible for running the new service since mid-June 1989, with Jiang's elevation to the top job.[21]

In the Jiang Zeming era, a myriad of "working leadership groups" (*gongzuo lingdao xiaozu*) emerged to address strategic and security issues: Taiwanese affairs, "the upholding of social stability", national security, and so on. Similarly, Zeng Qinghong restructured the Bureau for Foreign Affairs (*Zhongyang Waishi*). This body reported simultaneously to the government (the State Council) and the party, and was charged with defining the major axes of PRC diplomacy. The bureau was was also known by its English name, the Central Office for Foreign Affairs (COFA). It was no coincidence that, towards the end of the twentieth century, as China became increasingly prominent on the world stage, its organizations were adopting English titles. Some officials even found themselves having to reverse their names on business cards, putting their first name before their surname to "Americanize" their profile.

The COFA was not the only body to have overtaken the Ministry of Foreign Affairs in importance. It also collaborated with another political intelligence service, which had been founded back in the first days of the communist victory, and which increased in stature during the 1950s and 1960s under the aegis of Kang Sheng: the International Liaison Department of the Central Committee (*Zhonglianbu*), the ILD, originally modelled on the Soviet Comintern. We already know it from earlier chapters, and in the 1990s, under the guidance of its director Ms Li Shuzheng, it began to regain its stature.

Trained in communist youth movements in both Shanghai and later the USSR, Li had reached the top of the service over the course of twenty years. In the days of Mao, Zhou Enlai and Kang Sheng, the ILD had established links with other Marxist-Leninist parties. In time, it broadened its reach to associate with traditional communist parties; in 1983, it sent the head of its Europe section, Cao Junjie, to the *L'Humanité* Festival, organized by the French Communist Party. With the collapse of communism across Europe in 1989, the ILD began to make contact with parties across the political spectrum, with the goal of understanding the political dynamics of different countries. Today, the ILD has a representative in some forty international embassies. Its work is parallel to, and often intersects with, that of the Guoanbu, and some officials move between the two for different assignments. Similarly, it collaborates with the party's Investigation Bureau and the United Front Work Department.

In the manner of the Guoanbu, the ILD began setting up other cover associations, such as the China Association for International Understanding, which brings foreign academics over to China and houses them in the ILD-run Hotel Wanshou, in Beijing's Haidian district. While the ILD is located in a large, modern building constructed during the Jiang Zemin era, its "research offices"—the heart of political intelligence—remain at 4 Fuxing Street, an old building that it shares with a security services publishing house, Contemporary World Publishers *(Dangdai Shijie Chubanshe)*.

In recent years, Chinese leaders have sought to give the ILD new status by making its director a minister, and it is clear that there are multiple interwoven relationships and bridges between the various Chinese secret services. It is quite understandable that until very recently their counterespionage opponents—whether Western, Indian, Korean or Japanese—have had trouble compiling an authoritative Who's Who of its special agents.

The "Black Horse"

Jiang Zemin was now on the attack. On 18 March 1998, after thirteen years of loyal service as head of the Guoanbu, Jia Chunwang was forced to give up the State Security ministership—though not without seizing a portfolio that was significantly weightier, at least in terms of staff numbers. He now became head of Public Security, with hundreds of thousands of police officers under him. He was to oversee the full range of missions assigned to the Gonganbu, from traffic control—at a time when car sales were exploding in China—to the management of the Chinese gulag, the *laogai*, partially co-administered by the Guoanbu, given its responsibility for spies and dissidents.[22]

Jia was replaced at the Guoanbu by the 56-year-old Xu Yongyue, who had a crewcut and high cheekbones, a snub nose, dark sunken eyes, deep red lips, and a high forehead that gave him the look of an intellectual. His horse-like chin befitted his animal in the Chinese zodiac. He was born in July 1942 in the Year of the Horse, in Zhenping, Henan province. His father's given name for him was Yongyue, which means "eternal jumper". It is hardly surprising that he was nicknamed the "Black Horse" (*Heima*).

In 1962, after two years of service in the PLA, Xu entered the Beijing School of Public Security at the age of twenty, and then later became a teacher in the school's technical section. Having officially joined the party in 1972, he was appointed secretary within an office of the Academy of Sciences, a transfer that involved working in scientific intelligence.

In 1976, he became private secretary to the education minister, Zhou Rongxin, a friend of his father. It comes as no surprise to learn that his father, Xu Mingzhen, had a career as a secret agent, notably in the United Front Work Department and the Ministry of Defence, mainly working in Hong Kong and usually for missions against Taiwan. In 1992, six years before his son was made head of the Guoanbu, Old Xu was named Beijing's secret envoy to the Taiwanese authorities, and sent to meet President Lee Teng-hui in Hong Kong to warm the relationship between the "two Chinas".[23]

The younger Xu had earlier worked as secretary to Zhu Muzhi, the deputy director of propaganda in the CCP Central Committee (1976-82). There he had become acquainted with another important figure in the world of espionage: the extremely discreet Yu Wen, a deputy director and the wife of Qiao Shi, then coordinator of all the security services. Better still, Xu had been secretary to the head of the new Discipline Inspection Commission, the "Immortal" Chen Yun, in office from 1978.[24] Deng Xiaoping had chosen Chen, who was both the revolution's economist and co-founder of the Shanghai Teke in the 1920s, to lead the fight against corruption. Chen had also been Qiao Shi's mentor.

In other words, Xu was, if not a foreign intelligence expert, then at least an experienced insider to lead Jiang Zemin's Guoanbu. Before his promotion, he was the number two in Hebei province, at the beginning of what he believed was a political career. But he was stopped in his tracks, and the Taiwanese analysis of his appointment was astute:

> Xu Yongyue's leap to the post of Minister for State Security drew attention from all quarters. His successful entry into the central core of CCP power can be attributed to the following factors: 1) Xu had a strong background working in the public security system and had put in long years as secretary, to a range of CCP senior statesmen, who relied heavily on his services. In particular, during his term as Chen Yun's confidential secretary he had an early opportunity to establish a personal rapport with Jiang Zemin in Shanghai. 2) In the work arranged for him as deputy secretary of the Hebei Provincial Party Committee and head of political science and law work after Chen Yun faded from the political scene in 1993, Xu won the approbation of the Party Central Committee for his steady, restrained, down-to-earth work style and very low profile with regard to the mass media. 3) China's Ministry of State Security is in charge of secret service, espionage, and domestic and overseas intelligence work. It is the power that preserves the CCP's dictatorship and has long been a key posting vied for by members of all factions. Jia Chunwang had already enjoyed a long tenure as Minister of State Security. Xu's appointment to this weighty office and his inclusion among the members of the Central Committee Leading Group on Taiwan Work are an element of the CCP's changing-of-the-guard plan for carrying its dictatorship forward into the next century.[25]

But, above all, Jiang Zemin needed a reliable man to reorganize the foreign intelligence services.

Xu's overhaul of the Guoanbu

Robert Lawrence Kuhn, author of a rather hagiographic biography of Jiang Zemin, is nonetheless right when he explains that "Jiang quietly but radically expanded the Ministry of State Security, giving it broad powers to maintain public order and ferret out corruption, in addition to its stated roles in espionage and counterespionage. The Ministry's mission required it to monitor (and spy on if necessary) ordinary citizens, Party members, government officials, and foreign nationals. It did not go unnoticed that by building up the [PAP] and the [Guoanbu], Jiang was setting up his own independent base of assertive (and potentially intrusive) power that was outside the ring of control maintained by the Beijing Party organization, run by the combative Chen Xitong, and by the PLA general staff, with whom he was still not very close."[26]

Before expanding the prerogatives of the Guoanbu—which had played an important role during the Hong Kong handover the previous year, and had ramped up its operations against Taiwan and the rest of Asia, the new boss had to clean up the Augean stables. There was the dirty business of CICIR leader Qiu Guanghui's gambling, and the allied services that Jiang Zemin wanted to reclaim, such as the United Front Work Department. Many of the UFWD's agents carried out intelligence missions abroad, using cover provided by the Foreign Affairs Bureau within the Ministry of Foreign Affairs. These operatives found themselves lodged in embassies alongside Guoanbu spies. In July 1998, Prime Minister Zhu Rongji—like Jiang Zemin, a former mayor of Shanghai—revealed that the UFWD had been importing tens of thousands of cars, and had pocketed more than 2 billion yuan that had been shared between various leaders of the party and the army.

A purge was needed, along with an internal clean-up within the Guoanbu—in other words, the "deprivatization" of the secret service. In fact, during a Politburo meeting in July 1998, Jiang Zemin gave the green light for the process of separating the commercial enterprises then run by the police, the army and the security services. In the previous decade, when Deng Xiaoping had instructed the Chinese to make money, the trend had been both the privatization of the state sector, and the setting up of commercial enterprises dependent on public bodies. These initiatives, set in motion in tandem with the "socialist market economy", were at the origin of multiple scandals and a wide variety of corruption cases.

Meanwhile, those within Guoanbu had to be seen to be irreproachable. Qiu, who had gambled away secret service funds, was an example of the serious corruption that needed to be wiped out. A progress report presented to the new boss, Xu Yongyue, declared that the service must dispose of 112 companies, and cut ties with 144 more. A handful were allowed to remain attached to the service, but were to be duly accredited with the state registration chambers. In the following year, 110 of the 112 companies were abandoned.

This was not easy, for many directors of overseas and underground operations complained that they would be deprived of "necessary channels for professional security work"—in other words, many secret agents would lose their cover, both in China and abroad.[27] However, in the context of the fight against corruption, the service heads considered it vital that the secret services rebuild their image, in accordance with the party line. Under Xu, a mini decoupling committee was set up, with the deputy minister Ding Renlin, the Guoanbu's Central Commission for Discipline Inspection secretary, Yu Hongbao, and Liu Yiping, a deputy minister and head of corporate affairs. Under their leadership, a "rectification committee" was set up, with branches in all thirty-one of the Guoanbu's provincial offices.

The Guoanbu needed to lead by example, taking part in committees overseeing the "decoupling" of inter-administrations.[28] In practice, this meant that, in the Jiang era at the turn of the century, the Guoanbu arrogated to itself the lion's share of internal security, even though it had been originally created with the specific purpose of carrying out espionage operations abroad and conducting foreign counterintelligence.

During a video conference with the heads of the regional offices, Xu Yongyue persuaded his services to establish memoranda on "decoupling" operations. The question was which companies should be given up and which should be kept, and under what form of management. The Guoanbu needed to decide whether to close them down completely, or hand over their administration to local authorities or central government, in general the Economic and Trade Commission.

The operation was completed in June 1999. The Guoanbu "confidentiality committee" sent a directive to all sectors asking them to "guarantee confidentiality while the rectification of businesses was underway". It was imperative to avoid identification through overly curious or indiscreet "hostile forces"—either those businesses the Guoanbu had decided to keep under its direct control, or those that remained allied to the Guoanbu for the purposes of carrying out espionage abroad.

Tens of thousands of undercover agents abroad were thus posted to other welcoming business fronts with an established cover. The outcome of this highly original "decoupling" operation was that, although Xu was indeed pursuing reform of his services, he was obliged to ask Beijing to compensate for the loss of his private enterprises with substantial budgetary increases—if, that is, China was to continue to expand its intelligence community, which was certainly the goal of the globally ambitious Jiang era. In the second half of the 1990s, Xu validated the reshaping of his service along the lines shown in Appendix VIII, which I was able to draw up with the help of Chinese open sources and with many contributions from men and women—in the West, Japan and even the PRC—who knew details about its structure.

Of all the local offices, the Beijing office at 14 Dongchang'an Avenue was obviously the best known, especially since the Guoanbu was sharing its offices with the Gonganbu. Not only was this Beijing bureau in charge of controlling the operations in the capital itself, but it also oversaw international operations and kept an eye on expat communities—diplomats, journalists, businessmen—under the direction of Li Yintang, distant successor of the CIA defector Yu Zhensan. Like all the offices in major cities, it had to collaborate with another major administration, the Bureau of State Secrets, which was responsible for both the classification of state secrets, and the prevention of any leaks via contact with foreigners (*Li tong waiguo*), long prohibited but now less of an issue given the economic expansion and increase in trade underway in the 1990s.

MI6's former Beijing head of station, Nigel Inkster has explained that intelligence-gathering abroad is now largely dealt with by the regional State Security Offices (*Guoanju* and *Guoanting*): "Most of the foreign-intelligence collection within the [Guoanbu] is conducted by the State Security Bureaus ... The Shanghai [bureau] carries out collection against the United States and its main Western allies; the neighbouring Zhejiang [bureau] against northern Europe; the Qingdao [bureau] against Japan and the Koreas; the Guangzhou [bureau] against Hong Kong, Taiwan and Southeast Asia; and the Beijing [bureau] against Eastern Europe and Russia."[29]

Playing for high stakes in Afghanistan

Everything seems to be a state secret in the People's Republic of China. Every year, alarming reports by Amnesty International, China Watch and Reporters Without Borders list the number of journalists who have been expelled or arrested. Yet, at the same time, when everything is stamped "top secret", leaks are inevitable.

Take a sunny spring Sunday morning in Beijing's Panjiayuan flea market, during my 2007 trip to research this book. Nothing could be more enjoyable than rummaging around the market's bookstalls. They attract almost no tourists, since all the books are in Chinese. Sellers would fall over themselves trying to sell me books of photos, or magazines with pictures of scantily dressed Chinese girls. This particular Sunday, they showed no surprise when I expressed interest in what ought not to have concerned me in the slightest: the history of the CCP, the Lin Biao plot of the early 1970s, the mysteries of Hu Yaobang's rise and fall, the Gang of Four, salacious stories about Madame Mao or Jiang Zemin's Shanghai clique. The booksellers were unsuspecting because such stories fascinate plenty of readers, who lap up revelations that confirm or contradict the many rumours, which often turn out to be extremely precise and accurate. Imagine my excitement when, next to a stack of dusty old pamphlets by Mao, I came upon a 240-page document, with a stamp on its top right-hand corner: 秘密—*Mimi*, meaning "secret".

The toothless old woman to whom I handed over 20 yuan was so happy that she also tried to sell me the pile of Chairman Mao's writings: *On the Correct Handling of Contradictions among the People*; *Rectify the Party's Style of Work*; *Against the Cult of the Book*, and the rest. But I was very happy with my top-secret document, "Collection of World Strategic Reference Materials of the 4th Bureau", published jointly by military intelligence—the PLA2—and the Central Military Commission's Office of International Military Cooperation.

This text, which I sent ahead to France in order to avoid having it on me when I left the country, had a markedly historical flavour. Published internally by the PLA General Staff in March 1983, it dealt with current news topics of the time: the Falklands War, the Israeli invasion of Lebanon, and the Soviet invasion of Afghanistan. These reports from the PLA2 also covered technical and tactical capacity—for example, the use of Soviet helicopters in Afghanistan—and were used for training officers. They also drew on reports, translated into Chinese, by American and Soviet experts.

Above all, the document made clear the extent to which, since the war in Afghanistan (1979-89), Chinese military intelligence had grown beyond its traditional theatres in the Far East and Asia. The situation in Afghanistan took a singular turn under Jiang Zemin with the victory of the Taliban and the entrenchment of al-Qaeda, a major destabilizing factor in the region—and the PRC had certainly had a hand in these developments. Not only did it share a 75-kilometre border with Afghanistan, but in the aftermath of the Soviet invasion in late 1979, the Chinese—at the request of the Americans—had taken a major role in the arming, training and financing of the Afghan Mujahedin. They continue to support the Taliban today, hoping to play an important role in ending the long-running conflict.[30]

The armaments supplied by Beijing had offered the Taliban a distinct advantage against the invading Soviets: the Simonov machine guns and Kalashnikov assault rifles cloned by the Chinese used the same ammunition as the Soviet military. This meant that, if a group of Afghan underground fighters managed to steal weapons from Soviet troops, they would be able to use them. But the real prizes were the Chinese-made 107mm multiple rocket launchers that Beijing gave the Muhajedin at the Americans' request. The central location of aid to the Afghan resistance was in Peshawar, where the CIA and the Chinese services had weapons depots. Chinese advisors were also present in the Yasin region, while logistics operations were overseen by the Air Force general Zhang Tingfa.

An ideological problem had overshadowed Beijing's support, but Deng Xiaoping and his team were pragmatic. They would have preferred not to abandon Afghanistan's pro-China communist organizations, such as Shoaleye Djawid (Eternal Flame) or Sorha (The Reds), but the traditionalist warlords did not distinguish between these Marxist-Leninists and those supported by Moscow. All were secularists and atheists—infidels—and all were to be liquidated. Besides, romanticism was not the strong point of Chinese diplomacy. In the art of war, which they had had no small part in inventing, the Chinese understood that a wise ruler builds alliances with strong warlords. Thus, in 1980, the Diaochabu and the PLA2 backed a warlord named Rahmakoul, the general of a small army at the eastern end of the long Wakhan corridor, a strip of Afghan territory wedged between the USSR, China, Pakistan and India.

Similarly, it was easier to supply arms to these underground fighters than to secure the logistics of Maoist groups seeking to mount attacks in Kabul. Fundamentalist Islamist resistance leaders, like the fierce and increasingly powerful Gulbuddin Hekmatyar, benefited from this. Beijing was caught in a paradox: the Hezb-i-Islami Afghanistan (HIA) of Hekmatyar, jihadist hero and future ally of the Taliban, was liquidating pro-Chinese groups such as the Afghanistan Liberation Organization (*Sazman-i Rihayi Afghanistan*). ALO fighters were murdered in both Pakistan and Afghanistan. In November 1986, Dr Faiz Ahmad, founder and leader of the organization, was betrayed by a double agent and handed over to Hezb-i-Islami, along with several of his deputies.

Legend has it that, in August 1980, the PLA's engineering troops established an arms delivery route to guerrillas in the north of the country via the Karakorum Highway, the old Silk Road. In fact, the vast majority of Chinese weapons were airlifted to Islamabad, an operation overseen by the air general Zhang Tingfa, who was also first party secretary in the Air Force, and visited the area as early as 1979. Thousands of mules, the "strategic animals" of the Mujahedin, did take the Karakorum Highway. There was also talk of creating a Mujahedin office, to be set up jointly by Saudi Arabian and Chinese services.

The campaign against the Soviet invaders, backed by Beijing, provoked an inevitable response from the KGB, which organized diversionary operations in Afghanistan, the USSR and Xinjiang, far-west China, where they were carried out by Tajiks recruited in East Turkestan, which had been annexed by the PRC. Chinese border guards frequently arrested "infiltrated Soviet agents".

The ethnic revitalization plan waged against the centralized power of Beijing was even described in a 1979 book by Victor Louis, an extraordinary Russian-born journalist and expert on Soviet disinformation, who wrote for the Western press, including the *Evening News* and the *Sunday Express*. He was known to have close links to the KGB. In *The Coming Decline of the Chinese Empire*, Louis predicted the implosion of the People's Republic of China following uprisings by minorities like the Tajiks and the Uyghurs.

Mao's grandson, secret agent

In October 1983, General Eugene F. Tighe of the US Defense Intelligence Agency was sent to Beijing by President Ronald Reagan for talks with General Huang Zhengji, then deputy director of the PLA2. On the agenda were the practical aspects of operations to supply weapons to Afghan partisans.

Until 1984, the Chinese had been the Mujahedin's main suppliers; after that, it was the CIA and the Pakistani Inter-Services Intelligence (ISI). Everything always went through the embassies. Mohammad Yousaf, head of the ISI's Afghan Office, recounted this anecdote: "I never visited the US embassy; I never attended diplomatic functions or formal military occasions. The only exception was with the Chinese. Every year General Akhtar [Abdul Rehman Khan, head of the ISI] and I would go to the Chinese embassy for dinner after the official signing of the arms protocol, whereby China agreed to supply us with specified types of quantities of weapons and ammunition for the Mujahideen. This was typical Chinese. They always insisted on absolute accuracy in all their dealings. I remember the colossal fuss that was made, involving high-ranking embassy officials, when just one small box of ammunition among thousands went astray. We later recovered it, but very politely they had insisted we move heaven and earth to do so. What a contrast to everybody else."[31]

Naturally, the Chinese were seizing the opportunity to try and sell their equipment. The Afghan battlefield served as a showcase for newly created, outward-looking services like COSTIND. But, despite pressure from their US "comrades", the Chinese failed to sell their Red Arrow laser-guided portable missiles to the Pakistani army, which found them impractical. In 1985, the Pakistanis had the idea of suggesting that the Chinese transform their multiple rocket launchers (MBRLs), which were unfeasibly heavy, into portable ones (SBRLs). "We had already made this change at the request of the PLA, but by now it was considered an obsolete weapon," the Chinese military attaché in Islamabad, Colonel Zhou Jiang, told me. Nonetheless, 500 were ordered and sent to Rawalpindi, followed by another thousand in 1987. "This weapon greatly increased our ability to target Kabul," General Akhtar recalled.

What the head of the ISI did not say—and perhaps did not even know—was that there was an unusual officer in the military intelligence mission in Islamabad at this time. Deputy military attaché Major Kong Jining was none other than Mao Zedong's grandson, as I discovered and revealed in 2001 in the French magazine *Le Point*. This choice of envoy—the son of one of Mao's few children to have survived both the revolution and the Chairman's general lack of interest in his offspring—indicates just how important Beijing perceived its role in Afghanistan to be.

In 1936, He Zizhen, Mao's second wife, gave birth to a daughter named Li Min. This was after the Long March, and before she was dispatched to the USSR so that her place could be ceded to Jiang Qing. Nine years later, Li Min was sent back to China, where she was brought up by Jiang Qing alongside Jiang's own daughter with Mao, Li Na. Her mother He Zizhen, who was placed in a psychiatric asylum by Stalin, was allowed to return to China after the communist victory, on condition that she undergo electroshock therapy in Shanghai.

After gaining a science degree, Li Min worked in the laboratories that were developing the atomic bomb. Later, she worked at COSTIND under Nie Rongzhen, the so-called father of the atomic bomb. There she met a general's son called Kong Linghua. They married in 1959 and had two children: Kong Jining, born in 1962, and his younger sister Kong Dongmei. As children, they used to visit their grandfather Mao at the Zhongnanhai government complex. They would put on little Red Guard uniforms and chant their grandfather's sayings. The fall of the Gang of the Four was a far from glorious moment: Li Min was arrested, and she denounced her stepmother and guardian Jiang Qing as a counter-revolutionary. This allowed her to rejoin the privileged elite under Deng Xiaoping, while her husband, General Kong, was appointed head of PLA propaganda.

At twenty-one, their son Kong Jining went to Nanjing to study English with the other trainee cadres at the PLA's Institute of International Relations, where future special agents were trained. This was how the young Major Kong came to meet his baptism of fire in the late 1980s, when he was sent to Pakistan as assistant to the military attaché, helping supply weapons to the Mujahedin in liaison with the ISI.[32]

Ironically, it was the same teams of Chinese military intelligence agents—around 300 of them, according to the CIA—who later reversed the process with Pakistan's help, recuperating and sending back to China material that had originally been delivered to the Mujahedin, such as the Stinger portable air-to-air missile.[33]

According to US sources, there was little to be proud of in the final episode of Chinese aid to Afghanistan, the Battle of Jalalabad. This siege of the pro-government garrison by Islamist guerrillas, which lasted from March to June 1989, was a failure for the anti-Soviet forces. In addition to the rebel forces' poor strategy, the refusal of the Chinese to supply ammunition or help with logistics played a pivotal role.

A US source told me at the time that Beijing was sending a clear sign to Washington: it was at this time, in the midst of the Tiananmen protests, that the American embassy and CIA decided to grant asylum to Professor Fang Lizhi, and Deng Xiaoping was not happy about it. But this U-turn in Afghanistan also reflected the fact that Moscow's simultaneous thaw in relations with both Beijing and Washington was changing the rules of engagement. Not long afterwards, as we shall see, it would lead to the beginning of a close collaboration between the Chinese secret services and the KGB and, later on, the new Russian organs of intelligence—against the Americans and NATO.

When the Taliban took power in Kabul, however, the Chinese special services were still in the front row. In 2000, agents of the Guoanbu and its CICIR paid regular visits to Afghanistan's fundamentalist leadership. The following year, in March 2001, the large Chinese manufacturer Huawei installed communications systems in Kabul and Kandahar, just as it had in Saddam Hussein's Iraq. Even more extraordinary, after the 9/11 attack on New York's World

Trade Center that autumn, and the subsequent US offensive in Afghanistan, Beijing's secret services were able to recover an American missile thanks to their now besieged Taliban peers. It was duly sent to Beijing to be taken apart and analyzed.

Chinese military intelligence even managed to infiltrate Uyghur secret agents into the small Islamist group in Xinjiang led by Osama bin Laden and al-Qaeda—a few of whom were killed or captured by the Americans and interned in Guantanamo Bay as terrorists. Commandos of the NATO-led ISAF—the International Security Assistance Force, which had been in Afghanistan since the beginning of 2002—frequently found Chinese-made weapons in the storerooms of the al-Qaeda members they were hunting. In May 2007, an ISAF helicopter was shot down by the new HN-5 portable anti-aircraft missile launcher—*Hong Ying* (Seabird)—which the Chinese had sent via Iran to both the Taliban and the Iraqi Shiite resistance.

In June 2006, Afghan President Hamid Karzai went to Beijing and gave a speech at the China Institute of International Studies, in which he implored the Chinese to step up in the common fight against terrorism. Professor Li Wei, the Guoanbu's terrorism advisor, could only approve—as long as he ignored the fact that it was the Chinese, even more than the Americans, who had equipped and helped both the Taliban and future al-Qaeda members among the Muhajedin, as Jiang Zemin's global secret services grew and grew.

Afghanistan itself is a prime example of just how quickly and successfully these Chinese services staked their place in the geopolitics of the incoming twenty-first century. Before we continue following Chinese spies out of the old millennium and into the new, it is worth us considering this. Just fifteen years on from Karzai's trip to Beijing, thanks to the secret interventions of the Jiang era, the West's withdrawal from Afghanistan has found China and its intelligence services well placed in relation to the new Taliban regime.

In the summer of 2021, as the Americans withdrew from Afghanistan and the Taliban returned to power, the Chinese hoped to secure an important role for themselves in the new order. According to my sources, until the Taliban retook the country in a lightning offensive following the US withdrawal, the Guoanbu had been sharing intelligence with the government in Kabul. On 18 December 2019, a post on Twitter, accompanied by photographic evidence, revealed that the Guoanbu chief, Chen Wenqing, had met with Afghan National Security Advisor Hamdullah Mohib, to discuss the evolving situation in the country.

Mohib, however, was wary in his dealings with the Guoanbu; he knew perfectly well that the Chinese were playing a double game. During the period leading up to the Americans' departure, the Guoanbu was sharing information not only with the Afghan administration, but also with the Taliban intelligence service, which is organized into regional military commands; the Chinese were working with the Taliban not only against the Americans, but against ISIS and al-Qaeda as well.

One year after this meeting, in December 2020, Mohib's suspicions were vindicated, as the Afghan National Directorate of Security arrested ten Chinese secret agents in Kabul. All of them were handled by Li Yangyang and Sha Hung, from the Guoanbu's Xinjiang branch.[34]

The ten agents were accused of having set up a spy ring in collaboration with the Taliban and the Haqqani network—a powerful guerrilla group, and a longstanding ally of the Taliban and its late leader Mullah Omar. (The network has also been utilized by the ISI, the Pakistani intelligence service, with which Beijing is on excellent terms.) But under interrogation, the Chinese agents explained that, in fact, they were spying not for or with, but on the Taliban and al-Qaeda, and that they had only been in contact with the Haqqani network for information about rebels belonging to the Turkistan Islamic Party, an armed Uyghur group.

A special envoy was dispatched to Beijing, and tough negotiations ensued; the Chinese spies were repatriated on a government plane in February 2021. This incident passed without comment in the West, but it foreshadowed a significant diplomatic event that was to come six months later: the Xi government's swift political recognition of the Taliban's rule, officially called the Islamic Emirate of Afghanistan.

8

CHINA AND RUSSIA VS AMERICA

Just before midnight on 7 May 1999, the US conducted a series of test strikes on real targets using JDAM precision-guided missiles,[1] guided by GPS. Since 24 March, NATO had been bombing Belgrade—its first offensive in half a century of existence. The pretext was aiding the province of Kosovo in its defence against the Serbs, and supporting its separatist paramilitary organization, the Kosovo Liberation Army.

Three of the five missiles dropped by B-2 bombers hit the Chinese embassy, in the Neo Beograd municipality. In the smoking rubble, about thirty Chinese lay wounded. Three people were killed; they were, officially, journalists reporting on the war between NATO and Serbian forces: Shao Yunhuan, 48, attached to the Xinhua News Agency, and Xu Xinghu, 29, and his wife Zhu Ying, 27, both correspondents for *Enlightenment Daily* (*Guangming Ribao*).

There was no doubt that the attack was in violation of international law. During the hours that followed, a decade after the massacre of students calling for democracy, demonstrations were held in Tiananmen Square. People carried placards with reproductions of *Guernica*, Picasso's famous painting depicting the Nazi aerial bombardment of the Basque city during the Spanish Civil War, and slogans like "Down with American imperialism!" or "No, Clinton, we are not Monica!" A year on from the Lewinsky scandal, its shadow still hung over American politics.

In the White House, Clinton himself, overwhelmed by the escalating conflict, tried to reach President Jiang, who was refusing to take his calls and demanding a public apology. Was it really true that a certain Dr Folamour in the Pentagon had authorized the airstrike without the president's knowledge? In his memoirs, Clinton reiterated the official explanation: that the CIA had inadvertently used an out-of-date map of Belgrade, which showed the embassy as an old Serbian building used for military purposes. The embassy building, finished only three years earlier, appeared to have been rather easily overlooked.

A week passed. On 14 May, the US president finally managed to talk to Jiang Zemin: "I apologized again and told him I was sure he didn't believe I would knowingly attack his embassy. Jiang replied that he knew I wouldn't do that, but said he did believe that there were people in the Pentagon or the CIA who didn't favor my outreach to China and could have rigged the maps intentionally to cause a rift between us. Jiang had a hard time believing that a nation as technologically advanced as we were could make such a mistake. I had a hard time believing it, too, but that's what happened."[2]

It was a humiliating situation for Jiang Zemin. He had done everything he could to maintain a cordial relationship with the White House since Clinton had become president in 1993, including welcoming him on a state visit to China the previous year. In the upper echelons of the PLA, Jiang had come under a great deal of criticism for this stance. Now, Zhang Wannian, vice-chairman of the Central Military Commission, was expressing concerns—shared by several other generals—about Zhongnanhai's soft response to what had happened in Kosovo. But members of the Politburo Standing Committee asked General Zhang to allow cooler heads to prevail within the ruling circle of the PLA. A centrist position was presented on television by Jiang Zemin's heir apparent, Hu Jintao.

Hu expressed the government's anger, while at the same time threatening those who might seek to exploit the situation by encouraging rioting during anti-American demonstrations. It would serve no one's interests to see a rerun of Tiananmen, or, a more recent example, the 25 April demonstration by the Buddhist-Taoist Falun Gong movement, which had paralyzed the centre of Beijing with a peaceful siege of Zhongnanhai, residence of the ruling elite. The situation was complicated by the fact that the Falun Gong leader, Li Hongzhi, had gone to live in the United States, and Chinese intelligence claimed he was part of a CIA conspiracy.

General Zhang took this opportunity to develop his concept of the "New World War". He shared the opinion of the securocrats, who were using the CIA as a punching bag in their analysis of the Belgrade bombing, claiming that:

1. Senior NATO generals gave the order to strike.
2. Without seeking the agreement of the other NATO countries, the United States and Great Britain gave the green light to the attack in order to test both the Chinese government and the public reaction.
3. The CIA missile attack was part of a broader long-term campaign of hostility as part of its anti-communist campaign.
4. The CIA used the excuse of 'out of date maps' to conceal its real motives for the attack.
5. The CIA took advantage of this so-called 'accidental bombing' to pressure the US government and Congress to increase its budget.[3]

Meanwhile, General Chi Haotian, who had ordered the 1989 Tiananmen massacre and was now defence minister, outlined a different five-point list—the "five preparations" constituting the necessary response to this deliberate US attack. The Chinese needed to:

1. Win the hi-tech war;
2. Win via a blockade and a counter-blockade in the Taiwan Strait;
3. Wage a modern war following a military provocation by the US-Japan alliance;
4. Win a third regional world war launched by the United States and NATO against China and other countries;
5. Successfully protect China against a US-led nuclear offensive.

It was easy enough to say. But everyone knew that the Chinese army was a colossus with feet of clay. Faced with US technology, the PLA would be as paralyzed as the ancient Terracotta Army. That was why the Belgrade coup had triggered such an earthquake, comparable to the humiliation twenty years earlier when the PLA had been routed by Vietnamese forces.

Jiang Zemin had no desire to add fuel to the fire. He needed first to find out what had really happened in Belgrade. Various interpretations were possible, according to intelligence conveyed to Zhongnanhai. The Chinese special services, represented in Washington by General Chen Kaizeng—former military attaché in London and future head of military intelligence—believed that the purpose of the Kosovo war in general (1998-9) was to divert attention away from the Lewinsky affair, and that the embassy attack may well have been a genuine blunder. Jiang Zemin, the object of constant rumour-mongering regarding his many mistresses—including the beautiful singer Song Zuying—would certainly have understood. However, the total destruction of a foreign embassy demanded another explanation, perhaps a little less far-fetched and a little more rational.

Within an hour of the bombing, Jiang had convened the Standing Committee of the Politburo, to whom he advocated a moderate response to the United States. This contrasted with his thundering Kremlin counterpart, Boris Yeltsin, who—between gulps of vodka—unleashed the idea of a great Sino-Russian military alliance against NATO. But Jiang had every reason to avoid fanning the flames. As Beijing was getting ready to join the World Trade Organization, China and America had more to gain from commercial cooperation than from triggering a new Cold War.

Mission Save Milošević

Behind this realpolitik, there were also technical reasons for maintaining a conciliatory attitude. General Xiong Guangkai, who was close to Jiang and responsible for the PLA intelligence services, and his subordinate General Luo Yudong, head of the PLA2, briefed the country's seven leaders.[4] He explained that the Chinese embassy had actually been home to several top-secret joint Sino-Serbian operations, which NATO had uncovered. This collaboration between Belgrade and Beijing dated back almost two decades to 1977, when Belgrade service manager Stane Dolanc had accompanied Tito, president of the Yugoslav Federation, to Beijing. We know what happened five years later in 1983, just as the Guoanbu was being set up: Dolanc welcomed the deputy minister of Chinese security on a visit to Yugoslavia whose purpose was to strengthen the Chinese regional intelligence bases in Belgrade and Bucharest, Romania.

After Tito's death and the disintegration of the Yugoslav Federation, the Guoanbu had intensified its collaboration with the Serbian services. In November 1997, Serbian leader Slobodan Milošević and Jovica Stanišić, head of the SDB service (*Služba državne bezbednosti*), had made a visit to Beijing.[5] But it was principally military intelligence that was affected by the embassy bombing. Among the most seriously wounded was the military attaché Colonel Ren Baokai, in charge of liaising with the Serbian army and in particular with General Branko Krga's military intelligence service, the *Vojna obaveštajna služba* (VOS). The embassy wing where Colonel Baokai's office was located was one of the targets of the radio-controlled bomb, as the Chinese protested to their central command in a dispatch intercepted by the Echelon network, run by the US with the help of Australia, Canada, New Zealand and the United Kingdom. There was a good reason for this targeting: the wing housed a large system for eavesdropping and broadcasting secure signals. Not only did the Chinese track missiles in order to study what countermeasures might be feasible, but the radio system also enabled the Serbian army to track the missiles' communications and even to guide some of their operations. NATO's wiretapping system uncovered this on 23 April, when an air attack intended to strike Milošević interrupted shortwave broadcasts to the Serbian army. (These resumed some time later—from the Chinese embassy.)

"According to my sources, the Yugoslav army was using the Chinese embassy's antennae to broadcast their own shortwave messages," explained Miloš Vasić, a correspondent in Belgrade for *Vreme* magazine, who has studied the case. "They fired hundreds of metres of coaxial cable from their transmitter, which was located in another building in the neighbourhood. The Chinese had been repeatedly warned to stop broadcasting these messages, but they continued, which is why they were bombed. The same sources claimed that the embassy was housing the main base of Chinese intelligence, which meant that the Americans were able to kill two birds with one stone."[6]

Even as the ashes of the journalists killed were being repatriated to Beijing, the Chinese secret services remained focused. Ten days later,

Echelon again intercepted communications between the Guoanbu headquarters, headed by Xu Yongyue in Beijing, and what remained of its intelligence base in Yugoslavia. Their contents were summarized in a report by the US Defense Intelligence Agency: "Chinese embassy personnel in Belgrade were instructed ... to collect missile fragments from the bombed embassy building and send them back to China, probably aboard the aircraft chartered to evacuate injured embassy personnel."[7]

In addition, the Americans obtained evidence that this collaboration between the Chinese and the Serbians had been negotiated by Milošević's wife, Mira Marković. After a trip to China in 1990, she had openly expressed her admiration for the Chinese system, and in particular the way in which the Tiananmen movement had been so effectively crushed. Now, at the instigation of former prime minister Li Peng and his deputy Luo Gan, the Chinese secret services even drew up a plan to whisk the Miloševićs out of the country and grant them asylum, as they had done for the Cambodian king Norodom Sihanouk in 1979. (The reader may recall that the attempt in 1989 to do the same for the Romanian Ceauseşcus had failed.) Plans for the operation to rescue the Miloševićs had been in place since November 1998 between the Guoanbu and the SDB, whose new head, Radomir Marković, was a friend of the Miloševićs' son Marko, who also hoped to find refuge in China.

History, however, decreed otherwise; Slobodan Milošević was indicted in absentia by the International Criminal Tribunal for the Former Yugoslavia in The Hague in May 1999, and arrested two years later. He died in prison in 2006 before the trial ended. Rumour has it that his wife tried to reach China before settling in Russia. Her son, Marko, showed up at Beijing airport on 9 October 2000, travelling on a diplomatic passport, but was turned back because he didn't have a visa.[8]

Other war criminals remained on the run.[9] In 2007 a group of former Milošević collaborators and friends of his widow Mira were spotted in Shanghai, according to sources with knowledge of the hunt for Serbian warlords. Among them were former police chief General Goran Radosavljević ("Guri"), wanted in Europe for war crimes, and his intelligence officer, Dragan Filipović ("Fitcha"), known for his book—heavily influenced by Chinese ideology—*How to Fight the Globalist Stench*. In China, I was told that Filipović had links with one of the Shaolin martial arts schools, the cradle of *wushu* and *kung fu*, where commandos from the Chinese special forces train.

The PLA2 in Serbia

Jiang Zemin's Central Military Commission activated all its intelligence units and analysis centres to study the war in Kosovo. One might argue that this move was connected with the Chinese determination to build a GPS system to compete with NATO's JDAM, which had guided the missiles that hit the embassy in Belgrade, by developing a relay system to cannibalize the European Galileo programme, temporarily joining up with it. But that was clearly not all.

The aim was to examine the details of the conflict and analyze the consequences of US strategy, tactics, use of weaponry and new technologies. The same study had been made in relation to the US-led Operation Desert Storm—the operation to retake Kuwait after its invasion by Iraq in 1991. The Kosovo war was a strategic turning point, and this in itself was a reason for reflection on the part of PLA strategists. It was up to the PLA2 to study all the latest technical innovations, such as the use of helicopters to infiltrate special forces into the Kosovo Liberation Army. The results of this study led the Chinese to begin setting up similar units in 2000.

The researchers concluded that what made this war innovative was the use of hi-tech weaponry. Tactical and strategic attacks were coordinated from a command centre far from the battlefield and the enemy defence perimeter. Missiles were accurately triggered at a distance of up to 12,000 kilometres from Kosovo, just as cruise missiles were guided from a distance of 800 kilometres, and bombers flew at high altitude without having their targets in their sights. The Chinese reports were clear: this was "the first war without vision", a "contactless" war in which information systems and the control of airspace were determining factors.

In 1999, Chinese colonels Qiao Liang and Wang Xiangsui were given permission to publish a book whose thesis would revolutionize the field of military strategy. *Unrestricted Warfare* drew on the experience of the wars in the Gulf and the former Yugoslavia. Qiao and Wang argued that modern conflicts making heavy use of hi-tech weaponry were too costly for developing countries like the PRC. At the same time, Western democracies, under pressure of public opinion, no longer wanted to lose men in combat. This was a weakness that must be exploited, by developing new forms of urban guerrilla warfare that would sap the enemy's willingness to fight. This strategy would involve both economic warfare and the computerized destruction of the enemy's IT systems. These predictions were sufficiently influential to lead some US observers to suggest in 2001 that the Chinese colonels' concept of asymmetrical warfare had given Osama bin Laden the idea of attacking the World Trade Center.[10] Despite a certain reticence among some officers of the old guard, the PLA invited the two colonels to undertake a study on Kosovo based on their ideas.

Meanwhile, NATO strategists were conducting their own research: they believed that recent attacks, including the bombardment of its websites and those of the White House with spam, were allowing the PLA's 3rd Department (the PLA3, in charge of communications) to test the Americans' responsiveness in this new era of information technology warfare.[11] In the aftermath of the NATO strikes on Yugoslavia and the destruction of Beijing's embassy, the Chinese were questioning their own theory of a "world moving towards multipolarity". Once again, the United States had shown that—in their eyes at least—they were still the world's policemen.

Another consequence of the war was that General Xiong Guangkai set up a military technological research taskforce. On the political front, Jiang Zemin was particularly unhappy with the ultra-nationalist sentiments being expressed by many strategists affiliated with military think-tanks, but he was obliged to work with them. After a barrage of Chinese propaganda against "hegemonic American policies" and attacks on NATO's role in the Kosovo crisis, the Politburo ordered its strategists to analyze why NATO was so openly aligned with Serbian and Russian positions.

The problem for the leadership was this: on the one hand they had re-established a relationship with the Russians and Serbs, but on the other, they were afraid that Kosovar independence would set a bad example. They were, of course, thinking of the thorny issues of Tibet and Xinjiang. "We must remember the words of the late Deng Xiaoping, who said that China must keep a low profile in any international affairs that do not pose a direct threat to its vital interests and national security," concluded one report.

Officials drew a parallel with the Romanian revolution of 1989, when the Chinese services had wrongly predicted that Ceauşescu would retain his hold on power. Ten years later, in the summer of 1999, Jiang Zemin gave the green light for the creation of a new strategic think-tank, comparable to the White House National Security Council, which advises US presidents on national security and foreign policy matters.

Hu Jintao, who went on to become general secretary of the CCP in 2002, inaugurated this new Bureau of International Strategic Studies (*Guoji zhanlüe yanjiushi*), tasked with shaping strategy against the United States and NATO.[12] To do this, the new service had to provide the CCP Central Committee, the State Council (or government) and the Central Military Commission with in-depth analyses of intelligence reports, which would then be used as the basis for making policy recommendations. Its director was Jiang Zemin's protégé, Zeng Qinghong (director of the CCP's General Affairs Bureau), and among his choice of advisors was, of course, General Xiong Guangkai, supported by several experts on NATO, including General Zhang Changtai, who would be appointed military attaché in Paris in 2006. With eighty analysts in three departments studying US defence affairs and European issues, as well as NATO itself, this new centre for intelligence analysis and forecasting had its headquarters at the Xishan Military Command Centre, which also housed the Guoanbu headquarters. There is no doubt that, during this period, one man in particular stood out for his versatility: General Xiong Guangkai, head of military intelligence.

General Xiong Guangkai, intelligence star

Busy as he was in June 1999, Xiong would certainly have been interested in the apparent suicide of the German Sinologist Violetta Zhang, detailed in the previous chapter. He was a distinguished Germanist and fluent German-speaker, who often travelled to Munich to take part in seminars on terrorism and other strategic issues.

The baby-faced Xiong, with his large glasses, profuse head of hair and bulging forehead, was born in the Nanchang capital of Jiangxi in March 1939, in the Year of the Rabbit. This zodiac animal is considered *yin* (dark), which contradicted his given name, Guangkai ("luminous project"). This horoscope sign, which as we shall see fascinated him, is located in the west, and is distinguished by its prudence and discretion along with a desire to impose its way independently on the way matters progress.[13]

There is a reason for mentioning the meaning of the names given to children according to ancient traditions of the movement of the stars, the structure of the family and the horoscope. Even in the era of GPS-guided missiles, such details have genuine significance in Chinese lives. It is also valuable to know that in communist mythology, Nanchang, where General Xiong was born, was the birthplace of the PLA, after a failed uprising led by Mao on 1 August 1927. Xiong bore on his uniform a crest for this date, "8–1" (*Ba yi*); the date of the uprising had been chosen because this is a lucky number. Its significance became even more marked when the date and time were chosen for the opening ceremony of the Beijing Olympics: 8 August 2008 at 8pm.

After a long time spent on the benches of the Zhangjiakou (formerly Kalgan) Institute of Foreign Languages, Xiong Guangkai began his career as a translator and intelligence officer in East Germany, where he was posted from 1960 to 1967. Then, from 1974 to 1981, he was military attaché in West Germany. It was during these two periods, when he travelled a great deal around the two German republics, that he made many friends in the Warsaw Pact intelligence services. These friends included a young but experienced KGB officer named Vladimir Putin. Since this glorious era, when socialist regimes covered half of Europe, the two intelligence officers have remained in contact and regularly exchanged gifts to celebrate Russian and Chinese New Year.[14]

In 1982, Xiong joined the PLA2 General Intelligence Department under the command of General Wu Jinfa, and helped forge the new and reformed services of the Deng Xiaoping era. He was involved in the surprising Sino-American collaboration against the Soviets in the last years of the USSR—the joint interception of Soviet communications, and the provision of military support to the Afghan resistance.

In 1988, Xiong had taken over the leadership of the PLA2. Under him it remained responsible for military intelligence, while the PLA3, then led by General Shi Quan, dealt with signals intelligence (SIGINT) and other missions that were part of the information technology war. For this reason the PLA3 was also known as the Communications Department (*Tongxin Bu*), a sector it shared with the PLA4 (*Xibu*), in charge of electronic warfare (electronic countermeasures and radars, also called *Dianzi Duikang Leida Bu*).[15]

As we have seen, within the structure of the PLA, a deputy army chief of staff was named overall head of the various special departments; in Xiong's time, this was General Xu Xin. Xu had close links with President Yang Shangkun and his brother, General Yang Baibing, head of the PLA's General Political Department, and he had involved the military intelligence apparatus in the suppression of the Tiananmen protests in 1989. Xiong had showed no qualms about infiltrating the democratic movement in many different ways. Three years later, in November 1992, he took over from Xu Xin as deputy chief of staff, thus becoming head of the vast military intelligence conglomerate. He appointed a Red Prince in his place at the PLA2: General Ji Shengde, son of Ji Pengfei.[16]

Xiong was one of the few officer generals to have climbed, rung by rung, to the very top of the military intelligence career ladder. In 2007 he went on to play a major role as head of the China Institute for International Strategic Studies (CIISS), a PLA2 think-tank. He experienced one major career setback, when he unsuccessfully lobbied for Jiang Zemin to name him Guoanbu minister, which was deemed impossible: it was felt in the upper echelons of the service that he risked bringing an overly political tone to a ministry trying to maintain some neutrality in the struggle between political factions. Some felt that Xiong was using his trips abroad for his own personal publicity, in order to increase his standing within China itself. This was suggested in the American Defense Intelligence Agency's highly detailed dossier on him (its author also noted that he had two daughters with his charming wife Shou Ruili, an aeronautic engineer allergic to seafood).

At the time of the Belgrade affair in 1999, 2,000 analysts were employed on Bei Andeli Street, north of Beijing. From here, a daily intelligence bulletin instituted by Xiong was distributed to the top brass of the army, the government and the party. Hundreds of analysts were also working independently of the PLA2. Every ten days, the CIISS published an internal newsletter about the "movements of foreign troops" (*Waijun dongtai*). This might cover the Mexican army or the French navy, though it naturally tended to focus on the large regional armies of Asia. This secret document was sent to all PLA departments. During Xiong's leadership, it was Colonel Chen Xiaogong who managed the information base. Chen rose from intelligence strategist to military attaché in the United States, and then head of the PLA2. In the summer of 2007, he was named overall head of all the military special services.

Xiong Guangkai had an unusual and rather remarkable profile; he became a kind of itinerant super-diplomat for the PLA and was in contact with all the major foreign military representatives—American, Russian, French, British, German—and even international policymakers. As overall head of military intelligence, an ambassador for the army, and a sales representative for the arms industry, he frequently travelled to America and Europe, as well as consolidating relationships and fostering arms-trading agreements with South Africa, Syria and North Korea, where he knew Kwon Hui-Gyong, former ambassador to the USSR and head of the Research Department for External Intelligence.

In fact, some strategists were suspicious of the beliefs that lay beneath General Xiong's moderate and jovial appearance. In 1995 he threatened the Clinton administration after the US president expressed interest not only in making a state visit to Taiwan, but also in inviting the Taiwanese president, Lee Teng-hui, to the White House. Xiong warned the Americans of the "explosive" consequences of such a position. Challenged in the press, he claimed that he was merely quoting Deng Xiaoping—by then 91 years old—who had been intensely focused for twenty years on the return of Hong Kong to China: "The status of Taiwan is at the crux of Chinese–US relations. If this question is not handled properly, the result could be very explosive!"

In 1996, at the height of the Taiwan Straits crisis, when the PLA was testing new missiles, Jiang Zemin successfully defused the situation by sending an ageing secret agent, Xu Mingzhen—father of the Guoanbu chief Xu Yongyue—to meet with the Taiwanese president on a visit to Hong Kong. The meeting was encouraged by the Hakka networks, to which both Lee Teng-hui and Deng Xiaoping belonged.

In December 1997, after Deng's death and the handover of Hong Kong, Xiong Guangkai became—like his civilian counterpart Xu Yongyue—advisor to the Central Leading Group for Taiwan Affairs, chaired by Jiang Zemin, which was engineering a hardline strategy for bringing about the annexation of Taiwan. There were now 1,328 nuclear strategic missiles of the 2nd Artillery permanently aimed at the rebel island.

* * *

Considering the immense size of the PLA—2.2 million men—it was hardly surprising that the array of intelligence services linked to it was concomitantly massive. The Chinese had originally copied the Soviet GRU—a service that remained unchanged even after the implosion of the USSR—and only later diversified the structure. Thanks to its military attachés, the PLA2 was able to gather intelligence about foreign armies based on open sources and contacts between military attachés in different countries.

In recent decades, the PLA has also copied the former USSR's system of science and industrial intelligence services, in China brought together under the veritable "intelligence vacuum cleaner" COSTIND. In order to increase the PRC's technological potential, its firepower, and its tactical and strategic resources, military intelligence employs tens of thousands of agents—scientists, students, tourists, shopkeepers and businessmen.

There are, of course, many cover organizations known to the French DST and the FBI, such as the China Association for International Friendly Contacts (CAIFC), created in 1984. The CAIFC created a subsidiary that was also involved in international liaisons for military intelligence, the Centre for Peace and Development Studies. The CAIFC's general secretary in 2001–7 was Colonel Li Ning, whose focus was on establishing solid relationships in the field of economic exchanges. He was a former aide to General Xiong Guangkai and a former military attaché in London, specializing in the handover of technology secrets and arms sales to the Middle East. So much for "peace and development".

In autumn 2007, the CAIFC found itself in the eye of the storm. Wang Qingqan, a founding member of the organization, was sentenced to death in a closed hearing, for treason and spying for the Japanese. He was a PLA colonel and head of mission in Japan until the end of the 1990s, having been appointed first secretary at the Chinese embassy in Tokyo with a remit to widen the circle of "friendly" acquaintances. He took this mission so seriously that he was "turned" by the Japanese services, handing over confidential intelligence. He was arrested in the summer of 2007 by the Guoanbu in Beijing. The leaders of the PLA2, like secret services the world over, know only too well that contact work can be an excellent way of gathering large amounts of intelligence, but also has its risks.

Meanwhile, the PLA2 was busy setting up front companies and infiltrating bona fide businesses. Not only that, but the PLA2 had a consummate rival in the PLA's General Political Department, namely the Liaison Service, headed for a period by Deng Rong, daughter of Deng Xiaoping, and then from 1999 by General Liang Hongchang. Espionage and psychological warfare were the two mainstays of the Liaison Service. It has long been claimed, correctly, that the principal target of its secret agents is Taiwan. However, since the beginning of the twenty-first century, counterintelligence agencies have discovered the existence of more and more private companies set up as fronts in Europe and the United States. It is hardly shocking that the most powerful country in the world is also the most spied upon; nor does it come as any surprise that the United States is not best pleased at finding itself the principal victim in this high-stakes game.

The Cox Report: Chinese plunder in America

The extent of Chinese technological espionage was becoming apparent as the millennium turned (see Appendix III for the overall structure). On 1 October 1999, the French defence attaché saw the PLA march in Beijing and realized that the Red Flag (*Hongqi 7*) was an exact copy of the French Crotale missile. The Americans were in for an even more unpleasant surprise: the Chinese rocket *Dongfeng 31*, with nuclear warheads, was a shameless replica of US technology.

In spring 1999, a Taiwanese-born physicist named Wen Ho Lee was fired from the Los Alamos Nuclear Research Center, arrested, and charged with handing over information to Beijing. Professor Lee was eventually released, with an official apology from the court, in September 2000. He appears to have been the victim of a Chinese would-be defector, who had contacted the CIA in Taiwan in 1995 claiming to be in possession of documents implicating the Los Alamos physicist. The FBI eventually admitted that they had been tricked by a sham defector who was trying to feed the Americans false intelligence. Lee had in fact refused to hand over information to a group of Chinese scientists he had met at international conferences; they were asking about Trident missile W-88 nuclear warheads to be fitted to submarines, which the Chinese wanted to copy. Was this the Guoanbu trying to punish him for his non-cooperation, by labelling him a spy? In the book he later wrote about the affair, Lee revealed that he had indeed had dealings with two science "head-hunters", Zheng Shaotong and Li Deyuan. The latter had apparently tried to worm his way into French scientific circles working on "nonlinear hyperbolic equations".[17]

These discoveries confirmed the findings of the Cox Report, published coincidentally just two weeks after the Belgrade embassy bombing, on 25 May 1999. It had taken a long time to put together this 700-page dossier, which detailed the PRC's vast technological espionage of the United States.

Critics of the report—some possibly activated by the Chinese themselves—saw it as a clear attack on the Clinton administration, already undermined by the Lewinsky affair and the Chinagate scandal (the revelation that the Chinese had made financial contributions to the Democratic National Congress in the lead-up to Clinton's 1996 presidential campaign). In reality, though, the technical details in the report point the finger at the Bush and Reagan administrations, and it barely mentions Chinagate. For good measure, it was countersigned by four Republican representatives and four Democrats. This impressive bipartisan unanimity in itself suggests the enormous extent of Chinese technological theft.

The Cox Report concluded that China had managed to penetrate all the secrets of American defence, including rocket guidance computers, neutron bombs, multiple nuclear warheads and laser searches. It warned that, although the Chinese did not yet have the capacity to launch their own production of the prototypes they had copied, they would be able to do so by 2009 or 2010. The report also indicated that the Chinese services were not the only guilty parties: several American companies had handed over important technologies to the Chinese by means of their joint ventures. Others had had their patents or technical plans stolen through sheer naivety.

Twenty years on, the Cox Report remains burningly topical—we can't know if it is still pertinent in the list it provides of CCP demands for Chinese spies, but it is at least highly relevant today in its detailing of their working methods, particularly as the services' financial means are much greater now than when the report was written. It is also a useful reminder that the machinery of government was entirely under the control of the CCP Central Committee's general secretary and PRC president Jiang Zemin, who chaired the Politburo and its executive, the seven-member Standing Committee, supported by a powerful secretariat. At the head of the secretariat was vice-president Hu Jintao, who later succeeded Jiang. The Central Committee also included among its members Xu Yongue, head of the Guoanbu and so of counterintelligence. The State Council, equivalent to the government, was run by the prime minister, Zhu Rongji, also a high-ranking CCP official.

The PLA was under the direct control of the party's Central Military Commission (CMC). "The party commands the gun; the gun must never be allowed to command the party," as Mao used to say. Nothing had changed in the twenty years since his death. Thus Jiang Zemin also chaired the CMC, supported by two senior vice-chairmen, Generals Zhang Wannian and Chi Haotian, who were vehemently anti-American (or "anti-imperialist") during the Kosovo war. Everything was structured around this top-down power apparatus: the eight-member CMC controlled the army, the navy, the air force, the 2nd Artillery (strategic missiles), the spying operations of the PLA2, the PLA Liaison Office, and, after Tiananmen, the People's Armed Police (PAP).

While the CMC controlled the strategic axes of defence, the government was also directly behind several industrial organizations. Set up in 1982 by Deng Xiaoping and directed by his daughter, the science and technology research organization COSTIND had become more of a civil body since 1998, as it no longer officially reported to the CMC, but to the government-run Council of State Affairs. As we saw in the case of Hong Kong, COSTIND managed large state-owned companies.[18] These projects were in collaboration with a myriad of "scientific and technological leading groups"—research and development units, piggybacking on the Academy of Sciences and Military Sciences, and other academies within defence- and intelligence-related universities and research institutes. They all came under the umbrella of the State Council-controlled International Studies Research Centre (ISRC/*Guoji Wenti Yanjiu Zhongxin*), also dreamt up by Deng Xiaoping.

In March 1986, Deng had launched Programme 863, whose purpose was to raise the necessary funds for these projects. After ten years, with the help of 3,000 scientists, around 1,500 objectives had been attained in the fields of economics and defence. The most experienced scientists were chosen to reduce the gap between the West and China in advanced defence, aeronautics and space, information technology, lasers, automation, energy and new materials. Programme 863 focused on the following areas of military intelligence:

- Biological warfare (research on genes and genetic mutations)[19]
- Space technology (particularly spy satellites—seventeen of which were launched between 1997 and 1999—as well as launch modules for space exploration); China is equipped with an MIR space station copied from the Russians
- Information technology, in particular artificial intelligence, computing and image interpretation, all of which make it possible to develop "3CI" (Command, Control, Communications & Intelligence) systems to develop software for military applications
- Laser weapons (including plasma technology and spectroscopy)
- Robotics, smart weapons and robot soldiers
- Nuclear weapons (following the discoveries made by researchers at Tsinghua University's Institute of Nuclear and New Energy Technology, particularly its design for gas-cooled reactors that can assist in weapons manufacture)

- So-called "exotic" materials of all kinds, from rare metals, composites, materials from new energies and so on.[20]

The Cox Report details the many goals on intelligence services' "shopping lists", used to guide spies and obtain abroad the means necessary to accelerate research and develop specifically Chinese applications. The modernization objectives listed in the report mainly concern battlefield communications, reconnaissance (aerial or other), space weaponry, mobile nuclear weapons, attack submarines, aerial pursuit, remote-controlled weapons, and the training of rapid-action land forces.

The race for information technology and its applications had two arenas: civilian and military. The Cox Report focused on the military aspect because it appeared to be the most threatening. But of course, China was using identical methods to pirate blueprints for civil aviation, cars, renewable energy technologies, drug monopolies and new means to protect the environment, to take just a few examples. Indeed, the services rely on the guiding principles decreed by Deng Xiaoping in 1978, the "16 characters" policy, which specifically requires the mixing of "civil" and "military" in order to "erase the borders between state operations and commercial activities, between purely military and commercial interests":

> Combine the military and civil society—*Jun min jiehe* 军民结合
> Combine peace and war—*Ping zhan jiehe* 平战结合
> Prioritize military production—*Jun pin yousheng* 军品优生
> Civil society must support the military—*Yi min yang jun* 以民养军

After outlining the PRC's objectives in technological development, the Cox Report established the specific role of secret agents, based on the testimony of both China experts in the United States and several Chinese defectors:

> The primary professional PRC intelligence services involved in technology acquisition are the Ministry of State Security (MSS) [the Guoanbu] and the PLA General Staff's Military Intelligence Department (MID) [the PLA2].

> In addition to and separate from these services, the PRC maintains a growing non-professional technology-collection effort by other PRC Government-controlled interests, such as research institutes and PRC

> military-industrial companies. Many of the most egregious losses of U.S. technology have resulted not from professional operations under the control or direction of the [Guoanbu] or [PLA2], but as part of commercial, scientific, and academic interactions between the United States and the PRC.
>
> Professional intelligence agents from the [Guoanbu] and [PLA2] account for a relatively small share of the PRC's foreign science and technology collection. The bulk of such information is gathered by various non-professionals, including PRC students, scientists, researchers, and other visitors to the West. These individuals sometimes are working at the behest of the [Guoanbu] or [PLA2], but often represent other PRC-controlled research organizations—scientific bureaus, commissions, research institutes, and enterprises.
>
> Those unfamiliar with the PRC's intelligence practices often conclude that, because intelligence services conduct clandestine operations, all clandestine operations are directed by intelligence agencies. In the case of the PRC, this is not always the rule.

The Cox Report outlined the Guoanbu's activities in the highly specialized area of technological research, noting that, when spying on a particular domain, the State Security service might well come across other information of a civil or military nature. "The MSS relies on a network of non-professional individuals and organizations acting outside the direct control of the intelligence services, including scientific delegations and PRC nationals working abroad, to collect the vast majority of the information it seeks."[21]

Two years after the publication of the Cox Report, Paul D. Moore, head of Chinese counterintelligence at the FBI and witness to many cases of Chinese espionage, detailed the challenges facing investigators in the wake of the fragmented nature and so-called amateurism of Chinese espionage, with its highly complex divisions of labour:

> One of the problems the FBI and other U.S. counterintelligence agencies have long had with attempting to neutralize Chinese intelligence-collection operations in the United States is that the people who covertly gather intelligence for China normally don't look like spies, act like spies or pilfer large amounts of secret information.
>
> ... For most areas of Chinese intelligence collection, the actual work of locating and obtaining desired information, even very sensitive data, is carried out by academics, students, businessmen or journal-

> ists. Chinese intelligence officers typically do not direct or control the effort, because it is Chinese intelligence consumers who determine the nature and extent of Chinese collection operations, just as it is U.S. consumers whose purchases shape the U.S. economy.
>
> Since they are not intelligence professionals, Chinese collectors do not understand or make use of clandestine techniques such as "dead drops" under pedestrian bridges in parks; instead they tend to rely on simply sitting down with a knowledgeable friend or contact and asking confidentially for information or assistance. The normal consumer collects information for his own use or for his immediate co-workers, so his collection goals are very modest. Even when a collector pilfers sensitive or classified information, it is normally in small pieces.[22]

To put together these vast puzzles, China relies on a large number of correspondents to carry out this semi-clandestine work. In 2000, the FBI estimated that the Chinese had the third-largest number of espionage agents in the United States. Eight years later, the FBI estimated that China had now taken the lead and that the Guoanbu, the military spying services and the allied civilian research offices were now the best run in the world, despite the significant growth of the Russian services after Vladimir Putin had become president in 2000. The question was whether the FBI was exaggerating the dangers to justify demanding larger budgets.

According to the FBI, in 2000 there were nearly 2,000 Chinese government officials, diplomats and journalists based in Canada and the United States giving cover to the top layer of intelligence—mostly in "white" and "grey" areas, in other words largely using open sources. The presence of 15,000 Chinese students—even if only a minority were professional secret agents—offered considerable opportunities for targeting laboratories and research centres in, for example, Silicon Valley. Three thousand Chinese delegations visited the US and Canada every year. This figure does not include the large numbers of tourists, touring circuses and Beijing opera companies, all naturally accompanied by many agents, who keep their eye on more than the visiting performers during such visits.

There was also known to be infiltration of "deep-water fish" into the large Pacific Coast Chinese communities, in the Chinatowns of San Francisco and Vancouver (known as "Wang Cover"). In 1999, according to Charles Svoboda, former head of the Canadian Security Intelligence Service (CSIS), the PLA2 was using Chinese mafia networks, the Big Circle Boys, based in Vancouver, Toronto and Ottawa, to carry out intelligence missions. One of the largest foreign intelligence operations was run out of the Ottawa embassy, located in a former convent; CSIS set up a special counterintelligence unit with the sole purpose of protecting itself against the Chinese services.

Beyond this broad outline—embellished with numerous concrete examples, available in full online[23]—the Cox Report details the wide variety of approaches employed to acquire foreign technology:

- Reliance on the Red Princes, who exploit their political, military and commercial connections to acquire foreign technology
- Illegal transfers of US technology via third countries
- Lobbying of US commercial companies in order to effect the illegal transfer of licensed technologies through joint ventures
- Exploitation of dual-use products and services that have unsuspected military advantages
- Use of front companies to illegally acquire technologies
- Use of well-established commercial enterprises as covers for acquiring technology
- Acquisition of stakes in US technology companies
- Clandestine espionage carried out by personnel within ministries, commissions, institutes and military industries, independent of the PRC intelligence services.[24]

There are three remarks that should be made at this point. Firstly, the Cox Report covered the US, but this type of operation was equally underway in Europe, Australia, New Zealand, Japan and Korea. Secondly, these espionage techniques were also applied to Chinese economic intelligence in the US. Finally, the lines between the two sometimes blurred, with Chinese military intelligence agents carrying out civilian economic espionage missions, or picking up information of interest to large "patriotic" companies subsidized by the Chinese state. In short, the Cox Report confirmed that, at the turn of the millennium, the Chinese technological espionage operation in America and beyond was dizzyingly vast.

The Clintons and Chinagate

Among its many revelations, the Cox Report noted the fact that the PLA2 was headed by General Ji Shengde, son of the former foreign minister Ji Pengfei. This apparently minor detail was more significant than it might have seemed: as the Cox Report was published in late May 1999, Ji Shengde was about to be arrested—because of Bill and Hillary Clinton.

While the Monica Lewinsky affair was breaking, a potentially much bigger scandal was brewing: Chinagate. By 1996, the Democratic Party had received around $4.5 million in donations for President Clinton's re-election campaign from the Chinese-Indonesian group Lippo, the Chinese-Thai group Charoeun Popkhand, and San Kin Yip, based in Macao. The funds included some $300,000 paid at the direct request of the head of the PLA2—General Ji Shengde, Xiong Guangkai's deputy.[25] In September that year, the Los Angeles Times broke the story that the funding was of problematic origin; this was followed by a Washington Post piece stating that the Justice Department's investigation had discovered the involvement of Chinese agents.

The trap had been set in the 1980s, when Bill and Hillary Clinton dined regularly at the Fu Lin Chinese restaurant in Little Rock, Arkansas, owned by Charles (Yan Lin) Trie. Bill, who was introduced to Trie by Hillary, often went there for lunch, never paying a cent, and the boss soon became a "friend", as did one of his relatives, formerly of the Taiwanese air force, called John Huang. He worked for Lippo, a financial and commercial partner of several Chinese companies, and one of the donor organizations involved in Chinagate in 1996—by which time Huang was a fundraiser for the Democratic National Committee.

This tells us two important things: first, that the Chinese were adept, just as the KGB had been, at preparing the ground for long-term operations, betting on a few privileged young people to make their way to the top of the elite; and secondly, that the employment of Chinese-Americans and Taiwanese was considered vital, since this was a way to obscure the true identity of an operation's sponsors up in Beijing.

The planting of Huang turned out to be a wild success. After the first Clinton administration began in 1993, he was taken on in the US Department of Commerce, becoming deputy assistant secretary for international economic affairs and became advisor for China to Secretary of Commerce Ron Brown. In January 1994, with Brown's blessing, Huang was given unlimited access to confidential documents about economic and technological intelligence, even though in principle only a US-born citizen could be given such authorization.

Around the same time that John Huang joined the White House, the China Resources Group (*Huaren Jituan*)—a holding company subsidiary of the Hong Kong-based Ministry of Foreign Trade and Economic Cooperation (MOFTEC)—became a major shareholder in Lippo, with a 50 per cent stake in the company. China Resources also served as a front for General Ji Shengde's PLA2. The military implications of Chinagate became clear when it was revealed that the arms dealer Wang Jun, director of Poly Technologies—the subsidiary of the intelligence think-tank COSTIND—had also received an invitation to the White House in December 1996. This visit was organized by none other than Charles Trie, owner of the Clintons' favourite Little Rock Chinese restaurant, who had been raising funds for the Democrats for fourteen years.

Just before his trip to the PRC in June 1998, Clinton felt the scandal breathing uncomfortably down his neck. The media revealed links with Liu Chaoying, a PLA colonel and businesswoman with links to China Aerospace International Holdings (CASIL), a company set up by the Chinese military and listed on the Hong Kong stock exchange as a subsidiary of the China Aerospace Corporation.

The CASIL director Wang Meiyue has been named for his role in the Chinagate scandal and its links with the PLA2. His agent in the US was Johnny Chung, a Chinese-American who had introduced the attractive Colonel Liu into Democrat circles during Clinton's re-election campaign. The two were photographed together at a 1996 fundraising reception. Johnny Chung received a $360,000 donation to the Democratic Party, including a cheque for $50,000 handed over personally in March 1995 to the First Lady's chief of staff, Margaret Williams. Chung named Colonel Liu in his testimony to the FBI investigation charged with throwing light on the Chinese contribution to Clinton's re-election campaign. According to Chung, Liu had confirmed that the money came directly from the PLA and had even had him meet the PLA2 chief, Ji Shengde.

Far from being a free spirit of the Chinese elite, Liu was the daughter of Admiral Liu Huaqing, former head of the Chinese navy who had become first PLA chief, charged with modernizing the military, then a vice-chairman of the CMC. He was implicated in the 1991 French-Chinese frigate case in Taiwan, as one of the fortunate beneficiaries of illegal kickbacks. Jiang Zemin replaced him in September 1997 with General Wang Zhannian, the "hawk" of the Kosovo war. While Beijing denied any meddling in US democracy and Colonel Liu escaped the affair untouched, Chung and Johnny Huang were each given a five-year prison sentence, and the money was eventually returned. President Clinton, denying any knowledge of the funds' origins, stopped short of ordering an independent commission of inquiry, instead supporting a full investigation by the FBI.

In the United States, one of the most harmful consequences of Chinagate was probably the wealth of technology intelligence obtained by the Chinese lobby. The FBI compiled an exhaustive list of the companies who had engaged in this subterfuge, as well as establishing the ambiguous role of the Department of Commerce, in which John Huang had played a clandestine role facilitating transactions in favour of Beijing. The plot thickened further in April 1996, when a strange plane crash in Bosnia cost US Secretary of Commerce Ron Brown his life, shortly after the head of the White House administration, Leon Panetta, had asked him to "put to one side" some incriminating archives concerning the "Chinese connection".

The heat was taken off Chinagate by a cigar in the Oval Office. Monica Lewinsky supplanted Colonel Liu in the minds of most Americans, and then George W. Bush was elected in 2000. But later on, with the possibility—twice—of Hillary Clinton being elected to the White House, Chinese analysts knew that the buried scandal of hidden funding might well come back to haunt her. This might actually have suited them in the 2016 election.

Meanwhile in Beijing, a key figure regularly quoted in the American press took the hit for Chinagate. He was also implicated in a separate corruption scandal within China. In 2000, Ji Shengde, head of the

PLA2, was suspended and transferred to the Academy of Military Sciences, before being arrested, tried behind closed doors and sentenced to fifteen years in prison. This led his father, former foreign minister Ji Pengfei, to commit suicide.

The mysterious Dozorov dossier

Ji had been officially replaced as head of military intelligence in August 1999 by General Luo Yudong, director of the Nanjing espionage academy, the Institute of International Relations, and former head of intelligence at the Chengdu regional command, covering Tibet. Luo was at the centre of another international intrigue among the Chinese spies of the new millennium.

In May 1999, as the rubble of the Chinese embassy in Belgrade was still smoking, a mysterious man made a trip to Beijing. General Valentin Korabelnikov was head of the GRU, Russian military intelligence. The GRU had hardly changed since the Soviet era, except that it was now working closely with its opposite number in Beijing, the PLA2. Korabelnikov was in the PRC for discussions with his "Chinese comrades", principally his counterpart, the bald-headed General Luo. The US-led bombing of the embassy could only help relations between the Chinese and the Russians, which were in any case already good. Moscow seized the opportunity to exploit the surge in nationalist and anti-American sentiment that accompanied the NATO offensive, NATO being the great bogeyman of the Cold War era.

As we know, there had been an era when the Soviet services oversaw the Chinese, followed by an era of ideological disagreement that lasted until the end of the Cultural Revolution. Then had come a rapprochement orchestrated by Deng Xiaoping, though the two countries still regarded each other with distinct suspicion in that period. In the 1980s, Yuri Andropov's KGB knew that Deng was collaborating with the Americans, who had deployed "big ear" eavesdropping devices in the Pamir Mountains and helped the Chinese to arm the Afghan Mujahedin against the Soviet army. The Kremlin wondered whether Mao and Kang Sheng had been right during the Cultural Revolution to brand this man a "capitalist roader". This question—who was the real Deng Xiaoping?—has been one of the great mysteries confronting me in the writing of this book.

After appointing Vladimir Putin as prime minister in August 1999, Boris Yeltsin unexpectedly resigned as president in December of the same year. Putin, a former KGB counterintelligence officer, became acting president of the Russian Federation. In May 2000, after receiving the keys to the presidential residence, Putin discovered a cabinet in his office that contained a bulging file on a man three years dead: Comrade "Ivan Sergeyevich Dozorov", better known as Deng Xiaoping.

Every person who ever worked for the Soviet services received a Russian identity. The life of Deng was such a mystery even to KGB elders like Putin that the Dozorov file was still in his hands in 2007. It was filled with layers upon layers of information: medical records; documents about Deng's role in the Comintern under the alias "Krezov"; his role in Paris from 1923 to the end of 1925, with Comrade "Moskvin" (Zhou Enlai); his time in Moscow between January and August 1926; the grades he obtained in Russian and English in class 7 at Moscow's Sun Yat-sen University (which had 300 Chinese students); his relationship with Karl Radek, the provost of the university who was murdered in prison in 1939, and Radek's lover Larissa Reissner (who also had an affair with Liu Shaoqi in 1928); his contacts with Trotsky, who came to teach at Sun Yat-sen University; his links with the Comintern agent Jean Cremet ("Vainer") in France, the USSR and China, the man who had armed Deng's Guangxi underground fighters in 1929; his file, no. 233, as a Chinese member of the Soviet Communist Party; his certification by the Russian secret services and his military training with the GRU (weapons handling, encryption, disguise, espionage); his false passports; his links with pro-Russians such as the future Chinese president Yang Shangkun (imprisoned for wiretapping Mao on behalf of the KGB during the Cultural Revolution) and with Chiang Ching-kuo, Chiang Kai-shek's exiled son in Moscow; his romantic relationship with a 19-year-old student, Zhang Xiyuan; and even, quite extraordinarily, how, in the midst of the Cultural Revolution in 1969, on the run and under the protection of the Sichuan military district, he had been put in touch with an Asian-origin Soviet intelligence officer.

Everything was in there, an absolute cornucopia of information for historians. It was such an explosive file that the Chinese probably had no desire for it ever to see the light of day.

A Russian intelligence expert told me that he had examined the dossier, classified as “state secret, access forbidden”, and that it still remains in the hands of the Russian president, as one of Putin’s ultimate trump cards. Today, however Putin has noticeably warmer relations with Beijing than when he first became president in 2000. So why keep hold of this file now, after all this time? Perhaps Putin occasionally consults it in order to clarify what happened on 16 May 1989, when Mikhail Gorbachev went to Beijing to meet Deng in the middle of the Tiananmen protests and found himself snubbed, just as the Soviet empire was on the verge of collapsing.

Or perhaps Putin uses it to revisit the August 1991 diplomatic blunder that occurred during the attempted coup against Gorbachev, when the Chinese ambassador to Moscow, Yu Hongliang, expressed ardent support for the putsch. The irony was that, almost ten years previously, it was Yu who had been sent to Moscow to re-open channels, dropping hints to Piotr Kapitsa, a well-known academic specializing in China, that Beijing was keen to discuss certain issues it hoped to deal with regarding Vietnam, Mongolia and Afghanistan. Contact had been established with the Soviet ministries of defence and foreign affairs, as well as with the KGB, and it was decided that secret negotiations would be conducted twice a year, once in each capital.[26] Yu, who represented Deng Xiaoping’s position on the attempted coup, had to leave Russia in 1991 after it failed. But Sino-Russian relations were not adversely affected.

The Sino-Russian spy axis

Nature abhors a vacuum. The dismantling of the Soviet services after the collapse of the USSR left the field wide open to the globalized development of Chinese services. In the early 1990s, the Russians realized that their range of international intelligence activities was shrinking. Unlike military intelligence—General Yevgeny Timokhin’s GRU, which remained intact—the KGB was split up into at least four sections: border guards, wiretapping (FASPII), counterintelligence (FSB) and the 1st Directorate in charge of intelligence (PGU) within the foreign intelligence service (*Sloujba Vnechnoï Razvedki*), under the leadership of the academic spy and future prime minister, Yevgeny Primakov.

In the years that followed, these services signed agreements with most of the foreign intelligence services that had once been their enemies. But with the Chinese, the stakes were different. In the summer of 1992, Primakov, leader of the "Orientalist" clan within Russian intelligence and diplomacy, went to Beijing to sign a secret cooperation protocol between the four major services: the SVR and GRU on the Russian side, and the Guoanbu and PLA2 on the Chinese side. In November 1995, the Russian ambassador to Beijing Igor Rogatchev celebrated the good relationship between the services by honouring the memory of the Chinese spy Yan Baohang, who had informed Stalin of Hitler's plan to invade the USSR in June 1941.[27] A strategic partnership agreement signed in 1996 by Boris Yeltsin and Jiang Zemin—who had studied in the USSR—intensified this relationship.

In the spring of 1999, NATO's attack on Yugoslavia and the bombing of the Chinese embassy strengthened the China–Russia intelligence axis, signalled by the mutual visits of various notables from the services. In May 1999, General Valentin Korabelnikov, head of the GRU, was spotted in Beijing. The following month, General Zhang Wannian, first vice-chairman of the Central Military Commission, accompanied by General Xiong Guangkai, head of military intelligence, made the pilgrimage to Russia. On the first day of their visit to Moscow, on 9 June, Zhang and Xiong met with the then FSB head, Vladimir Putin. Beyond his role in strategic issues, Putin, we may recall, was a long-time friend of Xiong.

The following day, the Chinese held talks with their military counterparts: General Manilov and of course Korabelnikov, the master "bat" (symbol of Russian military reconnaissance). On the agenda was a plan to share intelligence about the missile defence system the Americans were hoping eventually to deploy in the Far East and Eastern Europe. There were also technicalities to be discussed around Russia's decision to sell its SIGINT intercept base at Lourdes, Cuba, to the PLA by January 2002, for budgetary as well as tactical reasons. The Chinese now had greater financial means than the Russians to run this type of system, and there was nothing stopping them from selling the Russians mutually beneficial information gathered through the base. Ultimately, the Chinese established an even greater presence there than the existing Russian apparatus, along with several other eavesdropping and transmission stations for spying on the United States.[28]

Meanwhile, in September 2000, Xiong Guangkai, together with the Gonganbu chief Jia Chunwang, welcomed to Beijing General Konstantin Totskiy, head of the Federal Border Guard Service. This is an extremely important agency, not only because of the historical Sino-Russian border conflict, but also because it is a key—if often underestimated—intelligence service, as explained to me by the China–Russia relations expert Iliya Sarsembaev. The focus of these three-way meetings was another area of cooperation: organized crime and illegal immigration, mainly from the PRC to the Russian Federation, as the flow of Chinese immigrants into the Russian Far East intensified, accompanied by the emergence of Chinese mafia organizations in Khabarovsk and elsewhere. The previous year, Chinese gangsters had murdered the head of the Russian mafia in Khabarovsk.

In 1999–2000, Russian media reported on this extension of the field of Sino-Russian cooperation. Under the headline "Old spies unite", the *Moscow Times* published an analysis by a former KGB officer specializing in Chinese issues, Konstantin Preobrazhensky. His remarks about the psychology governing the Sino-Russian alliance have been corroborated by all, both Russian and Chinese, with whom I have discussed it:

> The cooperation between Russian and Chinese spies is comfortable on the psychological level. After all, Chinese spies are communists. The Russians are all former members of the Communist Party and cultivate great nostalgia for the communist era, when both their salary and their status were much higher. They do not hide their communist sympathies. In Russia, they freely use the term "comrade", which dates back to the Stalinist era, as a term of affection. It is easy for Russians to find a common language with the Chinese. And Russian spies do not like America at all, blaming the country, as a stronghold of capitalism, for all the misfortunes that have plagued Russia since the fall of the KGB.[29]

Shortly after this, the monthly review *Segodnyia* pointed out something that was to become surprisingly common in the world of post-

Cold War intelligence: "The Russian security services are now taking lessons from their former Chinese students."[30]

On top of these published pieces, I was offered a third account of the Sino-Russian intelligence rapprochement. This one came direct from "Ivan", a former border intelligence officer who conducted exercises with Chinese counterparts answering to both the Guoanbu and the Central Military Commission: "I think that, with hindsight, we have to recognize that Mao was right in launching the Cultural Revolution against the 'Chinese Khrushchev'. At least he managed to safeguard the Communist Party. Because here, unlike in China, the party has collapsed and we have lost power. The only organizations that today are keeping up the tradition of socialism are the intelligence services, which are thus able to strengthen ties with the Chinese. That explains the excellent quality of the relationship between our services today."[31]

The Shanghai Club

In 2002, President Vladimir Putin was seeking to forge a triangular alliance with China and India to counterbalance US domination. But the decades-long outright hostility between New Delhi and Beijing had not faded. Moreover, India was beginning to grow closer to the United States, after decades of friendship with the USSR. Under Jiang Zemin (1989-2002), China's closest ally was neighbouring Pakistan, with whom it had commercial ties, especially in arms trading. So Putin and Jiang had to content themselves with a tactical alliance, each helping the other to deal with the deployment of US missile defence systems—the Russians in Eastern Europe; China facing Taiwan.

Intelligence exchange agreements—which included the sharing of technology intelligence—become paramount. Nonetheless, there was absolutely no question of the Chinese answering to the Russians as had been the case back in the 1920s and 1930s, or even of working in tandem, as had been the case between Russian and Chinese organizations when the PRC was first founded in 1949. Those days had been swept away for good in the whirlwind of the mid-century Sino-Soviet schism and the Cultural Revolution. Indeed, according to Chinese political scientists, this had been the one positive legacy of the terrible

Kang Sheng era: "At least, after having been the Soviet services' man within Chinese communism, he then became the architect of the rupture and the subsequent independence of our services."[32]

The Russians and Chinese initiated a basic programme of regional cooperation known as the Shanghai Club or Shanghai Cooperation Organization (SCO). Founded in Shanghai on 14 and 15 June 2001, this later evolved by bringing the former Muslim republics of the USSR into the Sino-Russian allied sphere of influence: Kazakhstan, Kyrgyzstan, Tajikistan and Uzbekistan. Today the Shanghai Club has an economic component, as well as a section for fighting "Islamist terrorism", established in the wake of the 9/11 attacks.

On 16 July 2002, *Pravda*—a newspaper that has changed a great deal now that it is no longer the mouthpiece of the Soviet Communist Party—revealed that the head of the Russian National Security Council, Vladimir Rushalo, had met with major figures in Chinese intelligence on a four-day visit to Beijing, with the intention of strengthening links between Russian organizations and the Chinese security services. The summit was of such significance that it was the acting Guoanbu and the Gonganbu ministers, Geng Huichang and Jia Chunwang respectively, who were there agreeing the expansion of security cooperation, within the framework of the Shanghai Club.

An underlying element of this strengthened alliance was the fight against Islamists, specifically the Muslim separatists of Chechnya and Xinjiang. In autumn 2005, deputy Gonganbu minister Meng Hongwei was chosen to head the "Security Group", one of the ten units organizing the Year of Russia celebrations being planned in China. The Security Group was an organization aimed at consolidating bilateral relations with the Russian FSB, a step towards the group being named to the rotating presidency of the Shanghai Club's anti-terrorist group—achieved after successfully inviting Mongolia, Pakistan, Iran and India to a summit for coordinating the national security forces and those of the Shanghai Club in the fight against Islamist fundamentalism.

This explains why it was so important for the Chinese to strengthen the Eastern axis of their international partnerships. For example, in March 2006, while chairing the Shanghai Club summit in Tashkent, the deputy Gonganbu minister Meng Hongwei announced a 2007-9 development plan for a regional antiterrorist department.[33]

In the run-up to the 2008 Beijing Olympics, inter-service coordination included training drills by counterterrorist forces. In September 2007, a brigade from the Snow Leopard Unit (*xuede feizhoubao*), headed by Captain Qu Liangfeng, went to Moscow to lead its men in the Domestic Counterterrorism "2007 Cooperation" exercises. This special unit of the PAP—which reported directly to the Central Military Commission—was headed by Hu Jintao himself, by then Jiang Zemin's successor as paramount leader of the PRC. Coming a year before the Games, this exercise focused attention on the commandos of the 13th Special Brigade of the PAP Corps, which had already taken part in about 100 operations—but these had only been in Beijing, where the Brigade was stationed.

This was all part of the Shanghai Club programme, and on the Russian side, it did not go unnoticed that the training exercises were taking place at a time when people were talking again about the failure of the special forces during a 2004 hostage-taking at a primary school in Beslan. Perhaps not entirely coincidentally, a little earlier that summer, the "2007 Peace Mission" manoeuvres on the borders of Kazakhstan—involving 6,000 men from the six Shanghai Club countries—revolved around a simulated hostage-taking by 1,000 Islamists.

What's a little espionage between friends?

Clearly, there was more than a cordial agreement developing in the early 2000s between the Chinese and Russian intelligence services. But this did not, apparently, prevent the Chinese from attempting to steal Russian technological secrets. Inter-service agreements were drawn up to make clear that, even if the Chinese did try to spy on the Russians, a protocol between Beijing and Moscow meant that everyone would remain discreet on the subject, and that the problem would be solved amicably.

Several Chinese espionage cases in Russia have nevertheless been hinted at in newspaper articles. There was the 2000 case of the Institute of Oceanology in Vladivostok, which saw the laboratory head Vladimir Shchurov trying to interest colleagues at the Chinese Institute in Harbin in his underwater listening devices. In 2002,

Valentin Danilov of the Krasnoyark Space Research Institute in Siberia, was caught by the FSB providing technical information about satellites to the Chinese. Russian counterespionage was extremely sensitive when it came to aerospace engineering, given that the Chinese were engaged in a vast operation of "cannibalizing" the MIR space station at this time. Initially this takeover was backed by a rather shaky Sino-Russian partnership agreement, whose aim was the conquest of the Moon for military purposes. The flight of the first Chinese astronaut, or "taikonaut", Colonel Yang Liwei, took place on 15 October 2003.

According to COSTIND, which manages manned flights as part of the Project 921 programme launched in 1992, Yang's space flight was the first step towards a Chinese Moon landing, with exploration to be followed by settlement of the Moon and, eventually, the conquest of Mars. The intention is that the red Chinese flag will fly on the "red planet" on 1 October 2049, the centenary of the People's Republic of China, by which time the PRC will have successfully established an inhabited settlement on Mars.[34]

Another known case of aerospace espionage was the Macheksport affair of November 2005, named after a company run by Igor Rechetin. Rechetin was arrested by the FSB along with two other executives and accused of spying for the Guoanbu, which was hoping through them to procure space technologies and components that could be used to arm intercontinental ballistic missiles. In this affair and the others of its kind that have not reached public attention, a double standard appears to be at play. While the Russian agents are either brought to court or placed under house arrest, their Chinese case officers (*Gongzuo dandang guan*) remain invisible after the scandal has broken. They are simply taken back to the border with a pat on the shoulder.

The Chinese secret service residents stationed in Moscow, officially in charge of liaison with Russian "organs", would be contacted directly in the event of a problem of this type and expected to solve it within three cell phone calls. Two such agents have made names for themselves as outstanding collaborators with FSB, SVR and GRU experts: General Zhu Da, the PLA2 military attaché in Moscow, and the Guoanbu's Moscow station chief, the "minister–advisor" Cheng

Guoping. Despite Cheng's importance within the Guoanbu, he has also remained a diplomat. When he was Chinese consul in Khabarovsk, he often served as an interface with the Russian secret services. Later, he became a Mandarin presenter on Radio Moscow.

This was in the era when Prime Minister Primakov, the "KGB peace lord", was promoting the idea of talks with Uyghur nationalists in Kazakhstan, to try to mediate between the Xinjiang separatist movement and the Chinese authorities. Radio Moscow's Chinese service highlighted these negotiations in broadcasts pushing the idea of peace. But after 9/11, the Chinese intelligence services' unified antiterrorist command became determined to do everything it could to eliminate the Uyghur separatists before the Beijing Olympics took place.

Given all we've seen in this chapter, it should be no surprise that they sought to do this with the help of their reconciled friends, the Russians. We know that this new special relationship between the Chinese and Russian secret services coincided with the rise of Chinese technological espionage. But the early 2000s was also an era of economic warfare.

9

SEA LAMPREY TACTICS

ECONOMIC WARFARE

Was Huang Lili really the innocent young woman portrayed in the French television broadcasts from her trial at the Versailles criminal court on 20 November 2007? Her defence argued that she was simply a naive young Chinese girl who was spying "against her will and without her knowledge". Were there not 30,000 Chinese students in France just like her who might have fallen into the same trap? Were some of them really Guoanbu secret operatives, under cover of being students?

By this point in our tale, the reader might feel able to form an opinion for themselves. Huang's conviction for "breach of trust" a month later changed nothing in terms of the fundamental problem facing counterintelligence detectives investigating Chinese conspiratorial methods. This was the first time since the conviction of Bernard Boursicot a quarter of a century earlier that a case of illicit intelligence-gathering for China had come before the French courts. Even now, Boursicot remained the only individual to have been convicted of treason, since as a French diplomat he was a part of the state apparatus. This did not arise again until 2018, when a number of DGSE agents were charged with committing treason by spying for China.[1]

We've already heard from Paul Moore, a longstanding veteran of the FBI's fight against Chinese moles, but it's worth repeating his point: "the people who covertly gather intelligence for China normally don't look like spies, act like spies or pilfer large amounts of secret information ... For most areas of Chinese intelligence collection, the actual work of locating and obtaining desired information, even very sensitive data, is carried out by academics, students, businessmen or journalists."

On 27 April 2005, 22-year-old Huang Lili was arrested in her office at the Heating and Passenger Compartment (air con) Division of the car parts manufacturer Valeo, in a town called La Verrière in the Yvelines region west of Paris. She had secured the internship at Valeo as part of her studies at the Compiègne University of Technology, working in the Research & Development department for computer-aided design. As she later admitted, she had copied some forty files onto her laptop, including two projects for BMW and Renault, and several others regarding defects of certain parts, as well as the company's charts regarding its planning and organization in China—all of which were unrelated to her internship. Since she came from Wuhan province, a region that was being developed by the car industry, it is possible that she was being guided remotely from there. The case was extremely sensitive, since BMW's new SUV model had just been hacked by other networks and the Smart car had been copied by the manufacturer Shuanghuan, which had received certification to sell its models in Europe. Citroën had already experienced this economic nightmare when its CX was counterfeited in 1993 by the Chinese manufacturer Greely, which sold its version for half the price of the original.

"One day, I was working on a Valeo PC, and I didn't have enough space for my work," Huang told *Libération*. "So I erased and copied these two files onto my personal disk. ... I took the documents to prepare my report. I loaded lots of files from the intranet, and then went through them. If I saw that the title could be useful for my internship, I copied the file. In total, I must have taken thirty or forty files." She had given the police the same explanation during her 53-day detention.[2]

Meanwhile, at the Chinese embassy on Rue Washington in Paris, which houses the offices of several intelligence services, people were getting a little worried. Madame Chen Li, assistant to Police Officer Wang Caizhu of the Gonganbu, was on the prowl. She was studying in her spare time, working on an MPhil about the Chinese mafia at Paris's Assas law school. Chen was doing everything she could to obtain information on Huang Lili's case, for back in Beijing certain people were getting very anxious that they were about to witness a wave of arrests in France. Even if Huang were to be acquitted, her case was surely going to complicate industrial espionage in both public and private laboratories in France, since it was bound not only to sensitize laboratory heads but also to alert the French counterintelligence services to Chinese ways of working. Though Huang was only indicted for "breach of trust" and "fraudulent intrusion into an automatic data system" she was still being accused of industrial espionage, in other words of hacking into confidential databases in a sensitive domain concerning future car designs.

"I needed to know generous things [she meant 'general'] about the company," she told the hearing on 20 November, apologizing for not having paid attention to the "confidentiality agreement" that she had signed at the beginning of her internship: "I read it quickly, without paying proper attention." She had similarly ignored the warnings of her co-workers at Valeo, who never saw her without her laptop and its 40-gigabyte hard disk. She also had a mobile phone, but the police investigation found that she had not used it to send any information to China—at least not this mobile phone—nor her email address.

Probably in order to avoid damaging its image, the company, through its CEO Thierry Morin and its lawyer, played down any damage it had suffered. Huang Lili was not the Mata Hari she had initially been painted as. From the point of view of a large company like Valeo, it made no sense to demand a prison sentence for an intern. Valeo had a large presence in China, with a technical centre in Wuhan (the Eldorado of the Chinese automobile industry and the province Huang hailed from), its 5 Axis school for training Chinese personnel, a Shanghai office that had enabled the company to spread across Asia from 2001, and a Beijing office, established in 1994, where it had begun its first three joint ventures in windscreen wipers and air-conditioning. Witnessing the impact of similar incidents, such as the special ops on Danone (see below), was all the persuasion that heads of victim companies needed to exercise caution in their response to such attacks.

Nonetheless, the prosecutor, Marie-Laure Boubas, worried the defence by evoking "active manipulation", "concealment", "bad faith and breach of trust", and by asking for a one-year jail sentence, including a ten-month suspended sentence to cover Huang's pre-trial detention. Thanks to support for Huang Lili from her student friends and some of her professors, as well as media coverage of the case—which managed to make her come across as the victim—her lawyer Raphael Pacouret hit a nerve when he criticized anti-Chinese hysteria in France: "All interns have the same methods. But they aren't all called [Lili], and they aren't all Chinese." He called Huang's actions professional malpractice rather than a punishable criminal act, and asked for his client to be acquitted. But the court was not swayed: on 18 December 2005, Huang was sentenced to a year in prison, with ten months suspended and two months to be served, and €7,000 in damages to be paid to Valeo.

She had not been exonerated, as broadcast media claimed, relying on courtroom dispatches summarizing the arguments of the defence. Nor was she was convicted of espionage, which is a different charge in criminal law. But she had been convicted of "breach of trust" for having dishonestly procured information. Moreover, it was clear that she had understood this when she was shown proudly brandishing her Chinese passport and complaining, "There is nothing I can do up against the legal system of another country", whilst making claims on French television that France had been influenced by the United States in believing that there was such a thing as Chinese spies on their territory. If that had really been the case, she argued, she would not have been allowed to stay on and finish her degree, but would instead have been expelled from the country.

From Huang Lili to a cure for Alzheimer's

I was curious to talk to experts close to the Valeo investigation, the subject of so much media speculation. An expert in protecting economic property explained to me a few months before the trial: "In this case, I believe that the Chinese already had knowledge of these files, but what interested them was, as is so often the case, the system of validation [confirmation or corroboration]. That is the challenge in this area. Can we really call this espionage? Thousands of post-doctoral students and highly qualified scientists are interviewed by experts upon their return, or while they are still abroad completing their studies. This hardly makes them secret agents At a pinch one might call them potential 'honorary correspondents', who might later be questioned if their research, their experiments or their dissertations catch the attention of the relevant scientific services. All countries do that. The difference between them and us is that they have so many more [informants] than we do."

In this context, counterintelligence experts perhaps don't judge that they need to be keeping an eye on all Chinese students who, without considering themselves to be spies, are nonetheless part of the huge apparatus set in motion by Beijing to hoover up intelligence: "Influenced by the British and the Americans, one day our bosses had the idea of making a list of all the Chinese students who had come to France to study. Apart from anything else this would be an impossible task, just in terms of the number of people we could allocate to the task. We also tended to agree with our German colleagues that it wouldn't really achieve anything, unless by chance we actually came across a real Guoanbu agent, some kind of foot-dragging permanent student, working undercover.

"Some high-ranking official must have realized what a useless idea it was. It was dropped. We could intervene only in specific instances where we had already identified intelligence agents operating on our territory, by studying their modus operandi and their contacts. Actually, we realized that we were more likely to spot the presence of the Chinese services by following some high-profile figure in the world of French industry or politics who was genuinely corrupt and eating out of the hands of the Chinese secret services."

She went on to offer me several examples of politicians and other prominent figures on regional and general councils, or the former top brass in the French foreign office who, immediately after leaving his post, set up a consultancy firm using all his contacts—this was most welcome to the Chinese—as well as a Hong Kong tycoon specializing in arms sales to the Middle East.

Beyond the counterintelligence community's view of the Chinese espionage problem, there also remains the delicate balance sought by the scientific community, which believes that breakthroughs on one side can benefit the other, and vice versa—only, of course, if they are shared.

On 8 April 2006, a French CNRS researcher based in Strasbourg was stopped by customs at Entzheim airport. He was on his way first to Paris, then to Canton. "Dr X" was Chinese-Cambodian, born in Phnom Penh in 1940. He spoke perfect Mandarin and was a naturalized French citizen. He travelled regularly to conferences in Asia on subjects that testified to the wide range of his knowledge and expertise: the chemistry of natural products, bio-organic chemistry, and neurochemistry. These subjects took in essential oils, insect brain proteins, healing and neurologically active plants, cell therapy, and the induction of neural stem cell differentiation via small synthetic and natural molecules—one of Dr X's fifteen patents.

Customs discovered that Dr X, an employee at the French Institute of Chemistry, was carrying several samples from his laboratory that he was taking with him to China. This brilliant researcher appeared to have isolated a molecule capable of activating stem cells in the brain with the potential to cure both Alzheimer's disease and multiple sclerosis. In other words, the stakes were rather high.

"The scientific advisor at the French consulate in Canton, who entirely understood the point of a research partnership, had invited me to visit in order to prepare a Franco-Chinese workshop on this research topic," Dr X told *Le Figaro*. "My mistake was to take a few samples with me without having thought to ask permission from the CNRS, in order to be able to show that our work is actually complementary."[3] The CNRS filed a complaint, on the grounds that any discovery resulting from research carried out in its laboratories belongs to it by right—and especially any discovery that might make a colossal fortune for the pharmaceutical company that marketed it. Dr X was automatically and swiftly retired, and the legal case was closed. The scientific research community managed to avoid a scandal.

In terms of counterintelligence, though, the Dr X case raised a rather more general question: would it be better in such instances for the West to intercept the offender, as part of an exercise to "protect intellectual property", giving a warning shot to the scientific community? Or would it be better in fact to give them free rein and then to keep them in their sights, hoping to coax their handling officer out of the woodwork, and so identify an entire network?

For a long time, Guoanbu officers used to bring their agents back to China to debrief them. But this has begun to change and a growing number of Chinese spies are being noticed in countries other than the one where they were first recruited. This means, for example, that a French agent who meets his Chinese handler in Bangkok—where the Guoanbu has a significant presence—will leave no trace when entering China, having committed no crime in Thailand.

While Chinese economic espionage has spread across the globe since the late 1980s, at home it has continued to exploit the naivety and generally nonchalant approach of Western entrepreneurs with no one but themselves to blame when they are stripped of their patents, prototypes and market in the Eldorado that is twenty-first-century China. That is why counterintelligence services make a point of raising awareness on the security front for all those trading, investing or even simply travelling in China.

The anti-espionage protection manual

The British boast a longstanding tradition of cooperation between the intelligence services and the City. The pragmatism of Her Majesty's Secret Service has been honed by long experience in Singapore and Hong Kong. In 1990, in response to the flourishing of Chinese intelligence, MI5 produced a protection manual for businesspeople visiting China, called *Security Advice for Visitors to China*.[4] This manual is a timely reminder that:

> The motive behind the Chinese Intelligence Service cultivation of Westerners is primarily to make "friends": once a "friendship" is formed the Chinese will use the relationship to obtain information which is not legally or commercially available to China and to promote China's interest. The information required may not be classified: it can range from comment and analysis of Western political and economic trends, to Western security and defence matters, com-

> mercial practices, negotiation positions and industrial developments. Information on Western scientific and technological progress is a high priority requirement of the Chinese Intelligence Service.
>
> A second objective of a "friendship" can be for "talent spotting", that is meeting other Westerners through the original contact who may have more political influence and better access to information of interest.
>
> *Characteristics of a Chinese Intelligence Approach*
>
> The Chinese Intelligence Service approach to Western visitors differs from the more familiar techniques and methods of intelligence services of other communist countries, for example the Soviet KGB. A Western visitor is more likely to be the subject of long term, low key cultivation, aimed at making "friends". This technique leaves those visitors with an appreciation of China and a love of Chinese culture particularly vulnerable.
>
> Cultivation of a visitor or contact of interest is likely to develop slowly: the Chinese are very patient. An initial business transaction may be followed up by friendly social contact, such as an invitation to a meal or tickets to a cultural or sporting event. The target of the cultivation may be invited to return to China, ostensibly to discuss further business ventures or to speak at learned institutions; businessmen may be offered advantageous commercial opportunities, students may be offered exceptional research facilities. In reality, the return visit will be for the Chinese Intelligence Service to assess the potential of the target.
>
> The aim of these tactics is to create a debt of obligation on the part of the target, who will eventually find it difficult to refuse inevitable requests for favours in return.

As this MI5 document was published in the early 1990s, it states that China does not have the means to pay agents as other countries do. By 2008, this was of course no longer true, thanks to the increased wealth of businesses and the emergence of private-sector research centres, which have substantial funds for recruiting sources.

The considerable financial resources at stake, in the world of espionage as well as in other economic and strategic domains, began to pose real problems for foreign services, which in the past were able to recruit agents in China fairly easily by means of cold, hard cash. Now the opposite began to be true, as was first reported in early autumn 2007 by the Taiwanese counterintelligence services. Red China was buying spies.

"The economic boom in mainland China is the cause of the huge difficulties facing the Taiwanese intelligence services," according to Shi Hwei-yow, head of the National Security Bureau (*Kuo An C'hu*), responsible for sending agents to mainland China. This is because sources have been getting more and more greedy, while the budget of the Taiwanese services has not increased at the same pace. Similarly, the Chinese have been able to "turn" Taiwanese agents as easily as flipping pancakes. At the end of September 2007, a Taipei court sentenced two spies working for the PRC, one of whom, Chen Chih-kao, was a former member of another service, the Taiwanese FBI (*Tiao Ch'a Pu*), and had become a businessman on the mainland.[5] He had been "turned" by the Shanghai Guoanbu bureau headed by Wu Zhonghai, who offered him substantial funds to help his floundering business.

MI5's anti-espionage manual, showing great familiarity with the psychology of Chinese handling officers (*Gongzuo dandang guan*), emphasizes a point that businessmen and commercial agents do not always fully recognize: "a relationship built first on a business and then on a social footing can gradually develop into a tacit agent recruitment, making the businessman a controlled source of information for the Chinese Intelligence Service."

In 2008, the Chinese services were using the most modern means of electronic surveillance, intercepting mobile phones, Blackberry calendars, and so on. But the monitoring of visitors to China has not fundamentally changed from the close surveillance practices of the 1990s, as described in the MI5 manual:

> The Chinese have extensive resources at their disposal. They can and do place listening devices in hotels, guest houses and restaurants. They can search luggage and hotel rooms, scrutinize mail, and mount surveillance operations against visitors. Although this type of attack is more likely to be used against targets of particular interest, its possible use against others cannot be ruled out.
>
> Visitors to China should be aware that all private and business papers are at risk if left in offices or hotel rooms (even if locked in a briefcase), and they should assume most hotel, domestic, bar and restau-

rant staff are subject to the influence and control of the Chinese Intelligence Service.

In conclusion, the British offer the following tips:

> Understanding how the Chinese Intelligence Service operates is the best protection a visitor can have. Remember that status, occupation and background afford no immunity from special attention. Be especially alert for flattery and over-generous hospitality. Be careful about personal behaviour and be alert to compromising situations. If arrested or charged with infringing local regulations, or caught in an embarrassing situation, always insist on being allowed immediately to contact either the British embassy in Beijing or the consulate–general in Shanghai. ... There are many cases on record where people have been compromised and left to think that their troubles were over, only to find themselves some years later subject to a threatening approach.

These warnings corresponded to the ramping up of economic intelligence in the Deng–Jiang era.

A brief history of economic intelligence

It was under Deng Xiaoping, in the early 1990s, that economic intelligence began to boom. This has led to a popular belief that such Chinese intelligence was born in that period. However, the first intelligence cells of this kind were actually formed as early as the 1930s, at the communist base in Yan'an. It was Chen Yun, one of Kang Sheng's assistants in the Shanghai Social Affairs Department (SAD), who really unleashed it. Throughout his long life (d. 1995), Chen Yun zigzagged between issues of discipline and security, and economic questions. Those who came after this "Immortal" continued along similar lines: this was how his son Chen Yuan, an expert in financial affairs and in particular the Central Bank, was implicated in the financing of US lobbies not only directly linked to Chinagate, but also to Republican Party representatives.[6]

Often, the history of intelligence is embellished with stories of spies, double agents and honey traps. But the SAD, and successive intelligence agencies affiliated with the CCP, equally embedded itself deep in major financial and commercial organizations, particularly in

Shanghai and Hong Kong. Networks were established, thanks to invisible connections (*touming guanxi*) within Kuomintang and foreign-based companies that came from the global Chinese diaspora. Similarly, copying the Russian system of *rabcors* (worker correspondents) within the unions, the CCP had established an important web of networks engaged in economic intelligence in China before 1949.

When Chen Yun launched his first five-year plan, he relied on the research and intelligence sectors linked to the early economic intelligence structures, integrated into SAD and other CCP special services. In the early 1960s, for example, the diplomat Yuan Lulin moved from the "Committee for the Promotion of International Trade" in Austria, to head of the foreign affairs intelligence service, and then, towards the end of the Cultural Revolution, to a position as a banking advisor at the embassy in Switzerland.

The CCP's Diaochabu (which replaced the SAD) has conducted economic intelligence operations abroad ever since these first networks were set up, despite the fact that it was partially dismantled within China itself after the founding of the Guoanbu. In the 1960s, the French counterintelligence service (the DST) closely monitored visitors to the Leipzig International Fair, an important hub of intelligence in Eastern Europe, where attempts were often made to recruit Western businessmen. The Chinese were very present and engaged in similar attempts at seduction, as well as setting up their own trade fair in Canton. In 1966, the DST demanded the expulsion of three interns who had been showing a suspicious amount of interest in Ohmic's electronic equipment factory in Le Mans; the same went subsequently for a Xinhua News Agency correspondent, Li Yannian, and Tian Yiching, head of the French embassy press office, accused of industrial espionage, taking advantage of the chaos in some factories around the general strike of May 1968.[7]

When the Diaochabu was absorbed into the Guoanbu, the new state security service turned an entire section of its economic research unit into an intelligence department. In 1985, its director Ling Yun, a specialist in political counterintelligence, was replaced by an engineer, Jia Chunwang, who had trained at Tsinghua University and would later become Gonganbu minister. The Guoanbu now began to employ other people from the highly reputed university, known for producing top-quality cadres. In Beijing, a school of economic intelligence opened its doors at the Guoanbu's instigation, followed by a new business school in Shanghai.

In 1987, the principal Guoanbu agents in the Chinese embassy in West Germany were a married couple, the husband undercover as a "commercial advisor". Twenty years later in 2007, they were still there, and the "commercial advisor" had become such an important part of intelligence operations that he began to be a real thorn in the side of General Zhang Changtai, the defence attaché in Berlin at the time (no relation to the Zhang Changtai posted to Paris in 2006). There was an amusing reason for the two men's mutual dislike: they had the same name, and embassy workers in Berlin were always bringing them each other's post.

Back in the 1980s, the great intelligence reform consisted of using traditional methods, inherited from the Japanese espionage campaign of the 1950s, but in far greater number and by way of innovative technical means. "Astonishingly, at this year's Bordeaux International [1988], the Chinese were photographing everything, and using up-to-date video cameras that allowed them to film explanatory panels in their entirety, even ones that were completely innocuous," according to Colonel Ferron, regional head of the DPSD, the French military security directorate.[8]

Another example was the famously comical affair of the neckties, which obviously belongs to the era before digital cameras. In 1985, counterintelligence services noticed that some Chinese visitors to the company Agfa—at the time far more advanced in certain development processes than Kodak—had contrived to "inadvertently" plunge their neckties into special developer baths. Back at their hotel, they cut off the ends of their ties and sent them to China for analysis. "Cleaners" from the French secret services found the remains of the ties in the wastepaper baskets.

In 1983, in parallel with the creation of Guoanbu, the Ministry of Foreign Economic Relations and Trade (MOFERT) was born, headed by Chen Muhua—a respected militant who had nearly died in the 1940s when Kang Sheng had her arrested in Yan'an as a Kuomintang spy. She was rescued just in time by Zhou Enlai, the "revolutionary mandarin" behind the "Four Modernizations" realized in this period by Deng Xiaoping. She was clearly the ideal choice to lead the way in trade modernization.

The establishment of a large foreign trade ministry, coupled with one for scientific and technological research, was much-needed, not least since Comrade Deng launched a major national hi-tech research and development programme between 1982 and 1988. This included Programme 863, launched in March 1986, which had a military as well as civilian component, and the Torch Programme (*Huoju*), which spawned fifty-three hi-tech industrial development zones whose mission was to siphon off technologies from the West, Korea, Japan, and elsewhere.

Under the auspices of MOFERT's international sector—and that of its successor, MOFTEC—various roaming Guoanbu operatives directly involved in espionage operations were offered covers, as per Deng Xiaoping's ideas. Madame Chen was seconded into this area, thanks to a former Diaochabu technician, Wei Jinfei, who was advisor to the minister of trade until his death in 1983.

Beyond the "black zone" of industrial espionage, there were also several economic intelligence cells playing extremely important roles in the Chinese development race. In 1984, the Sichuan Scientific and Technical Information Centre was founded, which included "a FAX information network, a network for sharing commercial intelligence, and a global network exchange for economic, scientific and technical intelligence", as well as a service for collecting and providing samples of foreign products. The SSTIC brought together 15 million items of data for an expected 50,000 users and developed a major documentation service by fax, specializing particularly in marketing intelligence.

By 1986, MOFERT, located at 2 Dongchang'an Avenue in central Beijing, was the driving force behind the establishment of an economic and commercial network that brought together regional, local and import-export business institutions, and was equipped with a satellite terminal (VSAT) and an electronic data interchange network. It intended to build 300 terrestrial stations for national and international networks within five years. This was comparable to the Japan External Trade Organization's system, and capable of transmitting any economic data both to a central database and to the companies involved, in order to facilitate their interventions abroad.[9]

Headquartered in Beijing, the national branch then included 200 stations that used Asian civilian satellites. The international branch had 100 stations serving South-East Asia via satellite, North America, Japan and Oceania by submarine cable, and Europe, Africa and Asia from satellites in the Indian Ocean.[10]

It is possible to trace the birth of Chinese economic surveillance back to this birth of MOFERT/MOFTEC. It was supported by services directly linked to the upper echelons of the CCP, such as the United Front Work Department, which, as we have seen, intervened with the Chinese diaspora abroad. The UFWD's 5th Bureau, responsible for economic intelligence, was headed from the late 1980s by Hu Deping, son of Hu Yaobang, the CCP general secretary ousted during Tiananmen, and director of the Chinese Society for Research into the Private Economy. Hu was later made head of China's international chamber of commerce, a role that sent him to different European countries to establish links with business groups hoping to invest in China.

Chinese systems of economic surveillance

"My services are not engaged in espionage operations, but rather in overt intelligence, and large-scale economic surveillance," Professor Liu Xiaoxi told me in 2007. He was then director-general of the Macroeconomic Research Department, part of the State Council's Research Bureau.[11] The occasion was a dinner with leaders of the China Reform Forum, linked to the CCP's Central School, followed by a wide-ranging discussion on the driving forces behind economic intervention abroad. There had also been a lengthy presentation of the major reforms in this area, covering every detail: the instigating role of Deng Xiaoping; the launch of major information technology programmes under Jiang Zemin; and the "theory of the three harmonies" conceived by President Hu Jintao (2003-13), who wanted to continue China's evolution into a superpower while avoiding conflict with other large nations.

However strong that desire may have been, the craving for energy deposits could and did trigger strategic and diplomatic conflict, as had happened in 2006 in Darfur, on Sudan's border with Chad. The

French DGSE's special forces, responsible for the security of the Chadian president Idriss Deby, had found itself surrounded by rebels armed by the Chinese. But the most important thing is to remain "friends". "The informative research of economic surveillance is organized into three channels," Liu explained to me, between spoonfuls of spicy soup. "They are officially institutes of economic research: non-governmental organizations and private institutions. Forty or so researchers are centralizing this information, in order to allow the government to plan for the next few years."

At the turn of the millennium, Liu was working with the CCP's Investigation Service (*Zhongyang diaoyanshi*), which had replaced the Diaochabu in 1983. It was headed at the time by Chen Jinyu, a former academic, who emphasized that research, and its centralization, was all done using open sources. A huge data flow was being processed, which was apparently posing a problem in terms of sorting and analysis. "Our managers receive a lot of information, and it is true that a coordinating body is missing. But to tell the truth, I am not sure that this would be possible in a country as vast as China. For at least two reasons: the regionalization of the economy and the undeniable size of the private sector since Deng Xiaoping's sea-change." This explains the existence of a myriad of intermediate-level information coordination and regulation commissions, which, according to Liu, are able to circulate information in a much more fluid way than in the past.

The interface between state, party and even military intelligence agencies and large, theoretically private companies, remains constant. "E-information, in other words information gathered on the internet, modelled on American and other systems, has become extremely important," Liu pointed out. "This is an area in which the Ministry of Information [which controls the internet through the security services] plays a pivotal role."

He also emphasized that the traditional vectors of information, part of the Chinese intelligence system since 1949, continue to be important: for example, the confidential economic reports produced by the Xinhua News Agency and various ministries now working online. Just a few days before we met, I had managed to get hold of a manual for how to gather intelligence on the internet, published by Tsinghua University's IT department. It illustrated the huge revolution of cadre training and technological surveillance in the new economy.

What Professor Liu explained to me was fairly comprehensive. All that was lacking was an explanation of how intelligence useful for state affairs and national security was coming out of the private sector in the first place—and the role of the army in a growing number of cases concerning commerce and industry.

Economic "research bureaus"

Following my meeting with Professor Liu, I wanted to find out a little more about the structure of the State Council's Research Bureau for which he worked, then headed by Wei Liqun.[12] This bureau, which had grown significantly under Jiang Zemin, has given up its role as a generalist and political intelligence agency, and is now confined to gathering strategic commercial and economic intelligence.

This reorientation was encouraged by Wei's predecessor, Gui Shiyong. The Research Bureau, located in the official government residence at Zhongnanhai, answers directly to the prime minister. Its mission is to collect, compile and analyze all intelligence of an economic and societal nature, both internally and abroad, to guide the leadership's decision-making. It simultaneously helps CCP leaders to document their activities and the government to consider what new reforms should be undertaken. But the Research Bureau is not simply a triage station; it is also a think-tank and a laboratory of ideas. As director, Wei used to accompany Hu Jintao's prime minister, Wen Jiabao, on his various trips abroad, just as he had accompanied Wen's predecessor Zhu Rongji while deputy director.

The bureau is made up of six departments; the first secretarial department also oversees the Department of Foreign Affairs. The other five are research departments, for global research; macroeconomics (Professor Liu's department); trade, transport and industry; rural economics; and social development. Wei further boosted his team by engaging the services of analysts specialized in "globalization", including Ms Jiang Xiaojuan, former general secretary of the International Investment Research Centre at the Chinese Academy of Social Sciences, which plays an important role in many areas of research and intelligence, including strategy.

The Research Bureau works in harmony with the two main ministries involved in strategic research on economic warfare: MOFCOM, the Ministry of Commerce (*Shangwubu*), which succeeded MOFTEC in 2003; and MOST, the Ministry of Science and Technology. Both have a powerful information research network that extends over the entire globe. MOFCOM's economic intelligence organisms are endowed with enormous manpower. The trade minister Bo Xilai (2004–7), son of Mao Zedong's finance minister Bo Yibo, benefited from a structure that had been refined by his predecessor at MOFTEC, Shi Guangsheng. Shi had a wealth of experience as a commercial attaché in Mali and Belgium, having already led MOFERT/MOFTEC's import-export division and participated in the delicate 15-year negotiations regarding China's entry into the World Trade Organization in 2001.

The mission of MOFTEC/MOFCOM's intelligence apparatus, expanded after 2003, was to replicate China's internal economic transformation in the global economy, making it a major player. Its positioning within the WTO, the negotiation of intellectual property treaties, the definition of commercial strategies, the acquisition of new technologies, the creation of joint ventures—all these activities and many others demanded the deployment of economic intelligence techniques and expertise at a national level. On the international stage, this apparatus was augmented by parallel structures in megacities like Shanghai, Chongqing and Canton, as well as in provinces such as Shandong, where "siphoning" systems particularly effective for economic intelligence had been implemented. Committees for twinning cities and other forms of exchange were also exploited by regional structures.

At the State Council, MOFCOM was overseen by Deputy Prime Minister Wu Yi, described in 2004 by *Forbes* magazine as the second most powerful woman in the world, after then US National Security Advisor Condoleezza Rice. This was a logical appointment, given that Wu had run the ministry in the 1990s and overseen the birth of its economic intelligence unit.

MOFCOM relies on specialized internal departments, such as the Department of Economic Affairs and International Trade, as well as a myriad of think-tanks and institutes that have emerged since the

1990s.[13] The Research Institute of International Trade, set up in 1994 by Shi Honghai, can be considered the original Chinese economic intelligence structure, in the sense that it is understood in the West. This clearly echoes the use of scientific research centres and think-tanks seen in the previous chapter.

The establishment of data banks, regional structures for economic research, and the provision of foreign intelligence to Chinese companies via the internal magazine *Foreign Trade Survey* all naturally exploit the diversified structures of government agencies with "research sections", such as the finance ministry and the Bank of China. However, MOFCOM's intelligence specialists also work in conjunction with the offensive counterintelligence of the Guoanbu, in particular its 17th Bureau, headed by Tian Gengren, and its "business" bureau, founded in 2000 by Chen Quansheng (later director-general of the State Research Council). Among the tens of thousands of Guoanbu "deep-water fish", vast numbers of intelligence agents are embedded within the economic networks of the Chinese diaspora around the world.

The Guoanbu's 10th Bureau, headed by an expert named Liu Zhisheng, covers the scientific and technological field and thus acts as the interface with the Ministry of Science and Technology, led in the early 2000s by an automobile industry expert who is not a member of the CCP, Wan Gang. The 10th Bureau has many highly aggressive structures responsible for collecting information, patents and reports, as well as for other active measures including the recruitment of scientists, of both Chinese and non-Chinese origin.

Subsidiary to the Executive Bureau headed by Li Chaocheng, MOFCOM's Research and Investigation Departments 1 and 2 are responsible for internet research carried out by the e-documentation division—online intelligence-gathering done via artificial intelligence.

Led by Jin Xiaoming, the International Cooperation Division is, of course, the most active abroad, establishing scientific research agreements between institutions and laboratories at global, inter-state and sub-state levels. It is split into seven departments: (1) Planning/general affairs; (2) Conference organization; (3) America/Oceania affairs; (4) Africa/Asia; (5) Europe; (6) Research policy; (7) Eastern and Central Europe. It guides research from the diplomatic posts where it is represented, in liaison with the Guoanbu and

COSTIND, which manages military technological research. In Paris, its coordination post is located in the Rue Washington embassy annexe, on the fourth floor.

At the beginning of 2006, the OECD estimated that China was about to become the second-largest research and development (R&D) investor after the United States, spending $136 billion in the field and surpassing Japan's spending of $130 billion. This means that China's R&D development was more intense over the decade than its economic expansion, which was then fixed at a steady rate of between 9 and 10 per cent a year. However, the science and technology ministry in Beijing has denied these figures, claiming that it spends only a quarter of this amount, and spent only $30 billion in 2005.

This suggests that, in the field of civil and economic technology, the Beijing authorities are downplaying the real figures, just as the PLA does for the annual military budget, veiling the boon represented by intelligence funding. It is important to avoid giving the impression that the Chinese state apparatus has a determining role in the private sector's R&D, if one wants to maintain the fiction that China is governed by the market economy. In reality, 55 per cent of the R&D budget is state-owned.[14] Within each of the structures mentioned above, a government steering committee determines its objectives and targets for technology research overseas, as part of a global policy.

Sea lamprey tactics

In 2006, at a conference in Paris, General Daniel Schaeffer, former defence attaché at the French embassy in Beijing, described in detail the "practices of Chinese economic intelligence in the acquisition of high technology".[15] After defining the main players in economic intelligence, he went through the "Chinese operating methods", much as this book has given multiple illustrations of secret service methods using both clandestine and open sources to capture the key intelligence information that feeds the Chinese economy. There were nine of these MOs in total, which might provide a useful summary at this point.

The first is the acquisition of open intelligence, particularly easy in the West and in democratic countries because of the profusion of sources and access to information (especially using the internet, as the Chinese services are increasingly doing). This can also be acquired during highly instructive visits to facilities and companies. The second is the exploitation of political relationships, particularly the kind that will lead to scandal. Chinagate in the United States is one example, as is the Taiwanese frigate scandal (see below).

The third method is international cooperation in the economic field, essentially meaning foreign investment. As Schaeffer put it, "The rush to China has opened up a veritable mine of technology, and has enabled it to make up in record time for the backwardness of the Maoist regime." By 2004, the CIA was warning that China was on its way to becoming the world's sixth economic power, even though its GDP (10,561 yuan, or €1106) would put it at the level of extremely weak economies, such as Honduras and Sri Lanka. Foreign investment was initially the engine of Chinese growth, worth $660 billion and involving half a million businesses. After a while, though, the opposite dynamic was brought into play: China began using its accumulated assets to purchase energy resources abroad. Depending on the mood of the forecasters, it would be either all good or all bad: some thought that, by 2010, because of massive income disparity, the bubble would burst or at least the country would experience considerable social unrest, while by 2035, it would have overtaken the United States as the biggest economy in the world. world. The CIA confirmed its own prediction in its 2018 "factbook", and the World Bank, the London School of Economics and the US Treasury are all agreed on this today. This is in spite of the slowdown in China's growth, the trade war with Donald Trump, and the growing sanctions and regulatory buffers around emerging technologies (as with Huawei's 5G networks in 2019).

The fourth method for economic intelligence is direct commercial acquisition. This is where China buys a few copies of a product for the purpose of dissecting it and then manufacturing its own version. The best-known example of this was the magnetic levitation train developed by the Germans, the Maglev. Berlin hoped to sell the entire Beijing–Shanghai route to the Chinese. Instead, the Chinese bought just the Shanghai stretch, from the airport to the city centre. In the meantime, in 2006, engineers at Chengdu's Southwest Jiaotong

University Industrial School of Engineering had fabricated their own Chinese Maglev train. In aeronautics circles, it was feared that the same process would happen with Airbus. Another way to gather economic intelligence through purchases is by buying "apartments", rather than the entire building, as was done in the mid-1980s. Aircraft manufacturers would order more engines than actual aircraft, for quite obvious reasons: the engine was the only element that the Chinese had not yet succeeded in copying.[16]

The reader has already encountered examples of the fifth method, scientific cooperation, as in the case of the anonymous CNRS researcher. Schaeffer was right to warn against paranoia and seeing all research cooperation as no more than a vast organized looting of knowledge. He pointed out that "the whole problem is knowing, when it comes to cooperation, where to set the bar for sharing knowledge, acknowledging that some might compromise our economic, technological and strategic interests, and to what extent our researchers ought to be alert to where the limits lie when it comes to the exchange of knowledge". His remarks were based on a particularly French issue: unlike in Britain or Germany, French counterintelligence has struggled to reach a consensus with the scientific community on how to define what constitutes the protection of intellectual property.

The sixth method is student cooperation. The Valeo affair was just the tip of the iceberg—the French security services' statistical analysis concluded that the Chinese did not consider French universities to be the best places to send their future elites to study, apart from the training of top state administrators and other territorial officials (managed in China by the CCP Central School). This must mean that there are many more Huang Lilis in other parts of the world.

The seventh method will take us right back to the beginning of our story, and the interwar era when Zhou Enlai and Deng Xiaoping had been student–workers in France: "returning from the West". Chinese researchers in the West, particularly those in private laboratories, were expected to put their acquired knowledge to good use when they returned to China. The network of Confucius Institutes established in 2004, in partnership with major Chinese technology companies and twinned with leading universities, required more refined analysis—especially since many foreign students now come to study and undertake internships in China. Beijing's hope is that these students will be won over to the cause of the Chinese economy.

The eighth method is exploitation of national pride. This primarily concerns the vast community of overseas Chinese, the *Huaqiao*, whose relationships with their country of origin remain strong. It can also be used to refer to the traditional web of regional relationships, or *guanxi*. These connections have a part to play in organized crime, as can be seen in some pockets of the Teochew or Wenzhou ethnic groups, though clearly not the majority of them. Such relationships have sometimes been exploited for the purposes of first-grade espionage, as we saw in the cases of the Guoanbu's CIA moles, Larry Wu Tai Chin (1986) and Jerry Chun Shing Lee (2018).

Finally, the services employ an infinite number of negotiating strategies, including lobbying, stand-offs with negotiating partners, using blackmail to gain access to the Chinese market, competitive pitching—in the course of which the Chinese get hold of technical files containing the knowledge they are after, without even needing to conclude negotiations—and partnerships that turn against Westerners participating in joint ventures, as in the Danone affair (see below).

So what does all this tell us? It is simple: large Chinese companies now have operating procedures and considerable financial resources that allow them easily to set up shell companies for siphoning off Western technology. They are now responsible for an extremely high volume of espionage, unmatched by any country since the implosion of the Eastern Bloc.[17]

Many of these techniques bring to mind the sea lamprey—a legendary snake-like fish known in China as the "eel with eight eyes" (*ba mu man*). Scientists can date its evolution into its current form to around 530 million years ago. Like twenty-first-century China, it has time on its side. The notion of the "sea lamprey strategy" (*ba mu man ji*) comes from the fact that this slippery, greenish fish blends in with the seascape, clinging to the rocks, and then, having waited patiently to select its prey, closes in and latches on, siphoning off its blood through its multiple orifices. It is the perfect metaphor for Chinese espionage techniques.

Huawei's business intelligence

The telecommunications empire Huawei Technologies was founded in 1987 by a former PLA officer, Ren Zhengfei, in the Shenzhen Special Economic Zone. It is an excellent example of a company that has mastered the "sea lamprey strategy", and the perfect symbol of China profiting from and buying up the rest of the world. One could write an entire book about the company, which has in fact published several books itself, celebrating its multiple successes; these can be found in any Chinese bookstore. Huawei has become a major player, as the laid-off employees of Alcatel-Lucent in Rennes, Brittany discovered when the company was forced to relocate following Huawei's decision to set up a factory in Lannion, also in Brittany.

By the early 2000s, Huawei counted thirty-one of the top fifty telecoms operators among its customers, including British Telecom, Telefónica, Orange, China Mobile and Vodafone. It had around 30,000 researchers worldwide, one of its largest teams, which commanded 10 per cent of its overall budget. 62,000 of its employees, half of its entire workforce, worked in research and development. By 2018, its manpower had tripled in size, to 180,000 employees worldwide, with 79,000 working in R&D. Not a week goes by without an announcement that it is opening up in yet another location. Its competitors are convinced that it exploits every kind of technological intelligence strategy, pointing out that it has shown little concern for geopolitical ethics since it signed lucrative contracts with Saddam Hussein's Iraq and the Taliban in Afghanistan in 2001 to set up both civilian and military communications networks. As Deng Xiaoping liked to say, it doesn't matter if a cat is black or grey—so long as it catches mice.

Huawei is visibly growing and expanding its offering. One of its triumphs was the $700 million contract it signed with China Mobile Communications Corporation, whose networks cover thirty Chinese provinces including Canton, Zhejiang, Fujian, Jiangsu and Shandong. Given these circumstances, it comes as no surprise to learn that Huawei has developed a gigantic business intelligence apparatus to unearth everything about its competitors, its potential markets and the research and development of other companies it is interested in acquiring. According to my information, this apparatus also works to the benefit of the state apparatus, including the PLA—in which Ren still serves as an officer in the reserves—and of course, unavoidably in China, the CCP.

According to its own documents, this business intelligence system—Huawei TopEng-BI—depends on the internal and external flow of information and information in liaison with all its subsidiaries and the following networks: a real-time data warehouse, an online analysis process, data-mining, an AI system, and a geographical information system. The complex interface of these sectors gives access from Huawei's massive headquarters in Shenzhen to analyses, information and market projections, an effective sales support, and detailed analyses of the company's clientele, which presumably also enables access to vast amounts of personal data. It is difficult to know what to make of this last point—especially if one thinks of the potential overlap with ministries like the Guoanbu and the PLA's 3rd Department, in charge of communications warfare.

Unlike the countries out of which other operators work, in China there is no control over data protection. It has unprecedented systems in place for analyzing millions of calls, clients, VIP customers, competitors, monitoring systems, automated reports on device use, customer profiles, and data to be exploited. Officially, all of this is used for marketing purposes, including breaking into new markets. But the reality is that Huawei's business intelligence systems, a programme like no other—except for the American NSA—represent one of the world's largest organizations dealing in technological intelligence.

Britain, thanks to research undertaken at the Government Communications Headquarters (GCHQ), has best understood the threat posed by Huawei due to its technological penetration of Western telephone manufacturers including British Telecom and Orange. Moreover, in 2013, the Joint Intelligence Committee, which runs British intelligence operations, warned that in case of cyber-attack, "it would be very difficult to detect or prevent and could enable the Chinese to intercept covertly or disrupt traffic passing through Huawei-supplied networks."[18]

In the following years, claims about Huawei's involvement in shady activities became part of the economic rivalry between Donald

Trump's America and Xi Jinping's China. In January 2019, Huawei's chief financial officer, Meng Wanzhou—founder Ren Zhengfei's daughter—was indicted by the US Ministry of Justice, together with Huawei Device US Inc. and SkyCom Tech., a Huawei subsidiary, on charges of money laundering and financial fraud. As she had been arrested earlier in Canada, and with the US exerting pressure for her extradition, Beijing authorities retaliated by arresting Canadian citizens in China.

At the same time there were numerous claims by counterintelligence agencies around the world that Huawei's operations increasingly presented a security threat. As Ms Sun Yafang retired as Huawei chairwoman in 2018, it was recalled that, before joining Huawei in 1989, she had been a leading technician in the Guoanbu telecoms department.

In Europe, Taiwan and Japan, national administrations opposed the use of Huawei mobile phones equipped with special devices that allowed automatic interception of communications and data, especially as the firm attempted to become dominant in the worldwide deployment of the fifth generation of cellular communications, 5G.

In the UK, MI6 director-general Alex Younger expressed concerns about the Huawei 5G system in December 2018. In France, Huawei was not allowed to erect 5G antennae close to the Paris headquarters of the Ministry of Defence, while the prime minister's SGDSN (General Secretariat for Defence and National Security) suspected Huawei of being a Trojan horse that provided Beijing with the ability to freeze 5G networks in case of conflict, which would thereby debilitate connected devices and internet-controlled autonomous vehicles.[19] French intelligence (DGSE) uncovered an attempt by Huawei agents to build up a private biographical data system on leaders of the French competitor company Orange, which ironically favoured a strategic alliance with the Chinese firm.[20]

Together with the Australians, German and other European security services agree that, despite disclaimers by its leaders, Huawei was intimately linked to the PLA interception and cyberwar effort (see chapter 11).

This brings us back to our question, which we can now answer: it is perfectly clear how the CCP—and so the PRC—benefits from economic intelligence. Not to mention the purely material gain generated by the corruption that is endemic at the highest state levels.

The Taiwan frigate scandal

It's time to talk about corruption. Scandals regularly break out in China, and the CCP's Discipline Inspection Commission, supported by the Guoanbu, leads investigations that often culminate in the execution of senior cadres who serve as fall guys. But not always. The front-page scandals of the Taiwanese frigates and the Clearstream affair simply would never have taken place were it not for the corruption of the CCP leadership during the time of Jiang Zemin and his Shanghai clique (1989-2002). This could also be said, though to a lesser extent, of the politicians and knights of industry in the entourage of French president François Mitterrand (1981-95). Above all, it was those in Beijing and the Taiwanese navy who averted their eyes while pocketing lavish bribes who were responsible for the sale of six La Fayette frigates to Taiwan for 6 billion francs by the defence contractor Thomson-CSF (now Thales).

In December 1991, once the contract for the frigates' sale had been signed, a Swiss front company sheltering two intermediaries in the pay of the oil company ELF, Alfred Sirven and Christine Deviers-Joncour, was demanding 160 million francs from Thomson-CSF for its participation in the negotiations. But Alain Gomez, CEO of Thomson-CSF, resisted. The "ELF network" argued that it had played a pivotal role not only in persuading the Taiwanese navy to accept the tender, but also in convincing the French state that it was worth the risk to its relationship with the PRC, and ensuring that the CCP did not consider it an act of hostility.

By August 1991, these three goals had been met, though less thanks to the ELF network than to another, set up by Alain Gomez with the help of his Chinese friend Lily Liu, and a third set up by an expert in arms trading, Andrew Wang. This victory paved the way for further arms sales. To arrive at this result, President Mitterrand had been persuaded to change some minds, convincing his foreign affairs minister Roland Dumas, who—sensitive to his ministry's arguments on the need to maintain mutual trust with Beijing—was not very supportive of the tender. Eventually, the Taiwanese admirals conceded that French vessels were better than Korean ones, even if they cost rather more. And the Chinese were satisfied with making a purely formal protest against the sale of military equipment to Taiwan.

The investigation of Thomson-CSF's complaint against the small ELF network later showed that these shifts of opinion had not been due to the strength of conviction among Thomson-CSF sales executives. After being heard by the judge, Renaud Van Ruymbeke, Foreign Minister Roland Dumas went on the record to claim that Mitterrand had authorized the payment of a "commission" of $400 million to the Taiwanese decision-makers, and $100 million to Chinese officials who were later revealed to be part of President Jiang Zemin's inner circle—the prime minister, Zhu Rongji (who visited Paris on 16 April 1991), Jia Chunwang, then head of the Guoanbu, and Wang Baosen, the former mayor of Beijing, who would commit suicide in 1995.[21] Bribes had also reportedly been paid to former Shanghai mayor Huang Jun, Admiral Liu Huaqing, head of the PLA, who would later be implicated in the US Chinagate; Foreign Minister Qian Qichen, and even Deng Pufang, the son of former president Deng Xiaoping and head of the China Disabled Persons' Federation.

Kickbacks were also paid to various French politicians on the left and right and to several Taiwanese officials. Just as the affair reached the French courts, with international arrest warrants issued and a Taiwanese commission of inquiry also seeking certain individuals, several of those involved seemed to vanish completely. Among them was Wang Chang Poo—otherwise known as Andrew Wang, the professional arms trading intermediary. According to Christine Deviers-Joncour, who claimed that the ELF network had been key to the success of the negotiations, Wang was no more than a figurehead, whereas Thales claimed that it was he who had opened the door to the negotiations. Whatever the truth of the matter, Wang, who held a flotilla of bank accounts in Asia and Europe through which at least 5 billion francs transited, was now nowhere to be found. The mysterious Lily Liu was similarly absent. Some claimed it was she who had pulled the strings in China, but Deviers-Joncour called her no more than a decoy persona, an amalgamation of three not very high-ranking Chinese women.

By cross-checking all the different leads and statements, in Beijing, Taipei and Paris, it is possible to work out who all these shadowy characters really were. First there was Li Tingting. Owner of a US-based business, she was quickly sidelined in the frigate affair, but she deserves mention, if only because she is the daughter of Liu Shaoqi, Chinese chairman during the Cultural Revolution—and she had proposed taking on a mediating role with Zhongnanhai in the affair.

Admiral Liu Huaqing's entourage was then—mistakenly—implicated. As we know, Liu's daughter, Colonel Liu Chaoying—deputy director of the PLA2's 5th Bureau—would play a pivotal role for military intelligence in Chinagate. That affair would later see her imprisoned along with her boss, General Ji Shengde, not helped by Jiang Zemin's outright hostility towards her father. The reason the admiral was named in the frigate affair was that he was a protector of the woman who had actually run the Beijing network for Thomson: Lily Liu (no relation). The latter was from Taiwan, the daughter of a nationalist air force officer, and apparently a former flight attendant.

Her sister, Liu Chuan, had set up a school for models in Shanghai, and then became a supermodel in Hong Kong, where she invited Lily to join her. Lily was a familiar face in Hong Kong circles, and became the girlfriend of one of the diplomats at the French consulate who had played a central role in the 1989 Hong Kong network helping Tiananmen dissidents to flee abroad. She also had close links to the Xinhua News Agency, China's main secret service cover in Hong Kong. For French counterintelligence, there was no doubt that Lily Liu was, at the very least, an "honourable correspondent" for the Guoanbu, under the protection of Jia Chunwang as well as Deng Xiaoping's son and Admiral Liu Huaqing, to whom she was particularly close. She was paid between 60 and 70 million francs to smooth out any difficulties between Paris and Beijing over the frigate deal. She used to travel frequently, but after the scandal broke in 1997, she restricted her movements to Shanghai, Beijing and Hong Kong, where she ran a company in liaison with the military commission COSTIND.

In her book about the affair, Christine Deviers-Joncour was not wrong to say that it was "thanks to Lily Liu [that] military equipment sold by Thomson [to the Taiwanese] contained nothing that Beijing didn't know about already. As for French corruption, Liu almost certainly knew all about the payment of bribes—which would be a very handy card to play in the event of regaining sovereignty over Taiwan. How could Paris object [when it had been so compromised itself]?

"So Lily Liu was kept under close surveillance after the story broke, primarily to ensure that she didn't try and disappear, and also so that there was no chance for anyone to "disappear" her permanently. Much like Sirven from the ELF network, she was in possession of perhaps not enough explosive information to blow the French Republic to smithereens, but at least enough detergent to air a great deal of dirty laundry in public."[22] What was to stop the Chinese services from applying indefinite pressure to the French politicians from across the spectrum who had been involved?

Lily Liu's role in the affair raises another question, one that has never really been examined: had all the frigates' technological secrets been offered up to the Chinese leadership at the same time as they were sold to its Taiwanese opponents? This makes sense when one recalls that Thomson-CSF had already played this double game earlier in the Mitterrand presidency, during the Falklands War: it had handed MI6 the secrets of the Exocet after having sold the same missiles to the Argentinians.

In these circumstances, it is perhaps not surprising to learn that several witnesses died before the presiding judge, Renaud van Ruymbeke, was able to hear their depositions. The first suspicious death connected to the case was that of Thierry Imbot, son of General René Imbot, former head of the DGSE (1985-7). According to his father, Thierry, who was stationed first in Beijing and later in Taiwan, had been intending to go to the press when he was found dead in October 2000 at the foot of his Parisian apartment building. According to the police, he had fallen while trying to close the shutters of his studio flat.

Then Jacques Morisson, the former Thomson-CSF executive who had negotiated the contract, "committed suicide" in May 2001 by throwing himself from the fifth floor of his apartment building in Neuilly-sur-Seine—his apartment was on the second floor. After him came Jean-Claude Albessart, representative of Thomson's international office in Taiwan, whose death in 2002 was attributed to an aggressive cancer; not to mention the unfortunate Captain Ying, found beaten and drowned off the coast of Taiwan, who had been about to publicly denounce corruption in his country's navy. Despite the case being classified military top secret, information continued to leak out.

In 2005, two investigating judges raided the offices of French Finance Minister Thierry Breton. The investigative weekly *Le Canard enchaîné* revealed that several sensitive files were found in the office of his principal private secretary, Gilles Grapinet. One concerned the Taiwan frigates, and listed the names of those who had received one of the famous kickbacks. Among the twenty beneficiaries "were several Chinese from Taiwan, as well as half of the Politburo of the Chinese Communist Party."[23] In France and the PRC alike, the cloak of secrecy enjoyed by the intelligence and security services also served to conceal corruption among the powerful.

The other form of corruption to emerge around the turn of the millennium, in which the Chinese secret services did intervene, was also at the heart of the economic war. It concerned state support for companies that were private but considered "patriotic", in the face of competition from Western businesses. At the beginning of summer 2007, a French company experienced a particularly far-reaching and devastating example of this kind of manipulation.

Special operations against Danone

The China story of the Danone Group is not merely a case of unfair competition suffered by the French company, similar to the experience of other foreign companies like the US giant Procter & Gamble. Rather, the standoff between Danone and its Chinese partner Wahaha involved mounting an operation, with the approval of the Chinese authorities, to exclude a foreign company from the market once it had done its work helping to develop a local version of itself. At least, that is what was suspected.

The case of Zong Qinghou, head of the Chinese company Wahaha, was clearly a remarkable use of *guanxi*—circles of Chinese influence—and also of the secret services, which allowed the multimillionaire businessman to turn against Danone—Wahaha's majority shareholder, with a 51 per cent stake. It all began in 1996, when Zong became a partner in the Danone Group, which develops energy and yoghurt drinks and bottled water, generally sold to hotels and foreigners. The company that Danone set up with Zong, Wahaha, benefited from the technical expertise of the French, particularly when it came to developing production lines. However, ten years later, without telling Danone, Zong set up several parallel companies in the same sector. Once Danone found out, it demanded that all the companies be legally brought into the shared parent company.

The situation deteriorated, all in the name of Zong's "Chinese patriotism". When Franck Riboud, Danone's CEO, decided to take the case to court, on 9 May 2007, Chinese customs conveniently discovered "bacteria" in samples taken from seized bottles of Danone-owned Evian water. For the many business leaders who were already complaining of harassment by the State Administration for Industry and Commerce, there was no doubt that this was an operation intended to destabilize the company. But it would be very difficult to prove.

It was certainly true that Zong enjoyed support at the highest levels of state. At the very top was Wu Yi, the former head of MOFCOM and all-powerful deputy prime minister, who was overseeing the trade sector for another few months. In addition to running economic intelligence organizations that aided "patriotic businesses" like Zong's, Wu also had access to those bodies charged with investigating and clamping down on certain companies, since in 2003 she had taken over responsibility for the Leading Group, in charge of rectifying and regulating the market, which worked closely with the security services.[24]

During a 2001 visit to Zong's business in Hangzhou, Wu Yi had been highly positive about the expansion of the Chinese group Wahaha. This was accompanied by unwavering support for its activities from the governor of Zhejiang, the regional secretary of the CCP and the party's secretary in Hangzhou. This already impressive show of support was strengthened even further after Zong was elected to the National People's Congress in the province of Zhejiang.

If any doubt remains about Zong's links to the most deeply concealed networks within the Chinese state, we need only follow the Paris newsletter *Intelligence Online*, and look at the man behind the subsidiary responsible for Wahaha's foreign exports, particularly to the United States. Among the products developed by Wahaha was a new kind of cola drink to compete with Pepsi and Coca-Cola in China, called "Future Cola" (*Feichang Kele*). The soft drink tycoon was not aiming to compete with the American giants in their mainstream home market, but to sell its products in Chinatowns across America. Zong commissioned the import-export company Manpolo International Trading to set up this positioning. But its main shareholder, Guan Liang, was—and remains—head of the "United Chinese Association Eastern US".

Very present on the business scene, Guan is on excellent terms with the Chinese consulate in New York, so much so that it recruited him in the war against the Falun Gong spiritual movement, long considered by the CCP to be an "anti-Chinese sect". Falun Gong even took Guan to court for assaulting some of its members at a meeting in 2003. In this ongoing case, Guan Liang, whose anti-Falun Gong speeches are in the public domain, denied having acted in concert with the Chinese consul in New York, Zhang Hongxi, who has since had to leave the country. He also denies having any links with the 610 Office, another secret service—it was founded in 1999 specifically to combat the dissidents and members of the vast Falun Gong organization, whose leadership is based in the United States, and which supports the overthrow of the CCP.

10

THE 610 OFFICE AND THE FIVE POISONS

On the night of 24–25 April 1999, hundreds of coaches from all over China converged on Tiananmen Square, where the police were on high alert as the tenth anniversary of the student massacre approached. Demonstrators from Beijing, carrying small plastic bags, joined the flood of protesters. By early morning, there were 10-15,000 men and women of all ages sitting on the ground on the western side of the square, encircling Zhongnanhai—not only the seat of the government, but also the residence of the ruling elite.

As far as President Jiang Zemin was concerned, there was no doubt: these peaceful demonstrators, from Falun Gong, were besieging both the state and the CCP. It was like a return to the events of 1989. And this protest felt like a "personal message": the president had begun his career in Changchun, Manchuria, in automobile production. Changchun was also where, in 1992, a former army musician and son of two intellectuals called Li Hongzhi had set up Falun Gong, of which he was the guru.[1] Li was by now in exile in the United States, and it was surprising that he had succeeded in organizing such a huge gathering from such a distance.

The demonstration had already been going on for five hours, without a sound; there was no chanting of slogans. Absolute silence reigned, while the growing mass of protesters, seated in the lotus position, now extended for 2 kilometres. They were simply asking for the release of some of the movement's leaders, who had been arrested several days earlier in Tianjin.

A reporter I met in Beijing while conducting my own research was also there that day. He explains why the Chinese leadership was in such a state of alarm at this development: "It was really disturbing. The protesters seemed to be in some kind of state of enlightenment. Their eyes were empty, their gestures jerky. It was as though they came from a different time, five centuries ago. It was not surprising that the CCP panicked. They were like ghosts from a distant past; or, to put it more simply, they were the generation that had been sacrificed by the Cultural Revolution. They saw younger people making money in present-day China, while they, whether former Red Guards, or the Red Guards' victims, were taking refuge in an ascetic philosophy."

Shortly before the demonstration, a physicist from the Academy of Social Sciences, He Zuoxiu, had published a vitriolic article entitled "Why young people should not practice Qigong", the traditional holistic and meditative practice adopted by Falun Gong. In his attack on the organization, he drew a parallel with the Boxer Rebellion, which had ultimately led to the fall of Empress Ci Xi after the siege of the foreign legations in 1900, thus bringing to an end the reign of the last dynasty, the Manchụ Qing. Falun Gong, according to He, were threatening to destroy China at the close of the twentieth century, just as martial arts practitioners had done at its beginning. Paradoxically, it was He's article that had provoked the protest in Tianjin where the Falun Gong loyalists had been arrested, leading in turn led to this demonstration on 25 April.

Other scholars compare Falun Gong with the Taiping insurgency movement of the 1850s against the Qing. The Hakka leader Hong Xiuquan has been described as a precursor of Li Hongzhi, the Falun Gong guru. For the Hong Kong academic Maria Hsia Chang, it is possible to detect a direct descendance from the fourteenth-century White Lotus, one of the most important ancient movements under the Ming and Qing dynasties.[2]

Jiang Zemin believed absolutely that Chinese emperors since time immemorial had feared such movements—and that such movements might equally overthrow a "Red Emperor". In 1989, during the student protests in Tiananmen, many Qigong associations, whose own ideals were also symbolized by the Goddess of Democracy, had offered their support to the students. When the president left the compound through the northern exit, he was driven to the edge of the small alleyway neighbourhoods called *hutongs*, towards streets where the Falun Gong followers were patiently lined up. Meanwhile, You Xigui, Jiang's former bodyguard from Shanghai, put his entire service on high alert.[3]

Prime Minister Zhu Rongji, more pragmatic and less ideological than Jiang, was refusing to make a drama out of the situation. He had already been down into the street to talk with the Falun Gong followers, and that evening, he tried to convince the Politburo to be lenient and allow a space for the movement to exist, insisting that "If people join Falun Gong, it is because they have been excluded from economic growth, and that's our fault!"[4] When the former Hong Kong governor Chris Patten later questioned him about the events of 25 April, Zhu told him that it was impossible to contain the movement. Patten's response in his memoir was to wonder, "Where were the security services and the police?"[5]

Luo Gan triggers the manhunt

Eventually, after a ten-hour sit-in, the Falun Gong followers left, as peacefully as they had arrived.

Jiang Zemin, however, was not going to let them get away with it. Unlike Zhu Rongji, he advocated harsh measures, because he imagined, and proclaimed, that Falun Gong's aim was to undermine authority in the same way as the Solidarity trade union in Poland had done in the 1980s, to the horror of Deng Xiaoping. Now the relationship between the two old friends, Zhu and Jiang, both former mayors of Shanghai, began to deteriorate. The president also took to task another member of the Politburo, Luo Gan, China's top policeman, demanding to know how it had come to this: why hadn't the Guoanbu warned them about Falun Gong, and where had the Gonganbu been? "How could it be that in one night the Falun Gong just appeared? Did they come from under the ground?" This was perhaps an allusion to Dixia Cheng, the underground city of Beijing, whose corridors still lay in wait for leaders to flee the capital in case of insurrection.[6]

There was a perfidious implication to Jiang Zemin's remarks. Might this event have been deliberately set up by the secret services, the better to repress the movement afterwards? The question arose because it had been discovered that the physicist He Zuoxiu, who had originally sparked things off with his anti-Falun Gong article, was none other than Luo Gan's brother-in-law.[7] Luo was the head of the party's political-legal commission (*Zhengfawei*), which coordinated the actions of the security services and had representatives from all the important services: this included the new Guoanbu minister, Xu Yongyue, as well as his predecessor, now Gonganbu minister, Jia Chunwang.

We have, of course, already met Luo Gan, the Kang Sheng of the 1990s, after the Tiananmen student massacre. But now that he is ten years older and wiser, it is time to detail his career path. Born in 1935 in the Year of the Pig in Shandong, Luo Gan was the son of one of the ten Red Army marshals—Luo Ronghuan, a hero of the Long March who had been responsible for its security, before becoming PLA chief of staff in 1949 at the founding of the PRC; he was also at one point commissar for another, more famous marshal, Lin Biao.

His son, though, did not do things strictly in the correct order. Luo Gan had climbed to the upper echelons of industrial technology and trade unions, which had enabled him to travel. He spoke French, English and German, which he had learned at the Karl Marx University of Leipzig.[8] It was during the Tiananmen protests in 1989 that his career took a dramatic turn. As labour minister under Prime Minister Li Peng, he helped Li carry out the severe crackdown in Beijing. When Jiang Zemin took control of the party, Li Peng and his "tough guy" faction imposed Luo Gan on the Politburo, and in 1998, Luo Gan took control of the political-legal commission, replacing Ren Xianjin, whose deputy he had been.

This commission was not all-powerful solely because of its control over the security services, but also because it controlled the offices of prosecutors and courts, and the labour re-education camps, the *laojiao*. Before 1989, several reformers—including the master spy at the time, Qiao Shi—had wanted to abolish it, for it was a powerful brake on any inclination towards the separation of powers and therefore the possibility of a democratic leadership. But in 1989, Luo Gan committed himself fully to repressing the student uprising. He is widely held to have been responsible for a fake video that circulated showing students throwing Molotov cocktails at a tank—we now know this was actually footage of two tanks' regiments battling it out during the crackdown.

Luo Gan was an unconditional supporter of the established order and of harsh measures and, at every meeting of the political-legal committee, he enjoined the police cadres and secret agents of the special services to protect national security a little more. *Yan Da!*—Strike harder!—was his favoured slogan: hit both criminals and dissidents hard. As far as he was concerned, they were one and the same.

After the Falun Gong protest in April 1999, Jiang Zemin's anger would not be soothed. It must be said that he had a fair amount on his plate that spring. In March, his trip to Europe had turned sour when pro-Tibetan demonstrators had heckled him in Switzerland. In May came the NATO air forces' destruction of the Chinese embassy in Belgrade. When it came to Falun Gong, the Chinese leadership wanted results. Luo Gan was given "100 days and 100 men"—special investigators, handpicked to clear up Falun Gong. Across the country, the Gonganbu was tasked with registering suspected members of the movement.

In June, Luo delivered his report. These were its main conclusions:

- The 25 April demonstration had been organized after the clandestine visit to Beijing by the Falun Gong guru Li Hongzhi, who had arrived on 22 April under an assumed identity. He left for Hong Kong on 24 April, just before the mass demonstration around Zhongnanhai.
- From Hong Kong, Li had made twenty-nine phone calls to Falun Gong's secret headquarters in Beijing to issue instructions.
- The Beijing leaders of the movement had been identified and arrested; among them was Li Chang, director of computer services at the Gonganbu in Beijing. At the organizers' trial, which began in late 1999, he was sentenced to eighteeen years in a labour camp.
- Falun Gong claimed to have 70 million members, but the security services estimated the number at only 3 million. The cult had spread to forty countries.
- Li Hongzhi had huge financial means, especially through the sale of meditation books and tapes used by his followers, as well as funds whose provenance was unknown.

- Residing in the United States, there was no doubt that he enjoyed the support of the CIA, especially in terms of his wide range of technical resources—radio, television, a weekly newspaper published in several languages, *The Epoch Times*, and above all his extremely well-designed website, which was used not only for propaganda purposes, but also for conveying internal information about China and the actions of its leaders.[9]
- It was vital to ban Falun Gong over the whole of the PRC's territory.
- It was also vital to set up a special intelligence service to monitor it and ensure effective propaganda against the movement as it sought support from Western countries, just as the Dalai Lama and Tibetan independence movement were doing.

Luo Gan's investigation also caused great concern when it revealed that various well-known figures had joined Falun Gong. Among them was Qian Xuesen, the father of Chinese missiles and the atomic bomb, who had been tempted back to the PRC by the intelligence services in the 1950s while working at an American research laboratory. Later on, Qian had sunk into a delusional mysticism, proposing to supply the western provinces of China with drinking water by detonating an atomic bomb under the ground in Tibet. Some time later, Qian was made to put his name to a call for the banning of Falun Gong.

Even some parts of the PLA were implicated. Luo's investigation revealed that Li Hongzhi, after founding the movement in 1992, had managed to lecture in various officers' messes and other closed groups within the 2nd Artillery, the most sensitive sector of the PLA. This was the Strategic Nuclear Weapons Corps, which had intercontinental and other missiles pointed at Japan and Taiwan. This revelation was even more delicate given that one of the main officers in charge of the 2nd Artillery was General Luo Dongjin, deputy political commissioner—and Luo Gan's own brother.

The 2nd Artillery was also affected by another incident at this time, carefully concealed by the authorities. It took place on 26 April 1999—the day after the Falun Gong demonstration—between 5.30am and 10.30pm. The central military command of the PLA in the Canton region found itself totally paralyzed following an attack by a computer virus. Communications were disrupted between this command centre—which oversees the South China Sea fleet as well as the units of the infamous 2nd Artillery—and the eighty-plus bases that it controls. While PLA computer scientists were struggling to fix the system, the leadership was torn between several hypotheses: was this a ramping up of Falun Gong aggression? Was the CIA behind it? Taiwan? Or all three?[10]

In the aftermath of the cyber-attack, orders were given for all PLA soldiers who were Falun Gong adherents to come forward, sign a declaration renouncing their faith, and hand over any sacred objects or philosophy books written by Li Hongzhi. Military security, led by General Zhang Zhenhua, focused particularly on the situation in the special forces units and the People's Armed Police (PAP), whose officers practiced martial arts (*wushu*) including Qigong gymnastics ("work of the breath"), which was at the heart of Falun Gong recruitment.

The problem was that these elite units of the PLA and the police numbered no fewer than 200,000 men. This was the fundamental challenge for the Chinese leadership: Falun Gong recruited ordinary Chinese citizens by word of mouth, many of whom practised Qigong, or Taijiquan, as part of their lifestyle. Former president Yang Shangkun, for example, practised Qigong with a master who also happened to be the Chinese doctor of French fashion designer Pierre Cardin. It was impossible to outlaw an age-old practice that was an integral part of Chinese daily life.

This was why Luo Gan's men proposed engaging in a programme of targeted monitoring and infiltration. This would include operations around the world in countries where there was a large Chinese community, such as Australia and France. The security services coordinated operations to begin in Beijing, then spread throughout all the regions of China, before sending representatives to embassies abroad. Comrade Luo's new 610 Office was about to become Falun Gong's designated nemesis.

The 610 Office divides up the globe

On 10 June 1999, the 610 Office (*liu-yi-ling*), charged with leading the crusade against the Falun Gong movement, was born. Its name is derived from this founding date. As a crisis coordinating body, it soon attained the status of a fully-fledged ministry, under the aegis of Luo's political-legal commission. Its small band of 100 elite investigators spawned 1 million policemen, from Beijing to deepest China, who were brought together to work for the 610. Its administration was put into the hands of Liu Jing, a deputy Gonganbu minister. In terms of logistics, he relied mainly on the Gonganbu's 26th Bureau, headed by Zhang Yue. Through Zhang's intervention, regional 610 Offices—charged with tracking, arresting and interrogating followers of the movement—were established within each regional Gonganbu office, in conjunction with its 5th Bureau—the one responsible for overseeing the Chinese gulag, the *laogai*.

The largest offices were set up in Beijing, headed by Zhang Xianlin; Shanghai, headed by Li Genlin; and Tianjin, headed by Zhao Yuezeng. All the satellite offices, including those in the most remote provinces, had to report back on their campaign against Falun Gong. This campaign was supported by a major propaganda drive, at the instigation of the deputy prime minister, another high-up overseeing the 610 Office. The propaganda included regular broadcasts on the state television channel CCTV and the publication of books detailing Li Hongzhi's supposed corruption and Falun Gong's responsibility for the apparent suicides of many of its followers. The most widely circulated of these books, by Ji Shi, was entitled *Li Hongzhi and his "Falun Gong": Deceiving the Public and Ruining Lives.*[11]

This text, which reflected the authorities' point of view, claimed that "Li Hongzhi's illegal organization, the Falun Dafa Research Society, was the highest body within Falun Gong, of which Li Hongzhi was the chairman. It had 39 general education offices and 28,000 practice locations across the country. Two million people joined Falun Gong."

Many of its members were sent to *laogai* camps, and an intense human rights struggle began. Falun Gong has several strange and complex aspects, with its fusion of Buddhism, Taoism and belief in the imminent arrival of aliens who will come to Earth and trigger the ultimate destruction of communism. The vast majority of its members are Chinese who dream of having more freedom. The nonviolence they displayed garnered them great sympathy abroad, especially in the English-speaking world, as a persecuted minority religion. Within its own media, the movement detailed the suffering, torture, abuse and harassment of its members, claiming, for example, that systematic organ harvesting and execution of Falun Gong prisoners was taking place.[12]

The 610 Office, which Falun Gong calls the "Chinese Gestapo", was monitoring the movement in Canada, Ireland, the United States and Australia, where several MPs spoke out in defence of the organization. In dozens of countries, its members were demonstrating daily in front of the Chinese embassies.

Because the movement was being guided by Li Hongzhi from the United States and had global ramifications, the 610 Office had for months been placing investigators in all Chinese embassies, which was creating tensions with the Guoanbu representatives already posted there for foreign intelligence, as well as those responsible for keeping an eye on Tibetans and separatist Uyghur Muslims in Xinjiang. Each believed their sector and their mission was the most important. Intelligence service officials dealing with security for the forthcoming Beijing Olympics believed that the links between al-Qaeda and certain Uyghurs posed a greater danger than non-violent Tibetans and Falun Gong devotees. These tensions continued into the Hu Jintao era. In Moscow in 2006, where a handful of Falun Gong devotees demonstrated with placards around the clock, the Guoanbu station chief Cheng Guoping complained that he was wasting a huge amount of time on the movement, when he should have been focusing on coordinated anti-NATO actions with allies from the Russian FSB and SVR.

Taking matters into its own hands, Luo Gan's political-legal commission in Beijing demanded—in view of upcoming major events such as the 2008 Olympics and the Shanghai World Expo in 2010—that the heads of all embassy services come together to support both permanent and roaming representatives of the 610 Office, and that they coordinate with each other in order to collaborate, sometimes at regional level. This meant representatives of the CCP, the Guoanbu station chiefs, the Central Committee's International Liaison Department (*Lianluobu*), the CCP Research Bureau (which had a disciplinary role within embassies), education advisors, police attachés and even military attachés. The political and legal departments of the embassies were also charged with studying the legal provisions in each country, to see if local laws against cults could be invoked to permit a ban on Falun Gong, which, from the outside, might resemble Scientology or other similar cults.

This was obviously a serious tactical error on the part of Luo Gan. By forcing these officials to come out of the woodwork, drawing attention to themselves and their close surveillance not only of Tibetans, Uyghurs and democratic dissidents but also of (often Western) Falun Gong adherents, he opened the way for the host countries' counterintelligence services to identify the structure of the Chineses networks. The Gonganbu police attaché in Paris regularly attempted to persuade both the French interior ministry and the head of Interpol in Lyon to allow the police to monitor Falun Gong followers as "criminal elements" and to share the results of their investigations with the Chinese. This was obviously out of the question. Similarly, it had recently been noted that Zhang Jinxing, the former press attaché at the Chinese embassy in Paris, had returned to the French capital, this time under cover of being a doorman, which was hardly a promotion. His true mission was to monitor Parisian Falun Gong devotees, under the guidance of the influential Song Jingwu, who represented the CCP's political services as minister counsellor, number two in the embassy.

With all of this activity emerging, European security agencies learned that the Chinese had set in motion a programme to list all members of martial arts associations practicing Taijiquan and Qigong gymnastics and so on, fearing that Western followers of the movement were entering China as tourists. Chinese people in the diaspora were joining Qigong clubs to investigate Falun Gong members, as well as setting up clubs from scratch to lure in members in Madrid, Brussels, Dublin, Berlin, London and Paris, and then manipulate them.

In western France, for example, the counterintelligence investigations focused on several clubs, in particular a Taijiquan circle, established four years after the birth of Falun Gong by a former NCO of the PLA, who had since acquired French nationality by marriage. The club organized pro-Beijing visits to China, which angered some members. The purpose was to prevent fans of Chinese meditative and martial arts from succumbing to Falun Gong's call. But this tactic was a double-edged sword. On multiple occasions, members of the Chinese security services themselves became fascinated by the principles of the movement, and became moles for it. Many operatives who joined Falun Gong for operational purposes ended up defecting.

Han, the "Chinese Schindler"

I met Ward Elcock, director of the Canadian Security Intelligence Service (1994-2004), at a 2002 symposium in Montreal on the judicial impact of the 9/11 attacks. His words on that occasion came back to me while I was writing this book: "In Canada, the Chinese intelligence services are becoming more active and aggressive. And that requires a new form of organization." He recounted to me a whole series of technical operations mounted by the Chinese.[13]

As far back as 1999, his predecessor as the head of CSIS, Charles Svoboda, had described how the PLA's special services were setting up intelligence cells in Canada with the help of Chinese mafia members, and embedding sleeper agents within the diaspora communities in Toronto and Vancouver. The CSIS has grown since Svoboda's day. In the 2000s, its counterintelligence section on China had eighty officials—a huge number that the German and French services could only dream of, although they too have expanded in size and expertise.

But what Elcock didn't tell me, of course, was that a few months previously his service had picked up a Chinese man in Toronto called Han Guangsheng, who turned out to be the first 610 Office policeman to throw in his lot with Falun Gong. According to the movement's website, he was a kind of "Chinese Schindler". After fourteen years of loyal service with the Gonganbu, Han had been catapulted to the leadership of the Shenyang City Judicial Bureau in Liaoning (Manchuria). In this capacity, he was responsible for running five *laogai* camps in the north-east, for five years. He witnessed the shocking treatment of the 500 Falun Gong adherents who were interned there during this period, including the rape of a 15-year-old follower by prison guards. He banned abuse in the camps under his command. Even more remarkably, he allowed 150 prisoners to escape without trying to recapture them, and drafted a memorandum against the use of torture practised in a further camp for which he was not responsible; he claimed torture was forbidden under the Chinese constitution. Methods used included caning and electric shocks, popularized during the Kang Sheng era.

In September 2001, while on a visit to Toronto, Han Guangsheng defected. He was not the only one to do so; some time later, another senior cadre in the Shanghai judicial services followed his lead, seeking asylum in France. Perhaps France simply did not have a budget comparable to that of the Americans—or perhaps it didn't wish to antagonize Beijing? Either way, the France of Jacques Chirac, a "great friend of the Chinese", was certainly not a wise choice for seeking asylum from the PRC, whatever its reputation as the birthplace of universal human rights.

The 610 Office moles confess

On the whole, Australia tended to be a better bet. This was where Chinese services lost another defector on 26 February 2005, when Hao Fengjun, a 32-year-old security officer, arrived in the country via Hong Kong with a 256-megabyte MP3 USB stick, filled with information about the Chinese secret services. Two days later, he sent in his visa application. For months, Hao awaited a summons from the Australian counterintelligence services, the Security Intelligence Organization (ASIO). He was not just anyone: he had been one of the top people at the Tianjin 610 Office. Surprised at the radio silence from the Australian services, he decided to go public. At the end of July 2005, ASIO finally invited him in for questioning.

Upon examination, his USB stick made it possible to identify many, but not all, secret agents; some code-names remained impenetrable. In addition, some of the data Hao supplied was hypersensitive, indicating that Chinese moles had infiltrated the very heart of Australia's Department of Foreign Affairs and Trade (DFAT). Could this explain officials' slowness to get in touch with Hao? Perhaps Australian diplomats had been reluctant to grant him refugee status because of the influence of these moles; or perhaps they had been concerned that such a move might harm the relationship between Prime Minister John Howard and the new Chinese leader, Hu Jintao?

In any case, the situation was far from straightforward. On top of Hao's defection to Australia, the Chinese ambassador Fu Yi lost face a second time. In early summer 2005, one of her diplomats at the consulate on Sydney's Dunblane Street, 37-year-old Chen Yonglin, defected. He applied for asylum and suggested that Han Guangsheng, whose asylum request to France had failed and whom he had met, do the same in Canada. But still no luck—both countries turned down their applications, in spite of public support for both men.

"It was totally incomprehensible," said David McKnight, an Australian intelligence historian who welcomed me to his charming bungalow near Bondi Beach a year after this extraordinary episode. "There was a strong anti-communist tradition here during the Cold War. I know what I'm talking about: once upon a time I belonged to the Australian Communist Party, before I switched sides. And today, we refuse to give political asylum to a communist dissident because we want to trade with China. Which is more important to us than the defence of human rights! That's why I published a furious article—'When money talks, left and right change sides'—about the Chen Yonglin case, to awaken people's conscience. I wanted to remind people that in 1954, when the KGB spy Vladimir Petrov defected to Australia, the Menzies government took the opportunity to educate the public about totalitarianism in the USSR. Today, when Chen Yonglin seeks asylum from a conservative government, he is denied it and told to return to China. Chen must be very disconcerted to see that we are going along with the Chinese government and telling citizens who want democracy to keep their mouths shut. This article might have earned me the congratulations of an old Taiwanese man who used to be associated with the World Anti-Communist League, the WACL, but certainly not of the young traders doing business on the Shanghai Stock Exchange!"[14]

Although he was denied political asylum, Chen Yonglin was interviewed by ASIO in mid-July 2005, a fortnight before his comrade Hao. But after his debriefing, the counterintelligence service made clear its disagreement with his statements about the existence of thousands of Chinese secret agents in Australia alone. (Hao later clarified this: there were thousands of sources working for the

Guoanbu in the Chinese diaspora.) Over time, however, the ASIO did begin to acknowledge the danger, expanding its Chinese section at the beginning of 2007 (as it happens, while I was in Australia), and recruiting dozens of Mandarin and Cantonese speakers.[15] Even so, I sensed clear embarrassment on the part of an ASIO spokesperson and an ASIO representative for Asia in charge of their national security council, the Office of National Assessment, whom I had asked for a briefing on the role of Chinese services in the country. Australian diplomats had no desire to quarrel with Beijing.

Meanwhile, Chen was under the protection of pro-democracy activists and Falun Gong followers; the movement was well established in Australia, and Chen became a follower. He was also debriefed by the CIA, which took his revelations rather more seriously than ASIO. Three months later, he testified:

> During my work at the Chinese consulate in Sydney, Wang Xiaoqiang and Yuan Ying, two deputy directors of the Central 610 Office, came to inspect our work rooting out the Falun Gong at the Chinese embassies in Australia and New Zealand. At the end of 2003, Yuan Ying told us about the situation of Falun Gong in China. He said that there were about 60,000 Falun Gong practitioners, of whom half were in labour camps and prisons while the other half were being closely monitored. Wang Xiaoqiang, another official from the 610 Office, came to the consulate in 2002. At the time, he said that the battle against Falun Gong was not going very well. Every day, hundreds of followers came to protest in Tiananmen Square, where of course the police were waiting to arrest them. Wang said he could not understand the Falun Gong followers. They were always non-violent. When arresting police officers asked them to get onto the buses, they almost always did. In fact, the government felt that it was losing face simply because so many demonstrators were coming to Tiananmen. Protesting in Tiananmen is a very sensitive business.[16]

Chen's information, like Hao's, was very precise. He explained that the consulate had recorded a list of 800 Falun Gong followers in the wake of a 2001 CCP directive to "Fight Falun Gong actively in all areas and gain the support and sympathy of the public".

In practice, the consulate officers would request an interview with someone applying for a visa or a visa extension for China. If it turned out they were Falun Gong practitioners—and their guru Li Hongzhi insisted that they must never lie!—their passport information would be taken and entered on the global blacklist drawn up by the two security ministries, Gonganbu and Guoanbu. Needless to say, these Chinese people would no longer be permitted to return to the land of their ancestors. It was more difficult for Chinese counterintelligence when it came to foreign followers of the movement, who travelled as tourists, a little like the "surveyors" who engaged in amateur espionage in 1960s China for Australian intelligence.[17]

When Chen Yonglin was asked why he had waited so long before defecting, he first explained it by saying that, since his father had been killed by the local authorities in his village after having written the calligraphy for a petition, he had hesitated to participate in the Tiananmen demonstrations in 1989. He had been studying at Beijing Diplomatic College. "But I must confess that I am not of a very brave nature," he admitted. However, he was working as a stringer and translator for an NBC television crew, which allowed him to see the full drama of the student massacre. After he graduated, he had joined the Waijiaobu, the Ministry of Foreign Affairs, and worked at the Chinese embassy in Fiji from 1994 to 1998. Three years later, he was posted to the consulate in Sydney. He began to notice how secret agents acted against Falun Gong followers, and before switching sides he erased the consulate's digital files on some 800 Falun Gong members.

Several of the counterintelligence officials I interviewed for this book believe that the revelations of these two defectors, Hao Fengjun and Chen Yonglin, were genuine, and revealed a number of methods used by the Chinese services. Were they to admit that the two men had been Chinese agents, Beijing's reputation would have suffered significant damage.

The details given by Hao Fengjun had been so precise because he had been part of the 610 Office itself, having been plucked from the staff of the Guoanbu's regional office. The Guoanbu's director in Tianjin had been relieved of his duties in February 2005—in my opinion for having let Hao abscond—and replaced by a new head, Zhong Wei.

Thanks to Hao, it was revealed how hundreds of agents working for the 610 Office had been sent to Canada, Australia, New Zealand

and the United States. In 2004, a different source had revealed that a couple of American Falun Gong practitioners in California were in fact 610 agents, operating under cover of a travel agency specializing in tourism to China. Though these networks were under the supervision of the Guoanbu, every day the 610 Office received information from the embassies and intelligence posts about the movements, lectures and media appearances of Falun Gong followers. And every day a summary classified *juemi*—top secret—was handed to the Chinese secretariat, president, State Council and CCP Politburo.[18]

The turn towards France and Germany

If the Chinese services thought they would be able to limit the number of defectors fleeing to English-speaking countries, they were to be disappointed. In autumn 2005, in Chinese embassies throughout Western Europe, there was deep concern that Falun Gong followers as well as other dissidents were either planning a campaign to boycott the 2008 Beijing Olympics, or thinking up protests to embarrass the authorities, for example during the Olympic torch's relay from Greece to Beijing, via various European cities.

In 2006, Liu Jing, head of the 610 Office, was given a mammoth task: to crush Falun Gong ahead of the 2008 Olympics. The Chinese were particularly worried that it would trigger a protest movement comparable to the Rose and Orange Revolutions in Georgia and Ukraine: "The Chinese came here to study the situation in the two former Soviet republics very closely, and they came to the same conclusions as the services of the Russian Federation," explained Iliya Sarsembaev, a specialist in the Russian services and their relationship with the Chinese. "Just like with Falun Gong, it was believed that the CIA was very active in fostering the emergence and development of these movements."[19]

For Liu Jing, it was vital to stop the haemorrhaging of defectors and to prevent links being forged between Falun Gong and other dissidents. The pressure increased in mid-October, when the Falun Gong newspaper *The Epoch Times* unexpectedly held a forum in Paris, where the two defectors Hao Fengjun and Chen Yonglin spoke. The event received little coverage in the media, but was closely followed by both Chinese diplomats and French intelligence. Even more surprisingly, in May 2006 a conference on Chinese dissent was held in Berlin. This was the first time there had been such an event since Tiananmen in 1989. Nearly 200 dissidents-in-exile attended the low-key five-day conference on 17-22 May, at the invitation of the Chinese Democratic Front, headed by Fei Liangyong. Diplomats from the Chinese embassy tried to get information on the conference participants out of the various German police services, but to no avail.

Zhongnanhai must have been seriously worried, for this meeting, largely funded by the Taiwanese, was the first time that traditional post-Tiananmen dissidents had joined forces with Falun Gong members. In Europe, Falun Gong seemed to be split into two tendencies: those who wished to coexist with the Chinese authorities, and those of a more political bent who were openly calling on CCP militants to split from the party, renounce their membership and overthrow the Beijing government. It seemed like a long time since devotees of Qigong had protested simply for the right to exercise their practice—now the movement was attacking the CCP head on. A controversial book popular with activists, *The Nine Commentaries*, delivered a radical reading of the party's history since its creation in 1921, and explained how it might be made to collapse. It turned out that cracking down on the Falun Gong movement had only served to radicalize it.

Also present at the Berlin Congress were Germany-based Uyghur Muslim delegates from Xinjiang, and Tibetan supporters of the Dalai Lama. In France, liaison officers from the Chinese police, in contact with the security services, besieged the headquarters of the intelligence services, wanting to obtain information on the Uyghurs, who were now organizing politically in exile. Simultaneously, the Chinese were trying to figure out the role of the new representative of the Dalai Lama in Paris, Jampal Chosang. It was claimed that he was being rather more active than his predecessor, trying to form a pro-Tibet parliamentary lobby and calling on athletes to demonstrate for human rights during the Olympics.

If the Guoanbu men stationed in Germany had thought they were done with the Uyghurs, they were wrong. At the end of November 2006, in Munich, the General Assembly of the World Uygur Congress (WUC) took place among Chinese Muslims from Xinjiang, as much the victims of Chinese brutality and repression as Falun Gong disciples or Tibetans. On this occasion, German counterintelligence took the opportunity to update its records of pseudo-diplomats within the Chinese consulate at Munich, which was headed by Yang Huiqun and some "deep-water fish" acting under cover of working in business and the restaurant trade.

German intercepts revealed that the Chinese services were closely monitoring Dr Hamit Hemrayev, director of the WUC "research bureau", which is considered a kind of Uyghur secret service and counterintelligence bureau. The reason for this surveillance, according to a Chinese diplomat who had recently defected, was the fear in Beijing of an alliance between the WUC and Falun Gong, which was by then well established in Germany.[20]

Meanwhile, another defection took place in February 2007: a teaching assistant at the University of Science and Technology of Macau, Wang Lian, fled to Australia where, still under Falun Gong's protective wing, he claimed that he had been recruited by the Guoanbu to monitor Falun Gong followers in Hong Kong, where the movement was somewhat tolerated because of the special constitutional status of the former British colony. This muddied the waters even further, at the very moment when Ernst Uhrlau, director of the German Federal Intelligence Service (BND), was warning his European colleagues about the risks of propaganda by unreliable defectors.

In March 2007, an embassy diplomat in Ottawa defected and revealed how the Chinese services were operating in this part of the world. Most damagingly, she made public internal documents from Liu Jing, Luo Gan and others that contained recommendations on the most effective means to battle against the "five poisons" threatening China: the Falun Gong "cult", Tibetan separatists, Islamists among Xinjiang Uyghur Muslims, democracy activists in Hong Kong, and independence activists in Taiwan.

History will tell if the avalanche of defections and Falun Gong's rise played a major role in the evolution of twenty-first-century China. An early analysis by Australian researcher Richard Bullivant detailed the conditions in which Chen Yonglin eventually obtained a visa and protection, after having been subjected to intimidation by the Chinese embassy. Most importantly, he showed that the Chinese were particularly effective at infiltrating the Australian Department of Foreign Affairs. In a senatorial investigation, an earlier defector, Wang Jiangping—an ASIO counterintelligence advisor in the fight against the Guoanbu—had sent a written report in which he explained that he "would not recommend that any defector provide information to that Department."[21]

Concluding his report, Bullivant, who based his analysis on specific documents, adds: "The Chinese Intelligence Services plan that, through perceptions management operations, influence operations in the media, universities recruiting consultants, intelligence officials, politicians and diplomats, Australia will slowly but steadily develop, in the words of Chinese strategists, as 'a second France'."[22]

In other words, Bullivant confirms what other experts have told me and what is revealed by the multiple defections explored in this book: Australia and France are the two countries where the heads of the Chinese secret services believe it is easiest to infiltrate and manipulate both institutions and people.

Embassies like no others

During the Cold War, two principal intelligence residences were housed in the Soviet embassy, the KGB and the GRU (military intelligence). In contrast to the Chinese, there was duplication within each service, with a multiplicity of networks and points of contact. Another difference between the two was that 20 per cent of Soviet diplomats were involved in intelligence, whereas the figure for Chinese diplomats was at least 40, if not, 60 per cent.

I once asked a Chinese diplomat about this. He seemed not to understand the question. Spying? "What nonsense! This is just American propaganda feeding a stupid belief." Intelligence, however, was something else entirely. The Chinese word *Qingbao* also means "open information": the Chinese government must be properly informed about what is happening in foreign countries in order to make decisions.

The Chinese embassy in Paris on Rue Washington, where the consular services are located, is the home of representatives of large organizations—mainly those answerable to the party, security bodies that answer to the State Council, and those that feed information to the PLA. There are other satellite organizations located in regional consulates as well as in delegations to international organizations such as UNESCO, also headquartered in Paris.

Conventional diplomatic intelligence reports to the Foreign Affairs Information Bureau (*Waijiaobu*), represented by a deputy chief of mission. Political intelligence is largely handled by the International Liaison Department of the CCP Central Committee, whose 8th Bureau is responsible for Western Europe. Its Beijing head, Gu Honglin, makes frequent visits to France, Italy (he speaks Italian and was lately a consul in Florence), Belgium, Germany and Portugal, to hold discussions with representatives of centre-left parties, Social Democrats, Greens, and others. We are a long way from the Kang Sheng era, when the ILD's only concern was setting up Maoist splinter parties. Today its diplomatic agents travel around different countries, opening exhibitions about China and introducing cultural events of all kinds that are an opportunity to spread the word of "friendship between peoples" and to discover new talents, within Chinese diaspora communities and beyond.

* * *

In this world of political intelligence, changes of personnel are frequent: co-option of ILD members by the Guoanbu and vice versa; exchange of cover between journalists and diplomats; military intelligence spies and businessmen dealing with economic surveillance; and so on. For the heads of security analysts in the Chinese embassy's host countries, it can be quite dizzying, and occasionally leads to quasi-theological arguments about the existence and precise role of certain special services.

Two basic questions divide American counterintelligence and its European counterparts: what is the exact role of the representative of the CCP's investigative department (formerly the Diaochabu, today the *Zhongban diaoyanshi*), and should this representative be seen as part of the more global Guoanbu? And why is military intelligence (*Qingbaobu*) also undertaken by agents from the PLA (General Political Department) Liaison Department (*Zongzheng Lianluo bu*), who are sometimes under cover as cultural attachés—as is the case in

Washington—or who take part in clandestine missions, for example under cover of working for private telecoms companies in Europe?[23]

Within the PRC's London embassy—first established in 1877 as the Chinese Legation—there is the same covert organization of the Chinese secret services under diplomatic cover. This will no doubt have been restructured after the embassy's 2018 move from Portland Place to a new address on the site of the old Royal Mint, near the Tower of London. It is worth recalling that when the CCP set up its first intelligence service in the 1930s, it was not only with the help of the Soviet services (the NKVD and the GRU). As well as exploiting the age-old roots of imperial Chinese espionage, the first red spies also drew inspiration from the two intelligence communities they fought in the concessions of Shanghai: the French and the British.

Today, the military attaché's roles are multiple. They make contact with foreign counterparts and with the army general staff, in order to establish the battle order of the armed forces and its projects and technical innovations, specifically regarding weapons, communications, strategy and battle plans. They must also maintain relationships with retired soldiers who are invited to Beijing and elsewhere in China to chair conferences or take part in symposia organized by various institutes linked to the PLA2. This is what is known as "contact intelligence".

Since the Chinese deny that the Guoanbu has agents in the embassy, liaison with the host country's intelligence services is organized through the defence attaché or the police attaché (Gonganbu). We may as well take France as an example, since we know it is a key target for Chinese infiltration. This arrangement pretending that the Guoanbu does not exist explains why in 1984—the year after the Boursicot affair—Colonel Wang Naicheng, stationed in Paris, was the one to organize a Chinese visit to meet with Raymond Nart and several of his deputies at the DST—in other words, with the very counterintelligence men who had arrested their agent. Wang's successor in Paris, Colonel Han Kaihe (who was later posted to London in 1994) knew France well, since he had lived there for ten years with his wife, also an officer. His mission had been to make contact with researchers, academics and intelligence agents known for their committed opposition to Soviet communism, in order to obtain information about the ideological transformations brought about by Mikhail Gorbachev. Colonel Han sounded out various politicians, police officers and journalists, including the far-right journalist Pierre de Villemarest, whose book on the GRU was published in Chinese in 1990.[24]

Similarly, General He Shide was in regular contact—as was the ambassador and General Xiong Guangkai, former PLA2 leader—with an ex-head of the DGSE, who were now bugging his phone. The French service was dismayed by his loquacity, no doubt a consequence of his naivety rather than malevolence.[25]

In Paris, another intelligence agency had been set up in the wake of the Tiananmen uprising in 1989, within the Chinese embassy's education section, whose offices were at 9 rue Glacière. The best known of its agents, Bai Zhangde, employed as a driver and second secretary, narrowly managed to avoid being expelled from France in 1990 because of his harassment of exiled student democrats. He left the country for a while before returning to Paris, this time as embassy advisor and head of the same service, for which he travelled all over the country, to Brest, Lyon, Marseille and Strasbourg, building relationships with politicians and educational leaders. Tellingly, technological surveillance, under the management of Wang Shaoqi, is housed on the same floor in the main Rue Washington embassy building as the police attachés and political intelligence specialists.

* * *

These structures evolve constantly, gaining personnel and refining their research techniques, particularly when it comes to exploiting the internet, which is not as restricted in Western countries like France as it is in China. The main problem, as several Chinese specialists have explained to me, is the coordination of information.

In the 1990s, Western counterintelligence identified an ambassador's wife working as an intelligence coordinator in France and the Benelux countries, whose role was more important than that of her husband. She was particularly active in operations directed against the Taiwan Representative Office (TECRO, the Taiwan nationalists' quasi-embassy). After her return to Beijing, she was given the responsibility of supervising the training of younger agents, particularly in language skills, before they were sent on mission. This was a field in which she excelled, having once worked as an interpreter for Deng Xiaoping.

As we saw with the 1989 Tiananmen movement, after which refugee dissidents in France came under close surveillance, several Chinese press correspondents were believed to be high-flying undercover Guoanbu officers. Of course, the Xinhua News Agency, which moved to its current office in Clichy-la-Garenne, just outside Paris, in 1988, and which I visited shortly after this move at the invitation of one of its directors, was doing the same work it always had. In Chevilly-la-Rue, buildings bristling with antennae and satellite dishes have attracted the attention of the French media. Echoing investigations conducted by the internal security directorate (the DGSI), the weekly magazine *L'Obs* revealed that Chinese teams involved in electronic warfare were engaged in intercepting communications (SIGINT). According to an investigation by journalist Vincent Jauvert, a secret centre of satellite eavesdropping in France was almost certainly reporting to the 8th Bureau of the PLA3.[26]

France is not alone. As we have seen in this chapter, and as we will continue to see in the next, Australia is another example of the several countries all over the world dealing with the issue. There, we find the same type of installation that engineers from GCHQ expected to see deployed after the Chinese moved in 2019 to their new embassy at Royal Mint Court by the Tower of London, the largest Chinese diplomatic representation in the world.

PART THREE

11

CYBER-WARRIORS OF THE PLA

Seen from the air, Pine Gap Base, south of Alice Springs, offers a view of satellite dishes and white domes no different from those of any ordinary satellite station. But in fact this is the jewel in the West's crown of technological espionage against China. Situated in the red land at the heart of Australia, it is marked on tourist maps as a "forbidden zone". The local telephone directory lists it as a "joint defence facility" with various social and medical centres. Built in 1966, the station is run jointly by the Australian ASD/DSD (the signals directorate) and the American NSA, and operates a major aspect of electronic warfare—the large-scale interception and interpretation of communications signals. In the world of signals intelligence, it has become customary to use the American abbreviation SIGINT.

This huge Australian station was originally set up at the time of the Cultural Revolution and the US war in Vietnam. Sixty years later, thanks to the development of new technologies, it has increased its operations tenfold. Pine Gap now records Chinese army communications in real time, as well as those of their North Korean and Vietnamese counterparts. A former employee of the Australian technical services told me in Canberra, "It's a network of underground tunnels where nearly 800 Australian and American technicians and analysts work. They are directly connected to the NSA HQ in Fort Meade, Maryland. Then Group B in charge of Asia interprets this information."

Nor is this interception centre isolated. It is complemented by a group of stations run in Australia by the Navy, the ASD (Australian Signals Directorate, formerly DSD), and other special services. Faced by the "Asia challenge", the New Zealand Government Communications Security Bureau has also joined the group. Together, these agencies forged an alliance with the NSA, the Canadians, and Britain's GCHQ, the largest Western intercept agency after the NSA. GCHQ began deploying its "big ears" technology in Hong Kong in 1947, with a station at Little Sai Wan with 140 Australian technicians; another at Tai Mo Shan in the New Territories; and one at Stanley Fort, on the Chung Hom Kok Peninsula, operated by the Royal Air Force and the DSD.

However, the British services had dismantled these stations in order to stop them being "cannibalized" by the PLA3, in charge of Chinese SIGINT, after the handover of the colony in 1997.[1] This was when GCHQ planted bugs in the British High Commission, within the consulate nicknamed "Fort Alamo". Similarly, the Australian DSD set up a listening cell in its Hong Kong consulate in direct communication with the Watsonia power plant near Melbourne. Just before the Chinese flag replaced the Union Jack in Hong Kong, the British had also embedded hundreds of bugging devices in the offices at the Prince of Wales Barracks, now PLA headquarters.

After the 1993 abandonment of Operation KITTIWAKE, run out of the Stanley Fort satellite station, it came under the management of the DSD/ASD, which has since run it from another station in Geraldton, Western Australia. It still performs the same functions: telemetry of Chinese missile ballistic tests, launch of satellites and recovery of satellite data collecting photographic information (PHOTINT), electronic information (ELINT), and other intelligence on China.

As part of the US–Canadian–British–Australian–New Zealand eavesdropping alliance, in place since the beginning of the Cold War, these operations came under the ECHELON system, which hit the headlines in Europe with the fear that "Big Brother" was intruding into the lives of ordinary citizens, listening in on their private telephone conversations and exploiting information mined from their electronic communications.

But in the middle of the Australian desert, technicians had no qualms about monitoring China night and day. The PRC is considered to be an unscrupulous dictatorship, and its military development and economic aggression is of great concern. Alice Springs is a good place from which to monitor the country. This small town, where tourists are as likely to encounter spy engineers as Aboriginal people, has a strong tradition of both communication and interception. The topography of the site lends itself to it.

In 1870 Charles Todd, who gave his name to the Todd River, founded a telegraphic station that connected Adelaide on the south coast to Darwin on the north coast, and well beyond—to the rest of the British Empire, including Hong Kong and the British settlements in Tianjin and Shanghai.[2] In the Victorian era, Chinese gold diggers from Fujian arrived here, as indicated by the name Chinaman's Creek, located on the road leaving Alice Springs in the direction of the ASD–NSA secret station. Today's subjects of ASIO surveillance are more recent arrivals: the dynamic Chinese immigrant community assumed to harbour some "deep-water fish", Guoanbu secret agents on a mission to recruit Chinese-origin engineers and linguists, baiting them with reminders that they are part of the large Chinese diaspora, the *Huaqiao*.

The location of the base was also chosen because of technical considerations, according to James Bamford, an expert on the history of the NSA: in the 1960s, a satellite could intercept unencrypted data and send it straight to the base, thus avoiding the risk of a Soviet spy ship in turn intercepting the communication and discovering what intelligence had been stolen. Back then, the Chinese themselves did not have the technical capacity to play this game, though it would not be long coming. Since Alice Springs is miles from anywhere, located right in the middle of Australia, patrolling spy ships were too far from the signal to identify the "footprint", as it is called. Engineers at Pine Gap could then encrypt the intercepted material and send it, via another satellite, to the NSA headquarters in Fort Meade.[3]

In the aftermath of Gough Whitlam's Labor Party election victory in 1972, followed by Australia's diplomatic recognition of the PRC, the CIA was convinced that the authorities in Canberra would decide to close Pine Gap. This would have been a disaster for the Anglo-

American intelligence community. Theodore Shackley, head of the East Asian Division at the CIA, even went so far as to encourage various destabilization operations against the Australian government, similar to those attempted in Britain against the Harold Wilson government.[4] In Western democracies, the secret services respect the government and the constitution—so long as their own prerogatives remain unquestioned. One suspects that some of their heads might prefer to live with the Chinese system: at least in Beijing, the secret services are in power, hand in glove with the party and the army.

Ultimately, however, Pine Gap continued to function and to prove its utility in the secret war: Canberra was informed about the 1975 invasion of East Timor by the Indonesians and was able to see right through the Chinese army's communications. Even if it failed to break the codes, it was able to study any significant stream of communication. The proof came on 17 February 1979, when Pine Gap was the first to know about the Chinese invasion of Vietnam led by General Yang Dezhi, the former commander of Chinese "volunteers" during the Korean War. Chinese communications were being scrambled by Soviet ships, since Moscow had signed a defence agreement with Hanoi the previous year. The offensive, aimed at taking the Vietnamese "from behind" while launching a blitzkrieg on Cambodia and capturing several thousand Chinese Khmer Rouge advisors, resulted in a blistering thrashing for the PLA. As we saw in Chapter 4, this was a humiliation for Deng Xiaoping, back in power after his woes during the Cultural Revolution. But Deng, as always, bounced back: it was by learning from this setback that he came to propose the major reform of the PLA in his era, starting with its intelligence and electronic warfare services. The rest is history.

The Oxford *caught in a storm, and Operation Oyster*

China's electronic surveillance was also carried out through operations of proximity. The Americans sent very daring means of reconnaissance and interception out towards the PRC. By the time the Pine Gap SIGINT base was built in 1966, the NSA was also using spy ships, such as the USS *Oxford* (AGTR-1), loaded with antennae and 11,000 tonnes capable of doing 11 knots, when it was not docked at Yokosuka in Japan. With 250 officers and men on board, it was sent out into the China Sea to track the turmoil of the Cultural Revolution by intercepting party and army communications. But the USS *Oxford* suddenly found itself in the eye of a typhoon, being propelled towards the Chinese coast. Perhaps there really is a god who watches over spies! By some miracle, the ship was driven back towards the open sea, where it drifted towards safety in Taiwan, having been on the very brink of either running aground or being captured—as indeed another spy ship was, two years later, in January 1968, when the USS *Pueblo* was taken by North Korea. The capture of the *Oxford* would have been to the delight of the Chinese, who were desperate to "cannibalize" such a ship—to take it entirely apart and study every detail to improve their own system. In the case of the *Pueblo*, the US had been double crossed by the Soviets, who had already obtained the secrets of the NSA's operation from their mutual friend Kim Il-sung.[5]

In 1967, the game was equally close: the USS *Banner*, the same type of ship as the *Pueblo*, was not far from Shanghai, just 25 nautical miles from Zhoushan Island, in international waters, when it found itself surrounded by fishing boats: "I had the impression that they were going to try to tow me or something similar," the captain, Major Charles Clark, later said. "They were only about five metres away. Two of the fishing boats had larger guns than ours, but although our guns were smaller, I thought we had the option of fighting them off."[6] Eventually, however, the Chinese forces were ordered to give up what was legally an act of piracy and the US spy ship was allowed to reach Japan without a shot being fired. The Americans were also using other, less risky means to listen in on China, co-administering terrestrial wiretapping stations with the Japanese, South Koreans and Taiwanese.[7]

But back to Australia. There is another straightforward way for the West to intercept Chinese communications: listening in on Beijing's embassy in Canberra. I went to the Australian capital in late 2006 to study the electronic warfare between the Chinese and their opponents. There I met the internationally renowned Professor Desmond Ball at the Strategic and Defence Studies Centre, Australian National University. He told me bluntly: "In our opinion, the [PLA3] has not installed a major listening station in the embassy in Canberra, because we can't see any satellite dishes or bundles of antennae. It is more likely the case that the Chinese community serves as the eyes and ears of Madame Fu Yi.[8]

The day after we met, on my way to Coronation Drive, I noticed that the British High Commission is located just one small street away from the Chinese embassy. The former has an impressive display of antennae, and the GCHQ team, posted there under diplomatic cover, was unashamedly intercepting the communications of their honourable neighbours. It is obviously easier to do this in Canberra than in Beijing, where Chinese counterintelligence—the Guoanbu, in charge of embassy surveillance—has built tall buildings around the foreign embassies grouped together in the Dongzhimen district to block listening systems, as well as a microwave tower for capturing British communications.[9]

In Canberra, although they were unable to intercept all external communications, Australian services did discover another trick when the Chinese embassy changed buildings in 1990. Assisted by thirty technicians from the NSA, the Australian Secret Intelligence Service—codenamed OYSTER—managed to embed bugs within the new embassy. However, after an Australian newspaper got wind of the affair, it took all the diplomatic skills of the head of ASIS to dissuade it from publishing the story, which would have been hugely damaging both for the intelligence services and for Canberra diplomats. It was a wasted effort, for *Time* magazine in the US revealed that Ambassador Shi Chunlai's embassy was riddled with bugs. Unsurprisingly, this type of operation has become increasingly frequent since the Chinese overtook the Russians in espionage in the first decade of this century.

China on the counterattack

In the 1990s, Deng Xiaoping, Yang Shangkun (who had been accused of placing listening devices in Mao's offices during the Cultural Revolution) and Jiang Zemin pushed for the establishment of what was then almost the most powerful electronic espionage structure in the world, second only to the Americans.

This immense Chinese listening realm was not built from scratch. As early as the 1930s, when Zhou Enlai was leading the secret war in

Shanghai against Kuomintang nationalists, his former comrade from Paris, Deng Xiaoping, was overseeing the establishment of technical units in communist bases in southern China. Their friend Nie Rongzhen, who had been in charge of liaison between militants in Paris ten years earlier, was commissioned to set up a secret radio post in Hong Kong, with wireless links to the Comintern in Harbin and Vladivostok. At the same time, another comrade from their Paris days, the future head of the party's secret services Li Kenong, was responsible for infiltrating the nationalists' radio systems.

It should come as no surprise, therefore, that in November 2006 the PLA feted the memory of this first communications school, that of its predecessor, the Chinese Workers and Peasants Red Army. In March 1933, Deng Xiaoping chose its location, Pingshangang, in Ruijin province. Nowadays, young SIGINT technicians and apprentice PLA radio operators come to pay homage at this historic site. What they are told during this pilgrimage is breathtaking: in the space of just a few months, 2,100 linkage systems were established that radiated out through the whole of China, communist and non-communist; the CCP's long march to power owes much to the long-obscured war of radio communication.

After the communist victory, Li Kenong became head of the party's secret service, the Social Affairs Department (SAD), in 1950. He was also serving as PLA deputy chief of staff, which meant that he was overseeing both major sectors of intelligence at the time: the PLA2, in charge of military espionage, and the PLA3, in charge of military SIGINT.[10] The system has barely changed today: in July 2007, while I was in Beijing, General Chen Xiaogong, son of a friend of Zhou Enlai, was appointed to this important Chinese intelligence post.[11] There was one difference, however: another, small section, the 4th Department (*Si Bu* or PLA4) was added in the late 1980s, covering the more recently developed sector of electronic warfare, and sharing with the PLA3 the immense responsibility of cyber-warfare, waged on a new battlefield of which Mao Zedong could never have dreamt: the internet.

* * *

From his top-secret headquarters in Xionghongqi, in the north-western Beijing suburb of Haidian—named for its ponds, which date back to the

Ming dynasty—General Qiu Rulin could contemplate his empire, established in 1950, where 20,000 technicians were at work. His PLA3 was primarily responsible for the interception of foreign army communications, but it had also considerably developed the field of Chinese military research and development.

Nearby, the Xibeiwang district was home to the PLA3's largest communications interception station, just one base among dozens whose goal was to collect and decode all signals emitted from Russia, the primarily Muslim former Soviet republics, India, both Koreas, and China's two "priority opponents", Taiwan and Japan—not to mention its main enemy, the United States.

According to specialists who have been able to seize a large number of satellite photos, each military region—Beijing, Shenyang, Chengdu, Guangzhou, Lanzhou, Jinan and Nanjing—has its own station. These PLA3 stations are organized according to their targets: the Chengdu station, for example, monitors Tibet and India, while the Shenyang station monitors Korea and Japan.[12] The other sites are located in north-east China, near Jilemutu and Kinghathu Lake; on the south coast near Shanghai; and in the military districts of Fujian and Canton, which are constantly mobilized against Taiwan. There are also stations situated near Kunming (north of Vietnam and Myanmar), as well as in Lingshui, on the southern tip of Hainan Island in southern China. The Lingshui base expanded in 1995 to cover the South China Sea, the Philippines and Vietnam, which is also monitored by stations dotted all the way along the border. In the 1980s, further stations were set up on two small islands in the Paracelsus archipelago. In addition to the Kashi and Lop Nor stations, two more were established in Xinjiang: the Dingyuanchen base, focused on Russia and the primarily Muslim former Soviet republics, is distinct from the Changli base, near the provincial capital Ürümqi, which intercepts satellite communications.

As Desmond Ball argued as far back as 1995, "China has by far the most extensive network of SIGINT intelligence of any Asia-Pacific country".[13] Needless to say, barely ten years later, China had become one of the major players in SIGINT anywhere in the world, alongside the United States, the United Kingdom, and the Russian Federation.[14]

The PLA3 shares with the PLA2 the management of a group of institutions and training schools where students of both departments receive training. The largest of these is the PLA Institute of Foreign Languages in Luoyang, under the administrative control of the PLA3. Technicians and cadets must complete linguistic internships not only abroad—perhaps truly as innocent students of the language and literature of linguistically interesting countries—but also in remote areas of China, Mongolia and Xinjiang, where listening posts are located, and where it is important both to know the local dialects and to learn to withstand the harsh mountain climate.

The PLA4 was transferred in 1991 from PLA3 headquarters at Xionghongqi to Tayuan, near the Summer Palace in Beijing. It is now much bigger. There is a straightforward reason for this: the PLA4, responsible for electronic warfare, carries out cyber-war operations with the aid of naval and air capacity, including new reconnaissance planes—specifically, Chinese AWACS planes of Russian origin, and Ilyushin II-76 airlifters equipped with (since 1997) an Israeli-made airborne early warning system.

On 1 April 2001, the service received an unexpected gift, when Chinese fighters forced a US navy spy plane to land on Hainan Island in southern China, leading to a standoff between Washington and Beijing. This was the first capture of its kind since the forcing down of CIA planes in the 1950s. EP-3E, code-named "Peter Rabbit", intercepted voice communications and radar signals on the mainland. The PLA took the plane to pieces in order to copy all its devices, and its technical departments managed to unlock all the secrets of the data-coding system, nicknamed "Proforma", on the border between intelligence and cyber-warfare.

The leader of the PLA4 at the time, General Dai Qingmin, could only rejoice. He is often considered one of the architects of cyber-warfare, who, along with other theorists, spearheaded its modernization, creating the concept of a "people's war in the era of information technology". This, to put it simply, includes electronic attacks aimed at camouflaging ongoing military operations; weakening the enemy's early warning system; scrambling communications; and blocking and paralyzing any attempts by the enemy to respond, in order to trick them wherever they turn. The PLA had reached a real turning point in its theory in the early 1990s, when it moved from a defensive posture to undertaking offensive operations in the realm of electronic warfare, in concert with the regional units of the PLA3 in the three armies of land, air and sea.

In order to be able to adapt constantly and modernize their systems where necessary, these departments are service providers for major spying structures located in foreign countries—not only the PLA2, but also the Liaison Service of the PLA Political Department (*Zhengzhi Lianluobu*) and the multiple research institutes, branches and front companies that have been created by "intelligence vacuum cleaner" structures like COSTIND.

The Chinese also sell on their technology in some of these fields, primarily to Middle Eastern and other Asian countries. The Chinese Electronics Import-Export Company (CEIEC) is responsible for these sales. As we shall see, around the turn of the millennium, the PLA3 and PLA4 began to cross a new threshold in the intelligence war, entering the online battlefield and becoming the principal country implementing wartime measures in cyberspace.

A helping hand from the CIA and BND

Before their launch into cyber-warfare, the Chinese had an extraordinary training school. It was the very people they were fighting against, the Americans, who came to their rescue. In 1979, the Chinese, as we have seen, were taken by surprise by Ayatollah Khomeini's Iranian revolution, just as the Americans were. The Americans lost their base in Mashhad, a large radio station run with the British, which intercepted communications from the USSR. From this shared blow emerged an unexpected "friendly" intelligence collaboration. As early as April 1979, US intelligence services received the green light from Jimmy Carter to negotiate with Deng Xiaoping on possible collaboration in this area.

The Anglo-American interception base was closed and its workers redeployed elsewhere. Admiral Stansfield Turner, head of the CIA, travelled incognito to Beijing, even going so far as to wear a false moustache so as not to be spotted by KGB agents.[15] In May 1979, Deng let it be understood by US senators that he would agree to install "big ears", on the condition that only Chinese engineers be responsible for the installation, even if intelligence was to be shared.

Negotiations continued, despite an angry dispute that flared up. On the eve of the US presidential elections, Cao Guisheng—the same secret agent who had disastrously declared the invincibility of the Khmer Rouge the previous year, and who had since become first secretary in the political section of China's Washington embassy—announced that Carter was certain to be re-elected.[16] The Chinese took their hopes in this matter for reality, much preferring to see Democrats—Carter, the Clintons—in the White House, generally the rulers of less hawkish administrations that would give Beijing's services more opportunities for penetration and advantageous negotiations. But it was Ronald Reagan, the former film actor and an FBI informer during the McCarthy witch-hunt of the 1950s, who was elected president in late 1980.

Yet Deng Xiaoping would have been wrong to despair. Reagan's arrival at the White House in January 1981, and the promotion of his friend Bill Casey to head of the CIA, actually strengthened the process of Sino-American cooperation: it turned out that the Chinese shared an obsession with the two conservatives. Both sides were hoping to trigger the collapse of the Soviet Union, particularly because, at the end of 1979, the Red Army had invaded Afghanistan. Geng Biao, the head of Chinese defence, finalized the agreement. Ten years previously, he had been appointed by Zhou Enlai as head of the CCP's International Liaison Department. He was a consummate intelligence specialist.

In a conversation about China's collaboration with the West, Desmond Ball told me, "Admiral Bob Inman, the NSA director who became number two at the CIA, whom I knew well at the time, brought in Chinese technicians to train them while we were building listening posts with the NSA in the furthest reaches of China." This was around the time of the Afghanistan war, when the CIA and the Chinese services were already working together to arm the Mujahedin. The dispatch of the first Chinese technicians to the United States was undertaken with the utmost discretion by David Gries, the CIA station chief in Beijing, who had learned Mandarin at the Taichung Language School in Taiwan, formerly the main base of the struggle against the mainland communists.[17]

Under the codenames SAUGUS and SAUCEPAN, the Qitai and Korla stations in Xinjiang were built by the CIA Science & Technology

Directorate, with technical materials provided by the CIA and NSA's Office of SIGINT Operations, and managed jointly with the Chinese for a decade. Originally these stations were required to perform telemetry tests on missile trials—to ensure that the SALT-2 arms control agreements were being respected, with supporting documentation—as well as on rocket launches and even nuclear tests near the Aral Sea. Subsequently, SIGINT's function has been extended to other communications intelligence and electronic SIGINT missions (COMINT and ELINT).

West German technicians from the BND, Helmut Kohl's federal secret service, began taking part in these operations after negotiations to that end, which began immediately after the appointment of the first BND resident in Beijing, Reinhart Dietrich, in 1982. In the aftermath of the events of Tiananmen in June 1989, in protest against the massacre of students and as part of a stealth embargo, the Americans decided to withdraw from the management of stations in China itself, opening one instead in Outer Mongolia, which was more politically correct.

The West Germans were alone in what was called Operation PAMIR, with the BND even expanding its presence. Better still, the training of Taiwanese engineers, for which it was responsible as part of the division of labour between allies, was cancelled. From now on, technicians from the PLA2 and PLA3 came to Munich to undergo training, at both the BND school of communications and the nearby Söcking listening station co-run with the West German military. At the time, the BND maintained relations only with the PLA general staff's departments. This was because the PLA2 head, General Xiong Guangkai, had special expertise in German affairs, having formerly been an attaché at the embassy in West Germany with his wife Shou Ruili, who was a scientific attaché. In the aftermath of the Tiananmen massacre, about fifty Chinese researchers had landed in West Germany for technical training. The problem was that a number of these agents were taking advantage of their leisure time to expand their networks across the country, contacting state-level branches of West German counterintelligence (the *Bundesverfaßungsschutz*) for information on Chinese dissident refugees.

Operation PAMIR, based in the mountains of Xinjiang, occasionally went through positively acrobatic contortions. There were one-off missions during which Chinese fighter planes made furtive incursions into Soviet airspace to test the reactions of their prey; these allowed BND technicians from PAMIR stations to record and analyze "enemy" communications. It was all the more interesting an exercise because, since it was run from Europe, it did not provoke a reaction from the Red Army. Mired in the war in Afghanistan, it simply sent spy missions to stations beyond the Chinese border. For this, it had to appeal for help to Afghan state security, the WAD, founded by the pro-Soviet president Mohammed Najibullah, which had around 70,000 agents.

"Dr Najibullah commissioned the WAD to set up intelligence and infiltration operations against the BND station in the mountains. I interviewed a former WAD captain operating in Tajikistan," explained Erich Schmidt-Eenboom, a historian of the BND, when we met at his research centre near Munich. "He told me that some agents had managed to rummage through the station's rubbish bins, which were carelessly left outside, before their contents were destroyed, and deduced that the Germans were not content to be working against the Soviet Union and Afghanistan and were also spying on Chinese telecommunications."[18]

Blinded by their hatred of the Soviet system, the Western powers were cooperating with the Chinese in other parts of the world beyond the Russian borderlands—for example, in Angola against pro-Soviet guerrillas, and in Cambodia, delivering weapons to the defeated Khmer Rouge, all the while allowing Beijing to continue pushing its pawns further out into the world.

The PLA3 exports its wiretaps

The PLA3 equally managed to export its eavesdropping systems to areas of political influence where the PRC had alliances with other authoritarian regimes. There was, as we have seen, an apparatus in their embassy in Belgrade, razed by the Americans via NATO in 1999. Similarly, in 2003, during the American invasion of Iraq, the Chinese had SIGINT systems in Baghdad, which remained in place until the defeat of Saddam Hussein. This explains why the Chinese embassy in Baghdad was mysteriously pillaged after the city's fall in April that year, as diplomatic personnel fled to Jordan, and thieves removed electronic equipment and computers.

On the PRC's own borders, the Chinese were most in tune with the regimes of Laos and Myanmar. The SIGINT station in Hop Hau, Laos, in use since the 1960s, was modernized and expanded in 1995. Similarly, in the early 1990s, Chinese technicians built a SIGINT station on the island of Grande Coco, 50 kilometres north of India's Andaman Islands. This enabled them to monitor the Straits of Malacca, through which thousands of ships pass, as well as Indian missile-testing in the Bay of Bengal. Soon afterwards, the Chinese installed half a dozen coastal stations in Myanmar.

But they did not only set up antennae to spy on the major regional powers and their neighbours. In 1997, they provided the Myanmar dictatorship—whose leader, General Khin Nyunt, was also the head of the secret services—with SIGINT-equipped vehicles, allowing Khin to intercept the communications of minority guerrilla movements fighting the military junta, such as the United Wa State Army, ensconced along the border of China's Yunnan province.[19]

Fake-real oceanographic ships

In the early 1980s, as part of the "Four Modernizations", Deng Xiaoping wanted to revive the "maritime spirit" of ancient China—hardly surprising for a Hakka man steeped in travel and trade. When he appointed Ye Fei in 1979 as the navy's political and military leader, everyone wondered why he was entrusting this position to someone who was not an experienced seaman. Ye Fei may have participated in the war against Japan alongside Deng, but his previous position had been minister of communications.

In fact, the one explains the other. Deng was specifically keen on modernization and development in the field of communications. The Chinese built information-gathering vessels which reported either to the PLA3 offices of the PLA coastal military regions or to central naval intelligence (*Haijun Qingbaoju*). This large network of wiretapping sea vessels also reported to the Department of Science and Technology within the defence ministry, run for several years by Wang Tongye and then by General Nie Li, a satellite and oceanographic intelligence specialist, who was also deputy head of COSTIND. General Nie was a chip off the old block: she was the daughter of Nie Rongzhen, Zhou Enlai's and Deng Xiaoping's old friend and the long-time scientific patron of the defence development programme.

The programme made it possible to arm a flotilla of a dozen spy ships developed along the Russian model, and spread it out over the entire Asian region. These are often presented as oceanographic vessels belonging to the Beijing Academy of Sciences, and they may indeed undertake topographical surveys of (theoretically) an entirely peaceful nature. This was the case, for example, of the *Yuanwang 1* and *Yuanwang 2* spy ships, built in Shanghai, which were first sighted in 1980 in the Pacific Ocean, where they were tracking and analyzing the intercontinental ballistic missile launch. In 1986, Beijing launched *Yuanwang 1*, commanded by Captain Zhu Pengfei, describing it as a "190 metre detection and surveying vessel capable of travelling at a maximum of 20 nautical miles an hour and of detecting traces of space navigation devices, collecting data, performing checks and recovery, and so on."[20] It turns out that "and so on" covered a multitude of secrets!

One of these spy ships was operating off the coast of Hong Kong in 1993 and was also, according to British sources, interfering with GCHQ's eavesdropping system. This was significant, for it was precisely at this time that the Stanley Fort base was being dismantled.[21] Over the next decade a third *Yuanwang* ship, built after the other two, was frequently sighted in the seas off northern Taiwan. Hong Kong, Taiwan and the Spratley Islands—where the Chinese were installing a mini-wiretapping station—were frequent targets for these electronic information-gatherers. Other ships—such as the intelligence-dependent *Xiangyang Hong 09*, *Xiangyang Hong 05* (SIGINT) in 1988, and *Xiangyang Hong 10* (COMINT)—appeared to be preparing operations against Vietnam. From the beginning of the twenty-first century, this flotilla, supported by new ships, was making more and more daring voyages, including occasional short incursions into the territorial waters of two neighbouring countries whose response capacity they were testing: Taiwan and Japan.

Without attempting to draw up a comprehensive map or a detailed chronology of the operations, it is clear that there were three distinct episodes in this war of nerves, which were intensifying every year, as the Chinese navy expanded its area of navigation.[22] Firstly, in May–June 2000, the *Haibing*, sailing north of the Sea of Japan and circling around the archipelago, passed through the Strait of Tsugaru, which is approved as an international strait for passing without restrictions, according to the law of the sea. It arrived in the Pacific at Honshu. According to the Japanese Self-Defence Forces, it was carrying out a military intelligence mission. Secondly, in April 2002, the Canton-based *Xianyang 14* patrolled within Taiwan's territorial waters. Finally, in July 2004, a Japanese P3-C aircraft spotted the oceanographic ship *Nandiao 411* ("Song of the South", a play on the double meaning *t'iao* or *diao*, both "to sing" and "to make intelligence") in waters off Okinotorishima Island. This vessel, run by the South China Sea Fleet headquartered in Zhanjiang, Guangdong province, was seen sailing not far from the same island again in May 2005.

But by the early 2000s, the PLA had succeeded in further expanding its eavesdropping capabilities far beyond this kind of regional coastal navigation.

Spy ships in the South Pacific

As we know, France is a particularly favoured target of Chinese intelligence, which is known to have operators in the DOM-TOM, the French overseas departments and territories. This is particularly the case in locations where there is a Chinese community, such as in La Réunion and Polynesia, where supporters of Taiwan and the PRC compete for influence. The French DGSE is also well aware that the CCP's International Liaison Department has often used Martinique and Guadeloupe as bases for its political intelligence activities in Africa, the Caribbean and Central America.

But the most spectacular operation of all took place in Polynesia. The services of the French senior defence clearance officer were concerned that Chinese ships such as *Yuangwang* and others in its class were making regular visits to the civilian port of Papeete, without authorization from the military authorities. Even though they figured most prominently in Commander Prezelin's "bible" *Les flottes de combat* (Combat Fleets), the Chinese insisted that they belonged to the Beijing Academy of Sciences and were on purely oceanographic research missions. Of course, naval experts knew that their satellite dishes and antennae served quite another purpose, for example the monitoring of missiles launches. As early as May 1980, the *Yuangwang 2* space observation structure, built in the Shanghai shipyards, had been seen tracking the firing of a Chinese ICBM in the Pacific. Its equipment said it all: a large rotating satellite dish for telemetry and remote control; a hemispherical dome containing optical tracking instruments; two small satellite dishes; laser-tracking equipment; two directional broadband radios for high-frequency transmissions, and last but not least a helicopter landing platform.[23]

The authorities knew perfectly well that these vessels were gathering intelligence, which they would then deliver to general communications interception missions; even just during stopovers, the devices would continue to function. They also knew that radio beacons were placed on Tahiti while the 400 sailors, engineers and technicians left the ship and spent time on land in the Chinese community—this mingling makes it difficult to be sure who really went back on board, and who remained on the island under cover.

The question was how to react. When the *Yuangwang 2* docked at Tahiti for a six-day break on 18 May 2007, an announcement was made that the "research ship" was being hosted by the Chinese community and the newly appointed Chinese consul Chang Dongyue. "After a month at sea, the stopover is being put to use for cultural exchanges, for the crew to rest and the ship to be refuelled. A tour of the island is planned for today, with a sporting day at AS Dragon, followed by a convivial meal."

In September 2007, the brand new *Yuangwang 5*, recently built in Shanghai, anchored at Papeete. This intelligence-gathering vessel was part of the large, growing electronic apparatus being built by the Chinese as part of the battle of interception and intelligence warfare.

Chinese "ears" in Cuba

In 1961, as a result of a dispute between the Soviet Union and Albania, the Chinese had seized four of the twelve Whiskey-class submarines docked in the Albanian port of Vlorë, which Khrushchev's navy had been forced to sabotage and abandon. Four years later, an extraordinary fact had come to light: Italian intelligence announced to NATO that Chinese-controlled submarines were engaged in exercises in the Adriatic Sea—in other words, in the Mediterranean.

Forty years later, the Chinese began taking over other former Soviet bases in different parts of the world. A quite different diplomatic pattern emerged in Cuba in the aftermath of the Cold War, one that was of even greater concern to the US. The Russians, now on good terms with the Chinese, decided to gift them their former sites in Castro's Cuba, beginning with the Cienfuegos base where Chinese submarines were anchored, and Isla de la Juventud, where Chinese spy ships had been spotted. The largest transfer was the 70-square-kilometre Lourdes listening post, constructed in 1964 in the province of Havana. Previously home to 1,500 technicians and under the jurisdiction of the GRU, which had set it up, it is now run by the PLA3. Announcing its closure on 17 October 2001, Chief of Staff Anatoly Kvachin said that the annual lease was costing Moscow $200 million. "For this price, we could send twenty military satellites into space," the Russian general explained.

Meanwhile, during a visit in early 1999, the Chinese defence minister Chi Haotian negotiated with the Cubans the establishment of a second station in Jeruco, 50 kilometres east of Lourdes, to eavesdrop on North American civil and military telecommunications. Raúl Castro, Fidel's brother, nicknamed "El Chino", was also facilitating the exchange of information between the Guoanbu and the Cuban service, the Dirección General de Inteligencia, headed by General Eduardo Delgado Rodríguez, from the joint-run Bejucal intelligence base.[24] With the signing of this agreement, three Chinese-Cuban generals—members of the small Chinese community that had participated in the Cuban revolution—were particularly singled out for praise: Armando Choy, Gustavo Chui and Moisés Sío Wong, president of the Cuba-China Friendship Association.[25]

It had perhaps been a mistake on the part of the US to have broken their SIGINT alliance with the Chinese in 1990. The turning of the tables in the early 2000s was quite extraordinary. Time and again, I have been witness to the ways in which the Chinese manage to keep two irons in the fire at all times. They monitored the Soviets in cahoots first with the US, then with the West Germans. Now they were monitoring the United States using techniques learned from them, having been given the means to do so by the USSR.

At the same time, another battlefield was being developed—that of cyber warfare, whose potential was growing thanks to an invention of the US military during the Vietnam war: the internet.

Chinese internet

By 1993, the Chinese government was looking to develop an information infrastructure to accompany the country's economic breakthrough. Prime Minister Zhu Rongji launched the "golden" projects: the Golden Bridge, a plan to computerize China's economic infrastructure and its links with the worlds of science and technology; Golden Cards, a means of payment in the form of a credit card for 300 million Chinese; and Golden Customs, which was to streamline foreign trade.[26]

The success of these projects led to an announcement by the State Council of three further projects: Government Online, Online Business and Family Online. The problem was that these networks theoretically existed on the internet, with all the dangers that implied for an authoritarian state seeking to control not merely its citizens' activities, but their very thoughts.

Afraid of the anarchy of the World Wide Web (*Wan wei wang*, 10,000 three-dimensional networks), in 1995 Jiang Zemin announced the launch of a central body to regulate business, while the Ministry of Telecommunications created a business network called ChinaNet. The following year, four state-dependent providers began offering global access: ChinaNet, using China Telecom's infrastructure; ChinaGBN, with the same infrastructure but for the Ministry of Industry and Electronics; CERNET, for the State Committee for Education; and the CSTNet of the Chinese Academy of Sciences (formerly CASnet), both using their own infrastructure. At the same time, Zhang Ping, director of CBnet, began offering a subscription service for the China Business Information Network, with an archive of *China Daily*, and an internet connection.[27]

Without going into the technical details, it should be noted that, as early as 1998, the existence of private networks outside the monopoly of China Telecom began to be considered a problem for "national security". Parallel networks, such as Unicom and China Netcom, were permitted. Despite the dangers posed by e-democracy, the Chinese government—whether the PLA, the CCP or the intelligence services—saw what there was to be gained from the internet. The field of propaganda was taken over in 2000 by an Office of Propaganda on the Internet. The Xinhua News Agency and PLA have developed very elaborate websites. The CCP Central Committee's International Liaison Department developed a website, as did the China Institute for Contemporary International Relations (CICIR), the think-tank under the aegis of the Guoanbu's 8th Bureau. Naturally, the Gonganbu, which is in charge of the police, also set up its own site, with regional differences and addresses enabling citizens to contact it directly. On all these sites, the Chinese pages contain far more information than those in English. There are some amusing contradictions to be found: the pages on Tsinghua University's website devoted to the history of intelligence and to Li Kenong, former head of the party's special services, have been heavily redacted in translation.

Fearing leaks of information useful to officials and researchers but prohibited to citizens and more importantly foreigners, the idea of creating a national intranet, parallel to the open internet, began to gain traction. As early as 1996, the China Internet Company was working on the idea of a virtual Great Wall, a closed-circuit China Wide Web that would guarantee a high level of security.[28]

The Guoanbu, in charge of spying operations abroad, was of course active in the new realm of digital security. In June 2001, its leading IT specialist, He Dequan, gave a special conference on the subject to members of the State Council, including Prime Minister Zhu Rongji, who explained at the end of the presentation that "the government will further increase the development of the digital industry. But at the same time, the relevant government departments are exploring ways to boost the development of technology to ensure intelligence security".

In fact, in terms of technical developments, the Chinese launched their fibre-optic communication programme as early as 1998, as part of their global cyber-warfare strategy, which was considered highly effective in dealing with attempted intrusions. For example, the Beijing military region uses a vast fibre-optic "military information highway", rendering the type of interception carried out by stations like Pine Gap almost impossible.

An army of cyber-warriors

The Chinese have been able to develop such inviolable encryption and undetectable transmissions on their highly-regulated "internet" because their services are in a engaged a global battle of intrusion, hacking, spam bombing, and virus infection of foreign websites and databanks.

Welcoming the German chancellor Angela Merkel to Beijing on 27 August 2007, Prime Minister Wen Jiabao expressed his regrets that hackers had attacked computers in the German Chancellery and several ministries in recent months. Trying not to lose face, Wen—known for his reforming and conciliatory spirit towards the West—had to acknowledge an unavoidable fact: the publication that same day of a special issue of *Der Spiegel*, whose entire front page was devoted to a dossier about Chinese espionage against Germany, in which it was claimed that the PLA had launched a computer intrusion programme using Trojan horses. *Der Spiegel* claimed that the Chinese were transmitting spyware via a Windows PowerPoint folder. This was just the tip of the iceberg. Thousands of private companies and government departments, including the police and the military, had been attacked by PLA cyber-warriors over the past eight years.

Merkel—who grew up in East Germany and studied at the Karl Marx University in Leipzig, just like the head of the Chinese secret services, Luo Gan—understood the double language of the communist system, as she had been quick to point out to the Beijing leadership in September 2007, while still agreeing to commercial activity with the Chinese. Meanwhile, the British, American and Italian intelligence services also claimed that ministries in their countries were being targeted by the PLA. The US claimed that several incursions had been carried out against the Pentagon. In early 1999, a Trojan horse (in the form of PICTURE.EXE or MANAGER.EXE) had circumnavigated the globe, attacking primarily AOL's subscriber computing systems, before returning to China with its looted data.[29] In

Asia, too, several intelligence agencies complained about the spread of such attacks in Japan, Taiwan, South Korea and India.

Perhaps the most disturbing examples of combined attacks are those carried out against Japan, which I wrote about for *Sapio* magazine in Tokyo in 2005. A first wave of attacks occurred on 15 April 2005, when several companies, including Mitsubishi and Sony's China subsidiary, were targeted. Other companies preferred not to make their cases public for economic reasons, stating only that they were used to these kinds of computer attacks, and that they were protected by their firewalls.

That morning, the heads of the two companies, as well as employees of Kumamoto University, arrived at work to discover anti-Japanese messages and the red Chinese flag embedded on their respective websites. More seriously, it was discovered that the Ministry of Foreign Affairs (*Gaimusho*) and the Japanese Defence Agency, which had been similarly attacked the previous summer, were once again the target of attacks that included being bombarded by spam and being sent viruses and Trojans, apparently by internet users furious with the way Japanese textbooks present the Sino-Japanese War. According to police experts, the Chinese cyber-warfare system was using so-called "rebound bases", which made it impossible to identify for certain the sources of the attacks, notably in the case of websites based in countries with large Chinese communities, such as Vancouver and Toronto.

The political nature of these attacks was familiar to the Japanese. In January 2000, several ministries had been attacked after statements made by politicians denying the reality of the 1937 massacre in Nanjing by the imperial army, in which 150,000 people (or 300,000 according to the Chinese) were killed. In each case, attacks involving systems to erase databases originated in China, and were then rerouted via internet service providers abroad.

The PLA's cyber-warriors, who were behind these operations, had begun their attacks in 1999. A taskforce was set up at the request of the Central Military Commission involving half a dozen services specialized in computer warfare. These were the PLA2, then led by General Luo Yudong; the Communications Department (*Tongxin Bu*), led by General Xu Xiaoyan; the PLA3 led by Qiu Rulin; the defence ministry's Department of Technological Intelligence; the Institute of Military Science's Department of Special Technologies, nicknamed "Department 553"; and the 10th and 13th Bureaus of the Guoanbu, responsible for communications. The taskforce was led by Xie Guang, deputy minister of COSTIND, who was one of the principal theoreticians of cyber-war.[30]

Trained technicians were needed, too. General Si Laiyi was charged with setting up the PLA University of Science and Technology, which involved the merger of a number of telecommunications research institutions to train cadres in cyber-warfare (*Xinxi Zhanzheng*). This involved a thorough practical and theoretical training, using books such as Qiao Liang and Wang Xiangsui's *Unrestricted Warfare* and various Western books including *Wars in Cyberspace* by the French journalist Jean Guisnel, which was published in Chinese in 2000.[31]

After they graduated, cadets and technicians of all ranks moved into action, taking part in internal simulations of war games and in real attacks such as those carried out against Japan and against the German Chancellery in 2007. But during the same period they also faced another invisible army actively fighting against China: the Hong Kong Blondes.

The Hong Kong Blondes

Blondie Wong's entire life had been marked by violence. As a child, at the tail end of the Cultural Revolution, he had witnessed the murder of his father at the hands of the Red Guards. In 1989, as a student in Europe, he had watched the Tiananmen massacre unfold on television. He felt an unquenchable hatred for the Zhongnanhai elite, who returned the sentiment. In the summer of 1999, a team of Guoanbu "cleaners" was sent to Saint-Nazaire in Brittany, to assassinate him.

This unusual exile was one of the principal figures behind the "Hong Kong Blondes", a group of highly trained cyber-dissidents involved in viral attacks against Chinese army computer systems. Luckily for Blondie Wong, by the time the "cleaners" set out to try and "service" him, he was no longer in the west of France, if indeed he ever had been—he was nothing if not a master of disinformation and fake news. He may have been warned to leave for Canada, where he would remain under armed guard.

The Hong Kong Blondes were a group of obsessive hackers who proved that, with a computer, it was possible to defeat a huge system designed to control an entire national population. For the PLA and its huge empire of cyber-warriors, the boot was now firmly on the other foot. Since 1989, the Blondes had been circulating stories on the internet to create a smokescreen for their continued attacks on government networks, even after the handover of the region to the PRC—rather daring, bearing in mind that the Chinese special services had now taken control of the Hong Kong police. The hackers were threatening communist installations in the name of human rights. They were said to be around fifty computer engineers, both within China and abroad, some in high-ranking positions of power, who vowed to avenge the massacre of their friends and relations at Tiananmen Square.

This was one of the strengths of their strategy: Zhongnanhai and the security services simply did not believe it was possible to hack their systems from within. Like the famous dissident Fang Lizhi, who was smuggled out of China by the Americans in June 1990, Blondie Wong was an astrophysicist, and well versed in many of the scientific programmes that had been developed at the request of Deng Xiaoping and, later, Jiang Zemin.

Guoanbu agents flew out to Vancouver and Toronto to continue their pursuit. Again they discovered that Wong had already left, with a female member of the group, Lemon Li, who had been imprisoned and later exiled for a period in Paris. It was in fact she who had settled in Saint-Nazaire, not Wong. They had made for India. "This was no coincidence," a specialist in telecommunications and cyber-war, not fond of the Hong Kong Blondes, told me in Beijing. "They must have been under the protection of the Indian services, which were much more advanced than we were in this area. Their secret service, the RAW, and the Indian army, were having fun with these frenetic war games against China."

A subsidiary of the Hong Kong Blondes, called the "Yellow Pages", decided to intensify their attacks on China's communications infrastructure, and on the multinationals helping Beijing both to strengthen their anti-hacker protection and to use the internet to spy on the population. The only true blonde in this mysterious group was a woman called Tracey Kinchen, a former MI5 technician who was helping the Blondes and the Yellow Pages. The implication here was that MI5 was also in on the game, helping the group to conduct small-scale cyber-guerrilla attacks against a numerically superior army, by focusing attacks on its weak points.[32] Because Kinchen was apparently active in Hong Kong, the local security services conducted an investigation, but failed to identify her. Some investigators even went so far as to claim that the Blondes did not really exist. According to certain US sources, they had relocated to Bangkok.

The Blondes had begun with a campaign sending personalized emails to leaders of the PLA and various organisms that were part of the Chinese military-industrial lobby. Nothing too nasty, but it had been enough to alert military security, which failed to explain how so many email addresses and intranet mailboxes had fallen into the group's hands. Then the Blondes had downloaded confidential codes, including information on satellite guidance, which was rather more ingenious. In the process, they carried out targeted attacks by erasing databases, followed by disinformation campaigns and bombarding websites to make them freeze—displaying denial of service messages—just as the PLA's cyber-warriors were doing to other sites.

Today, armies and security services in every industrialized country, as well as large private companies, are used to these kinds of attacks, but at the time—the dawn of the internet era, which began around 1995 in Asia—the PLA3's laboratories could not believe their eyes. It was even claimed that the Blondes were able to install codes to monitor and send warning signs to Chinese computers. In 1999, 228 cyber-attacks were launched from Hong Kong, according to Lo Yik Kee, head of the new Computer Crime Section of the Hong Kong police's commercial crime bureau, set up in early 2000, whose first task was identifying the cybercafés from which the attacks on the PLA were being launched. Never short of statistics from the other side of the Bamboo Curtain, the Gonganbu in turn denounced 72,000 attacks, of which 200 had hit their targets.

Meanwhile, Tracey Kinchen, the MI5 operative, was discovered to be living in Bangkok by a journalist, but she kept her cool:

"Blondie Wong and the Hong Kong Blondes would never want to hurt anyone. They follow Gandhi's and Martin Luther King's worldview of non-violence."[33]

In spite of Kinchen's protestations, the Chinese were convinced that this was a large-scale sabotage campaign that had been going on since 1998, when one of their communication satellites had been hacked. To prevent further attacks, in autumn 1999 the PLA organized an anti-hacker war game. The scenario was that "black intruders" (*Heike*, which sounds like "hacker"), had managed to hack the CCP's websites and hijack their content.[34] Soon, under the leadership of Chen Zhili—the education minister and Jiang Zemin's Shanghai-born mistress—the Guoanbu, Gonganbu and propaganda service began mobilizing their resources at Shenzhen University, to refine a system of filtering and tracking the email inboxes of Chinese students abroad.[35]

Monitoring internet users

While undertaking multiple intrusions into external networks, the Chinese secret services had also been given a mission to organize a vast system of control of the Chinese population, starting with the younger generations who were now surfing the internet while increasingly avoiding cybercafés.

In 1995, at the point when the internet really began to take off in East Asia, there were only a few thousand academics who wanted to maintain links with foreign colleagues. They were obliged to register with the Ministry of Posts and Telecommunications, which controlled the China-Pack link to the World Wide Web. Initially, control was vested in the State Council's Information Office, headed by Zeng Jianhui, a propaganda specialist and international editor at the Xinhua News Agency. After having investigated closely Singapore's methods of controlling the internet, in 1996 Zeng was replaced by the former ambassador to Great Britain, now deputy minister of information, Ma Yuzhen.

Ten years later, a highly sophisticated surveillance system had been set up. For example, the Public Information Bureau (PIB) of the Office of Public Security (*Gonganju*) in Lhasa had developed a system to control all internet users. It is probably no coincidence that Tibet serves as a laboratory for computer surveillance techniques, ahead of extending these methods to other parts of China. From early 2004, both Chinese and Tibetan residents of Lhasa seeking to access the internet in cybercafés received a registration number with a password, which they could use to surf sites or exchange emails. The user was then able to buy an inexpensive "navigation map", on condition that they fill in a "citizen identification form" (*shenfen zheng*).

These cards were distributed by the PIB, which was headed by "Luobu Donzhu" (whose Tibetan name was Norbu Dondrub). The PIB was also responsible for licensing cybercafés. The avowed goal of this service was "to fight internet crime", but its sister agency, the Guoanbu's Lhasa office, charged with counterintelligence operations against India, also intended to monitor coded emails that might be exchanged between Tibetan resistance networks and the Dalai Lama's Research and Analysis Centre in Dharamsala.

This monitoring system appeared to be very effective, since it required the individual user to register rather than the computer system used. The smooth functioning of this repression went so well behind the virtual Great Wall that it made sense to exploit the complacent help of any external systems ready to make a deal with the CCP in exchange for a commercial leg-up into the much-coveted Chinese market.

Cyber-dissidents were imprisoned, with the help of foreign accomplices of the Chinese state apparatus such as the search engine Yahoo, which provided the Gonganbu with the emails and IP addresses of people who went on to be arrested. The most famous case to date is that of Wang Xiaoning, sentenced in September 2003 to ten years in prison—and two of losing his civil rights—for "inciting the subversion of state power". He had been behind email newsletters advocating a democratic opening up of China. Similarly, Shi Tao, editor of an economics newspaper based in southern China, was sentenced in April 2005 to ten years in prison, for allegedly leaking state secrets by posting online a Chinese government statement to the media, forbidding any marking of the anniversary of the Tiananmen crackdown. In 2007, Reporters Without Borders counted over fifty online reporters imprisoned in the *laogai*, the Chinese gulag.

Between 2002 and 2004, several tens of thousands of the PRC's 110,000 officially registered internet cafés were closed down. The rest were obliged to equip themselves with software for monitoring and bookmarking the URLs visited by customers, which then blocked those that were prohibited. Between 30,000 and 40,000 operatives from security agencies were responsible for monitoring internet traffic, while the number of internet users doubled in three years, increasing from 80 million internet users in 2004 to 162 million in 2007.

The two security ministries, the Gonganbu and Guoanbu, recruited talented computer scientists, including IT graduates from US universities. They were obliged to offer them excellent salaries to keep them from going into the private sector. They also recruited the occasional genius hacker, just as the Western counterintelligence agencies were doing. This was the case of one of the stars of Chinese internet security, an ex-hacker recruited in Shanghai in 2003.[36] The Guoanbu was particularly interested in foreigners, whether those suspected of espionage or simply journalists, diplomats and most particularly businessmen and traders whose emails and email attachments might contain important commercial secrets. These foreigners would frequently be asked for their passport before being assigned a computer in a cybercafé or the business centre of their hotel, in order to keep track of their online activity. As an internet specialist in Beijing explained to me, new teams were created and others greatly expanded in time for the 2008 Olympics.

The Golden Shield

With the public launch of the Golden Shield (*jindun*) programme in April 2006, the Gonganbu further expanded its surveillance methods, which were under the technical direction of the computer scientist Fang Binxing, head of the Beijing University of Posts and Telecommunications.[37] The Gonganbu was congratulating itself on being able to root out websites that threatened China, thanks to the 640,000 computers in the Golden Shield network, organized into twenty-three systems across China (with the exceptions of Hong Kong and Macao). Its system was so advanced that the Gonganbu was also able to solve crimes online and thus reduce the crime rate, by better controlling internet users.

The Golden Shield, which cost $10 million, was a kind of giant intranet run by the Chinese security services, allowing them to block some sites, spy on others, and monitor users. Its innovation lay in the programming of keyword filtering in Chinese cyberspace, which triggered surveillance, automatic blocking of communications, or both. It was a system similar to what the American NSA had developed with the ECHELON network and its "dictionaries", which could sample conversations in which pre-programmed words appear. The difference was that, with a few exceptions such as violent Islamist sites, the blocking of websites, blogs or chatrooms was not the very purpose of the ECHELON operation.

In China, a semantic analysis of a thousand forbidden keywords reveals the concerns of power and the fantasies of the Gonganbu, at this time under Meng Jianzhu. At the top of the list were the "Great Poisons": 20% of the words were to do with the Falun Gong movement, 15% to do with Tibet, Taiwan and Xinjiang. Another 15% were related to Chinese leaders and their families (including security chiefs Zeng Qinghong and Luo Gan, as well as historical figures like Deng Xiaoping, Mao Zedong and his wife Jiang Qing); 15% to do with politics and corruption, with the word "democracy" considered just as subversive as "dictatorship", even if it is a word specific to the proletariat; 10% concerned the police and national security; 10% were the names of dissidents and political exiles (including Chai Ling, face of the 1989 Tiananmen student movement, who had spent time as a refugee in Paris); and 15% were words about sex: night club, orgy, porn video, and so on.

But the Chinese language being what it is—a sequence of syllabary phonemes presented in characters that can give rise to various interpretations—the Gonganbu computer park also managed to ban official texts and comments about them that included words such as "National Security" (*Guojia anquan*). In the end, only economic expressions were able to slip through the cracks.

Commonly used and even mythical words like Dragon-Tiger-Leopard, (*Long Hu Bao*) when joined together, become suspect—this is the title of a Hong Kong erotic magazine, as well known as *Playboy* (itself a forbidden word). The expression "a band of pigeons" (*ge pai*) was held to be a covert attack on the communist leadership. Even worse for the authorities, an expression like "the great law" (*dafa*) had to be permanently censored, because it refers to the principles of Falun Gong.

Without a doubt, the Golden Shield procedure became less and less effective in tracking "counterrevolutionary criminals". Even were computers really able to scan the entire Chinese computer system, young people on the internet use thousands of common words related to everyday life and slang to encode their intimate conversations, which are already naturally very figurative and allegorical in Chinese characters. Soon, the Gonganbu had to revise its Orwellian programme, whose linguistic-political and psychological consequences were already obstructing the system.

In 2004 the authorities had published draconian guidelines for sending text messages, entitled *Self-Discipline Rules Regarding the Content of Text Messages*, to prevent the dissemination of pornographic, fraudulent or illegal messages. Similar instructions were prominently displayed in cybercafés. SMS had played a significant role during the country's SARS outbreak the previous year, and the security services were planning to block a number of words including "Tiananmen" as they approached the anniversary of the 1989 student massacre.

The problem was that internet usage in the PRC was on a exceptionally massive scale, given a population of over 1.3 billion. China Mobile, the country's largest provider of cell phone services, signed an agreement to participate in the tracking of unacceptable text messages. Nonetheless, even with the best intercept system in the world, in 2003 the Gonganbu and the various interception services of the PLA can only have processed 220 billion text messages, or 55 per cent of all that year's traffic—a real headache for special services analysts.

The PLA intensifies its cyber-warfare

In 2009-12, the Hu Jintao era was coming to an end, moving towards Xi Jinping's replacement of Hu first as general secretary in 2012, then as president in 2013. During these transition years, the already expanded intelligence services of the PLA went through a significant period of technological growth, including satellites, communications interception, drones, submarines, and oceanographic vessel intelligence-gathering. The development of Chinese SIGINT interception bases in Africa was testimony to this, alongside the development of an African presence in Beijing, in partnership with Chinese telephone equipment manufacturers. This project was not limited to economic relationships, contrary to what the Chinese might have wanted us to believe.

This was the thesis posited by Didier Huguenin, a French researcher specializing in Chinese information manoeuvres in Africa. His Master's dissertation on economic intelligence states, "It is worth drawing attention to a particularly strong interest in electromagnetic intelligence (ELINT, SIGINT), as evidenced by the setting up under cover of assistance to local services of an interception centre and appropriate equipment. This was particularly the case in Djibouti, Mali, the DRC and Zimbabwe."[38]

There had definitely been an increase in the duplication of structures, between those reporting to the actual general staff (the PLA2, PLA3 and PLA4) and those who reported to the General Political Department (including military security and the International Liaison Department). In the summer of 2007, the choice of General Chen Xiaogong to oversee the sector as deputy chief of staff was not insignificant, since he was a strategist specializing in relations with the United States who had experience on the ground in Afghanistan and Pakistan. The PLA3 and PLA4, as well as the formal Communications Department, had been attracting a good deal of attention, because—as we know—Western, Indian, Korean, Taiwanese and Japanese agencies suspected them of being behind a series of cyber-attacks targeting websites around the world. And of course these services were also responding with their own counter-intrusion operations. Thus the PLA's intelligence services had no choice but to adapt.

The perfect illustration of this extension of the field of combat was the appointment in spring 2009 of General Yang Hui as head of the PLA2. Prior to this he had been deputy director of the PLA3, with a solid technical background in communications interception and cyber-warfare. Some experts went so far as to claim that his appointment was part of the cyber-warfare strategy lobby's wholesale takeover of military intelligence.

Be that as it may, faced with the intensification of the cyber-war, several other powers, primarily neighbouring Asian countries, set up new services to counter the Chinese threat. This was the case in April 2008 for India, after websites and databases linked to its foreign ministry were attacked by Chinese hackers, identified through Indian counterintelligence's analysis of IP addresses. Even more seriously, the computer systems of the Indian National Security Council, headed by Mayankote Kelath Narayanan, had been hacked.

Narayanan was given the task of commissioning an audit of the National Technological Research Organization (NTRO), the Indian equivalent of the NSA, which worked closely with the RAW and the Indian army's special services, as well as the economic intelligence body responsible for raising awareness within private companies under constant attack by the Chinese in 2007-8. The conclusion these analysts arrived at could just as well be applied to all the other countries falling prey to these attacks: it was vital to create a cyber-warfare counterstrike force, namely a coordinated structure of cooperating services—in India's case, this would include the NTRO, the Army Cyber Security Establishment and the Economic Intelligence Bureau.[39]

India's experience was of concern to two other major regions also being specifically targeted by Chinese cyber warriors: North America and Europe. At this point, virtually every individual on the planet ought to have begun feeling concerned: in 2009, once again, the Chinese hacking apparatus had infiltrated a messaging system, in this instance belonging to Google, which drew attention to the activities of the PLA's intelligence-gathering laboratories. Indeed, leaving aside the commercial dispute that made it clear to the Chinese that Google wanted to topple the Chinese internet provider Baidu and its affiliates, the US security services were convinced that civilian agencies and groups of ghost hackers alone would not have been able to penetrate Gmail's encryption without the help of specialist units, brought in by the PLA3. This led a French specialist to conclude: "This was not just a commercial battle, but a 'dry run' for a cyberwar, conducted by the PLA3. Not one aspect of this war escaped them."[40]

It also explained why one of these operational divisions—Chengdu's Bureau of Technical Reconnaissance (BRT3), covering operations against Xinjiang, Tibet and north-east India—was congratulated by the army for the "exceptional qualities of its work in the field of computerization, information-gathering in a hostile environment, and its research supporting academic structures and other ministries that work to protect state secrets." Meanwhile, there were also attacks being carried out in the other direction: Ji Guilin, editor-in-chief of the Chinese defence ministry's new website, launched in August 2009, complained just six months later that the United States had already carried out some 230 million attacks against the site (www.mod.gov.cn).

But the emerging war of communications was not only a battle of cutting-edge computer technology; it was simultaneously being fought in the shadows, by individuals finding their own ways to penetrate the enemy system. This became evident in the case of a Chinese network that was dismantled in Louisiana, which gave the FBI and others a clear idea of the Chinese secret services' new MO and intensive use of the internet for sending encrypted messages.

A bit of background: in early February 2008, the FBI published the conclusions of a lengthy investigation into Kuo Tai Shen, a Chinese-American from Taiwan, Kang Yuxin, his female liaison and a Chinese citizen, and Gregg Bergersen, the US agent they had recruited, who was a specialist arms dealer to Taiwan at the Defense Security Cooperation Agency in Arlington, Virginia. Some of the more noteworthy aspects of this case included the use of a furniture shop in a town called Houma as the network's cover, and the recruitment of a Taiwanese operative, which was becoming more and more frequent thanks to the United Front Work Department—the CCP's special service for rallying Chinese in the diaspora to Beijing's cause. The new Taiwanese president at this time, Ma Ying-jeou, was favourable to the idea of a rapprochement with Beijing.

The other unusual aspect of the affair was the massive use of inboxes hosted by Bellsouth.net, Hotmail and Gmail.[41] Thanks to them, Ms Kang had been able to correspond with "Mr X", a Chinese intelligence officer who was based first in Canton and then in Hong Kong. Kuo, the network manager, also received emails telling him to call certain numbers, which subsequently revealed the role of the Chinese services using Hutchicity, an internet provider based in Hong Kong. The FBI also noted that, during their exchanges, Kuo and

"Mr X" had used a coding system purchased commercially in February 2007, PGP Desktop Home 9.5 for Windows—but then discussed its use on the phone! The description of the investigation gives as much information about the workings of the FBI, in liaison with the US Pacific Command intelligence service, as about the methods the Chinese were using. For example, it tells us that on 4 June, "Mr X" used FedEx to send Kuo a new internet address for sending secret information obtained through Bergersen and transferred via encrypted attachments. This detail suggests not only the use of countless wiretaps, but also the interception of emails and conversations in Hong Kong, undoubtedly with the help of both the local NSA branch in the US consulate and Britain's GCHQ, which continued to have a presence in its former colony.

* * *

The services in Beijing did not appreciate the fact that their activities were being unveiled. This was evident in the fury of the Chinese authorities in November 2009, after global security corporation Northrop Grumman's publication of an analysis of China's cyberwarfare techniques. Packed with information provided by the American intelligence community (although officially provided by the private sector), the report pointed the finger at certain specialist departments of the PLA general staff—the PLA2, PLA3 and PLA4.

Most importantly, for the first time, groups of hackers were formally identified as having links with Chinese security services. Some were shown to have been involved in attacks against foreign governments, including the group Hack4.com, which targeted French embassies in China and in various English-speaking countries, including the United States and Canada in December 2008. This was a coordinated attack to "punish" President Nicolas Sarkozy, who had shaken hands with the Dalai Lama during a trip to Poland a month earlier. Though they chose not to publish their report for "diplomatic" reasons, the French special services had been able to detect the link between Hack4.com and the Guoanbu.

The Northrop Grumman report did not mince its words: these groups of hackers were linked not only to Guoanbu, but also to the 1st Research Bureau of the Gonganbu. In contrast, PLA3 preferred to call on graduates of cyber-warfare training academies. One case highlighted in the report particularly stood out: the Black Eagle Base, members of which had been arrested in Henan by the Gonganbu for hooliganism. Six months later, they had been released and went on to form the Black Eagle Honker Base, a group of hackers who began working for the presumably more pragmatic Guoanbu. This group, and several others, had links with the School of Information Security Engineering at Shanghai's Jiao Tong University, whose dean, He Dequan, was the former head of the Guoanbu's science and technology department. This made it clear that the Guoanbu was still active on all "underground fronts", *Yinbi zhanxian* (荫庇 战线).

12

BEIJING 2008

CHINA WINS THE ESPIONAGE GOLD

During the flight to Athens on Sunday, 24 March 2006, Geng Huichang might well have reflected on the astonishing epic of the Olympic Games. As deputy Guoanbu minister, he must have recognized the link between the performances of superb naked athletes on the race-tracks of ancient Olympia and the consummate, no-less-elite ancient art of Chinese espionage, with an equally storied legacy. In the eighth century BCE, around the time of the First Olympiad (776 BCE), epic battles were taking place between the secret agents of different Chinese states, similar to the ancient Greek city-states. The period of major economic and military clashes between 770 and 475 BCE is described in the famous *Zuo Zhuan*, the "Spring and Autumn Annals".

This heroic era was marked by the adventures of Xi Shi, a kind of Chinese Mata Hari—a legendary beauty who precipitated the fall of King Wu of Nanking using "the beautiful woman stratagem" (*meiren ji)*—the timeless art of erotic seduction employed by Chinese spies. These episodes were codified in the Chinese text best known in the West, Sun Tzu's treatise *The Art of War*, which began circulating in China in 510 BCE. In the final chapter, the great strategist uses his calligraphy brush to describe the different kinds of spy. "There are five kinds of secret agents that can be employed, namely: native agents, moles, double agents, provocateurs and peripatetic informants. When these five types of agents are all at work simultaneously and nobody knows their processes, they constitute the 'sovereign's treasure'."[1]

So was Professor Geng, as he was known, a native, a mole, a double agent or a provocateur? It seems he was a "peripatetic", not to mention highly literate, a man who certainly knew his classics. He was also the public face of the famous secret service football team, the Goan. Geng was a round-faced man, with large glasses and slicked-back, jet-black hair. Flying over Piraeus as the plane approached the airport, perhaps he was taking stock of his strange career, constantly on the move.

In 2006 he was in his fifties; born in Hebei in 1951 in the Year of the Rabbit, he was an important geopolitical specialist and head of the intelligence think-tank China Institute for Contemporary International Relations (CICIR), a position that had naturally led to him becoming second in command at the Guoanbu. On top of this, he would go on to have a remarkable role in the nuclear negotiations that the Americans and North Koreans were planning, as well as becoming increasing specialized in economic intelligence. By September 2007, he would be named overall head of the Guoanbu.

The noisy Athens airport was decorated with giant photos of *Evzonoi*—an elite guard sporting distinctive white kilts and pompom-topped shoes. Geng Huichang was greeted by the Chinese ambassador, Tian Xuejun, who took him the following day to see three high-ranking officials: the minister of public order Vyron Polydoras, the head of the National Intelligence Service Ioannis Korantis, and the police chief Anastasios Dimoschakis. After discussing Prime Minister Constantin Karamanlis's recent visit to Beijing, they got straight to the heart of the matter, the purpose of Geng's mission: the security strategy for the 2008 Olympic Games. After all, not only was Greece the birthplace of the ancient games, but it was also the first and only country to have hosted the Olympics since the 9/11 attacks. Professor Geng's expertise was limitless, and this was the new mission that had fallen to him: to protect the Olympic torch.

The Beijing Olympics: "One World, One Dream"

"The Central Party School has an important role in developing the theories that govern the current international strategy: for example, the 'theory of peaceful development', on China's rise and on diplomatic activities that have led to our soldiers now taking part in peacekeeping operations in Africa under UN control."

These were the words of Li Junru, head of the CCP school for training cadres. Li, a close friend of Hu Jintao, was keen to explain to me the genesis of current policy, which is still based on a Marxism-Leninism for the twenty-first century: "In terms of the outside world, the theory that we have developed for training communist party cadres corresponds to the theory of 'social harmony' in China, developed by President Hu. We believe that the Chinese Communist Party must continue to rule this country, which now has a population of 1 billion, 300 million. But having analyzed the experience of the USSR and its collapse, we understand that different systems have to coexist, just as socialism coexists with the market economy in our country. This is what we mean by the policy of harmonies that we have put in place since our 16th Congress. China wants to be a leader of world peace, and the Olympics will be a marvellous showcase for getting that message across."

This is, of course, merely a brief summary of my much longer conversation with Li, also an influential member of the China Reform Forum. Li even agreed to answer my more technical questions about the flow of information within the party and the government, the role of the intelligence services, and many other topics that proved extremely useful to me while I was writing this book. I am all the more aware that in the world of Chinese intelligence, starting with the Guoanbu, the CCP Central Committee and its political commissioners play just as important a role as during Mao's time, even if the political theories driving policy have evolved. In Chinese embassies all over the world, I have seen that it is often the party representative who coordinates intelligence activities.

It was clear from Li's words that there were many challenges facing Hu as president, the wider leadership of the CCP, and the State Council. They were walking a tightrope: wanting the international community to adopt the policy summarized by the slogan of the Beijing Games—"One World, One Dream" (*Yige Shijie, Yige Mengxiang*)—whilst avoiding people abroad politicizing the Olympics by drawing attention to a number of problematic issues: the energy conquest of China across the globe; its role in Africa, particularly in Sudan and Darfur; the flow of its cut-price exports; large-scale counterfeiting; the policy supporting proliferation of weapons of mass destruction; the weakness of the yuan; the pervasive corruption impacting on foreign companies; all-out espionage including computer-hacking; and the build-up of a large army which was adopting hacking technology and was primarily a threat to Taiwan—which would remain the case into the Xi era, in spite of Taiwan's attempt at rapprochement with Beijing after the Kuomintang's electoral victory in 2008.

There were also plenty of issues related to China's domestic politics, including everything to do with human rights, in particular freedom of expression, crackdowns on dissent, the difficult questions of Xinjiang and Tibet, and the repression of religious and philosophical movements such as Falun Gong. Could the excitement of sport make the rest of the world forget all this? That was the dream of the CCP and the PLA's security services, which were in a state of alert rarely seen before in modern China, to ensure that these issues did not surface, erased from people's minds by the athletes' performances. This was how the leadership hoped China would finally, head held high, enter the modern world of the twenty-first century.

* * *

China was expecting 100 heads of state, 20,000 athletes and 2 million visitors. Four billion fascinated viewers would be witnessing China taking its place, for the first time, at the centre of the world—where, as far as the Chinese were concerned, it had always stood. Everything, from the choreography of the events to the splendour of the stadiums and the beauty of the athletes' performances, had to reflect an image of the PRC triumphant. But, to borrow one of Deng Xiaoping's famous precepts, one must conquer with modesty. For the organizers of Beijing 2008, nothing could be allowed to disrupt the ceremonies and the events.

In the run-up to the games, it sometimes seemed, when talking to the Chinese, that they were exaggerating the risks so as to reassure themselves, or to prove that they were truly experts in security. It was unclear why the colossal PRC would be unable to manage what a country as small as Greece had achieved—unless it fell victim to bureaucratic management problems, a natural disaster, the massive flow of spectators, or organized criminal activity involving ticket-touting. Still, 1.3 billion Chinese losing face would make for rather a lot of sad faces—not least among the CCP leaders, first and foremost President Hu.

Alongside weather engineers and pollution cleaners, security agents played a key role in the games. This was a golden opportunity for the Chinese services to become officially part of the international arena dominated by the major intelligence, security and counterterrorism communities. It was vital that they succeed in protecting the athletes, the public, and most particularly the regime, which was more vulnerable within its own borders than it cared to admit, both socially and economically, given the multiple minority nationalities and risk of insurgencies on the margins of its empire.

This explains why the cluster of security services was closely monitoring both the Chinese population and foreigners as the Olympics approached. The leadership at Zhongnanhai was hoping to see Chinese athletes win large numbers of medals, but they were also going for gold in another field—espionage. China was attempting to square a huge security circle: ensuring complete safety for both the local population and foreign visitors to the games, without insisting on stifling levels of security. How was the leadership to ensure that security would be 100 per cent guaranteed, without preventing journalists from doing their work freely and positively?

How was it going to be possible to avoid infringing the rights and principles held dear by both tourists and journalists, when the media was restricted, journalists were monitored, emails and text messages were intercepted, bugs hidden in hotel rooms, suitcases rifled through, address books stolen, and every sound, from a scream to a whisper, recorded, from the suites of the Beijing Hotel and rooms of the Friendship Hotel to the a small *hutong* guest-houses? How could China be seen to respect its citizens' rights when those same *hutong* neighbourhoods had barely escaped being destroyed to make way for Olympic construction and a clean-up of Beijing's centre?

The Lives of Others, the beautiful 2006 film by the German director Florian Henckel von Donnersmarck, tells the story of a Stasi agent in

East German spying on a couple who work at the theatre. As elsewhere, it was a smash hit in China, with one significant difference—it was officially banned. Nonetheless, pirated DVDs of the film circulated for a year all over the country, for everyone recognized themselves in this film—the ordinary citizen, constantly spied on by the regime, by the communist party, by State Security, by the ladies from the neighbourhood committee with their red armbands.

It so happens that *Guoanbu* in Chinese, State Security, translates exactly to *Staatssicherheit*—Stasi—in German. And let us not forget the terror felt by the CCP leaders in 1989 when, just months after they had faced down their own uprising at Tiananmen, the Berlin Wall was torn down with pickaxes. They were right to be afraid of disturbances during the Olympics, while the world was watching.

"What the Chinese special services were asked to do," a journalist who has lived in Beijing for years explained to me, "was to ensure that no movement demanding any kind of recognition, no uprising like Tiananmen, be allowed to take place in front of 4 billion television viewers. In comparison to that, the risk of a Uyghur or Tibetan terrorist attack was just a pretext to ensure that people in Beijing, indeed all Chinese people who have any contact with foreigners, think only about the games, and nothing else!"

Nonetheless the political activities of all "five poisons", as the 610 Office called them—Tibetans, Uyghurs from Xinjiang, Falun Gong adherents, other dissidents, and Taiwanese separatists—remained an issue of great concern for the CCP. The extraordinary safety procedures set up for the Olympic Games were shaped entirely in response to them.

The secret services in Olympic training

Up until the seventeenth party congress, which took place in October 2007, it was Luo Gan, head coordinator of the services as chair of the party's political-legal committee, who was in charge of preparing the intelligence and security protocol for the Olympics. As we know, Luo—who had been close to Li Peng, "the butcher of Beijing"—had enthusiastically backed the repression of the Tiananmen massacre, and had coordinated the fight against the Falun Gong movement in

1999 and the creation of the 610 Office. The Gonganbu minister Zhou Yongkang played a key role by Luo's side, before taking over from him on the Politburo Standing Committee in October 2007, as coordinator of the security and special service work section (*tewu gongzuo*). He was replaced at the Gonganbu by Meng Jianzhu.

Zhou was given the most important task: coordinating all the intelligence agencies abroad and the repression within China, following in the footsteps of his namesake Zhou Enlai, Kang Sheng the "shadow master", and Qiao Shi, "the Chinese Andropov". But his presence on the Standing Committee testified to the fact that Hu Jintao had not entirely succeeded in getting rid of Jiang Zemin's old Shanghai clique, led by Zeng Qinghong, who was also active in the security field and was Zhou Yongkang's brother-in-law. Zeng continued to be influential from the shadows, following Chinese tradition, at the intersection of the military lobby (his brothers and sisters were all PLA generals) and what was already being dubbed the oil mafia—a lobby that had begun to play a crucial role, including in the domain of intelligence, because of China's need for a massive supply of energy.

With ten months to go before the Olympics, Zhou Yongkang needed to prioritize the smooth organization of population control and the security of the games. If a terrible accident or attack did take place, he was not going to be able to blame Luo Gan, whose retirement and handover to Zhou had been something of a poisoned chalice. The CCP and the government carried out several major operations with the "Leading Group of National Security" (*Guojia Anquan Lingdao Xiaozu*), led by President Hu himself.

The Beijing Organizing Committee for the Olympics had been set up in December 2001, strongly overshadowed by the 9/11 attacks that had taken place three months earlier. Risk assessment structures were put in place, which bolstered existing government structures—notably the Security Command Centre set up to ensure public safety during the games. One principal structure was kept in place beyond August 2008, a body headed jointly by the Guoanbu and Gonganbu, called the Counterterrorism Bureau. Unsurprisingly, its head, Professor Li Wei, was one of the deputies to Geng Huichang, head of the Guoanbu.

Professor Li was also director of the Centre for Counterterrorism Studies at the CICIR. In a report he validated Beijing's decision to set up China's first counterterrorism agency, to collaborate with Westerners, Russians and members of the Shanghai Club, which also included the majority-Muslim former Soviet republics of Central Asia. He proposed major changes in the Chinese approach to tackling terrorism, including the establishment of the new agency, which should be specific and autonomous. His conclusion made clear what the real issues were: "Antiterrorism measures are vital to ensure a climate of social harmony." In other words, the new measures were not only aimed at averting hypothetical attacks by al-Qaeda, but equally at diverting attention from the various enemies within, whether the Falun Gong movement, spontaneous uprisings such as the peasant revolts recurrent in central China's history, or insurgencies taking place on the country's furthest frontiers—Tibet, Xinjiang and Mongolia—not to mention social movements in major urban centres.

One of the first full-scale counterterrorism exercises took place in Inner Mongolia, involving 2,700 men from various units of the PLA Special Forces and the People's Armed Police (PAP), and "blue-haired dogs" from the Gonganbu. The large industrial centre of Baotou served as the location; the scenario was a workers' uprising and a subsequent explosion of terrorist activities. The joint exercise was a success. As head of the new joint Guoanbu/Gonganbu Counterterrorism Bureau, Professor Li, who had overseen the operation with his deputy Zhao Yongchen, was extremely pleased, claiming that thanks to this anti-terrorist effort, "local security and social stability would be guaranteed".

The blurring of responsibilities did not stop there. At the same time, the highly discreet Counterterrorism Working Group (CTWG) came into being. With a lightweight structure of just a few dozen analysts, it was able to bypass the more weighty administrations such as the Gonganbu, and had direct access to Hu Jintao, his rival and vice-president Zeng Qinghong (dismissed from office in October 2007), and the office of Prime Minister Wen Jiabao.

More of a think-tank than a coordination committee, the CTWG brought out regular reports and made recommendations on how to assess the risk of attack, especially in anticipation of the 2008 Olympics and the 2010 Shanghai Expo. As is often the case with the Chinese, in order to maintain institutional balance, the group had not one single head, but two deputy directors: one was a career counter-intelligence official, Xiong Desheng; the other was Professor Li.

This heavyweight counterterrorism expert had been a key figure in the field since his 2004 report. This had led to the setting up of the CTWG in June that year. "The government needs to increase its efforts in several areas," he had written, "including legislation, institutional structures, technological research, training personnel, and increasing public awareness of the danger of terrorism."

The kidnapping of two Chinese engineers abroad at the end of 2004 accelerated the CTWG's activities in protecting Chinese executives in certain high-risk areas abroad where they were increasingly present, particularly the Muslim Arab world and sub-Saharan Africa. Then came the Islamist 7/7 attacks in London on 7 July 2005. Li Wei drafted another report, warning of the risk of similar attacks in Beijing and detailing the northern capital's weak points: "In Great Britain, as in Spain the year before [the 2004 Madrid train bombings], a small group of people were able to spread terror in an urban area. This must be taken into account for Beijing."

The CTWG's reports and proposals went to the numerous security coordination agencies reporting respectively to the State Council, the Presidency and the CCP. However, to avoid any administrative backlog, the analysis always went first to the Leading Group on State Security, led by Hu Jintao, the Gonganbu chief Zhou Yongkang and the Gonganbu chief Geng Huichang.

The result was clear: for the first time in the history of the Chinese secret service, a technocratic lobby—influenced as much by the theories of American neoconservatives around George W. Bush as by the most conservative elements of the CCP—was in charge of the first steps in China's counterterrorism strategy, and also of the security of the Olympic Games. Professor Li was credited with having played a role in the appointment of his colleague Geng as head of the Guoanbu, since he had Hu Jintao's ear.

A home-grown Orange Revolution?

Liu Jing, deputy Gonganbu minister, was given a diabolical role: to crush the Falun Gong movement in time for the Olympics. Since

2006, the Chinese leadership had grown increasingly afraid of a home-grown "orange revolution" akin to the one that had taken place in Ukraine at the end of 2005, and which the Russian and Chinese services had directly attributed to the CIA. The Polish Solidarity movement had posed a similar threat to Deng Xiaoping twenty years previously.

In 2005, Liu Jing was commissioned to report on the Orange Revolution in Ukraine and the Rose Revolution in Georgia. The objective was to determine whether China was at risk of a similar upheaval because of the non-violent opposition of Falun Gong and other, growing social movements that were causing great anxiety to the CCP elite. Political scientists and security experts were tasked with analyzing the use of NGOs by the CIA in both ex-Soviet countries.

As always, the Guoanbu was never far from these delicate operations. Three analysts from the CICIR, Xu Tao, Feng Yujun and Li Dong, were dispatched to Kiev and Lvov to conduct "sociopolitical surveys" and draw up profiles of the Ukrainian movement's leaders, Viktor Yushchenko and his ally Yulia Tymoshenko, who were seen as being in the pay of the United States.

This resulted in Geng Huichang presenting a report to Hu Jintao. The Guoanbu had managed to get hold of a list of the Oranges' financial supporters, which included Freedom House—an NGO chaired by former director of the CIA James Woolsey. The Hungarian-born American billionaire George Soros and his Open Society Institute were also on the list, accused by the Guoanbu of having been a principal backer of the 1989 Tiananamen protests. Specifically, the ministry charged Soros with supporting the entourage around both Zhao Ziyang, the reformist general secretary at the time, and his friend, the dissident businessman Wan Runnan, who escaped to France after the 4 June massacre.

When it rains, it pours: in late summer 2007, another foreign movement began causing concern among the Zhongnanhai leadership: the "Saffron Revolution", a series of anti-government protests in Myanmar, led by Buddhist monks. The CCP leaders were concerned about the possibility of the unrest spreading to Tibet.

* * *

As number two at the Gonganbu, Liu Jing did not want to take any risks with Falun Gong, whose guru Li Hongzhi was in exile in the United States. He thought it vital to continue chasing down the movement. As we have seen, the 610 Office abroad was under Luo Gan's leadership. It clearly also had bodies in China, which did the same work as the mainstream security services and poached their personnel. Liu Jing relied on the Gonganbu's 26th Bureau, headed by a man called Zhang Yue, using its services to set up "610 Offices" within every regional Gonganbu office, in conjunction with the 5th Bureau (which administered the huge Chinese gulag, the *laogai*). The purpose of these offices was to track down, arrest and interrogate sympathizers of the Falun Gong movement.

Because the Gonganbu was tasked with dealing with mass revolts, rather than the targeted terrorism carried out by small, seasoned groups, Liu was also joined by an antiterrorist police force set up in August 2005. This was a new special force equipped with the most effective technical facilities for coping with mass urban unrest. Until then, the crushing of demonstrations, strikes and riots—including Tiananmen Square in 1989—had been carried out by the PAP, created in 1983, and the PLA. The PAP, under the overall command of General Wu Shuangzhan, had some 800,000 police officers. Reformed as a result of its disastrous performance during Tiananmen, it was still not considered effective enough to deal with the new problems brought about by the transformation of Chinese society in the twenty-first century.

"The new squadrons of this new force will be better able to deal with terrorist incidents, demonstrations and other critical situations," said Zhou Yongkang, during a presentation of the corps in his last few months as Gonganbu minister. Naturally, people were imagining all sorts of horrendous scenarios that might take place in the massive crowds at the Olympics, moving between different stadiums, as well as the possibility of increased unrest. Already, according to Gonganbu statistics for 2004, some 74,000 demonstrations and "disturbances" had taken place, involving almost 4 million Chinese.

The new special police units were to be spread across thirty-six cities, with a nucleus of 600 specialists, equipped with helicopters and light-armoured personnel vehicles, in each major city—Beijing,

Shanghai, Canton, and Chongqing, the largest with over 32 million inhabitants. But the PAP had not spoken its last word: commandos from its 13th Special Brigade would also be on the scene. They had already taken part in 100 or so operations in the capital, where they were stationed, and it was their Elite Snow Leopard unit that had gone to Russia to rehearse collective hostage-taking exercises, seen in real life when Chechen commandos stormed a school in Beslan in September 2004.

The PLA, too, was involved in this massive exercise in the run-up to the Olympics. Without attempting to unravel the labyrinth of all the different corps and units involved, I shall highlight just a few. The Olympic Games Security Committee was linked to an important military command. This command, responsible for overall games security, was led by Tian Tixiang, who reported to General Chen Xiaogong's PLA2 intelligence department and to military security, a subsidiary of the PLA General Political Department. The military was given eight missions that paralleled the "civil" security operations: the air defence of Beijing and other host cities including Qingdao, where water sports were being held; maritime safety, dealing with entry points to coastal areas; the response to nuclear, biological and chemical terror attacks (some of the bunkers in the underground city, Dixia Cheng, were modernized in view of this, as was the underground command of the Central Military Commission to which they connected); and finally tactical support, with its own special forces in case of terrorist attacks and hostage-taking. During the year that preceded the games, the PLA carried out some twenty-five full-scale disaster simulations.

Although a wide-ranging Olympics Security Committee had been set up, with links to both the Beijing Olympic Committee and the Beijing Municipal Government, a thorny issue remained unresolved. It led to the special services spending time visiting foreign intelligence agencies and soliciting visitors even a little bit in the know—including academics and journalists such as myself, as I described at the beginning of this book. The problem was a basic difference of opinion between two lobbies and two theories of Chinese security. One, represented by Professor Li Wei of the Guoanbu, saw al-Qaeda commandos everywhere among other terrorists, including, in his classification, Uyghurs and Tibetans. The other side, which was represented by the Gonganbu's Liu Jing, expected mass demonstrations that risked degenerating into violent protests, or a resurgence of Falun Gong along the lines of its 1999 peaceful sit-in.

Paranoia was on the rise as the fateful date 8/8/2008 approached. In November 2007, the special services suggested that security be strengthened to prevent the possibility of a bacterial attack during the Olympics. They recommended monthly monitoring of the capital's twenty-seven laboratories, to check that no viruses, bacteria or disease-carrying agents had been stolen. According to Liu Jing, this was the type of attack most to be feared around the time of the games. The question was to what extent he agreed with the theories of his rival Li Wei on who might perpetrate unrest.

There was only one solution that would ensure that everyone agreed on the real risks: total surveillance, with no breaches and no exceptions.

The Olympic Games Security Command Centre

The deputy at the Beijing mayor's office, Qiang Wei, handed Hu Jintao a progress report on the security for the forthcoming games in mid-February 2007. He assured the president that all was progressing smoothly. The Olympic Security Command Centre, set up in June 2006, was key. There was rather more discretion around the "Intelligence Centre" that had been specifically conceived for the games, whose objective was to pursue, both in China and abroad, the regime's opponents—Uyghurs, Tibetans and Falun Gong, as well as foreign spies disguised as sports journalists.

Before being named director of the Beijing's Gonganbu bureau (*Beijing Gonganju*), where he remained until 2001, Qiang Wei (b. 1953) had a career in the chemical industry, and had been elected to various political posts in the Beijing municipality. His role in the Communist Youth League while the future president Hu was its head had obviously played a part in his appointment as head security honcho for the Olympics, just as it had when he was appointed to the Beijing mayor's office in December 2007.

With a budget of $1.3 billion, Qiang requested special help from the American, Russian, German, British and French security services, as well as advice from Europol, after having looked closely at the security procedures for the 2004 Athens Olympics. Qiang considered that the biggest threat to the games came from from al-Qaeda, via Uyghur separatists. Private US and European security companies provided state-of-the-art equipment to supplement purchases from the MILIPOL homeland security fair, held every year in Paris.

As director of the Security Coordination Group, Qiang Wei announced the launch of the games' Security Command Centre, which would guarantee a real-time response to any risk arising from the large-scale events. He appointed five deputy directors: Ma Zhenchuan, his successor as director of municipal public security, specifically in charge of video and computer surveillance (including interception of emails, text messages and mobile phone communications); the deputy Gonganbu minister Liu Jinguo, responsible for liaising with his boss Meng Jianzhu and not to be confused with his fellow vice-minister Liu Jing; Zhu Shuguang, deputy PAP commander; Li Binghua, vice-president of the Olympic Committee, in charge of dealing with security issues related to invited sports federations; and finally Niu Ping, about whom little was communicated. There was a good reason for this—he was a counterintelligence veteran and deputy Guoanbu minister.

It was because of Niu Ping that the Guoanbu was given the mission of running the other branch of the coordinating committee, the Intelligence Centre (*qingbao zhongxin*). This organization had been set up without fanfare in June 2006, to gather intelligence about any dangers threatening the Olympics. It relied on Guoanbu intelligence agents posted abroad, but was also willing to seek information from foreign intelligence services.

Special Guoanbu departments were established in Xinjiang and Tibet to anticipate the threat of subversive movements, as well as any possible activities by the Taiwan secret services, which were present in Fujian and Shanghai and which, Beijing officials thought, might attempt to give insurgents a helping hand. According to surprising but reliable intelligence, special teams from the Guoanbu and PLA3, led by General Chen Xiaogong, went to Pakistan and Afghanistan to make contact with al-Qaeda, through their longstanding contacts in the

Taliban as well as among cadres of the Pakistani ISI service, with which the Guoanbu was on good terms. Their message for al-Qaeda's leaders was clear: it would not serve their interests to attempt to disrupt the Beijing Olympics. It has even been claimed that the Chinese knew the whereabouts of bin Laden in 2008, but were careful not to share this information with the Americans. Geng Huichang's agents were certainly active in the field.

According to Western security sources, despite the collaboration sought and obtained by the Chinese services, the Olympics Intelligence Centre played a role in detecting foreign service agents attempting to pry in Beijing, under cover of being there for the games. The centre dealt with registering all journalists, athletes and spectators who were entering China on tourist visas, and were therefore the most difficult to force to conform to regulations.

In addition to all of this, the Olympics Intelligence Centre was also responsible for protecting the Olympic torch. After being lit in Olympia, Greece on 25 March, then transported to the Panathinaikos stadium, the torch was to be flown to Beijing on 31 March. From there the relay would begin, with the mottos "Journey of Harmony"—which recalled Hu Jintao's slogans—and "Light the sacred fire, propagate our dream", which echoed the CCP's Olympic slogan "One World, One Dream", which had been plastered on walls all over Beijing for months. Over 130 days, nearly 20,000 torchbearers were to travel 137,000 kilometres across the whole of China—the longest distance ever run in the entire history of the modern Olympic Games.

There was always a real danger of the torch being hijacked, stolen, or used for propaganda purposes by some Tibetan, Uyghur or Falun Gong-affiliated Qigong group. To deal with this risk, each province established strict measures, overseen by the security services. Only the most trustworthy police and soldiers were chosen to represent the lofty ideals of Pierre de Coubertin, inventor of the summer Olympics, and carry aloft their flaming symbol.

Registering journalists and tourists

Under the pretext of organizing Olympics security, the Chinese services launched the largest-ever operation of registering foreign nationals, in addition to the reinforcement of their longstanding strategies for controlling the Chinese population.

A special committee was set up, theoretically to facilitate access to the games for sports journalists, in conjunction with the International Olympic Committee. But it imposed the usual draconian conditions for visiting foreign journalists, who were to be granted visas provided that they had an invitation from an official body and were able to detail all the people they would interview and all the places they would be visiting. This, of course, made it possible for the Guoanbu's international relations department, which was responsible for journalists, to trail them more easily than if they had entered the country on a simple tourist visa. Anyone who did try this was at risk of provoking retaliation against themselves as an individual, or their editorial board.

Journalists were obliged to provide extremely elaborate documentation in order to obtain visas and permits for entering the stadiums themselves. According to the authorities, this was aimed at preventing "fake journalists" from operating on Chinese soil. The Chinese authorities pledged to relax restrictions on journalists explicitly covering the Olympics or covering stories in the lead-up to the games. This led to an extremely strict registration protocol being adopted by the Guoanbu, the Gonganbu and the Ministry of Information—to take just three principal departments out of the twenty involved in the Olympics Security Committee.

These were the identification codes entered into both the Guoanbu system as well as that of the Press Service of the Beijing Olympic Committee, in liaison with the press centre of the National Olympic Committee:

– (E) Journalist, editor, photo editor, generalist dependent on media or freelance under contract.
– (Es) Sports journalist: specializing in one particular Olympic sport.
– (EP) Photographer category.
– (EPs) Specialized sports photographer.
– (ET) Technician.
– (EC) Auxiliary (clerks, secretaries, interpreters, drivers, couriers). These had access only to the Beijing Olympic Committee's Press Service. To be attached to press groups, newspapers/journals and

the National Olympic Committee after reservation of a private Press Service office.

– (ENR) Member of a non-rights-holding radio and/or television organization (granted only by the International Olympic Committee).

– (Ex) Local press. Access only to the Olympic facilities (Zone 4) of the co-organizing cities during the football, sailing and horseback events. No access provided to facilities in the capital, including the Press Service.

– (Epx) Local photographer. Again, access only to the Olympic facilities (Zone 4) of the co-hosting cities during football, sailing and horseback events, and no access to facilities in the capital, including the Press Service.

As this registration and categorization was taking place in China, teams were being set up in every Chinese embassy abroad to identify sports journalists and pinpoint the nature of their media outlets, in order to define whether they expressed an "antagonistic" or a "friendly" attitude towards China. This work was linked to that of the diplomatic intelligence organizations: the Foreign Affairs Information Department, the 610 Office, the Guoanbu, the United Front Work Department, the CCP International Liaison Department, the Party Political Investigation Bureau, the police (Gonganbu liaison officers), the PLA Liaison Department and the PLA2 defence attachés. Deputy minister Li Junru even pointed out to me the existence of some CCP Central Party School positions, for example, at the Washington embassy.

Naturally, the purpose of all of this was to ensure security in the Chinese sense: to prevent journalists at the Olympics on the pretext of covering sporting events from reporting on problematic subjects, whether internet censorship or the situation for Uyghurs in the capital. Moreover, since the Chinese systematically use their state media as cover for intelligence activities, most significantly with the Xinhua News Agency, they inevitably assumed that the CIA, the German BND, MI6 and the French DGSE would be bound to send battalions of "honourable correspondents" to the games. On the other side, MI5 was warning British visitors to the Olympics to be wary of attempts to recruit them as "friends of China", a warning that was equally pertinent to other foreign nationals.

Apart from foreign spies, it was human rights activists that the security services wanted to prevent from disrupting the smooth running of events. A banner unfurled with "Long live free Tibet!" during a Rebecca Adlington swimming race would have been as unacceptable for the Gonganbu's "blue-haired dogs" as an attack blamed on the Uyghurs, like the one in May 2007 in which Mao Zedong's giant portrait on Tiananmen Square was blackened.

This explained the putting on file, as we saw in Chapter 10, of Qigong and other martial arts associations, not only in China but also in countries such as France, Germany, Australia and Canada, which were believed to be harbouring Falun Gong supporters or members. Nationals of these countries who were involved in the movement might come to the games to whip up non-violent protests, or even hold press conferences, such as the one organized by a team from Reporters Without Borders near Beijing's Olympic Press Centre in the autumn.

One of the organizations responsible for setting up these data banks was the CICIR, which carried out an extensive file compilation programme targeting different NGOs, particularly those working in Darfur, as well as the international organizations that were arguing for a boycott of the Olympic Games. One of its challenges was to try and establish relationships between these groups and the CIA. Once again, as throughout their history, the Chinese special services were caught between two stools: on the one hand they had to go cap in hand to ask for help from the Americans with both technology and know-how in the fight against terrorism; and yet at the same time they were seeking to score points against the United States, their number one rival, by firming up and expanding their twenty-first-century espionage programme.

The Danes on camera

We cannot close this chapter without pointing out that the Olympics saw the emergence of new practices within existing services, and even some new ad hoc services: namely, the establishment of an unprecedented "sports intelligence" department, targeting all rival foreign teams, which was engaged in operations either independently or with a team of personnel from the Guoanbu, the PLA and the National Sports Administration. This strategy was overseen at the highest level by Liu Peng, minister of the General Administration of Sport of China (*Guojia tiyu congju*, GASC), who chaired BOCOG, the Beijing Organizing Committee of the Olympic Games.

According to a French "sports intelligence" source, since the Athens Olympics if not earlier the GASC had been training peripatetic teams of professionals, both civil and military, to focus on the three main sporting disciplines: athletics, swimming and other water sports. These teams benefited, no doubt, from logistical support as well as the Guoanbu's technical expertise, particularly in terms of wiretapping and intercepting communications. They not only engaged in sports surveillance missions, but also in the selection of athletes to be sent abroad for training, and recruitment of foreign coaches, generally dismissed after their use was exhausted. Some of these coaches came from the former Eastern Bloc—former East Germany, Romania, Hungary—where they were ideologically more reliable, had links with the old secret services such as the Stasi, and were expert in the intensive use of doping.

There were also various special operations in individual disciplines, such as ping-pong, where it was particularly important that the Chinese not be outdone by foreign teams. In a number of countries, including Sweden, the Chinese had been spying on rival athletes' training habits in order to train clones into the same strengths and weaknesses, against whom their own champions could train. Similar operations had been conducted for three years against Italian and French fencers—which did not, however, prevent them from ultimately excelling at Beijing.

Project 119 was set up in 2001 as a huge profiling enterprise, including the individual registration of foreign athletes. Its declared aim was for the PRC to win 119 gold, silver and bronze medals—the target was later increased to 122. China had won thirty-one medals at Athens in 2004. This work was boosted by technical teams sent all over the world to film the sports teams considered the most "dangerous", or, alternatively, niche sports that they thought were neglected—and therefore a weak point—in certain countries. These were often women's sports, which traditionally received less financial support in the West than in the East, such as women's weightlifting and women's wrestling.

This explains why several cases of espionage—no doubt only the tip of the iceberg—emerged ahead of the games. Danish female footballers were filmed in their hotel room in Beijing by technicians spying on them behind a two-way mirror; they were caught red-handed in a small adjoining storage room. The explanation provided by hotel management, who smuggled out the secret agents, was that they had been in the closet not to spy, but to get a glimpse of the athletes ahead of the games. Honour saved! Another example was the computer hacking of the British canoe and kayak teams and the British boxing federation, which had been uncovered by MI5. This operation had obtained access to the athletes' Sports Federation files, which contained their medical records, professional records, and personal data.

Naturally, several European security services returned some parries to ensure security of communication between Beijing and their countries, or within Beijing, or between athletes, their families, their coaches, and so on during the games. Several episodes that came to light after the games—such as the case of Prime Minister Gordon Brown's advisor, whose Blackberry was stolen in Shanghai by a young Chinese woman—showed that the Guoanbu's technical services were exploiting weak points such as unencrypted laptops and cell phones, as well as tourists' private lives. It was even feared that the Chinese might break into the Downing Street server and siphon off emails. Jonathan Evans, director-general of MI5 at the time, warned that "China was carrying out state-sponsored espionage against vital parts of Britain's economy, including the computer systems of big banks and financial services firms."[2]

For the Chinese, putting aside the security aspect, the outcome of the Beijing Olympics was positive. Though they did not succeed in their ambition of winning 119—or 122—medals, they came away with a total of 100 medals, including fifty-one gold. The special services' antics during the games did not go unanswered. The 2012 London Olympics provided an excellent opportunity for British intelligence to take revenge, and for the Chinese to attempt further improvement of their sporting success. Chinese sports intelligence had many days ahead of it.

* * *

Contrary to the promises made to the International Olympic Committee and world opinion, the 2008 Olympics had not led to any softening of domestic policies, nor to opening the door even a chink toward democracy. If anything, the games saw another turn of the screw for Tibetans, Xinjiang Uyghurs, Mongolians, trade unionists and cyber-dissidents, who suffered further crackdowns, the likes of which had rarely been seen since the Tiananmen Square massacre twenty years earlier.[3]

The Olympics went wonderfully well from the point of view of Chinese security and intelligence officials. Apart from the Tibetan crisis and the battle against Uyghur separatists, the challenge launched by China had had a most successful outcome. The various agencies known as "special working bodies" (*tewu gongzuo jigou*) benefited from considerable resources and budgets thanks to the games. Their image was strengthened in the Chinese media, in the eyes of the local population, but also, paradoxically, among the foreign intelligence agencies that cooperated with Beijing on counterterrorism security for the games.

The Chinese intelligence community experienced the Olympics as an unprecedented test, one that allowed it to shift to a higher level and take its place alongside China's strategic and economic powerbrokers. It was an opportunity to make great changes both for population control in the digital era, and in creating tools to gain strategic knowledge of the outside world. After the games ended, Geng Huichang, head of the Guoanbu, was able to reposition himself in his favoured fields of strategic and economic intelligence. Another notable result of the Olympics had been the collaboration of mixed Gonganbu/Guoanbu teams in the exploding field of counterterrorism, their activities often blurred with counterinsurgency tactics in civil society. Similarly, the PAP—which had distinguished itself in London and Paris with the Olympic torch relay led by its own Zhao Shi—now possessed both a counterintelligence and a counterterrorism department.

In 2010, a similarly massive security operation was undertaken for the Shanghai Expo. The operation was supervised by Cai Xumin, a Shanghai native and head of the local Guoanbu, and the newly appointed vice-president, Xi Jinping; the latter had already coordinated security for the Olympics two years earlier. Xi's ambition, with the backing of the Shanghai clique and the relative goodwill of Hu Jintao himself, was to succeed Hu as general secretary, head of the Central Military Commission, and president of China.

This was a major challenge, because guaranteeing the security of the Shanghai Expo would be far more complicated than it had been with the Olympics—not only because the Expo took place over six months, from 1 May to 31 October 2010, but also because the numerous exhibition venues, pavilions and stands were scattered over a large area of the city, rather than in a relatively small number of hyper-protected stadiums. Thus the PLA requested assistance from security bodies, who agreed to undertake training exercises once again, in spite of the evident tension between certain cadres representing the Shanghai military region and those who came to share the expertise they had gained from the Olympics—such as the introduction of ground-to-air missiles for destroying projectiles or hostile aircraft.

General Xie Dezhi, second-in-command of the Shanghai garrison since 2008, coordinated the exercises, whilst introducing some innovations. These included cooperation with the Gonganbu, the decision to fly PLA-piloted EC 135 helicopters over the Expo sites, and the training of special units for street fighting, in replica settings of the Bund and other Shanghai neighbourhoods, constructed out of cardboard in Mongolian villages. Most significantly of all, after having studied the November 2008 Mumbai terrorist attacks by Islamist maritime commandos, the marine units carried out security and civil protection exercises similar to those carried out at the mouth of the Yangtze River in Shanghai, with five ships and helicopters. Guoanbu operatives mounted their own various operations—honeytraps, blackmail and censorship—against foreign visitors during the Expo, as was the tradition at all major fairs and international exhibitions.

Two years later, when he replaced Hu Jintao as general secretary, Xi Jinping set about establishing a new programme for coordinating the intelligence community (see Chapter 14). But before that, two men whose image had benefited from their successful roles in securing the Olympics and the Shanghai Expo found themselves at loggerheads. They were Zhou Yongkang, coordinator of the security services, and Xi Jinping himself, who was now hoping to become paramount leader of the PRC. Not since the Cultural Revolution and the days of Kang Sheng, head of Mao's secret service, had the battle of the Beijing factions played such a devastating role.

13

ZHOU'S FAILED COUP

THE GUOANBU SAVES XI JINPING

Every morning, as the sun tried to pierce the dusty pollution haze, Comrade Geng Huichang would leave for work in north-west Beijing, going from Zhongnanhai, the village of rulers that backs onto the Forbidden City, towards the Beijing Zoo. His destination was a large, drab building recalling the communist architecture of the 1950s. Over the lintel of the monumental gateway, an eloquent symbol is carved into the stone: the sword and shield of the CCP, overlaid by the hammer and sickle, hanging above the image of an imperial palace. This is the Western Garden district, headquarters of the Ministry of State Security, otherwise known as the Guoanbu.

Geng would head up to the seventh floor, perhaps adjusting his customary blue tie—polka-dot or striped depending on the day—before entering his office, where he would greet the heads of various departments: espionage, counterintelligence, cybersecurity, and so on. Since 2007 and the Olympic Games, when he had been responsible for the event's security, he had risen to become overall head of the sprawling secret service.

Like its old-school model, the Russian KGB, the Guoanbu is responsible for both internal security and counterintelligence, and for foreign intelligence covering the entire planet, its main enemy naturally being the CIA. As we have seen, the Guoanbu has been responsible for orchestrating the theft of digital technology from other countries, in collaboration with the PLA. Liaising with the police, it has intercepted the emails of dissident internet users, tracked down militant Tibetans, and spied on foreign businesspeople, whose numbers had been steadily increasing since China opened up to international trade under Deng Xiaoping.

Geng's challenge was to ruthlessly apply the rules of an increasingly hegemonic twenty-first-century CCP, at the same time as continuing to pursue the achievements of Chinese capitalism. This was not merely a motto; it was a real conundrum that seemed to him to be becoming more of a headache than ever. On one cold winter morning in 2009, he received a report that—although he didn't realize it at the time—was going to change the face of China.

This top-secret file (绝密的 or *Jiumide*) incriminated Bo Xilai, a major regime figure who was hoping to take the helm at the next party congress, scheduled for autumn 2012. A former trade minister, he was part of the fifth generation of leaders since Mao Zedong had brought the CCP to power in 1949, a Red Prince who wanted to turn China into a superpower, even daring to hope that the country would overtake the US economically by 2030. The affair was even more delicate given that Bo was the brother-in-law of Jia Chunwang, the Guoanbu minister from 1985 to 1997.

Taking his place in the family line, the ambitious and undeniably charismatic Bo Xilai was mayor of Chongqing, a megacity with 30 million inhabitants. He was the son of Bo Yibo, a veteran of Mao's Long March, who had been a minister under Deng Xiaoping. Bo Junior took after his father. He managed to unite the two Chinese communist traditions, having built up a considerable fortune during his city's rapid development and having profited from the inevitable cronyism that came with it, while still promoting neo-Maoist ideology, recalling the tormented period of the Cultural Revolution, when Mao dispatched hordes of Red Guards to attack party leaders deemed too reformist. As an adolescent, Bo Xilai had been a member of the most rabid faction of the Red Guards. By the twenty-first century, in the new, all-conquering China, people were beginning to wonder if he was dreaming of repeating the feat—of taking over the leadership of the party and the state, by force.

Prime Minister Wen Jiabao, fearing the irresistible rise of the Chongqing mayor, had ordered a Guoanbu investigation. The very security of the country was at stake, because Bo himself was circulating distasteful rumours about not only Wen, the head of the government, but also Hu Jintao, the outgoing president, and the man who was the favourite to inherit the presidency, the Shanghaian Xi Jinping.

The result was this explosive, hand-written document—to avoid leaving any trace on a hard drive—which Geng Huichang read avidly that morning, gulping down cup after cup of tea to hone his concentration. The dossier was filled with detail and drew attention to Bo Xilai's weakness. This was his wife, the international lawyer Gu Kailai.

Gu was an alluring, canny businesswoman, who took advantage of her numerous business trips to set up covert networks that she used to invest a good chunk of the couple's massive fortune on foreign financial markets. She might well have had her eye on the position of Chinese First Lady, but prudence dictated that she discreetly place her money aside abroad, in case of the collapse of Chinese communism. Like many members of the Chinese elite, she made sure that their son, Bo Guagua, received a perfect international education, at Oxford. A British businessman, Neil Heywood, both tutor and financial advisor to the young student, had suggested that the family make some investments in various tax havens, and purchase apartments in the United States and France. The Guoanbu investigation now confirmed that Heywood was rather more than a friend of the Bo family. He was also Gu's lover.

"We need some more details about this Mr Heywood," Geng Huichang demanded. Thanks to the sheer number of agents Chinese services were able to throw at a case, it took less than a month to complete this investigation. In early 2010, Qiu Jin, the deputy minister in charge of counterintelligence—the Guoanbu's 8th Bureau—stated categorically that, unsurprisingly, it turned out Heywood was an agent for MI6. Geng's response was, "How can we be sure?"

In principle, a high-profile professional like Geng Huichang did not need to know the source of such information. However, given the importance of the case, Qiu Jin revealed that the Guoanbu's source was Wang Lulu, Heywood's Chinese wife, who was only too happy to spy on her unfaithful husband and her rival Gu Kailai.

Once he had been made aware of these findings, Wen Jiabao had a trump card to block Bo Xilai's rise. Hu and his eventual successor Xi Jinping were rapidly informed.

But Wen was not the only one in on the secret. A Guoanbu official who was not part of Wen's entourage warned Bo Xilai that he and his wife were in the sights of the secret service, and that Neil Heywood was now believed to be an MI6 agent. This leak was about to set in motion an unexpected tragedy.

The assassination of Neil Heywood

The second act of this highly charged drama took place a year later in Chongqing. Alerted to the fact that the Guoanbu was monitoring their activities, Bo Xilai warned his wife Gu Kailai that she was too close to Neil Heywood. Did he know that she was being unfaithful? For this fairly liberated couple, that would have been considerably less serious than the revelation that her lover was an MI6 spy. In hindsight, it is likely that Bo's revelation panicked his wife, triggering the drama that drew to its climax exactly one year before the highly anticipated 18th Congress of the Chinese Communist Party, when a new leader was expected to emerge.

On 15 November 2011, Wang Lijun, local Gonganbu chief and deputy mayor of Chongqing (thus Bo Xilai's deputy), was woken in the middle of the night. The body of the British businessman Neil Heywood had just been discovered in a room at the Lucky Holiday Hotel. "Don't touch anything, I'm on my way!" Wang, originally from Mongolia, hurried to the hotel, about 10 kilometres away. It was palatial, a favourite of wealthy couples on romantic weekends. Above the cloud of pollution that hangs over Chongqing, the air in this mountainous suburb to the south was clean and pure.

Wang knew Heywood, having met him many times in the company of his boss. Wang had been helping Bo Xilai refine his image as a modern politician, despite the "neo-Maoist" veneer of his politics. The media-friendly "super-cop" was leading the fight against the mafia in Chongqing, which was understood to comprise not only criminal gangs but also troublesome political rivals. He had even had a number of them killed. One particular slogan summed up the situation: "In

Chongqing, we sing red" (songs from the time of Mao), "and we hit black" (hard against the local mafias).

The "incorruptible" Wang could expect eternal gratitude if he agreed to bring a speedy end to this highly embarrassing episode for Gu Kailai. The dossier was immediately closed: "Mr Heywood died of a heart attack after consuming too much alcohol," the express autopsy concluded three days later, on 18 November. Neither Wang Lulu, Heywood's Chinese widow, nor the British embassy disputed this version of events, preferring to keep a low profile in the case. But Deputy Mayor Wang was suspicious. He decided to take the precaution of having a vial of blood drawn for analysis before the corpse was cremated—this was how he discovered that Gu, in the great tradition of Chinese opera, had poisoned her English "friend" with cyanide.

Who was Heywood? An unscrupulous businessman? An over-demanding lover? A troublesome spy working for MI6? A clumsy blackmailer? Or all of the above?

On 28 January 2012, Wang told Bo Xilai what he had discovered, and how he planned to protect his wife. Questioned by her husband, Gu Kailai yelled at him that it was a setup. The next day, Bo called the police chief. "You bastard! You want to compromise my wife, my family, my career!" He spat at Wang, and then punched him. We know about this because it was witnessed by Wang's deputy, who testified later. Upset, humiliated and fearing for his life, Wang Lijun decided to spill the beans. But to whom?

To his bosses in Beijing? Impossible. The Gonganbu, to which Wang reported, had been headed between 2002 and 2007 by Zhou Yongkang, the regime number three, now Luo Gan's successor as head of the political-legal commission that coordinated the security and intelligence services. Zhou was one of Bo Xilai's principal allies, and he was hoping that Bo would be promoted to first secretary and Chinese president at the party congress coming in eleven months' time—or, failing that, to his own post of overall head of the secret services after his official retirement. As per tradition in the services, Zhou was then expected to retain significant influence behind the scenes. Wang perhaps considered going to the rival agency, the Guoanbu—but that tack would not be without its risks either.

Troop movements and Comrade Wang's defection

The Guoanbu boss, Geng Huichang, had earned a reputation for avoiding factional battles in order to maintain professional neutrality for his spies, under the aegis of the State Council, the central government, where prime minister Wen Jiabao held the reins of power. In the Neil Heywood assassination, he was playing Chinese chess—he liked to remain several moves ahead of his opponent. Clearing up the mystery of Neil Heywood would allow him to take Bo Xilai's "queen", Gu Kailai—a fatal blow. However, even more disturbing information was flowing into the Western Garden.

At the time of Heywood's death, unexpected and significant troop movements were taking place that had not been programmed by the general staff; these started in Sichuan province, whose capital, Chengdu, was the headquarters of the military region that dealt with insurgencies in Tibet. These PLA exercises, though unplanned, were understandable. Sichuan had formerly been under the leadership of Zhou Yongkang, and he had positioned representatives there before becoming head of security. Meanwhile, in Chongqing, which had also been under Sichuan's administration before gaining province status itself, Bo Xilai had organized military exercises for the 14 November. The timing was all the more remarkable as the manoeuvres took place not only at the time of the Heywood affair, but also while the president, Hu Jintao, was out of the country, attending an Asia-Pacific Economic Cooperation summit in Hawaii. Was this a show of force, or a dress rehearsal for a takeover in the near or distant future? Or was it a way to show that Bo Xilai was untouchable?

The question arose because General Xu Caihou, second in command at the Central Military Commission headed by Hu Jintao, was on the move. He seemed to be more than happy to be seen at Bo Xilai's side. Rather more discreetly, Zhou Yongkang also met with the two men, and other general officers. In the corridors of Zhongnanhai, the government compound in Beijing, there was talk of strange meetings of generals favourable to a joint leadership under Bo Xilai and Zhou Yongkang, primarily heads of the navy and 2nd Artillery—the body responsible for intercontinental strategic missiles capable of striking Taipei, Tokyo or Washington. Zhou, for the first time, was being identified as pulling the strings of all these different interests. This was how a specialist in CCP factional battles explained it to me: "The problem in China is that rumours have such consequences that they end up coming true!"[1]

Zhou Yongkang was thus a choice target for the Guoanbu, sword and shield of the party. But its boss, Geng Huichang, prefers to rely on facts, not rumours. As the case appeared to be picking up speed, he discreetly summoned Qiu Jin, his head of counterintelligence, to one of the Guoanbu's many hotel–restaurants, in search of more solid information.[2]

Meanwhile, in Chongqing, Wang Lijun increasingly feared for his life. As Chinese New Year approached, heralding the arrival of the Year of the Dragon—traditionally a year of great upheaval—he made the decision to defect. This dramatic development, in early 2012, had a global impact. Not since the end of the Cold War had a defection taken place in the open like this. The steps taken behind the scenes to avoid catastrophic consequences were similarly unprecedented.

On 6 February, Wang Lijun visited the US Consulate in Chengdu, having first sent an emissary to warn of an imminent courtesy call. Facing a dumbfounded consul, he asked for political asylum. In Chongqing and in Zhongnanhai, the leadership compound in Beijing, just as in the US embassy, there was universal consternation, not helped by the fact that Ambassador Gary Locke was preparing for the arrival of Secretary of State Hillary Clinton, visiting for a diplomatic summit. The embassy's CIA station, headed by Jean-Paul Ebe, was given the task of convincing Wang to surrender to the Chinese authorities, in order to avoid a serious diplomatic crisis between Beijing and Washington. Ebe trusted the Guoanbu for one simple reason: it was the only counterintelligence service that was not under Zhou Yongkang's control.

"This was what distinguished this highly professional service from the other, more political intelligence organs of the Central Committee." This was the view offered me by "Bill", a Hong Kong-based CIA analyst who followed the case day after day. "Since the 1980s, there has been a liaison mission between our agency and the Guoanbu, and in this case, our station chief was playing a very delicate game. Everyone, on the American side and the Chinese side, was delighted to see him resolve this thorny situation." Qiu Jin, the counterintelligence chief who had first investigated Bo Xilai and his wife, flew out to Sichuan. With the agreement of the CIA, his mission was to recover the very talkative Wang Lijun, ideally before he revealed too many secrets.

But the situation in Chengdu had degenerated. At the exact moment Wang entered the consulate, a Guoanbu official in Sichuan alerted Beijing, and Zhou Yongkang was informed. Convinced that the defector was about to hand over all his secrets to the CIA, he telephoned Bo Xilai: "We must recover Wang at all costs!"[3]

Bo easily convinced the mayor of Sichuan—previously run, we should remember, by Zhou Yongkang—to send special troops to surround the US consulate, claiming that there was a terrorist inside who was about to explode a bomb on diplomatic premises. The scene on Linshiguan Street, a stone's throw from Sichuan University, was quite surreal. Armed to the teeth, Chinese commandos stood facing the US marines responsible for protecting the building, while American and Chinese special agents tried to intervene and calm everybody down.

At last, Qiu Ji, deputy head of the Guoanbu, arrived. Trusting him, Wang surrendered. He was transferred to the Western Garden headquarters in Beijing, where he told all: how Gu Kailai had ordered the assassination of Neil Heywood; how Bo Xilai had covered it up, just as he had covered up innumerable shady deals; and how Bo had plotted with Zhou Yongkang to seize power and destabilize the man on track to become the next Chinese president: Xi Jinping. It was Zhou who had leaked information to the American press about Xi's hidden fortune. A French family friend of Bo Xilai, the architect Philippe Devillers, was arrested in Cambodia on Beijing's demand and extradited to the PRC; his testimony largely confirmed Wang's statement. Devillers was released, and remained silent, fearing reprisals.

The fall of Bo Xilai was now inevitable. In the spring of 2012, he was removed from his position as mayor of Chongqing and expelled from the CCP leadership. He did attempt one last coup in March, declaring a state of siege in his city, while in Beijing special forces were mobilized from the People's Armed Police (PAP), leading to several attacks on the elite troops of the 38th Army led by General Wu Zhenli, which had crushed the student protests on Tiananmen Square in 1989. This time, the troops had a different goal: to storm the government's "forbidden city". And who was the chief political commissioner of these PAP special forces? None other than Zhou Yongkang.

The legal consequences for Gu Kailai and Bo Xilai are well known. Betrayed by Wang, they were sentenced at large show trials. During the first, on 20 August 2012, Gu denounced her husband and even accused Zhou of being an evil genius. She was given a suspended death sentence, meaning life imprisonment. Her husband, tried the following year for "corruption, embezzlement and abuse of power", also managed to save his head by claiming his innocence and taking care not to reveal the leadership's secrets—a deal had obviously taken place.

In November 2012, during the CCP's 18th Congress, the road was opened for Xi Jinping to take over from Hu Jintao as the general secretary, chairman of the Central Military Commission, and ultimately president of the People's Republic of China. A new era had begun.

Except for one small detail—in the seaside resort of Beidaihe, where the select inner circle of the leadership meets at the end of every summer, the decision was made to target Zhou Yongkang. He was seen in public for the last time in October 2012, during a meeting of the Alumni Association of Beijing's China University of Petroleum, where he had begun his career half a century earlier.

From this point on, the Guoanbu investigators and those involved in the fight against corruption began looking closely into the case of "Big Tiger" Zhou. He had been the only person in the Politburo that spring to oppose the prosecution of the Bo Xilai faction. He had perhaps even been fomenting a slow-moving coup d'état when his own vertiginous rise had begun; it would have been the first in China since the 1960s.

Zhou Yongkang: from fisherman's son to king of oil

This is the dark tale of Zhou Yongkang, the son of a modest eel fisherman who became the head of China's biggest oil consortium, then number three in the CCP, overall head of the secret services and leader of the political police force of the world's largest autocratic state.

Born in December 1942 in Wuxi, Jiangsu province (north of Shanghai), he was given the name Zhou Yuangen. One day, however, his teacher asked him to change his name, on the grounds that another schoolboy shared not only his surname, Zhou, but also his first name. His father chose Yongkang (永 康), "eternal quietude"—which turned out to be somewhat less than prophetic.

In 1964, young Zhou joined the CCP. Two years later, he completed an engineering degree at the China University of Petroleum in Beijing, with a special focus on "geological research and exploration". He was a hard worker. Even during the Cultural Revolution, which saw every institution swept clean, technicians were still needed. At the height of the political storm, when different squadrons of Red Guards were battling it out, the young engineer was already drilling for oil. Mao died in 1976, by which time Zhou Yongkang had three years' experience of exploration in the largest oil fields belonging to the Chinese National Petroleum Corporation (CNPC), in Liaoning province. Over the next decade, his skills and expertise, as well as his legendary severity when it came to managing personnel, led him to take over as head of the CNPC, one of the most powerful Chinese companies at the time. His position saw him prospecting in Asia, Latin America and Africa—wherever he could establish energy development for this new China on the move. In Sudan, for example, people remember seeing Zhou himself working on CNPC oil wells.

During the Deng Xiaoping era in the 1980s, Zhou Yongkang switched to political management, both as minister of planning and natural resources, and as party secretary in Sichuan province. His rise was remarkable, but not unstoppable: at the turn of the century, following an investigation for corruption, the "Godfather of Sichuan" was sacked, at the instigation of National People's Congress deputies.

Given this career, and especially the unfortunate episode of his dismissal, no one expected that in 2002 he would stage a comeback and take on the unlikely public security portfolio. The Gonganbu's gigantic domain covered road traffic as well as urban security, the criminal police brigade, the hunting down of dissidents and management of the *laogai*. Comrade Zhou excelled in the role. His empire also extended in part to counterespionage, sometimes outside the country, thus enabling him to encroach on the Guoanbu's turf—to the great irritation of that ministry's head, Geng Huichang.

On top of all this, Zhou also oversaw the terrifying 610 Office, with its 15,000 police officers. We have seen how this office pursued the underground adherents of the Falun Gong movement across the globe. In addition, Zhou served as political commissar of the PAP, which numbered some 800,000 officers actively involved in crushing the separatist rebels of Tibet and Muslim Xinjiang. His political influence was clearly significant, because he joined the Politburo—the first security minister to have done so in a quarter of a century.

Zhou took this opportunity to develop a parallel diplomacy service, meeting with interior ministers from all around the world: Bakirdin Subanbekov from Kyrgyzstan, the Zimbabwean Kembo Mohadi, the Bavarian Günther Beckstein, and the future French president Nicolas Sarkozy. With them, he sought to devise the best way to fight corruption and organized crime. Soon, Zhou Yongkang could be seen as a special envoy at the side of his closest ally, the North Korean leader Kim Jong-il. How had Zhou, a fisherman's son, managed to reach this apex of global politics?

The answer is that he was a member of the Shanghai clique led by former president Jiang Zemin. Vice-President Zeng Qinghong (2003-8), Jiang's closest advisor, was general secretary of the famous political-legal commission that oversaw the secret services as well as the judicial administration. He imagined that, when it was time for him to retire, Zhou Yongkang would take over from him. Zhou was so close to this circle that he even married Jiang's niece. Agnès Andrésy, a Beijing-based French analyst who has studied Chinese power networks, explains this family imbroglio in her book:

> Zhou was married from the 1970s to Wang Shuhua, a former oil plant worker, with whom he had two sons. ... They divorced in 2000. A few months later, Wang died in an accident: on the outskirts of Beijing, not far from the Ming tombs, she was run over by an army car transporting two policemen. Zhou was strongly suspected of having ordered the assassination of his ex-wife (the policemen confessed a few months later), and his son Zhou Han subsequently cut all ties with him.
>
> In 2001, Zhou Yongkang, then head of the Sichuan branch of the party, invited Zeng Qinghong and Jiang Zemin for a vacation in Chengdu. Zhou told him that he was a widower, and Zeng decided

> to introduce him to Jia Xiaoye, Jiang Zemin's wife's niece, a reporter for the television channel CCTV, who was twenty-eight years younger than Zhou.[4]

Zhou, newly minister of the Gonganbu, married the young Jia. When Jiang Zemin stepped aside for his successor Hu Jintao, Hu's compromise with Jiang's Shanghai clique was to promote Zhou to the highest security rank in 2007. In other words, he was at last able to head the political-legal commission, and thus supervise the entire security community.

We're already familiar with the hugely important task he was assigned: the security of the Olympic Games, taking place the following year. At the same time, Hu announced the new leader of the Guoanbu, Geng Huichang, an economist specialized in US affairs, and a former director of the China Institute for Contemporary International Relations (CICIR). Geng, who lived more simply than most of his colleagues, was a reformer, in favour of strict respect for the law in the service of the state. He loathed the party bigwigs who grew rich at the expense of the people.

Hu had deliberately sought to strike a balance between the two men, who were far from having a good relationship, but were obliged to work together. To make the 2008 Olympic Games a triumph, it was vital to build a "united front" against the "imperialist enemy" and its spies, who were about to swarm into the country during the games. At the time, Zhou Yongkang said, "The international situation is so acute that antiterrorism is one of our major concerns." This was his reason for announcing the establishment of special units to protect the stadiums and sports teams.

As we saw in Chapter 12, there was a secret service delegation to al-Qaeda ahead of the games, warning the terrorist organization off trying anything at the Olympics via Uyghur separatists. A small number of the latter had become involved in jihad in Afghanistan, just as hundreds more would join the ranks of ISIS in the 2010s. From the authorities' point of view, this shift justified the intensification of population control and repression in Xinjiang.[5] Experts I spoke to in Asia in winter 2014 believed that Zhou had taken advantage of these initiatives at the time of the Olympics to form special units that might, in due course, play a role in a revolution in Zhongnanhai.

During 2011, the last year during which he was responsible for overseeing the security services, Zhou managed to obtain an increase in their budget, which meant that they now had greater financial resources than the PLA. He did this by raising the spectre of popular revolt in China, inspired by the Arab Spring. Incidentally, some funds earmarked for the "preservation of the social order" in China were later discovered to have disappeared into his personal kitty.

The Yellow Men's Band hunts the Tiger

The advantage of being located near the big children's playgrounds in Beijing is being surrounded by plenty of greenery. But the hundreds of party officials hard at work opposite the park, at 41 Pinganli Xi Dajie (West Peace Avenue), were not having much fun at all. This was the address of the Central Commission for Discipline Inspection (CCDI, *Jilu Jiancha Weiyuanhui*), which had recently spearheaded the launch of a major campaign of "crushing flies" and "hunting tigers", focusing on the corruption among cadres endemic all over the country. The Bo Xilai investigation had begun in April 2012. There was also a taskforce led by Liu Jianguo, a former deputy Gonganbu minister with close links to Xi Jinping, which was planning a major offensive against Zhou Yongkang.

As soon as he came to power at the end of 2012, Xi set up a new centre of gravity, in order both to purge the old Zhou Yongkang system and to retake control of the CCP, the PLA and the secret services. This was nothing like Jiang Zemin's Shanghai clique or the Communist Youth League's circle of elders around Hu Jintao.

Xi Jinping relied on another regional group to form his praetorian guard, which he deployed in his anti-corruption fight and against all those who had tried to keep him from coming to power. Both Chinese and Taiwanese experts interviewed by this author have mockingly called it "The Hebei Yellow Men's Band". This is a play on words, referring to the fact that the eastern province of Hebei, which encircles Beijing, is north of the Yellow River. In fact, the creation of this web of invisible relations (*touming guanxi*) dates back to 1982, when Xi Jinping was secretary to Defence Minister Geng Biao, formerly head of the CCP's International Liaison Department, and deeply implicated in political intelligence abroad. Xi later began his rise through the party in Zhengding, Shijiazhuang prefecture, in Hebei province.

The Hebei Band was made up of the following figures:

- Li Zhanshu, head of the CCP Central Committee's powerful Bureau of General Affairs and of the Office of State Secrets, who was in effect Xi Jinping's power behind the throne. His father, Li Zhengxiu, had been an intelligence officer under Mao in the 1940s.[6]
- Wang Jiarui, head of the party's International Liaison Department—the political intelligence service whose representatives in embassies abroad, including in London, were responsible for coordinating intelligence research.
- Wang Jianping, the new commander of the PAP.
- Madame Sun Chunlan, appointed in early 2015 to run the United Front Work Department (the other political intelligence service still responsible for trying to engage with Chinese and Taiwanese citizens living abroad).
- Liu Jianguo, facilitator of the CCDI anti-corruption taskforce.
- Wang Shaojun, appointed head of the Central Guards in 2015, responsible for protecting ministers and senior party leaders.

But the most notable member of this dream team was another Hebei native already familiar to us: none other than Geng Huichang. The head of the Guoanbu rallied to Xi Jinping, and by early 2013 he had become the figurehead of an invisible club brought together to precipitate the fall of Zhou Yongkang, having already played a central role in Bo Xilai's demise.

Nonetheless, before launching his final deathblow, Xi Jinping went to Shanghai to pay his respects to Jiang Zemin, by now an old man. He addressed his predecessor roughly along the following lines: "If Zhou Yongkang and his acolytes are prosecuted, there will be no need to go further in the fight against corruption." The implication of this was that the Shanghai clique would be spared, and neither Jiang nor his vice-president Zeng Qinghong would be implicated—even if they had been in any way involved in the conspiracy hatched against Xi. Jiang Zemin consented.

Some 200 men from the CCDI taskforce organized the rout and arrested Zhou Yongkang, who was put under house arrest—or perhaps was locked in a gilded cage. During my research for this book, I discovered that during 2014 he spent most of his time in Beijing, imprisoned within the red lacquered ramparts of Zhongnanhai. There are luxury houses there that no one leaves, except to be taken to an austere detention centre that is part of the "bamboo gulag". With a swimming pool, tennis court, Taoist garden, and breathtaking view of the lake, it is a stylish residence for a fallen dignitary. Zhou's butlers were commandos from the CCP Central Guard, and the former party number three—once overlord of the security services and, according to *Forbes* magazine, the twenty-ninth richest person in the world—was treated humanely, if somewhat strictly.

The only people to visit him were anti-corruption detectives from the party and members of his family during police interrogations. And, of course CIA agents sometimes filmed him, stooped under the burden of his troubles, as he walked through the meandering Zhongnanhai gardens, not far from the Guards Office and the lavish "Chrysanthemum-Scented Pavilion".

For eighteen months, the CCDI worked to untangle the multiple networks created by Zhou Yongkang over the past thirty years—not only those established by the security services, but also an equal number of others set up with the oil money he had earned over a long period. Naturally, he had placed members of his family and his inner circle of friends in a variety of state-owned businesses. Similarly, he had played an important role in the provinces: in his childhood home Jiangsu, where his brothers still lived—one, who was suffering from cancer, had died when the Guoanbu agents turned up to arrest him; in Liaoning, where he had worked in the oil business; in Sichuan, where he had led the party; and in Beijing, where he had been first a minister and then the coordinator of the security services.

A team of investigators, headed by Liu Jianguo, had arrested over 300 people who were now waiting to be judged as accomplices of China's most famous prisoner. The most high-profile were Guo Yongxiang, Zhou's former aide-de-camp and ex-deputy governor of Sichuan; Li Chuncheng, deputy general secretary of the Sichuan branch of the CCP; Liang Ke, former head of the Beijing Guoanbu bureau (presumably the mole who had alerted Bo Xilai that he was being investigated); and Shen Dingcheng, Zhou Yongkang's former private secretary, responsible for coordination with the secret services—at the time of his arrest, he was vice-president of PetroChina International. Among the other leading figures were a dozen deputy ministers; Jiang Jiemin, former president of CNPC and its subsidiary PetroChina (listed on the stock market since 2000); and the former vice-governor of Hainan Island, a major Chinese tourist destination.

The most interesting character within these hybrid networks was Li Dongsheng, former deputy Gonganbu minister and one of the 610 Office's experts at tracking down Falun Gong adherents. After becoming deputy director of the CCTV state television channel, Li had made a name for himself by interviewing his former boss Zhou, the young female journalists forced to become Zhou's mistresses, and various call girls and chambermaids who worked at the hotels where he stayed during his tours of the provinces. This led to accusations of "abuse of power for sexual favours", which were among the charges against Zhou in December 2014.

Li Dongsheng was also close to a young CCTV reporter, Jia Xiaoye: Jiang Zemin's niece who had become Zhou Yongkang's wife, and who now also found herself in prison for multiple financial malpractices, and possibly even complicity in the murder—disguised as a traffic accident—of Wang Shuhua, Zhou's first wife. One of their sons, Zhou Bin—who had remained close to his father—was also accused of corruption, along with his wife, Huang Wan.

The anti-corruption taskforce searched the homes of many hundreds of people throughout the country, seizing some 90 billion yuan (around $13 billion) belonging to Zhou, his family, friends and associates. Astronomical sums were made public via the Hong Kong media. Xi Jinping was showing the "little people" that the fight against corruption was having an impact at the highest levels of society. However, according to the scarce information that filtered through during the winter of 2014–15, Zhou Yongkang refused to cooperate with CCDI accountants and officials during his interrogations, declaring, "I am the victim of persecution, of a battle between factions, of a political conspiracy."

Analysis of the now-frozen Zhou family bank accounts shows that 37 billion yuan remain, on top of 51 billion yuan in shares, the bonds seized in the family's sumptuous homes in Beijing, Shanghai, Tianjin,

Chengdu and elsewhere—not to mention collections of artworks, sixty luxury sports cars, and massive quantities of cash in foreign currencies and gold ingots. Investigators even discovered, during a 2014 house search of someone suspected of being part of Zhou's gang, a large, solid-gold statue of Chairman Mao.

The army purged, the secret services remodelled

The PLA did not escape scrutiny in Xi's anti-corruption offensive. Several heads rolled over the course of 2014, starting with General Xu Caihou, former deputy leader of the powerful Central Military Commission. Not only was the campaign now targeting senior members of the Hu regime, but some, like Xu, were suspected of having participated with Bo Xilai and Zhou Yongkang in a conspiracy to destabilize Xi Jinping during his ascent to power. Xu was arrested, but fell ill and died on 15 March 2015.

Still others were convicted of aggravated corruption, for instance of selling ranks, decorations and promotions. Among them was General Guo Boxiong, another leader of the Central Military Commission; the captains of the 2nd Artillery, responsible for intercontinental nuclear missiles; and naval bosses including Admiral Ma Faxiang, the navy political commissar who committed suicide in September 2014 after being interrogated by CCDI investigators, throwing himself from the top of the PLA headquarters building in Beijing.

Others swore allegiance in March 2014 to the new president, after he summoned officers to remind them that "the party commands the gun", as Mao used to say. In the wake of this, eighteen army chiefs and heads of military regions publicly announced their support of Xi Jinping. Many were preparing for early retirement. Of course, the anti-corruption campaign grew well beyond the Bo Xilai–Zhou Yongkang affair. But the ghost of this conspiracy remained the driving force behind the elimination of corrupt cadres as well as those seen as political nuisances. In 2014, according to official figures, 72,000 cadres from the PLA and the Ministry of Defence—sixty of whom had the rank of minister—and sixteen generals were dismissed and charged with corruption. For perspective, the army had a total of 2 million soldiers in active service.

"By the winter of 2014–15, Xi Jinping had completed the great purge," Arthur Ding, director of the Institute of International Research of Taipei, told me. "President Xi managed to break up Jiang Zemin's 'Shanghai clique', to which Zhou Yongkang belonged, as well as dismissing several military leaders who were close to [Zhou], including Xu Caihou and Guo Boxiong. He was sending a clear message to all the 50-year-old officers whom he had placed in key positions, and to the leaders of the principal ministries: in our reforms, we are preserving the middle managers, so long as they share our convictions. Basically, the same old tradition: slit the chicken's throat to terrorize the monkey."

Professor Ding, who had a broad and mischievous smile on his face for the entire duration of our conversation, is without a doubt one of the connoisseurs of the secret world of Chinese politics. He had first walked into the building of National Chengchi University in the Taipei hills thirty years ago, during my first visit there in 1986, when I was researching the first biography of Kang Sheng.[7] He was showing his old-fashioned side that day, with a teapot bigger than his computer sitting in the middle of a pile of documents. I wondered how he could be so certain. He had a thousand sources in his small office, both from mainland China and from nationalist Taiwan. I had to take my hat off to him when, a week after our meeting, an unforeseen development confirmed every detail of the analysis he had shared with me.

Zhou in Madame Mao's cell

On 5 December 2014, the heads of the CCDI came to inform Zhou Yongkang, still in his gilded cage, of the charges he would be answering in court in 2015: "The investigation is over. You can no longer be called 'comrade', now that you have been expelled from the party and charged with the following crimes: embezzlement in collusion with your family, serious infringements of good governance and self-discipline, nepotism, bribery, innumerable adulterous liaisons, the abuse of power to obtain sexual favours—all things which have damaged our reputation. And even more serious charges of disclosing party and state secrets, as in treason."

That same evening, the Xinhua News Agency broadcast the extraordinary news. This was the first time since the 1970s and the end of the Cultural Revolution that a leader of China's supreme assembly, the Politburo Standing Committee, had been accused of such crimes.

A few days later, the journalist Eric Meyer, who has long been writing about the developments in Chinese power for his newsletter *Le vent de la Chine*, wrote, "Now a party taboo has been broken: according to an unspoken rule, which up until now has been universally respected, once a party cadre reached the rank of deputy minister (a much lower rank than that held by Zhou), he became untouchable. But now Zhou faces the death penalty—which may or may not be suspended. More than anything, his downfall shatters the conservatives' 'steel square', which has frozen political reform in China for the last twenty years. Indeed, since the announcement of Zhou's indictment and expulsion from the party, all his former allies have rushed to rally around Xi Jinping and to show submission in the name of 'party unity'."

On the day he was formally charged, Zhou Yongkang was transferred to Qincheng Prison, high on a hill to the north of Beijing, where Pu Yi, the last emperor of China, had been incarcerated in the 1950s, and where Jiang Qing, the widow of Chairman Mao, had been imprisoned in 1976 for an attempted coup. The cell she had occupied, number 1, now housed Zhou. The wolfish grin of the man once known as the "great tiger" was frozen. Geng Huichang, his rival as head of the "other" service (the Guoanbu), must have been rubbing his hands in glee.

But the "shadow battle" against Zhou Yongkang did not leave the Guoanbu entirely unscathed. Internal investigations led to the dismissal of Qiu Jin, the counterintelligence chief, on the grounds that he had been sent to recover Wang Lijun from the US consulate—which had also in itself constituted an inappropriate politicization of the 8th Bureau, responsible for counterespionage. Liang Ke, the head of the local Guoanbu office in Beijing, was also fired, accused of being Bo Xilai's mole in the service and of having accepted bribes from Zhou Yongkang. The arrest of his collaborators, all cadres in the Beijing office, gives an idea of the extent of the purge carried out within the Guoanbu itself.

During that winter, the boss Geng Huichang was planning a restructuring of the service. He poached hundreds of special agents, originally recruited by Zhou Yongkang, from the Gonganbu's 1st Department, and had them retrained in counterintelligence in a more professional and less ideological way. In 2014 and 2015, several of Geng's deputies, including the heads of counterintelligence, were dismissed, including Qiu Jin, who was alleged to have failed to properly control Liang Ke. In autumn 2014, Ma Jian, Qiu Jin's successor, was removed from office upon his return from Pakistan, where he had been engaged in bilateral exchanges with the ISI, aimed at ending the conflict in Afghanistan and dealing with the fight against ISIS. The grounds invoked for Ma's dismissal were blatant corruption.[8] The case of the deputy minister Lu Zhongwei was unusual, because while he was also dismissed, the reason given was the claim that his secretary had been recruited by the CIA (see Chapter 14).

Dysfunction within his own ministry did not stop Geng, the figurehead of the "Hebei Yellow Men's Band", from being named secretary general of the new National Security Committee, modelled on the US National Security Council. "In two years, Xi Jinping has managed to cumulate all the powers," Andrew Yang, former Taiwanese deputy minister of defence, told me at the end of 2014. His think-tank, the Chinese Council of Advanced Policy Studies, analyzes the balance of power between security and defence. By the time we spoke, Xi was chairing no fewer than eighteen taskforces, as well as several expert commissions, including on Taiwan. "He even shaped the National Security Committee, which coordinates all the security services. Its function is to identify the central issues to be addressed by intelligence. Its prerogatives are mixed with those of the services, but this time it's Xi Jinping personally directing all the different domains." No wonder the American media was already announcing that Xi Jinping might become the "Chinese man of the century", as Mao Zedong and Deng Xiaoping had been before him.

There was a stunning epilogue to this rebalancing of power: on 6 December 2014, with the announcement in the media of Zhou Yongkang's expulsion from the CCP and the appalling crimes of which he was accused, the *People's Daily* published an opinion piece by Geng Huichang, which seemed to have nothing to do with the story of the day—though it had finally broken thanks to him. In a highly political article, the Guoanbu chief explained why China had to undergo profound reform—under President Xi Jinping, it was implied—and become a society that respected rule of law, free of ideological constraints, one that guaranteed the independence of the legal system and permitted lawyers to freely defend its citizens. It was an extremely unexpected article to have come from the head of the powerful Guoanbu. But it was no doubt a harbinger of things to come.

This was not necessarily a reform that would benefit Zhou Yongkang, imprisoned in the Beijing hills in Madame Mao's old cell. In the back alleys where the wildest of rumours run rife, as well as in the palaces he used to frequent, people were saying that Zhou was bound to be condemned to death—quite possibly without any chance of a reprieve.

The new Gang of Four

Given the extraordinary conflict that was simmering in Beijing, it is easy enough to see why Xi Jinping, once his power was strengthened, intended to take control of the newly reorganized intelligence community, with the help of his Hebei comrades.

The new president had suffered a great deal from Kang Sheng's abuses in the 1960s, and still held deep feelings of bitterness and profound mistrust towards the omnipotent heads of the security and intelligence services. Xi was duly briefed on this issue by Yu Zhensheng, number four in the Politburo and responsible for its reform, who was also the brother of Yu Zhensan, the Guoanbu agent who defected to the CIA and was behind the arrests of Larry Wu Tai Chin and Bernard Boursicot. As we have seen, Xi had been ruthless in his handling of Bo Xilai, who was accused not only of corruption while mayor of Chongqing, but also for having attempted a coup with Zhou Yongkang.

New strategic directions were also emerging from an international perspective. China no longer wanted to be the world's factory, but its bank. Hence the development of large financial and economic intelligence structures around the creation of the Asian Infrastructure Investment Bank, as well as the deepening of economic ties with Europe and, via Central Asia, the development of the "new Silk Road", both terrestrial and maritime, in the One Belt One Road initiative. All this required a constant regeneration of orientation and

MO for the Guoanbu, the PLA2 and the PLA3 in charge of cyberwarfare, which was expanding rapidly. In March 2015, for example, Jason Pan, a specialist in secret service investigations for the *Taipei Times*, identified no fewer than twelve new offices within the PLA3, specifically working on the online war.[9]

At the beginning of his tenure as head of state, party leader and chairman of the very important Central Military Commission, Xi Jinping took some major steps in the field of security. He downgraded, for example, the post of head of the political-legal commission, held by Meng Jianzhu, the ex-head of Gonganbu and Zhou Yongkang's former deputy. For the first time in the history of the CCP, this position no longer came with a seat on the Politburo Standing Committee.

Similarly, at the end of 2013, Xi created a National Security Committee in the image of the US National Security Council, with the difference that he himself was its president. Senior members of the committee—whose relative effectiveness it is too early to judge—were several pivotal figures of this new generation, members of Xi's Hebei Band. These included the general secretary—none other than the Guoanbu head Geng Huichang—and Li Zhanshu, head of the Office of State Secrets and Xi Jinping's power behind the throne. These were the faithful, the men who had helped the president develop his anti-corruption campaign and the renewed crackdown on dissidents. In the spring of 2015, new national security laws were put into place, including one major new component: an anti-espionage law (*fan jiandie fa*), which they masterminded together.

Once again we saw the heads of services on the frontline of the secret war, having crushed the so-called "New Gang of Four" (*Xin Xirenbang*): Ling Jihua (former director of the CCP General Office, in charge of internal party security), General Xu Caihou, Bo Xilai, and the most formidable of these "tigers", Zhou Yongkang.

However, despite the services' key role in bringing Xi to power and consolidating his position, Xi went on to centralize all the power into his hands and those of his inner circle. In October 2017, just after the CCP's 19th Congress, Xi Jinping was able to replace the head of the Guoanbu, perform an internal purge in the ministry, and simultaneously carry out a reorganization of the PLA and a remodelling of its intelligence services. It was quite some programme.

14

XI'S MOLE HUNT AND THE BIRTH OF THE STRATEGIC SUPPORT FORCE

On 20 May 2017, *The New York Times* caused a sensation with the publication of an explosive investigation into the CIA, which had reportedly "lost" dozens of Chinese sources, either volunteers or paid informants, who'd been furnishing valuable intelligence about the PRC since 2010. These sources, having been manipulated by the CIA, had now been arrested by Chinese counterintelligence and tried on camera, charged with spying for the "imperialist services". Their fortunes varied; most were handed sentences of varying weight, depending on whether they agreed to collaborate during interrogation or, preferably, to return to spying, this time feeding the Americans false intelligence. Some were executed. *The New York Times* described a cadre shot in cold blood in front of his colleagues.

In its assessment of the roots and consequences of this disaster, the CIA tried to get to the bottom of how its agents and informers in the enemy camp had come to be identified in such large numbers. Had they been badly managed by their handling officers, or were some of their Chinese recruits in fact double agents, who had managed to pull the wool over the Americans' eyes by pretending to work for the US while really being in the pay of the Chinese services? Had their communications been intercepted? Were coded instructions embedded in documents attached to emails?

Tactical blunders were also cited, including the possibility that CIA case officers had made the mistake of meeting their informants in unsecured locations, for example hotels studded with hidden microphones, such as the Hilton in Beijing, near the huge US embassy on An Jia Lu Street. However, the report of former CIA analyst Gregary Levin, now regional security officer in the US embassy, suggests that this hypothesis is unlikely. This document, entitled *Crime and Safety Report* and still accessible in 2018 via the US embassy website, clearly warns American businesspeople gallivanting in China:

> All visitors should be aware that they have no expectation of privacy in public or private locations. All means of communication, including telephones, mobile phones, faxes, emails, and text messages, are likely monitored.
>
> There are regular reports of the human and technical monitoring of American businesspeople and visiting U.S. citizens. Activities and conversations in hotels, offices, cars, and taxis may be monitored onsite or remotely. Overt placement of microphones and video cameras are common in taxis. All personal possessions in hotel rooms, residences, and offices may be accessed without the occupants' consent/knowledge. Elevators and public areas of housing compounds are under continuous surveillance. Business travelers should be particularly mindful that trade secrets, negotiating positions, and other business sensitive information may be shared with Chinese counterparts, competitors, and regulatory/legal entities.
>
> The areas around U.S. and other foreign diplomatic facilities and residences are under overt physical and video surveillance; dozens of security personnel are posted outside of facilities and around residences, while video cameras are visible throughout the diplomatic offices and residential neighborhoods of Beijing. Embassy employees are warned not to discuss sensitive information in their homes, vehicles, or offices, and members of the private sector should take precautions to safeguard sensitive personal and/or proprietary information. In 2016, U.S. Embassy employees reported an increase in the tampering of locks on the front door of their residences, suggesting forced entry. In some cases, the tampering led to door locks that no longer operated as intended.
>
> The Chinese government has publicly declared that it regularly monitors private email and internet browsing through cooperation with the

> limited number of internet service providers (ISPs) and wireless providers in China. Wireless access in major metropolitan areas is becoming more common. As a result, Chinese authorities can more easily access official and personal computers. U.S. Embassy employees have reported seeing unknown computers and devices accessing their home networks. These intrusions likely required advanced computer knowledge and network password hacking to enable such a connection.
>
> Many popular services and websites (Google, Twitter, Facebook) are blocked.

Holden Triplett, the FBI attaché at the US embassy in Beijing, officially in charge of liaison with the Chinese security services, sounded the same warning.

Back at CIA headquarters in Langley, Virginia, they feared the worst, and with good reason. Though the focus in recent years had been on PLA hackers and cyber-warfare, human intelligence had continued to be vital. But, as evidenced by the China file bequeathed by Paul Brennan, the outgoing CIA director, to his successor Mike Pompeo in early 2017, this had been gravely compromised.[1] The CIA's internal counterintelligence service and the FBI set up a multidisciplinary team, located for security reasons in another part of Virginia. Its purpose was to conduct a "retrospective analysis", called Operation Honey Badger, to try and work out what had led to this serious intelligence failure. The possibility that there were traitors within the US services could not be ruled out.

Meanwhile, the Chinese media applauded what they saw as an homage of vice to virtue: the US "imperialist" services finally recognizing the superiority of their Chinese opponent. What they conveniently ignored was the fact that the disaster had been brought to light because American journalists, unlike them, enjoyed freedom from state intervention.

This game of smoke and mirrors was highly reminiscent of that between the KGB and the CIA at the height of the Cold War. The Chinese intelligence community was working hard at tracking down traitors both within and without the state apparatus, which is what had led to the loss of so many of the CIA's sources.

This Chinese mole hunt had begun under Hu Jintao in 2008. On taking over in 2012, Xi Jinping had set up a taskforce, which he himself chaired, to "strengthen national security". In 2017, the counter-intelligence services launched a vast campaign to raise awareness of the problem of foreign espionage, with dedicated websites, animations explaining how to spot a spy, and TV soap operas glorifying the heroes of this "special work" (*tewu gongzuo*). It was journalists, academics, and Chinese-American and Taiwanese businesspeople who were to bear the brunt of the campaign. In April 2016, the Guoanbu promised a reward of up to $77,000 to any citizen who helped to uncover "a lead that played a decisive role in enabling the prevention or shut-down of spying activity."

None of the names of the lost CIA agents were published by *The New York Times* in 2017. However, it was clear from the focus of the Chinese investigation that moles had been recruited from the highest levels of diplomacy and government, and even in some cases the Chinese secret services. The Guoanbu was at the heart of this crisis, for two reasons. Firstly, a substantial number of its top-level managers and operatives had been recruited by foreign secret services; secondly, its internal counterintelligence service had been tasked with detecting "double agents" within either the Guoanbu or other parts of the state apparatus.

Although the CIA had probably lost many informants, it had not been responsible for recruiting all these agents. Recruitment took place as little as possible within China itself, despite the fact that the main CIA station was located in Beijing. CIA satellites, located under diplomatic cover in consulates in Guangzhou, Chengdu, Shanghai, Shenyang and Wuhan, were under permanent surveillance. The station chief in Beijing was officially "accredited" through his counterpart at the Guoanbu office in Beijing, Li Dong, and his bosses at the East Gardens headquarters. This was part of the limited cooperation dating back to the days when the Chinese and Americans had worked together against the Soviets in Afghanistan.

Because of this scrutiny, the CIA resorted to using operatives who were entirely clandestine and NOC (under "non-official cover"), and who sometimes made contact with their agents. Most of their recruits were Chinese—diplomats, scientists and special agents—from within China itself. Other foreign services allied with the CIA helped to recruit these agents, whom they then either "shared" or passed on to the Americans, who had the largest budgetary and logistical capacity, not least when it came to offering these agents new homes if they decided to defect. These foreign services were primarily the Japanese, Taiwanese and South Korean, as well as British MI6 and the German BND, both of which had a strong presence in Singapore and Hong Kong.

Moles at the top of the Guoanbu

An extraordinary episode took place in Hong Kong, beginning in 2010, when Li Hui, secretary of one of the Guoanbu's deputy ministers, fell under the spell of a Chinese-American woman while visiting the semi-democratic city, still swarming with foreign secret agents. Li, a 40-year-old graduate from Beijing University and a specialist in the English-speaking world, agreed to work for the CIA. Thanks to information he provided, the FBI arrested several Chinese spies in the United States.[2] Now on the alert, the Guoanbu unmasked Li in March 2011, and realized that he had handed over many secrets about its internal workings. But meanwhile he had also recruited other colleagues, including his boss, the deputy minister Lu Zhongwei. This Shanghai native, an expert in the secret economic war being conducted in Japan and the rest of East Asia, was sacked in June 2012, if not for treason then for the neglect that had allowed Li to turn.

This was a serious blow for the Guoanbu boss, Geng Huichang, himself a specialist in US affairs, whose career rise had gone without a hitch since his 2007 appointment to oversee the security of the Olympic Games. Geng was an unusual figure in the services, having chaired the well-known CICIR think-tank, home to hundreds of researchers and analysts who travel the world attending international symposia. They constitute, of course, the Guoanbu's 11th Bureau, and this was where Geng had recruited his friend Lu Zhongwei, a specialist in North-East Asia and specifically Japan, who was named head of the CICIR himself in 2000.

At this point, it is worth adding an important detail to Geng Huichang's biography. Critics in Beijing have tended to claim that, until he became first deputy minister and then minister of state security, he had not done anything particularly impressive. There are indeed several notable lacunae in his CV. But the facts yet to be revealed, though the CIA is well aware of them, challenge the legend propagated by the Chinese: before becoming deputy minister in 1998, Geng, like his colleague Cai Ximin (head of the Guoanbu in Shanghai), disappeared for several years. According to some sources, the two men were working as undercover officers in various foreign countries, notably in the United States, conducting a series of complex and successful operations.

This explains why Geng could not be dismissed, even after the identification of a succession of traitors that made the very foundations of the Guoanbu tremble. The case of his friend Lu Zhongwei was not the only one to strike at the very top level of the ministry. As we already know, a few months later it was the turn of the Guoanbu's number two, Qiu Jin, the deputy minister responsible for counterintelligence. He was accused of being a double agent—*shuang mian jiandie*, literally a two-faced spy. Then, in late 2014, Liang Ke, head of the Beijing office, was arrested along with dozens of his colleagues. He was accused not only of having worked for foreign services but also, by implication, of having participated in the attempted coup led by Bo Xilai and Zhou Yongkang by wiretapping the new president, Xi Jinping.

From the outside, with Qiu's replacement as deputy minister by another senior figure in counterintelligence, Ma Jian, who oversaw operations in North America, everything appeared to be back to normal. A Guoanbu cadre for thirty years, Ma was said to be so effective that he could even have replaced Geng, who was soon due for retirement. In early winter 2014, Ma made a tour of China's allies among foreign services, including Pakistan's ISI. But in January 2015 he suffered a surprising change of fortune: he was imprisoned for corruption and spying. The prosecution claimed that he had received funds from a Chinese businessman who had fled to the United States in October 2014—Ling Wancheng, brother of Ling Jihua, the principal private secretary of former president Hu Jintao. The Chinese special services were determined to do whatever it took to bring Ling back to China.

Obviously, the hunt for moles continued with unabated frenzy on both the Chinese and the American side. Ma was replaced by Su

Deliang, political commissar and deputy minister of the Guoanbu.[3] In April 2016, Beijing uploaded a film to YouTube in which Ma Jian confessed, explaining that he needed a lot of money to maintain his six mistresses! Though he made no mention of his job as a spymaster, no one in the world of international intelligence was deceived by this footage. Ma was jailed for life in December 2018.

Ma Jian had been put through the wringer by the Central Commission for Discipline Inspection (CCDI), the legal arm of the "tiger hunt" against corruption, whose head, Wang Qishan, was both Xi Jinping's closest advisor and his vice-president from the nineteenth party congress in October 2017. As far back as December 2014, a Taiwanese counterintelligence specialist told me: "The mainland Chinese are using the front of the fight against corruption to perform a purge which is really about their hunt for moles. In this case, the CIA could not have known the real reason for the dismissal of one of its agents." So was this a tiger hunt, or a mole hunt?

The shake-up within the Guoanbu was considerable, but other sectors of government had also been infiltrated. Witness the case of Ambassador Ma Jisheng, who presented his credentials to Icelandic president Ólafur Ragnar Grimsson on 12 December 2012. The following month he had returned to China with his wife, Zhong Yue, to celebrate the Chinese New Year—it was the Year of the Snake. As soon as they got off the plane, they had been arrested by the Guoanbu and taken to a secret prison for interrogation. A colleague, another diplomat, had been arrested in Japan, where he had served with Ma—it turned out that the ambassador had first been recruited by the Naicho, the intelligence service that reports directly to the Japanese prime minister, during his posting as embassy advisor in Tokyo, from 2004 to 2008.

During that period, Ma Jisheng had narrowly avoided a tricky situation when one of the first secretaries of the embassy, Wang Qingqian—in fact a military intelligence colonel under diplomatic cover—was unmasked and sentenced to death for spying. A similar situation had emerged in Seoul, where the Chinese ambassador Li Bin was identified as an American agent. Non-diplomatic figures had also been accused of spying for the United States. In November 2008, a biochemist called Wo Weihan, whose daughters lived in

Austria, had been arrested on spying charges by the Guoanbu, condemned to death and executed in Beijing. In 2014, the CCTV reporter Rui Chenggang was targeted. Interrogated about his work for the CIA, he was also charged with corruption, for which he received a six-year prison sentence.

It seems clear that, under Hu Jintao, the secret services had been seeking to test the Obama administration. The secret war between China and the US certainly intensified during Obama's two terms as president, and even more so after Xi Jinping came to power in 2012. During this period, Ma Jisheng was caught up in this growing tussle, used first by both the Naicho and the CIA, and later, during his posting to Iceland, by the CIA alone.

The Chinese espionage offensive was ramping up, as evidenced by the large number of spy networks dismantled in the United States and the cyber-attacks led by the PLA3, against well-chosen targets such as the US Office of Personnel Management—the hacking of which in 2015 forced the CIA to withdraw several of its officials from its embassy in Beijing. This further weakened the agency's manpower, already greatly affected during this decade by the loss of so many of its sources. By summer 2017, after *The New York Times* broke that story, some experts were wondering if the CIA was not in fact embarking on a new strategy in its psychological warfare tactics, leaking information about its woes to the media.

This was clearly, for the CIA, a terrible series of unfortunate events. However, it was also extremely damaging to the Guoanbu's credibility, its reputation damaged not only by this mole hunt, but also by a series of corruption cases that had done great harm to the entire Chinese administration. The result was that the Guoanbu's role in counterintelligence (via its 8th Bureau) was restricted, only resuming in early 2018. Its rival ministry, the Gonganbu, now run by Guo Shengkun, saw its own counterintelligence department grow, along with its cyber-security service, which was distinct from that of the PLA.

This renewal of counterintelligence activity, alongside anti-corruption tracking abroad, indicated the important, albeit slightly forgotten, role of the Gonganbu's 1st Bureau, which had increased its responsibilities in the fight for national security and counterintelligence since 2012, as had been the case at the founding of the PRC sixty years earlier. This was the internal security bureau, whose full title was *Gonganbu Guonei Anquan Baoweiju*—Guoba for short. It was now as active as the Guoanbu when it came to interventions abroad.

This provoked a mini-scandal soon after Donald Trump's election in autumn 2016, when the FBI arrested Sun Lijun, head of the Guobao, who had the rank of a deputy minister. He and his deputy had flown to the US to try and obtain the extradition of Guo Wengui, who Beijing claimed was a corrupt billionaire. The FBI seized their computers and mobile phones before putting the "Pandas" (as the service's agents were called) on the first plane back to China.

Meanwhile, the FBI was continuing its investigation of the Chinese infiltration of the CIA. Within the next six months, two CIA operatives, Kevin Mallory and Jerry Chun Shing Lee—stationed in Beijing until 2007—were charged with espionage. Other Western services had not been immune to the Chinese intrusion. In 2015, after the NSA contractor Edward Snowden's defection, some of MI6's agents in China narrowly avoided having their cover blown—which suggested that the Chinese and Russians had intercepted communications from the American NSA.[4] In May 2018, it was revealed in France that two former DGSE operatives, Henri Manioc and Pierre-Marie Winterat, had been arrested and accused of spying for a foreign power—China—in December 2017.

The situation of Colonel Henri Manioc was unusual because he was a former DGSE chief of station under diplomatic cover at the French embassy in Beijing. He had defected in 1998 after having fallen in love with a Chinese woman he later married, who worked for the PSA car company in China. He went on to open a restaurant on Hainan Island, at which point Su Deliang was sent to monitor his handling. Su, formerly head of the Guoanbu in Shanghai—from where operations against the French and British were conducted—went on to be named overall head of the Guoanbu's counterintelligence service (the 8th Bureau).

Manioc later returned to France and set up a consulting firm with offices in Paris and London. He was convinced that the DGSE, after having questioned him, had decided to pardon his defection, since he had not revealed any key secrets to the Chinese. Nevertheless, in the intelligence community his actions were considered a betrayal. It was not until Emmanuel Macron's election as president in 2017 and the appointment of a new DGSE director that the affair resurfaced, and with it an understanding of the extent of the attacks carried out by the Guoanbu against the allied British, French and American services.

Manioc's case, if it makes it to trial in 2019–20, will be the first of its kind since the Boursicot case of the 1980s. It should also bring to light the secrets passed to the Guoanbu by the two retired DGSE agents, not least concerning the internal workings of the French counterintelligence service.

Chen Wenqing and the purging of the Guoanbu

After using the Guoanbu to overthrow Zhou Yongkang's network, Xi Jinping decided to remodel the service yet again, both purging it and curbing its powers. The main leaders around Geng Huichang were fired or arrested and charged with cooperating with foreign intelligence services.

In 2016 the command of the service was split between Geng Huichang, who was due for retirement, and a political commissioner called Chen Wenqing, who was preparing to take over as head of state security. At the time of his appointment in November 2016, the media drew attention to the fact that he had come to the job from the CCDI, which had just led the "tiger hunt" against corruption to target the faction around Zhou Yongkang, under whom he had in fact once served.

However, Chen had already worked for the Guoanbu, after he gained a law degree in 1983 from the Southwest University of Political Science and Law, along with two fellow students who also climbed the Guoanbu ladder: Niu Ping, who headed the Olympic Games Security Committee, and Ma Jian, the head of counterintelligence who had just been arrested. In the 1990s, Chen headed the service's regional department in Sichuan province, where he was born in 1960. Later, he joined the all-powerful CCDI, where he was deputy secretary until 2015. In the great communist tradition, he had been asked to carry out the arrests and investigations for the downfall of his former friend Ma Jian, as a way of proving his absolute loyalty to the Xi Jinping faction.

It was true that Geng Huichang had been about to retire on the grounds of age, but it was also the case that an investigation to continue to identify moles was opened by a "special agent", Tang Chao, appointed by the new director Chen. Rumours began to circulate in diplomatic circles that have since been confirmed: Geng Huichang was now the subject of an investigation. In addition to the dismissals of various counterintelligence heads, the main grievance against him was that four years earlier, at Zhou Yongkang's instigation, the Guoanbu had begun electronically monitoring party leaders, including Hu Jintao and Xi Jinping. Ultimately, the CCDI's investigation exonerated Geng: Zhou Yongkang had short-circuited the Guoanbu counterintelligence hierarchy in Beijing, bypassing even its head Liang Ke, in order to eavesdrop on the Chinese leadership.

Despite this "political acquittal", Xi Jinping decided to retire Geng and replace him with Chen from the CCDI. In addition, he decided to reduce the influence of the Guoanbu and rebalance it with the role of the Gonganbu's 1st Bureau, which also operated abroad.

Some time earlier, on Xi Jinping's orders, there had been a major change of leadership within the Guoanbu's regional offices, already underway before Chen's appointment. On 10 September 2015, the *Beijing Youth Daily* announced changes in leadership at the Guoanbu regional offices in Shanxi, Guizhou, Shandong, Xinjiang, Shanghai, Hainan and Henan. Indeed, following Zhou Yongkang's failed coup in 2013, transfers, arrests and purges began to multiply rapidly in 2015 under Chen's leadership.

I have been able to identify the main Guoanbu regional directors, who will no doubt remain in their positions for years to come unless they, in turn, become the victims of denunciations. In alphabetical order of provinces and megacities: Hebei (Liu Zengqi), Heilongjiang (Chen Donghui), Hubei (Zhang Qikuan), Hunan (Liang Jianqiang), Jiangsu (Liu Yong), Liaoning (Wei Chunjiang), Shandong (Jiang Lianjun), Shanghai (Dong Weimin), Shanxi (Wang Xiuwen), Sichuan (Zhao Jian), and Zhejiang (Huang Baokun). In Beijing, Li Dong, a specialist in Russian affairs, has replaced Liang Ke, who is now in prison.

On 7 November 2016, Chen Wenqing was officially named overall head of the Guoanbu, and his predecessor Geng was named advisor to the Central Leading Group for Taiwan Affairs at the Central Foreign Affairs Commission; he also remained on the political-legal commission overseeing security and the coordination of the security and intelligence services.

Chen's appointment was an indication of how much things had changed since the time when the Guoanbu was reluctant to include a branch of the CCDI within its structure, arguing that it had its own system of internal scrutiny, and fearing that a team examining operational expenses in such an extremely sensitive ministry risked leaking sensitive information regarding intelligence and counterintelligence.

During the CCP's nineteenth congress in October 2017, from which Xi Jinping emerged supreme leader of the PRC, it became clear that he intended to reinforce the political-security structure with a network of his own people—in other words, officials who had already worked with him in his different fiefdoms. We shall see over the next few years whether the Guoanbu will manage to regain the strategic importance it had in the past. Early indications, as this book goes to press, suggest that its new minister will not be content with just carrying out mole or tiger hunts.

One particular episode from early 2018 is very telling. After much internal debate, it was eventually decided that Chen Wenqing would be responsible for the partnership with foreign intelligence services to develop the strategic security of the One Belt One Road initiative. Along with Meng Jianzhu, the security coordinator at the executive level of the CCP, it was decided that the head of the Guoanbu, rather than the head of the Gonganbu, would handle relations with the foreign security services of all the countries traversed by this gigantic project—twenty-eight to date.

Naturally, a first counterterrorism circle was to be set up with close allies from the Shanghai Club, including Russia and the Muslim republics of the former USSR. In January 2018, a meeting was held in Uzbekistan, organized by the Regional Anti-Terrorist Structure (RATS), part of the Shanghai Club. A Russian counterintelligence expert, Yevgeniy Sysoyev, formerly number two at the FSB, presided over the meeting, seconded by Chinese representatives linked to the

Guoanbu: the permanent representative Xu Chuangong and the RATS deputy director, Ms Zhou Qing. At the same time, Chen Wenqing was developing relationships with Asian allies including U Thaung Tun, Myanmar's national security advisor, and General To Lam, Vietnam's minister of public security. The recurrent theme was the fight against terrorism—for the Chinese, primarily the battle against Uyghur separatists, whose jihadist elements were beginning to dwindle after the strategic defeat of ISIS in the Levant in 2017.

In the spring of 2018, Chen Wenqing resumed his campaign, and went to meet officials from countries as disparate as Saudi Arabia, Pakistan, Spain, Germany and Turkey. With the latter, there was the pressing issue of Turkish-speaking Uyghur separatists, active in both Xinjiang and ISIS, and often supported by the MIT, the Turkish secret service.

The convenient mystery of Flight MH370

In recent years, a number of events have changed how Chinese leaders think about the utilization of military intelligence. We have seen the importance of the First Gulf War, the Kosovo War, the wars in Afghanistan and Iraq, and the emergence of ISIS in Iraq and Syria. But according to information from a senior PLA officer, one particular event precipitated this shift of perspective, just as Xi Jinping and his advisors were preparing a huge overhaul of the army and its intelligence services.

On 8 March 2014, Malaysian Airlines Boeing flight MH370, flying from Kuala Lumpur to Beijing, disappeared off the radar with 239 passengers and crew on board, including 153 Chinese nationals. Among the various conspiracy theories, the most frequent was that put forward by Western intelligence services, who accused the much-weakened Guoanbu of a disinformation campaign implicating all outposts of Chinese state media, in particular CCTV television—the first to broadcast it worldwide, before it was taken up by Fox News. This was the false claim that the plane had been brought down in a terrorist attack by the East Turkestan Independence Movement, the Uyghur nationalist movement in Xinjiang, whose spirit had been somewhat broken by the killing of passengers in Kunming station,

Yunnan, the week before.[5] To back up the rumour, the Chinese services leaked information from Hong Kong that two individuals on the flight had been travelling on fake European passports. Shortly after, Beijing even suggested that a Uyghur suspect—an artist from Xinjiang—had also been a passenger on Flight MH370. The implication was that the plane might have been brought down by a Uyghur suicide bomber.

We should remember that, during its restructuring in the globalizing 1990s, the Guoanbu had expanded its special section for broadcasting fake news, the *Wuchuan Teke*, modelled on the *disinformatsia* section of the former Soviet KGB. The Chinese character *wu* (误) means "the word that has fallen from the sky", and today is taken up by a battalion of internet users obviously non-existent back in the 1990s.

According to a source, whose information has proved highly reliable over the years, in autumn 2014 the intelligence services sent President Xi a surprising report that explained the considerable diplomatic cooling between Kuala Lumpur and Beijing—not helped by the fact that, of the 227 passengers on Flight MH370, 153 were Chinese.

Since June that year, the Chinese services had been following a line of enquiry suggesting the plane had disappeared during an attempt to hijack it. They were investigating effectively two alternative versions of the same scenario. The first hypothesis was that the hijacking had taken place on the approach to Vietnam, and that having forced the plane to turn around and return to Malaysia, the hijacker(s) were demanding the release of the ex-prime minister Anwar Ibrahim, leader of the Malaysian opposition. Prosecutors initially claimed that the pilot, Zaharie Ahmad Shah, had been at Ibrahim's trial a few days earlier, but this has subsequently been refuted. Under this scenario, Prime Minister Najib Abdul Razak refused to enter into negotiations, and the plane crashed.

But Guoanbu and PLA2 investigators tended towards an alternative hypothesis, presumably drawing on evidence from surveillance carried out in the region by the PLA: they believed that Royal Malaysian Air Force fighters (either Sukhoi SU-30 or F/A-18D Hornet) had been tasked with shooting down the plane, once it had begun to be seen as a real danger. Such a decision on the prime minister's part would have been somewhat surprising—although the report included the fact that that he was implicated in the murder of an interpreter who had become his mistress, during a 2005 trip to Paris while he was minister of defence; she was allegedly planning to reveal information about bribes paid during negotiations over the purchase of a French submarine. In this scenario Razak, known for being both implacable and irascible, convinced himself that the Americans, whose base at Diego Garcia was threatened by the Boeing's flight path, would cover up his decision. But none of this explains why no trace of the plane has ever been found, despite the vast resources employed by Chinese military intelligence, including detection vessels and reconnaissance satellites. Meanwhile, the naval intelligence service (*Haijun Qingbao*) and the PLA's combat fleet both took the opportunity to increase their sphere of intervention, particularly in the Indian Ocean.

It is highly likely that the new military intelligence systems put in place in 2015 will prove more effective in the future. Besides the virtually free publicity given to the PLA3 (responsible for SIGINT), showing that its satellites could play a useful role in air safety, the PLA fleet naturally found itself on the frontline when it sent a missile-launching frigate and an amphibious landing ship (whose potential utility might be questioned) to the search areas. But Admiral Yin Zhuo drew perhaps the greatest propaganda feat out of the mystery when he explained that this affair proved it was in China's strategic interest to establish a permanent naval base in the Spratly Islands.

The SSF and the PLA's new intelligence

In the aftermath of a major series of purges within the PLA, related to multiple corruption cases and the failed attempted coup of 2012, Xi Jinping, as chairman of the Central Military Commission (CMC), finalized the structure of the new army. On 31 December 2015, it was reorganized along three major lines, with the establishment of the Army Leadership Organ, the PLA Rocket Force—which replaced the former nuclear missile corps, the 2nd Artillery—and the Strategic Support Force (SSF, or *Zhanlue Zhiyuan Budui*).

To summarize, the leadership now consisted of a Joint Staff Department (*Junwei lianhe canmo bu*), managing five "war zones" or "theatre commands" (north, east, south, west, and central) to replace the seven military regions that had existed previously.

The Special Support Force is of particular interest, since it now integrates most of the Chinese military's intelligence and specifically cyber-warfare departments.[6] According to its new head, General Gao Jin, the SSF is an "informational umbrella" (*xinxisan*), in other words an assembly of resources bringing together the Aerospace Reconnaissance Bureau (*tianjun bu*), a cyber-army (*wangjun*), and electronic warfare troops (*dianzizhan budui*). The SSF controls the Beidou communications satellites copied from the European Galileo system, the hacking stations of the former PLA3, aerial reconnaissance, satellite imagery and, above all, an army of drones of every shape and size, which tail foreign vessels in the international waters of the China Sea. The drones (UAV) used to be under the PLA2's jurisdiction.

The SSF, which groups together the new Chinese information warfare service, has its own intelligence centre (*qingbao zhongxin*), with four main departments: (a) an intelligence collection department; (b) an intelligence processing department; (c) a dissemination management department; and (d) a technical support department. At the same time, most of the intelligence functions of the former PLA2 are now spread out over several different sectors, as American experts Peter Mattis and Elsa Kania explain:

> The available Chinese sources suggest that the former General Staff Department's (GSD) intelligence functions have been divided between three new organizations, the Joint Staff Department (JSD), the Strategic Support Force (SSF), and perhaps also the PLA Army leading organ (i.e. national-level headquarters). The structural logic and organizational dynamics associated with these changes allow for certain initial inferences about the future of PLA intelligence.
>
> The JSD appears to have responsibility for strategic-level intelligence and to have taken over the human intelligence mission associated with the former GSD Second Department (2/PLA). The GSD deputy chief responsible for intelligence and foreign affairs, Admiral Sun Jianguo, is now a JSD deputy chief and continues to represent the PLA to foreign audiences in Beijing and at forums like the Shangri-La Dialogue in Singapore. Sun also still serves as the president of the China Institute for International and Strategic Studies (CIISS), a position with some

> authority in the military intelligence community. The JSD includes a subordinate Intelligence Bureau (*Qingbaoju*), which is most likely a renamed 2/PLA, which was known as the Intelligence Department (*Qingbaobu*). Unofficial sources identify the previous head of 2/PLA, Major General Chen Youyi, as chief of the Intelligence Bureau.

A full list of the new heads of this organizational structure encompassing military intelligence and cyber-warfare can be found at the end of this book.

It should also be noted that the new intelligence department, within the SSF, now competes with the Guoanbu and the 1st Bureau of the Gonganbu regarding strategic intelligence abroad, with its own handling officers under civilian cover. In addition to this, along with officials from the traditional International Liaison Department and the Central Committee's United Front Work Department, there is another military structure that, contrary to various rumours, has not disappeared—the Liaison Bureau (*Lianluoju*—now a bureau rather than a department), part of the Central Military Commission's new Political Work Department (*Junwei zhengzhi gongzuo bu*). This military espionage service continues to send "deep-water fish" around the world to propagate its own version of the "Chinese Dream".

In short, this is not merely a cosmetic reform, but a large-scale integration of China's counteroffensive resources. In evaluating its significance, it is worth quoting Moscow's reaction—for it was, after all, the Russians who helped launch the Chinese communist secret services a century ago. An article published by the Sputnik news agency on 19 January 2016 stated:

> China has established a new combat force to safeguard its national security: the Strategic Support Force (SSF). This unique structure will bring together the whole scope of capacities of the Chinese People's Liberation Army in waging special operations and information warfare.
>
> Apart from the former Departments of the PLA General Staff Headquarters, which were responsible for the technical reconnaissance, cyber intelligence, electronic warfare and offensive cyber operations, the new forces will be responsible for the military intelligence at large and for the psychological operations in particular. Additionally, the newly formed Forces could include Special Operations Units.

Thus, the Strategic Support Force is a structure with no equal in the world.

The most effective intelligence community of the century?

Today the community of Chinese security and intelligence services is the largest in the world, at least in terms of the sheer numbers of their officials, officers and agents. Since the first French edition of this book came out in 2008, they have attained the technological competence of the US and Russian services, particularly in the field of intercepting communications and the use of spy satellites. The numerous cyber-attacks attributed to the PLA's special units are evidence of this, although they are not the only ones to engage in this kind of operation.

Similarly, China is today involved in the massive siphoning of economic, scientific and technological intelligence, described under the generic term "sea lamprey tactics" in Chapter 9. Military and technological intelligence has gained considerable prominence as the Chinese develop their weapons and capabilities on land, at sea, beneath the sea, in the sky, and in space, towards Mars. Their strategic intervention in the search for possible energy sources has led to their activities on continents from which they have long been excluded, with Xi Jinping's extraordinary One Belt One Road project.

Africa and Latin America, where Mao tried in vain to foment revolution in the 1960s, have now become significant zones of Chinese economic and cultural influence. Africa is such an important area for twenty-first-century China that it is on the way to supplanting the European Union as the continent's number-one partner in trade and development. Two facts alone bear witness to this: the setting up of a strategic base in Djibouti, which means that for the first time expeditionary forces from the US and China find themselves side by side in a third country; and, for the first time since decolonization, there are more French-speaking African officers applying to train in China, at the Nanjing Academy and elsewhere, than at the prestigious French military academy of Saint-Cyr.

The strategy of cultural seduction, called "soft power", is also playing an unexpectedly important role. This has included the creation of a network of Confucius Institutes for the promotion of Chinese language and culture internationally (also supported by large multinationals like Huawei Technologies and ZTE, whose goals are not only cultural).[7] The 2008 Olympic Games, with its slogan "One World, One Dream", and the 2010 Shanghai World Expo, were also part of this powerful strategy.

* * *

Chinese services have begun to be better recognized, although the number of historians, journalists, academics and special service analysts closely studying the way they function remains relatively small. The word "Guoanbu" will probably become as familiar in the twenty-first century as the acronyms MI6, CIA and KGB were in the twentieth.

The significance of this is related to the likely evolution of Chinese society for decades to come. As in the former USSR—and to a certain extent in the Russian Federation of Vladimir Putin—the security and intelligence services are not simply an organ of information-gathering, or even of influence and limited action, as in democratic countries. They are an essential pillar of power, alongside the army and the single ruling party.

In the Chinese system, the special web of relationships known as *guanxi* has always played a decisive role in the rise or fall of this or that faction or clan, as has been seen in various tortured episodes in the history of the CCP in the People's Republic. Regional networks, generational relationships, the fact of having studied at places such as Tsinghua University, the Shanghai clique around Jiang Zemin, the network of Communist Youth League leaders around Hu Jintao, and the oil lobby supported by Zeng Qinghong and Zhou Yongkang have all played a role that is being reproduced down the generations. The networks around Xi Jinping were detailed in 2016 by Cheng Li in his remarkable book *Chinese Politics in the Xi Jinping Era*.[8] I myself have also investigated and demonstrated the importance of the Hebei Band in the special services.

But there is also a generational phenomenon specific and new to this fifth generation of CCP leaders. At the end of the 19th Congress of the Chinese Communist Party in October 2017, Xi Jinping not only emerged more powerful than ever, but the ideological and economic orientations established in that moment of triumph will give even greater weight to the role of intelligence and security administrations in the PRC.

The importance of this new generation of senior cadres in the intelligence field can be measured by their entry into the 204-strong CCP Central Committee. Wang Qishan, head of the powerful CCDI, has ceded his place to a new figure: Zhao Leji. This does not mean that Wang has retired—he remains one of the most important of Xi's confidential advisors, effectively a de facto vice-president. Zhao's deputy is Yu Zhongfu, also on the Central Committee, a former air force commissar.

Chen Wenqing, the Guoanbu chief formerly of the CCDI, has also come onto the Central Committee. Almost more significant politically—China still functions with a dual leadership system shared between a technical director/minister and a political commissar—Song Tao is now minister of the important International Liaison Department, in charge of political intelligence and contacts with political parties abroad. In terms of domestic security, Cai Qi is deputy director of the National Security Council chaired by Xi Jinping; Wang Xiaohong is director of the Beijing office of the Gonganbu; and, finally, General Zhong Shaojun, who runs the General Office of the Central Military Commission, is head of military security.

Cai Qi and Zhao Leji have also joined the upper echelons of the Politburo, alongside Guo Shengkun, the Gonganbu minister, elected at the 18th Congress in 2012. His Guoanbu counterpart Chen has not achieved this rank, indicating that his position has less political influence. At an even higher level, Zhao Leji is one of the seven members of the Politburo's Standing Committee that leads China, and has been awarded the portfolio of overseeing the security services as a whole.

Thus, under Xi Jinping no less than under his predecessors, with the CCP as the sole political party, the key role of the intelligence services remains as important in Chinese politics—in organization of internal affairs and control of the people, and in the eternal battle of the clans in power—as it is at the level of the vast global, economic, political and military strategy that is now known worldwide as the "Chinese Dream".

15

COVID-19

CHINA'S SECRET WAR

"The spymaster Dong Jingwei has defected to the Americans, and he's taken the secret of Covid's origins with him." In June 2021, this was the gist of the information spreading across those corners of social media that are interested in such matters.[1] But was this just another ploy in the psychological war between China and the US? The different views that have emerged on this question are revealing in themselves, giving us a view of the war waged by the Chinese secret services during the pandemic.

Dong Jingwei: a new Magician Gu?

Dong Jingwei was born in 1963 in Hebei province, where he would become regional director of the Guoanbu in the 1990s. He married a nurse and worked for the People's Bank of China before entering the secret services. He is not part of the elite Red Princes caste, hailing instead from a modest background; but he joined the ministry with the support of Li Zhanshu, then head of the CCP.

In 2012, Li served as chief of staff to China's new leader and his friend of thirty years, Xi Jinping; in that year Li also became director of the CCP General Office, which oversees the Bureau of State Secrets.

He was the one who summoned Dong Jingwei to Beijing, appointing him as a deputy Guoanbu minister, responsible for the 7th and 8th Bureaus (counterespionage).

On 10 February 2021, Dong reportedly boarded a plane in Hong Kong with his daughter, destined for California—where he was allegedly picked up by Lieutenant General Scott D. Berrier's Defense Intelligence Agency.[2] Over the next few weeks, however, Beijing would claim that Dong was still in China. On 18 June, the South China Morning Post reported that the deputy minister had made a public statement, encouraging his agents to "hunt down foreign agents and insiders who collude with 'anti-China' forces."[3] The next day, the Central Commission for Discipline Inspection produced a document from the Bureau of State Secrets: Party Communiqué No. 223, dated 21 May 1931, which ordered Gu Shunzhang's expulsion from the party for treason (see Chapter 1). The symbolic unearthing of this record in the summer of 2021 obviously echoed Xi Jinping's recent declaration during the CCP centenary celebrations, threatening those who betray the party.

A couple of days later, on 21 June, the FBI issued assurances that it was not holding Dong. Of course, this didn't rule out the possibility that Dong was in the US, but under the protection of the DIA or CIA. On 25 June, the CCP's political-legal commission offered apparent photographic evidence of Dong's presence at the Shanghai Cooperation Organization's 16th Session, also attended by the Gonganbu minister. But the image could have been doctored—it was a virtual conference, so the foreign delegates didn't see their counterparts in the flesh.

In other words, it's impossible to say with certainty where Dong Jingwei was in the summer of 2021; Beijing's insistence that he remains in China is far from definitive. But we can at least get a sense of the operations run by the Chinese spies under Dong's command—the files he could have passed to the West if he has in fact defected. They concern the question of a link between the outbreak of Covid-19 and Chinese biowar research; cyber-ops aimed at spying on the medical and pharmaceutical industries; and, finally, the use of Covid measures to bring Uyghurs, Hong Kongers and any other dissidents back into line.

Chinese biological warfare: what we know

Was Covid-19 a Wuhan laboratory experiment gone wrong? Were Chinese scientists making dual use, military as well as civilian, of biological research, and was Wuhan the epicentre of this strategy?

The Xi government refutes all such allegations of scientific experimentation, denying that the pandemic could have resulted from the novel coronavirus accidentally leaking out of a lab. The World Health Organization itself has been slow to confront this possibility; in January 2020, when Beijing was under fire for its lack of transparency about the pandemic's origins, Director-General Tedros Adhanom Ghebreyesus came to China's defence.[4] Yet, far from accepting and agreeing to the demands for an international inquiry, including by the WHO, Chinese diplomats instead chose to accuse the Americans of having caused the pandemic.

In early 2021, the incoming President Joe Biden asked his intelligence services to get to the bottom of it all. Despite China's insistence that it is not engaged in biological or bacteriological research for military purposes, several questions remain within Western intelligence communities:

- Why are Taiwanese spies convinced that the coronavirus broke out of the Wuhan Institute of Virology's Biosafety Level 4 (BSL-4) laboratory?
- The Wuhan lab was originally sold to China by France—are the French, and more broadly the Europeans, correct in their identification of three other Chinese labs as further BSL-4 facilities,[5] copied from the Wuhan laboratory after its foundation in 2017? (Given the origins of the Wuhan lab, France's secret services are obviously well placed to evaluate intelligence on this question.)
- Assuming the answer is yes, what then is the purpose of these 'cloned' BSL-4 labs? And what is the purpose of China's mobile BSL-3 veterinary labs, such as those similarly gained via Sino-French cooperation agreements?
- Why did General Chen Wei, head of biotechnology at the Academy of Military Medical Sciences, turn to running Wuhan's BSL-4 lab in February 2020, when the latter is supposed to be a civilian facility? Was she simply there to help get a vaccine developed, as with the previous SARS and Ebola pandemics?[6]

To get at any kind of possible answer to these questions, we need to turn to the history of biological warfare, and to the roots of the PLA's ideas today about biowarfare in the twenty-first century. We must return briefly to the days of the USSR.

Flashback to the Soviet days

The biowar machinery that we know and fear today came out of two events of the twentieth century, the first being the Japanese experiments carried out during the occupation of China, Manchuria and Korea (1937-45). Japan's infamous Unit 731 was responsible for lethal human experimentation during the Second World War. The second event was the capture of these army experts—by US secret services, according to a common narrative. It has been alleged that the US used these scientists' knowledge to deploy viruses and bacteria as weapons of war against the communists during the Korean War of 1950-3.

As we shall see, that theory is really a case of smoke and mirrors. Stalin's Soviets had already intervened in this matter prior to the Korean War, to help out the Chinese. The Russians had also captured scientists and seized the findings of Unit 731, and used these records to design weapons of mass destruction. They actually put the unit's leaders on trial,[7] and certain Soviet scientists on the jury were key players in the Sino-Soviet alliance—including the microbiologist Nikolai N. Zhukov-Verezhnikov, who was a KGB scientist, affiliated with the USSR's Academy of Medicine.

The leading officers and heads of the Japanese medical and veterinary services, responsible for Unit 731, were each given prison sentences ranging from three to twenty-five years. One of them, Kiyoshi Kawashima, had described to the jury how, in 1941, the unit dropped porcelain bottles of plague-infected fleas over the city of Changde, causing an epidemic. This use of biological agents was based on experimentation with 3,000 human guinea pigs.

Ten years later, General Efim Smirnov of the 15th Principal Directory of the General Staff sent a Soviet delegation to meet with Mao Zedong's scientists. According to a declassified CIA report from 24 July 1951, the man leading the delegation—the bacteriologist Professor Kakovsky—oversaw the setting up of a "large agency ... established in [Beijing] for research in bacteriological warfare". The

"Chinese personnel working on this project [were] former students who returned from England and the US". A second report, from late in the same year, reveals the creation of a special training school for handling biological and chemical weapons. Located outside the Manchurian village of Chinghochen, "The class numbers more than 170, of which 40 are women. Administrators and instructors are all Soviet. Lectures are given on which trainees take notes; field practices are conducted."[8]

Thus was born the PLA's nuclear, biological and chemical warfare apparatus, both offensive and defensive, and engaged in epidemiological research; as well as vaccine development in conjunction with civilian scientific organizations, such as the Chinese Academy of Sciences, the health and agriculture ministries, and so on.

The Korean War: a quid pro quo

In February 1952, two years into the Korean War, the Chinese and North Koreans announced that they had discovered "biological bombs", dropped by the American forces commanded by General Matthew Ridgeway to spread plague, typhoid and anthrax.

There are well-known records of the communication about this between Mao Zedong and Nie Rongzhen, then the Central Military Commission's chief of staff. On 18 February, Nie told Mao that the enemy had overflown the lines where the 20th, 26th, 39th and 42nd Corps of the People's Liberation Army were stationed, dropping insects. Experts were dispatched to the front, and the insects sent back to Beijing for analysis. The scientists concluded that they were infected with the bacteria that cause cholera, typhoid, plague and relapsing fever.

There was international outcry against viral warfare, with protests against "Ridgeway Plague". But, with echoes of the situation in 2020-1, China opposed a commission of inquiry run by the International Red Cross. In April 1952, the PRC set up its own "International Scientific Investigative Commission Concerning Biological Warfare in Korea and China", led by the British doctor Joseph Needham, future founding president of the Society for Anglo-Chinese Understanding; also appointed to the commission was Zhukov-Verezhnikov, the same expert who had sat on the jury of the Unit 731 trial.

The Commission found that biological weapons had in fact been used, citing the interrogation of US Air Force prisoners of war. Chairman Mao issued the following directives: "Be mindful of hygiene! Reduce sickness! Improve health! Crush the enemy's germ warfare!"[9] Today, however, we have access to reports sent back to Lavrentiy Beria, the Russian internal affairs minister, by the Soviet delegation to the North Korean army. These reveal that, in fact, documentation was falsified to incriminate the Americans.[10] In September 1997, Dr Wu Zhili, director of the Chinese Volunteers in Korea's medical division, composed a detailed report, made public after his death in 2013, explaining that the allegations of biological warfare had been false.[11]

Nevertheless, 1952 saw the PRC's first vaccination campaign, with the slogan "Sanitation is patriotism!"—and since this time, PLA training has included defence against germ warfare. Today, frameworks are starting to be set up with a view to developing not only defensive, but offensive capabilities in biowarfare.

The founding father of Chinese biological warfare

To recap, then, Marshall Nie Rongzhen became chief of staff at the start of the Korean War; and he is heavily implicated in China's development of biological weapons.[12] In the late 1950s, he became head of the State Council Science Planning Commission (which coordinates with the PLA), with the help of Kang Sheng, the spy chief responsible for repatriating Chinese scientists from abroad. Nie oversaw the PRC's military committee for developing strategic weaponry, and from 1958 ran the State Science and Technology Commission, which covered nuclear as well as chemical and biological warfare. During the Cultural Revolution, according to a circular from 16 May 1966, Nie's scientists were protected from the Red Guards; transferred to report to the Ministry of Defence and Marshall Lin Biao, they were able to continue their experiments.[13] That same month, Western secret services learnt that the PLA was building clandestine bioweapons factories in Yunnan, including a facility erected either close to or underneath Erhai Lake.[14]

Fearing that the USSR might strike northern China if Sino-Soviet tensions erupted into conflict, the Chinese also set up a working group there for the prevention and treatment of illness. After the armed clashes with Soviet forces along the Amur border river in 1969, Mao even became concerned about an attack on Beijing itself; this is why the underground city described in Chapter 3 was built, to protect the capital's residents in the case of nuclear, chemical or biological strike. Yet the American and Soviet archives are clear: Leonid Brezhnev and his chiefs of staff were averse to using bioweapons. The scientists of the USSR's 15th Directory advised against the deployment of germ agents to start epidemics in enemy territory (smallpox or anthrax, for instance), since this strategy would come back to bite the Soviets in their Far Eastern territories.

The 1980s: a treaty and an epidemic

In 1984, China acceded to the Convention on the Prohibition of the Development, Production and Stockpiling of Bacteriological (Biological) and Toxin Weapons and on their Destruction, which was first signed by the US, the USSR and the UK in 1972—but the PRC did not ratify its accession, and continued its bioweapons research. Two years later, in 1986, Xinjiang province saw an epidemic of haemorrhagic fever, which broke out not far from the nuclear site at Lop Nor. The former Soviet scientist Ken Alibek has published his account of the USSR's assessment that this was an accidental escape out of a bioweapons factory.[15] In 1989 there was a similar incident in Tibet: an anthrax epidemic, towards the end of a two-year uprising which, at the time of the outbreak, was being mirrored on Tiananmen Square in Beijing.

Another key event of this decade was the 1986 foundation of the 863 Programme, designed to catch China up in science and technology—including via biological espionage. Those behind the programme included "Colonel Professor" Cao Wuchu, a Cambridge-educated bioterrorism advisor and epidemiologist who, in 2020, was holding a key post at the Wuhan Institute of Virology. By the 1990s, the bioweapons proliferation specialist Eric Croddy could identify biowarfare research institutes at twelve separate sites across China.[16]

Today, we can build on Croddy's research to get a view of the full, somewhat complex organizational hierarchy involved. At the top of the pyramid is the CCP's Central Military Commission, led by Xi Jinping himself. The commission steers the State Administration of Science, Technology and Industry for National Defence, and this agency in turn runs overseas intelligence with a view to developing special biological weapons of war. There is also the Special Weapons Office of the PLA's General Armaments Department, which manufactures materiel for the dissemination of bioweapons.

The PLA Academy of Military Science, including its Academy of Medical Military Sciences, reports to both the Central Military Commission and the PLA's Logistic Support Department. These two academies are connected to the health and agriculture ministries (the latter housing China's veterinary administration), as well as to many laboratories answering to the State-Owned Assets Supervision and Administration Commission (SASAC). According to the Israeli researcher and former IDF intelligence officer Dany Shoham,

> A main body of SASAC is the China National Biotech Corporation (CNBC). The latter has an R&D centre in Beijing and various manufacturing sites affiliated with a system called "Institutes of Biological Products" (in principle, vaccines and blood derivatives, officially), which are strategically located in various cities across China. Included are Changchun Institute of Biological Products, Chengdu Institute of Biological Products, Lanzhou Institute of Biological Products, Shanghai Institute of Biological Products, Wuhan Institute of Biological Products, and the National Vaccine and Serum Institute, Beijing. The CNBC is apparently linked to the SASAC exclusively owned "China Poly Group Corporation" and its subsidiary, that is, "Poly Technologies", a defence manufacturing company.[17]

All this is complicated enough; but to truly get an idea of the vast stakes China has invested in this substantial initiative, you have to read the country's modern biowar theorists. Colonel Guo Jiwei of the Third Military Medical University[18] is the author of *The War for Biological Dominance*, which describes the decline of traditional military thinking, in favour of a strategic revolution centred on the theatre of "non-contact warfare" and on the "underground front"—the latter concerning cyber-warfare as well as biological warfare.

Colonel Guo has made his meaning clear in an article co-authored with the biotechnologist Yang Xueyen. His array of examples of how this vision might work prove that he is interested in biowarfare well beyond the use of bacterial agents:

> We can use many modern biotechnologies directly as a means of defense and attack, and with further development, they probably will become new weapons systems ... Direct-effect weapons can be used on human bodies to alter their biological features ... As a result, we might soon be able to design, control, reconstruct, and simulate molecules in living beings ...
>
> When attacking an enemy with biotechnological military weapons, we could choose targets from a nucleotide sequence or protein structure. We could cause physiological dysfunction by producing an ultramicro damaging effect to a gene's or a protein's structure and functioning ... As the application of viral vectors in gene therapy shows, the stable expression of the exogenous virulence gene transfected to targeted people via retrovirus, adenovirus, or an adenoassociated virus can cause disease or injury. As transfection technology develops, more viral vectors or other organismic vectors will be found, which will enable vector transfer to be more suitable for war.[19]

Subscribers to these ideas populate the highest levels of the Chinese command—including He Fuchu, former president of the Academy of Military Medical Sciences and now vice-president of its umbrella organization, the PLA Academy of Military Science; as well as the retired General Zhang Shibo, former commander of the Hong Kong garrison, whose 2017 book *New Highland of War* contemplated the use of biotechnology in "ethnically targeted genetic attacks" against the PRC's enemies—Uyghurs, Tibetans, Hong Kong dissidents.

The Wuhan labs

In October 2002, the Chinese delegation to the International Biological Weapons Convention made assurances that the PRC was not carrying out military-purpose biological research, was not manufacturing bioweapons, and was not stockpiling dual-purpose biological materiel. Yet the PLA's command structure in Wuhan suggests the opposite. That city is home to China's largest network of civil–military hybrid organizations specialized in biology; thanks to the SARS and H5N1 avian flu epidemics, Wuhan has become a military-scientific hub in the fields of virology, epidemiology, bacteriology and other biological research.

With the 2016 reorganization of the PLA (see Chapter 14), Xi Jinping set up "decentralized" joint-army command structures, and one of them came to Wuhan: the general headquarters of the PLA's Joint-Army Logistical Support Force (*Lianqin Baozhang Budui*), which oversees both the PLA health department and the Academy of Military Medical Sciences. The latter, being a PLA academy, also answers to the defence ministry—but in late January 2020, as the academy stepped in to take control of Wuhan's BSL-4 lab under General Chen Wei, it was reporting directly to the Logistical Support Force that had set up shop in the city four years previously.

This very public takeover by Chen was misleading, however; the lab was already under military control, as it has been ever since its foundation. It's not worth us going over the details of the Wuhan Institute of Virology's purchase of the lab from France;[20] but we should remember that the French security services had even been uneasy about the prior sales of lower-security BSL-3 labs, because orders placed with the French biotech firm Labover were coming down jointly from "the Chinese health ministry and the Chinese defence ministry".

In *France and China: Dangerous Liaisons*, the journalist Antoine Izambard explains that the construction of the Wuhan lab fell to a PLA company, though fifteen French businesses were also involved.[21] Izambard was one of the few able to visit the site, and his prescient book, published just a few months before coronavirus struck in late 2019, described the lab's security deficiencies. In April 2020, he wrote a piece in the French business weekly *Challenges*, underlining the French authorities' quiet suspicions about China's opacity in relation to the facility:

> These concerns, raised by the French and US intelligence services, are backed by very strong suspicions of the existence of a Chinese biological attack programme. Such a programme is made possible by the PLA's hold over every BSL-3 lab in China (handling less dangerous pathogens than BSL-4 labs), and by China's lack of transparency about measures put in place domestically to prevent a lab leak of biological agents ... In June 2004, four months before the signature of an international agreement, [French foreign intelligence] informed the authorities that China was seemingly planning the construction of five

more BSL-4 labs (three civilian, two military). At the same time as France's spies were sounding the alarm about this, several French businesses indeed found themselves being wooed by China to construct BSL-4 labs separate from the one at Wuhan.[22]

That year, 2004, the French Prime Minister Jean-Pierre Raffarin authorized the export of four mobile BSL-3 labs to China; the BSL-4 facility would be constructed via the same arrangement. But twelve years later, in 2016, France's interdepartmental commission on dual-purpose goods blocked exports to the Wuhan lab of spacesuits adapted for researchers in low-oxygen environments. This was meant to be a simple upgrade of the version of the suits that had been delivered in 2010; but the quantities ordered made clear that this batch was intended for other, undeclared sites.

It's understandable that Western intelligence is trying to identify these phantom labs. Everyone wants to know whether the novel coronavirus is of simple "natural" origin, transmitted to humans from an animal reservoir, or if it started life as an "enhanced" virus, created in a lab for civil or military research purposes, before escaping into the community. The risk of such an accident was a real cause for concern prior to the pandemic, including for the Chinese themselves, given the number of different biological research sites now in operation in Wuhan.[23] This network of organizations is made vulnerable by its complexity. There is:

- The Wuhan Institute of Biological Products (CanSino Biologics), which has been involved in the development of Covid vaccines alongside the groups Sinopharm and Sinovac.
- The Wuhan Institute of Virology (WIV), which has links to both the PLA and the Chinese Academy of Sciences.
- The WIV's BSL-4 lab, run by two French-speakers: Professor Yuan Zhiming, and Dr Shi Zhengli (said to have first identified SARS-CoV-2, the virus that causes Covid-19).
- The BSL-3 lab at the Central Hospital of Wuhan, whose Emergency Department director Ai Fen was one of the first to sound the alarm about Covid-19, before "disappearing".[24]
- The BSL-3 lab linked to the WIV, close to the Wuchang university campus—a 200-metre walk from the food market where pangolins have been identified as the source of the Covid epidemic.

- The BSL-3 lab attached to the university, where security issues have been flagged in the handling of samples.
- The BSL-4 lab linked to Hubei province's Center for Disease Control, which is known to have sent Tian Junhua and a team of bat-hunters to collect samples of novel viruses the bats may carry.
- A more recent BSL-3 facility, based on the French BSL-4 lab, within Wuhan's technological park (12 kilometres from the city centre), working in partnership with a monkey-supplier—the ambiguity here of the Level 3/4 distinction has posed security problems, and French intelligence has detected a growing "consumption" of test animals, suggesting that research is ramping up.
- And, finally, these "phantom" mobile BSL-3 labs. The Western intelligence services are trying to work out if they are the same as the rest—whether they have been supplied with test animals, and whether they are permanently based in Wuhan. (The French foreign intelligence agency has even raised concerns that at least one of them might in fact be located beyond China's borders, in an allied country such as Pakistan).[25]

The Harbin lab, the Taiwanese theory and the Covid hackers

In early 2020, the Taiwanese secret services went in search of intelligence on the BSL-4 lab in Harbin, which is linked to the veterinary research institute there. The result was a press conference given by Chiu Kuo-cheng, head of the National Security Bureau, confirming that there was evidence of a Level-4 lab being "cloned" in the northern Chinese city. Taipei's spies are the best informed in the world when it comes to activity inside mainland China, and Fang Chi-tai, an epidemiologist at National Taiwan University, knows it. In February 2020, he went public with a worrying question: did the Wuhan lab have samples of the novel coronavirus, since it is known to have been stockpiling a collection of lethal pathogens that might spread SARS or Ebola into human populations?[27]

Whatever the truth, the CIA and European intelligence agencies are digging into the workings of at least three other BSL-4 labs copied from the Wuhan facility, as well as the mobile labs. These investigations may soon discover where the coronavirus really came from—

either from a secret agent still on the ground in China, or else from a defector (the Dong Jingwei scenario). But states are not the only ones on the hunt for information related to Covid-19. The pandemic has provoked a global medical intelligence drive among civilian and military agencies alike, not only in terms of interceptions of confidential data, but also in terms of the theft of pathogens.

In July 2020, for instance, the FBI's cyber division accused two Chinese individuals of infiltrating the IT systems of biotech companies working on anti-Covid research, and infecting them with ransomware. These alleged hackers were acting for their own financial gain—but they were also working for the Guoanbu. According to the Justice Department's indictment, Li Xiaoyu, 34, and Dong Jizhi, 33, carried out their operations for the Guoanbu station in Guangzhou, using the China Institute of International Studies as a cover. The Guoanbu boss in Guangdong, Zhou Yingshi, made a similar cover claim when he took office in 2016, saying that he was part of the United Front Work Department.[28]

The indictment alleged that Li and Dong had managed to hack into systems relating to various areas, including Covid-19:

> 60. On or about January 25 and 27, 2020, LI searched for vulnerabilities at a Maryland biotech firm. That firm had announced less than a week earlier that it was researching a potential COVID-19 vaccine.
>
> 61. On or about January 27, 2020, LI conducted reconnaissance on the computer network of a Massachusetts biotech firm publicly known to be researching a potential COVID-19 vaccine.
>
> [...]
>
> 64. On or about February 1, 2020, LI searched for vulnerabilities in the network of a California biotech firm that had announced one day earlier that it was researching antiviral drugs to treat COVID-19.[29]

Hong Kong crackdown: the Covid pretext

The duo accused by the US also appear to have performed other services for the Guoanbu in Guangdong, the southern province bordering the Hong Kong "Special Autonomous Region". Since a draconian National Security Law was passed in the former British colony in the summer of 2020, the Guoanbu has been working with the CCP's newly installed security apparatus there, tasked under the NSL to watch everything that Hong Kong's pro-democracy opposition does. It's no coincidence that the new security chief in Hong Kong, Zheng Yanxiong, used to be the party boss in Guangdong.

The DoJ indictment against the two alleged hackers includes counts related to surveillance of pro-democracy dissidents:

> 69. On or about June 13, 2020, LI conducted reconnaissance on Hong Kong protestor communication methods.
>
> 70. On or about June 13, 2020, LI conducted reconnaissance on the network of Hong Kong webmail provider Netvigator.
>
> 71. On or about June 13, 2020, LI conducted reconnaissance on a U.K. messaging application frequently used by Hong Kong protestors.

The PRC's muscling into Hong Kong since 2019 has not happened in isolation from world events. China has been using Covid to repress dissidents, just as it did during the SARS crisis. Back then, Beijing had to deal with the sudden rise of mobile phones, and the birth of social networks. In 2003, there were 350 million mobile phones in China, and the Chinese sent 200 billion texts that year—the equivalent of 651 per user, or 7,000 every second. The Guoanbu warned the party leadership that these communication networks had already stoked revolution in Georgia, Ukraine and Kyrgyzstan. Surely they also posed a threat to the People's Republic?

By the time the SARS epidemic began in late 2002, the Chinese government had lost its monopoly on information. According to Dean Cheng, author of *Cyber Dragon*, when state media banned any coverage of the crisis, the news simply circulated from phone to phone, via email, and over the internet. Public confidence was eroded further when Dr Jiang Yanyong, a retired army surgeon, emailed television stations saying that the health ministry was lying about having SARS under control. Jiang's claim was picked up by the global press, which then fed the news back into China.[30]

Beijing learnt from this lesson: in the years following SARS, the PRC's gargantuan intranet scheme, the Golden Shield Project—best known for operating the Great Firewall of China—established a system of total surveillance over websites, emails, text messages and social networks like WeChat. Artificial intelligence, and its use in social control tactics like facial recognition, began developing at an exponential rate. It was in this context that the next pandemic arrived: Covid-19.

During the coronavirus crisis, Chinese tech companies have been vying to outdo each other with ingenious means of tracking the virus's spread. Baidu—the Chinese Google—has been using its resources to establish total state control over the Covid vaccination campaign; and its Covid security system at Beijing's Qinghe station has used facial recognition software to detect—through the face mask—anyone with a temperature over 37.3 degrees Celsius. The software can get through 200 people every minute. Similarly, in the Beijing metro, the deep-learning AI company Megvii found a way to check for a fever with only the forehead exposed; this testing system was used to filter travellers from Wuhan or its province, Hubei.

Since 2018, Xi's China has extended this vast techno-security apparatus to Hong Kong—part of a gradual revocation of the fundamental freedoms guaranteed by the Basic Law, which has preserved Hong Kong's political and economic difference from mainland China since the British handover in 1997. Hong Kongers have not met these developments with passivity. Their single biggest show of defiance against China's policies came on Sunday 16 June 2019, with 2 million of Hong Kong's 7.4 million inhabitants taking to the streets. This took place against the backdrop of a takeover by the Chinese secret services, which would ultimately be a year in the making.

In May 2020, the new National Security Law was put on the books of China's rubber-stamp parliament, the National People's Congress. The bill banned "actions to split the country", "terrorism" and "subversion of state power" in Hong Kong. The political commentator Willy Wo-Lap Lam warned at the time that "the new law could allow state security agencies such as the Ministry of State Security", the Guoanbu, "to set up branches" in Hong Kong. Bruce Lui, a journalism lecturer at a Hong Kong university, agreed: "State Security agents could carry out tasks such as investigation, intimidation and even secret arrests in Hong Kong."[31]

The law came into effect on 1 July, and Beijing's services promptly took over policing in Hong Kong, openly setting up a National Security Office in Causeway Bay. This bureau, formally known as the

Office for Safeguarding National Security of the Central People's Government in the Hong Kong Special Administrative Region, is run by Cheng Yanxing, seconded from the Gonganbu, and Sun Qingye, on loan from the Guoanbu. The first day of the new regime was timed to coincide with Hong Kong's annual rally commemorating the 1989 Tiananmen Square crackdown, which was banned, supposedly due to the Covid risk. Two months later, Carrie Lam—the leader of Hong Kong's China-controlled administration—sought to vaccinate at least half of the population; but scarcely 600,000 people came forward. PCR testing was also being shunned by a large majority of Hong Kongers. The pro-democracy leader Joshua Wong explained protesters' fear that their personal data would be taken and sent on to Beijing; he called the mass testing programme an excuse for "large-scale DNA collection", paving the way for "a China-style surveillance regime" in Hong Kong.[32] DNA samples were already being taken from arrested protesters, and Hong Kongers feared that a vast database was being set up like the one in Xinjiang, where Uyghurs have served as guinea pigs for a techno-surveillance system.

During the pandemic, repression in Hong Kong has intensified, with hundreds arrested—including, in January 2021, fifty-three high-profile democracy activists taken in for "inciting subversion". They were followed in April by the press magnate Jimmy Lai, whose arrest was the nail in the coffin for his independent-minded tabloid *Apple Daily*. At the time of writing, anti-Covid measures have been softened on the Chinese mainland, but remain severely restrictive across the water. As *Le Monde*'s Hong Kong correspondent put it in July, "The public health crisis has been weaponized wholesale as a way to tighten security. Three applications were made to hold the 1 July protest march, a long-established Hong Kong tradition, but these were rejected by police, citing the risk of contagion—even though there have been hardly any cases of local transmission in Hong Kong for several weeks now."[33]

Covid and concentration camps: the Uyghurs' pandemic

While Beijing has used the Covid crisis to shut down political opposition in Hong Kong, the secret services up in Xinjiang have spent the pandemic expanding the concentration camp system there. Across China, between 5 and 8 million citizens are detained in around 1,000 camps—but the complex of camps in Xinjiang is now the single largest on Earth. The province's overwhelmingly peaceful population has fallen victim to the pretext cited by China for its security crackdowns: the few hundred Uyghurs who have joined Islamist movements in Syria or Afghanistan. The Xinjiang Guoanbu, run by Tian Yong, has been hunting them down. Meanwhile, the Chinese government has had to admit to the world that it is running about thirty internment camps in Xinjiang, where 1.3 million people are being held—a full tenth of the total population in the Chinese "Far West".

Beijing calls these camps "vocational training centres" for individuals who need help to overcome their incorrect ideas; they are not only incarcerated, but subject to forced labour and "re-education". But the camp detainees are not the only Uyghurs in the grip of China's security system. As reporter Bruno Ripoche puts it, Beijing holds the entire province in a "digital straitjacket": "Every single vehicle is fitted with a transmitter, so that Baidu [which runs China's GPS equivalent] can track locations, smartphones have spyware installed," and "DNA is collected during routine medical exams".[34] On top of this, surveillance cameras linked up to facial recognition software work to identify and single out those of Uyghur ethnicity; these systems were built by Alibaba, sometimes known as "Chinese Amazon", and Huawei, of 5G fame. For "free" Uyghur citizens who have so far escaped the camps, QR codes on their front doors give the authorities instant data on who lives inside.

The pandemic has only worsened the situation in Xinjiang's concentration camps. Not only does the virus spread easily in such cramped, enclosed conditions, but detainees have been serving as deliberate fodder in China's fight against Covid. The Uyghurs are often used as slave labour, in industries including Western fashion—since the start of the crisis, they have been manufacturing PCR test kits and face masks. This is the equipment that has been pouring into ports all over the world as part of China's "pandemic diplomacy". In spring 2020, the number of mask manufacturers in Xinjiang jumped from just four to fifty-one, a quarter of them using camp labour.[35] Other Muslim minorities in China have also been put to work manufacturing personal protective equipment. And, most sinister of all, Uyghurs in the Xinjiang camps have been used as guinea pigs in Covid vaccine trials.

The Guoanbu's post-Covid dream

As we've seen in previous chapters, the Guoanbu's intelligence strategy think-tank, the China Institutes of Contemporary International Relations (CICIR), is very active indeed. It dispatches its analysts to battlefields, organizes conferences, and sends delegates to symposiums run by its counterparts; its staff are experts in geopolitics, analyzing the world order as it is today—the same order that Xi's China aspires to dominate in the twenty-first century, through economic, cultural and military might. It's fitting, then, to end this new edition of *Chinese Spies* with a look at the CICIR president's assessment of the post-pandemic world.[36]

In his 2020 report "The Coronavirus Pandemic and a Once-in-a-Century Change", Professor Yuan Peng offers his analysis that "The pandemic is as bad as a world war", and "the existing international order will be difficult to maintain". He points to the ways Covid has weakened the institutions that, until now, have upheld this order: the UN, the IMF, the World Bank, the World Trade Organization and the WHO. As Yuan sees it,

> The outbreak and spread of the coronavirus pandemic has plunged the entire world into mourning, as countries locked down and borders closed, economies ground to a halt, stock markets plunged, oil prices collapsed, exchanges were broken off, insults were traded and rumors proliferated. The shock of the impact has been in no way less than a World War, which is yet another attack on the existing international order. The old order is perhaps unsustainable, but a new order has yet to be built [and this] is the basic feature of a once-in-a-century great change … the root cause of the crisis roiling the contemporary international scene.[37]

This detailed analysis, which considers the pandemic response and current status of every world region, should be read widely and in its entirety. Here, however, we will limit ourselves to a passage that hints at the internal discussions now taking place within Xi Jinping's inner circle:

> Broadly speaking, China is in a relatively favorable position in terms of its strategic relations with great powers. This is in part due to China's continuous efforts in recent years to promote a great power diplomacy with Chinese characteristics, but it is also a position earned by serving as the great "rear base area"[38] in the war against the pandemic, and assuming the responsibility of supplying the world with public health goods. But a favorable position is not the same thing as a strategic advantage, and there are many variables at play: the evolution of the pandemic, strategic and tactical planning, the use of diplomatic contacts, and changes in domestic politics in various countries.

For secret service theorists like Yuan, the Chinese leadership must now seize the opportunity that has arisen, in the name of the regime's "total national security" doctrine:

> Faced with the virus, China quickly controlled the epidemic through centralized leadership, unified command, coordinated action, central–local integration, mutual assistance, public medical care, community management, and taking the people as the base. China took the [global] lead in restoring work and production, displaying unique institutional advantages, in stark contrast to the institutional shortcomings we saw in the United States and Europe—party antagonism, the abuse of ideas of "freedom," and political polarization. Not wanting to admit system failures and policy errors, the West indulged in denouncing and slandering China to cover up its own inadequacies, for instance blaming China for having "covered up the virus," or for using pandemic diplomacy to "carry out their regional strategic ambitions," claiming "ideological victories," etc.

Yuan closes by emphasizing that

> The issues of biosecurity exposed by the coronavirus pandemic, as well as various questions of national security included in the concept of total national security, all illustrate that development requires security. Without security, externally there is always the risk of an attack in the night, and internally, all of our economic accomplishments could disappear in the blink of an eye. Development is indeed the only path to follow, but after 40 years of development under reform and opening [up], we need to add a prefix: "secure development" is the only correct path.

After all that has been revealed in the pages of this book, readers should expect nothing less than this bold determination from Yuan, who is one of the great thinkers of Xi Jinping's China. These intellectuals are centre-stage in the fight to build the PRC's future on the ever-shifting sands of our world, and they have been quick to understand that the pandemic can be used as an excuse to remove all liberty from the Chinese people. Meanwhile, in the wings, we can glimpse their comrades in the Guoanbu fighting the same war around the world, in the shadowy realm of secret services—just as those first Chinese spies resolved to do in Shanghai 100 years ago, back when it all began.

APPENDIX I

GLOSSARY OF ORGANIZATIONS

The Chinese terms are explained in the text. These are the organizations that appear most frequently.

Central Security Bureau (*zhongyang jingweiju* 中央警卫局)—under the CCP, in charge of protection of leaders (similar to the US Secret Service).

CICIR – China Institute for Contemporary International Relations, an intelligence "think-tank" overseen by the Diaochabu and then, after its creation in 1983, the Guoanbu.

CIISS – China Institute of International Strategic Studies, another intelligence "think-tank" under the PLA2.

COSTIND – Commission for Science, Technology and Industry for National Defence.

Diaochabu (调查部) – CCP investigation bureau under the party's Central Committee, partly merged into the Guoanbu after 1983. Replaced at CC level by a smaller organ known as the Investigation and Research Office (*diaoyanju* 调研局).

Gonganbu (公安部) – Ministry of Public Security. Its full name is the Gonganbu Guonei Anquan Baoweiju.

Guoanbu (国安部) – Ministry of State Security. Its full name is the *Guojia Anquanbu* (国家安全部).

Guoba (国保, pronounced Guobao: "national jewel") – 1st Bureau of the Gonganbu. Its full name is the National Security Guard Bureau of the Ministry of Public Security (*gonganbu guonei anquan baojingju* 公安部国内安全保卫局).

APPENDIX I

ILD (*Zhongyang Lianluobu* 中央联络, abbreviated to *Zhonglianbu* 中联部) – International Liaison Department of the CCP Central Committee, dealing with political intelligence and liaison with political parties abroad.

Intelligence Centre (*qingbao zhongxin* 情报中心) – under the PLA Joint Operations Command Centre (*Lianhezuozhan zhihuizhongxin* 联合作战指挥中心).

ISRC – International Studies Research Centre, an intelligence "think-tank" under the State Council.

PAP – the People's Armed Police, overseen first by the Gonganbu and later by the Central Military Commission.

Political-Legal Commission – oversees all the Chinese security services.

PLA2 – the People's Liberation Army 2nd Department (*Zongcan erbu* 总参二部, also written 2/PLA), a PLA general staff department (GSD)) equivalent to *Qingbaobu* (below).

PLA3 – the People's Liberation Army 3rd Department (*Zongcan sanbu* 总参三部, also written 3/PLA), a PLA general staff department in charge of intercepts and cyberwarfare.

PLA4 – the People's Liberation Army 4th Department (*Zongcan sibu* 总参四部), a PLA general staff department in charge of radars and countermeasures.

Qingbaobu or *Zongcan Qingbaobu* (总参情报部) – military intelligence bureau; same as the PLA2.

SAD – Social Affairs Department (*Zhongyang Shehuibu* 中央社会部, abbreviated to *Shehuibu* 社会部 or *Zhongshebu*), the communist secret service (1937–61).

Strategic Support Force (SSF – founded in 2016, regroups China's information warfare service, cyber troops, electronic warfare forces, space troops (Aerospace Reconnaissance Bureau) and the former PLA2 (including UAV), under the overall leadership of General Gao Jin 高津.

State Council – equivalent to the government of the PRC.

Teke (特科) – "Special Section", CCP intelligence service in Shanghai (1928 to 1934) or *Zhongyang Teke* 中央特科 (special section of the Central Committee).

Tewu (特务) – "special affairs", a general term for intelligence matters.

UFWD (*Zhongyang Tongyi Zhanxian Gongzuobu* 中央 统一战线工作部, abbreviated *Zhongyang Tongzhanbu* 中央统战部) – United Front Work Department of the CCP Central Committee, in charge of political influence and intelligence.

APPENDIX II

LEADERS OF THE CCP AND PRC INTELLIGENCE COMMUNITY

Secretaries of the Central Commission of Political Science and Law or Central Politics and Law Commission (*Zhongyang zhengfa weiyuanhui* 中央政法委员 会, abbreviated to *zhengfa*):

1958: Peng Zhen, 彭真
1958–1960: Luo Ruiqing, 罗瑞卿
1960–1966: Xie Fuzhi, 谢富治
1969–1980: Ji Dengkui, 纪登奎
1980–1982: Peng Zhen, 彭真
1982–1985: Chen Pixian, 陈丕显
1985–1992: Qiao Shi, 乔石
1992–1998: Ren Jianxin, 任建新
1998–2007: Luo Gan, 罗干
2007–2012: Zhou Yongkang, 周永康 (jailed 2015)
2012–2017: Meng Jianzhu, 孟建柱
2017–: Guo Shengkun, 郭声琨

CCP Special Service Section (*Zhongyang Tewuke* 中央特务科, abbreviated to *Teke*) founded by Zhou Enlai on 11 November 1927:

1927–1928: Luo Yinong, 罗亦农
1928–1931: Chen Geng, 陈赓
1931: Gu Shunzhang, 顾顺章, later defects to Kuomintang

Social Affairs Department (SAD):

1938–1946: Kang Sheng, 康生

1946–1959: Li Kenong, 李克农
1959 under Soviet influence, the SAD is closed

Diaochabu (CCP Central Investigation Department):

1955–1961: Li Kenong, 李克农
1961–1966: Kong Yuan, 孔原
1966–1967: Zou Dapeng, [邹大鹏] (assassinated by Red Guards in 1967?)
1966–1969: Luo Qingchang, 罗青长
[Summer 1978, the Diaochabu is re-established]
1978–1984: Luo Qingchang, 罗青长
[In 1983: The Diaochabu is merged with the new Guoanbu, while two smaller sections remain at Central Committee level: the Investigation and Research Office (*diaochaju* 调查局) and the Research and Study Office (*diaoyanju* 调研局).]

International Liaison Department (ILD):

1951–1966: Wang Jiaxiang, 王稼详
1959–1960: Wu Xiuquan, 伍修权
1966–1970: Kang Sheng, 康生
1971–1979: Geng Biao, 耿飚
1979–1982: Ji Pengfei, 姬鹏飞
1982–1983: Qiao Shi, 乔石
1983–1985: Qian Liren, 钱李仁
1985–1993: Zhu Liang, 朱良
1993–1997: Li Shuzheng (f.), 李淑铮
1997–2003: Dai Bingguo, 戴秉国
2004–2016: Wang Jiarui, 王家瑞
2016–: Song Tao, 宋涛

United Front Work Department (UFWD):

1938–1942: Zhou Enlai, 周恩来
1942–1947: Wang Ming, 王明
1947–1948: Zhou Enlai, 周恩来
1948–1964: Li Weihan, 李维汉
1964–1966: Xu Bing, 徐冰
Interruption during the Cultural Revolution (1966–1975)
1976: Li Dazhang, 李大章
1977–1982: Ulanfu or Ulanhu, 乌阑夫
1982–1985: Yang Jingren, 杨静仁
1985–1989: Yan Mingfu, 阎明复

End of 1989–22 November 1990 no director (following Tiananmen crisis)
1990–1992: Ding Guangen, 丁关根
1992–2000: Wang Zhaoguo, 王兆国
2002–2007: Liu Yandong (f.), 刘延东
2007–2012: Du Qinglin, 杜青林
2012–2014: Ling Jihua, 令计划
2014–2017: Sun Chunlan (f.), 孙春兰
2017–: You Quan, 尤权

Gonganbu:

1949–1959: Luo Ruiqing, 罗瑞卿
1959–1972: Xie Fuzhi, 谢富治
1972–1973: Li Zhen, 李震
1973–1976: Hua Guofeng, 华国峰
1977–1983: Zhao Cangbi, 赵苍壁
1983–1985: Liu Fuzhi, 刘复之
1985–1987: Ruan Chongwu, 阮崇武
1987–1990: Wang Fang, 王芳
1990–1997: Tao Siju, 陶驷驹
1997–2002: Jia Chunwang, 贾春旺
2002–2007: Zhou Yongkang, 周永康
2007–2017: Meng Jianzhu, 孟建住
2012–2017: Guo Shengkun, 郭声琨
2017–: Zhao Kezhi, 赵克志

Gonganbu 1st Bureau—National Bureau for the Protection of State Secrets

1949–1950: Yang Qiqing, 杨奇清 (arrested in 1968 during the Cultural Revolution)
1950–1953: Chen Long, 陈龙
1953–1964: Ling Yun, 凌云
1964–1966: Mu Fengyun, 募丰韵 (demoted in August 1966 during the Cultural Revolution)
1980–1982: Tao Siju, 陶驷驹
1982–1990: Tan Songqiu, 潭松裘
1990–2002: Chen Fangfang, 陈芳芳 (Tao Siju's wife)
2003–2009: Chen Zhimin, 陈智敏
2011–2012: Li Jiangzhou, 李江舟
2012–2013: Bai Shaokang, 白少康
2013–: Sun Lijun, 孙力军

APPENDIX II

Guoanbu:

1983–1986: Ling Yun, 凌云
1986–1997: Jia Chunwang, 贾春旺
1997–2007: Xu Yongyue, 许永跃
2007–2016: Geng Huichang, 耿惠昌
2017–: Chen Wenqing, 陈文清

People's Liberation Army deputy chiefs of staff (i/c intelligence):

1950s: Li Tao, 李涛
1953: Li Kenong, 李克农
1975–1980: Wu Xiuquan, 伍修权
1980: Yang Yong, 杨勇
1982–1992: Xu Xin, 徐信
1992–1996: Xiong Guangkai, 熊光楷
1999–2006: Luo Yudong, 罗宇栋
2006–2007: Zhang Qingsheng, 章沁生
2007–2009: Chen Xiaogong, 陈小功
2009–2012: Sun Jianguo, 孙建国
2012: Ma Xiaotian, 马晓天 replaced by Qi Jianguo 戚建国
2015: Wang Guanzhong, 王冠中
2016: A deputy chief of the new Joint Staff Department, Admiral Sun Jianguo [孙建国] is put in charge of strategic intelligence.

PLA2:

1932: Wu Xiuquan, 伍修权
–1938: Luo Ruiqing, 罗瑞卿
1938–1946: Kang Sheng, 康生
1948–1949: Li Kenong, 李克农
1950–1953: Li Kenong, 李克农 Head of new General Intelligence Department (*zongqingbaoju*) dissolved; at the same time the PLA2 was directed by…
1950–1951: Liu Zhijian, 刘志坚
1952–1954: Yan Kuiyao, 阎揆要
1954–1967: Liu Shaowen, 刘少文
1967–1969: Shen Shazi, 渗砂子
1970–1975: Zhang Ting, 张廷
1975–1978: Peng Mingzhi, 彭明治
1978–1982: Liu Guangfu, 刘光甫
1982–1985: Zhang Zhongru, 张中如

1988: Wu Jinfa, 戊进法 (or Cao Xin 曺信?)
1988–1992: Xiong Guangkai, 熊光楷
1993–1995: Luo Yudong, 罗宇栋
1995–1999: Ji Shengde, 姬胜德 (jailed for corruption)
1999–2001: Chen Kaizeng, 陈开曾
2001–2003: Luo Yudong, 罗宇栋
2004–2006: Huang Baifu, 黄柏富
2006–2007: Chen Xiaogong, 陈小功
2007–2011: Yang Hui, 杨晖
2011–2015: Chen Youyi, 陈友谊
2015: Wang Xiao, 王肖
2016: The PLA2 is renamed the Intelligence Bureau (*Qingbaoju* 情报局) under the new Joint Staff Department of the Central Military Commission, led by Chen Youyi.

PLA3:

1949: Kong Yuan, 孔原
1950s–1960s: Wang Zheng 王诤
1954–1959: Li Tao, 李涛
1959–1967: Peng Fuqiu, 彭富九
1967–1969: Hu Bingyun, 胡病云
1969–1974: Hu Beiwen, 胡备文
1974–1975: Peng Fuqiu, 彭富九
1975–1982: Dai Jingyuan, 戴镜元
1982–1984: Jiang Zhong, 姜钟
1984–1990: Gu Zhaoqun, 贾朝群
1989–1992: Wei Chongbao, 卫崇保
1993: Wang Jianren, 王健仁
1993–1996: Shi Quan, 时权
1996–1999: Zhang Xiaoyang, 张小阳
2000–2005: Qiu Rulin, 邱如林
2006–2010: Wu Guohua, 吴国华
2010–2014: Liu Xiaobei, 刘晓北
2014–2015: Meng Xuezheng, 孟学政
2015: Huang Jiwen, 黄继文
2016: The PLA3 becomes the core unit of the new Strategic Support Force (SSF).

PLA4:

2000: Dai Qingmin, 戴清民
2005: Zeng Zhanping, 曾占平

2015: Yang Shuai, 杨帅

2016: The PLA4 is transferred to the new Strategic Support Force (SSF).

PLA5 (5th General Staff Department in charge of communications, *Zong canmo bu Tongxin Bu* 总参谋部通信部; renamed the Information Department, *Zong canmo Xinxihua Bu* 信息化部, in June 2011):

1930s: Pan Feng

1961–1968 and 1977–1979: Jiang Wen, 江文

1981: Cui Lun, 催伦

1999–2005: Xu Xiaoyan, 徐小岩

2006: Zhang Xuncai, 张训才

2008: Chen Dong, 陈东

2015: Yang Liming, 杨黎明

2016: The PLA5 is transferred to the new Strategic Support Force (SSF).

PLA GPD (General Political Department) Liaison Department (*Zongzheng Lianluo bu* 总政联络部—responsible for undercover intelligence work abroad, with Taiwan as prime target; originally part of the PLA Enemy Work Department; its cover was the China Association for International Friendly Contacts or CAIFC):

1955–1966: Zhang Zizhen, 张梓桢

[dissolved and re-established after the Cultural Revolution]

1975–1984: Yang Side, 杨斯德

1985–1990: Jin Li, 金黎

1990–1998: Ye Xuanning, 叶选宁

1999–2007: Liang Hongchang, 梁宏昌

2007–2012: Xing Yunming, 邢运明

2012–: Zhang Yang, 张阳

2016: Renamed the Political Work Department under Central Military Commission, headed by Miao Hua 苗华 with a new Liaison Bureau (*Lianluoju* 联络局).

PLA GPD Security Department (*Zongzheng baowei bu* 总政保卫部):

1930s: Luo Ruiqing, 罗瑞卿

1980–: Shi Jinqian, 史近前

1990: Yang Baibing, 杨白冰

1993: Zhou Ziyu, 周子玉

1994–1999: Zhang Zhenhua, 张振华

1999–2005: Li Guang, 李光

2005: Zhang Hui, 张辉

2010–: Yu Shanjun, 于善軍

APPENDIX III

CHINESE INTELLIGENCE STRUCTURE, 1921–2019

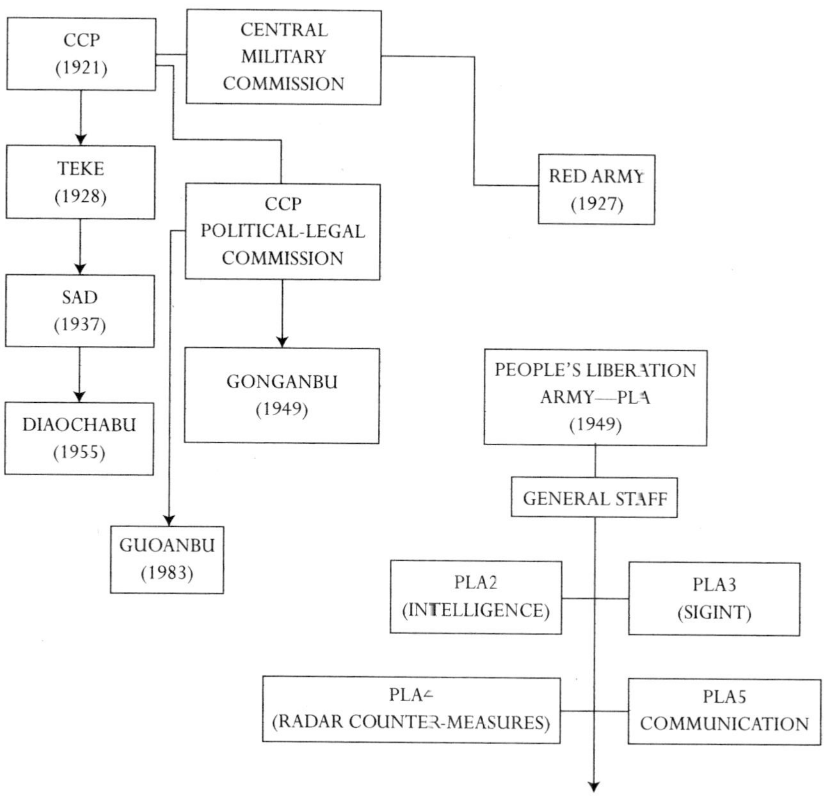

APPENDIX IV

PLA CHAIN OF COMMAND INCLUDING MILITARY INTELLIGENCE (IS)

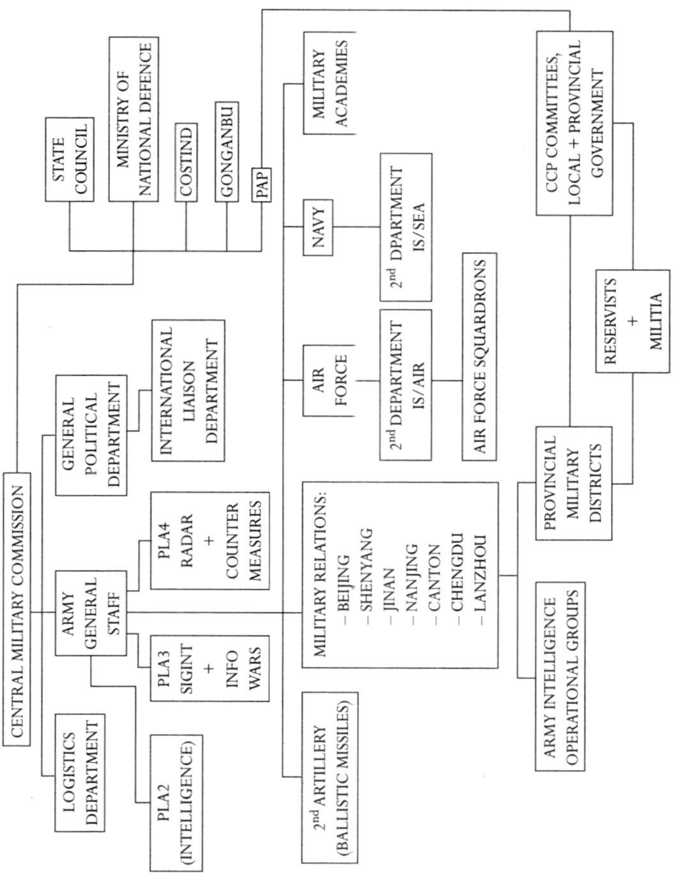

APPENDIX V

PRINCIPAL COMPANIES REPRESENTING THE CHINESE MILITARY-INDUSTRIAL LOBBY IN HONG KONG

AT THE TIME OF THE 1997 RETROCESSION

APPENDIX VI

STRUCTURE OF THE CHINA INSTITUTE FOR CONTEMPORARY INTERNATIONAL RELATIONS

Director: Chen Qurong

Deputies: Xu Dan (journal editor), Song Baoxian,

Lu Zhongwei (Japan expert and, since 2000, director),

Geng Huichang (sole remaining member of the previous team, in post since July 1986)

1. Institute of Eastern European and Central Asian Studies
2. Institute of North American Studies
3. Institute of Western European Studies
4. Institute of North East Asian Studies
5. Institute of African and Middle Eastern Studies
6. Institute of Latin American Studies
7. Institute for the Study of Major International Figures
8. Institute of International Social Studies
9. Institute of International Studies
10. Institute for the Study of China on the World Stage
11. Institute for the Study of International Change

APPENDIX VII

PRINCIPAL CASES INVOLVING CHINESE SPIES IN THE UNITED STATES

February 1984	Kuang Shi Lin and four other Chinese people arrested for attempting to export electronics.
December 1987	deputy military attaché Hou Desheng and consul in Chicago Zhang Weichu arrested by the FBI and deported for spying.
1992	Bin Wu, a former Guoanbu "deep-water fish", recruited into dissident circles after Tiananmen. Originally a professor of philosophy, he was "turned" by the FBI but was later sentenced to ten years in prison for theft of military technology.
December 1993	Kao Yenmen, a North Carolina restaurant owner, tries to buy missile components for sale in Beijing. He is deported and sent to Hong Kong.
March 1998	Peter Lee, a Taiwanese-American researcher at Los Alamos, sentenced to twelve months on bail for having passed secrets to the Chinese about lasers that can be used to simulate detonations of atomic bombs in 1985.
May 1999	arrest of Wen Ho Lee, physicist at Los Alamos, accused of providing information on nuclear weapons in 1988; he is tried for espionage, acquitted, and released in September 2000 with an official apology.
March 1999	Yao Yi, who reports to the PLA2, arrested in Boston along with Xu Zhihong; both men charged with trying to steal secret techniques for manufacturing gyroscopes with optical fibre that can be used for missiles.

June 2000	the Xinhua News Agency accused of trying to buy a building in Washington to spy on the Pentagon.
April 2001	two Chinese men from the PRC (Lin Hai and Xu Kai) and a Chinese-American (Cheng Yong-Qing) arrested by the FBI for stealing software from a company called Lucent (they had set up a joint venture to market it in China).
May 2003	arrest of Katherine Leung, described in the media as a Chinese Mata Hari and accused of having played an active role in the stalemate of the FBI's investigation into the Chinese financing of Bill Clinton's election committee. Like Lee, she is acquitted.
2004	a couple arrested and charged with selling $500,000 worth of electronic components to the Chinese for their missile system.
June 2006	trial of Ronald Montaperto, former head of the China Section of the Defense Intelligence Agency, who was recruited by the air attaché, General Yu Zhenghe.
March 2007	Chi Mak, a Chinese-American, found guilty of stealing technology concerning the US Navy. He is sentenced to twenty-four years in prison in 2008.
2008	Tai Shen Kuo, Gregg Bergesen and Yu Xin Kang each sentenced in three separate trials to fifteen years' imprisonment, for passing information to the Chinese about the technical data of precision weapons and their sale to Taiwan.
2010	Dongfan "Greg" Chung, an Orange County (California) Boeing engineer, sentenced to fifteen years in prison for handing over technical secrets to China, including data about the Space Shuttle.
April 2011	Xiang Dong Yu, also known as Mike Yu, and his wife Shanshan Du, both Ford engineers in Detroit, sentenced to three years and one year respectively, for passing confidential economic data about the company to the Chinese.
February 2012	computer company CYBERsitter (California) signs a transaction agreement for $2 billion (settlement for a $2.2 billion suit) after suing Lenovo and several other companies for code theft in 2010.

September 2014	US military contractor Benjamin Bishop sentenced to seven years for furnishing national defence secrets about the military command in Hawaii to his Chinese girlfriend online.
March 2017	diplomat Candace Claiborne of the State Department accused of treason; she reportedly provided information to the Shanghai Guoanbu, for payment in money and gifts, on the US government's stance regarding economic negotiations with China.

APPENDIX VIII

REORGANIZATION OF THE GUOANBU UNDER XU YONGYUE, LATE 1990S

Minister: Xu Yongyue
Chief of Staff & Director of General Affairs: Liu Yiping

Deputy Ministers:
Sun Wenfang, Zhan Yongjie, Wang Fuzhong, Niu Ping, Ding Renlin, Tang Jiyu, Yu Enguang, Hu Shaopo, Yu Fang, Hui Chun, Hui Ping.
Bureau of General Affairs: Qi Shuquan

1st Bureau Secret Services – Taiwan, Hong Kong, Macao: He Liang

2nd Bureau of Intelligence – Taiwan, Hong Kong, Macao: Zhan Yongjie

3rd Bureau of Intelligence – Taiwan, Hong Kong, Macao: Tian Jian

4th Bureau – technical support: Li Keyun

5th Bureau – illegals department

6th Bureau – counterintelligence & research: Jia Ruixiang

7th Bureau – internal Chinese affairs (intelligence circulation)

8th Bureau – planning, regional Guoanbu offices

9th Bureau – counterintelligence in China, counter-defection

10th Bureau – scientific & technical espionage: Liu Zhizheng

11th Bureau – Institute of Contemporary International Relations: Geng Huichang, Xue Qiao, Ms Lu Yaokun

APPENDIX VIII

12th Bureau – agent handlers abroad: Mao Guchun

13th Bureau – information technology service: He Dequan (+ Hong Kong bureau)

14th Bureau – communications, radio broadcasts: Liu Yushi (+ Macao bureau)

15th Bureau – agent handlers in Taiwan: Chen Yicun, Cai Daren (Centre of Operations)

16th Bureau – archives, analyses: Wu Zhuo (Bureau for the Study of Espionage: Bi Xiansheng)

17th Bureau – industrial and commercial intelligence: Tian Gengren

18th Bureau – Beijing Institute of International Relations (BIRI): Zhu Jishan

Beijing Institute of International Politics (BIPI); Suzhou Institute of Cadre Management (mail service)

Bureaus of personnel, inspection and discipline – finances, cadres: Yu Hongbao

Beijing Bureau: Li Yintang

Shanghai Bureau: Cai Xumin

Canton Bureau: Shen Hongying

APPENDIX IX

MAJOR SIGINT SITES

SIGINT Interception stations in China (source: Desmond Ball).

APPENDIX X

PLA3 CYBER-BASES

THE TWELVE CYBER-BASES OF THE PLA3

1st Bureau (Unit 61786): responsible for PLA security.

2nd Bureau (Unit 61389): specializing in cyber-attacks against Anglophone countries (US, UK, Canada, Australia).

3rd Bureau (Unit 61785): specializing in intercepting intelligence communications in neighbouring countries, including Taiwan and Korea.

4th Bureau (Unit 61419): Japan and North and South Korea.

5th Bureau (Unit 61565): Russia.

6th Bureau (Unit 61726): South and South-East Asia (particularly Taiwan, from the Wuhan station in Hubei province).

7th Bureau (Unit 61580): responsible for the coordination of a dozen regional satellite offices within China.

8th Bureau (Unit 61046): covering Europe, Africa, the Middle East and Latin America.

9th Bureau (Unit 61221): analysis of strategic intelligence, monitoring of the PLA's IT equipment.

10th Bureau (Unit 61886): Russia and Central Asia, with a special role for missile surveillance.

11th Bureau (Unit 61672): a third bureau monitoring Russian communications.

12th Bureau (Unit 61486): interception of intelligence particularly from branches of European, Japanese and Korean companies.

These bureaus are distinct from the TRB, the PLA3's Technical Reconnaissance Bureaus (*jishu zhencha ju*), which provided interception and communications for seven military regions before being regrouped into the five new theatres of combat and integrated into the Strategic Support Force (SSF) under Xi Jinping's reorganization in 2016. These include Unit 78006, which is the TRB of the former Chengdu military region covering Tibet and Xinjiang (see Chapter 14).

They are also distinct from internet spying stations like Unit 61398, located in Pudong, Shanghai, which had its moment of glory in 2013, when the US authorities held it responsible for multiple cyber-attacks in the United States.

Sources: Mark A. Stokes, Jenny Lin and L. C. Russell Hsiao, *The Chinese People's Liberation Army Signals Intelligence and Cyber Reconnaissance Infrastructure*, Project 2049 Institute, 11 November 2011; Dean Cheng, *Cyber Dragon*, *op. cit.*; interview with intelligence specialist Jason Pan, *Taipei Times*, March 2015.

APPENDIX XI

2008 BEIJING OLYMPICS SECURITY/ESPIONAGE STRUCTURE

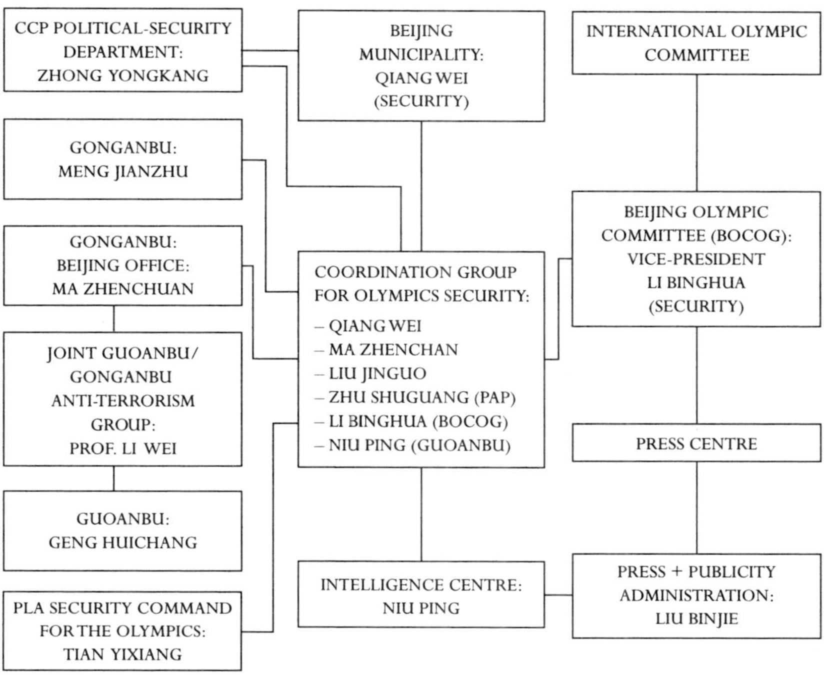

NOTES

INTRODUCTION: OLD RED SPIES NEVER DIE

1. See "Ex-Party intelligence Division Celebrates 90th Anniversary", *Global Times*, 24 May 2017.
2. A list can be found at the end of this book giving the names of the main Chinese intelligence services, as well as those of their principal leaders.

1. THE BATTLE FOR SHANGHAI

1. For further reading on the Green Gang and Du Yuesheng, see Roger Faligot and Rémi Kauffer, *The Chinese Secret Service: Kang Sheng and the Shadow Government in Red China* (trans. Christine Donougher), London, Headline, 1989; Roger Faligot, *La mafia chinoise en Europe* [The Chinese Mafia in Europe], Paris, Calmann-Lévy, 2001; Brian G. Martin, *The Shanghai Green Gang, Politics and Organized Crime, 1919–1937*, Berkeley CA, University of California Press, 1996.
2. From the biography of Luo Yinong, in Hu Hua (ed.), *Zhonggongdang shirenwuzhuan* [The Dictionary of Historical Personalities of the Communist Party], vol. 8, Research Centre of Historical Figures of the CCP [*Zhonggongdang shenwu yanjiuhui*], Xi'an, Shaanxi renmin chubanshe, 1983.
3. The future communist mayor of Saint-Denis, Jacques Doriot, actively collaborated with the Nazis during the Second World War. As a result, Russian and Chinese sources often avoid mentioning that he was present in Shanghai in July 1921. This is made apparent, however, in the archives of the Paris Police Prefecture (carton BA 40). See Jacques de Launay, "Dossiers de police des socialistes" [Police dossiers of socialists], *Histoire pour tous*, April 1975; and Hans Heinrich Wetzel, *Liu Shao Chi, le moine rouge* [The Red Monk], Paris, Editions Denoël, 1961. Doriot took part in a further political mission to China in 1927.
4. The GRU was and still is the armed forces' Main Intelligence Directorate (*Glavnoye Razvedyvatel'noye Upravleniye)*. The Cheka was replaced in 1922 by the GPU, and then in 1934 by the NKVD (People's Commissariat for Internal Affairs). The INO (Foreign Intelligence Department) remained throughout these metamorphoses.

5. This information is available in the archives of the French and International Concessions in Shanghai, as well as in Russian archives and the memoirs of Chinese revolutionaries who subsequently broke with communism, which are particularly eloquent on the subject. Official Chinese sources are more circumspect, because even today CCP leaders do not want to admit publicly that these services were entirely created by the Russians.
6. Vladimir Nikolayevitch Uzov, "Le renseignement soviétique en Chine, 1925–1927" [Soviet intelligence in China, 1925–1927], *Communisme*, N°65–66—2001. This article provides an excellent overview of the Soviet apparatus in China, based on recently opened archives.
7. Ibid.
8. According to documents in V.N. Uzov's Russian archive, the College's president, Tan Pin-san (1886–1959), had at his disposal an entire service with several branches set up by Fu-Li, his deputy in charge of counterintelligence and financial questions. A certain Yan-li was in charge of the informer network and the fight against organized crime, while somebody called Chen was head of counterintelligence in the Kuomintang army. The entire organization was overseen by the Soviet advisor Pozdneev.
9. Élisée and Onésime Reclus, *L'Empire du Milieu* [The Middle Kingdom], Paris, Hachette, 1902. Higher numbers have been cited, but they include the indirect victims of the violence triggered by the revolt and its subsequent repression, as is always the case during a civil war. See also the book by their son and nephew, Jacques Reclus, *La révolte des Taïping (1851–1864). Prologue à la révolution chinoise* [The Taiping Revolt (1851–1864): Prologue to the Chinese Revolution] (preface by Jean Chesneaux), Paris, Le Pavillon Roger Maria Éditeur, 1972.
10. Chen Yi (1901–72), who studied art at the Grande Chaumière Academy of Painting, was expelled from France along with fellow agitator Ye Jianying (1898–1986), who was from Canton and whose name means "heroic spear". He was the son of a wealthy Singapore merchant. Zhu De ("Red Virtue", 1886–1976) arrived in Marseille in autumn 1922 at the age of 36, a former warlord and opium addict turned communist. He went on to join the Chinese network in the Weimar Republic.
11. See more about Cremet in Roger Faligot and Rémi Kauffer, *L'hermine rouge de Shanghai* [The Red Ermine of Shanghai], Rennes, Les portes du large, 2005.
12. Nigel West, *GCHQ, the Secret Wireless War 1900–86*, London, Coronet Books, 1987.
13. The embassy archives were published by the White Russian N. Miraevsky, *World Wide Soviet Plots, as disclosed by hitherto unpublished documents seized at the USSR Embassy in Peking*, Tianjin Press (1927).
14. French military attaché report by Major Roques from Beijing, dated 18 February 1928, Service historique de l'armée de terre à Vincennes, France, 7 N 3284.
15. Archives from the Shanghai Municipal Police (MAE, E 515, cartons 458, 459, 460–465). Report N°33 mentions an assassination attempt on Chiang Kai-shek planned by Luo Yinong, with help from the GPU's Achinin, secretary at the Soviet consulate in Shanghai.
16. Statement by Gu Shunzhang after his desertion, Shanghai Municipal Police, Special Branch archive N°2911/8, 1931.
17. Captain Eugène Pick, *China in the Grip of Bolsheviks*. The incredible story of "Captain Pick", circus performer, petty criminal and spy for the Japanese navy in Shanghai, who vanished in a Taiwanese prison in 1950 after having been tried and sentenced by the

Americans, is at the heart of Bernard Wasserstein's *Secret War in Shanghai*, London, Profile Books, 1998.

18. Vladimir N. Uzov, "Le renseignement soviétique en Chine" [Soviet espionage in China], *op. cit*.
19. For a full account of Kang's life see Roger Faligot and Rémi Kauffer, *The Chinese Secret Service: Kang Sheng and the Shadow Government in Red China* (trans. Christine Donougher), London, Headline, 1989; and John Byron and Robert Pack, *The Claws of the Dragon: Kang Sheng, the Evil Genius behind Mao and his Legacy of Terror in People's China*, New York, Simon & Schuster, 1992; in Chinese, Lin Qingshan, *Kang Sheng waizhuan*, [biography of Kang Sheng], Hong Kong, Xinchen Chubanshe, 1987.
20. Pierre Broué, in his monumental history of the Comintern, listed the following aliases used by Zhou Enlai: Chen Kuang, Du Bisheng, Hu Fu, Kuan, Kuan Sheng (which may have been a confusion with Kang Sheng), Shao Shan, Siu, Te Ren, Wei Hen, Wu, Wu Hao and Moskvin. Pierre Broué, *Histoire de l'Internationale communiste (1919–1943)* [History of the Communist International, 1919–1943], Paris, Fayard, 1997.
21. Author interview with Guan Shuzhi in Taipei, 20 June 1986. Professor Guan was a communist in Shanghai during the 1930s, where he knew the team around Zhou very well, particularly Kang Sheng. He then crossed over to the opposing camp and became a supporter of the Kuomintang.
22. Quoted in Jacques Guillermaz, *Histoire du parti communiste chinois* [History of the Chinese Communist Party], vol. 1, Paris, Petite bibliothèque Payot, 1975.
23. Australian historian Matt Brazil suggested to me that the Shanghai structure was not in fact set up by Zhou Enlai, but rather that, a few years earlier, at the end of 1926, the military commission of the CCP created a Special Operations Bureau (*Tewu Gongzuo Chu*) in Wuhan, which constituted the other element of the developing structure. It was from this original service that the 2nd Department of the army, charged with military intelligence (PLA2), was born. But it is likely that Zhou borrowed this title for the "Bureau" whose embryonic foundations he laid in Shanghai in spring 1927, and then more concretely the following year after he returned from the USSR. See Matthew Brazil, "China", in Rodney P. Carlisle (ed.), *Encyclopedia of Intelligence and Counterintelligence*, Armonk NY, M. E. Sharpe, 2004.
24. Han Suyin, *Eldest Son: Zhou Enlai and the Making of Modern China*, London, Jonathan Cape, 1994.
25. Chen Lifu was head of the Investigation Section of the Kuomintang's Organization Department. Ascetic, almost mystical in his anti-communist beliefs, he set up a service in the Kuomintang for intelligence and psychological warfare, called the Central Bureau of Investigation and Statistics (*Zhong Tong*), headed by his cousin, Xu Enzeng, who like him had trained in America in radio communication. The second organization overseen by Chen Lifu, the AB or anti-Bolshevik line, specialized in infiltrating the communist underground in rural areas, and used psychological operations to provoke clashes between different groups of communists. The "turning" of prisoners was particularly prevalent, as suggested in a report by the Deuxième Bureau dated January 1935, signed by Colonel Bonavita, military attaché in Beijing: "When the Reds are arrested or surrender, they are not executed, but they are sent to concentration camps called "re-education camps" where they learn about the errors that they have made". Archives du Service historique de l'Armée de Terre [Archives of the History Service of the Army], Vincennes, France.
26. Yu Maochun, *OSS in China: Prelude to Cold War*, New Haven CT, Yale University Press,

1996; Frederick Wakeman Jr, *Spymaster: Dai Li and the Chinese Secret Service*, Berkeley CA, University of California Press, 2003.

27. John Byron and Robert Pack retrace the details of this episode in *The Claws of the Dragon, op. cit*. I uncovered the details of Luo Yinong's arrest in the Shanghai police archives: in dossier 205, 30 April 1928, "Lou-Ye-Nong" is described as being an "important member of the CCP's counterintelligence … This was a serious loss for the CCP". Byron and Pack also reveal that, in 1983, the Chinese executed He Zhihua's son as part of a general crackdown on corruption.
28. Nie Rongzhen, *Inside the Red Star: the Memoirs of Marshal Nie Rongzhen* (trans. Zhong Renyi), Beijing, New World Press, 1984.
29. Jean Cremet resurfaced in Europe, helped Malraux in Spain, and took part in anti-Nazi resistance in northern France. He lived under a false name, Gabriel Peyrot, until his death in Belgium in 1973, as Rémi Kauffer and I discovered after a lengthy investigation twenty years later. See Faligot and Kauffer, *L'hermine rouge de Shanghai* [The Red Ermine of Shanghai], *op. cit*.; and Roger Faligot, *Les tribulations des Bretons en Chine* [The Tribulations of Bretons in China], Rennes, Les Portes du large, 2019.
30. Jonathan Haslam, *Near and Distant Neighbours: A New History of Soviet Intelligence*, Oxford, Oxford University Press, 2015.
31. Unpublished memoir about Jean Cremet, given to the author and Rémi Kauffer in January 1989 by his daughter, Mme Frontisi-Ducroux.
32. Nie Rongzhen, in *Inside the Red Star, op. cit*., claims that special agents had time to go to Gu's apartment, where they found a letter addressed to Chiang Kai-shek in which Gu said that he was planning to change camp. This strikes me as an ex post facto attempt to blacken Gu's character, and there is no other evidence to confirm this version of events.
33. See Byron and Pack, *The Claw of the Dragon, op. cit*.
34. Author interview with Professor Guan Shuzhi, *op. cit*.
35. I have delved deeply into archives of the Noulens affair, in which Ho Chi Minh features under his alias "Fernand", a variation of the pseudonym "Ferdinand" he used in France (ARCH DMP). See also: Dennis J. Duncanson, "Ho Chi Minh in Hong Kong 1931–32", *The China Quarterly*, Jan–March 1974, and Sophie Quinn-Judge, *Ho Chi Minh: The Missing Years, 1919–1941*, Berkeley/Los Angeles CA, University of California Press, 2002. Incidentally, a document with his photo, found in the Comintern archives (Тибо in Russian), confirms that when in the USSR Cremet often used the pseudonym Thibault (both his wife's and his mother's surname); this contradicts a doubt expressed by Quinn-Judge.
36. Dispatch No. 159 from the French Consulate, dated 26 November 1931 (MAE), which also mentions the Noulens case and that of Comintern agent Joseph Ducroux, arrested in Singapore.
37. In addition to my book with Rémi Kauffer, *The Chinese Secret Service*, *op. cit*., I have relied both on archives and recent books published in China, including Hao Zaijin, *Zhongguo mimi zhan—zhonggong qingbao, baowei gongzuo jizhi* [The Secret Chinese Battle: The truth about CCP intelligence and protection], Beijing, Zuojia Chubanshe, 2004.
38. In fact, they called him "head of the 2nd Section of the GPU"—a reference not to the Russian service, but to Chinese/CCP intelligence. They didn't know exactly how the Chinese services functioned, but did know that many of the intelligence cadres had been trained in the USSR.

39. Published in 1934 in Moscow, in Paris by the CDLP and in New York by Workers Library Publishers.
40. André Malraux, *La Nouvelle Revue Française*, April 1931.
41. Kang Sheng was vehement in his denunciations of Trotskyists, even though at the beginning of his stay in Moscow some thought he had secret sympathies for the left opposition and for Trotsky himself. The latter was assassinated five years later in Mexico by the NKVD.
42. Quinn-Judge, *Ho Chi Minh: the Missing Years, 1919–1941*, *op. cit.*; Robert Turner and Victor Usov, "Kang Sheng—Chinese Beria", *Far Eastern Affairs*, N°4, 1991; William J. Duiker, *Ho Chi Minh: A Life*, New York, Hyperion, 2000.
43. For more about Kang Sheng's time in Paris, see the testimonies of French Maoists such as Jacques Jurquet in Kauffer's and my biography of Kang Sheng, *op. cit.*, chapter 3, "May 68 and the small Comintern of Kang Sheng". These testimonies have since been confirmed by documents in the Russian archives.

2. MAO'S SECRET SERVICE

1. Interview with Yan Mingfu published by the New China News Agency (Xinhua), "Chinese intelligence agent contributes to WWII Victory", 4 May 2005.
2. The use made of Yan Haobang's information in 1945 is quite clear. In terms of the information he provided in 1941, it is much less clear, for Stalin does not seem to have made much use of the plethora of information he received warning him of Hitler's imminent attack. Why would he believe the Chinese spy and not agents from his own GRU, like Richard Sorge, Leopold Trepper, Kim Philby and Alexander Rado? According to the Russians, General Filipp Golikov, head of the GRU, received a total of eighty-eight warnings of the Nazi attack without acting on them (Andrew and Gordievsky, *KGB: The Inside Story of its Foreign Operations, from Lenin to Gorbachev*, London, Hodder & Stoughton, 1990).
3. Zeng Shan, the leader of the first Jiangxi *soviet* (1927–35), was the father of Shanghai's vice-president Zeng Qinghong, Jiang Zemin's *éminence grise* and the rival to his successor as president, Hu Jintao. See his biography by Su Duoshou and Liu Mianyu, *Zeng Shan Zhuan*, Jiangxi Chubanshe, 1999.
4. Matthew Brazil, "China", in Rodney P. Carlisle (ed.), *Encyclopedia of Intelligence and Counterintelligence*, Armonk NY, M. E. Sharpe, 2004. To complete the story, it should be added that after the creation of the SAD, a new protection section of the CCP came into being, led by Zhou Xing, under the aegis of Kang Sheng. Zhou Xing distinguished himself in 1931 with the assassination of a number of Trotskyist dissidents.
5. Without actually naming him, Jean-Luc Domenach evokes Fu Hao's career as a "strange diplomat" in his thought-provoking book *Comprendre la Chine aujourd'hui* [Understanding China Today], Paris, Perrin Asies, 2007.
6. Warren Kuo, *Analytical History of the Chinese Communist Party*, vol. 4, Institute of International Relations, Taipei, 1971. In addition, Report No. 4508/S of the Shanghai Police Service, dated 25 November 1939 and signed by police chief Louis Fabre, points out that "for the overseas Chinese there is a special section in Hong Kong run by Pan Han, in conjunction with the Comintern." He further identifies "Kang Sheng aka Chao Yun, as head of the GPU in Yan'an".
7. Author interview with Park Sang-soo, Paris, 2 April 2000. For more detail on the

relationships between the CCP and secret societies, see the history section of my book *La mafia chinoise en Europe* [The Chinese Mafia in Europe], Paris, Calmann-Lévy, 2001.

8. For further details on the functioning of the SAD and biographical details of its main cadres, see Roger Faligot and Rémi Kauffer, *The Chinese Secret Service: Kang Sheng and the Shadow Government in Red China* (trans. Christine Donougher), London, Headline, 1989.
9. See Liu Jiadong, *Chen Yun yu diaocha yanjiu* [Chen Yun and the Search For Investigation], Beijing, Zhongguo wenxian chubanshe, Beijing, 2004. See Chen's article published in N°11 of the internal magazine *The Communist*, 1 October 1940, entitled "Some Questions about the Party's Secret Organisations". See also *Selected Works of Chen Yun, (1926–1949)*, Beijing, Foreign Languages Press, 1988.
10. John Byron and Robert Pack assert that General Wang Zhen, from Hunan, commanded this elite regiment (*The Claws of the Dragon: Kang Sheng, the Evil Genius behind Mao and his Legacy of Terror in People's China*, New York, Simon & Schuster, 1992). However, the German Sinologist Wolfgang Bartke of the Institute of Asian Affairs in Hamburg claims that he led anti-Japanese guerrilla operations first in the Canton region, and later in the north-east until the Japanese surrendered (*Who's Who in the People's Republic of China*, Brighton, Harvester Press, 1981). We will meet General Wang Zhen later, during the 1989 Tiananmen massacre (Chapter 5).
11. Peter Vladimirov, *The Vladimirov Diairies*, New York, Doubleday, 1975.
12. Byron and Pack, *The Claws of the Dragon, op. cit.*
13. Han Suyin, *Eldest Son: Zhou Enlai and the Making of Modern China*, London, Jonathan Cape, 1994.
14. Jean-Luc Domenach, *Chine: L'archipel oublié* [China: The Forgotten Archipelago], Paris, Fayard, 1992. Even the least lenient historians of the period, such as Jung Chang and Jon Halliday in their book *Mao: The Unknown Story* (Jonathan Cape, 2005), claim that only a few thousand died. Clearly, this was not so much a mass massacre as an experimental terror device, which would later be applied by other regimes in the East: North Korea, Burma, Laos and Cambodia, under the influence of Chinese communism.
15. Wang Ming's life was saved by Orlov and Vladimirov. He left China for the USSR in 1950. Five years after his death in 1974, a Moscow publisher brought out a book under his name in several languages: Wang Ming, *Mao's Betrayal*, Moscow, Progress Publishers, 1979.
16. Iris Chang, *Thread of the Silkworm*, New York, Basic Books, 1995.
17. Bruno Pontecorvo, brother of the *Battle of Algiers* filmmaker Gillo Pontecorvo, was a member of Service B, the French communist intelligence service linked to the Red Orchestra, the famous spy network that drove the Soviet GRU. Meanwhile Qian Sanqiang was linked during the war to Pao Xienju, the press officer of the Chinese nationalist embassy in Bern, who worked under the alias "Polo" (as in Marco Polo) for the Red Orchestra's Swiss branch. See Roger Faligot and Rémi Kauffer, *Service B*, Paris, Fayard, 1985.
18. In 2004, the PLA published an astonishing book entitled *Investigation of the First Chinese Nuclear Bomb*, containing much new information (Liang Dongyuan, *Yuangzidan Diaocha*, Jiefangjun Chubanshe, Beijing, 2005).
19. General Jacques Guillermaz, military attaché of the Free French in Chongqing, who knew Dai Li well, wrote to me on 10 April 1986: "Kang Sheng had nothing to do with the plane crash that caused the death of Dai Li on 17 March 1946. The aircraft that was

transporting him flew through a very heavy storm between Shanghai and Nanjing before crashing during a forced landing in the middle of the countryside."

20. Shen Zui's book (written with the help of his daughter Shen Meijuan) is published in English as *A KMT War Criminal in New China*, Beijing, Foreign Languages Press, 1986. In Chinese: Shen Zui, *Wo zhe san shi nian*, Hunan renmin chubanshe, 1983.
21. Peter Conn, *Pearl S. Buck: A Cultural Biography*, Cambridge, Cambridge University Press, 1998. Buck would continue to support Zhou and Mao during the Korean War in 1953, but fell out with them later during the Cultural Revolution.
22. See Sterling Seagrave, *The Soong Dynasty*, London, Sigwick & Jackson, 1985; and *Lords of the Rim*, London, Corgi, 1995. Also see Bernard Brizay, *Les trois sœurs Soong (Une dynastie chinoise du XXe siècle)* [The three Soong sisters: A 20th Century Chinese Dynasty], Paris, Éditions du Rocher, 2007.
23. *The Blue Lotus* was first published in Great Britain by Methuen Children's Books in 1983.
24. See Pierre Assouline's biography, *Hergé, the Man who Created Tintin*, Oxford, Oxford University Press, 2011.
25. Pat Givens, head of the Special Branch, was an officer of the Shanghai Municipal Police from 1906 to 1936. He organized a protective force with two Irish inspectors like himself, Mr Ganley and Eugene Hugh Lynch. All three were admirers of Michael Collins, the ex-head of the IRA's secret services, who later became defence minister of the Irish Free State.
26. In their delightful biography *Chang!*, Jean-Michel Coblence and Zhang Yifei, Zhang's daughter, mention his friendship with Tong, without specifying who he was (Brussels, Editions Moulinsart, 2003).
27. In 1949, the head of the Academy was Li Weihan, a close associate of Zhou Enlai from their Paris days. On 13 June 2002, his distant successor, Wang Zhaoguo, head of the United Front Work Department, celebrated the centenary of Tong Dizhou's birth in Beijing.
28. Gérard Lenne, *Tchang au pays du Lotus bleu* [Chang in the Land of the Blue Lotus], Paris, Librairie Séguier, 1990.
29. Ibid.
30. Benoît Peeters, *Hergé, Son of Tintin*, Baltimore MD, Johns Hopkins University Press, 2012.
31. See Chen Yi's article in Lucien Bianco et al. (eds), *La Chine. Le Dictionnaire du mouvement ouvrier international* [Dictionary of the International Workers' Movement: China], Paris, Les Presses de Sciences Po, 1985.
32. Christopher Andrew and Vasili Mitrokhin, *The KGB and the World: the Mitrokhin Archive II*, London, Penguin Books, 2005.
33. Figure cited by Domenach in his study of the *laogai*: *Chine: l'archipel oublié, op. cit.*
34. Author interview, Paris, 29 November 1986.
35. Xiaobing Li, *A History of the Modern Chinese Army*, Lexington KY, University Press of Kentucky, 2007.
36. See Iliya Sarsembaev's doctoral thesis, *La question territoriale: enjeu géopolitique dans les relations sino-russes* [The Territorial Question: Geopolitical strategies in Sino-Russian relationships], under the direction of Dominique Colas, Paris, Institut d'Études politiques, 2005.
37. Account by Miklós Lengyel, Hungarian state radio correspondent, 18 April 1996.

NOTES

38. William Blum, *The CIA: A Forgotten History*, London, Zed, 1986.
39. James Lilley (with Jeffrey Lilley), *China Hands: Nine Decades of Adventure, Espionage, and Diplomacy in Asia*, New York, Public Affairs, 2004.
40. Timothy Kendall, *Ways of Seeing China: From Yellow Peril to Shangrila*, Freemantle, Curtin University Books, 2005.
41. Richard Hall, *The Secret State: Australia's Spy Industry*, Melbourne, Cassell Australia, 1978.
42. Jean-Luc Domenach, *Mao, sa cour et ses complots, derrière les murs rouges* [Mao, His Circle and Its Plots: Behind the Red Walls], Paris, Fayard, 2012.
43. These cases of espionage around pro-Japanese leader Wang Jingwei provided the material for Ang Lee's film *Lust Caution* (2007), which was inspired by the real-life story of a spy infiltrating the entourage of Ding Mocun.
44. See Chang and Halliday, *Mao, op. cit*.
45. Zhang Yun, *Pan Hannian Zhuan* [Pan Hannian: A Biography], Shanghai, Chubanshe, 2006. In 1998 the Gonganbu monthly magazine, *China Police*, devoted several issues of the magazine to a biography lauding Pan Hannian.
46. Wendell L. Minnick, "Target: Zhou Enlai—was America's CIA working with Taiwan agents to kill the Chinese premier?", *The Far Eastern Economic Review*, 13 July 1995.
47. Kai Cheng, *Li Kenong: Zhonggong Yinbi Zhanxiande Zhaoyue Lingdaoren* [Li Kenong: The CCP Hidden Battlefront's Remarkable Leader], Chinese Friendship Publishing Company, 1996.
48. Dr Li Zhisui, *The Private Life of Chairman Mao* (trans. Tai Hung-chao, foreword by Andrew J. Nathan, with the editorial assistance of Anne F. Thurston), New York, Random House, 1994.
49. Richard Deacon, *'C': A Biography of Sir Maurice Oldfield, Head of MI6*, London, Futura, 1984.
50. See Faligot and Kauffer, *The Chinese Secret Service, op. cit*.
51. I have heard Chinese functionaries use the abbreviation *Zhongdiaobu* as well as *Diaochabu* when talking of the Central Investigation Department.

3. THE SPIES' CULTURAL REVOLUTION

1. See John Barron, *KGB, The Secret Work of Soviet Secret Agents*, New York, Readers Digest Press, 1974. The book was published ten years later in Chinese, translated by Shen Enqing (Liaoning Renmin Chubanshe).
2. See Jean Marabini, *Mao et ses héritiers, Ombres chinoises sur le monde* [Mao and his heirs, Chinese shadows on the world], Paris, Robert Laffont, 1972.
3. Quoted in John Byron and Robert Pack, *The Claws of the Dragon, op.cit*.
4. Stephen Fitzgerald, *China and the World*, Contemporary China Paper N°11, Canberra, Australian National University Press, 1977. The Australian embassy opened in Beijing in 1973.
5. For more details on the role of Wang Dongxing, former deputy to Kang Sheng at the SAD in Yan'an, see Dr Li Zhisui, *La vie privée du camarade Mao, op.cit.;* Jung Chang, Jon Halliday, *Mao: the unknown story, op.cit*.; P. H. Chang, "The Rise of Wang Tung-hsing: Head of China's security apparatus," in *China Quarterly*, N°73, March 1978; "Wang Tung-hsing—The Head of Peiping's Undercover agents", in *Issues & Studies*, Taipei, August 1976.

6. Several studies and memoirs have been published in Russia on the role of Soviet agents in China, including Viktor Usov, *Kitayskiy Beria, Kang Sheng (The Chinese Beria Kang Sheng*, Moscow, Olma-Press, 2003, and, by the same author, *Sovietskaya Razvedka v Kitae* [The Soviet intelligence service in China in the 20th Century], Moscow, Olma-Press, 2002.
7. This newspaper is today available online in both English and Chinese (more detailed): http://english.chinamil.com.cn/
8. Alexei Antonkin, *Les chiens de faïence (témoignage d'un correspondant de l'Agence Tass à Beijing)* [The memoirs of a Tass news Agency correspondent in Beijing], Paris, Editions de l'équinoxe, 1983.
9. Quoted in Christopher Andrew, Vasili Mitrokhin, *The KGB & the World—The Mitrokhin Archive II*, London, Penguin, 2006.
10. Some of these KGB officers published their memoirs in Russian, including Arkadi A. Zhemchugov (who worked in China, Burma, Indonesia and Malaysia): *Kitayskaya Golovolomka* [Chinese Puzzle]. During the 1990s, Turchak was reappointed bureau chief.
11. Mitrokhin Archive, file MITN 2–14–1.
12. Mitrokhin Archive, file MITN 2–6–1.
13. John Byron, Robert Pack, *The Claws of the Dragon, op.cit*.
14. The imprisoned deputy ministers were Yang Qijing (released in 1973), Wang Jinxiang, Liu Fuzhi, Ling Yun (the top counterintelligence expert), and Yang Yumin. The three who died in prison were Yu Sang, Xu Zirong and Xu Jianguo. The latter's case is a perfect example of how the Cultural Revolution ripped right through the top echelons of the security services: an expert on military security, Xu had been Mao's bodyguard during the Long March, and later Zhou Enlai's. He was transferred to Kang Sheng's SAD in 1936, where he headed the Security Division. After the "Liberation" of 1949, he became head of the Gonganbu in Tianjin and Shanghai. He was appointed ambassador first to Romania and then to Albania, where he set up collaborations with the respective local secret police, Securitate and Sigurimi.
15. Pu Qiongying was the real name of Deng's wife, Zhuo Lin. Kong Yuan's wife was called Xu Ming. For more details about this double wedding, see Deng Maomao, *Deng Xiaoping, My Father*, New York, Basic Books, 1995.
16. This detail is taken from Zhou Enlai's memoirs, a two-volume work: *Zhou Enlai Nanpu, vol. 2 1949–1976*, Beijing, Renmin Chubanshe, 1989.
17. Matt Brazil, "Mao Zedong", in *The Encyclopaedia of Intelligence and Counterintelligence*, Armonk, M. E. Sharpe, 2004.
18. The editor of this CIA report added the following names to the list of key leaders in the security sphere: "Zhang Yunyi and Xiao Hua from the Central Control Board; Xie Fuzhi and Yu Sang of the Ministry of Public Security [the Gonganbu], supported by Wang and Yang. Chen Boda, Political Research Bureau; and Kang Sheng, of the 'five man group'; the presumed successor (never identified) to Peng Zhen as the supervisor of the central Political Departments; and as an unattached, free-floating, doubly dangerous figure, Mao's wife, Jiang Qing."
19. CIA: Communist China, The Political Security Apparatus, 11. Destruction and Reconstruction, 1965–1969, (Reference Title: POLO XXXVII), 28 November 1969, RSS No. 0037/69. I have reinstated the transcription of proper pinyin names for consistency with the rest of this book, whereas the CIA editors originally used the Wade-Giles-CIA system.

20. See R. Faligot, R. Kauffer, *Kang Sheng & the Chinese Secret Service, op.cit.*; Yao Ming-Le, *Investigation of the Death of Lin Biao*, preface by Simon Leys, Paris, Robert Laffont, 1983.
21. CIA archives declassified in May 2007, Intelligence report, ref. POLO XXXI; *Mao's Red Guard Diplomacy*, 1967.
22. Markus Wolf with Anne McElvoy, *Man Without a Face: The autobiography of Communism's greatest spymaster*, New York, Random House, 1997.
23. For more on purges in the ILD, see CIA Intelligence Report, The International Liaison Department of the Chinese Communist Party, (Reference Title: POLO XLIV), RSS No. 0054171, December 1971.
24. CIA Intelligence Report, "The Chinese Communist impact on East-Germany", ref. ESAU VII-60, from CIA archives declassified in May 2007.
25. Author interview, Paris, December 1986.
26. Letter from Raymond Casas to the author, 2 December 1987.
27. Ironically, Frêche, alias "Georges Lierre", was accused by his FCML comrades on 5 June 1964 of being an "agent of the US secret services" (PCF archives). There are many documents about IDL links with Maoist groups around the world in Faligot and Kauffer, *Kang Sheng & the Secret Service op. cit.* Since it was first published, many archives have been opened confirming this central role of the IDL in Australia, New Zealand, Canada and the UK.
28. Nicolas Poliansky, *MID (12 ans les services diplomatiques du Kremlin)* [Twelve Years in the Kremlin diplomatic service], Paris, Belfond, 1984. In fact, Poliansky was mistaken: the RML was not Maoist but Trotskyist, originating with the Fourth International.
29. See Danièle Martin, "Les cordonniers 'suisses' du KGB", *Espionnage*, N°6, December 1970.
30. Bob de Graff and Cees Wiebes, *Villa Maarheeze, De geschiedenis van de inlichtingendienst buiteland* [Villa Maarheeze: The History of the Intelligence Service Abroad], The Hague, Sdu Uitgevers, 1998.
31. Xiong Xianghui, *Wode qingbao yu waijiao shengya* [My Career in Intelligence and Diplomacy], Beijing, Zhonggongdang Shi Chubanshe, 2006.
32. In Shanghai Pat Givens, head of the British Special Branch, had compiled a large file on Snow, the "communist agent", after he published an article revealing that Chen Duxiu, former head of the CCP, had been tortured by Givens while detained in the International Concession.
33. See Roger Faligot, *Les seigneurs de la paix* [Lords of Peace], Paris, Le Seuil, 2006.
34. National Security Archive, Memorandum for Henry Kissinger, by Winston Lord, "Memorandum of your conversation with Zhou Enlai", 29 July 1971.
35. James Lilley with Jeffrey Lilley, *China Hands, Nine Decades of Adventure, Espionage, and Diplomacy in Asia*, New York, Public Affairs, 2004.
36. Another version of Lin Biao's death posited that he was assassinated in a Beijing restaurant on the orders of Kang Sheng and Madame Mao; see Faligot and Kauffer, *Kang Sheng & the Chinese Secret Service, op.cit*; Yao Ming-Le, *Investigation of Lin Biao's death*, *op. cit.*
37. Having only just replaced Xie Fuzhi at the head of Gonganbu, Li was arrested and imprisoned by the service. Months later, he committed suicide by a drug overdose. Xie's widow, Liu Xiangping, then health minister, was, like her late husband, close to the faction around Madame Mao. Had she dispensed with her husband's successor, as rumour had it? Mao's doctor, Dr Li Zhisui, performed Li Zhen's autopsy; he confirmed drug overdose as the cause of death.

38. POLO archive XLVIX, August 1972, RSS N°0058/72.
39. Interview with Étienne Manac'h, December 1986. The ambassador published these diary entries in Volume 3 of his *Mémoires d'Extrême Asie* (Memoirs of Far East Asia), Paris, Fayard, 1977.
40. Interview with Ting Wang, Hong Kong, July 1986; see also Byron and Pack, *The Claws of the Dragon, op. cit.*, and Philip Short, *Mao Tsé-toung*, Paris, Fayard, 2005.
41. The "third force" was led by Kang Sheng and included members of the Politburo including Hua Guofeng, Wang Dongxing, Ji Dengkui, Wu De, Li Desheng, Chen Xilian and Saifudin. Its leading members had been closely associated with the security services. Before his death in December 1975, Kang Sheng was party vice-president and head of the security apparatus. Hua was appointed head of the Gonganbu in January 1975, and Wang was both responsible for the security of the CCP elite and commander of Unit 8341. Ji Dengkui joined the security services and was now in charge of the Political-Legal Group of the Central Committee, while Chen Xilian and Li Desheng were members of the "Investigative Group concerning Lin Biao's anti-party faction". At one time or another, they had all worked for Kang Sheng. See Ting Wang, *Chairman Hua, Leader of the Chinese Communists*, London, C. Hurst & Co./Queensland, University of Queensland Press, 1980.
42. Roger Aimé, head of the SDECE in Beijing, sent a despatch to headquarters in Paris suggesting precisely this scenario. Interview with Alexandre de Marenches, SDECE director (1969–81), June 1993.
43. Ting Wang, *Chairman Hua, Leader of the Chinese Communists, op. cit.*; Wojtek Zafanolli, *Le Président clairvoyant contre la Veuve du Timonier. Mécanismes de l'idéologie et pratique politique en Chine maoïste* [The Clear-Sighted President Versus the Great Helmsman's Widow: Mechanisms of Ideology and Political Practice in Maoist China], Paris, Payot, 1981.
44. Among the men who arrested Madame Mao was Marshal Ye Jianying's own bodyguard, Cao Qing, who in September 2007 became head of the Central Guard's Bureau.
45. Serge Thion, Ben Kiernan, *Khmers rouges!*, Paris, J.-E. Hallier/Albin Michel, 1981. For further details on the relationship between Pol Pot and Kang Sheng, see Faligot and Kauffer, *Kang Sheng and the Chinese Secret Services, op. cit.*
46. Vita Chieu, *The Khmer Rouge and Red China: My Untold Story*, Taipei, Bookman Books, 2010.
47. Enver Hoxha's notebooks (*Reflections on China*, Tirana, 1979) are filled with interesting comments on the Chinese secret services. He was particularly critical of Geng Biao, who replaced Kang Sheng as head of the ILD.

4. DENG XIAOPING'S DEEP-WATER FISH

1. A year after the publication of this book in French, revealing the role of Ying Ruocheng, his memoirs were published; these confirmed the claims herein. They also revealed that he was recruited by Peng Zhen, the mayor of Beijing, as a secret service agent (Ying Ruocheng and Claire Conceison, *Voices Carry: Behind Bars and Backstage During China's Cultural Revolution*, Lanham MD, Rowman & Littlefield, 2009).
2. See Chapter 3. A local Gonganbu bureau is called a Gonganju. Similarly, a provincial office is called a Gonganting. But the reader has enough names to remember, so I have chosen to call it the Gonganbu in all cases, for the sake of simplicity.

3. *A Great Trial in Chinese History: the Trial of the Lin Biao and Jiang Qing Counter-revolutionary Factions, November 1980–January 1981*, Beijing, New World Press, 1981. Byron and Pack, *The Claw of the Dragon, op. cit.*
4. Author interview with Li Junru, Beijing, July 2007.
5. The translation of this speech was published by the short-lived but interesting magazine *Paris-Beijing*, N°1 September–October 1979.
6. According to official reports, Madame Mao committed suicide in prison in May 1991.
7. See the biography of Ye Jianying in Maitron, *Biographical Dictionary of the International Labor Movement*, *China, op. cit.*; for a biography of Liu Fuzhi, see J. de Golfiem, *Personnalités chinoises d'aujourd'hui* [Major Chinese Figures of Today], Paris, L'Harmattan, 1989; Wolfgang Bartke, *Who's Who in the People's Republic of China, op. cit.*
8. CIA Directorate of Intelligence—*Directory of Chinese Officials: National Level Organizations, a reference aid*, CR- 85–12068, June 1985.
9. Appointed in 1985 by his father General Imbot—who was head of the DGSE at the end of the *Rainbow Warrior* affair (the destruction of the Greenpeace ship in New Zealand by a underwater DGSE team)—Thierry Imbot specialized in Chinese affairs before apparently committing suicide during the 2007 Franco-Chinese frigate scandal in Taiwan. One of his main contacts in Beijing was Zhu Entao (1938–2015). Officially head of the Gonganbu's Foreign Affairs Office, Zhu was an Interpol agent who often travelled to France. However, the FBI had banned him from visiting the US because of spying during the Larry Wu-Tai Chin affair. Zhu published his somewhat pared-back memoirs in 2006. His British counterpart Nigel Inkster was deputy head of the MI6 station in Beijing in 1983 and in Hong Kong, where he reorganized the British services during the handover of the colony. In 2001 he became a deputy director of MI6, in the role of chief operating officer. He is now director of future conflict and cyber security at the International Institute for Strategic Studies and the author of *China's Cyber Power* (Adelphi Series, 2016).
10. See Roger Faligot, "La sûreté de l'État fait peau neuve en Chine", *Le Monde diplomatique*, August 1984.
11. *The China Letter*, September 1984.
12. At the head of the international department of the MOFERT were Bu Zhaomin (head of relations with international organizations) and Zhang Xianliang, deputy director of the International Bureau.
13. Interviews recorded in summer 1986 during research for our biography of Kang Sheng.
14. Roger Faligot, *La Piscine: The French Secret Service since 1944*, Oxford, Basil Blackwell, 1989.
15. According to Nicholas Eftimiades (*Chinese Intelligence Operations*, Annapolis MD, Naval Academy Press, 1994), other hotels under surveillance were the Palace Hotel (run by the PLA), the Great Wall Hotel, the Xiang Shan Perfumed Hill Hotel, and the Kunlun Hotel, owned by the Gonganbu. Additionally, the Jianguo Hotel, the Bamboo Garden Hotel (former residence of Kang Sheng), the Hotel Beijing, and the Hotel Qianmen were run by the Guoanbu. The Friendship Hotel in Haidian even had offices of various state institutions and "research offices".
16. Ross Terrill, *Madame Mao: The White Boned Demon* (revised edition), Stanford CA, Stanford University Press, 2000.
17. Luo Bote, "Yu Zensan de teshu quanshi" [The Extraordinary Existence of Yu Zhensan], *Zhenming*, Hong Kong, October 1986.

18. *Les Arcanes de Chine*, N°15, bimonthly edition 25 February–10 March 2005. See www.arcanesdechine.com. This superbly researched newsletter was edited by Agnès Andrésy, author of *Princes Rouges. Les nouveaux puissants de Chine* [Red Princes: China's New Rulers], Paris, L'Harmattan, 2003.
19. I. C. Smith, *Inside: A Top G-Man Exposes Spies, Lies and Bureaucratic Bungling Inside the FBI*, Nashville TN, Nelson Current, 2004.
20. See Roger Faligot and Rémi Kauffer, *Kang Sheng and the Chinese Secret Services, op. cit.* Born in Tokyo, the head of the Xinhua News Agency was Liao Chengzhi (1908–83), a specialist in the United Work Front, and vice-president of the National People's Congress. He died in September 1983. See "Liao Chengzhi, un grand patriote et révolutionnaire" [Liao Chengzhi, a great patriot and revolutionary], *La Chine en construction*, September 1983. The obituary confirms that, between 1928 and 1932, Liao worked in Germany for the International Seafarers' Union, led a Chinese sailors' strike, and was arrested and deported from both the Netherlands and Germany. In Jan Valtin's book, *Without Fatherland and Border* (1947), he appears under the name of Leo Tchang as a leading member of the Comintern (M-Apparat) responsible for military activities in Rotterdam.
21. I. C. Smith, *Inside, op.cit.*
22. See more about the case in Tod Hoffman, *The Spy Within: Larry Chin and China's Penetration of the CIA*, Hanover, Steerforth Press, 2008; and I.C. Smith, *Inside, op.cit.*
23. Former Canadian intelligence service officer Tod Hoffman mentions him in *The Spy Within, op. cit.*
24. Interview with the author, Rennes-le-Château, 23 October 1998. Several other interviews allowed me to reconstruct the details of the case, along with counterintelligence records whose details correspond precisely with what Bouriscot told me. I was able to cross-check his testimony with the two former DST officers who had conducted the interrogations, as well as a former CIA agent who had followed the Yu Zhensan case. Bernard Boursicot agreed to allow me to evoke further details of his private life that make it possible to understand what happened.
25. Anthony Grey published a memoir about this period, *A Hostage in Peking*, London, Michael Joseph, 1970.
26. The Chinese secret service had "given" Shi Peipu a Uyghur baby from Xinjiang, the same ethnic group as the Turks, whose physical appearance was similar to that of a baby of mixed Asian and European heritage.
27. Author interview, Paris, 10 April 1998.
28. Joyce Wadler, *Liaison: The gripping real story of the diplomat spy and the Chinese opera star*, New York NY, Bantam Books, 1993. The medical and psychiatric reports in my possession are obviously considerably more detailed, but these quotations efficiently sum up the case, and tally with Boursicot's account thirty years later.
29. Quotations taken from court reports of the case.
30. Jacques de Golfiem, *Personnalités chinoises d'aujourd'hui, op. cit.* See also the official biography of Jia Chunwang in *Who's Who in China, Current Leaders*, Beijing, Foreign Language Press, 1989.
31. For a description of the various structures active at the end of the twentieth century, see "Comment les dirigeants chinois sont informés sur l'étranger", *Perspectives chinoises* No. 37, Hong Kong, September/October 1996; and David L. Shambaugh, "China's National Security Research Bureaucracy", *The China Quarterly*, June 1987.

NOTES

5. 55 DAYS AT TIANANMEN

1. This information, like other details about the KGB's activities in this chapter, has been cross-checked with several sources from both Russian and Western intelligence, as well as with journalists and diplomats who were stationed in Beijing at the time.
2. A reference to the 55-day Boxers' siege of the foreign legations in Beijing in 1900, an event that ended with the fall of their ally, the Empress Manchu Ci Xi. In 1964, Nicholas Ray took this episode to the screen in *55 Days of Beijing*, starring Charlton Heston, Ava Gardner and David Niven.
3. Robert Lawrence Kuhn, *The Man Who Changed China: The Life and Legacy of Jiang Zemin*, New York, Crown Publishers, 2004.
4. See Gordon Thomas, *Chaos Under Heaven: The Shocking Story Behind China's Search for Democracy*, New York, Birch Lane Press Books, 1991. Thomas was part of the press corps in Beijing at the time.
5. With the exception of Jean-Luc Domenach, few China-watchers in Europe realized how important Qiao Shi was. Rémi Kauffer and I wrote about him in the early '80s, and mentioned him at the end of our biography of Kang Sheng in 1986. A biography has been published about him in Chinese: *Gao Xin, Zhonggong Jiao Qiao Shi* [Qiao Shi, the Tycoon of the Communist Party], Hong Kong, Shijie Shuju, 1995.
6. This was how he was described by Graham Hutchings, Beijing correspondent for *The Daily Telegraph*, who interviewed him in August 1988 and profiled him when Qiao became the party no. 1 ("Party Promotes Loyal Secret Policeman with a 'merciless' smile", *The Daily Telegraph*, 8 June 1989). See also Roger Faligot, "Qiao Shi, l'homme des chiens bleus", *Le journal du dimanche*, 11 June 1989; and Roger Faligot & Rémi Kauffer, "Le chef des services secrets vise le fauteuil de Deng", *Le Figaro Magazine*, 1 July 1989.
7. Qiao Shi's wife may have given up her surname "Wang", which hinted at family ties with Kuomintang leaders, when she was arrested as part of the anti-rightist campaign of 1957. She is now called Yu Wen. See Gao Xin, *Zhonggong Jiao Qiao Shi*, *op. cit.*
8. Biography of Liu Changsheng, in Jean Maitron (ed.), *Dictionnaire biographique du mouvement ouvrier international. La Chine*, Paris, Les Éditions ouvrières, 1985.
9. The appointment of Qiao Shi completed the overhaul of the ILD leadership. His assistants were Qian Liren, Zhu Liang and Ms Li Shuzheng. His advisors and political intelligence experts who had particularly distinguished themselves in Africa and Asia were Tang Mingzhao, Zhang Zhixiang, Li Yimang, Ms Ou Tangliang, Feng Xuan, Liu Xinquan and Zhang Xiangshan (*China Directory*, Tokyo, Radiopress Inc., 1983).
10. Author interview with James Yi, Hong Kong, 4 July 1986.
11. For a full description of all these movements, see Andrew G. Walder, *Popular Protest in the 1989 Democracy Movement: The Pattern of Grass-Roots Organization*, Hong Kong, Hong Kong Institute of Asia-Pacific Studies, 1992.
12. Andrew J. Nathan and Bruce Gilley (eds), *China's New Rulers: The Secret Files*, London, Granta Books, 2002.
13. Excerpts from CCP Central Office Secretariat, "Minutes of the May 17 Politburo Standing Committee meeting", document supplied to Party Central Office Secretariat by the Office of Deng Xiaoping, quoted in Andrew Nathan and Perry Link (eds), *The Tiananmen Papers*, New York, Little, Brown and Company, 2001. This book is an aston-

ishing documentation of the minutes of Chinese leadership meetings during the events of 1989. I have also quoted from the meeting on 3 June when it was decided to send in the army. A certain number of American specialists on China suggest that the document is fake, because of the positive image it lends to Zhao Ziyang, but the broad thrust of the leadership conversations at this critical time have been ratified by many other documents and testimonies.

14. Xiaobing Li, *A History of the Modern Chinese Army*, Lexington KY, University Press of Kentucky, 2007.
15. Michael D. Swaine, *The Military & Political Succession in China: Leadership, Institutions, Beliefs*, Santa Monica CA, Rand Corporation, 1992. According to Nicholas Eftimiades (*Chinese Intelligence Operations*, Annapolis MD, Naval Institute Press, 1994), Deng Xiaoping did succeed in establishing a liaison with the regional centres of PLA2, military intelligence.
16. Transcript available at http://folk.ntnu.no/ronda/kk-f/fra081100/0444.html.
17. See Chapter 11.
18. Gordon Thomas, *Chaos Under Heaven, op. cit.*
19. Donald Morrison (ed.), *Massacre in Beijing: China's Struggle for Democracy*, New York, Time Books, 1989.
20. Iliya Sarsembaev, *La question territoriale: enjeu géopolitique dans les relations sino-russes, op. cit.* US defence attaché Larry Wortzel said he had heard rumours of tank battles, but did not believe it, although he admitted that, at the time, soldiers were attacking journalists, tourists and even Western diplomats, who, unlike the Soviets, were obliged to take refuge in diplomatic residences.
21. *Libération*, 7 June 1989. Sabatier published a remarkable biography of Deng Xiaoping (*Le dernier dragon* [The Last Dragon], Paris, J.C. Lattès, 1990), in which he goes into great detail about the Tiananmen massacre.
22. Xiaobing Li, *A History of the Modern Chinese Army*, Lexington KY, University Press of Kentucky, 2007. The author lists the following as among the general officers dismissed in the wake of the Tiananmen massacre: Hong Xuezhi, deputy secretary general of the CMC; Guo Linxiang, deputy director of the PLA Political Department; Li Desheng, political commissioner of the National Defence University; Li Yaowen, navy political commissioner; Zhou Yibing, commander of the Beijing Military Region; Xiang Shouzhi, commander of the Nanjing Military Region; Wan Haifeng, political commissioner of the Chengdu Military Region; Li Xianxiu, commander of the PAP; Zhang Xiufu, political commissioner of the PAP; and of course Xu Qinxian, commander of the 38th Corps. For an exhaustive list, it would obviously be necessary to go all the way down the ranks of the armed services.
23. Jacques de Golfiem, *Personnalités chinoises d'aujourd'hui, op. cit.*
24. Roger Faligot, "Chine: les espions manifestent" [In China, the spies are demonstrating], *Le Journal du dimanche*, 7 May 1989.
25. Guan Yecheng, *Zhongnanhai bingnian tai si fu zhong* [Attempted coup d'état in Zhongnanhai], *Zhenming* N°146, Hong Kong, December 1989; Wei Li, "The Security Service for Chinese Central Leaders", *The China Quarterly* N°143, September 1995.
26. *The Independent*, 27 December 2017.
27. James Lilley with Jeffrey Lilley, *China Hands: Nine Decades of Adventure, Espionage, and Diplomacy in Asia, op. cit.* In contrast to the absurd story of the CIA station chief going

on holiday, his assistant, Martha Sutherland, saw the PLA pepper her Beijing apartment with bullets.

28. See Roger Faligot, *La mafia chinoise en Europe* [The Chinese Mafia in Europe], *op. cit.*
29. Hong Kong is a cursed place for Swiss diplomats. In 1956, the wife of another Swiss Federation consul was burned alive in her car during riots between nationalists and communists.
30. Nicholas Eftimiades, *Chinese Intelligence Operations*, *op. cit.*
31. See Roger Faligot and Pascal Krop, *DST. Police secrète*, Paris, Flammarion, 1999.
32. Roger Faligot, "Des 'espions' chinois à Paris pour surveiller les dissidents" [Chinese spies in Paris keeping watch on dissidents], *Le Journal du dimanche*, 22 April 1990.
33. Donald Morrison (ed.), *Massacre in Beijing: China's Struggle for Democracy, op. cit.*
34. He was notably accused of involvement in the 1992 return of two dissidents to China, Xu Gang and Ma Qianbo, which was made possible thanks to contacts within the Chinese secret services.
35. Renseignements Généraux, *Activités associatives et commerciales de dissidents chinois*, 29 March 1993. Since none of these people have been the subject of legal proceedings, I will not name them. What is important here is to understand the penetration mechanism of the Chinese services. One of their agents involved in this affair, a journalist named Wang, was in 2007 company secretary of a business involved in Sino-European trade, run by well-known members of the Benelux business community.
36. The fact that Ma Tao possessed an up-to-date passport was highly unusual. With the banning of the FDC on 7 January 1990, "a spokesman for the Office of Arrivals and Departures in the Public Security [Gonganbu] announced the very same day that the passports of Yan Jiaqi, Wan Runnan and Chen Yizi had been cancelled by law, because of the role that they had played in the establishment of the FDC abroad and because of their continued activities that put the security, honour and interests of China at risk." *Beijing Information*, 15 January 1990.
37. MfS report, ZAIG, Nr.321/89, Berlin, 30.6.1989. *Information über die Durchführung kirchlicher Solidaritätsveranstaltungen im Zusammenhang mit den konterrevolutionären Ereignissen in der VR China* [Information on the Leadership of the Church Solidarity Events Connected With Counter-Revolutionary Events in the PRC], in Armin Mitter and Stefan Wolle (eds), *Befehle und Lageberichte des MfS—Januar-November 1989* [Orders and Reports of the Guoanbu: January–November 1989], Berlin, BasisDruck Verlagsgesellschaft mbH, 1990.
38. Ion Pacepa, *Red Horizons: The Extraordinary Memoirs of a Communist Spy Chief*, London, William Heinemann, 1988.
39. In 2007, Ivan Vladimirovich Grigorov was appointed a commercial tribunal judge in Moscow.

6. OPERATION AUTUMN ORCHID, HONG KONG

1. Author interview in Tokyo, March 1996.
2. Robert Delfs, "Death in the Afternoon", *The Far Eastern Economic Review*, 2 May 1991.
3. Ruth Price's remarkable biography *The Lives of Agnes Smedley* (Oxford, Oxford University Press, 2005) describes in detail Smedley's relationship with the Comintern and Soviet intelligence.
4. A little later another scandal emerged involving the Japanese prime minister. Hashimoto

Ryutaro (1937–2006), a victim of the "beautiful woman stratagem" (a honeypot sting), was forced to testify before the Japanese parliament that his mistress—who remained unnamed—was a Chinese spy who had became a Japanese citizen. Born in 1955, her name was Li Weiping, and she first met the future prime minister when she was working as a translator during his visit to China in 1980. She was then posted to the Chinese embassy in Tokyo as part of the CCP's intelligence service, the Diaochabu. Later she worked for the Gonganbu's Beijing bureau, which was responsible for counterintelligence and for the recruitment of foreign agents. According to one of my journalist contacts, she also tried to seduce the president of the *Yomiuri Shimbun* press group.

5. See Lo Ah's history of the Political Department: Lo Ah, *Memories of Special Branch, RHKP* (published in Chinese with the title *Zhengzhibu Huijilu*), Overseas Chinese Archives, Hong Kong Institute of Asia-Pacific Studies, Chinese University of Hong Kong, 1996.
6. Hong Kong Police Report, Special Branch Summary, November 1950, Public Record Office, London, CO537/6075—6450. The document also details the many Taiwanese intelligence networks in Hong Kong. (Shing Sheung Tat's Cantonese name is spelled Cheng Xiangda in pinyin.)
7. See Roger Faligot and Pascal Krop, *La Piscine: The French Secret Service From 1944*, Oxford, Basil Blackwell, 1989.
8. James Lilley with Jeffrey Lilley, *China Hands: Nine Decades of Adventure, Espionage, and Diplomacy in Asia, op. cit.*
9. *Citations du président Liou Chao-chi* [Thoughts of President Liu Shaoqi] was published in France in 1969 by Pierre Belfond, translated from the Chinese by Yves Dulaurens, with preface by Maurice Ciantar. The publisher claimed that "only one pirated edition had been published to date in Hong Kong, a translation of this edition."
10. The journalist Duncan Campbell was the first to describe this set-up, in "Hong Kong: A Secret plan for dictatorship", *New Statesman*, 12 December 1980.
11. See Roger Faligot, *British Military Strategy in Ireland*, Dingle/London, Brandon/Zed Press, 1983.
12. I published a number of articles on the subject at the time, including "Veillée d'armes à Hong Kong" [Armed vigil in Hong Kong], *Politique internationale* N°73, Autumn 1996.
13. See *Far Eastern Economic Review*, 16 November 1995. Prior to this, Shen Hongying was head of the Office of Protection of Secrets in Beijing (*Guojia baomiju*).
14. Nicholas Eftimiades, *Chinese Intelligence Operations*, Annapolis MD, Naval Institute Press, 1994.
15. Xu Jiatun, *Xianggang Huiyilu* [Hong Kong Memoirs], Taipei, Lianjing Chubanshe, 1993. Xu recounts how he suggested to the CCP that they open a discreet line of communication with the major capitalists of Hong Kong, who should no longer be considered "class enemies", but rather as potentially useful allies.
16. Among candidates put forward as potential future leaders of the Hong Kong executive was lawyer T.S. Lo (Lo Tak-shing), who had already announced that he was ready to take up the post. This member of the Royal Hong Kong Jockey Club, of mixed Chinese and European heritage, was close to Li Peng, especially since he had been the first businessman to go to Beijing to shake his hand after Tiananmen. But public opinion was so hostile to him that he quickly withdrew from the race; the support he had been receiving went to another lawyer, Judge Simon Li.
17. Agnès Andrésy, *Princes rouges, les nouveaux puissants de Chine* [Red Princes: The New

Chinese Power-Brokers], Paris, L'Harmattan, 2003. The newsletter *Arcanes de Chine* can be read online at www.arcanesdechine.com.

18. Two of Goldspot's three shareholders were not resident in Hong Kong but in Beijing: Wu Wei and Wu Yu, both living in the elite neighbourhood of Diaoyutai, where Qiao Shi, head of the secret service, also lived until 1989. The third shareholder, Zhang Yong, lived in Sino Plaza, Gloucester Road, Hong Kong, but was still a national of the PRC. Document of the Chamber of Commerce of Macao: Private Notary's Office in Macao, from the Notary António J. Dias Azedo, *Ao de maio de mil novecentos e noventa e nove*, Agência Turística e Diversões Chong Lot, Limitada.
19. Lo Ping, "Secrets About CCP Spies—Tens of thousands of them scattered over 170-odd cities worldwide", *Chen Ming*, No. 2311, January 1997, pp 6–9; FBIS (Foreign Broadcast Information Service, an open-source CIA outfit), *Journal Discloses "Secrets" about PRC Spy Network*, FBIS-CHI-97–016, 1 January 1997.

7. GLOBAL INTELLIGENCE: FROM JIANG ZEMIN TO AFGHANISTAN 2021

1. Armin Witt, *Violetta: Ein Tatsachenroman über chinesische Spionage im Westen* [Violetta: A True Story of Chinese Espionage in the West]. See the associated website: www.violetta-zhang.de.
2. Letter from Armin Witt to the author, 21 November 2007.
3. Lu Yaokan, "'*Xide' Zhenbang dongfangxue yu guoji wenti yanjiusuo 'jianjie'*" [A brief introduction to the German Federal Institute of Orientalism and International Studies], February 1987. See also a memorandum published in the CICIR's journal: Lu Yaokun and Feng Zhonglin, "*Deguo dui yazhou of zhanlue kaolu ji zhengce taozheng*" [Strategic considerations of Germany and policy adjustment towards China], *Xiandai guoji guanxi*, N°5, 1993, pp. 15–20.
4. Feng was also the Chinese translator of Uli Franz's biography of Deng Xiaoping.
5. Yue Shan, "Inside China Mainland", *Cheng Ming*, N°241, 1998.
6. Some historians trace the creation of the CICIR's predecessor to the period of conflict with the Japanese, when Zhou Enlai set up an institute in contact with the American OSS Mission Dixie and a Comintern satellite spy station in Yan.
7. David L. Shambaugh, "China's National Security Research Bureaucracy", *The China Quarterly*, N°110, June 1987. In 1999, the CICIR returned to being under the CCP's control as at its founding, though it continued building a semi-open intelligence organization.
8. Nicholas Eftimiades, *Chinese Intelligence Operations, op. cit.*
9. One of the reports by Professor Li Wei and Ms Gao Ying was officially published by the CICIR in 2004, co-authored by Yang Mingjie, Chen Jiejun, and Shi Gang, under the title "International Counter-Terrorism: Inspiration from Current Predicament". It was essentially a summary compilation of what had been written in the West in the aftermath of the 9/11 attacks in the United States.
10. See the special report "Chine-Afrique", *La lettre de l'Océan indien* [China and Africa: Letter from the Indian Ocean], November 2006, and other articles on the Chinese in Africa since 1992, on the website www.AfricaIntelligence.fr.
11. David Wise, *Tiger Trap: America's Secret Spy War with China*, Boston MA/New York, Houghton Mifflin Harcourt, 2011.

12. Author interview in Beijing, 29 June 2007.
13. The CICIR now also has an (English-language) website: http://www.cicir.ac.cn.
14. Chen Fengyi (ed.), *Guoji Zhanlüe ziyuan diaocha* [Global Strategic Resources Review], CICIR, Beijing, Shishichubanshe, 2005.
15. Author interview in Beijing, 20 June 2007.
16. The Hong Kong-based journalist Willy Wo-Lap Lam details Deng's thinking at this time in *China after Deng Xiaoping: The Power Struggle in Beijing since Tiananmen*, Hong Kong, P.A. Professional Consultants Ltd, 1995.
17. "La Chine investit massivement dans l'espionnage" [China is investing massively in espionage], *Le Soir*, 19 December 1991. Since 2008, Eric Meyer has published an online newsletter called *Le vent de la Chine* [China Winds]: www.leventdelachine.com.
18. Murray Scot Tanner, "The Institutional Lessons of Disaster: Reorganizing the People's Armed Police After Tiananmen", in James C. Mulvenon (ed.), *The People's Liberation Army as Organization*, Washington DC, RAND, 2002.
19. Further details can be found in his biography: Su Duoshou and Liu Mianyu, *Zeng Shan Zhuan*, Jiangxi, Jiangxi Chubanshe, 1999; and in that of Zeng Qinghong: Wu Kegang, *Zeng Qinghong—Zhongong Xiang'ao da guanjia*, [Zeng Qinghong: Guardian of Hong Kong and Macao], Hong Kong, Xinhua Publishing, 2004.
20. Zeng Qinghong's assistants in the department were: Yang Dezhong (from 1982); You Xigui (who replaced him in 1997); Wang Ruilin (1983); Hu Guangbao (1993); Chen Fujin (1994); Wang Gang (also 1994)—who replaced Zeng in 1999 as general affairs director of the CCP; and Jiang Yikang (1996).
21. Teng Wensheng was a real political player, as is clear from the fact that he sometimes wrote speeches for Deng Xiaoping and then became a minister at the turn of the century, when he was replaced at the head of the service by Wang Huning.
22. For further details, see Hongda Harry Wu, *Laogai: The Chinese Gulag*, Boulder CO, Westview Press, 1992.
23. See "Biographical sketch of Xu Yongyue", Archives of the 3rd Bureau China Department of the intelligence services of the Office of the Japanese Prime Minister; as well as the author's personal archives (Japan, 2000). See also Agnès Andrésy, *Princes rouges, les nouveaux puissants de Chine*, *op. cit.*
24. The expression "the Immortals" is used to refer to the group of historical leaders who had participated in the Long March.
25. Yale Y. Chen, "New Minister of State Security Xu Yongyue", *Inside China Mainland*, Taiwan, June 1998.
26. Robert Lawrence Kuhn, *The Man Who Changed China: The Life and Legacy of Jiang Zemin*, New York, Crown Publishers, 2004.
27. *Jianshao anquan yewu gognzuo qudao* is the Chinese term. I have relied for my account of this operation on the analysis carried out (based on published information) by Michael S. Chase and James C. Mulvenon, "The Decommercialization of China's Ministry of State Security", *International Journal of Intelligence & CounterIntelligence*, 15, 2002.
28. The Guoanbu leaders on the committees of these nine regions were: Zhao Baowen (Hebei); Zhang Shengdong (Shanxi); Geng Zhijie (Liaoning); Cai Xumin (Shanghai); Chen Yunlong (Zhejiang); Wang Jiashan (Anhui); Wang Guoqing (Shandong); Yaomin (Henan); Shen Xingfa (Shaanxi). Chase and Mulvenon believe that Guoanbu people were also present in sensitive provinces like Tibet and Xinjiang, but that their names remain unknown.

29. Nigel Inkster, *China's Cyber Power, op. cit*.
30. Farhan Bokhari, Kiran Stacey and Emily Feng, "China courted the Afghan Taliban in secret meetings", *Financial Times*, 6 August 2018.
31. Mohammad Youssaf and Mark Adkin, *The Bear Trap: Afghanistan's Untold Story*, London, Leo Cooper, 1992.
32. During the following decade, Colonel Kong Jining worked in Beijing with the strategic analysis group led by General Luo Renshi, former military attaché in Paris. He was then posted to London, where he was put in charge of technological intelligence before joining the military intelligence staff in 1997. (For further detail, see my article "The secret history of Mao's grandson", *Le Point*, 6 July 2001.) Kong went on to found, with his mother Li Min, a commercial enterprise: the Beijing Eastern Kunlun Culture Propagation Co, which publicized the "thought" of his grandfather, Chairman Mao. In 2018, he was head of a Christian NGO called China Mercy, providing aid to the poor of the country.
33. *The Far Eastern Economic Review*, 28 October 1993.
34. Then under the leadership of Tian Yong (田勇), the Guoanbu's Xinjiang bureau—based in the provincial capital Ürümqi—has trained Muslim agents for action in the Middle East, and for surveillance of Uyghurs living in exile around the world.

8. CHINA AND RUSSIA VS AMERICA

1. Joint Direct Attack Munitions.
2. Bill Clinton, *My Life*, New York, Knopf, 2004.
3. *Cheng Ming*, Hong Kong, June 1999.
4. The seven members of the Standing Committee of the CCP Politburo, elected on 19 September 1997, were: Jiang Zemin, Li Peng, Zhu Rongji, Li Ruihan, Hu Jintao, Wei Jianxing, and Li Lanquing. Wei Jianxing was the security coordinator. Qiao Shi finally retired, though as we know he had already left this sector to become speaker of the National People's Congress in 1992. Not long afterwards, Wei was replaced as head of the secret services by Luo Gan, who was close to Li Peng.
5. Stanišić was ousted the following year, in November 1998. Milošević was afraid that he was planning a coup against him.
6. Letter to the author, 2 December 2007.
7. Quoted in Bill Gertz, *The China Threat: How the People's Republic Targets America*, Washington DC, Regnery Publishing, 2000.
8. In an article entitled "Yougoslavie—les amitiés en panne" [Yugoslavia: stalled friendships] in the online newsletter *Le vent de Chine*, 16 October 2000, journalist Eric Meyer suggests that the emotion in Beijing following the fall of Milošević on 5 October 2000 was even more intense than the elation following Suharto's fall in Indonesia (1998), or the Kuomintang's loss of power in the Taiwan elections of March 2000. In the case of Taiwan, ultimately the CCP leadership would have preferred to see their longstanding enemy remain in power in Taipei than face a new, potentially pro-independence president.
9. See Jacques Massé, *Nos chers criminels de guerre. Paris-Belgrade-Zagreb en classe affaires* [Our dear war criminals: Paris-Belgrade-Zagreb in business class], Paris, Flammarion, 2006.
10. Qiao Liang and Wang Xiangsui, *Unrestricted Warfare: China's Masterplan to Destroy America*, Pan American Publishing Company, 2002.

11. Stéphane Marchand, *Quand la Chine veut vaincre* [When China Decides to Conquer], Paris, Fayard, 2007 offers a clear explanation for the war between the old and new guard of the PLA in the wake of the traumatic Kosovo war.
12. See the newsletter *Très Très Urgent (TTU)* [Very, Very Urgent], October 1999.
13. The character Xiong, meanwhile, signifies the word 'bear'.
14. According to *The Far Eastern Economic Review*, 8 August 2002.
15. For further details see Chapter 11. David Shambaugh is correct to point out that, according to US military documents, drawn from contradictory Chinese sources, this structure also features another communications department, independent of the 3rd and 4th (*Modernizing China's Military, Progress, Problems, and Prospects*, Berkeley CA, University of California Press, 2002). I noticed the same problem in Japanese defence sources.
16. Ji Pengfei was a CCP diplomacy veteran, former foreign minister and negotiator over the future of Hong Kong; he was also another friend of Qiao Shi, now speaker of the National People's Congress. General Ji appointed as his deputy Colonel Kong Jining—the same Kong who had served in the Afghanistan campaign, Mao's grandson.
17. Wen Ho Lee, *My Country Versus Me*, New York, Hyperion, 2001; Notra Trulock, *Code Name Kindred Spirit: Inside the Chinese Nuclear Espionage Scandal*, San Francisco CA, Encounter Books, 2003.
18. Including the China Aerospace Science and Technology Corporation (CASC), the China National Nuclear Corporation (CNNC), the China North Industries Group Corporation Limited (NORINCO), the Aviation Industry Corporation of China (AVIC) and the China State Shipbuilding Corporation (CSSC).
19. This explains rumours that the outbreaks of both SARS and bird flu in China began near the PLA laboratories outside Canton, where research into bacteriological and biological warfare was being conducted. In 1984 China had signed up to the international convention on the prohibition of bacteriological warfare (Bacteriological and Toxin Weapons Convention—BTWC), but this did not put an end to research that had begun during the Korean War.
20. Since the beginning of the twenty-first century, some of COSTIND's research departments have focused on means of destroying enemy systems through the use of intelligent weapons to attack radars and radio transmitting stations; the jamming of enemy communications by electronic warfare; attacks on communications centres and naval command centres; the destruction of electronic systems with electromagnetic pulse weapons; the destruction of computer systems with viruses; and so on.
21. US House of Representatives Select Committee, "U.S. National Security and Military/Commercial Concerns with the People's Republic of China, Volume 1", *op. cit.*, Chapter 1 'PRC Acquisition of US Technology', pp. 19–20.
22. *The Washington Post*, August 2001. This description does not only apply to the United States. The case of the Valeo student (Chapter 9) is a good illustration of this system and explains the difficulties facing counterintelligence services and companies when it comes to prosecution and obtaining convictions.
23. US House of Representatives Select Committee, "U.S. National Security and Military/Commercial Concerns with the People's Republic of China, Volume 1; submitted by Mr. Cox of California, Chairman", 3 January 1999 (declassified in part 25 May 1999), https://www.gpo.gov/fdsys/pkg/GPO-CRPT-105hrpt851/pdf/GPO-CRPT-105hrpt851.pdf.

24. The section of the Cox Report dealing with Chinese theft of technological secrets was confirmed two years later by another defector in December 2001: Colonel Xu Junping, director of strategy at the Ministry of Defence. Colonel Xu had worked in liaison with General Xiong Guangkai. According to my British colleague Gordon Thomas, who had access to part of his debriefing, Colonel Xu reportedly told the FBI that the Chinese were funding the higher education of students in America at leading universities, including Harvard and Yale, as part of a long-term intelligence plan. Xu revealed everything that the Chinese knew about CIA operations in the Far East; that the Chinese now have the largest number of spies of all services operating clandestinely in the United States; how China had bypassed sanctions against Iraq to help Saddam Hussein rebuild his nuclear potential; how a Chinese service team had gone to Belgrade to extract Milošević just before his arrest and referral to the ICTY; that Osama bin Laden had links with the Chinese special services; how China was intending to exploit Europe's recurring "problem" with (Chinese) immigration, and so on. In short, Xu's defection and the revelations of his debriefing came at just the right time to confirm every neoconservative fantasy about China, just as the testimonies of some KGB defectors had been exploited during the Cold War for domestic political purposes.
25. This is the amount given by Shambaugh in *Modernizing China's Military, op. cit*. In 1999, Johnny Chung testified before the inquiry that he had received $300,000 directly from General Ji Sheng, but handed over only $35,000 to the Democratic National Committee (*The International Herald Tribune*, 6 July 1999). In September 2007, the *Wall Street Journal* revealed that the Hong Kong-based Norman Hsu—linked to the same networks and convicted of fraud—had contributed $850,000 to Hillary Clinton's 2008 presidential primary campaign.
26. Iliya Sarsembaev, *La question territoriale: enjeu géopolitique et idéologique dans les relations sino-russes, op. cit*.
27. See Chapter 2 for details about the Yan Baohang affair.
28. For further detail, see Chapter 11.
29. *Moscow Times*, September 1999.
30. *Segodnyia*, May 2000.
31. Details of this interview cannot be supplied, to protect the source's anonymity.
32. Interview with Professor Meng Changlin, China Reform Forum, June 2007.
33. *Intelligence Online*, N°521, 7 April 2006 (www.IntelligenceOnline.fr). Meng was later promoted to president of Interpol, based in Lyon, but was recalled to Beijing in 2018 to be tried for corruption.
34. See Philippe Coué, *La Chine veut la lune* [China Wants the Moon], Paris, A2C médias, 2007; and Brian Harvey, *China's Space Program*, London, Springer & Praxis Publishing, 2004.

9. SEA LAMPREY TACTICS: ECONOMIC WARFARE

1. For more details of this case, see Chapter 14.
2. "J'avais accès à tout l'intranet, je ne pensais pas que c'était confidentiel" [I had access to the entire intranet, I didn't think it was classified], interview with David Revault d'Allonnes, in *Libération*, 21 June 2005.
3. Cyrille Louis, "*Le chimiste du CNRS se défend d'être un espion*" [CNRS research scientist defends himself against accusations of spying], *Le Figaro*, 20 April 2006.

4. The excerpts cited here are taken from the four-page MI5 manual, first written about by *Times* journalist James Adams in his book *The New Spies*, London, Hutchinson, 1994. These tips remain valid and are pertinent to visitors from all countries. See also Roger Faligot, *"Renseignement économique: la guerre fait rage en Asie"* [Economic Intelligence: The War Rages in Asia], *L'Asie*, December 1997.
5. Modelled on the FBI in the USA, the Ministry of Justice Investigation Bureau (MJIB or *Fa Wu Pu Tiao Ch'a Pu*), which deals with counterintelligence, reports directly to the Taiwan Ministry of Justice.
6. For details on all these affairs, and the influence of the Chen Yun clan, including the role of special agent Dai Xiaoming—a friend of both Chen Yuan (Chen Yun's son) and Robert Huang (Hillary Clinton's interlocutor during Chinagate)—see Agnès Andrésy, *Princes rouges, les nouveaux puissants de Chine, op. cit.*
7. See Roger Faligot and Rémi Kauffer, *Kang Sheng and the Chinese Secret Services, op. cit.*
8. Author interview, 12 May 1988.
9. The Chinese had obviously studied the Japanese system, as discussed in a highly technical article by Qihao Miao and Zuozhi Zhang, "Anatomy of JETRO's Overseas Technology Monitoring: Bibliometrical and Content Analysis", *Scientometrics*, 1990.
10. *Beijing Information*, 1 February 1993.
11. Author interview, Beijing, 27 June 2007.
12. Before taking over in 2001, Wei had been deputy of the previous director, Gui Shiyong. In 2018 Huang Shouhong took over from Wei.
13. These include Beijing's National Institute of Economic Research, the Economic Research Centre in Shanghai, and several others.
14. *China Daily*, 5 December 2006.
15. Daniel Schaeffer, *La pratique de l'intelligence économique chinoise dans l'acquisition des hautes technologies* [The practice of economic intelligence in the acquisition of advanced technologies], Proceedings of Conference on Economic Intelligence and International Competition, IECI, 16 November 2006, Paris La Défense.
16. Juan Antonio Fernandez and Laurie Underwood, *China CEO: Voices of Experience from 20 International Business Leaders*, Singapore, John Wiley & Sons (Asia), 2006.
17. The Indian intelligence service's Research & Analysis Wing (RAW), increasingly present around the world and of course one of the principal enemies of the Chinese services, is itself beginning to undertake something similar. By 2017, India had become a fully-fledged member of the SCO, as had its arch-enemy Pakistan. One of Beijing's aims is obviously to end New Delhi's support for Tibetan refugees, principally of course the most important of them all, the Dalai Lama.
18. *Taipei Times*, 8 June 2013.
19. *Le Canard enchaîné*, 6 February 2019.
20. *Le Canard enchaîné*, 8 March 2017.
21. See *"Beijing: Clearstream et frégates"* [Beijing: Clearstream and Frigates], *Intelligence Online*, 26 May 2006.
22. Christine Deviers-Joncour, *Opération Bravo, où sont passées les commissions de la vente des frégates à Taiwan?* [Operation Bravo: What became of the sales commissions of the frigates destined for Taiwan?], Paris, Plon, 2000.
23. *"Des camarades chinois bien arrosés"* [Well-greased Chinese comrades], *Le Canard enchaîné*, 3 May 2006.

24. Its full name is the Leading Group in Charge of National Rectification and Standardization of Market Economic Order.

10. THE 610 OFFICE AND THE FIVE POISONS

1. Falun Gong means "work of the wheel of the law". Qigong means "work of the breath".
2. For more on the Taiping movement, see Chapter 1; about Falun Gong's roots, see Maria Hsia Chang, *Falun Gong, secte chinoise. Un défi au pouvoir* [Falun Gong, the Chinese Sect: Challenge to Power], Paris, Editions Otherwise, CERI, 2004.
3. You Xigui later became leader of the Zhongnanhai elite's special security troops, the Jingwei Budui, and the 57003 elite unit.
4. Andrew J. Nathan and Bruce Gilley, *China's New Rulers: the Secret Files, op. cit.*
5. Chris Patten, *Not Quite the Diplomat: Home Truths About World Affairs*, London, Allen Lane, 2006.
6. Robert Lawrence Kuhn, *The Man Who Changed China: The Life & Legacy of Jiang Zemin*, *op. cit.*
7. Jennifer Zeng, *Witnessing History: One Woman's Fight for Freedom and Falun Gong*, Crows Nest, Australia, Allen & Unwin, 2005.
8. Jacques de Golfiem, *Personnalités chinoises d'aujourd'hui*, *op. cit.*
9. *The Epoch Times* can be accessed online: www.epochtimes.com.
10. Experience shows that attacks by cyber-warriors often occur when a country is in crisis. It is an opportunity for attackers to test the response capabilities of the targeted country. See Chapter 11.
11. Ji Shi, *Li Hongzhi & His "Falun Gong": Deceiving the Public and Ruining Lives*, Beijing, New Star Publishers, 1999.
12. Bruce Pedroletti, "*Des membres du Fa Lu Gong seraient victimes d'un trafic d'organes en Chine*" [Falun Gong members reportedly victims of organ trafficking in China], *Le Monde*, 18 August 2006.
13. Author interview, Montreal, 25 March 2002.
14. Author interview, Sydney, 26 December 2006. David McKnight is the author of *Espionage and the Roots of the Cold War: The Conspiratorial Heritage*, London, Routledge, 2001. His article "When Money Talks, the Right and Left Swap Sides" was published in the *Sydney Morning Herald*, 9 June 2005.
15. Cameron Stewart, "Spy drive to tackle Chinese," *The Australian*, 28 December 2006.
16. Statement by Chen Yonglin in *The Epoch Times*, 30 October 2005.
17. See Chapter 2.
18. In September 2005, a staff member at the Canadian embassy in China, Yang Jianhua, defected with his family. He was a hairdresser, but as we have seen, a junior job is not necessarily evidence of a minor role in the Chinese security apparatus.
19. Author interview, location concealed, 28 July 2007.
20. See *Intelligence Online*, N°536, 8 December 2006.
21. Wang Jianping, *Written submission to the Senate Foreign Affairs, Defence and Trade References Committee's Inquiry into Asylum and Protection Visas for Consulate Officials*, 26 July 2005.
22. Richard Bullivant, "Chinese Defectors Reveal Chinese Strategy and Agents in Australia", *National Observer*, N°66, 2005.
23. As we know, the origin of these two distinct military intelligence services goes back to

the 1940s in Yan'an, when Zhou Enlai set up a service independent of the one headed by Kang Sheng (see Chapter 2).

24. Pierre de Villemarest, *GRU, le plus secret des services soviétiques, 1918–1988* [The GRU: Most Secret of the Soviet services, 1918–1988], Paris, Stock, 1988. In Chinese: *Ge Lu Wu—Su jun qingbaobu neimu pilu*, (trans. Xiao Lianbing), Beijing, Huaxia Chubanshe, 1990.
25. He was replaced in 2006 by Zhang Chantai, who had been posted to Paris in the 1980s as deputy to the military attaché.
26. Vicent Jauvert, "Les "grandes oreilles" de Pékin en France" [Beijing's big ears in France] *L'Obs*, April 2014.

11. CYBER-WARRIORS OF THE PLA

1. Li Kenong's Diaochabu managed to infiltrate a Cambridge-educated secret agent. John Tsang was unmasked in 1961, at Hong Kong's Little Sai Wan station (run by GCHQ and the DSD). See Duncan Campbell, "The Spies Who Spend What They Like", *New Statesman*, 16 May 1980.
2. See Doris Blackwell and Douglas Lockwood, *Alice on the Line*, Alice Springs, Outback Books, 2001.
3. James Bamford, *Body of Secrets: How America's NSA and Britain's GCHQ Eavesdrop on the World*, London, Arrow, 2002.
4. Brian Toohey and William Pinwill, *OYSTER, The Story of the Australian Secret Intelligence Service*, Melbourne, Mandarin Australia, 1990. Labor's return to power at the end of 2007, led by former Beijing ambassador Kevin Rudd, was obviously in a less fraught context than the Cold War.
5. By the summer of 2007, the *Pueblo* was once more the subject of negotiation. Kim Jong-il, feeling magnanimous, was ready to return it to the Americans, in return for certain advantages in nuclear negotiations.
6. Bruce Swanson, *Eighth Voyage of the Dragon: A History of China's Quest for Seapower*, Annapolis MD, Naval Institute Press, 1982.
7. For further details about the Japanese spy system, see my book: Roger Faligot, *Naisho, Enquête au cœur des services secrets japonais* [Naisho: A Journey into the Heart of the Japanese Secret Services], Paris, La Découverte, 1997.
8. Author interview with Desmond Ball, Canberra, December 2006.
9. This system is described by a former employee of the Canadian Communications Security Establishment (CSE). See Mike Frost and Michel Gratton, *Spyworld: Inside the Canadian and American Intelligence Establishments*, Toronto, Doubleday, 1994.
10. Several senior intelligence officials have been appointed to this post. We have already met some of them; others—including generals Kong Yuan, Xu Xin, Xiong Guangkai and Chen Xiaogong—feature only at the end of this book (see Appendices).
11. See the article on his appointment in *Intelligence Online*, 23 August 2007.
12. With Xi Jinping's reform of the PLA in 2015, these bureaus fell under the Strategic Support Force (SSF). See Chapter 14.
13. Desmond Ball, "Signals Intelligence in China", *Jane's Intelligence Review*, August 1995.
14. Also included within the group of organizations governing military communications and interception is the PLA Communications Department, headed by General Yang Liming,

which is in charge of liaison between the Central Military Commission, the army general staff, and various units that ensure the protection of the most sensitive government lines. In 2011, this department was renamed the Informatization Department.

15. Bob Woodward, *Veil: The Secret Wars of the CIA, 1981–1987*, New York, Simon & Schuster, 1987. The celebrated *Washington Post* reporter explains how the Soviets would have keeled over if they had known the extent of the intelligence the Chinese and Americans were trading, and not just through the wiretapping stations.
16. Bill Gertz, *The China Threat: How the People's Republic Targets America*, Washington DC, Regnery Publishing, 2000.
17. His successor as CIA station chief, Keith Riggin, later became chairman of a consulting group called Pamir Resources & Consulting, Inc, which was named, curiously enough, after the SIGINT Operation PAMIR.
18. Interview with Erich Schmidt-Eenboom, 14 August 2007. This former Bundeswehr officer wrote a history of the BND, *Schnüffler ohne Nase, Der BND* [Sniffers With No Noses: The BND], Düsseldorf, ECON Verlag, 1994. See also Michael Müller and Peter F. Müller with Erich Schmidt-Eenboom, *Gegen Freund und Feind*, Reinbek, Rowohlt, 2002.
19. Desmond Ball, *Burma's Military Secrets—Signals Intelligence (SIGINT) from 1941 to Cyber Warfare*, Bangkok, White Lotus Press, 1998.
20. *Beijing Information*, 13 January 1986. See also the report by Yu Qingtian, "Deux villes scientifiques flottantes" [Two floating scientific cities], *La Chine en construction*, May 1987.
21. *The Far Eastern Economic Review*, 3 August 1993.
22. See in particular the ships *Xing Fengshan (V856)*, *Beidiao N ° 841*, and the *Yanha 519*, modified and renamed the *Yanha 723*. For more details, see Bernard Prézelin, *Les flottes de combat* [Combat Fleets], Rennes, Éditions maritimes et d'Outre-mer, 1995.
23. Prézelin, *Les flottes de combat* [Combat Fleets], *op. cit*.
24. See *Intelligence Online*, N°529, 25 August 2006.
25. See Armando Choy, Gustavo Chui and Moises Sio Wong, *Our History Is Still Being Written: The Story of Three Chinese-Cuban Generals in the Cuban Revolution* (ed. Mary-Alice Waters), New York, Pathfinder Press, 2005.
26. Details of these and other operations can be found in the dissertation by Second Lieutenant Sebastian Manzoni, *L'infrastructure nationale de l'information en République populaire de Chine—une illusion de liberté* [The National Information Infrastructure in the People's Republic of China: An Illusion of Freedom], under the direction of Catherine Sarlandie de la Robertie, Social and Political Sciences Division, Ecole Spéciale Militaire de St-Cyr, Military Training School, Military School of the Technical and Adjudicative Corps, June 2003.
27. Letter from Zhang Ping to the author, including a technical dossier, Beijing, 10 November 1994.
28. The results of this research were given to a provincial body, the Sichuan Zhongcheng Network Development Company Ltd. See Manzoni, *L'infrastructure nationale*, *op. cit*.
29. See the article by Michel Alberganti, "Le dernier virus informatique envoie son butin en Chine" [The latest computer virus sends its booty to China], *Le Monde*, 16 January 1999.
30. According to Indian sources, the 1999 taskforce also included the following figures: General Fu Quanyou, the PLA chief of staff, Generals Yuan Banggen and Wang Pufeng,

Wang Baocun, Shen Weiguang, Wang Xiaodong, Qi Jianguo, Liang Zhenxing, Yang Minqing, Dai Qingmin, Leng Bingling, Wang Yulin and Zhao Wenxiang.

31. Jean Guisnel, *Guerres dans le cyberspace. Services secrets et internet* [Wars in Cyberspace, Secret Services and the Internet], Paris, La Découverte/Poche, 1997. In Chinese: Jang. Jinei'er (Jean Guisnel), *Huliangwang shangde jiandiezhan* (trans. Xu Jianmei), Beijing, Xinhua Chubanshe, 2000.
32. MI5 was indeed at the forefront of the battle against Chinese cyber-attacks: in December 2007, *The Times* revealed that the head of MI5 at the time, Jonathan Evans, had warned the heads of some 300 businesses and banking/financial institutions of Chinese operations targeting Britain and Germany (Rhys Blakely, Jonathan Richards, James Rossiter and Richard Beeston, "MI5 alert on China's cyberspace spy threat", *The Times*, 1 December 2007).
33. Interview with WorldNetDaily correspondent Anthony C. LoBaido, who wrote in his article on the Blondes that they were using engineering cells in the US at Cal Tech Laboratories, MIT, Baylor, Texas A & M, West Point, Liberty Baptist and even the Air Force Academy in Colorado. This no doubt explains why the Chinese complained that the CIA was behind this offensive.
34. *Soldier's Daily (Zhanshibao).*
35. *Mingbao*, 27 February 1999.
36. Willy Wo-Lap Lam, *Chinese Politics in the Hu Jintao Era: New Leaders, New Challenges*, New York, M. E. Sharpe, 2006.
37. What follows is a summary of the Chinese system of cyber-control that has been the subject of several books, including the following: William Hagestad II, *Chinese Cyber Crime, China's Hacking Underworld* (2nd edn, CreateSpace Independent Publishing, 2016); Nigel Inkster, *China's Cyber Power, op. cit.*; and the most complete, Dean Cheng, *Cyber Dragon: Inside China's Information Warfare and Cyber Operations* (Santa Barbara CA/Denver CO, Praeger Security International, 2017).
38. Didier Huguenin, "Manœuvres et pratiques d'Intelligence autour d'une stratégie Sud-Sud" [Chinese Strategic, Business and Competitive intelligence in Western and Central Africa], Master IIDC, Intelligence économique, Institut francilien d'Ingénierie des Services, Université de Marne-La-Vallée, 2008–9.
39. This decision was equally brought about by the Chinese attacks against the IT system of the Dalai Lama, whose government in exile is based in India.
40. Paris-based French newsletter *Très Très Urgent*, N°743, 20 January 2010.
41. Gmail was attacked the following year by the Chinese.

12. BEIJING 2008: CHINA WINS THE ESPIONAGE GOLD

1. The term "espionage" in the title of *The Art of War*'s final chapter is expressed by the character "*jiàn*", which denotes a ray of sunlight coming through a half open door: 间 in simplified Chinese. At the time the text was written, it was the moon shining through a shuttered doorway: 閒. It is still used in the word "spy": *Jiàndié* 间谍. I personally retranslated (into French) the quotation from the Chinese text. My version is less poetic than those that spread in the West from the first translation, published in Paris in 1772 by the Jesuit priest Jean Joseph Marie Amiot, a friend of Emperor Qianlong. I prefer the term "sovereign's treasure", closer to the original than the phrase "divine labyrinth", which still

appears in the published French translation. It turns out that the technical terms used by Sun Tzu are actually quite close, in my opinion, to the intelligence vocabulary still in use in twenty-first-century China.

2. "Gordon Brown aide a victim of honeytrap operation by Chinese agents", *The Sunday Times*, 20 July 2008.
3. See Fabien Ollier and Marc Perelman, *Le livre noir des JO de Pékin* [The Black Book of the Beijing Olympics], Paris, City Editions, 2008.

13. ZHOU'S FAILED COUP: THE GUOANBU SAVES XI JINPING

1. See my article, "The Tiger Conspiracy", *Vanity Fair*, April 2015.
2. The Bamboo Garden in north Beijing is one.
3. This telephone conversation was brought to light by two exiled Chinese investigative journalists, Pin Ho and Wenguang Huang, in *A Death in the Lucky Holiday Hotel*, New York, Public Affairs, 2013.
4. Agnès Andrésy, *Xi Jinping, la Chine rouge, nouvelle génération* [Xi Jinping, Red China, and the New Generation], Paris, Éditions L'Harmattan, 2013.
5. See Nick Holdstock, *China's Forgotten People: Xinjiang, Terror and the Chinese State*, London/New York, I.B. Tauris, 2015.
6. Agnès Andrésy, *Xi Jinping, la Chine rouge, nouvelle génération*, *op. cit.*
7. Roger Faligot and Rémi Kauffer, *Kang Sheng and the Chinese Secret Services, op. cit.*
8. See "*Le Guoanbu amputé du contre-espionnage?*" [The Guoanbu cut off from counterespionage?], *Intelligence Online*, N°729, 11 February 2015; and Peter Mattis, "The Dragon's Eyes and Ears: Chinese Intelligence at the Crossroads", *The National Interest*, 20 January 2015.
9. Jason Pan, "PLA Cyberunit Targeting Taiwan Named", *Taipei Times*, 10 March 2015.

14. XI'S MOLE HUNT AND THE BIRTH OF THE STRATEGIC SUPPORT FORCE

1. Pompeo was appointed by Donald Trump, and subsequently named secretary of state in 2018.
2. See the box in Chapter 8 listing the principal cases involving Chinese spies in the United States.
3. As we have seen, in China, the organization of espionage is two-pronged: the technical director's role is parallel to that of a representative of the CCP, whose job is to maintain ideological discipline.
4. Reuters, "Britain pulls out spies as Russia, China crack Snowden files: report", 14 June 2015.
5. See Nick Holdstock, *China's Forgotten People: Xinjiang, Terror and the Chinese State, op. cit.*
6. For details see John Costello, "The Strategic Support Force: China's Information Warfare Service", *China Brief*, Jamestown Foundation, 8 February 2016; and Dean Cheng, *Cyber Dragon: Inside China's Information Warfare and Cyber Operations*, Santa Barbara CA/Denver CO, Praeger Security International, 2017.
7. See "Soupçons sur les Instituts Confucius" [Suspicions about the Confucius Institutes], *Intelligence Online*, N°558, 15 November 2007; and Fabrice de Pierrebourg and Michel Juneau-Katsuya, *Nest of Spies: The Startling Truth About Foreign Agents At Work Within Canada's Borders*, Montreal, Éditions Stanké, 2009.

8. Cheng Li, *Chinese Politics in the Xi Jinping Era: Reassessing Collective Leadership*, Washington DC, Brookings Institution, 2016.

15. COVID-19: CHINA'S SECRET WAR

1. SpyTalk, Jeff Stein and Matthew Brazil, "Rumors of U.S. Secretly Harboring Top China Official Swirl", *The Daily Beast*, 17 June 2021; Matthew Brazil and Jeff Stein, "Chinese Defector Mystery Deepens", *SpyTalk*, 21 June 2021.
2. On 29 April 2021, Berrier told the US Senate Armed Services Committee that "China and Russia ... are using the COVID-19 environment to conduct information warfare to undermine Western governments". Scott Berrier, Lieutenant General, U.S. Army, Director, Defense Intelligence Agency, "Statement for the Record: Worldwide Threat Assessment", Armed Services Committee, United States Senate, April 2021, https://www.armed-services.senate.gov/imo/media/doc/.
3. William Zheng, "Top Chinese spy catcher Dong Jingwei warns agents to look out for those who collude with foreign forces", *South China Morning Post*, 18 June 2021. This article cited a communiqué posted on the political-legal commission's website.
4. It's worth noting that Tedros, who has headed the WHO since 2017, was elected to the top job with Chinese support. Beijing also supported the Marxist-Leninist Tigrayan People's Liberation Front in Tedros's native Ethiopia in the 1980s; the director-general was a member of the movement. See *Le Canard enchaîné*, "La Chine démasquée", *Les dossiers du Canard*, No. 157, 2020.
5. The three labs in question are based in the north-eastern city of Harbin; in Kunming, capital of Yunnan province; and in Beijing.
6. SARS, or Severe Acute Respiratory Syndrome, is an infectious disease caused by a coronavirus, SARS-CoV-1 (the novel coronavirus that causes Covid-19 is known as SARS-CoV-2). Insectivore bats are the natural reservoir of the SARS virus—the population in which it usually lives and reproduces. The transmission of the virus from bats to humans occurred via an intermediary host: the civets sold in markets and consumed widely in China's south, particularly in the Cantonese region.
7. The judicial records were published in 1950 by the Foreign Language Publishing House, entitled *Materials on the trial of former servicemen of the Japanese Army charged with manufacturing and employing bacteriological weapons*.
8. CIA-Archives, Bacteriological Warfare School near Peiping, 26 July 1952, CIA-RDP82-00457R013100370001-9.
9. Mao's slogan was *Fencui Xijunzhan* (粉粹细菌战), literally 'crush germ warfare'.
10. See Milton Leintenberg, "New Russian Evidence on the Korean War Biological Warfare Allegations: Background and Analysis", *Cold War International History Project*, 11, Winter 1998.
11. Wu Zhili, "The Bacteriological War of 1952 is a False Alarm", September 1997, available at the Wilson Center Digital Archive, https://digitalarchive.wilsoncenter.org/document/123080.
12. According to Peter Mattis and Matthew Brazil, Nie had sent hundreds of intelligence officers to the North Korean forces, in which case he would have known that there were no US bioweapons. See *Chinese Communist Espionage: An Intelligence Primer*, Annapolis MD, Naval Institute Press, 2019.

13. Nie himself was also 'saved' from the Red Guards; he had been Lin's commissar during the war with Japan.
14. Also known as Dali Fu, or Tali Fu, this body of water drains into the Mekong River.
15. Ken Alibek, Biohazard: *The Chilling True Story of the Largest Covert Biological Weapons Program in the World—Told from Inside by the Man Who Ran It*, New York, Random House, 1999.
16. Eric Croddy, "China's Role in the Chemical and Biological Disarmament Regimes", *The Nonproliferation Review*, 9:1, Spring 2002, p. 13.
17. Dany Shoham, "China's Biological Warfare Programme: An Integrative Study with Special Reference to Biological Weapons Capabilities", *Journal of Defence Studies*, 9:2, April 2015, p. 141.
18. Now known as the Army Medical University.
19. Colonel Guo Ji-wei, The People's Liberation Army, China, and Xue-sen Yang, "Ultramicro, Nonlethal, and Reversible: Looking Ahead to Military Biotechnology", *Military Review*, July–August 2005, pp. 76–7.
20. In 2020, a French journalist who covers bioterrorism revealed some troubling facts about the BSL-4 lab, which he had unearthed for the investigative journalism site Mediapart. See Jacques Massey, "Wuhan–L'inévitable question de la prolifération" [Wuhan: The Inevitable Possibility of Breakout"], Mediapart, 28 May 2020; Jacques Massey, "Labo P4 à Wuhan: l'usage militaire au coeur des doutes" [Wuhan's BSL-4 Lab: Suspicions of Military Use], Mediapart, 28 May 2020; and Jacques Massey, *Bioterrorisme, l'état de l'alerte* [Bioterrorism: State of Alert], Paris, L'Archipel, 2003.
21. Antoine Izambard, *France–Chine. Les liaisons dangereuses* [France and China: Dangerous Liaisons], Paris, Stock, 2019.
22. Antoine Izambard, "L'histoire secrète du laboratoire P4 de Wuhan vendu par la France à la Chine", *Challenges*, 30 April 2020.
23. US diplomats were raising this concern well before the pandemic began; at a UN meeting of scientists on 30 July 2019, both the WIV director Wang Yanyi and the Wuhan director of the Chinese Academy of Sciences, Yuan Zhiming, were forced to outline the precautions taken to ensure security in the lab. See Yihan Zhang and Han Zhang, "Capacity building of biosafety Laboratories, a 2019 side event of expert meeting on biological weapons convention, was held in UN Geneva [sic]", *Journal of Biosafety and Biosecurity*, 2019.
24. Fang Fang, *Wuhan, ville close. Journal* [Wuhan, Locked Down: A Diary], Paris, Stock, 2020.
25. In late 2005, two researchers from Pakistani military labs were invited by Beijing's zoology institute to join a working group. The institute, like the lab in Wuhan, answers to the powerful Chinese Academy of Sciences; at the time it was led by Li Zhiyi, a former scientific attaché at the Chinese embassy in Paris. See Izambard, op. cit.
26. Jason Pan, "Virus Outbreak: NSB outlines Wuhan intelligence", *Taipei Times*, 1 May 2020.
27. Professor Fang cited French researchers' assertion that there were samples in the Wuhan lab of the horse-bat coronavirus RaTG13, which has been found to share 96% of SARS-CoV-2's genome sequence.
28. Alex Joske, "The Party speaks for you: Foreign interference and the Chinese Communist Party's united front system", policy brief, Australian Strategic Policy Institute/International Cyber Policy Centre, Report 32, 9 June 2020.

29. United States District Court for the Eastern District of Washington, *United States of America v. Li Xiaoyu and Dong Jiazhi*, indictment filed 7 July 2020, pp. 21–2, available at https://www.justice.gov/opa/press-release/file/1295981/download.
30. Dean Cheng, *Cyber Dragon: Inside China's Information Warfare and Cyber Operations*, Santa Barbara CA/Denver CO, Praeger Security International, 2007.
31. Willy Wo-Lap Lam, "Beijing Announces Its Intention to Impose a New 'National Security' Law on Hong Kong", Early Warning Brief, The Jamestown Foundation, 26 May 2020.
32. BBC News, "Hong Kong embarks on mass Covid testing amid criticism", 1 September 2020.
33. Florence de Changy, "Hong Kong tétanisé par un 'état de peur'" [Hong Kong paralysed by fear], *Le Monde*, 1 July 2021.
34. Bruno Ripoche, "La Chine impose la camisole de force aux Ouïghours" [China has the Uyghurs in a straitjacket], *Ouest-France*, 1 June 2019.
35. Muyi Xiao, Haley Willis, Christoph Koettl, Natalie Renau and Drew Jordan, "China Is Using Uighur Labor to Produce Face Masks", *The New York Times*, 19 July 2020.
36. The CICIR website states that Professor Yuan has four vice-presidents, identified as "research professors"—Fu Mengzi, Hu Jiping, Fu Xiaoqiang and Zhang Li—as well as two assistant presidents, Wang Honggang and Zhang Jian.
37. Yuan Peng (trans. David Ownby), "The Coronavirus Pandemic and a Once-in-a-Cenutry Change", *Reading the China Dream*, 17 June 2020.
38. This turn of phrase recalls the great rear base set up by the communists in Yan'an at the end of the Long March, thus evoking Mao Zedong's theory of a "protracted people's war".

NOTE ON SOURCES

1. Roger Faligot and Rémi Kauffer, *The Chinese Secret Service: Kang Sheng and the Shadow Government in Red China* (trans. Christine Donougher), London, Headline, 1989.
2. Peter Mattis, *Analyzing the Chinese Military: A Review Essay and Resource Guide on the People's Liberation Army*, Washington DC, Jamestown Foundation, 2015.
3. Xiong Xianghui, *Wode qingbao yu waijiao shengya* [My Career in Intelligence And Diplomacy], Zhonggongdangshi Chubanshe, 2006.

NOTE ON SOURCES

Since publishing my first article on this subject over thirty-five years ago—a piece in *Le Monde diplomatique* about Deng Xiaoping's establishment of the Guoanbu—I have written hundreds more such articles. With my co-author Rémi Kauffer, I published the first biography of Kang Sheng, the co-founder of the notorious special service set up in Shanghai in 1927 under the auspices of Zhou Enlai. *Kang Sheng and the Chinese Secret Service* has been translated into over a dozen languages.[1] It was followed by hundreds of articles, further books—notably on organized crime in China and the Hong Kong triads—and finally this book, now in its fourth edition, which has been entirely revised and updated for its publication in English.

Over the years I have been able to observe at first hand the considerable evolution of access to information necessary for undertaking research in the region. This research has been enriched by dozens of interviews with both key players and analysts or observers, principally in Asia and Europe. I have interviewed men and women who are still active in intelligence, as well as those who are now retired, many of whom are quoted in this book. Some have chosen to remain anonymous, which does not of course prevent me from thanking them here.

Since the early 1990s, I have been reporting on China for *Intelligence Online*, a bimonthly newsletter based in Paris, for which I have written more than 700 articles, around a third of which are biographical pieces on PLA functionaries, China's security services and intelligence organizations, its political influence structures, economic warfare and soft power. It has been a mammoth undertaking to identify, follow and analyze, using both online and traditional Chinese media, the reassignments and changes of personnel within the Gonganbu and Guoanbu services, the CCP, and all the organizations within the PLA.

But during this time, there has been a real transformation in the ease with which source material can be obtained. During the 1980s and 1990s, I used the *China Directory*, an administrative directory published in Tokyo by analysts connected to the Foreign Ministry, which helped me establish the nomenklatura. Researching in Hong Kong, a haven for China observers, was similarly invaluable. The Union Research Institute in Kowloon, recommended by David Bonavia of the *Far Eastern Economic Review*, was a mine of information, as was the work of a group of Jesuits, led by Father László Ladány, who later were to join the Jesuit priest Dominique Tyl in Taiwan. Similarly, in France, the *Missions Etrangères* newsletter, published by Father Léon Trivière, revealed his exceptional knowledge of CCP arcana. Dozens of magazines are published in Taiwan, in both Chinese and English, such as *Inside China Mainland* and academic journals like *The China Quarterly*. In the past it was difficult to get hold of PLA newspapers, whereas today much of the material can be found on the PLA's own website (although the multiple examples of disinformation remain a serious concern).

Going back further in time, it is now possible to look through the CIA's POLO archives, containing despatches from and fascinating analyses of the Cultural Revolution. For the period covering the 1920s and 1930s, I was able to comb through the archives of the French Concession in Shanghai (at the Quai d'Orsay in Paris) and of the Shanghai Special Branch (in London).

The 1990s saw the publication of the first memoirs by CCP leaders, including Yang Shangkun's. I brought dozens of copies of the latter back from China when I was there in 2008 to research this book, ahead of the Olympic Games. Such books can often be purchased online.

Many well-researched books on the secret war of espionage have been published in recent years. Some rely on a document produced in the 1950s for internal purposes at the request of the head of the secret service, Kang Sheng's deputy, Li Kenong. This kind of research has been made considerably easier by overviews of the available literature, such as that by the brilliant Chinese intelligence specialist Peter Mattis of the Jamestown Foundation.[2]

A personal anecdote: I was fourteen in 1966, and keen to understand what was happening in China during the Cultural Revolution. Was this the youth of China rising up against the old world? Or a war that had sprung up between factions, like the one I read about in one of my favourite novels, André Malraux's *Man's Fate*?

I started to teach myself a little basic Chinese. The following year I did a language exchange and went to live for a short time with a family in London. One day I went to the Chinese embassy in Portland Place, which was surrounded by huge numbers of police officers, to see if I could get hold of some documentation. I was fobbed off with propaganda magazines like *China Reconstructs*. A passing diplomat, sporting a Mao badge on his lapel, took pity on me and handed me his own Chinese copy of Chairman Mao's *Little Red Book*, which I have still. As a result of the breakdown of diplomatic relations between China and the UK, the ambassador in London had been called home and replaced by a chargé d'affaires called Xiong Xianghui. Might the book in my possession have belonged to him, or one of his colleagues?

Twenty years later, while researching my biography of Kang Sheng, I became convinced that this very Xiong was an important figure in the intelligence service. I had to wait another decade before I spotted Xiong's autobiography in a Beijing bookshop. It was published by the CCP and entitled *My Career in Intelligence and Diplomacy*.[3]

Even today, I sometimes flick with a certain nostalgia through my own typed index cards, containing biographies of members of the Chinese special services, which I began collating at the end of the 1970s from books and interviews. Today regional newspapers and administrative documents are available online and for the French edition of this book I put together biographies of regional directors of the Guoanbu (to take a single example), using websites like *China Vitae* (which contains up-to-date biographies in English) and most of all *Baidu Baike*, a sort of Chinese Google through which it is possible to access many biographical details.

The book ends with the rebuilding of the secret services, such as the Guoanbu, at the initiative of Xi Jinping in 2015. The purge of the Guoanbu was notable for the arrest of its head of counterintelligence, Ma Jian, who was jailed for life in December 2018. He was accused of corruption, but his arrest was also, undoubtedly, linked to the struggle between his service and MI6, the CIA, and the French DGSE. Ma Jian's confession—a nice exercise in propaganda—was filmed and broadcast on YouTube. We have come a long way from the secrecy that marked the era of the 102-year-old spy Yao Zijian, who fought the "underground war" on Mao's secret service.

INDEX

INDEX

INDEX

INDEX

INDEX

INDEX

INDEX

INDEX

INDEX

INDEX

INDEX

INDEX

ABOUT THE AUTHOR

Roger Faligot is an investigative journalist and author of many books on European and Asian intelligence, including *The Chinese Mafia in Europe* and *La Piscine*, the first history of France's secret services. He has been a correspondent for *The European*, and the Far East correspondent for *Intelligence Online* (1993–2018).